SUPERMAN
FOR TOMORROW

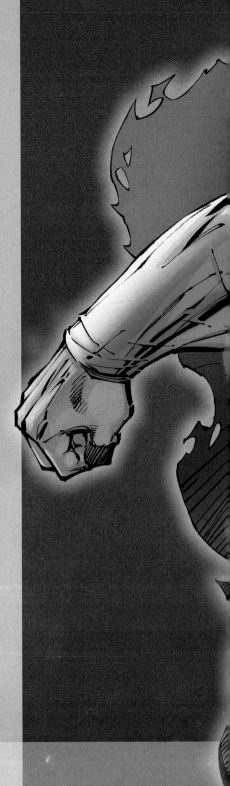

BRIAN AZZARELLO
+ WRITER +

JIM LEE
+ PENCILLER +

SCOTT WILLIAMS
+ INKER +

ALEX SINCLAIR
+ COLORIST +

RICHARD FRIEND

SANDRA HOPE

MATT BANNING

ERIC BASALDUA

JIM LEE

DANNY MIKI

TREVOR SCOTT

TIM TOWNSEND

JOE WEEMS

+ ADDITIONAL INKERS +

ROB LEIGH

NICK J. NAPOLITANO

+ LETTERERS +

SUPERMAN
FOR TOMORROW

SUPERMAN CREATED BY
JERRY SIEGEL + JOE SHUSTER

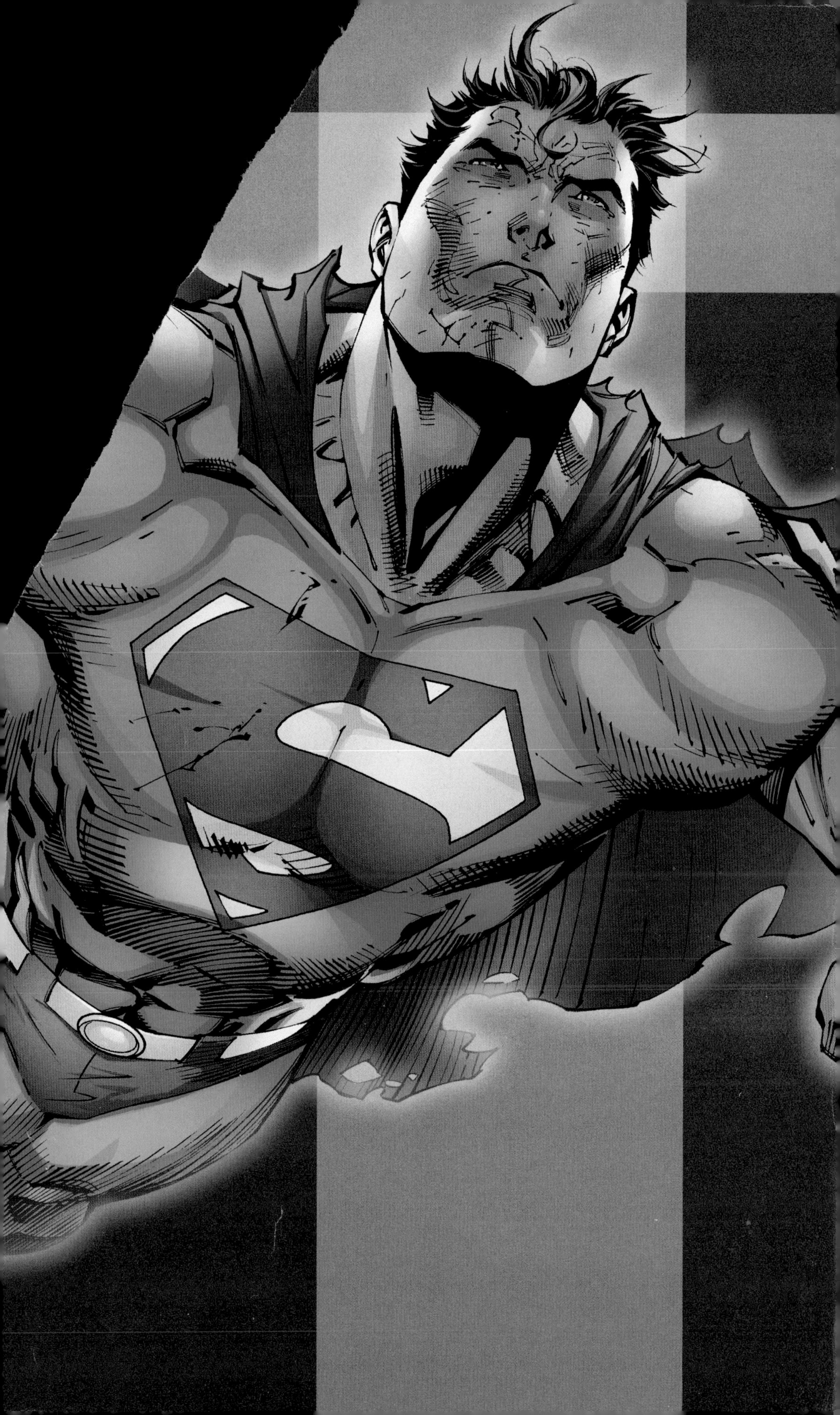

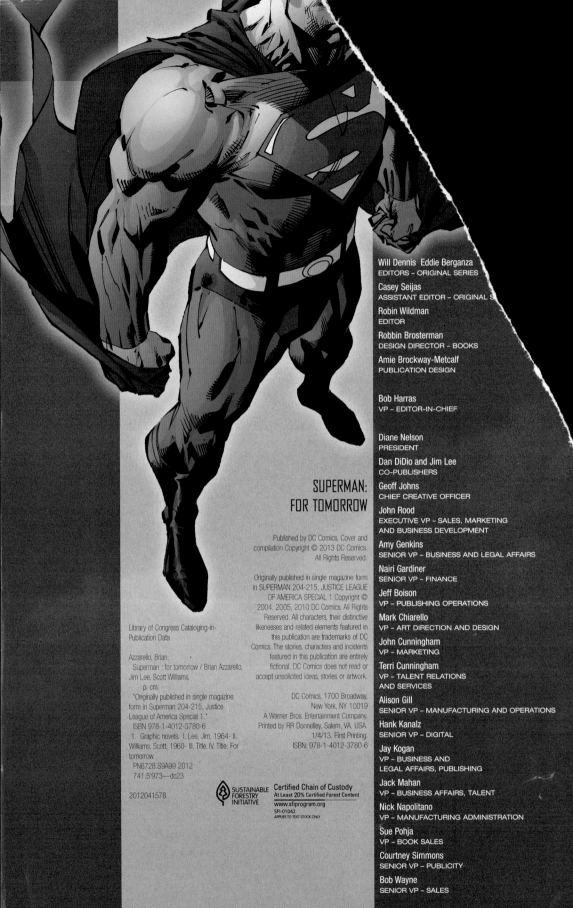

SUPERMAN:
FOR TOMORROW

Published by DC Comics. Cover and
compilation Copyright © 2013 DC Comics.
All Rights Reserved.

Originally published in single magazine form
in SUPERMAN 204-215, JUSTICE LEAGUE
OF AMERICA SPECIAL 1 Copyright ©
2004, 2005, 2010 DC Comics. All Rights
Reserved. All characters, their distinctive
likenesses and related elements featured in
this publication are trademarks of DC
Comics. The stories, characters and incidents
featured in this publication are entirely
fictional. DC Comics does not read or
accept unsolicited ideas, stories or artwork.

DC Comics, 1700 Broadway,
New York, NY 10019
A Warner Bros. Entertainment Company.
Printed by RR Donnelley, Salem, VA, USA.
1/4/13. First Printing.
ISBN: 978-1-4012-3780-6

Library of Congress Cataloging-in-
Publication Data

Azzarello, Brian.
  Superman : for tomorrow / Brian Azzarello,
Jim Lee, Scott Williams.
  p. cm.
  "Originally published in single magazine
form in Superman 204-215, Justice
League of America Special 1."
  ISBN 978-1-4012-3780-6
  1. Graphic novels. I. Lee, Jim, 1964- II.
Williams, Scott, 1960- III. Title. IV. Title: For
tomorrow.
  PN6728.S9A99 2012
  741.5'973—dc23

2012041578

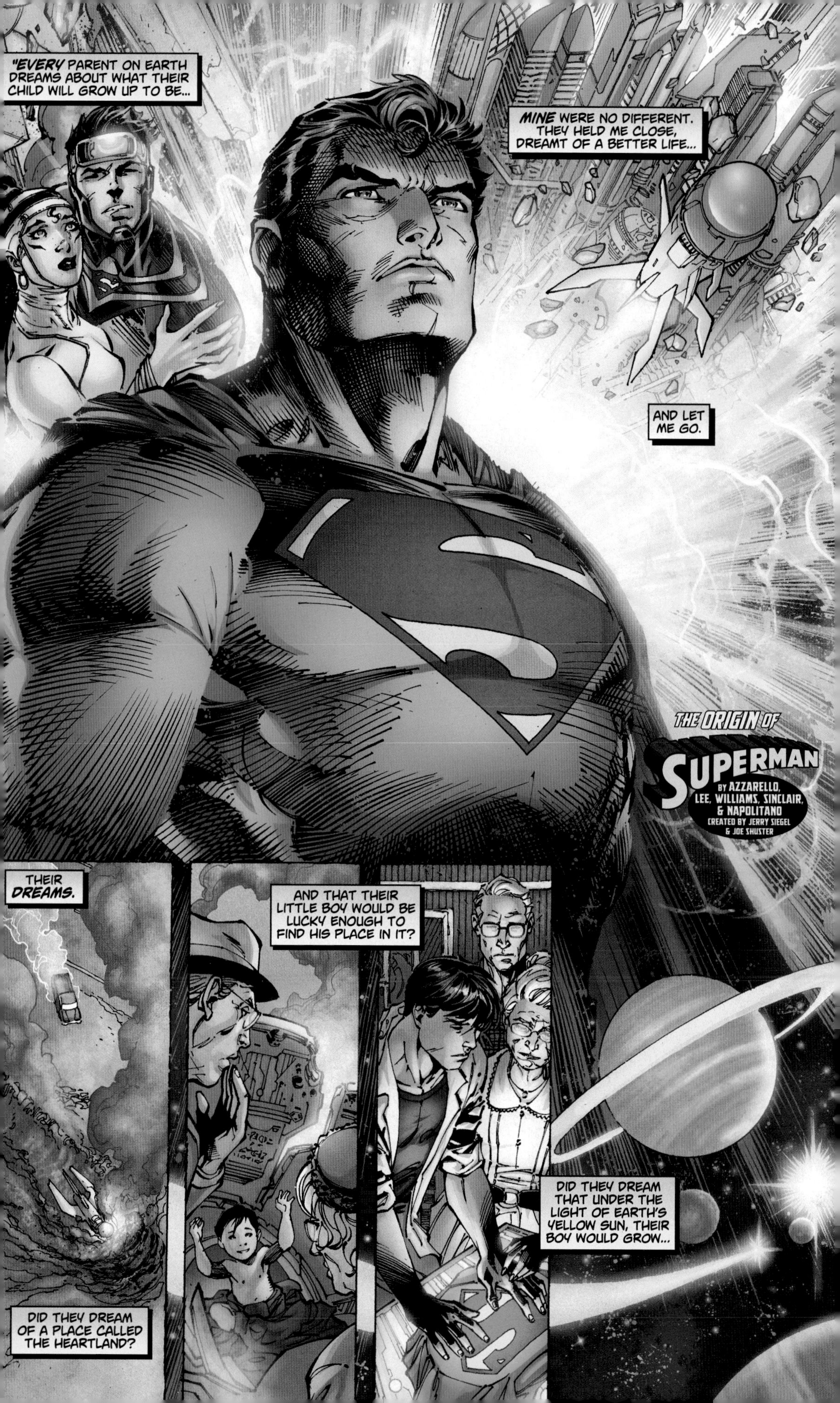
"EVERY PARENT ON EARTH DREAMS ABOUT WHAT THEIR CHILD WILL GROW UP TO BE...
MINE WERE NO DIFFERENT. THEY HELD ME CLOSE, DREAMT OF A BETTER LIFE...
AND LET ME GO.
THE ORIGIN OF
SUPERMAN
BY AZZARELLO, LEE, WILLIAMS, SINCLAIR, & NAPOLITANO
CREATED BY JERRY SIEGEL & JOE SHUSTER
THEIR DREAMS.
DID THEY DREAM OF A PLACE CALLED THE HEARTLAND?
AND THAT THEIR LITTLE BOY WOULD BE LUCKY ENOUGH TO FIND HIS PLACE IN IT?
DID THEY DREAM THAT UNDER THE LIGHT OF EARTH'S YELLOW SUN, THEIR BOY WOULD GROW...

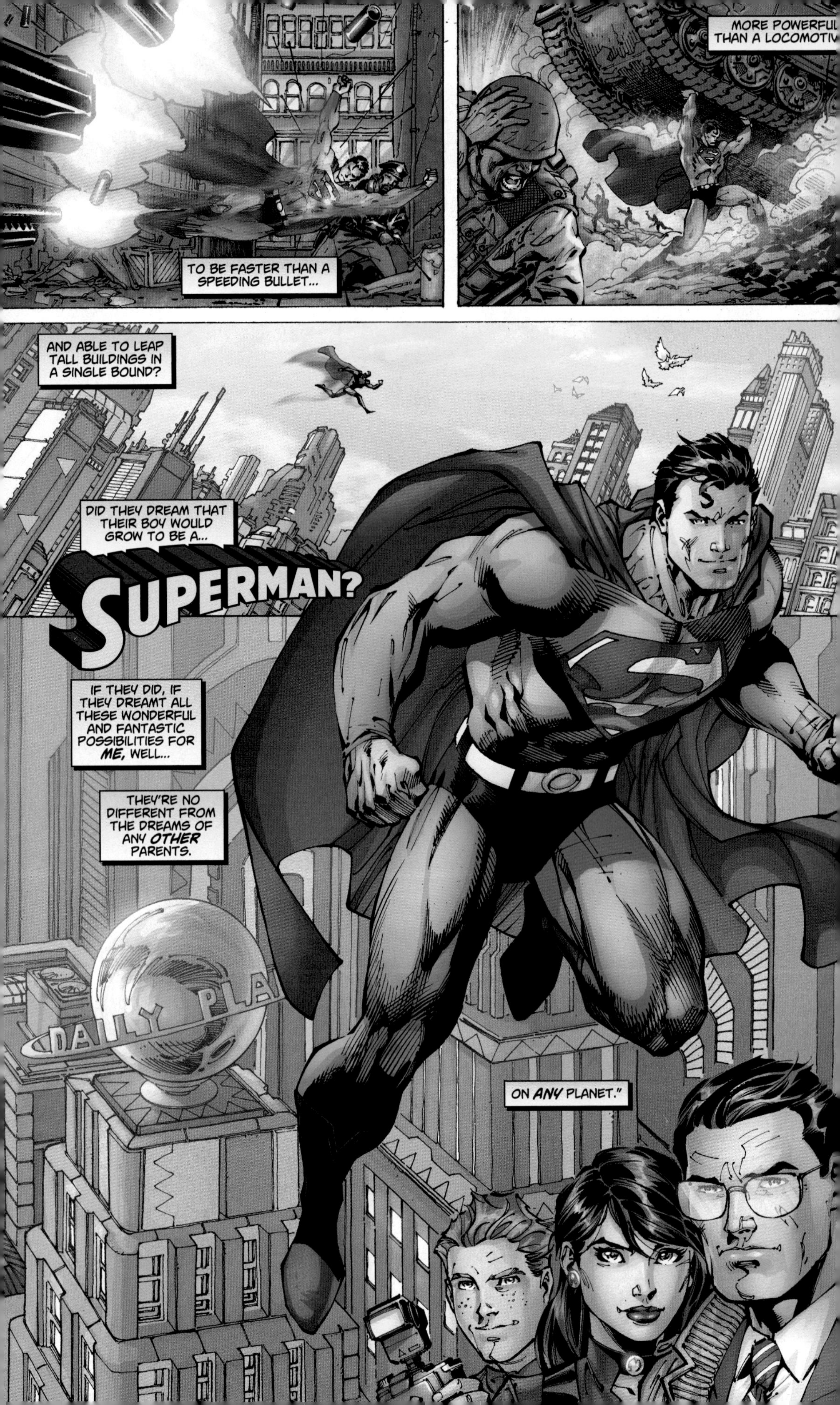

TO BE FASTER THAN A SPEEDING BULLET...
MORE POWERFUL THAN A LOCOMOTIV
AND ABLE TO LEAP TALL BUILDINGS IN A SINGLE BOUND?
DID THEY DREAM THAT THEIR BOY WOULD GROW TO BE A...
SUPERMAN?
IF THEY DID, IF THEY DREAMT ALL THESE WONDERFUL AND FANTASTIC POSSIBILITIES FOR ME, WELL...
THEY'RE NO DIFFERENT FROM THE DREAMS OF ANY OTHER PARENTS.
DAILY PLA
ON ANY PLANET."

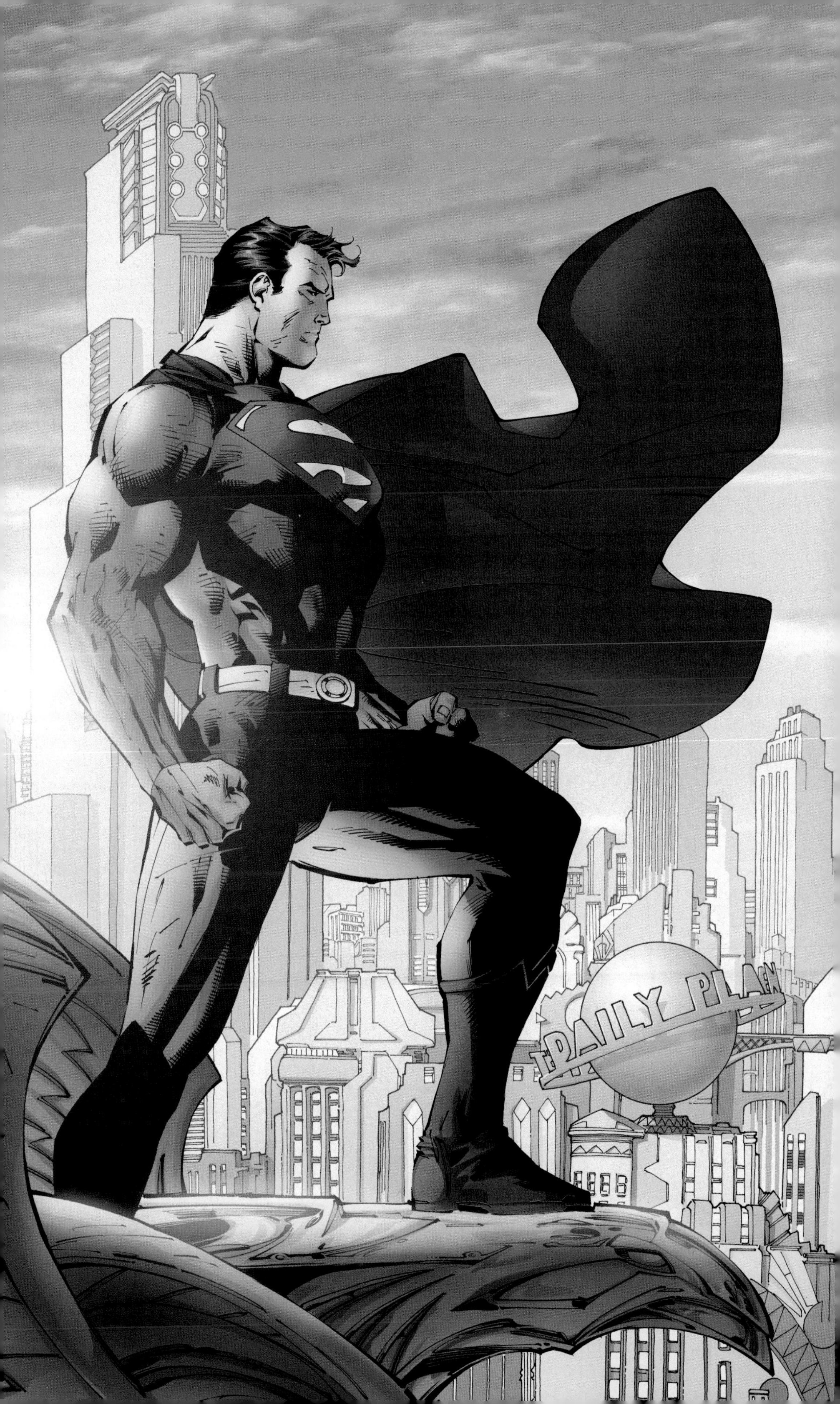

SUPERMAN 204

(2nd printing) cover pencils by Jim Lee

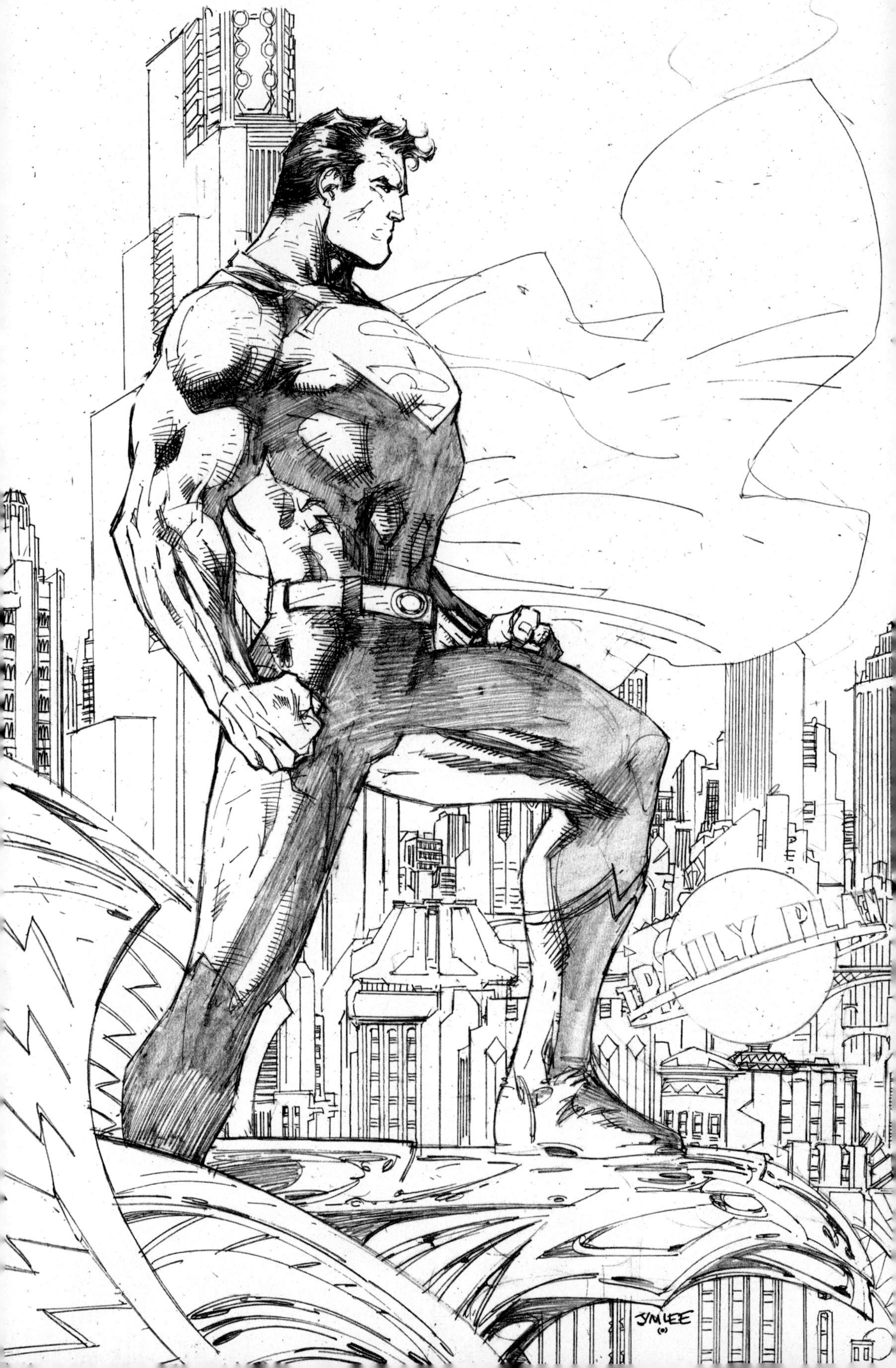
DAILY

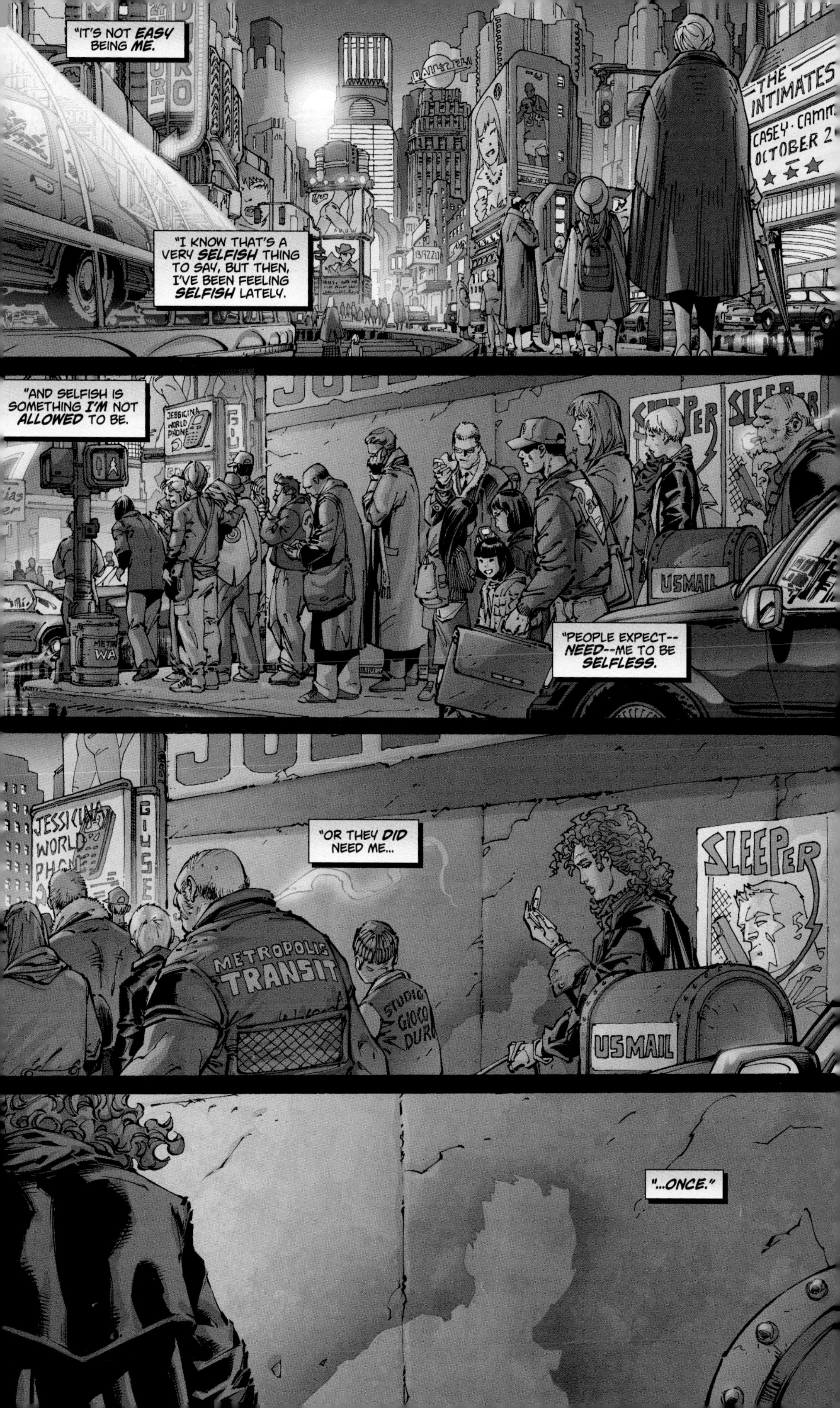
"IT'S NOT EASY BEING ME.
DAILY PLANET
THE INTIMATES
CASEY · CAMM
OCTOBER 2
"I KNOW THAT'S A VERY SELFISH THING TO SAY, BUT THEN, I'VE BEEN FEELING SELFISH LATELY.
"AND SELFISH IS SOMETHING I'M NOT ALLOWED TO BE.
JESSICINA WORLD PHONE
SLEEPER
US MAIL
"PEOPLE EXPECT--NEED--ME TO BE SELFLESS.
JESSICINA WORLD PHONE
GIUSE
"OR THEY DID NEED ME...
METROPOLIS TRANSIT
STUDIO GIOCO DURO
SLEEPER
US MAIL
"...ONCE."

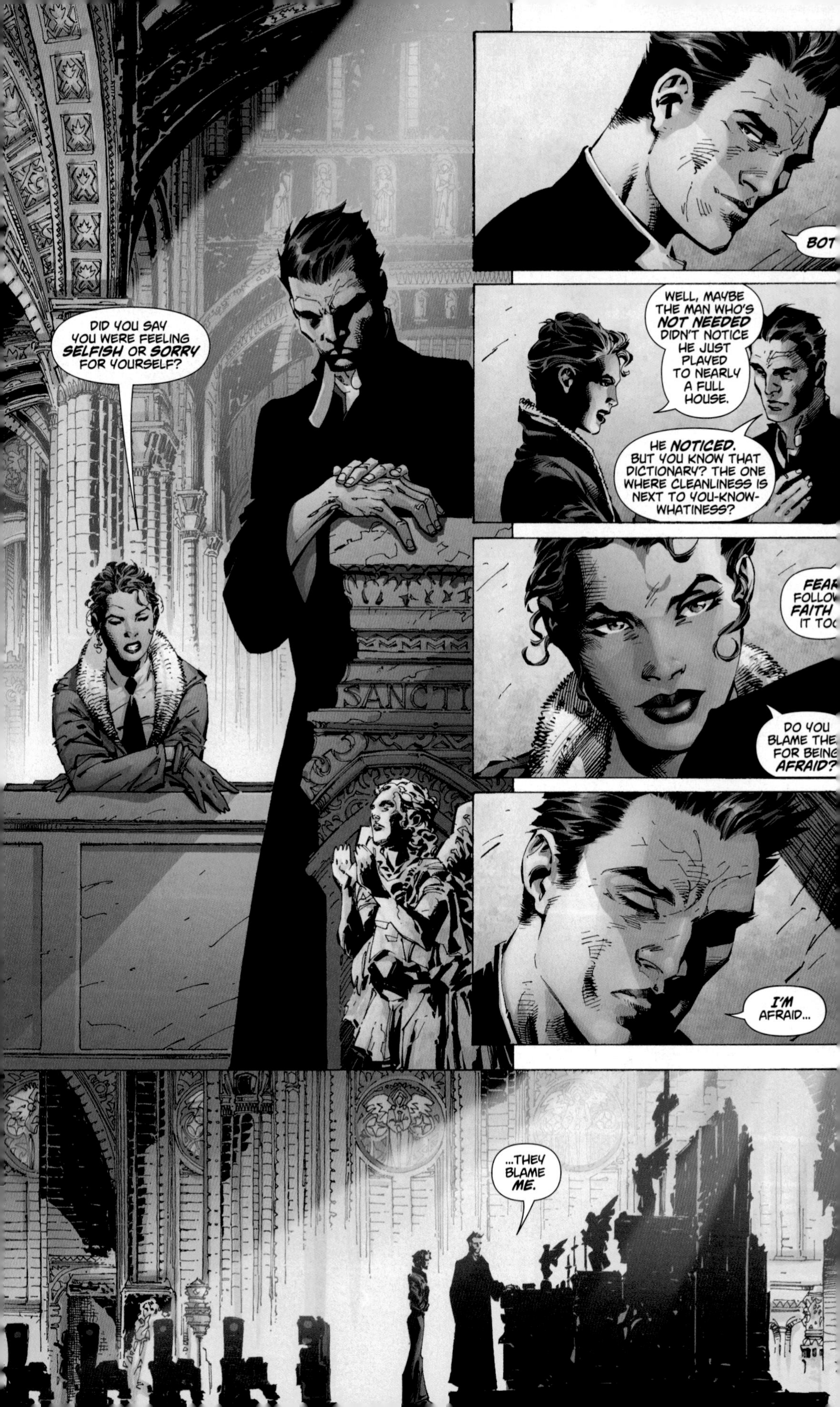

BOT
DID YOU SAY YOU WERE FEELING SELFISH OR SORRY FOR YOURSELF?
WELL, MAYBE THE MAN WHO'S NOT NEEDED DIDN'T NOTICE HE JUST PLAYED TO NEARLY A FULL HOUSE.
HE NOTICED. BUT YOU KNOW THAT DICTIONARY? THE ONE WHERE CLEANLINESS IS NEXT TO YOU-KNOW-WHATINESS?
FEAR FOLLOW FAITH IT TO
DO YOU BLAME THE FOR BEING AFRAID?
I'M AFRAID...
...THEY BLAME ME.

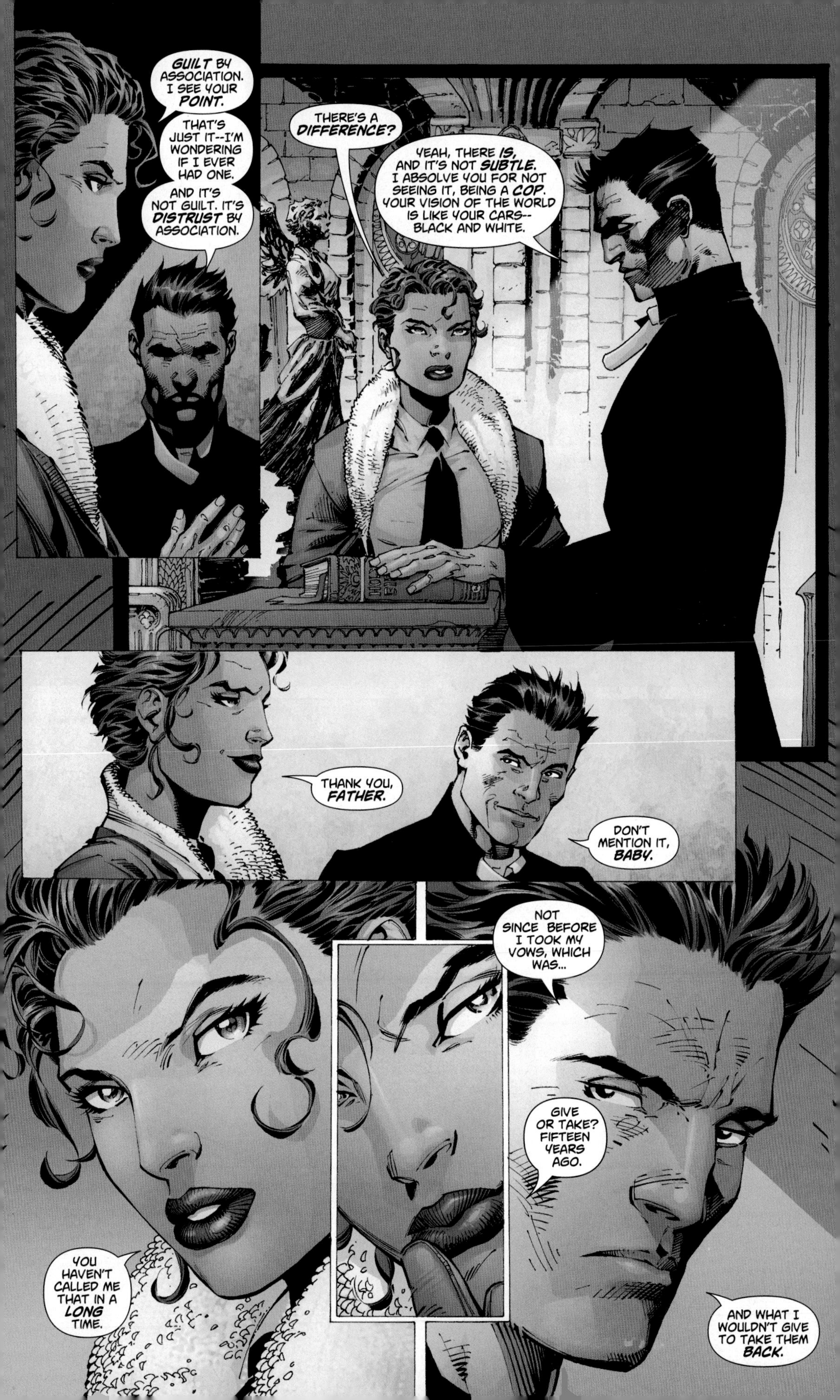
GUILT BY ASSOCIATION. I SEE YOUR POINT.
THERE'S A DIFFERENCE?
YEAH, THERE IS, AND IT'S NOT SUBTLE. I ABSOLVE YOU FOR NOT SEEING IT, BEING A COP. YOUR VISION OF THE WORLD IS LIKE YOUR CARS-- BLACK AND WHITE.
THAT'S JUST IT--I'M WONDERING IF I EVER HAD ONE.
AND IT'S NOT GUILT. IT'S DISTRUST BY ASSOCIATION.
THANK YOU, FATHER.
DON'T MENTION IT, BABY.
YOU HAVEN'T CALLED ME THAT IN A LONG TIME.
NOT SINCE BEFORE I TOOK MY VOWS, WHICH WAS...
GIVE OR TAKE? FIFTEEN YEARS AGO.
AND WHAT I WOULDN'T GIVE TO TAKE THEM BACK.

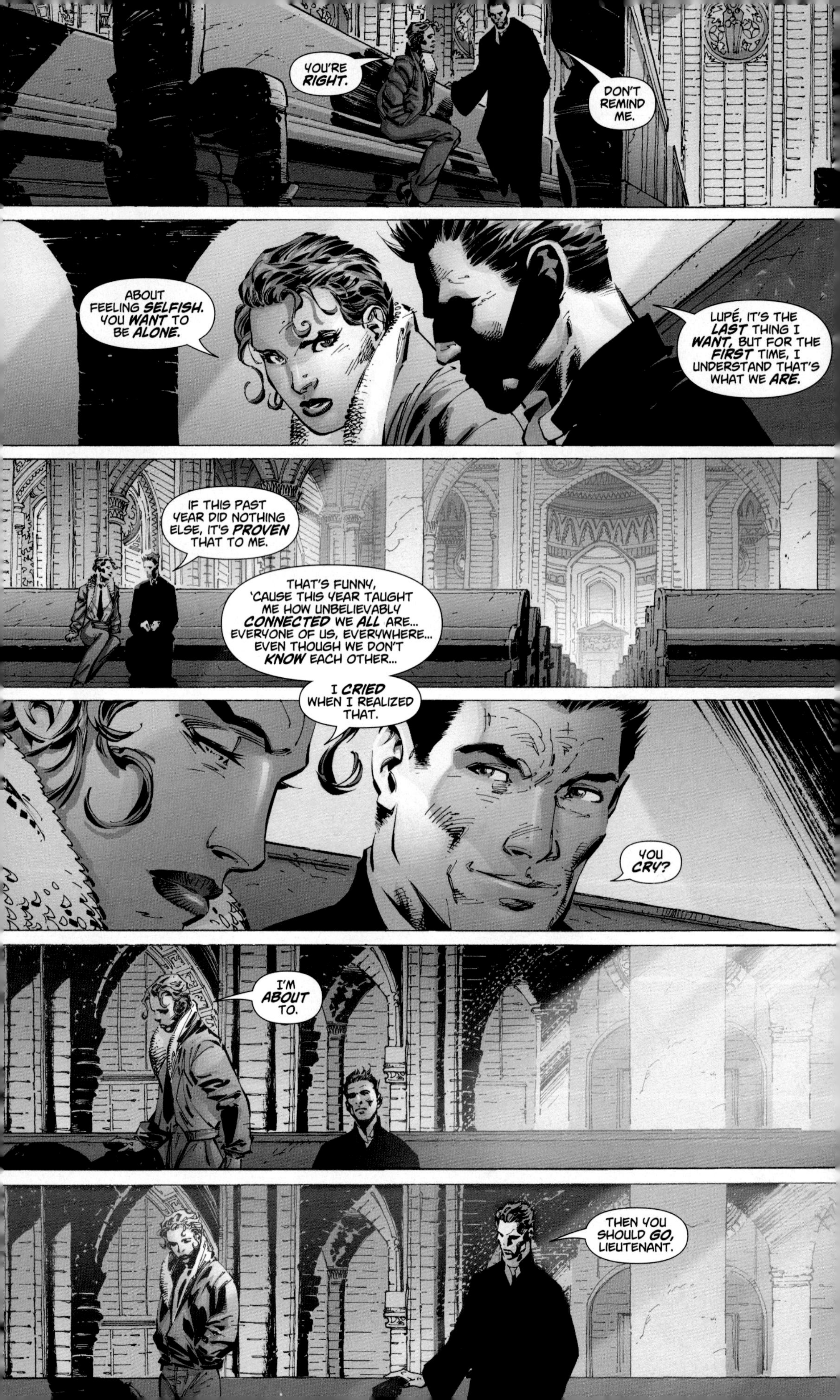
YOU'RE RIGHT.
DON'T REMIND ME.
ABOUT FEELING SELFISH. YOU WANT TO BE ALONE.
LUPÉ, IT'S THE LAST THING I WANT, BUT FOR THE FIRST TIME, I UNDERSTAND THAT'S WHAT WE ARE.
IF THIS PAST YEAR DID NOTHING ELSE, IT'S PROVEN THAT TO ME.
THAT'S FUNNY, 'CAUSE THIS YEAR TAUGHT ME HOW UNBELIEVABLY CONNECTED WE ALL ARE... EVERYONE OF US, EVERYWHERE... EVEN THOUGH WE DON'T KNOW EACH OTHER...
I CRIED WHEN I REALIZED THAT.
YOU CRY?
I'M ABOUT TO.
THEN YOU SHOULD GO, LIEUTENANT.

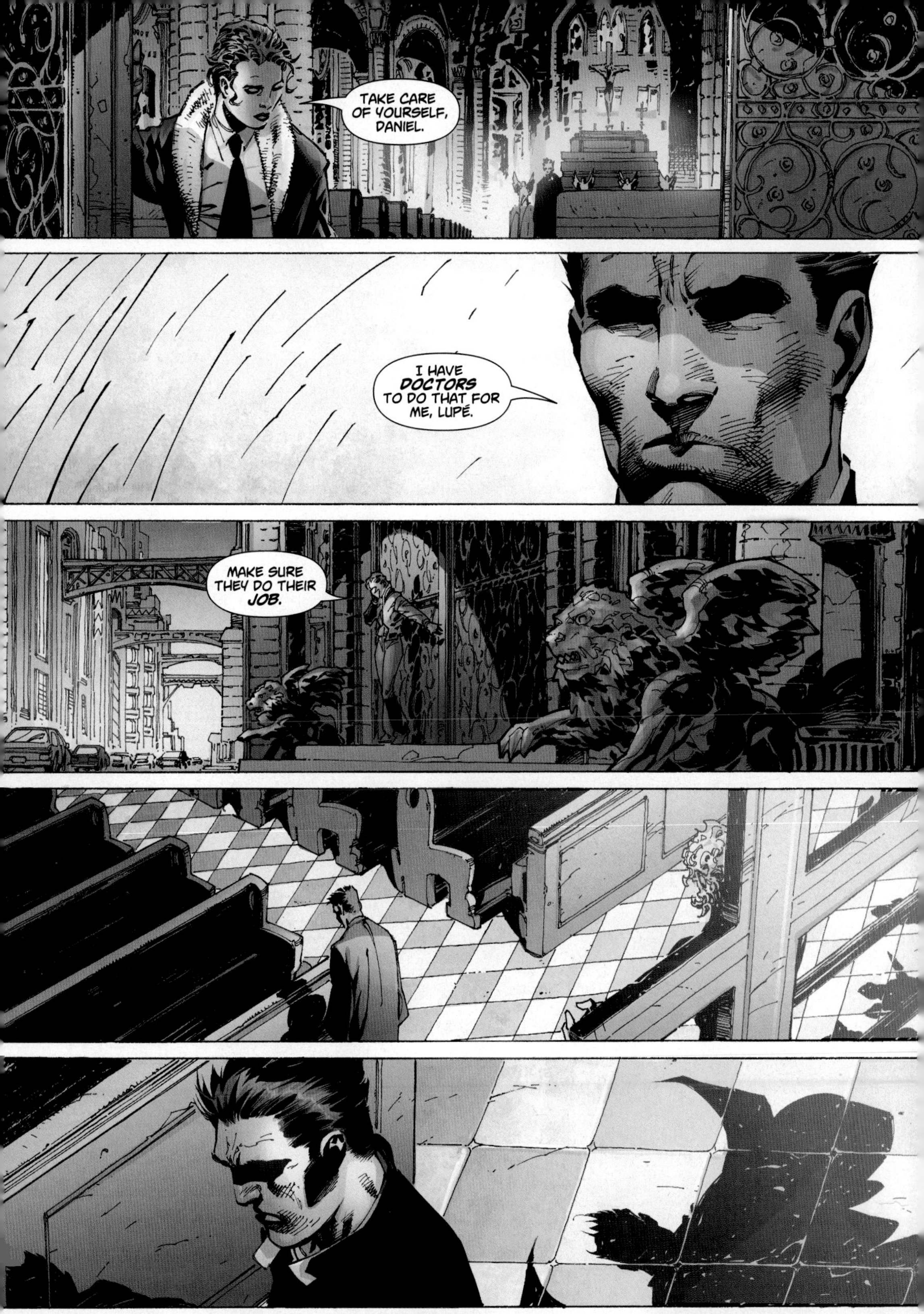
TAKE CARE OF YOURSELF, DANIEL.
I HAVE DOCTORS TO DO THAT FOR ME, LUPÉ.
MAKE SURE THEY DO THEIR JOB.

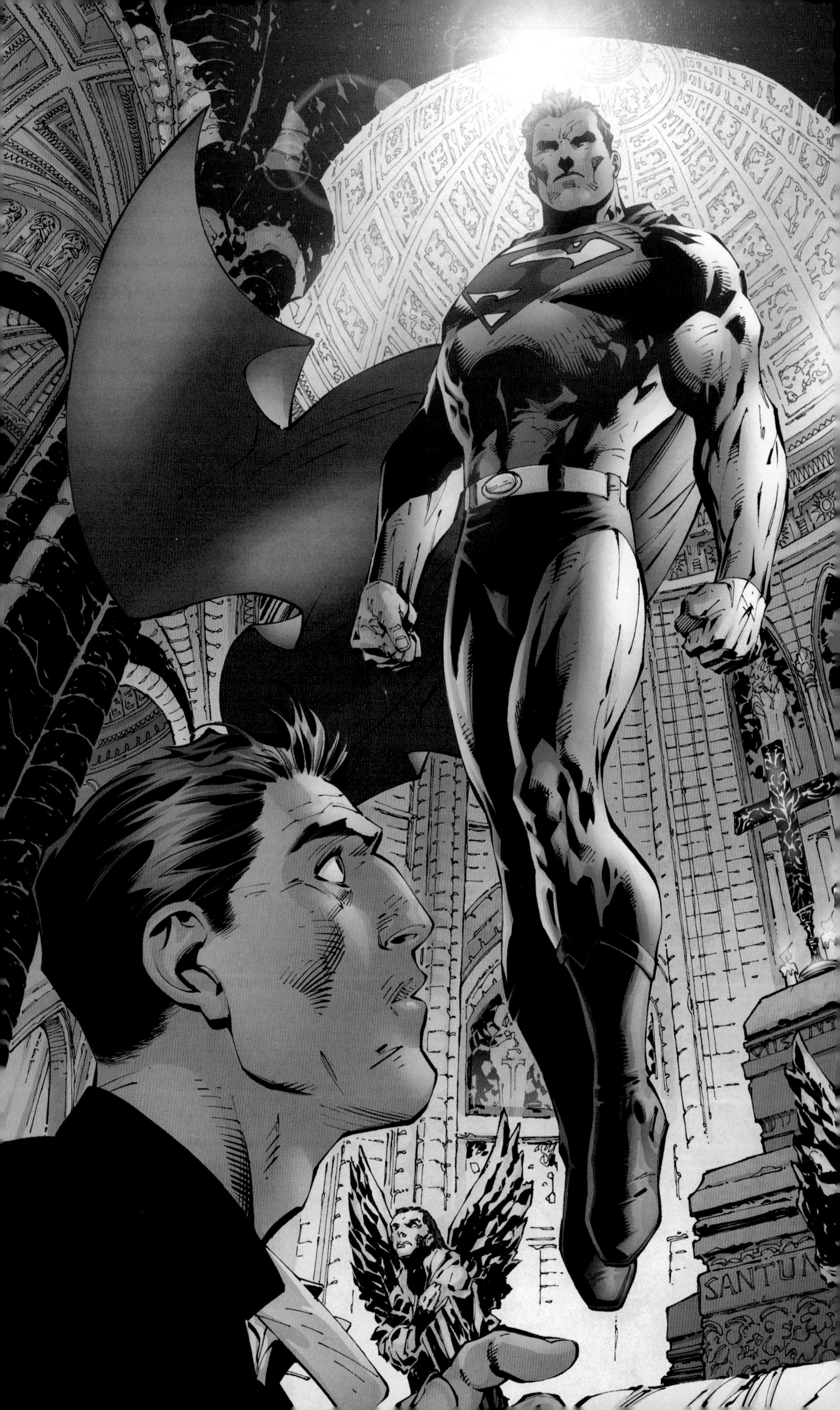
SANTUN

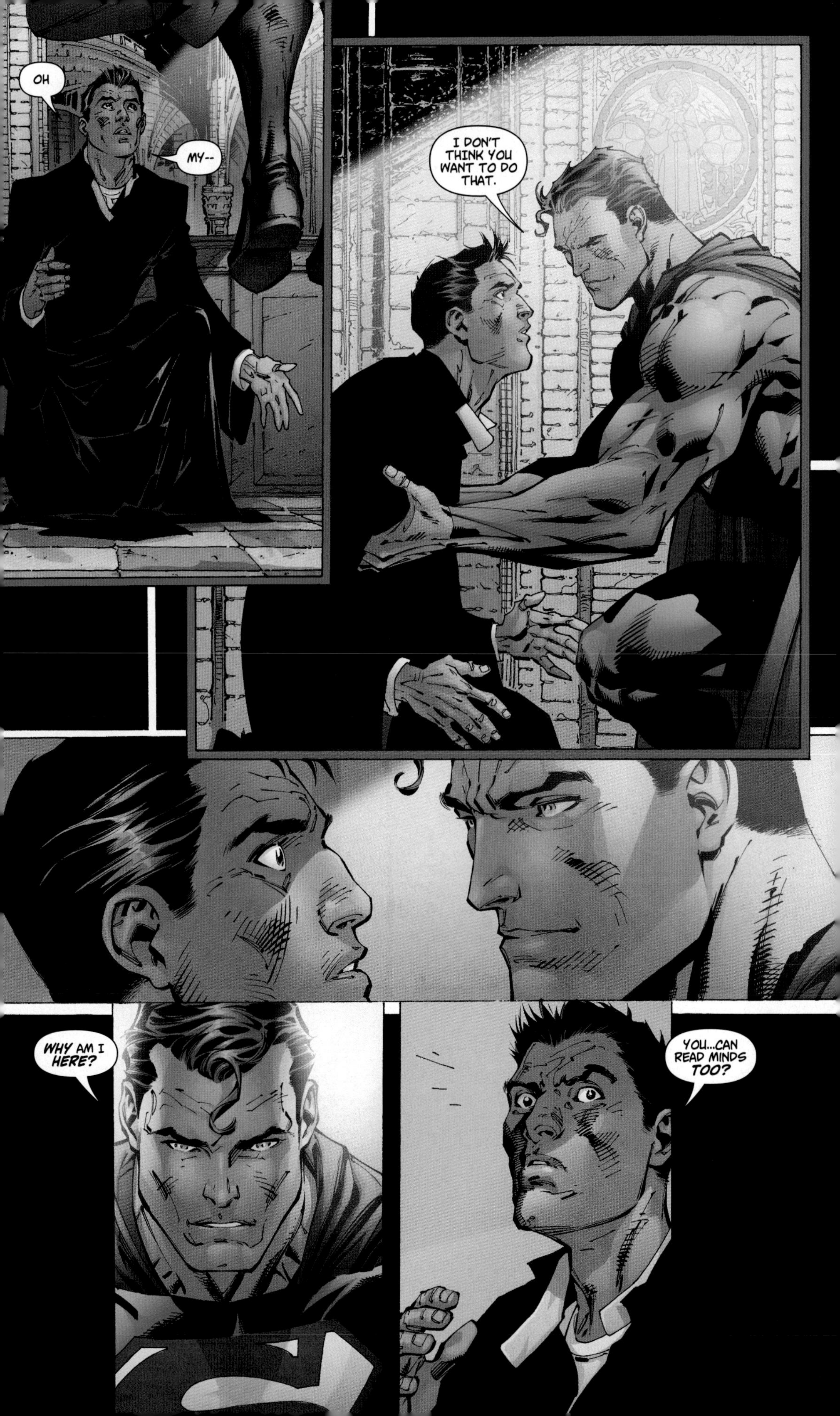
OH
MY--
I DON'T THINK YOU WANT TO DO THAT.
WHY AM I HERE?
YOU...CAN READ MINDS TOO?

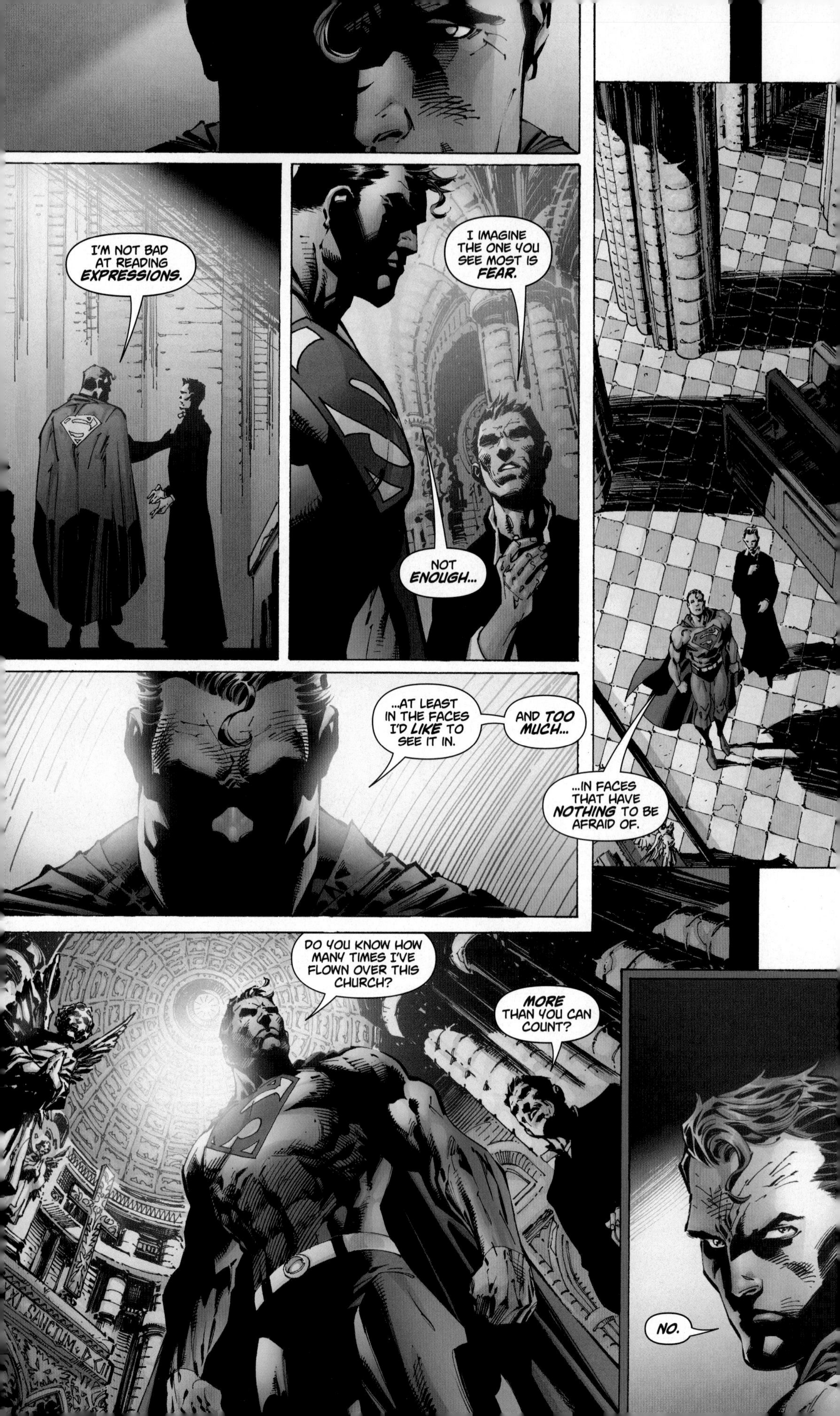
I'M NOT BAD AT READING EXPRESSIONS.
I IMAGINE THE ONE YOU SEE MOST IS FEAR.
NOT ENOUGH...
...AT LEAST IN THE FACES I'D LIKE TO SEE IT IN.
AND TOO MUCH...
...IN FACES THAT HAVE NOTHING TO BE AFRAID OF.
DO YOU KNOW HOW MANY TIMES I'VE FLOWN OVER THIS CHURCH?
MORE THAN YOU CAN COUNT?
NO.

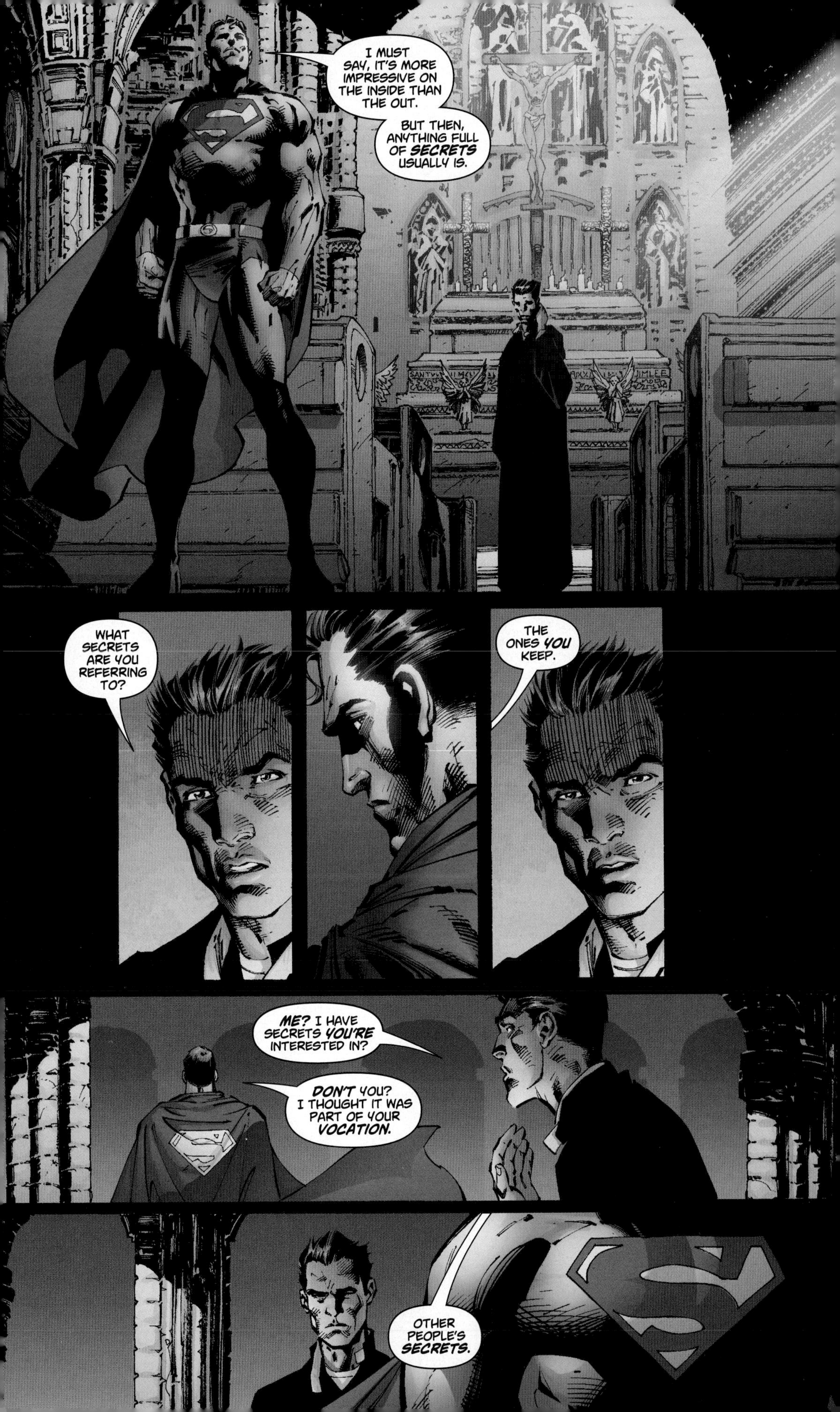
I MUST SAY, IT'S MORE IMPRESSIVE ON THE INSIDE THAN THE OUT.
BUT THEN, ANYTHING FULL OF SECRETS USUALLY IS.
WHAT SECRETS ARE YOU REFERRING TO?
THE ONES YOU KEEP.
ME? I HAVE SECRETS YOU'RE INTERESTED IN?
DON'T YOU? I THOUGHT IT WAS PART OF YOUR VOCATION.
OTHER PEOPLE'S SECRETS.

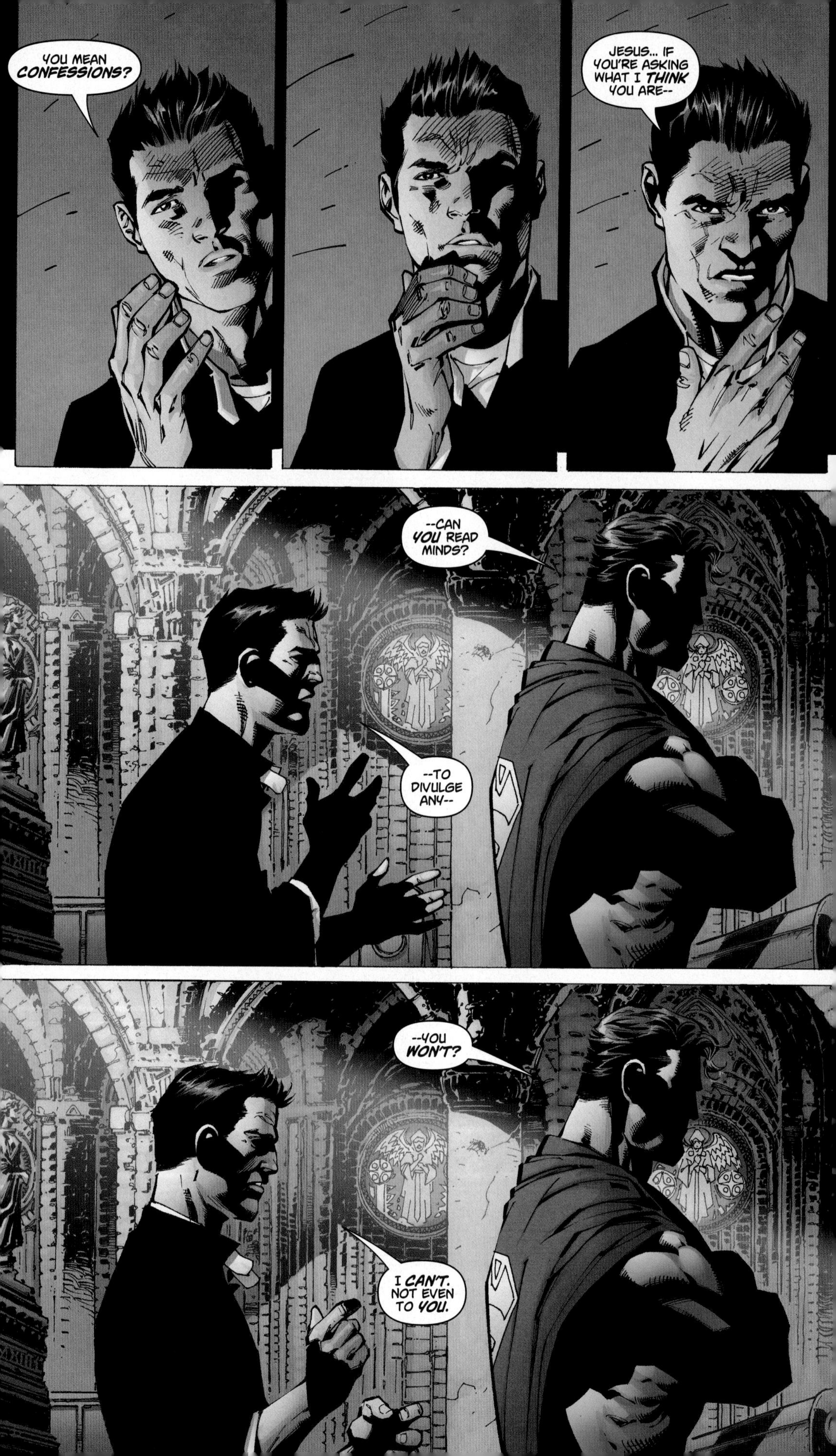

YOU MEAN CONFESSIONS?
JESUS... IF YOU'RE ASKING WHAT I THINK YOU ARE--
--CAN YOU READ MINDS?
--TO DIVULGE ANY--
--YOU WON'T?
I CAN'T. NOT EVEN TO YOU.

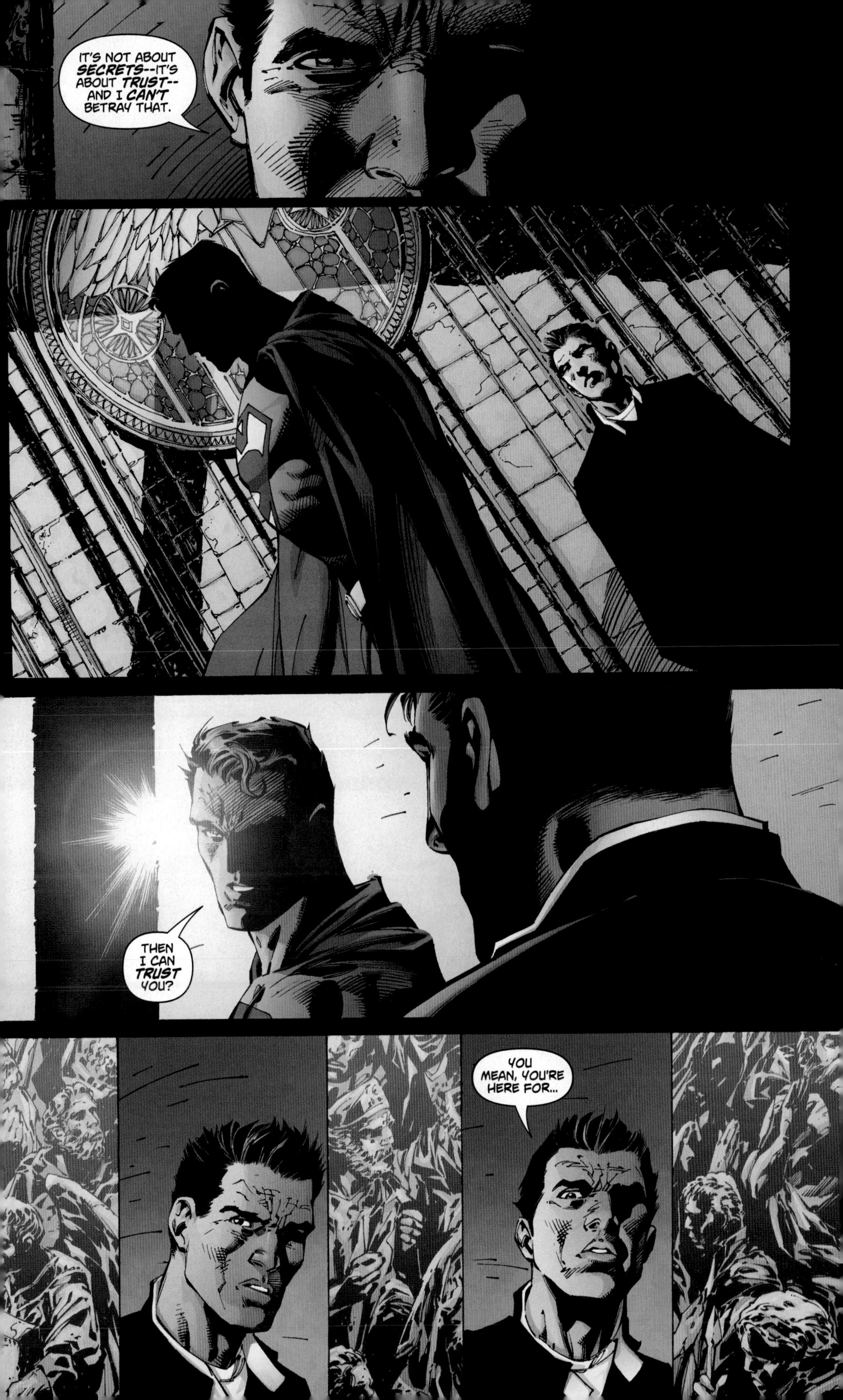
IT'S NOT ABOUT SECRETS--IT'S ABOUT TRUST--AND I CAN'T BETRAY THAT.
THEN I CAN TRUST YOU?
YOU MEAN, YOU'RE HERE FOR...

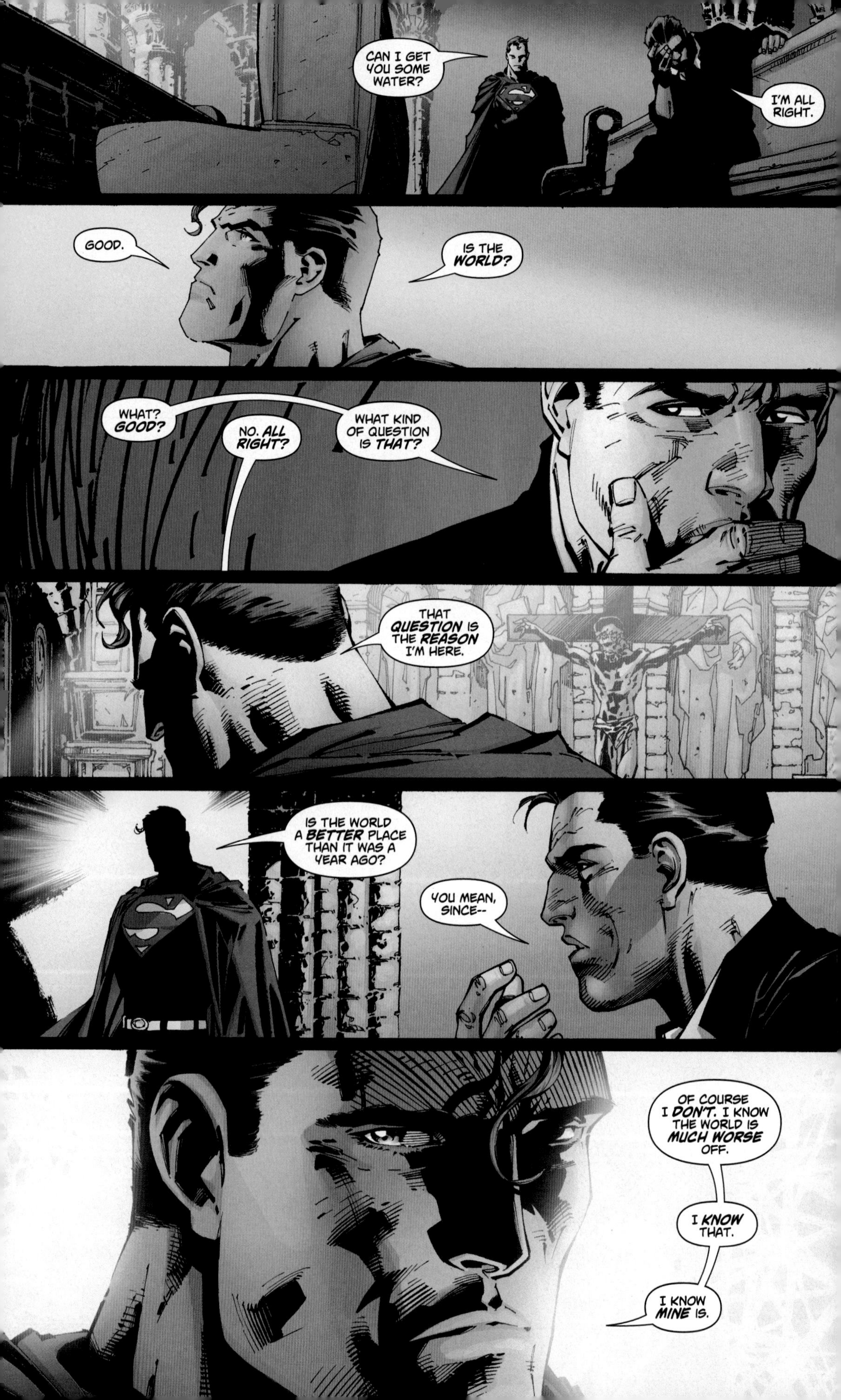
CAN I GET YOU SOME WATER?
I'M ALL RIGHT.
GOOD.
IS THE WORLD?
WHAT? GOOD?
NO. ALL RIGHT?
WHAT KIND OF QUESTION IS THAT?
THAT QUESTION IS THE REASON I'M HERE.
IS THE WORLD A BETTER PLACE THAN IT WAS A YEAR AGO?
YOU MEAN, SINCE--
OF COURSE I DON'T. I KNOW THE WORLD IS MUCH WORSE OFF.
I KNOW THAT.
I KNOW MINE IS.

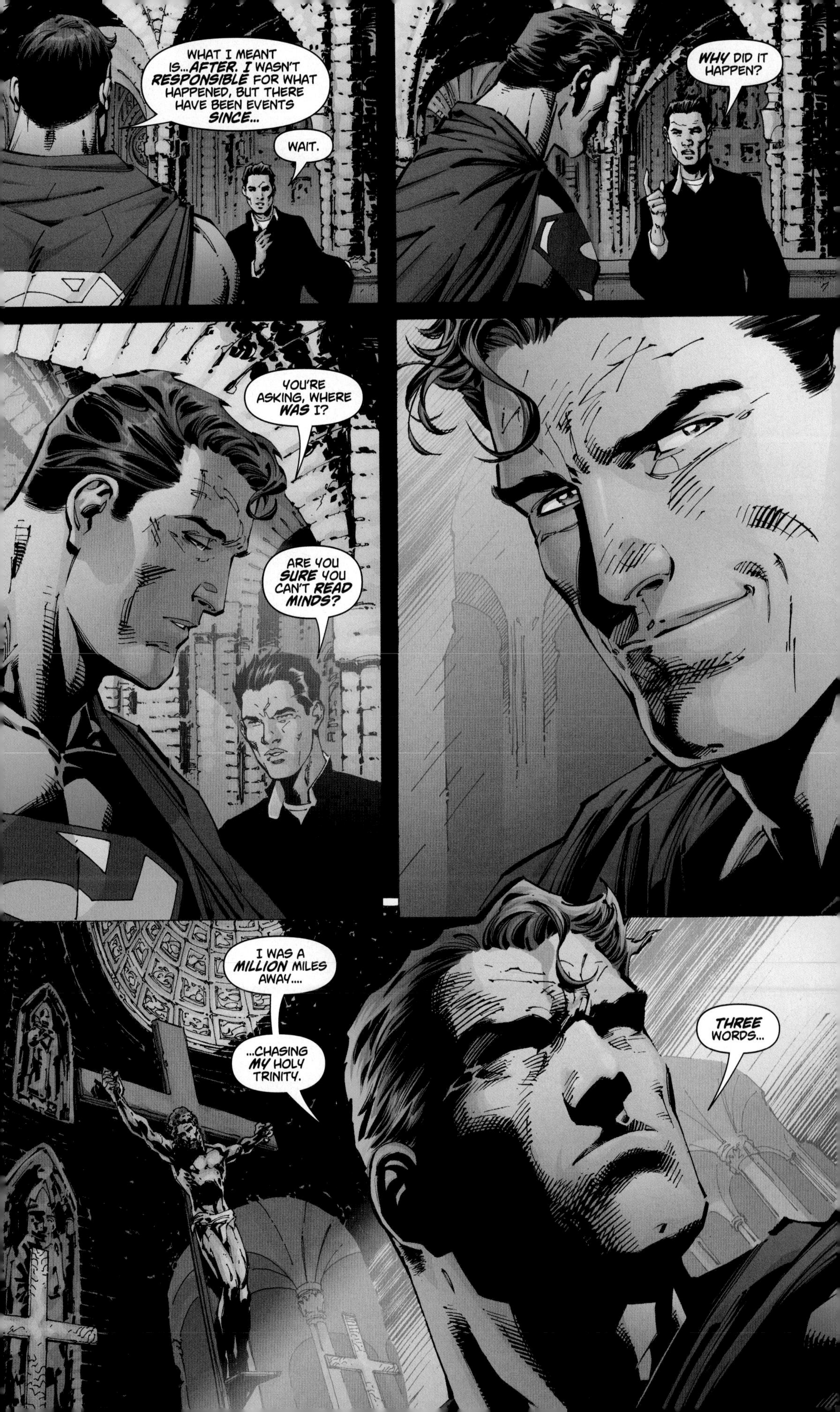
WHAT I MEANT IS...AFTER. I WASN'T RESPONSIBLE FOR WHAT HAPPENED, BUT THERE HAVE BEEN EVENTS SINCE...
WAIT.
WHY DID IT HAPPEN?
YOU'RE ASKING, WHERE WAS I?
ARE YOU SURE YOU CAN'T READ MINDS?
I WAS A MILLION MILES AWAY....
...CHASING MY HOLY TRINITY.
THREE WORDS...

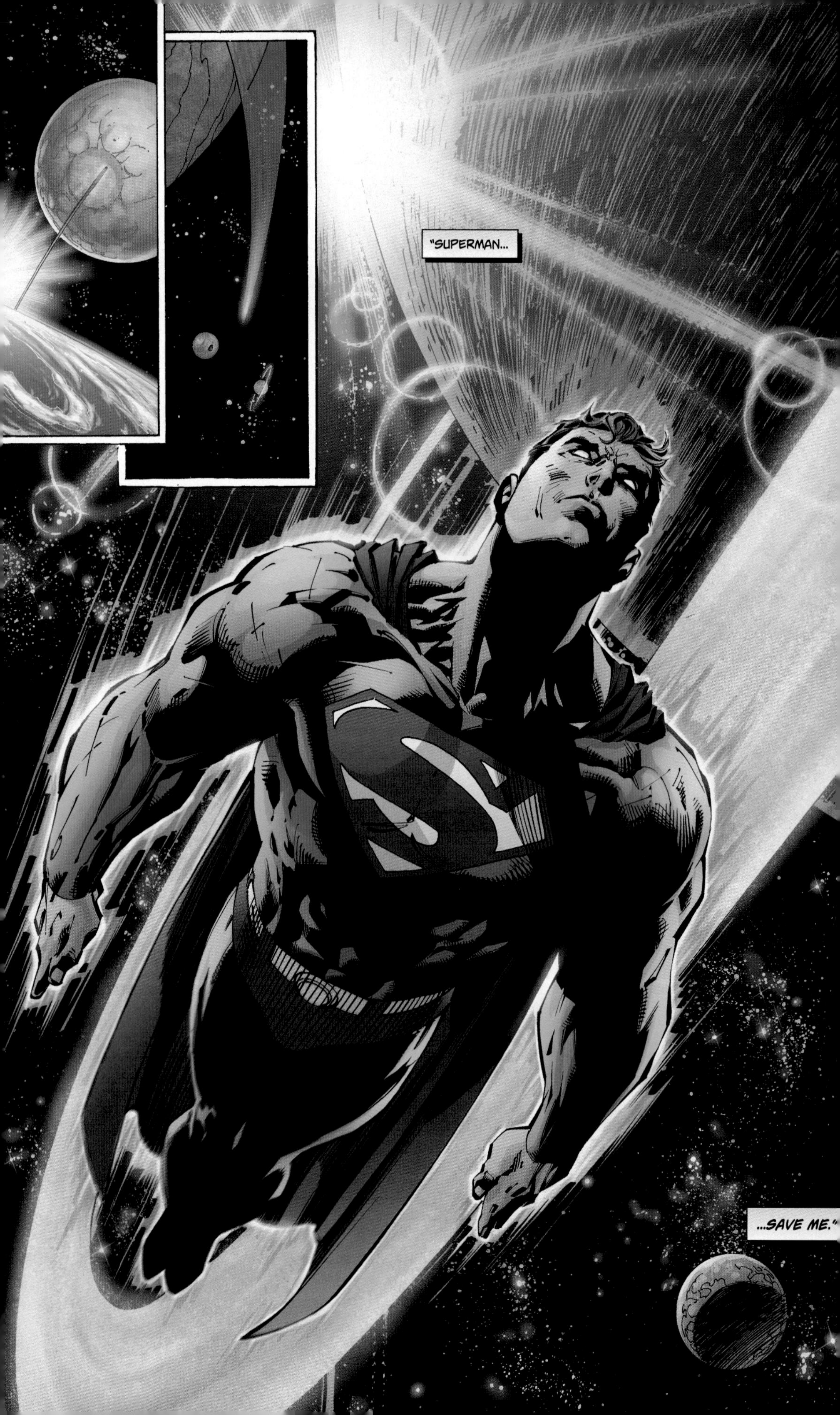
"SUPERMAN...
...SAVE ME."

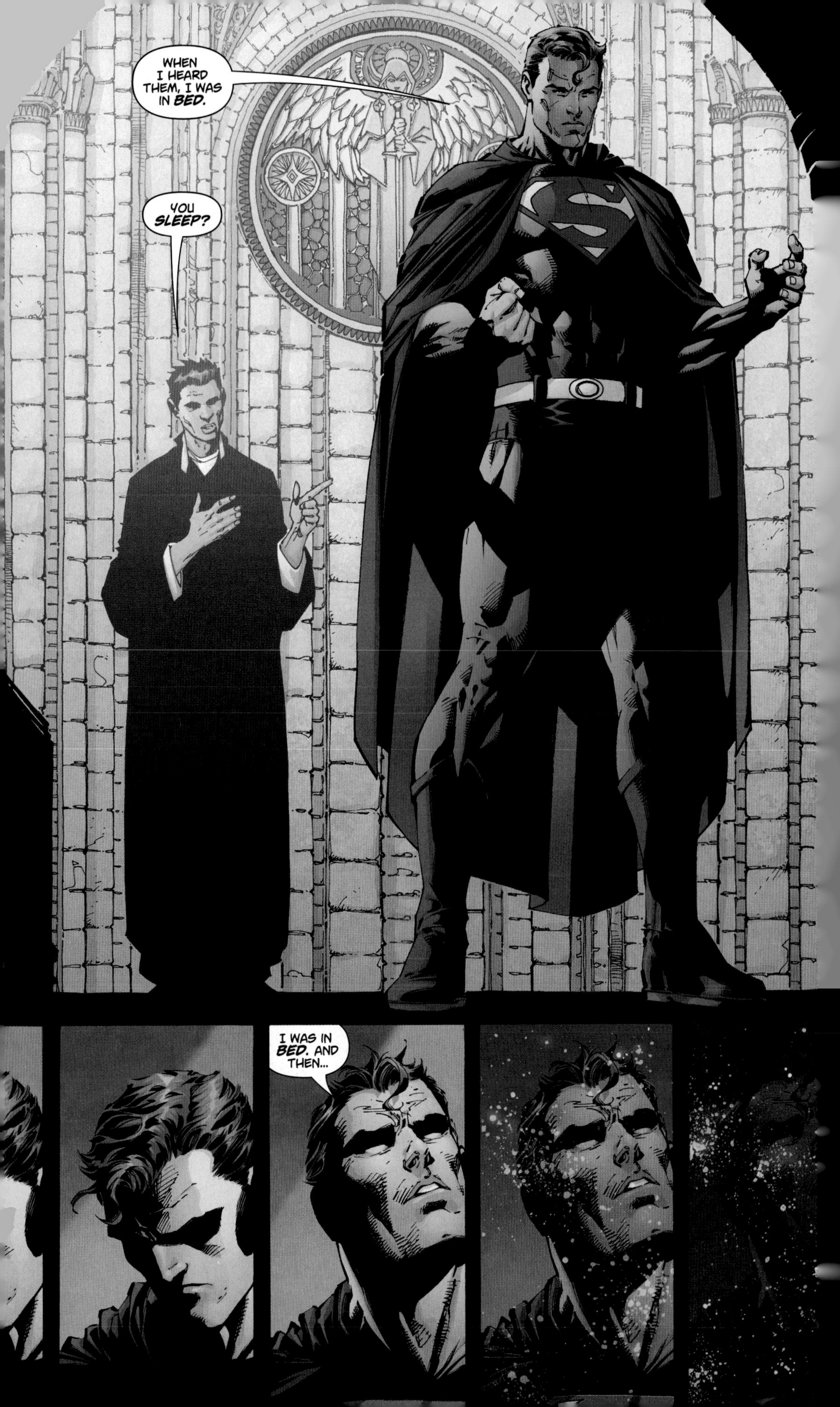
WHEN I HEARD THEM, I WAS IN BED.
YOU SLEEP?
I WAS IN BED. AND THEN...

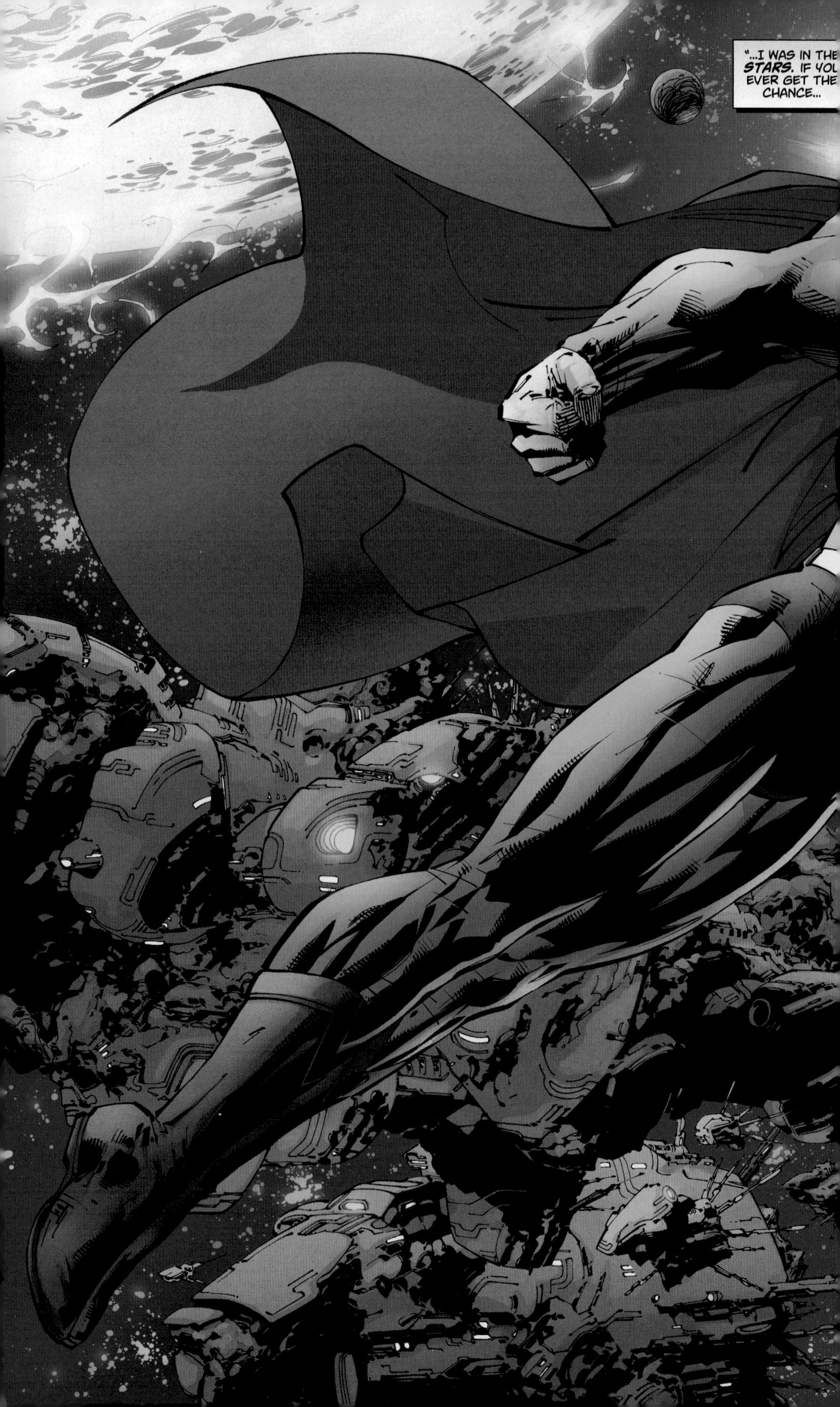
"...I WAS IN THE STARS. IF YOU EVER GET THE CHANCE...

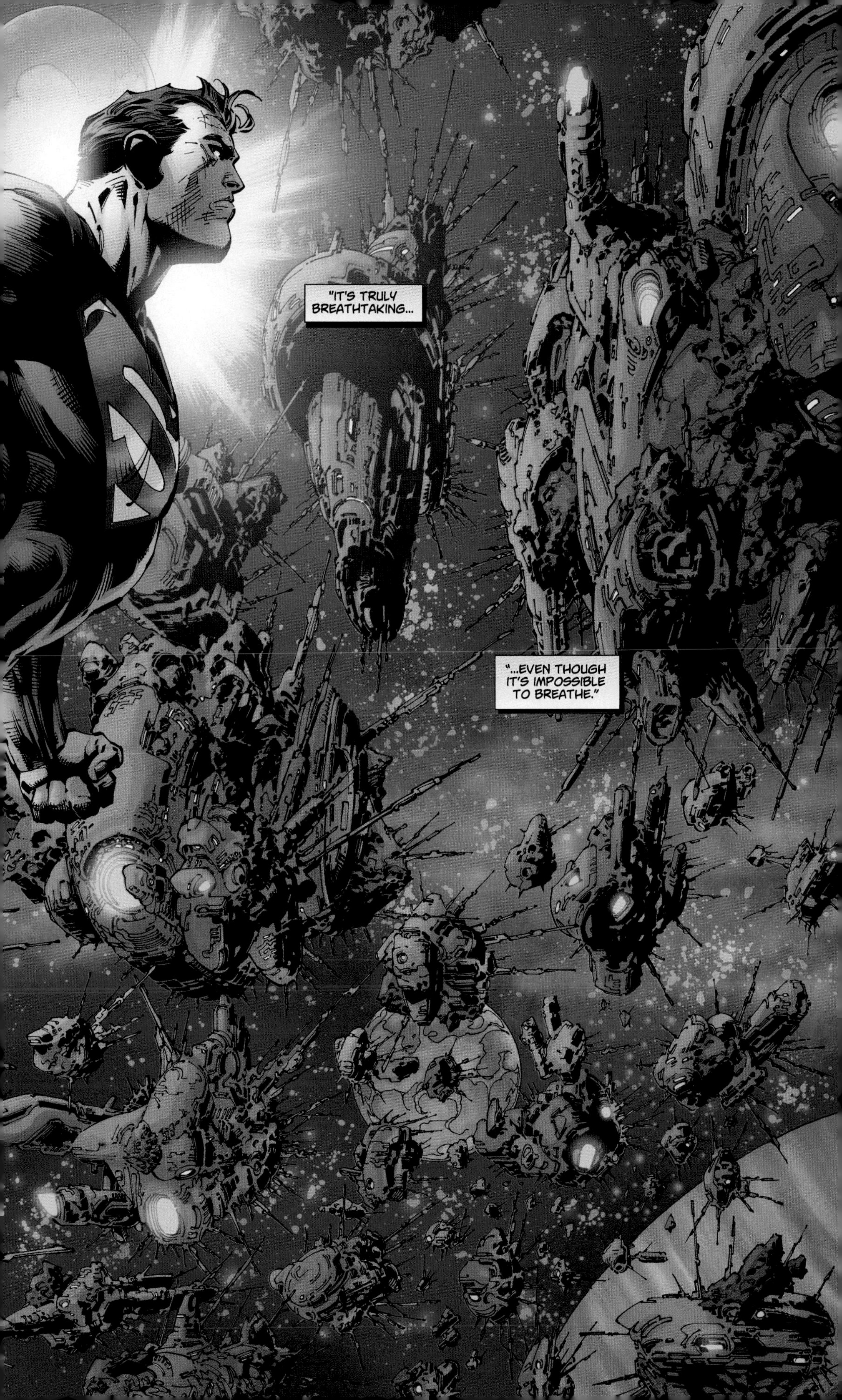
"IT'S TRULY BREATHTAKING...
"...EVEN THOUGH IT'S IMPOSSIBLE TO BREATHE."

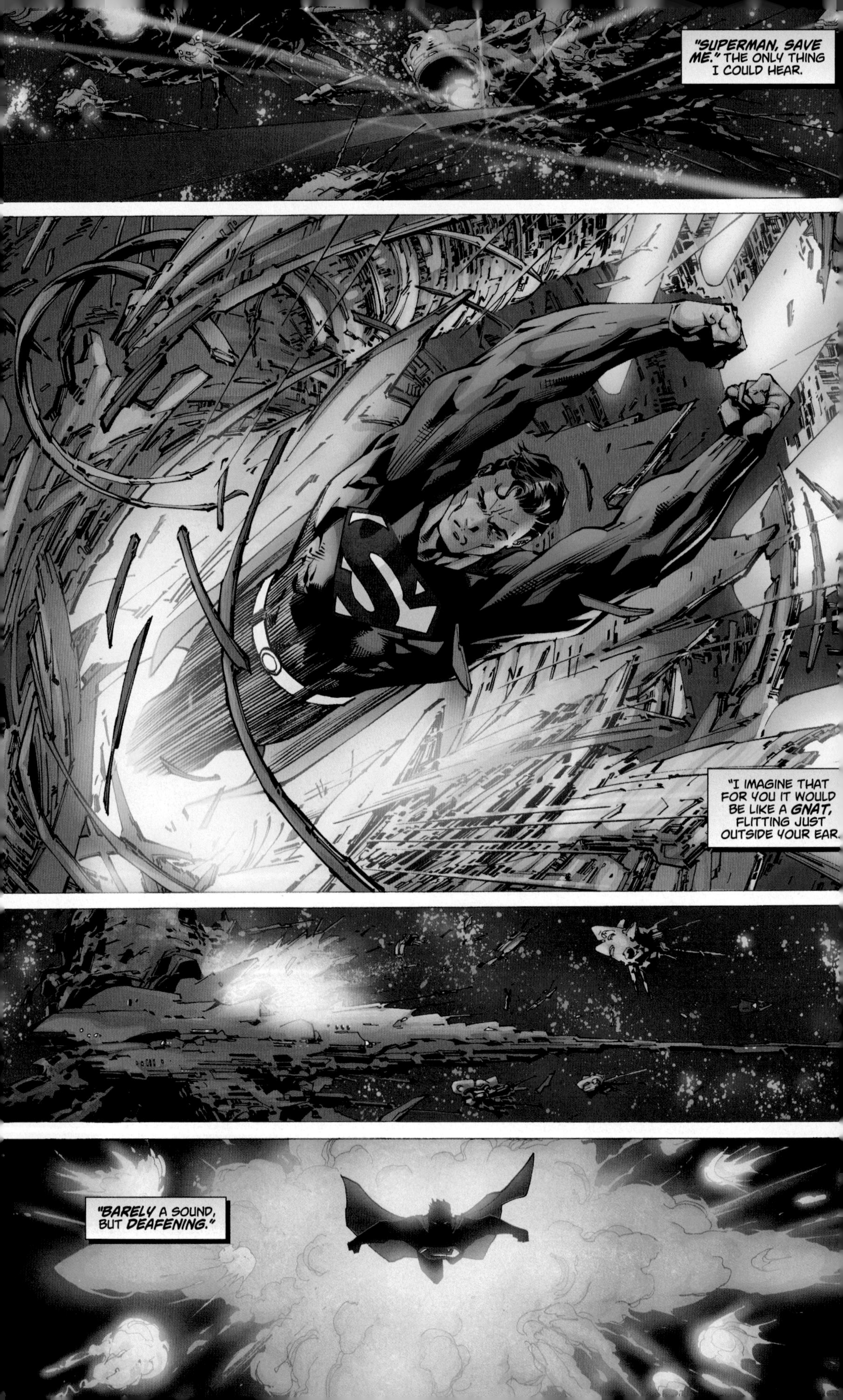
"SUPERMAN, SAVE ME." THE ONLY THING I COULD HEAR.
"I IMAGINE THAT FOR YOU IT WOULD BE LIKE A GNAT, FLITTING JUST OUTSIDE YOUR EAR.
"BARELY A SOUND, BUT DEAFENING."

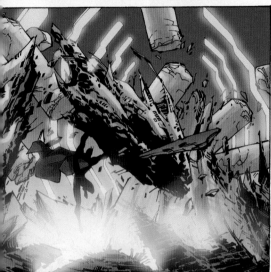

"SUPERMAN...

"SAVE ME."

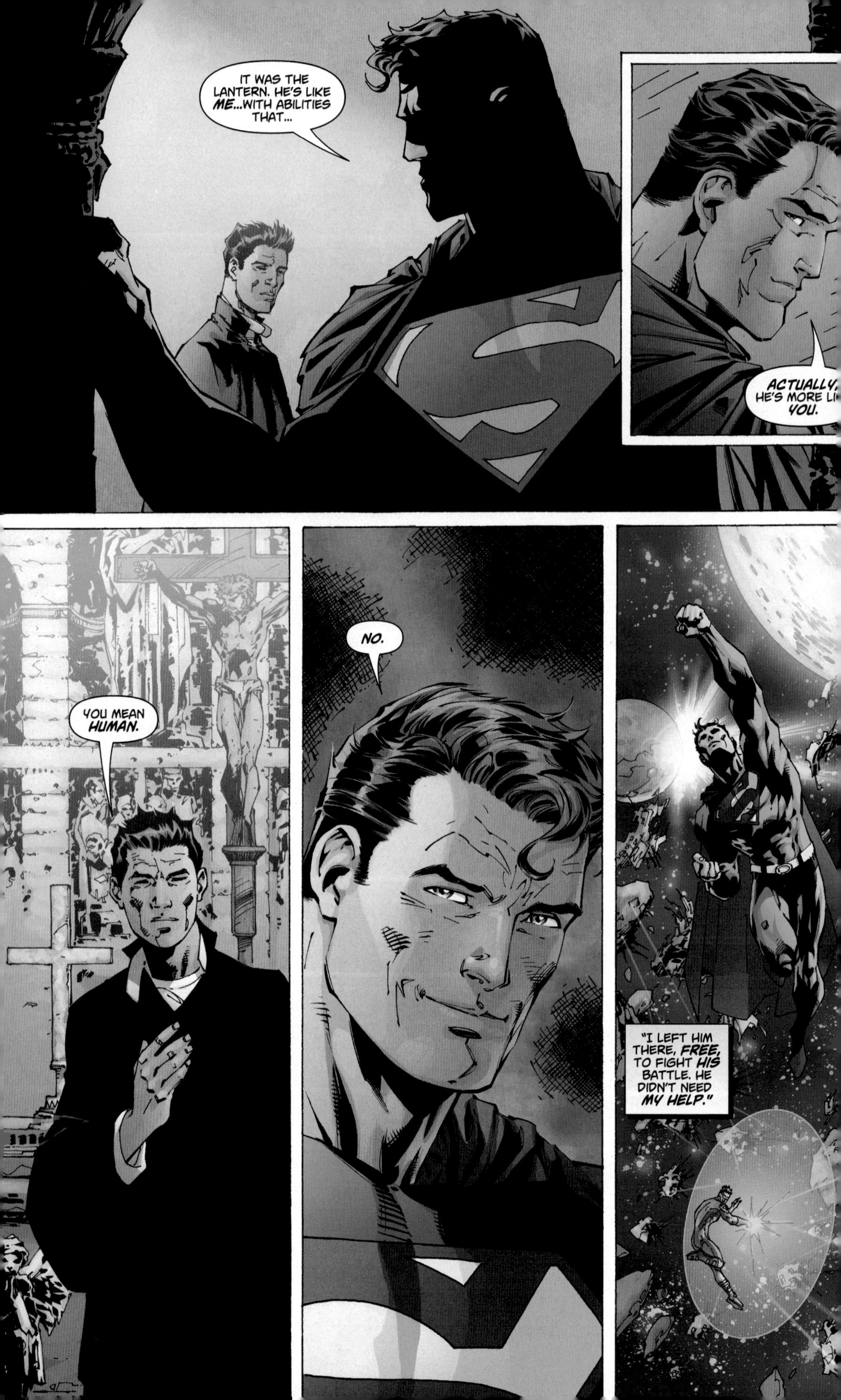
IT WAS THE LANTERN. HE'S LIKE ME...WITH ABILITIES THAT...
ACTUALLY, HE'S MORE LI YOU.
YOU MEAN HUMAN.
NO.
"I LEFT HIM THERE, FREE, TO FIGHT HIS BATTLE. HE DIDN'T NEED MY HELP."

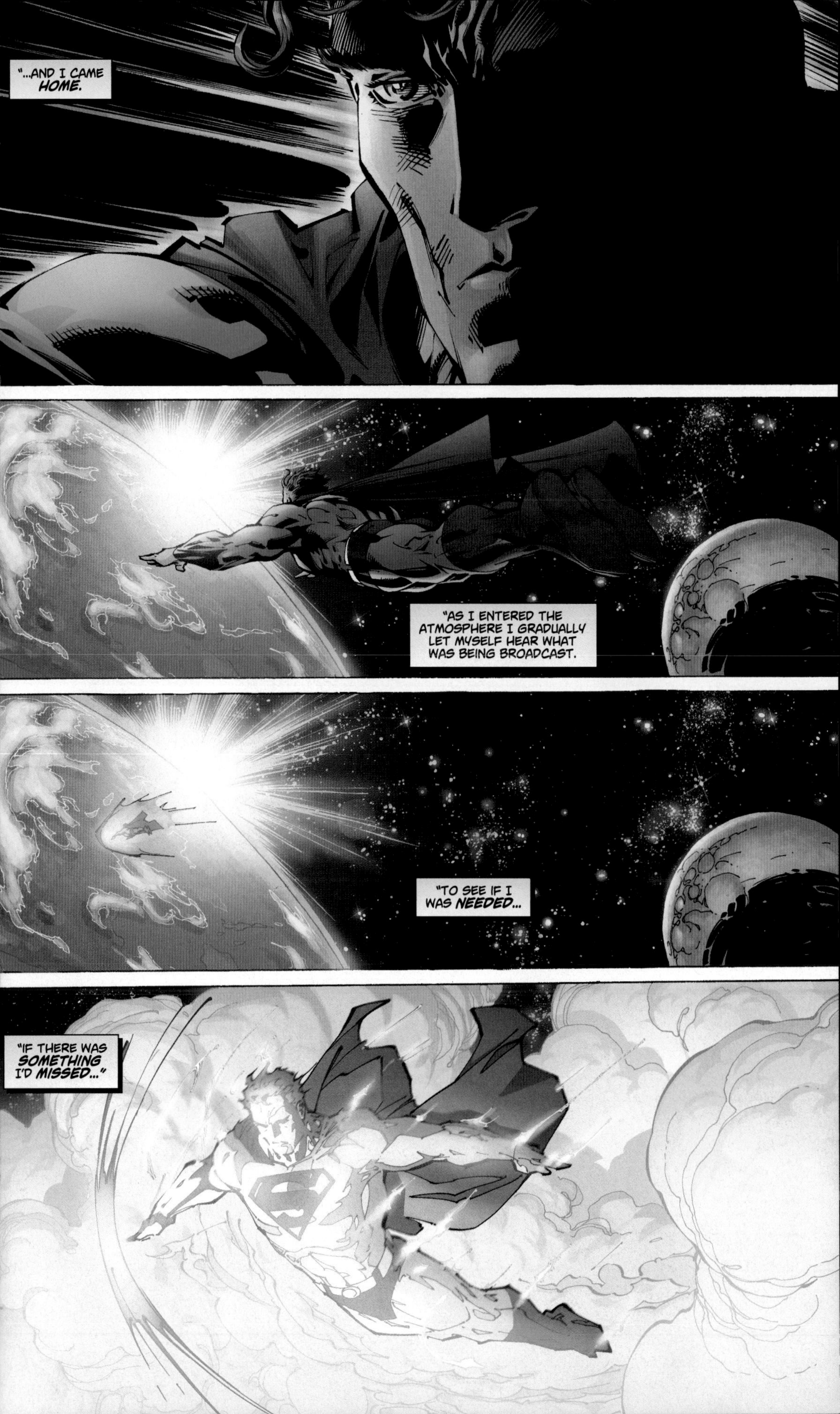
"...AND I CAME HOME.
"AS I ENTERED THE ATMOSPHERE I GRADUALLY LET MYSELF HEAR WHAT WAS BEING BROADCAST.
"TO SEE IF I WAS NEEDED...
"IF THERE WAS SOMETHING I'D MISSED..."

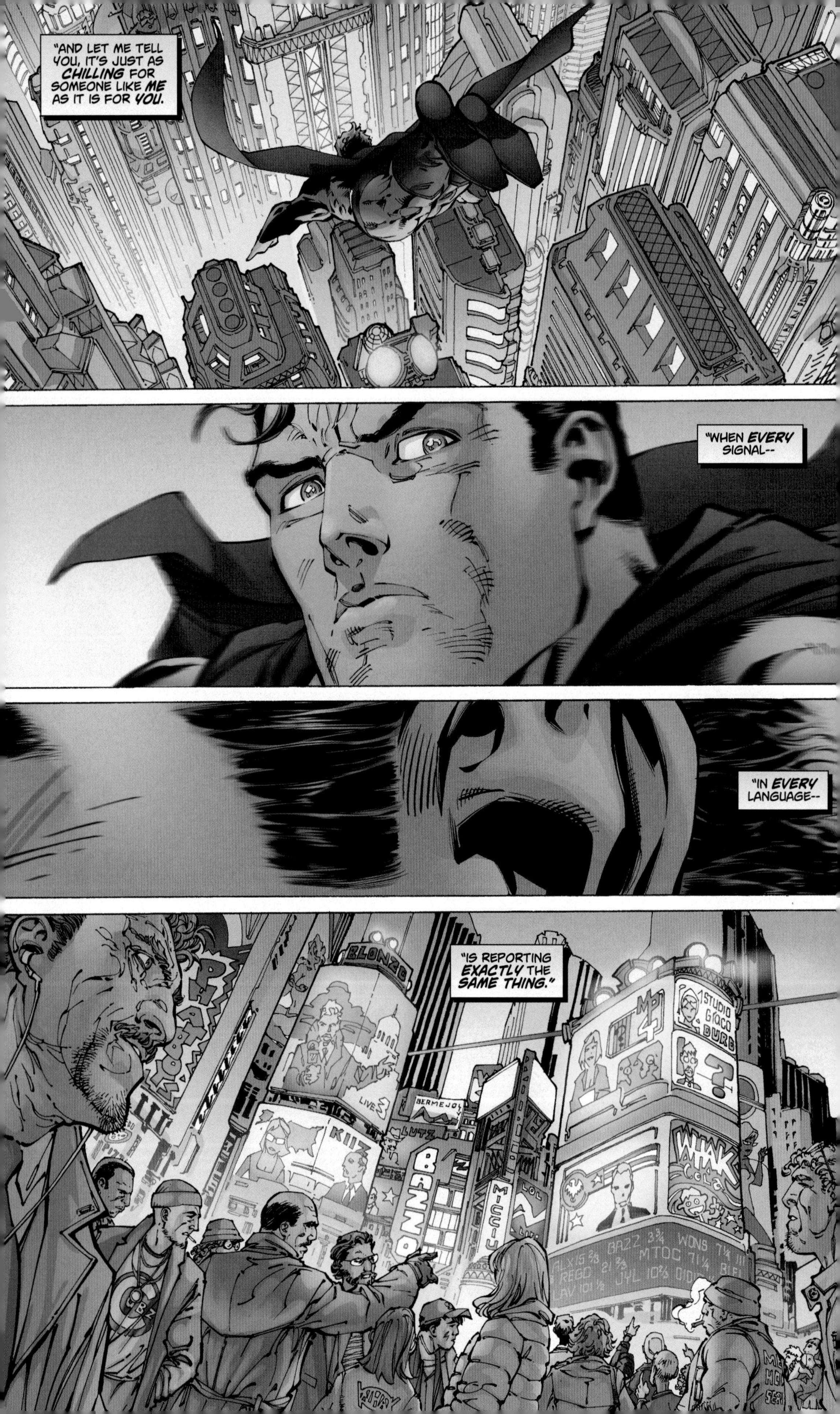
"AND LET ME TELL YOU, IT'S JUST AS CHILLING FOR SOMEONE LIKE ME AS IT IS FOR YOU.
"WHEN EVERY SIGNAL--
"IN EVERY LANGUAGE--
"IS REPORTING EXACTLY THE SAME THING."
BLONZO
LIVE 3
BERMEJO
LUTZ
KUZ
BANZO
STUDIO GIOCO DURB
WHAK COLA
BAZZ 3¾
WONS 7¼
MTOC 7¼
REGO 21
JYL 10⅝
LAV 101½

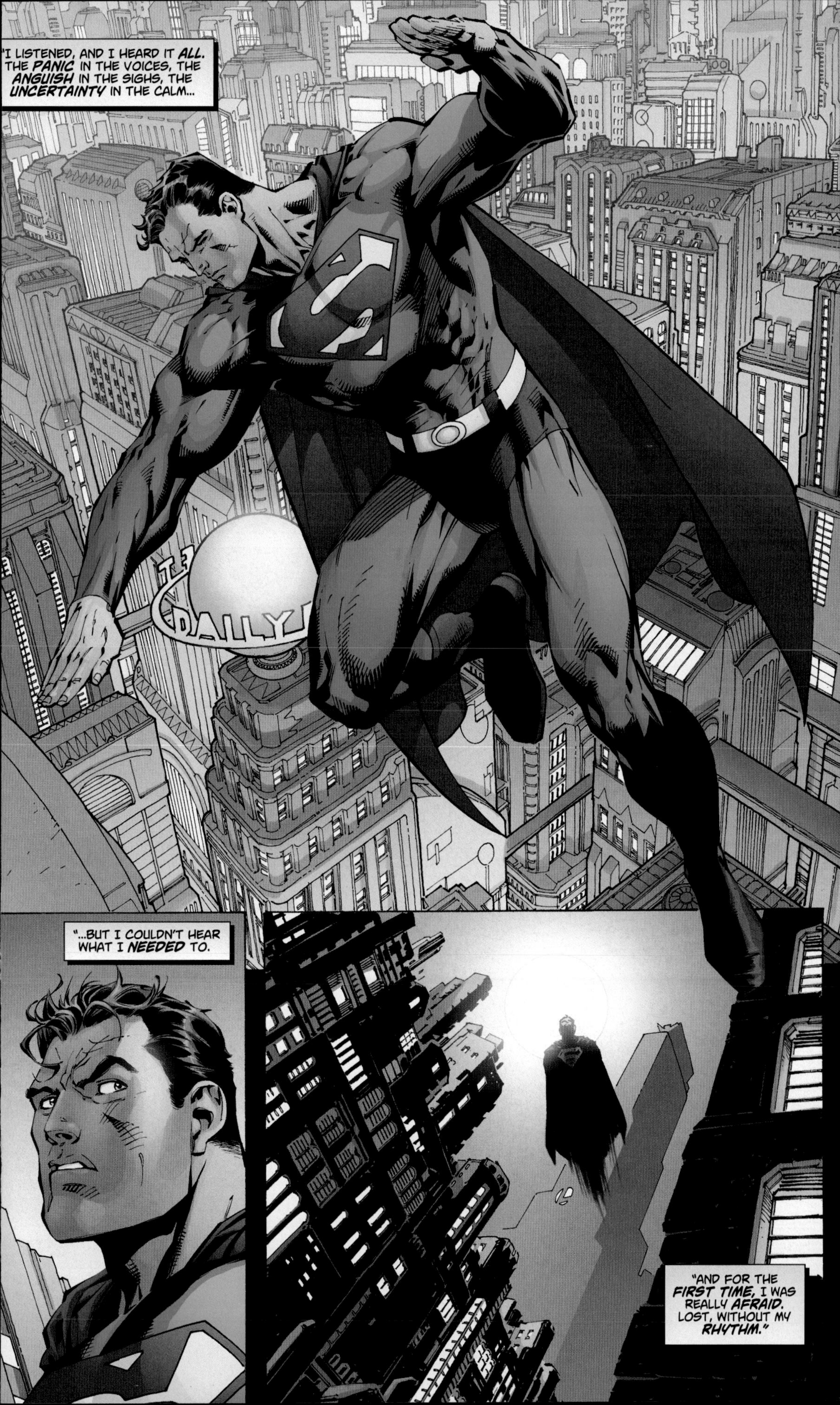
"I LISTENED, AND I HEARD IT ALL. THE PANIC IN THE VOICES, THE ANGUISH IN THE SIGHS, THE UNCERTAINTY IN THE CALM...
"...BUT I COULDN'T HEAR WHAT I NEEDED TO.
"AND FOR THE FIRST TIME, I WAS REALLY AFRAID. LOST, WITHOUT MY RHYTHM."

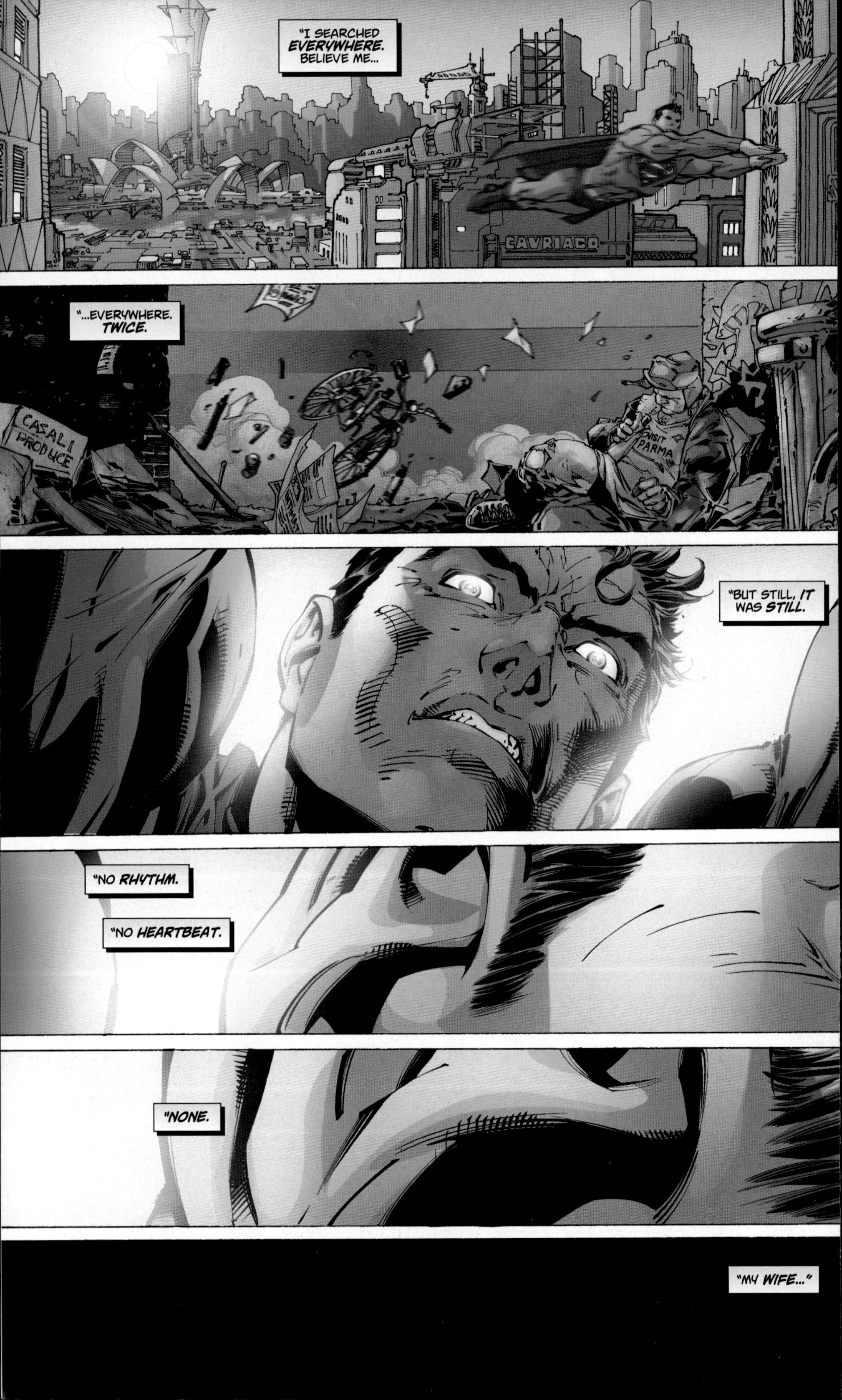

"I SEARCHED EVERYWHERE. BELIEVE ME...
CAVRIACO
"...EVERYWHERE. TWICE.
CASALI PRODUCE
VISIT PARMA
"BUT STILL, IT WAS STILL.
"NO RHYTHM.
"NO HEARTBEAT.
"NONE.
"MY WIFE..."

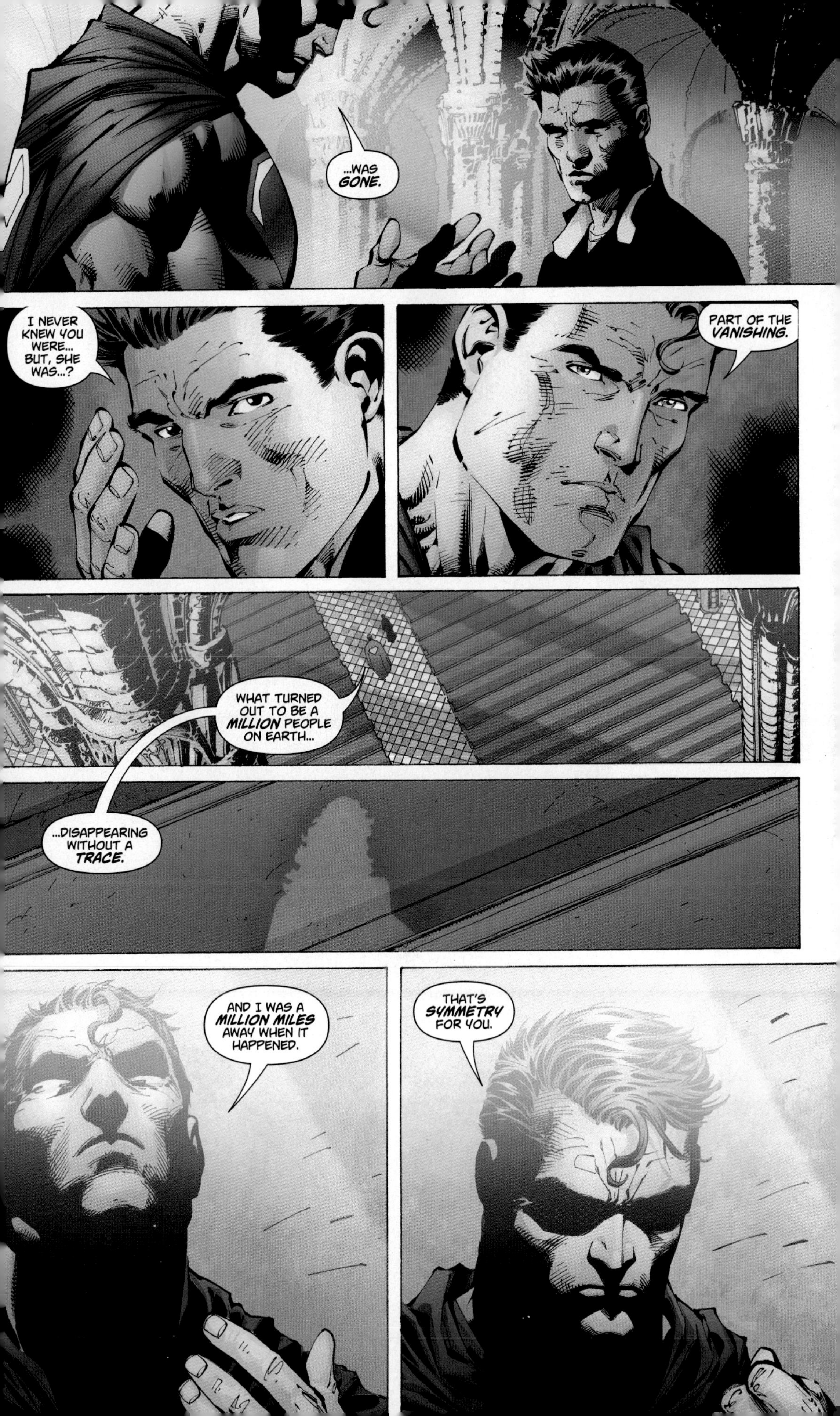

...WAS GONE.
I NEVER KNEW YOU WERE... BUT, SHE WAS...?
PART OF THE VANISHING.
WHAT TURNED OUT TO BE A MILLION PEOPLE ON EARTH...
...DISAPPEARING WITHOUT A TRACE.
AND I WAS A MILLION MILES AWAY WHEN IT HAPPENED.
THAT'S SYMMETRY FOR YOU.

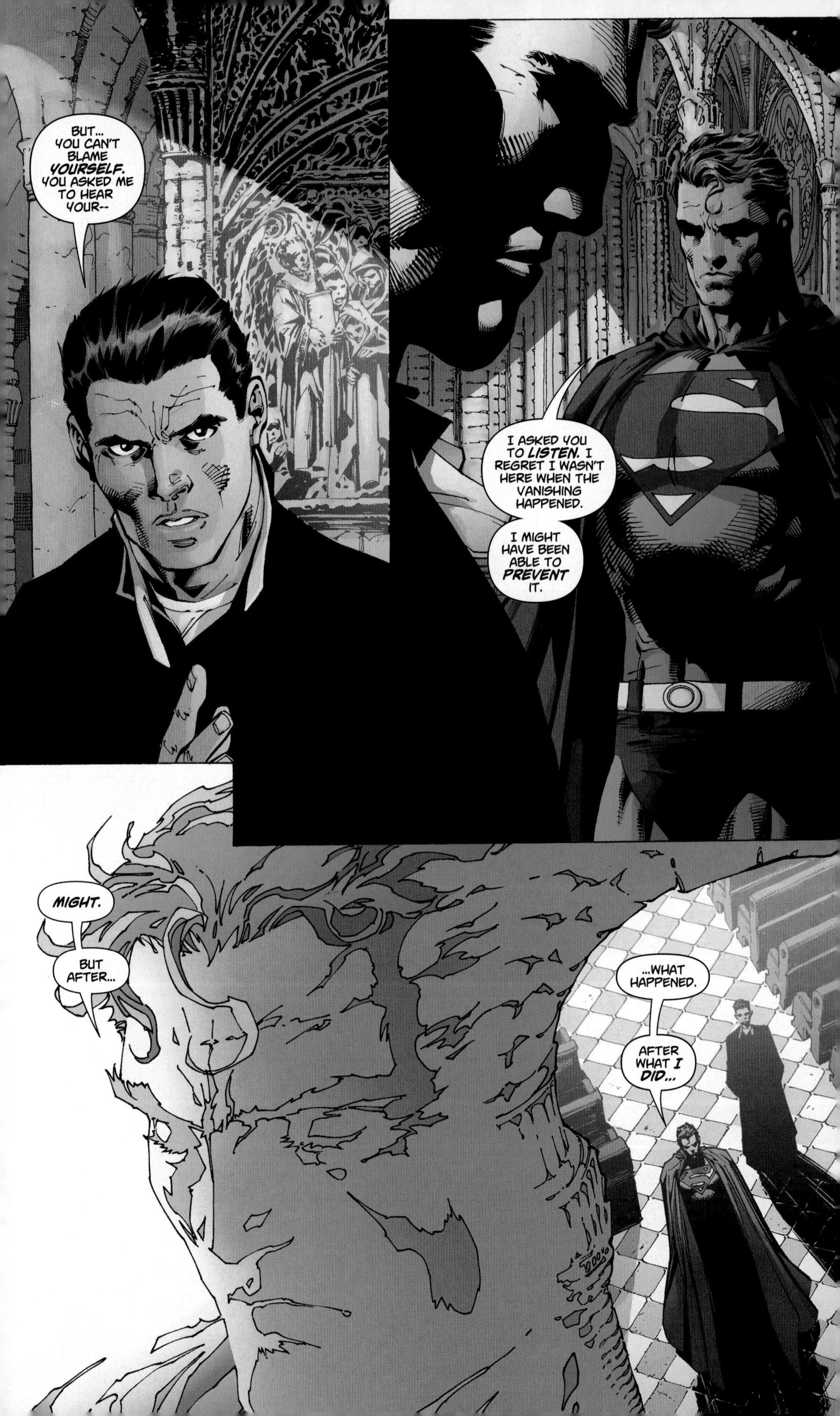
BUT... YOU CAN'T BLAME *YOURSELF*. YOU ASKED ME TO HEAR YOUR--
I ASKED YOU TO *LISTEN*. I REGRET I WASN'T HERE WHEN THE VANISHING HAPPENED.
I MIGHT HAVE BEEN ABLE TO *PREVENT* IT.
MIGHT.
BUT AFTER...
...WHAT HAPPENED.
AFTER WHAT *I DID*...

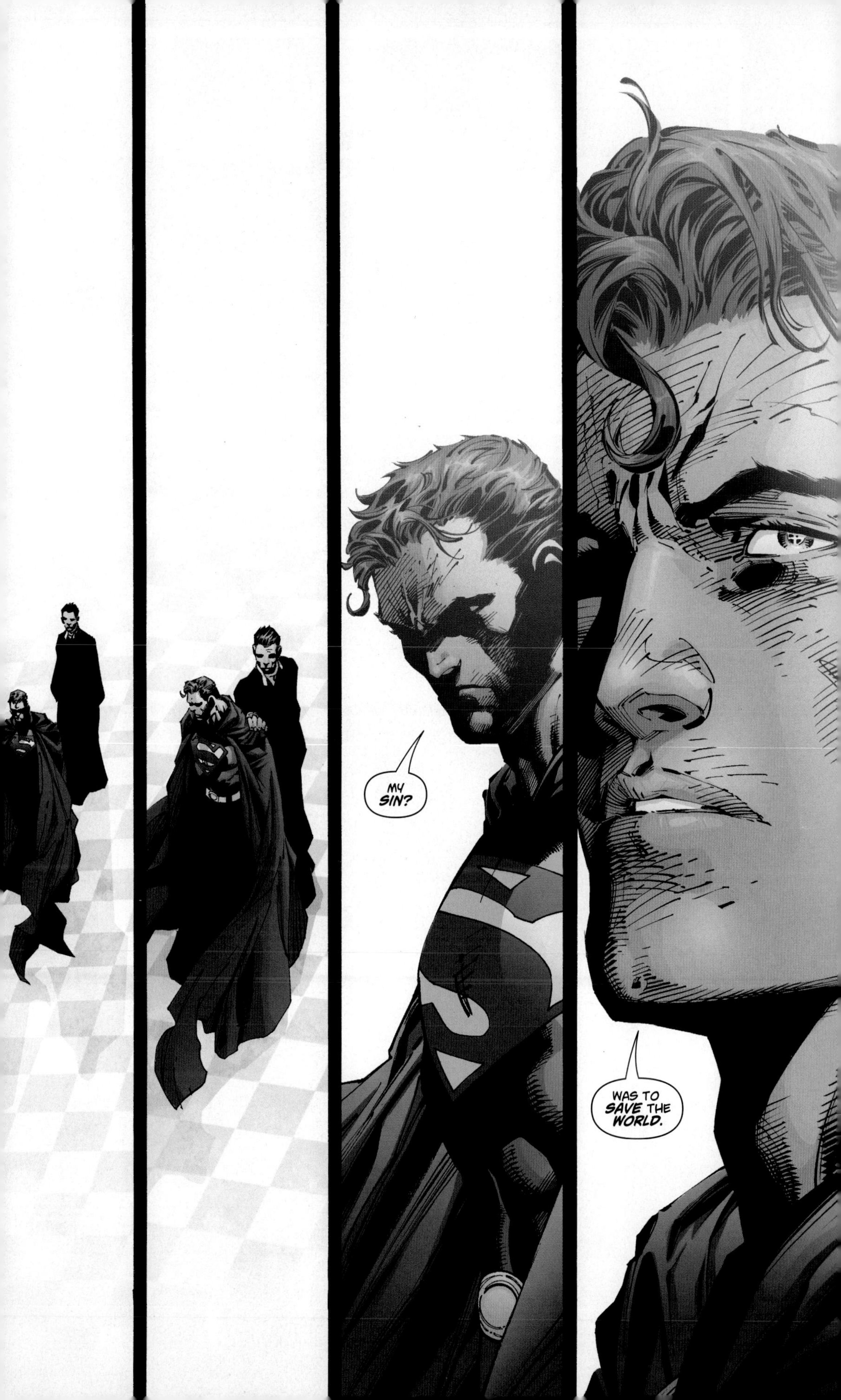

MY SIN?
WAS TO SAVE THE WORLD.

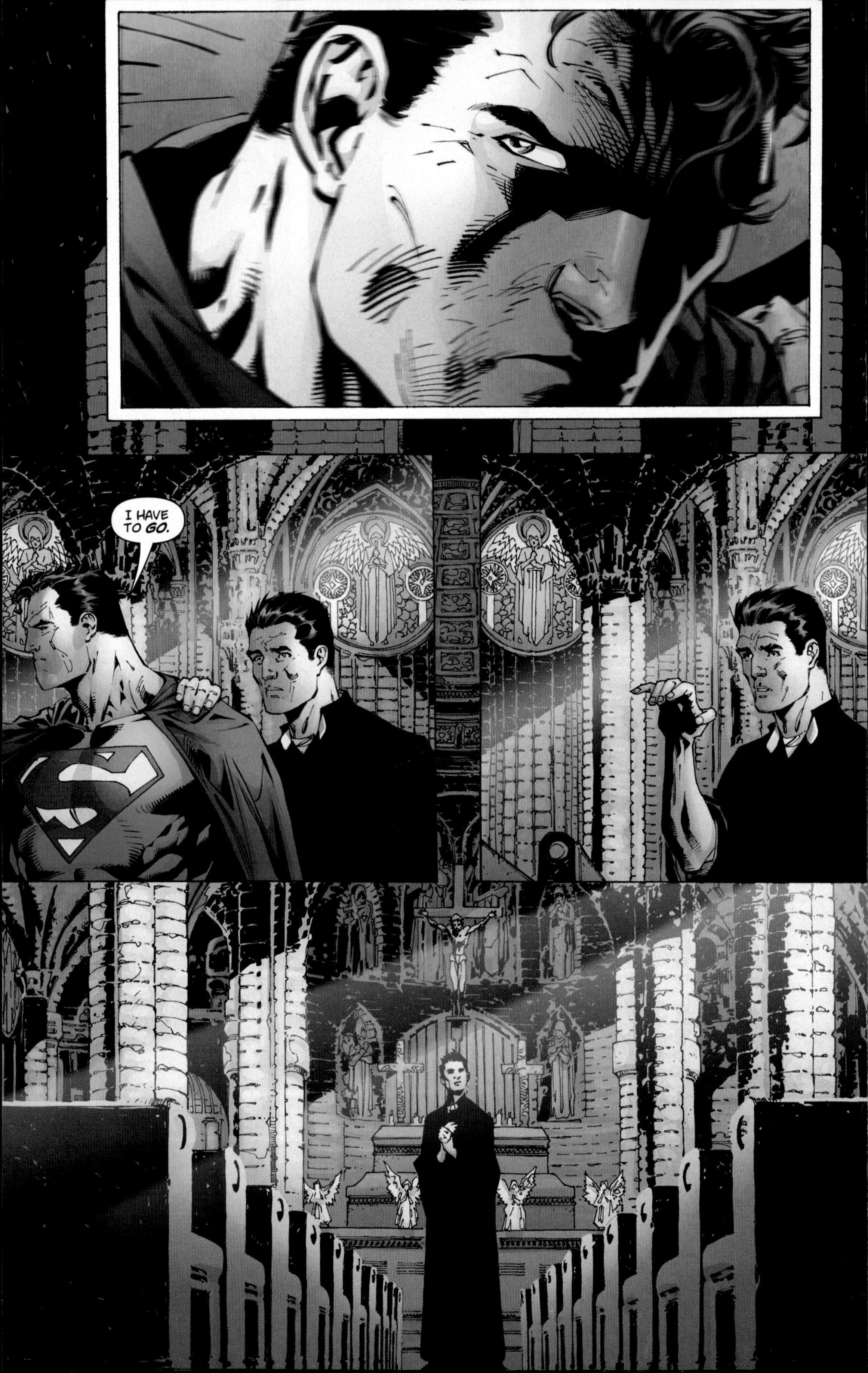
I HAVE TO GO.

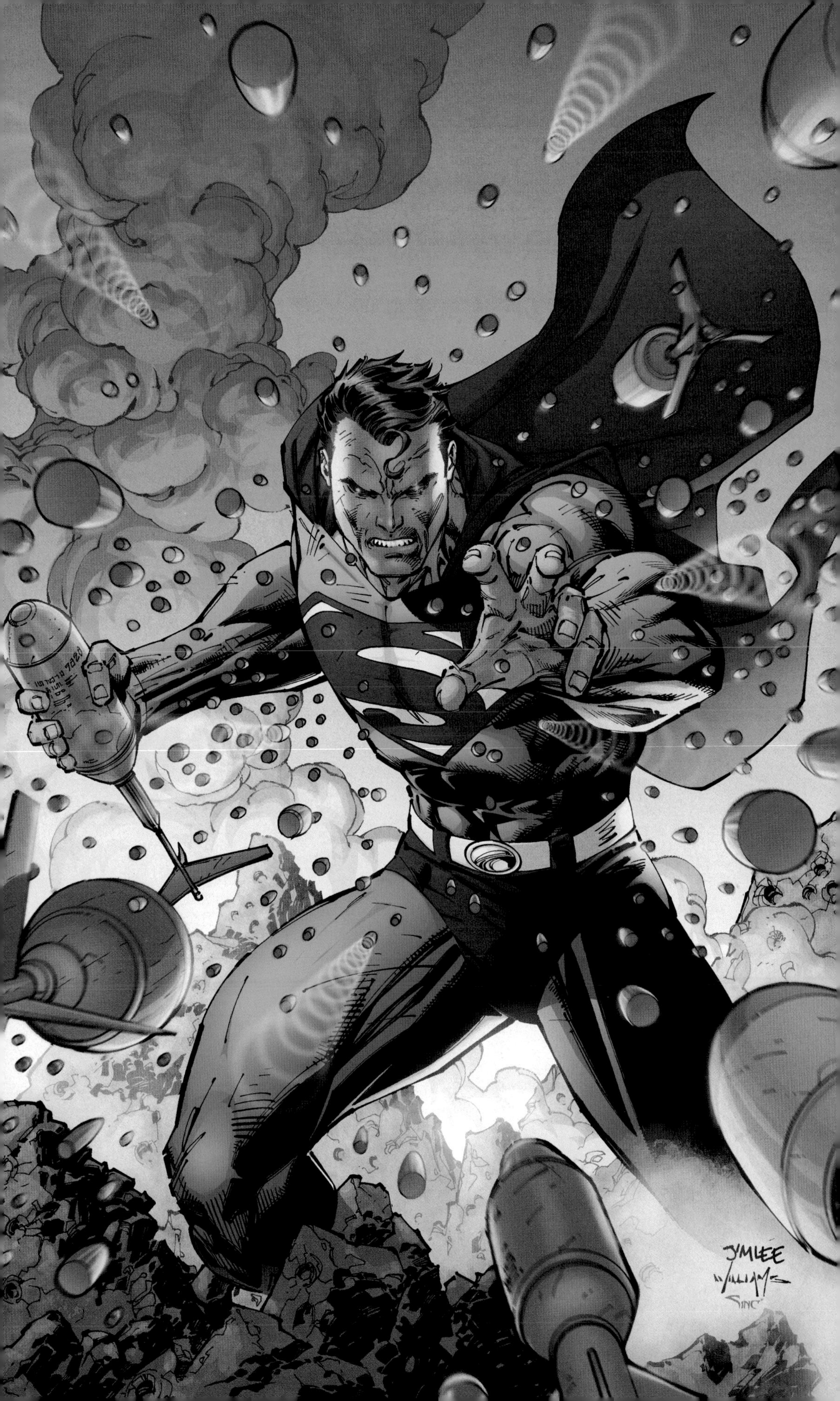

SUPERMAN 205
variant cover art by Michael Turner
with Peter Steigerwald

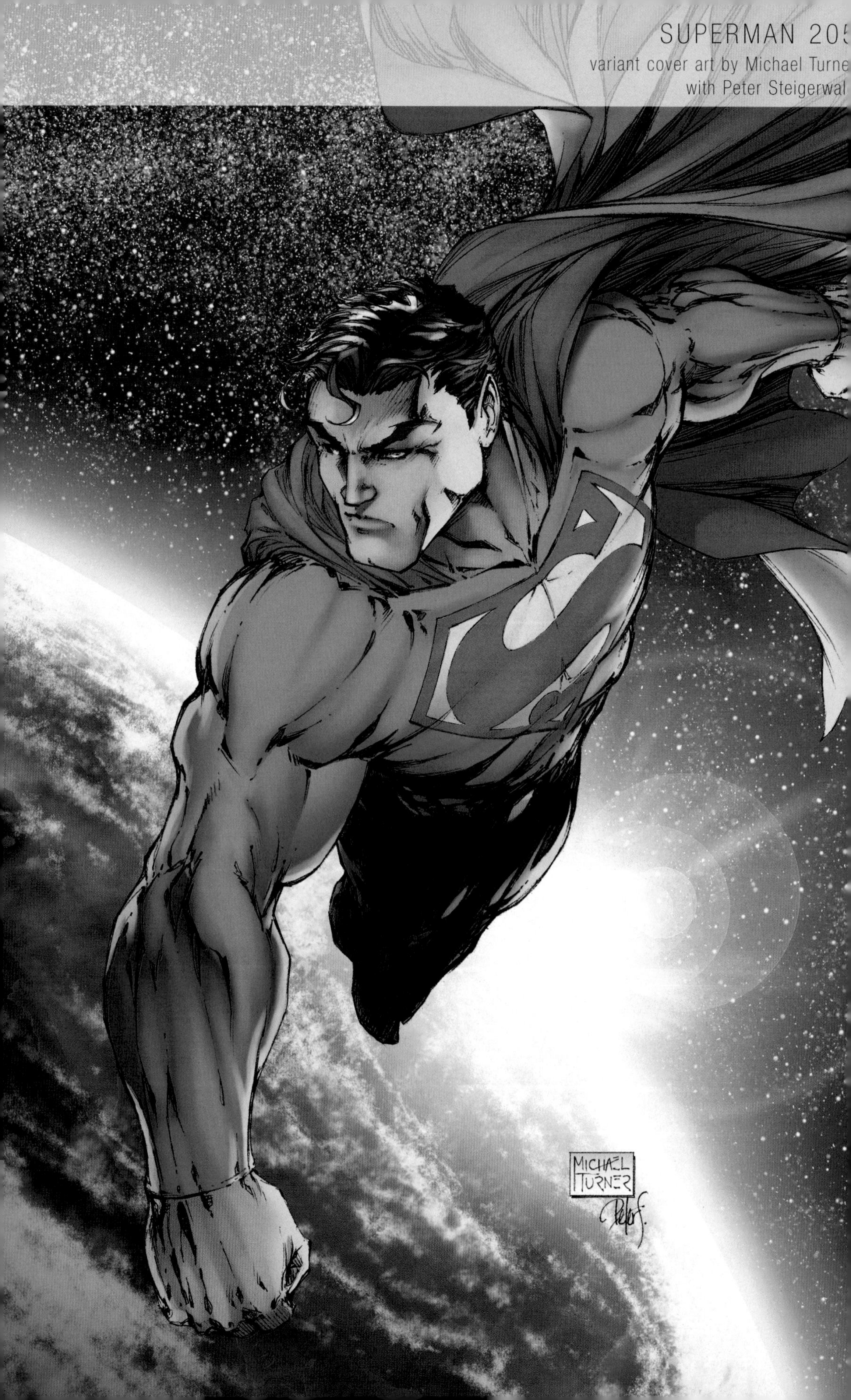
MICHAEL TURNER

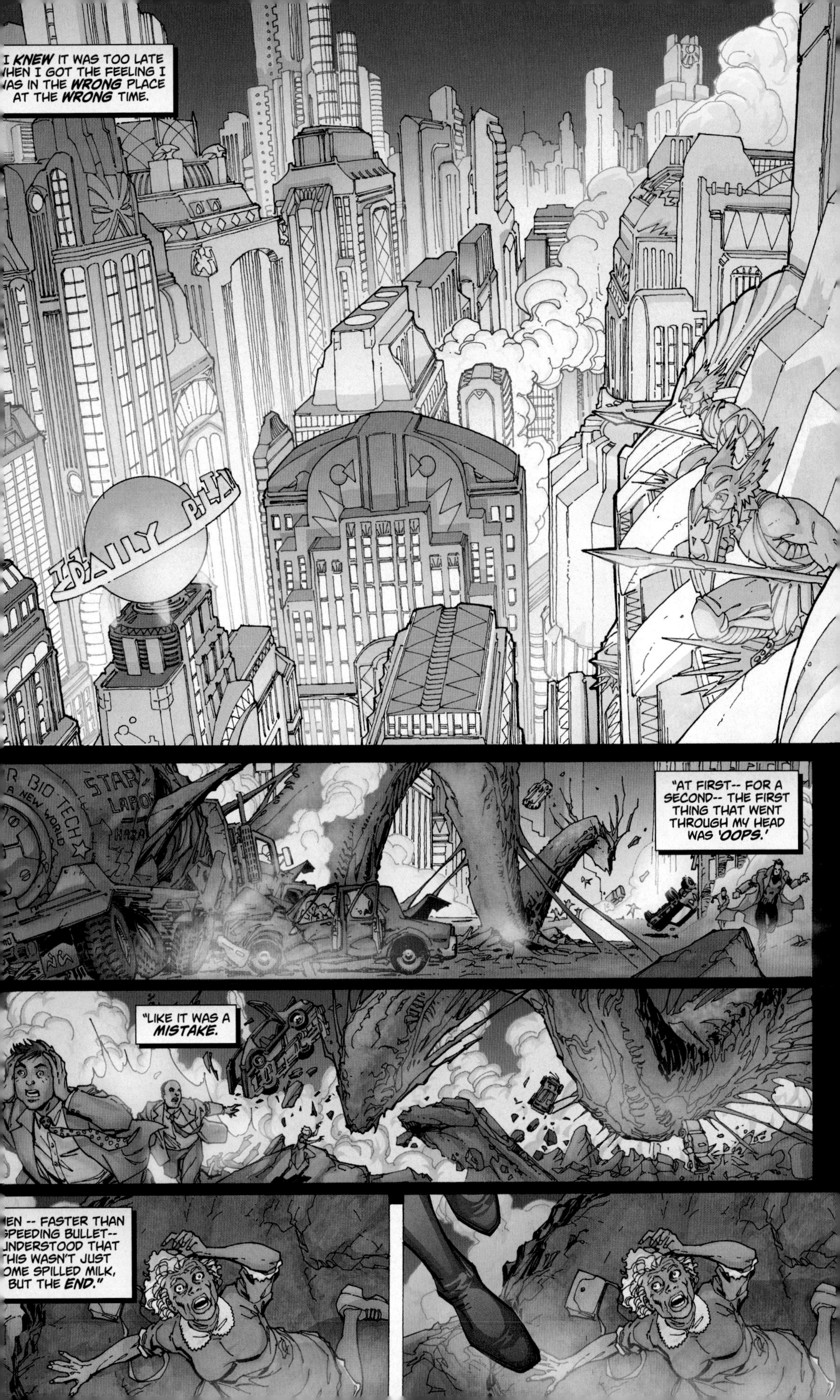
I KNEW IT WAS TOO LATE WHEN I GOT THE FEELING I WAS IN THE WRONG PLACE AT THE WRONG TIME.
"AT FIRST-- FOR A SECOND-- THE FIRST THING THAT WENT THROUGH MY HEAD WAS 'OOPS.'
"LIKE IT WAS A MISTAKE.
EN -- FASTER THAN SPEEDING BULLET-- UNDERSTOOD THAT THIS WASN'T JUST OME SPILLED MILK, BUT THE END."

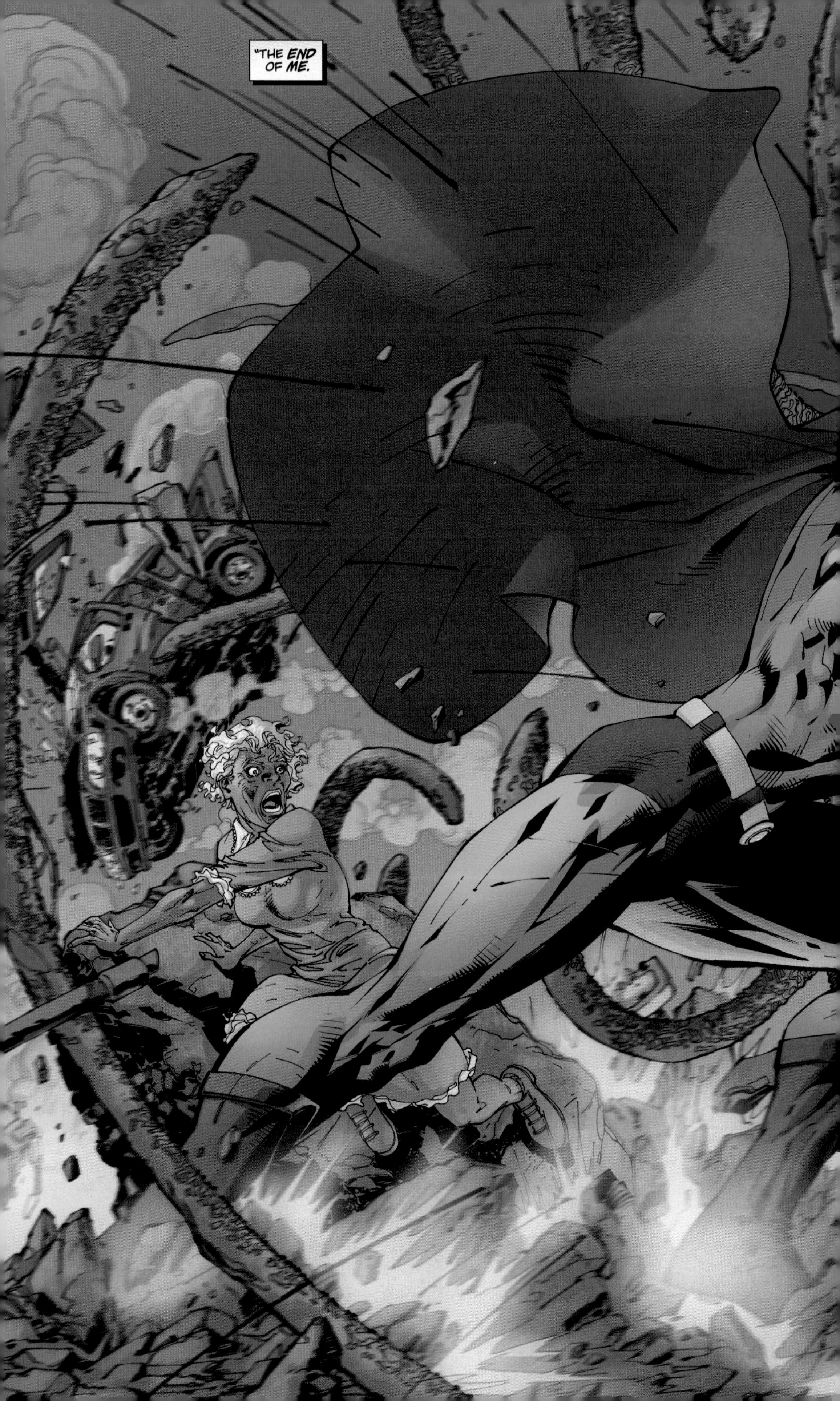
"THE *END* OF *ME*.

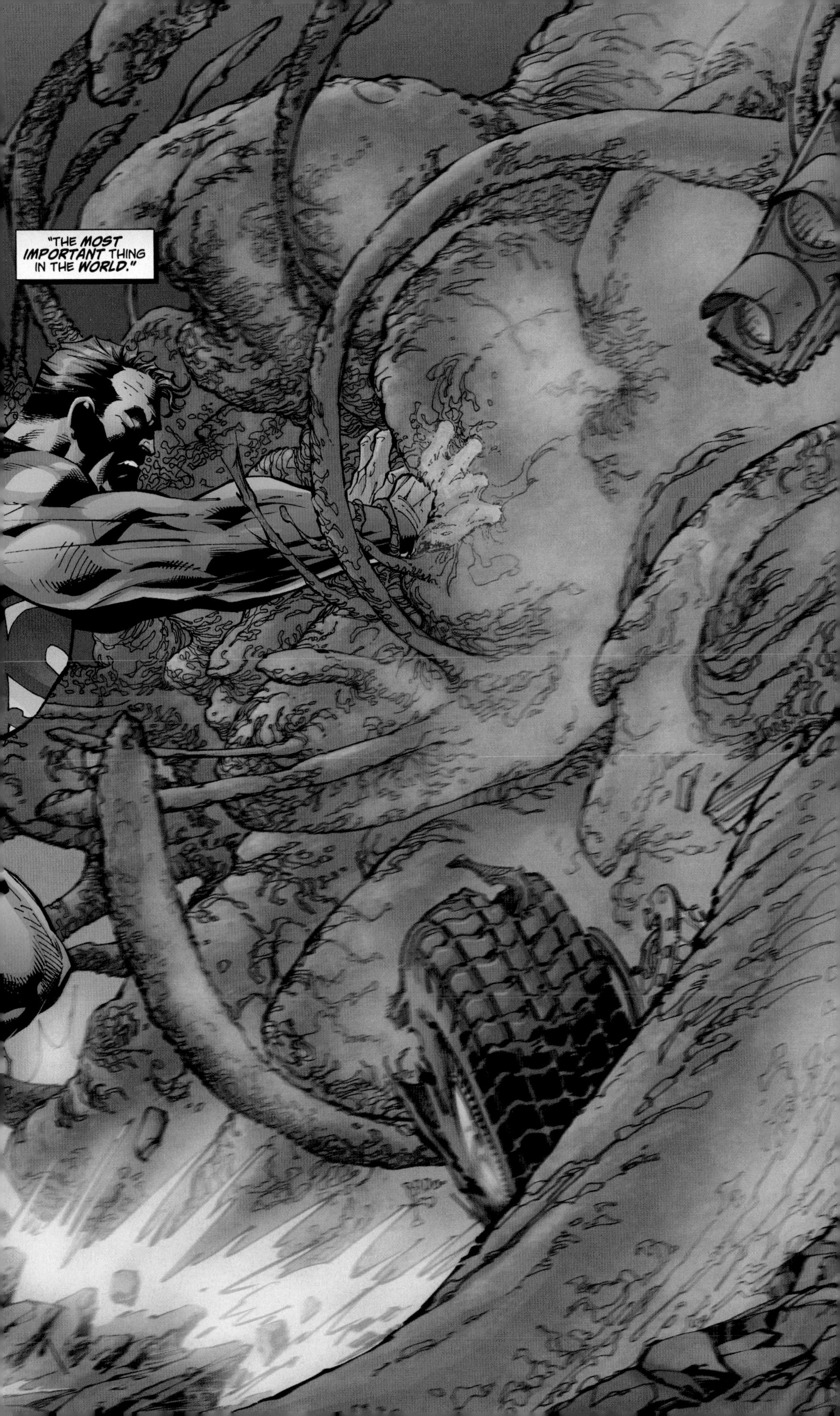
"THE MOST IMPORTANT THING IN THE WORLD."

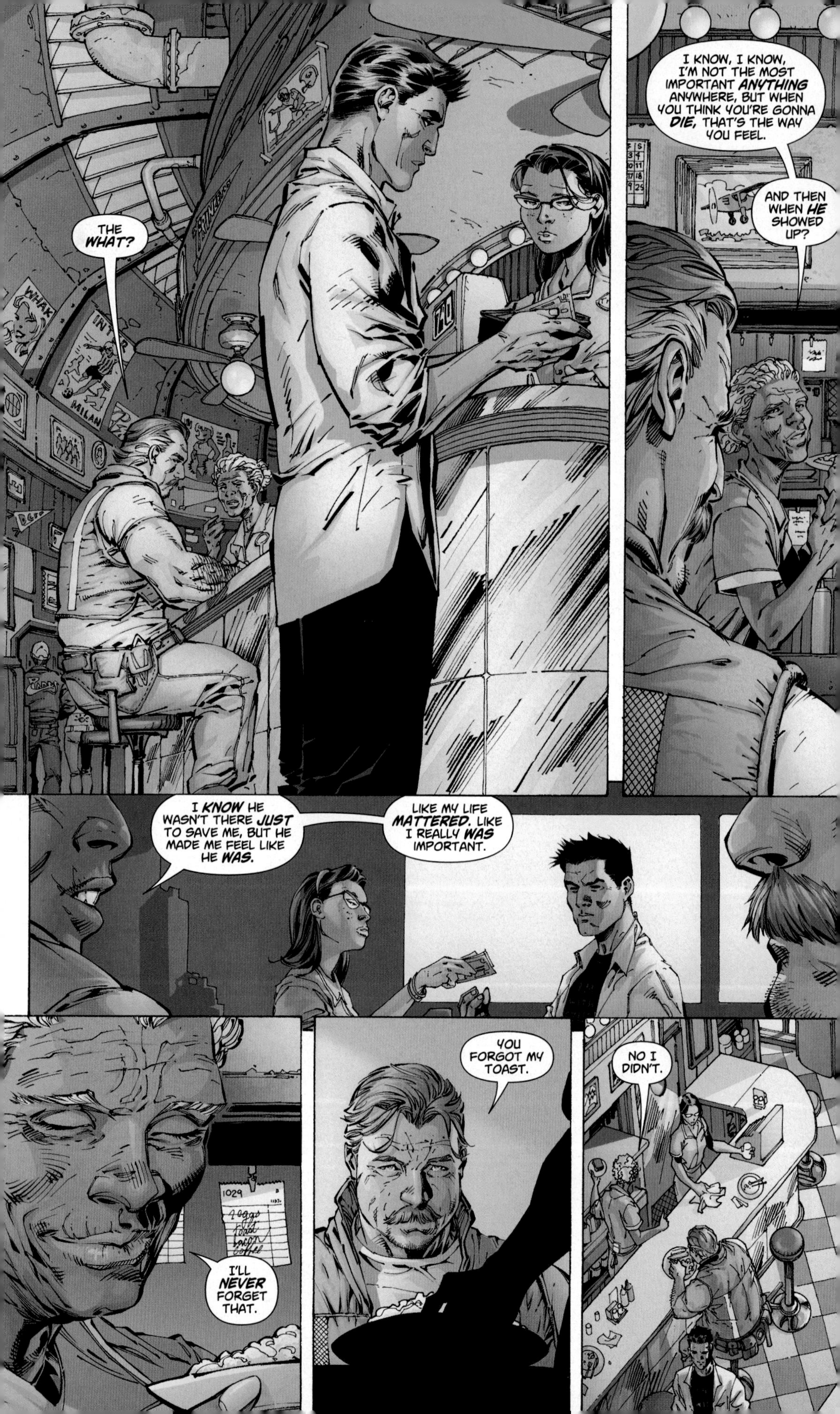
THE WHAT?
I KNOW, I KNOW, I'M NOT THE MOST IMPORTANT ANYTHING ANYWHERE, BUT WHEN YOU THINK YOU'RE GONNA DIE, THAT'S THE WAY YOU FEEL.
AND THEN WHEN HE SHOWED UP?
I KNOW HE WASN'T THERE JUST TO SAVE ME, BUT HE MADE ME FEEL LIKE HE WAS.
LIKE MY LIFE MATTERED. LIKE I REALLY WAS IMPORTANT.
I'LL NEVER FORGET THAT.
YOU FORGOT MY TOAST.
NO I DIDN'T.

HI, JOHN.

HEY, FATHER LEONE. WHAT CAN I GET FOR YOU? THE PEACHES-- OUT OF THIS WORLD.

CASALI'S MARKETPLACE
APPLES   79
GRANNIES   64
MACINTOSHS 64
PEACHES   39
BANANAS   40
ORANGES   47
NECTARINES 39
TANGERINES 30
STRAWB.   9

SPECIALS
BEEF   =
CHICKEN   =
WA FISH
BLENDS   =
SMOOTHIES
DWICH
SALAD

HOW'S RANDY?

AH! Y'KNOW... KIDS.

HE'S NOT SICK IS HE?

NO...

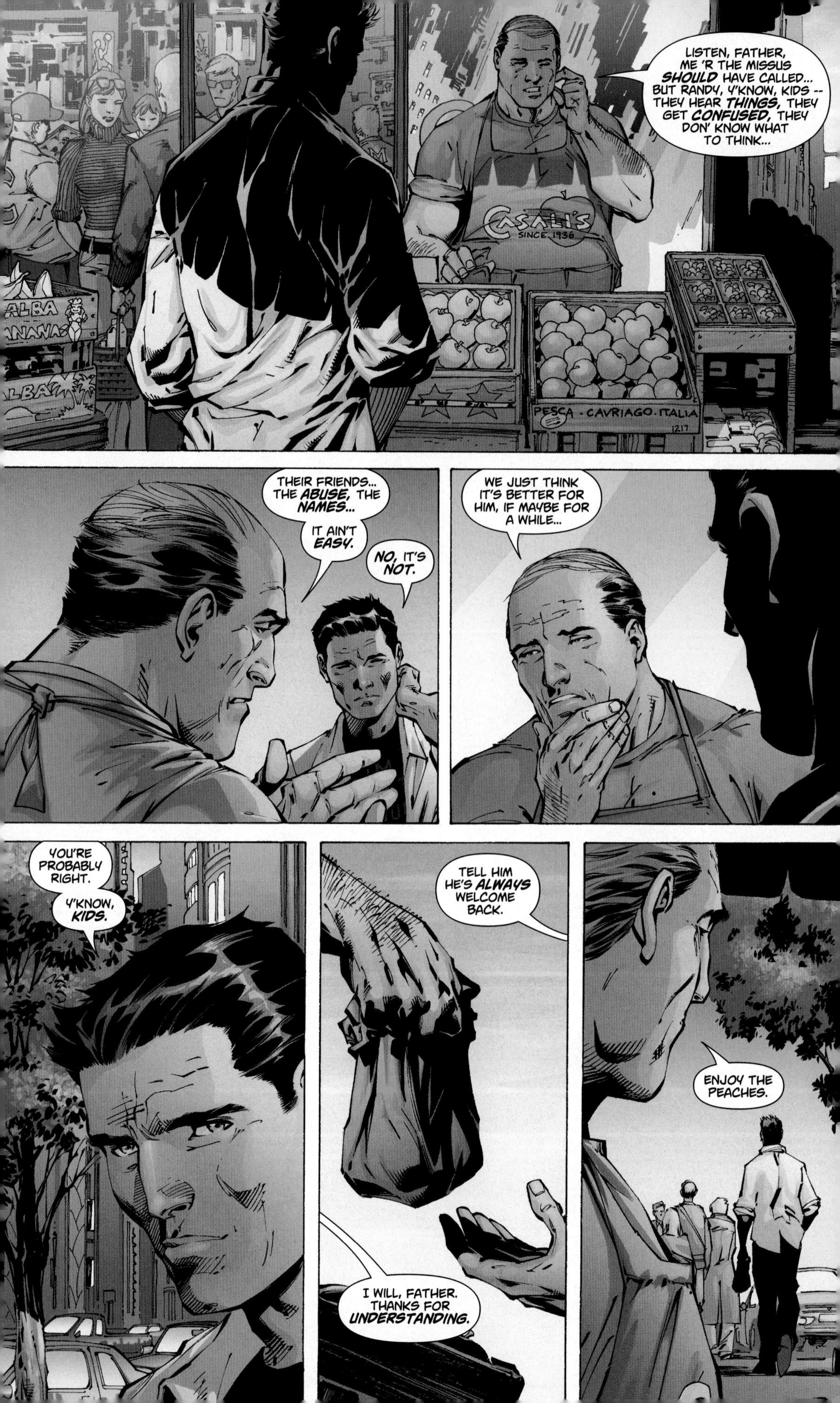
LISTEN, FATHER, ME 'R THE MISSUS SHOULD HAVE CALLED... BUT RANDY, Y'KNOW, KIDS -- THEY HEAR THINGS, THEY GET CONFUSED, THEY DON' KNOW WHAT TO THINK...
CASALI'S SINCE 1936
ALBA
ALBA
PESCA - CAVRIAGO. ITALIA
1217
THEIR FRIENDS... THE ABUSE, THE NAMES...
IT AIN'T EASY.
NO, IT'S NOT.
WE JUST THINK IT'S BETTER FOR HIM, IF MAYBE FOR A WHILE...
YOU'RE PROBABLY RIGHT.
Y'KNOW, KIDS.
TELL HIM HE'S ALWAYS WELCOME BACK.
I WILL, FATHER. THANKS FOR UNDERSTANDING.
ENJOY THE PEACHES.

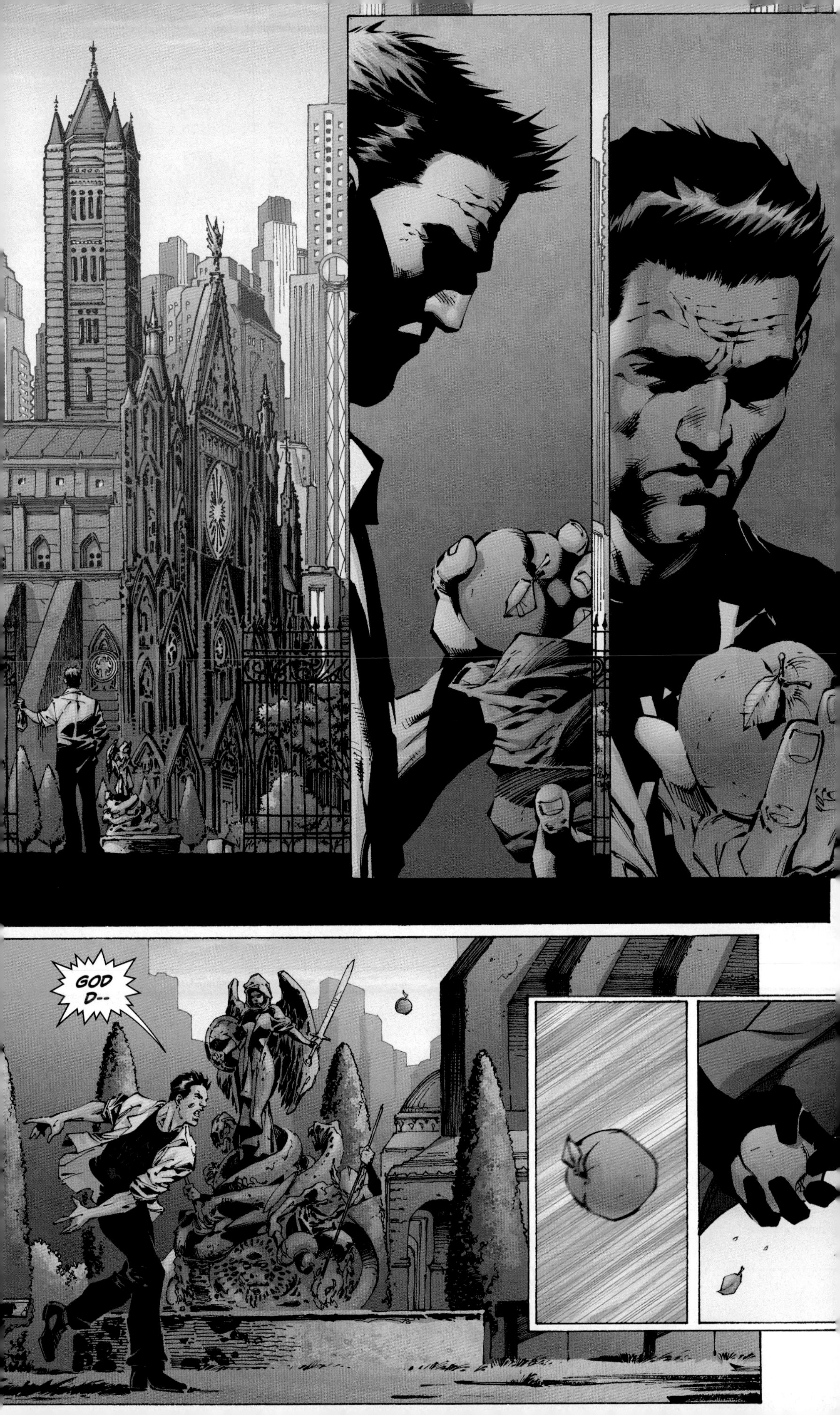
GOD D--

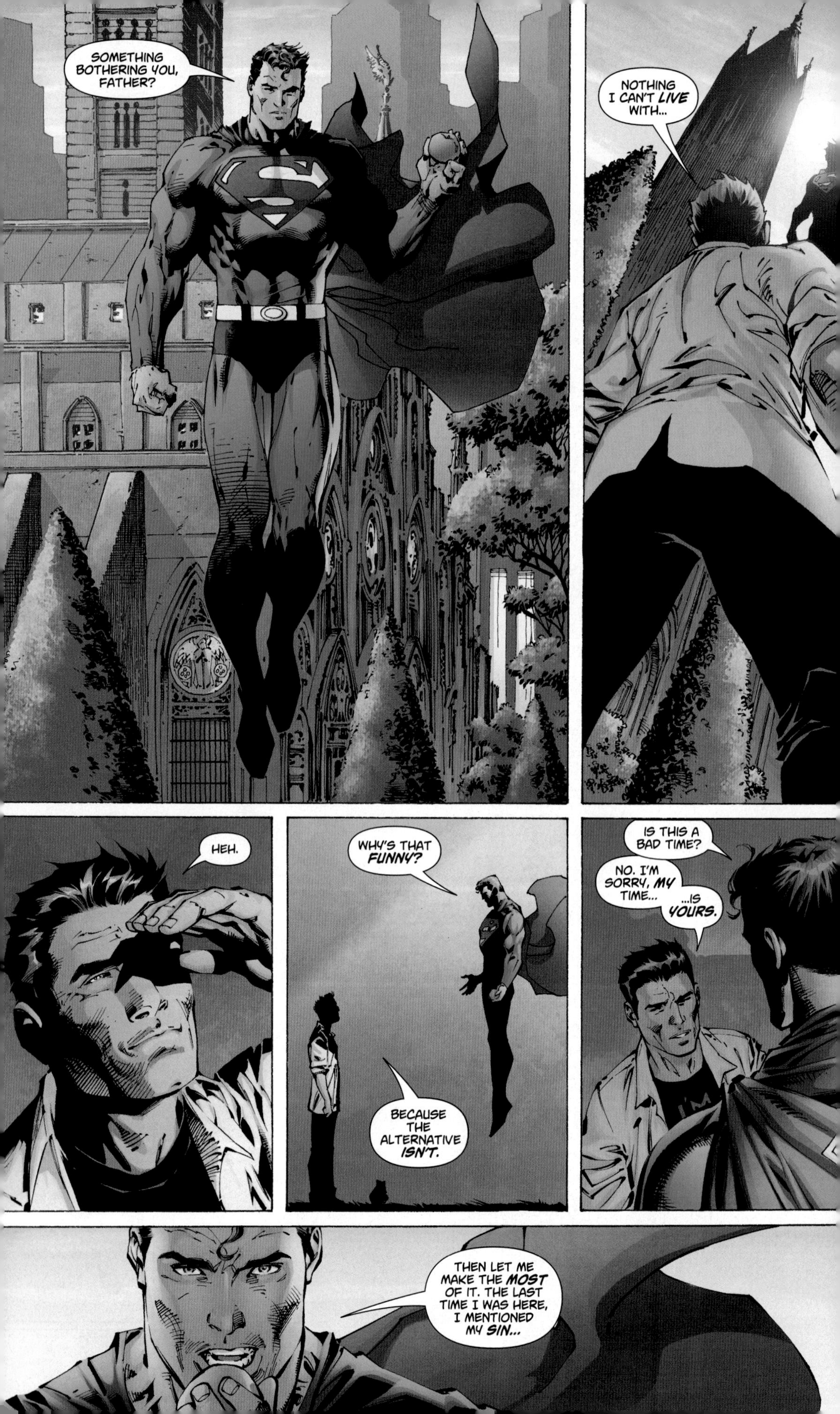
SOMETHING BOTHERING YOU, FATHER?
NOTHING I CAN'T LIVE WITH...
HEH.
WHY'S THAT FUNNY?
BECAUSE THE ALTERNATIVE ISN'T.
IS THIS A BAD TIME?
NO. I'M SORRY, MY TIME...
...IS YOURS.
THEN LET ME MAKE THE MOST OF IT. THE LAST TIME I WAS HERE, I MENTIONED MY SIN...

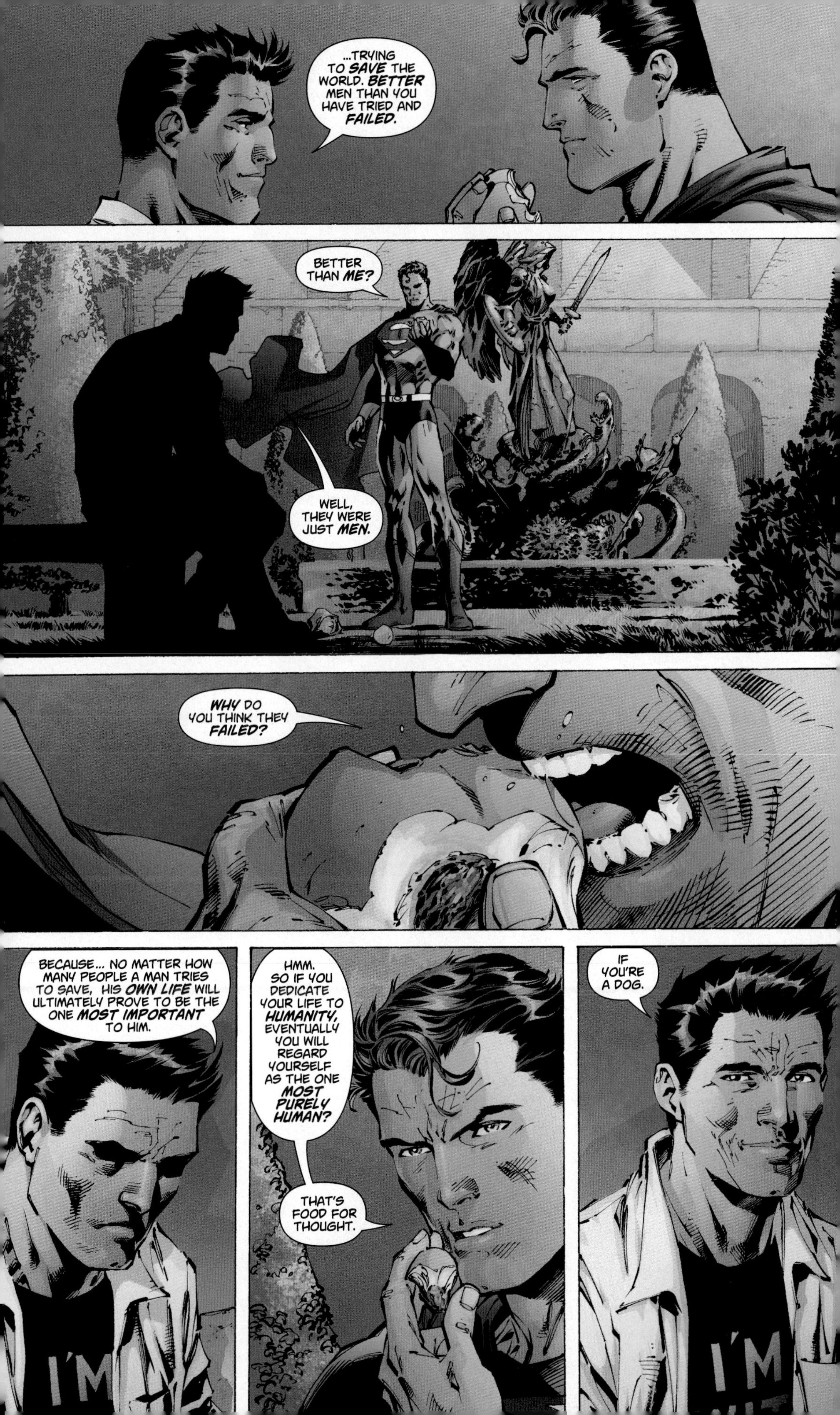
...TRYING TO SAVE THE WORLD. BETTER MEN THAN YOU HAVE TRIED AND FAILED.
BETTER THAN ME?
WELL, THEY WERE JUST MEN.
WHY DO YOU THINK THEY FAILED?
BECAUSE... NO MATTER HOW MANY PEOPLE A MAN TRIES TO SAVE, HIS OWN LIFE WILL ULTIMATELY PROVE TO BE THE ONE MOST IMPORTANT TO HIM.
HMM. SO IF YOU DEDICATE YOUR LIFE TO HUMANITY, EVENTUALLY YOU WILL REGARD YOURSELF AS THE ONE MOST PURELY HUMAN?
THAT'S FOOD FOR THOUGHT.
IF YOU'RE A DOG.
I'M
I'M

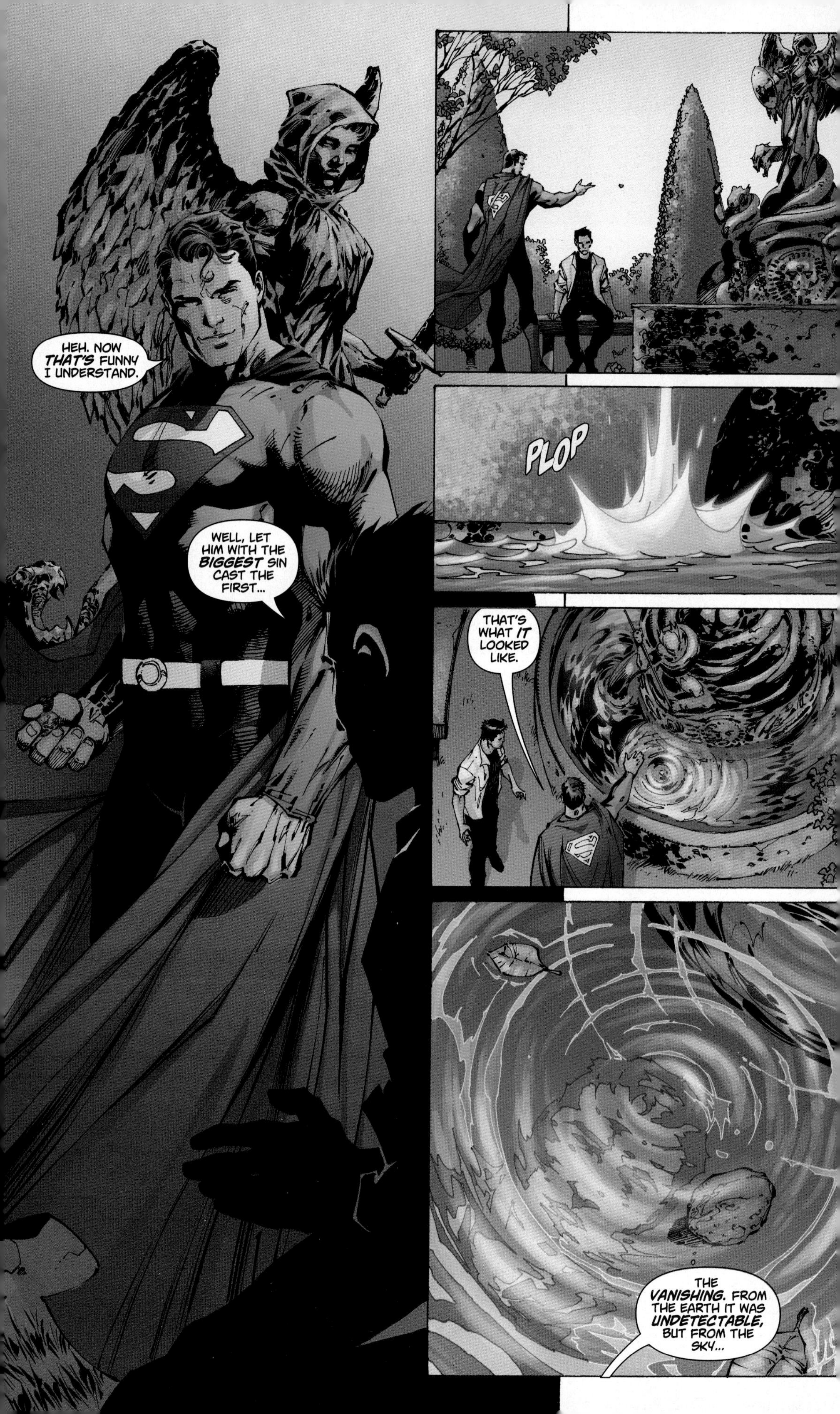
HEH. NOW THAT'S FUNNY I UNDERSTAND.
WELL, LET HIM WITH THE BIGGEST SIN CAST THE FIRST...
PLOP
THAT'S WHAT IT LOOKED LIKE.
THE VANISHING. FROM THE EARTH IT WAS UNDETECTABLE, BUT FROM THE SKY...

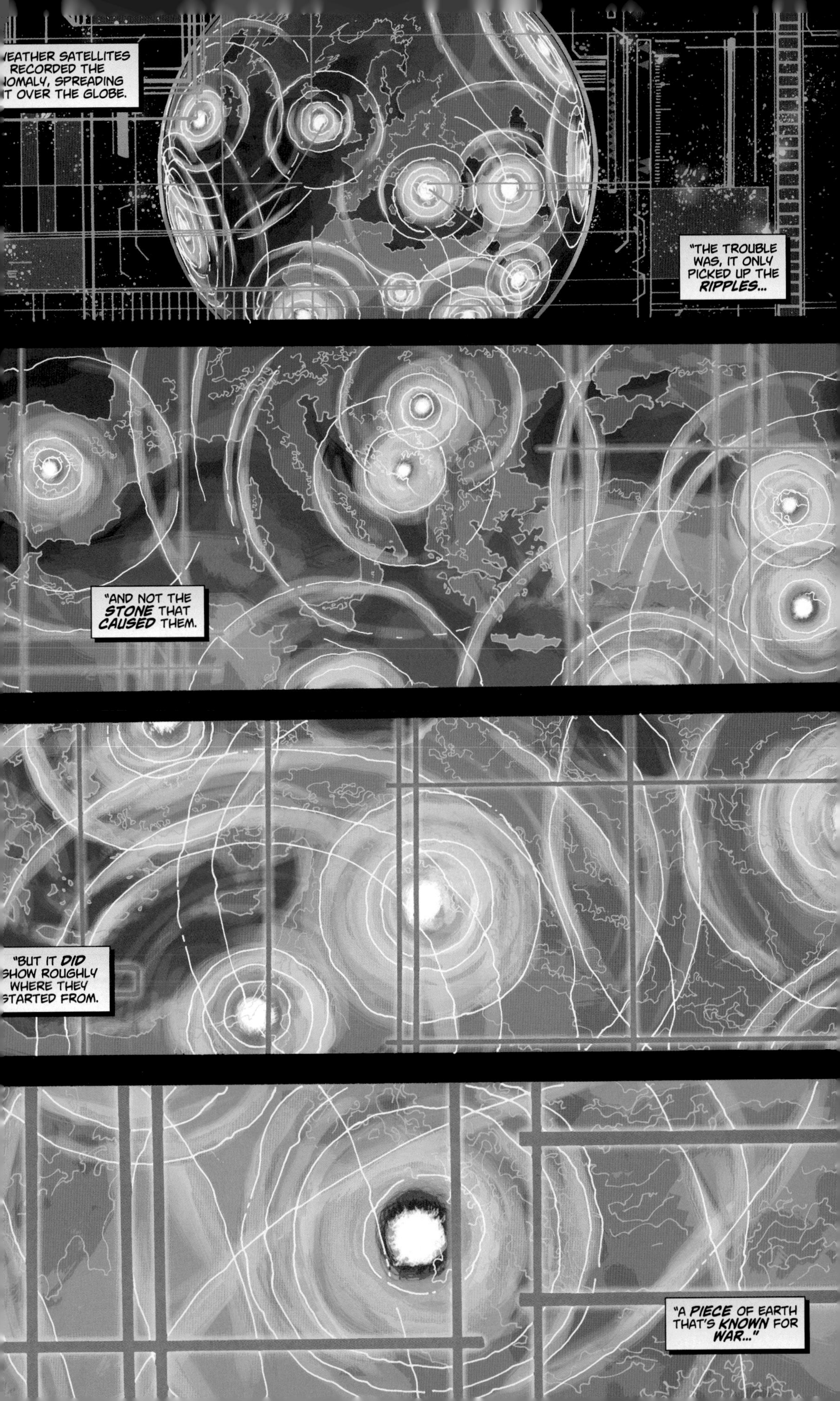

WEATHER SATELLITES RECORDED THE ANOMALY, SPREADING IT OVER THE GLOBE.
"THE TROUBLE WAS, IT ONLY PICKED UP THE RIPPLES...
"AND NOT THE STONE THAT CAUSED THEM.
"BUT IT DID SHOW ROUGHLY WHERE THEY STARTED FROM.
"A PIECE OF EARTH THAT'S KNOWN FOR WAR..."

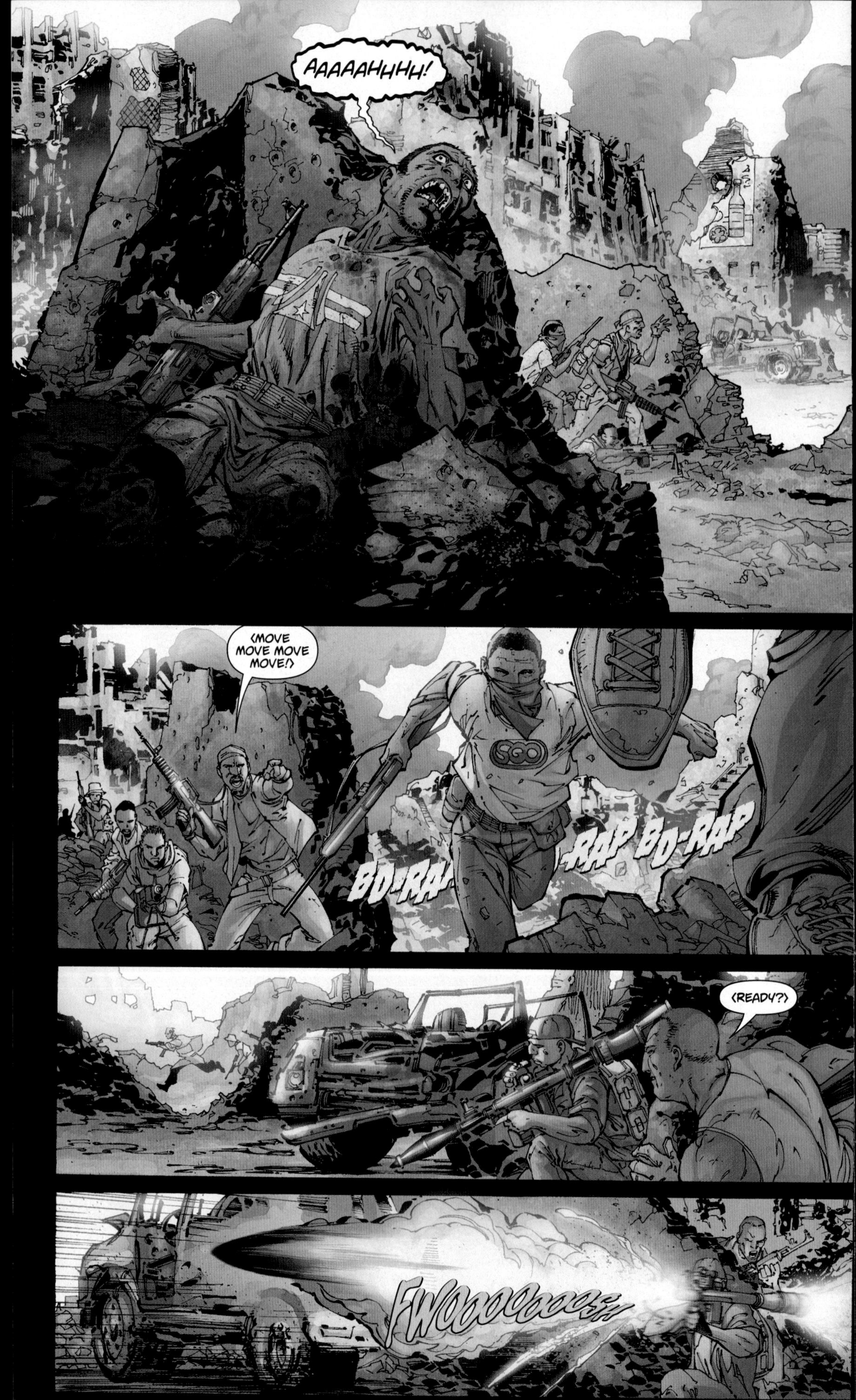
AAAAAHHHH!
<MOVE MOVE MOVE MOVE!>
BD-RAP
-RAP BD-RAP
<READY?>
FWOOOOOOOSH

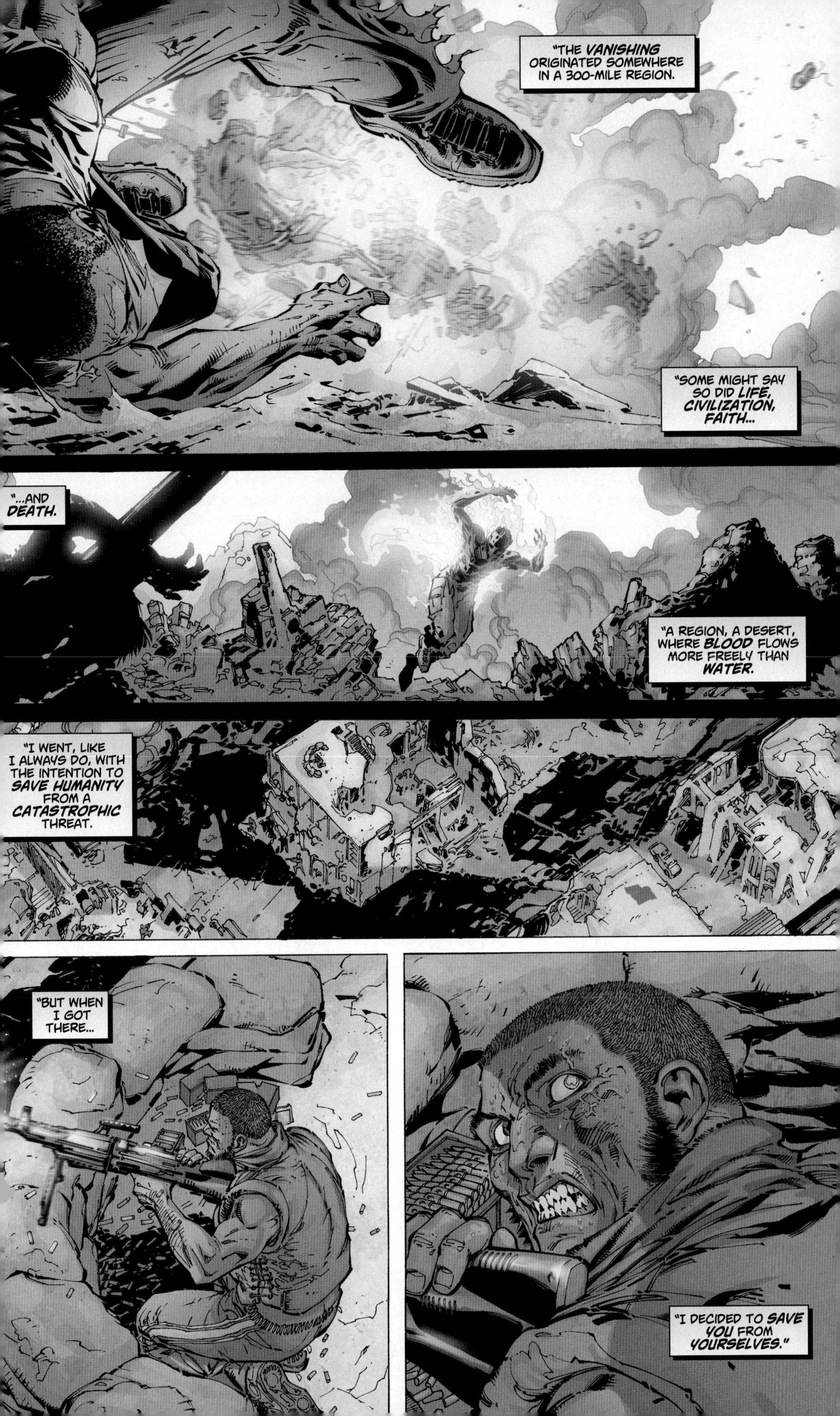
"THE VANISHING ORIGINATED SOMEWHERE IN A 300-MILE REGION.
"SOME MIGHT SAY SO DID LIFE, CIVILIZATION, FAITH...
"...AND DEATH.
"A REGION, A DESERT, WHERE BLOOD FLOWS MORE FREELY THAN WATER.
"I WENT, LIKE I ALWAYS DO, WITH THE INTENTION TO SAVE HUMANITY FROM A CATASTROPHIC THREAT.
"BUT WHEN I GOT THERE...
"I DECIDED TO SAVE YOU FROM YOURSELVES."

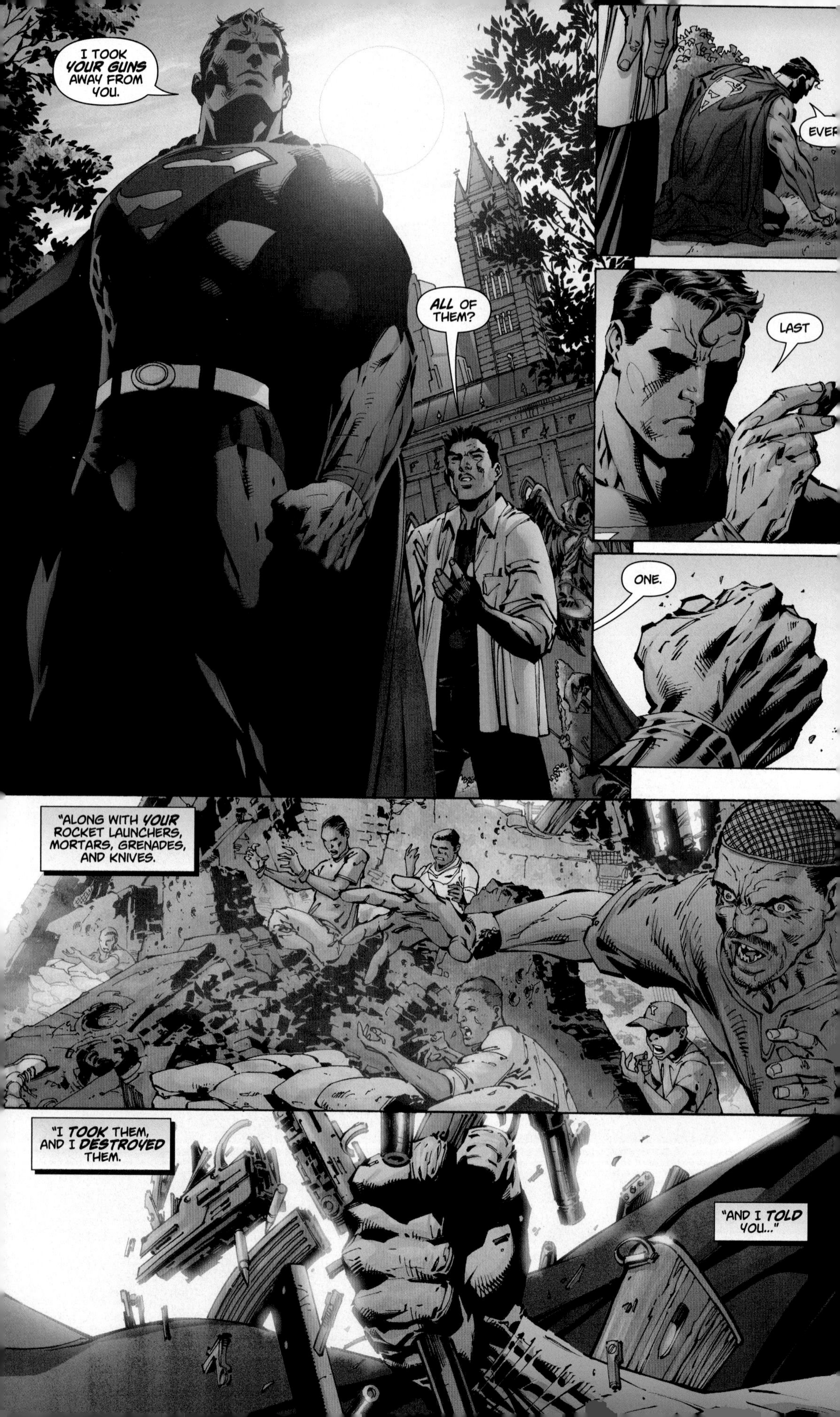
I TOOK YOUR GUNS AWAY FROM YOU.
ALL OF THEM?
EVER
LAST
ONE.
"ALONG WITH YOUR ROCKET LAUNCHERS, MORTARS, GRENADES, AND KNIVES.
"I TOOK THEM, AND I DESTROYED THEM.
"AND I TOLD YOU..."

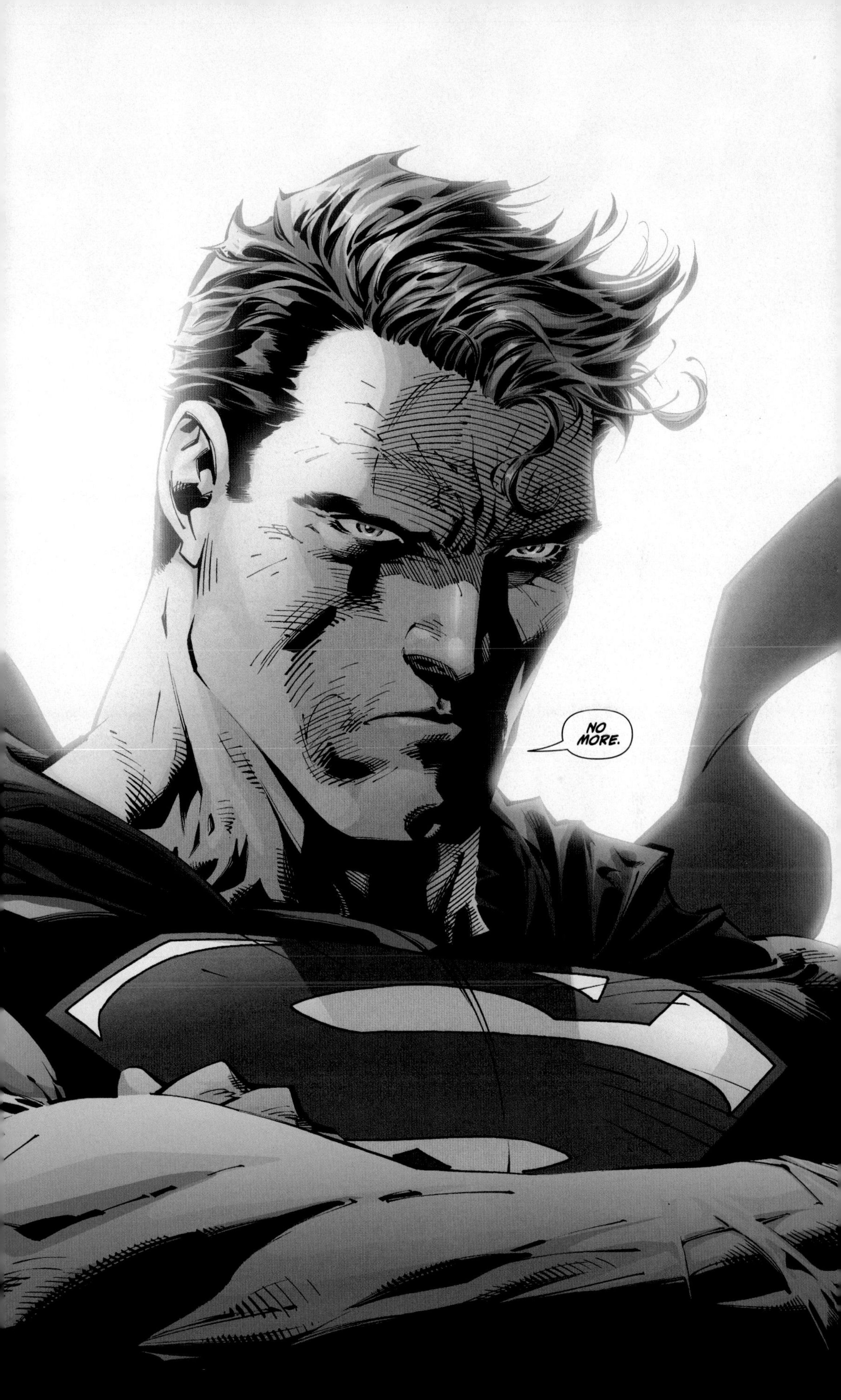
NO MORE.

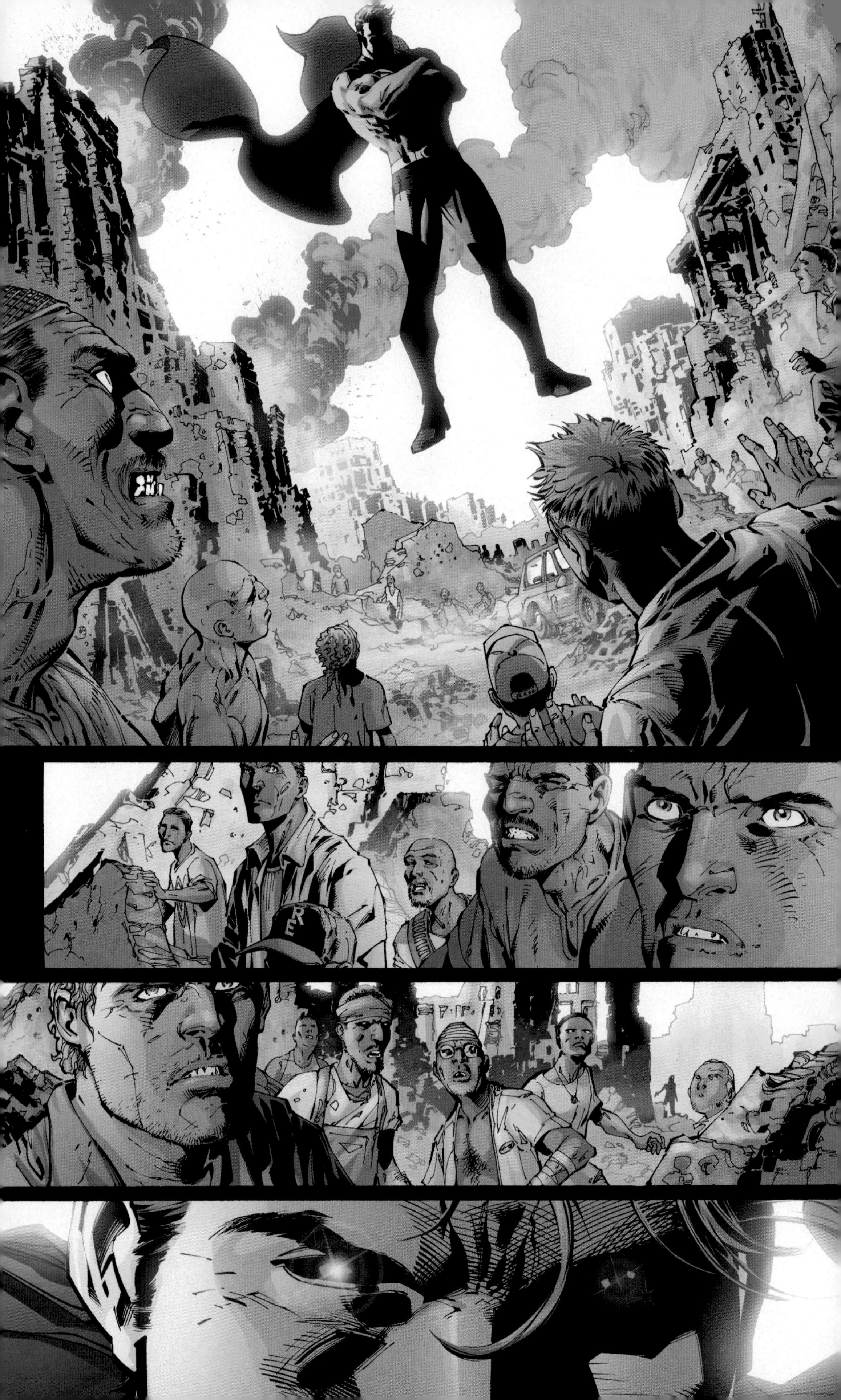

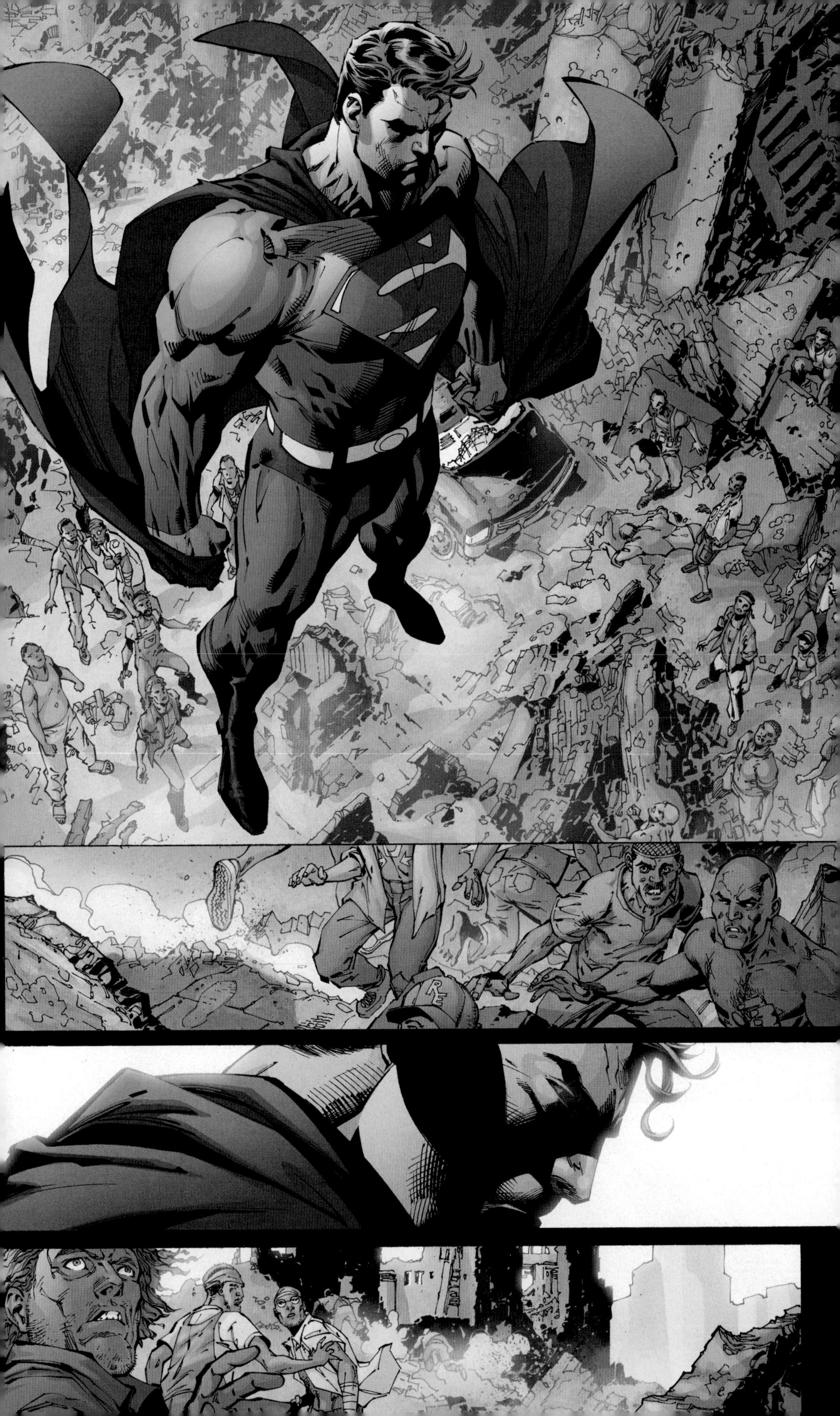

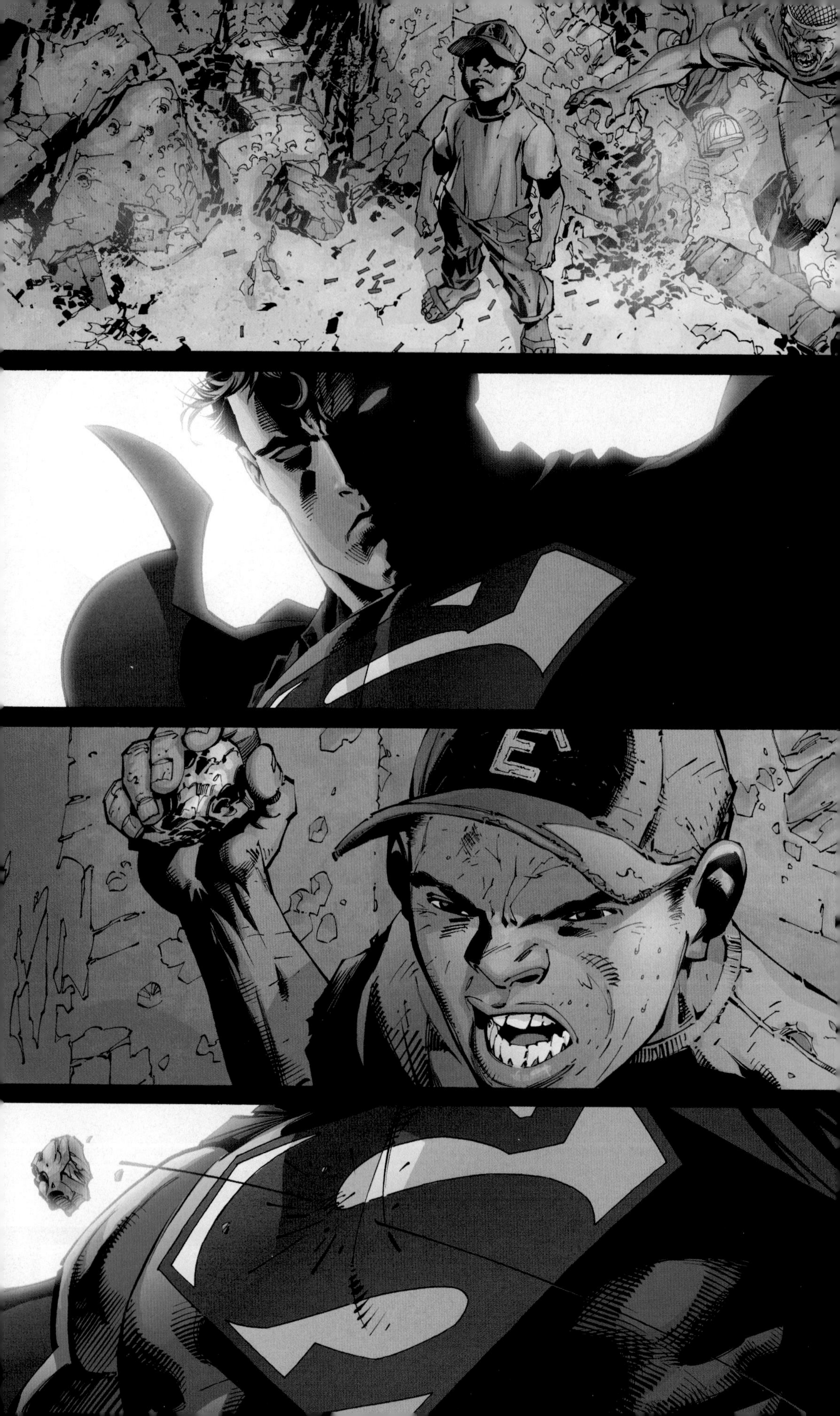

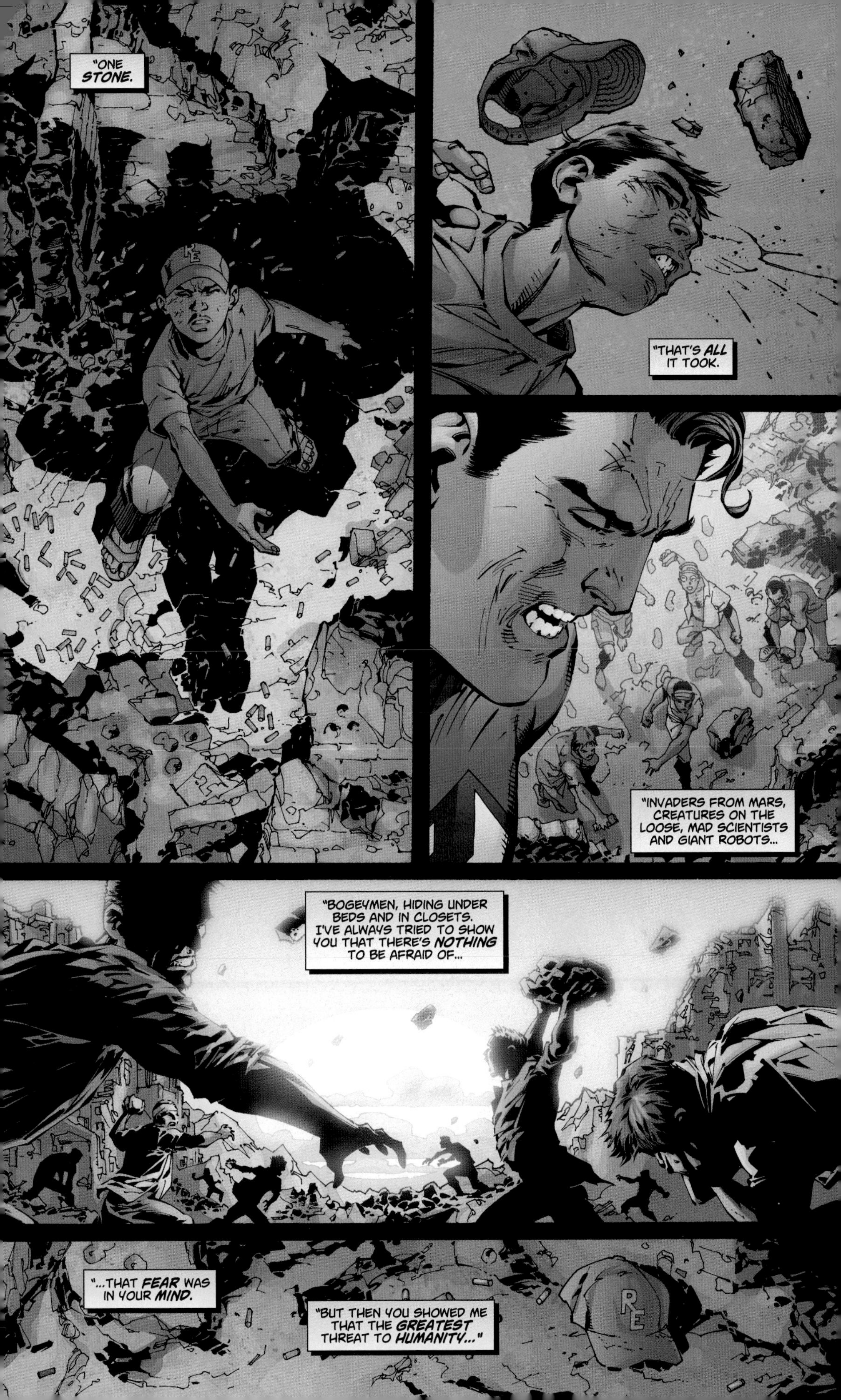
"ONE STONE.
"THAT'S ALL IT TOOK.
"INVADERS FROM MARS, CREATURES ON THE LOOSE, MAD SCIENTISTS AND GIANT ROBOTS...
"BOGEYMEN, HIDING UNDER BEDS AND IN CLOSETS. I'VE ALWAYS TRIED TO SHOW YOU THAT THERE'S NOTHING TO BE AFRAID OF...
"...THAT FEAR WAS IN YOUR MIND.
"BUT THEN YOU SHOWED ME THAT THE GREATEST THREAT TO HUMANITY..."
RE

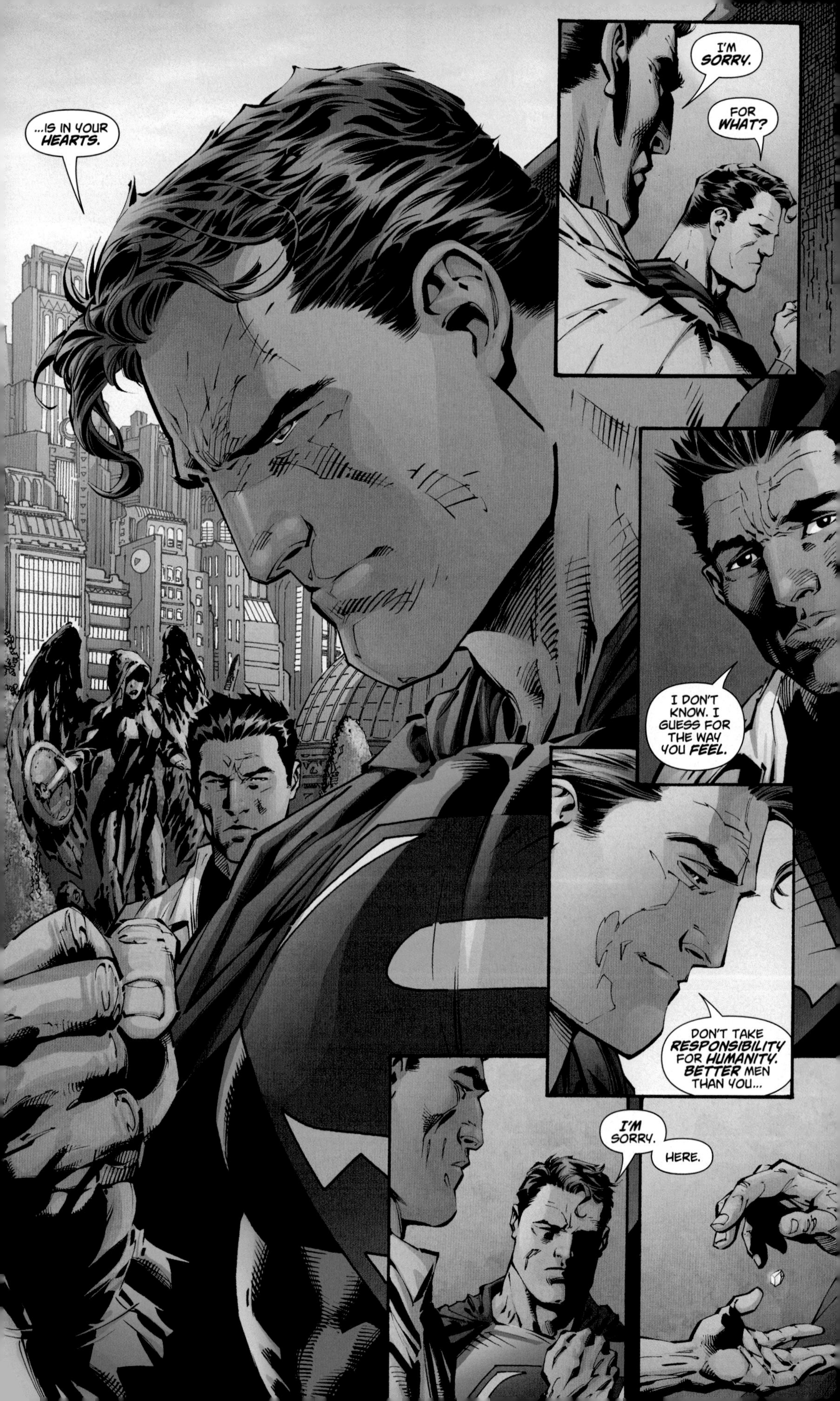
...IS IN YOUR HEARTS.
I'M SORRY.
FOR WHAT?
I DON'T KNOW. I GUESS FOR THE WAY YOU FEEL.
DON'T TAKE RESPONSIBILITY FOR HUMANITY. BETTER MEN THAN YOU...
I'M SORRY.
HERE.

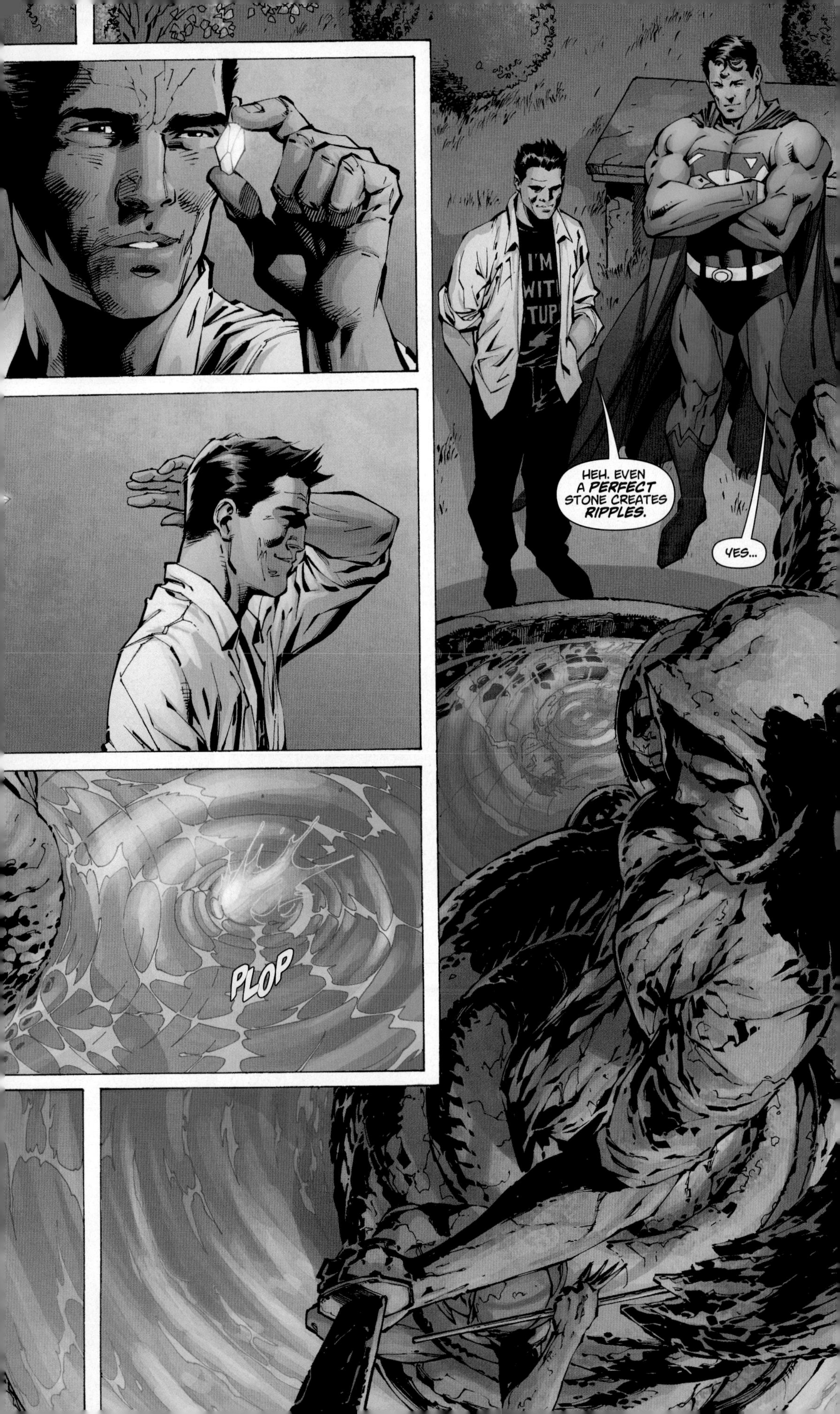
PLOP
I'M WITH STUPID
HEH. EVEN A PERFECT STONE CREATES RIPPLES.
YES...

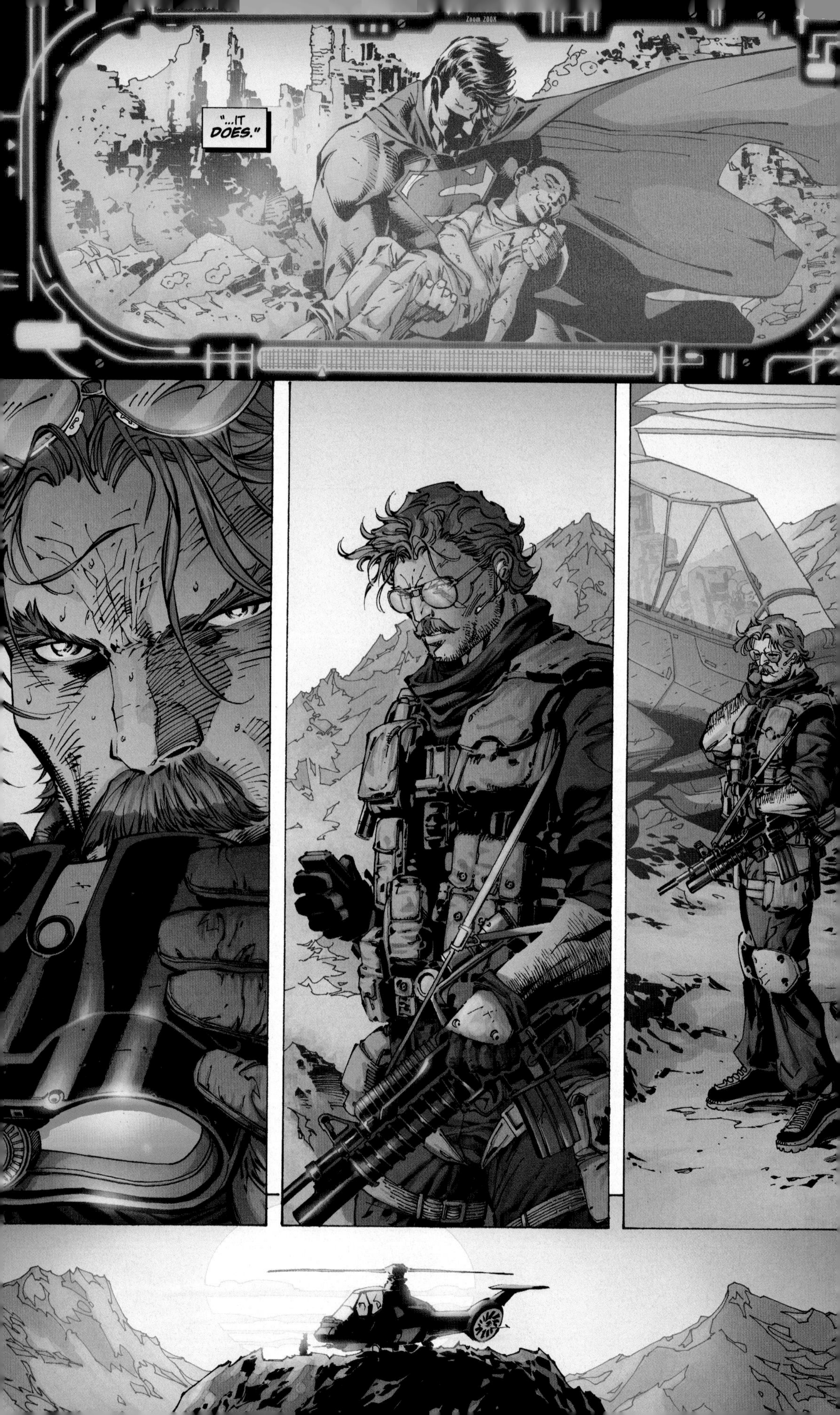
"...IT DOES."

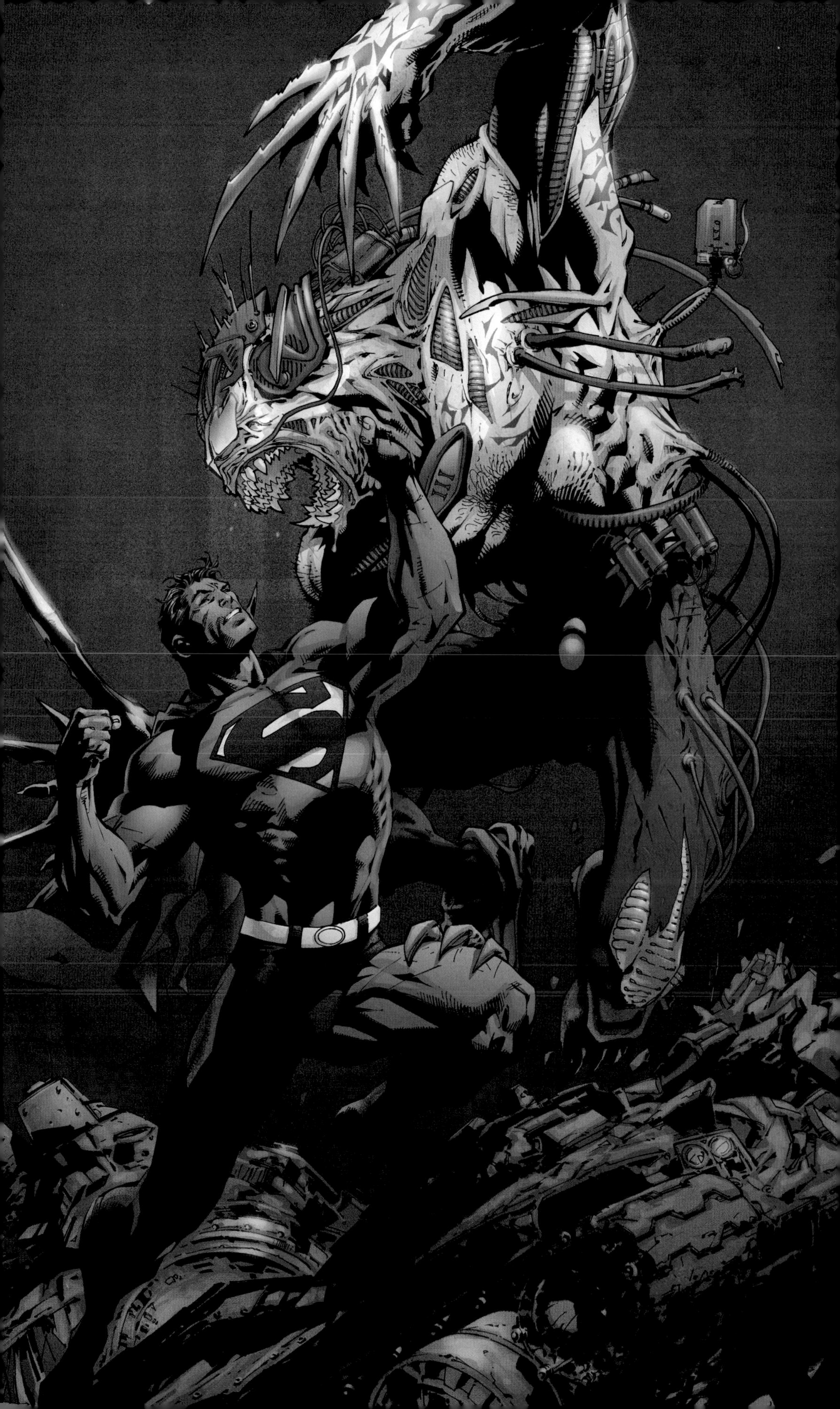

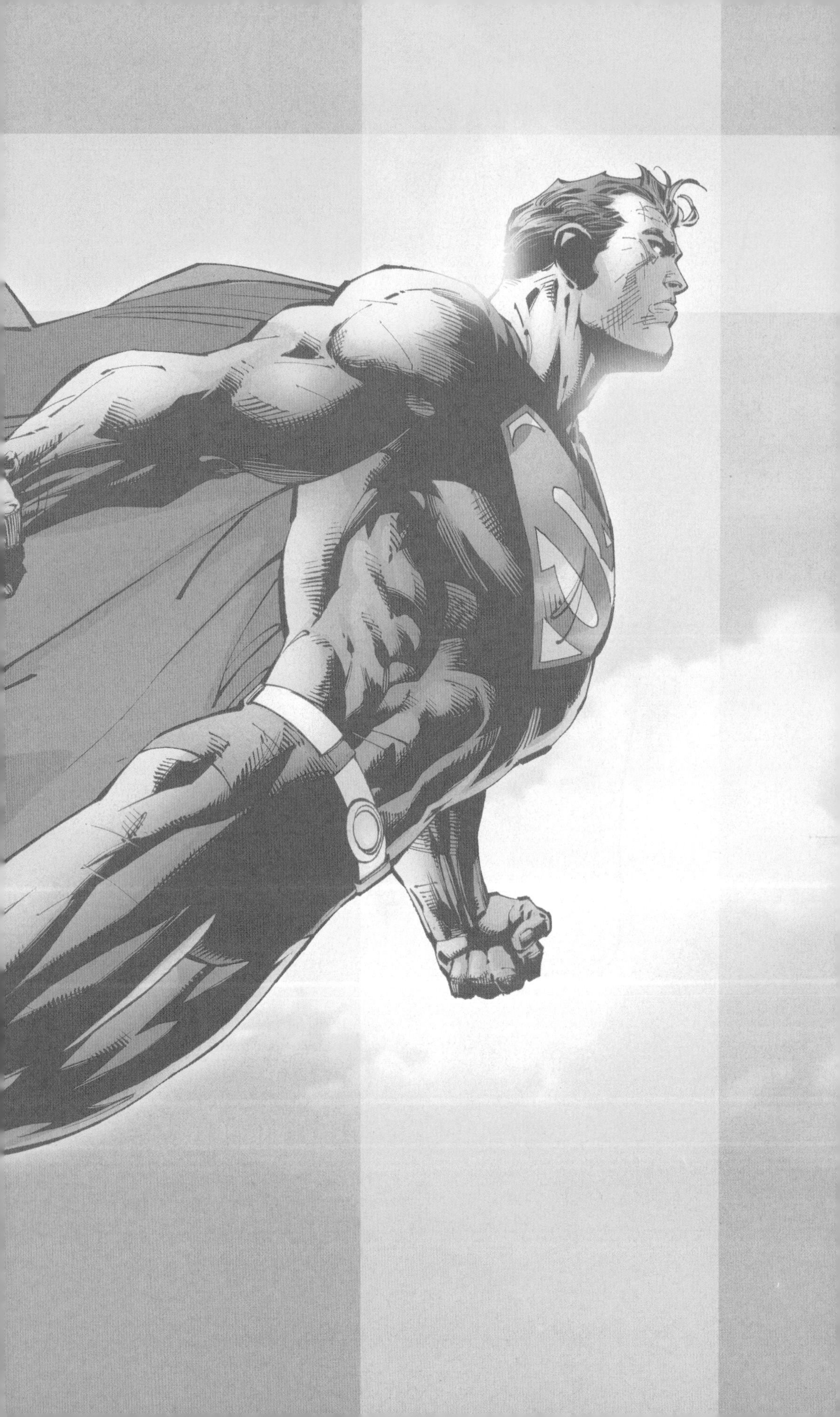

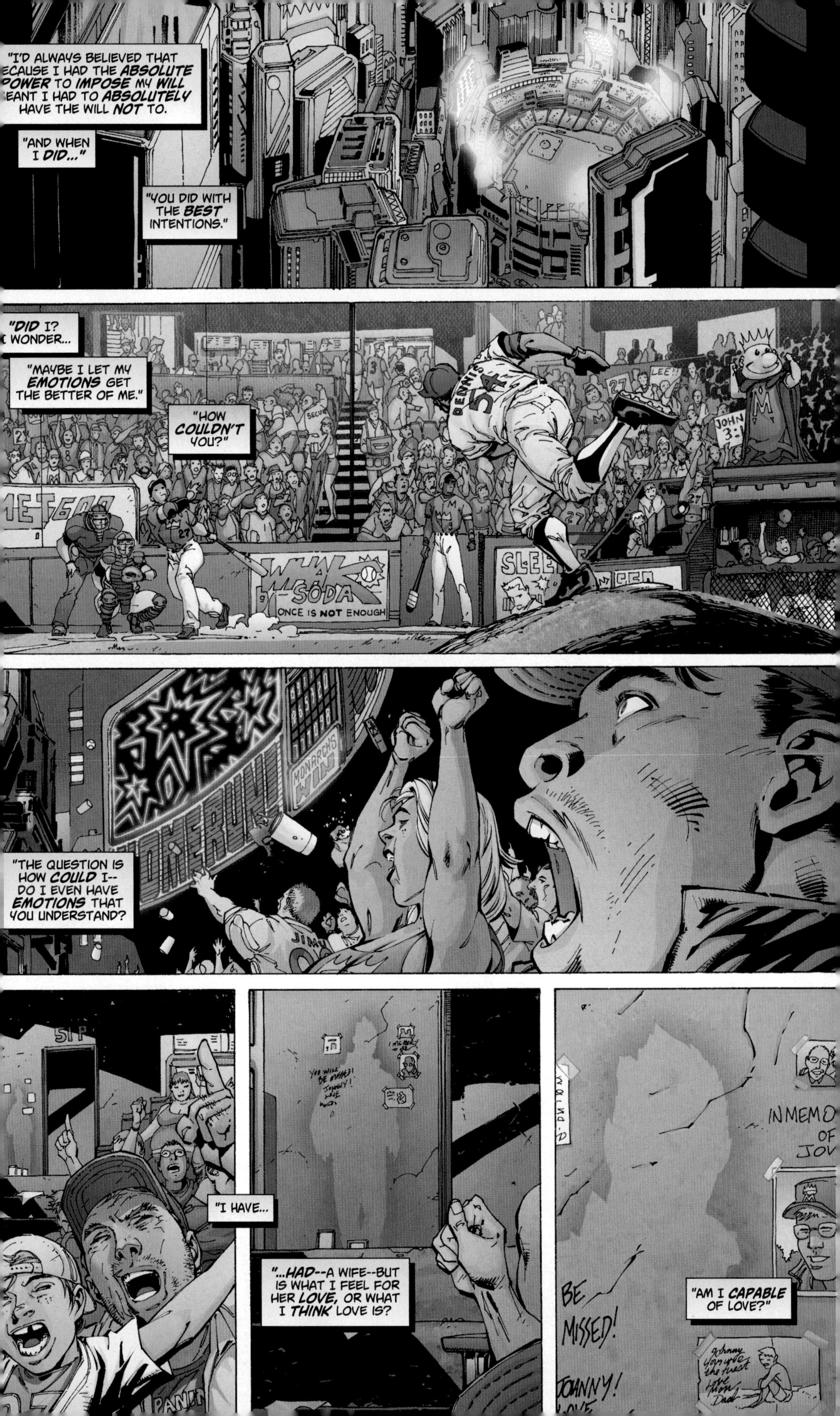
"I'D ALWAYS BELIEVED THAT BECAUSE I HAD THE ABSOLUTE POWER TO IMPOSE MY WILL MEANT I HAD TO ABSOLUTELY HAVE THE WILL NOT TO.
"AND WHEN I DID..."
"YOU DID WITH THE BEST INTENTIONS."
"DID I? I WONDER...
"MAYBE I LET MY EMOTIONS GET THE BETTER OF ME."
"HOW COULDN'T YOU?"
SODA
ONCE IS NOT ENOUGH
MONARCH'S WIN
"THE QUESTION IS HOW COULD I-- DO I EVEN HAVE EMOTIONS THAT YOU UNDERSTAND?
"I HAVE...
"...HAD--A WIFE--BUT IS WHAT I FEEL FOR HER LOVE, OR WHAT I THINK LOVE IS?
IN MEMO OF JO
BE MISSED!
JOHNNY!
"AM I CAPABLE OF LOVE?"

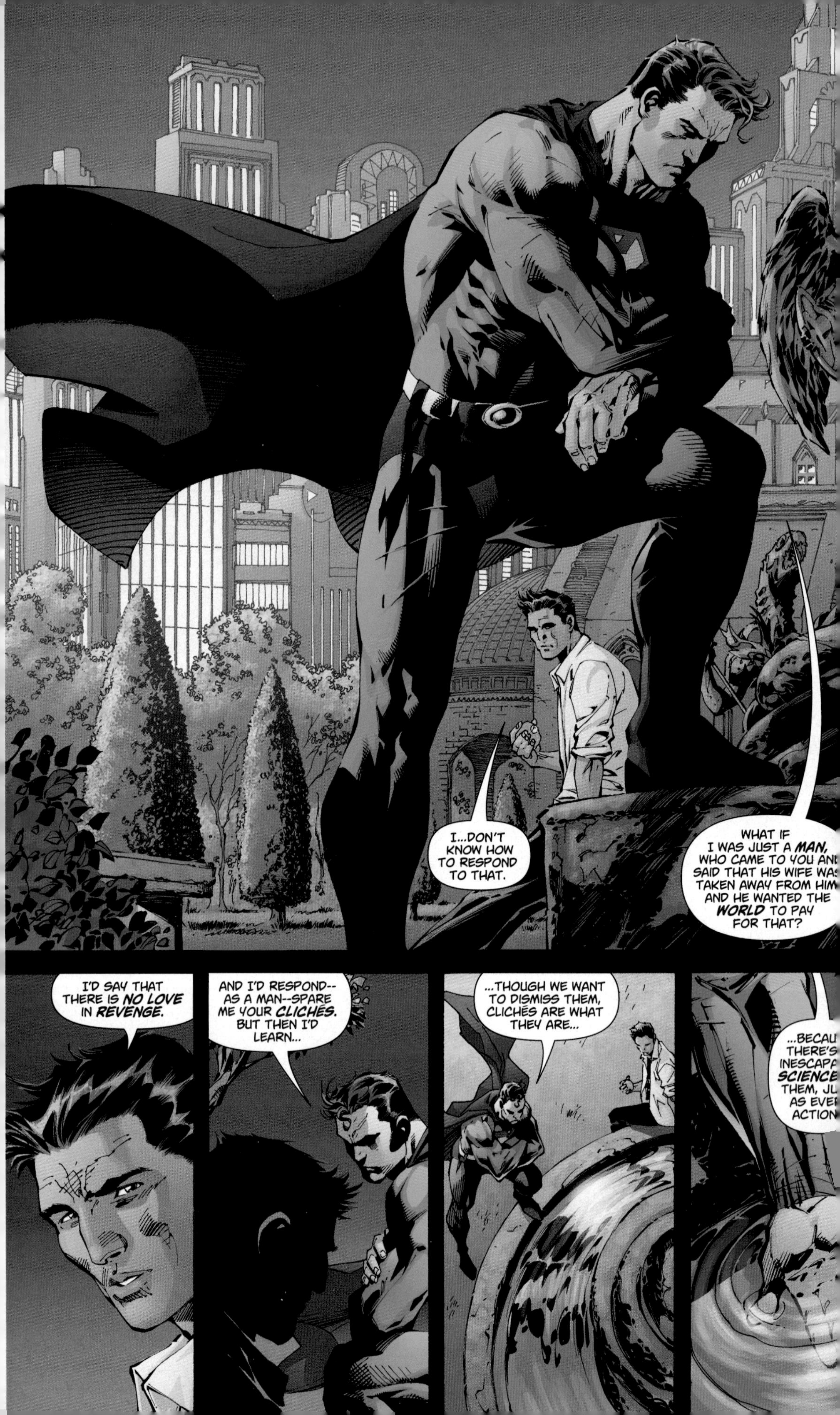
WHAT IF I WAS JUST A MAN, WHO CAME TO YOU AN SAID THAT HIS WIFE WA TAKEN AWAY FROM HIM AND HE WANTED THE WORLD TO PAY FOR THAT?
I...DON'T KNOW HOW TO RESPOND TO THAT.
I'D SAY THAT THERE IS NO LOVE IN REVENGE.
AND I'D RESPOND-- AS A MAN--SPARE ME YOUR CLICHÉS. BUT THEN I'D LEARN...
...THOUGH WE WANT TO DISMISS THEM, CLICHÉS ARE WHAT THEY ARE...
...BECAU THERE'S INESCAPA SCIENCE THEM, JU AS EVE ACTION

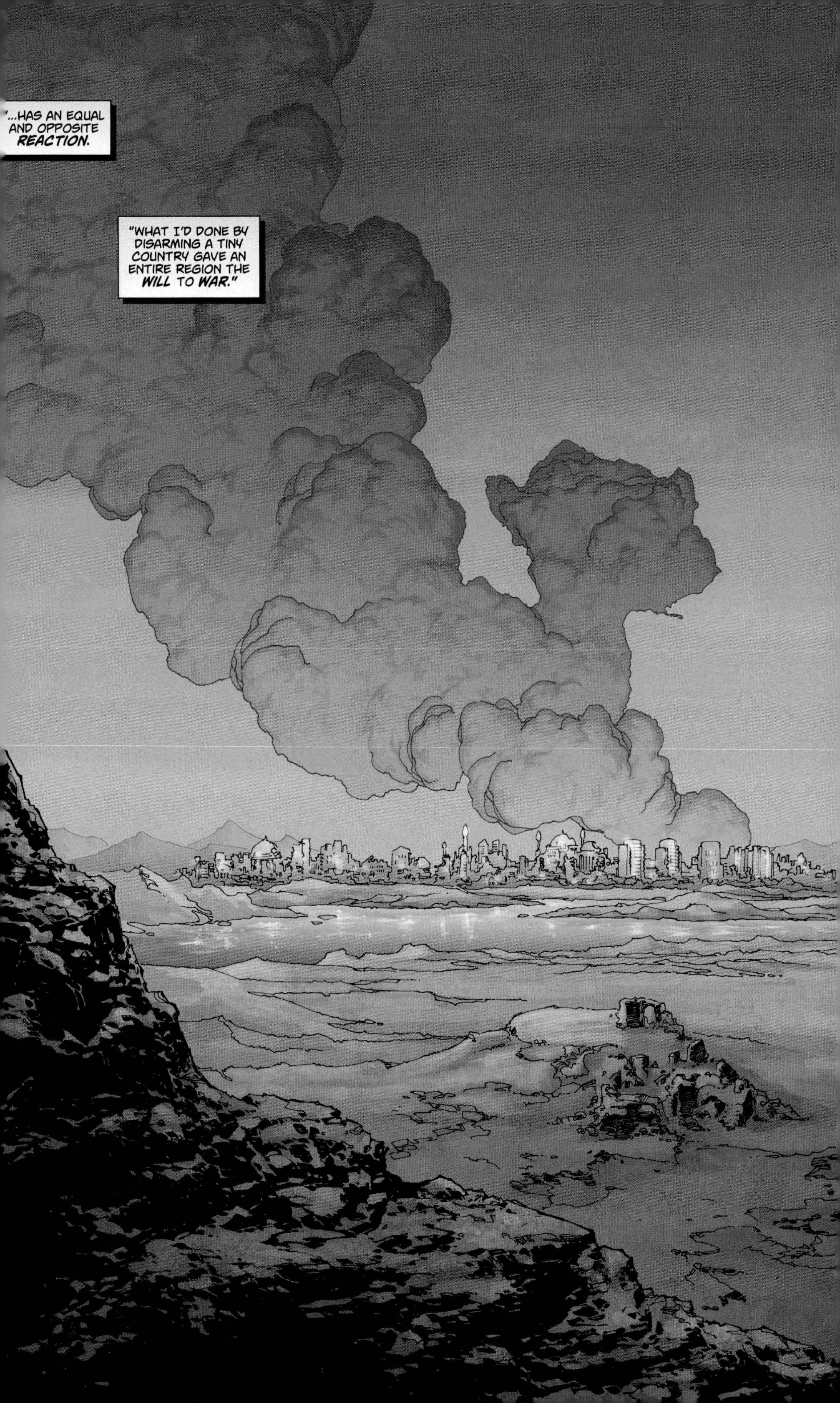
"...HAS AN EQUAL AND OPPOSITE *REACTION*.
"WHAT I'D DONE BY DISARMING A TINY COUNTRY GAVE AN ENTIRE REGION THE *WILL* TO *WAR*."

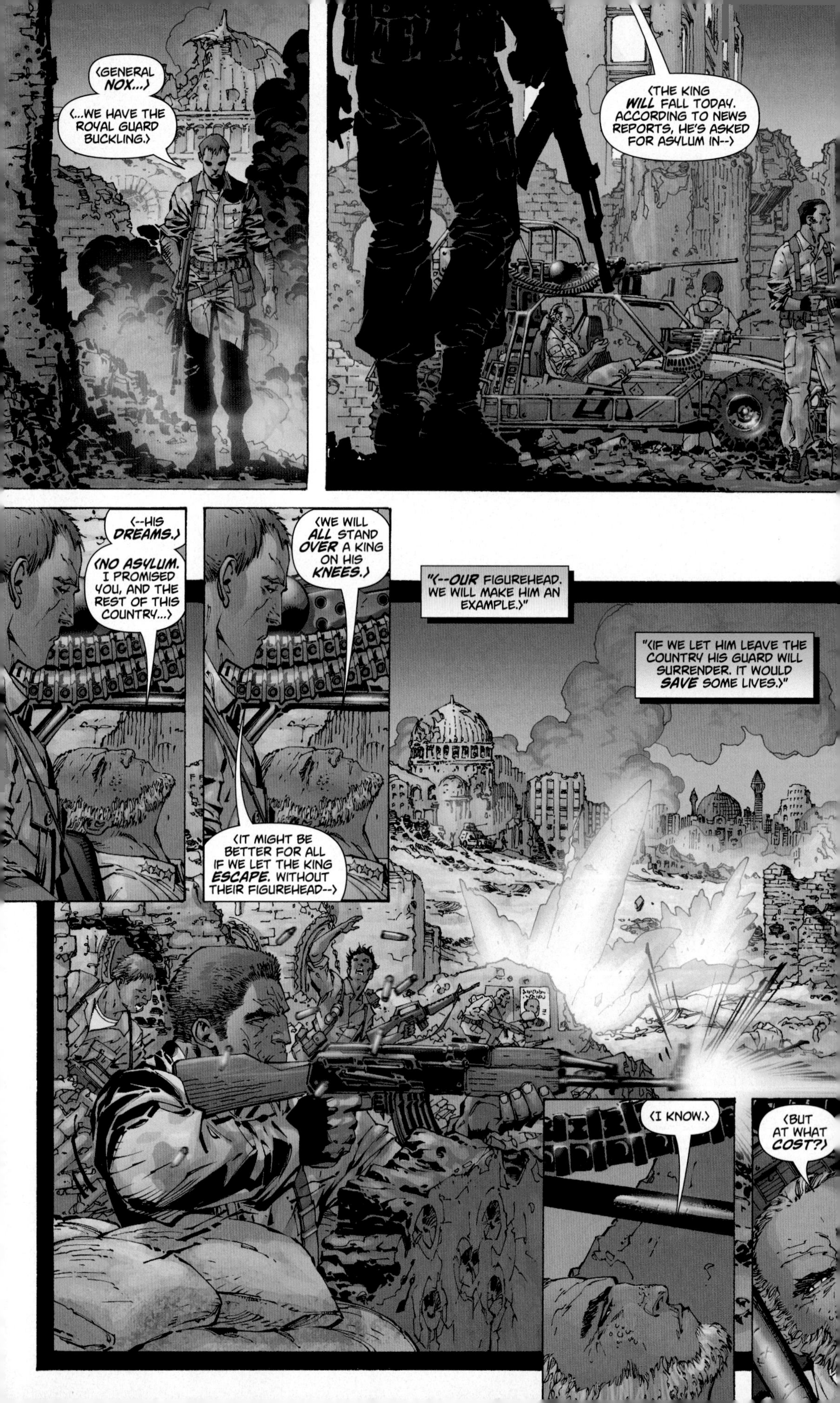

⟨GENERAL NOX...⟩
⟨...WE HAVE THE ROYAL GUARD BUCKLING.⟩
⟨THE KING WILL FALL TODAY. ACCORDING TO NEWS REPORTS, HE'S ASKED FOR ASYLUM IN--⟩
⟨--HIS DREAMS.⟩
⟨NO ASYLUM. I PROMISED YOU, AND THE REST OF THIS COUNTRY...⟩
⟨WE WILL ALL STAND OVER A KING ON HIS KNEES.⟩
⟨IT MIGHT BE BETTER FOR ALL IF WE LET THE KING ESCAPE. WITHOUT THEIR FIGUREHEAD--⟩
"⟨--OUR FIGUREHEAD. WE WILL MAKE HIM AN EXAMPLE.⟩"
"⟨IF WE LET HIM LEAVE THE COUNTRY HIS GUARD WILL SURRENDER. IT WOULD SAVE SOME LIVES.⟩"
⟨I KNOW.⟩
⟨BUT AT WHAT COST?⟩

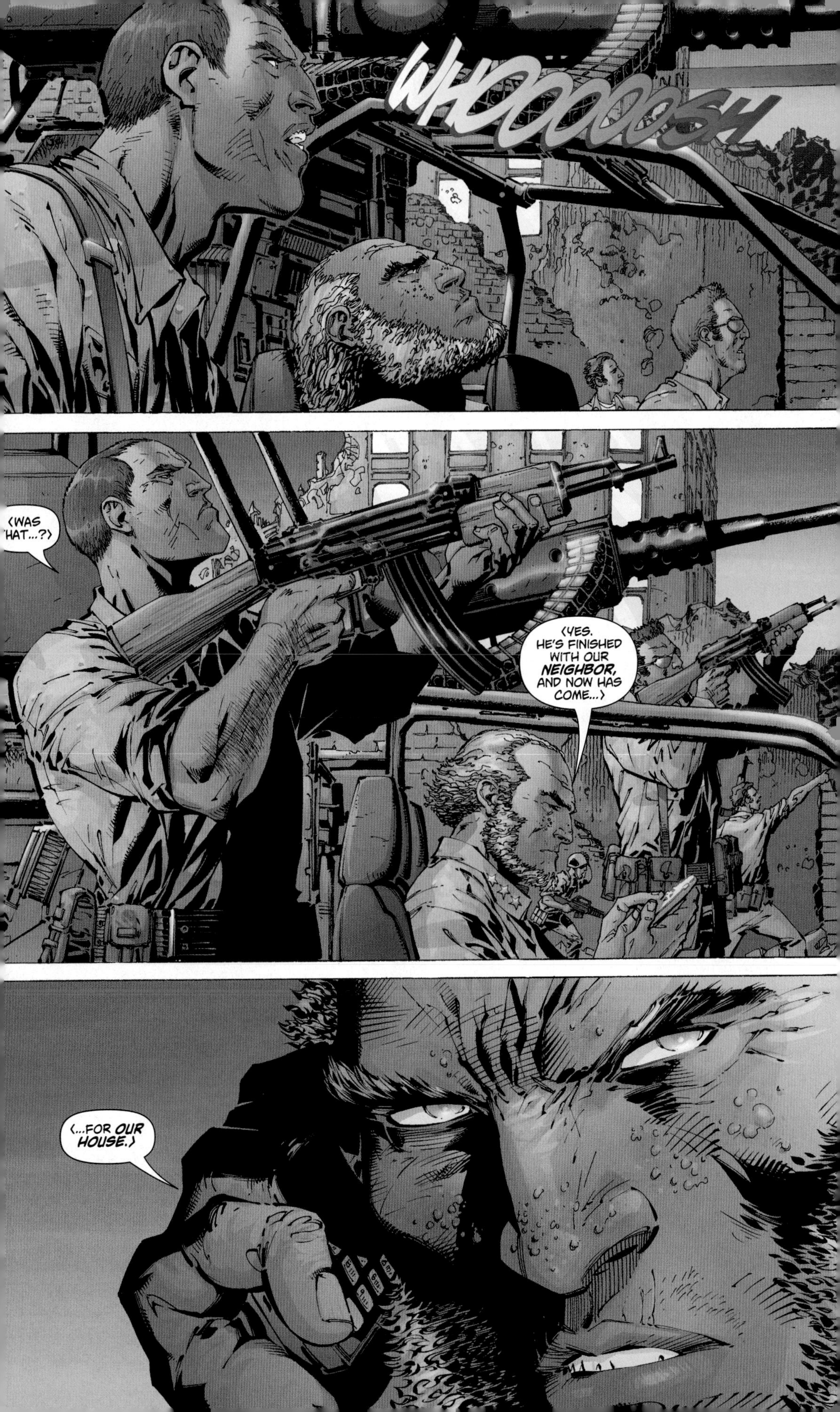
WHOOOOOSH
‹WAS
HAT...?›
‹YES.
HE'S FINISHED
WITH OUR
NEIGHBOR,
AND NOW HAS
COME...›
‹...FOR OUR
HOUSE.›

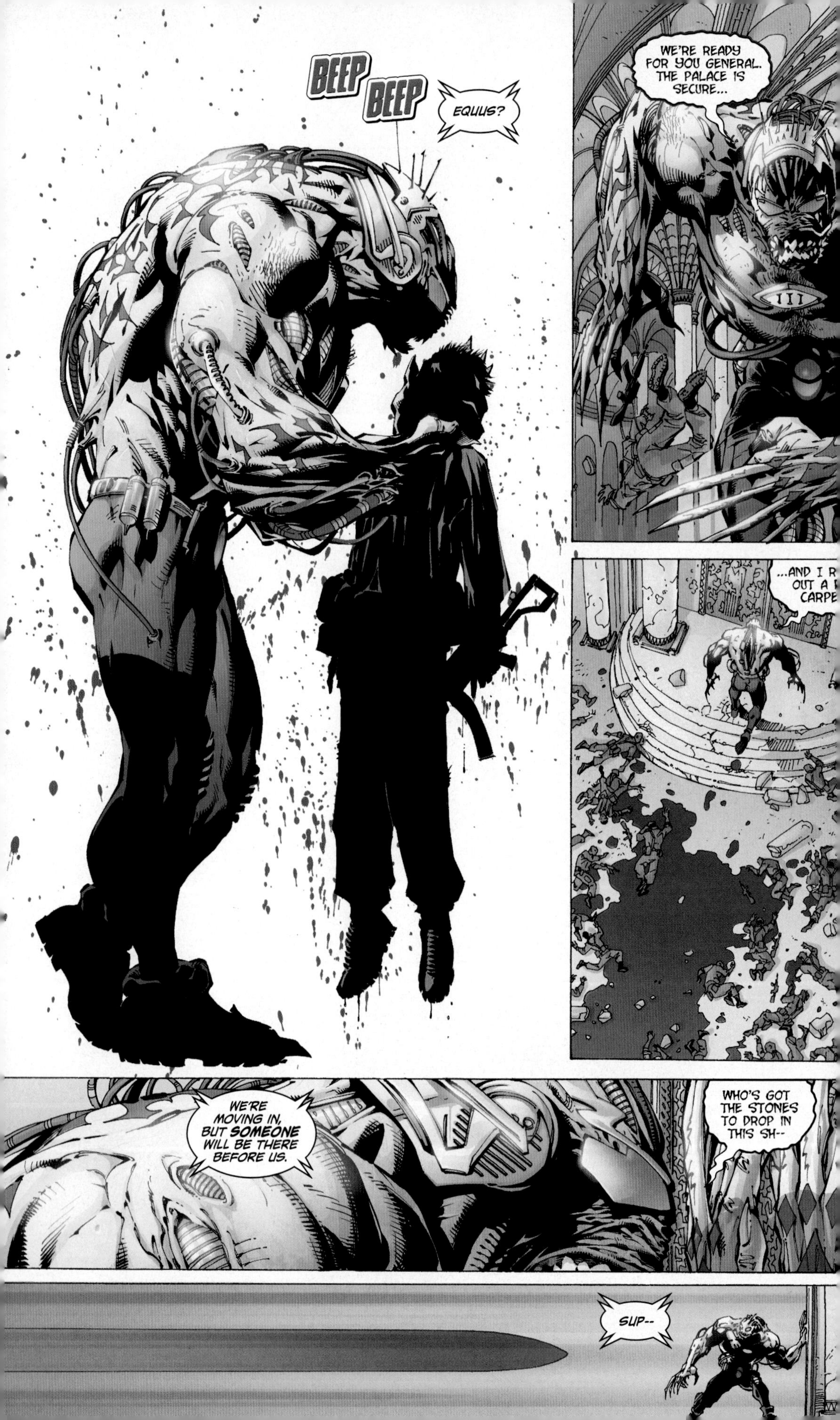
BEEP BEEP
EQUUS?
WE'RE READY FOR YOU GENERAL. THE PALACE IS SECURE...
...AND I R OUT A CARPE
WE'RE MOVING IN, BUT SOMEONE WILL BE THERE BEFORE US.
WHO'S GOT THE STONES TO DROP IN THIS SH--
SLIP--

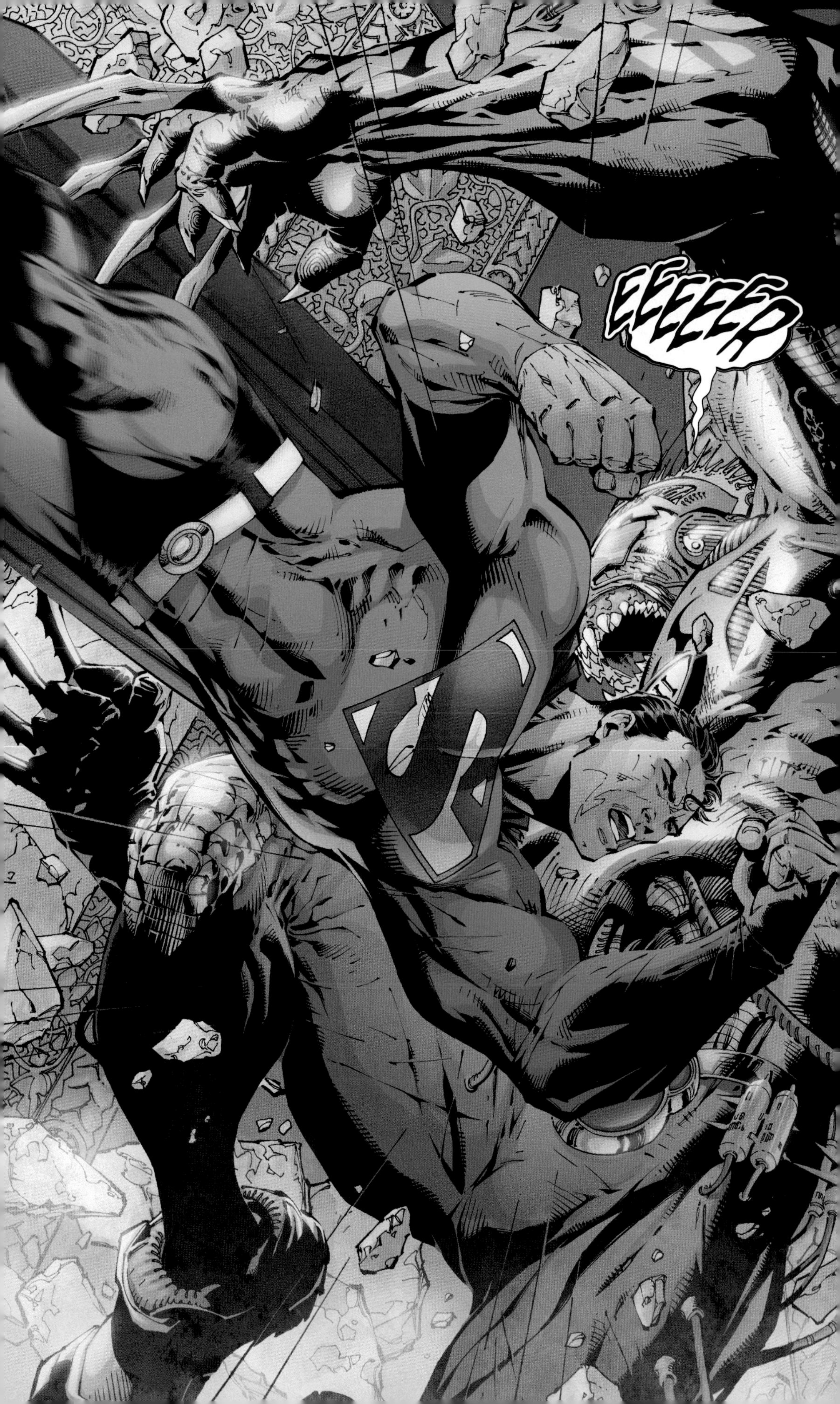
EEEEEA

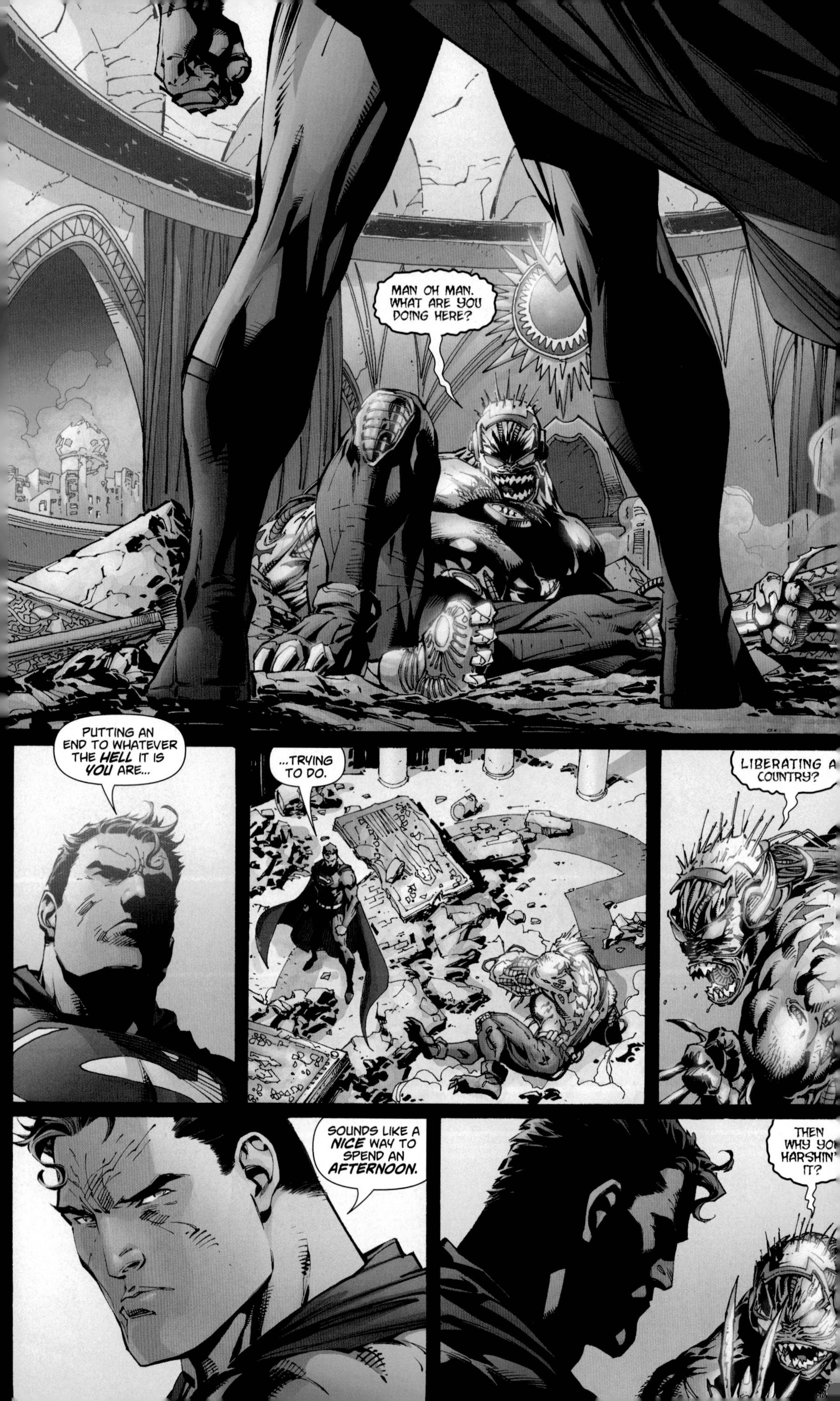
MAN OH MAN. WHAT ARE YOU DOING HERE?
PUTTING AN END TO WHATEVER THE HELL IT IS YOU ARE...
...TRYING TO DO.
LIBERATING A COUNTRY?
SOUNDS LIKE A NICE WAY TO SPEND AN AFTERNOON.
THEN WHY YO HARSHIN' IT?

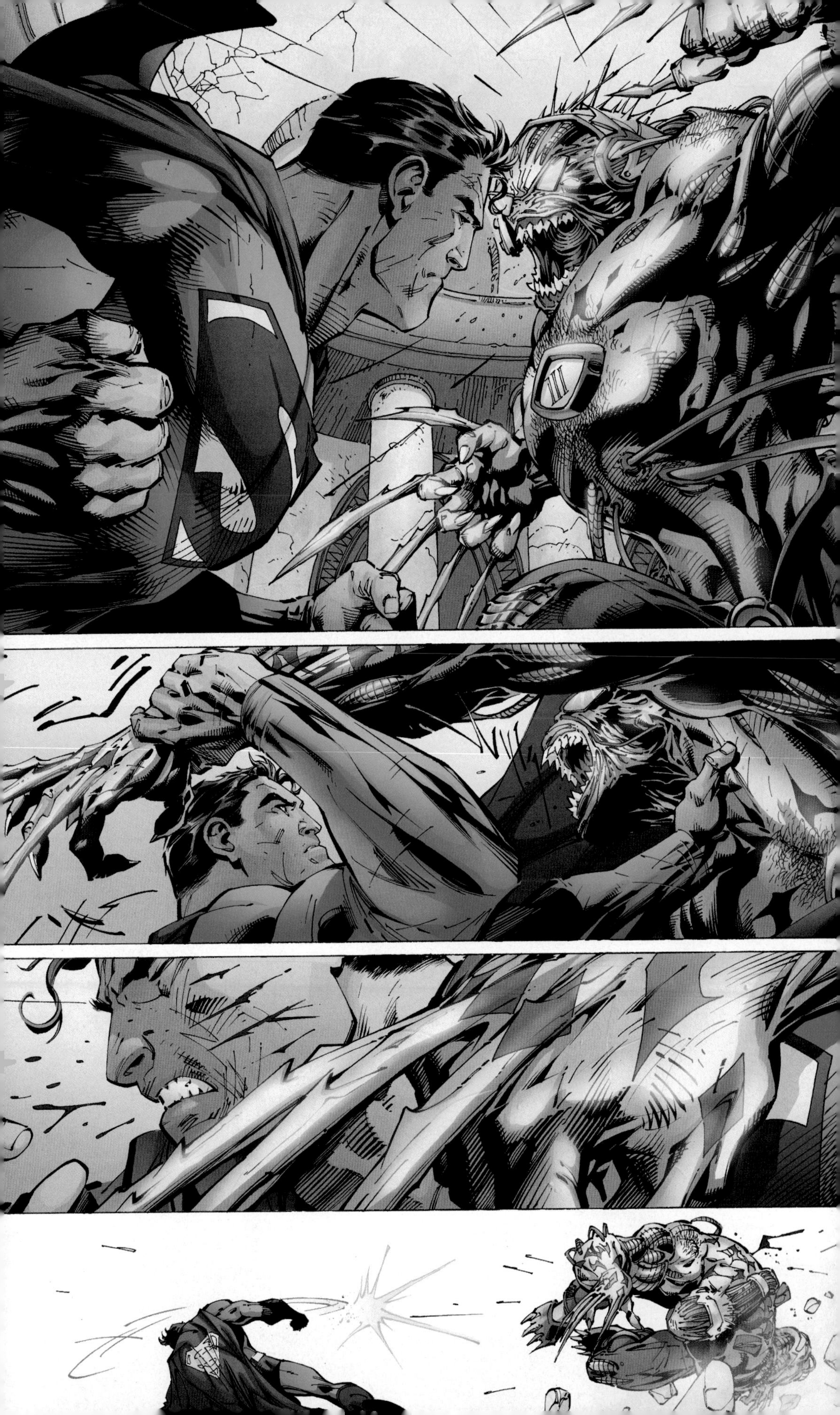

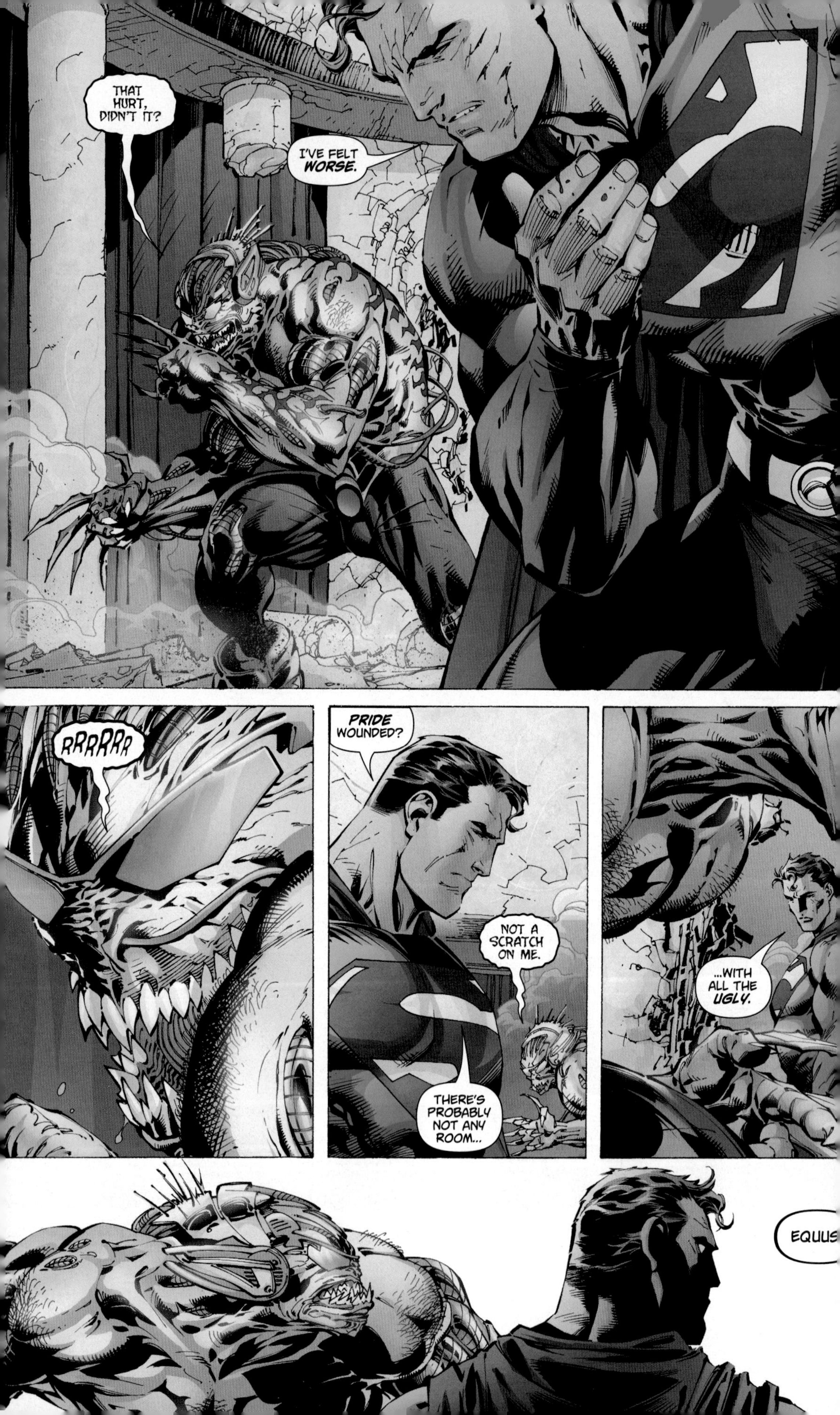

THAT HURT, DIDN'T IT?
I'VE FELT *WORSE*.
RRRRRR
PRIDE WOUNDED?
NOT A SCRATCH ON ME.
THERE'S PROBABLY NOT ANY ROOM...
...WITH ALL THE *UGLY*.
EQUUS

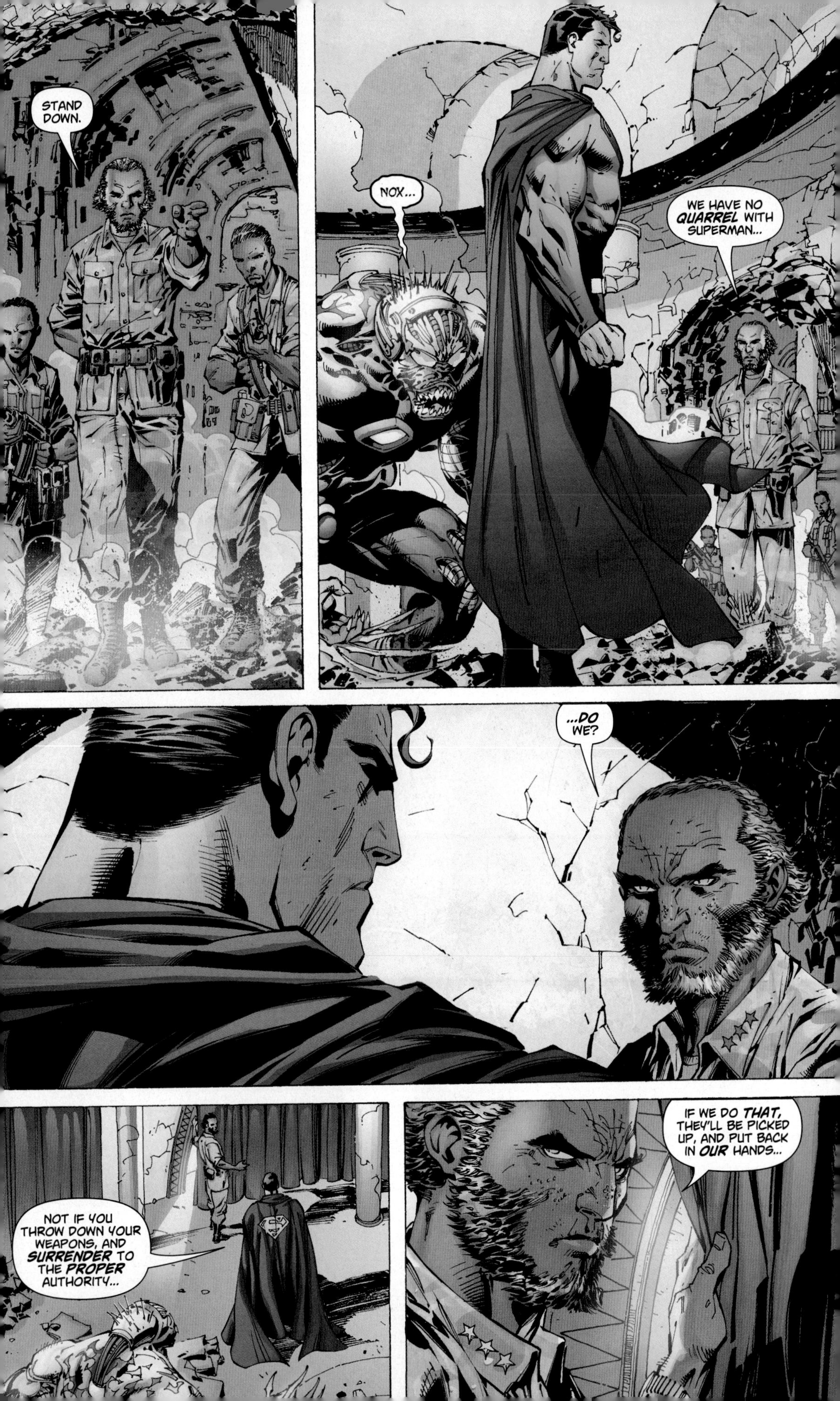
STAND DOWN.
NOX...
WE HAVE NO QUARREL WITH SUPERMAN...
...DO WE?
NOT IF YOU THROW DOWN YOUR WEAPONS, AND SURRENDER TO THE PROPER AUTHORITY...
IF WE DO THAT, THEY'LL BE PICKED UP, AND PUT BACK IN OUR HANDS...

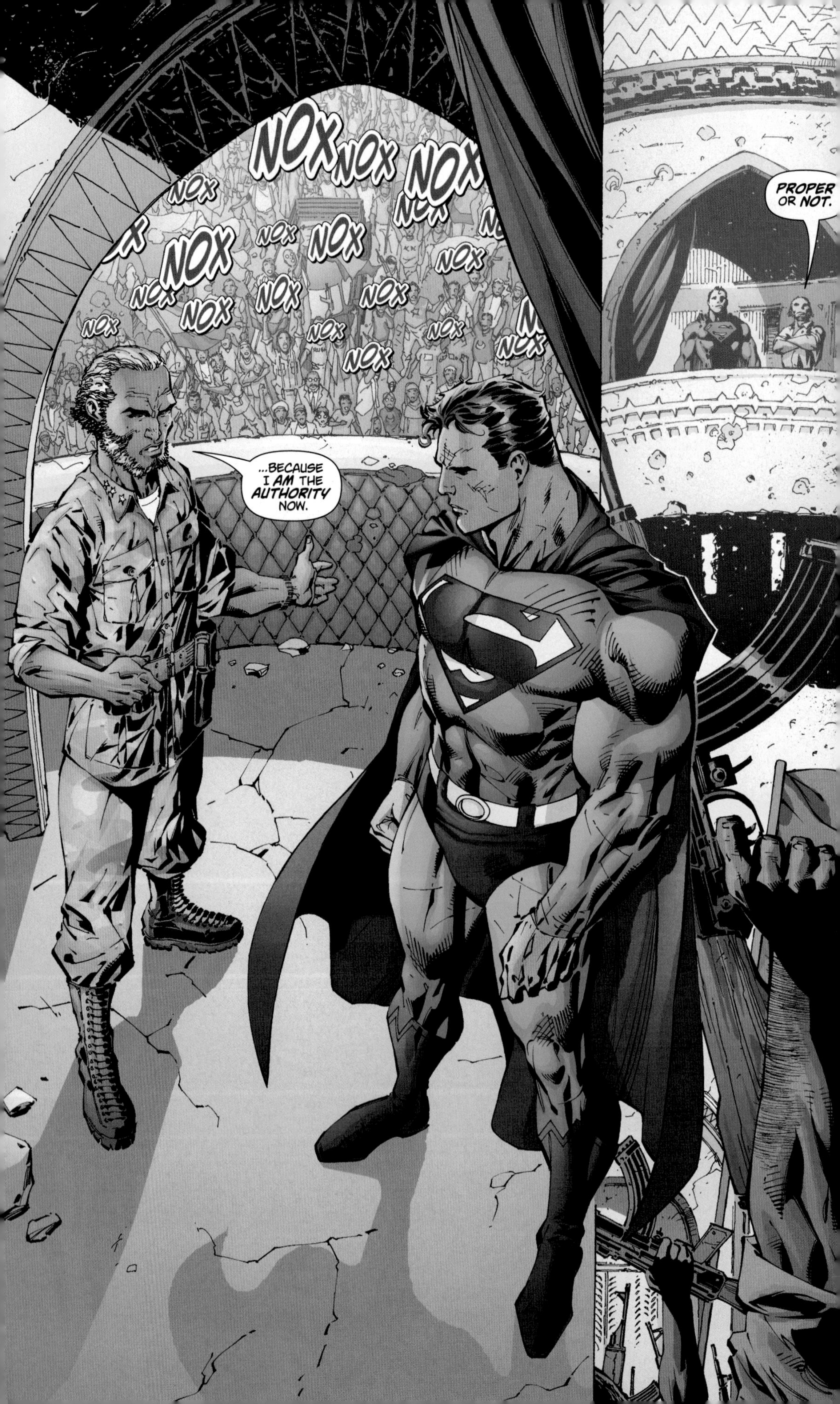
NOX NOX NOX
NOX
NOX
NOX
NOX
NOX
NOX
NOX
NOX
NOX
NOX
NOX
NOX
...BECAUSE I AM THE AUTHORITY NOW.
PROPER OR NOT.

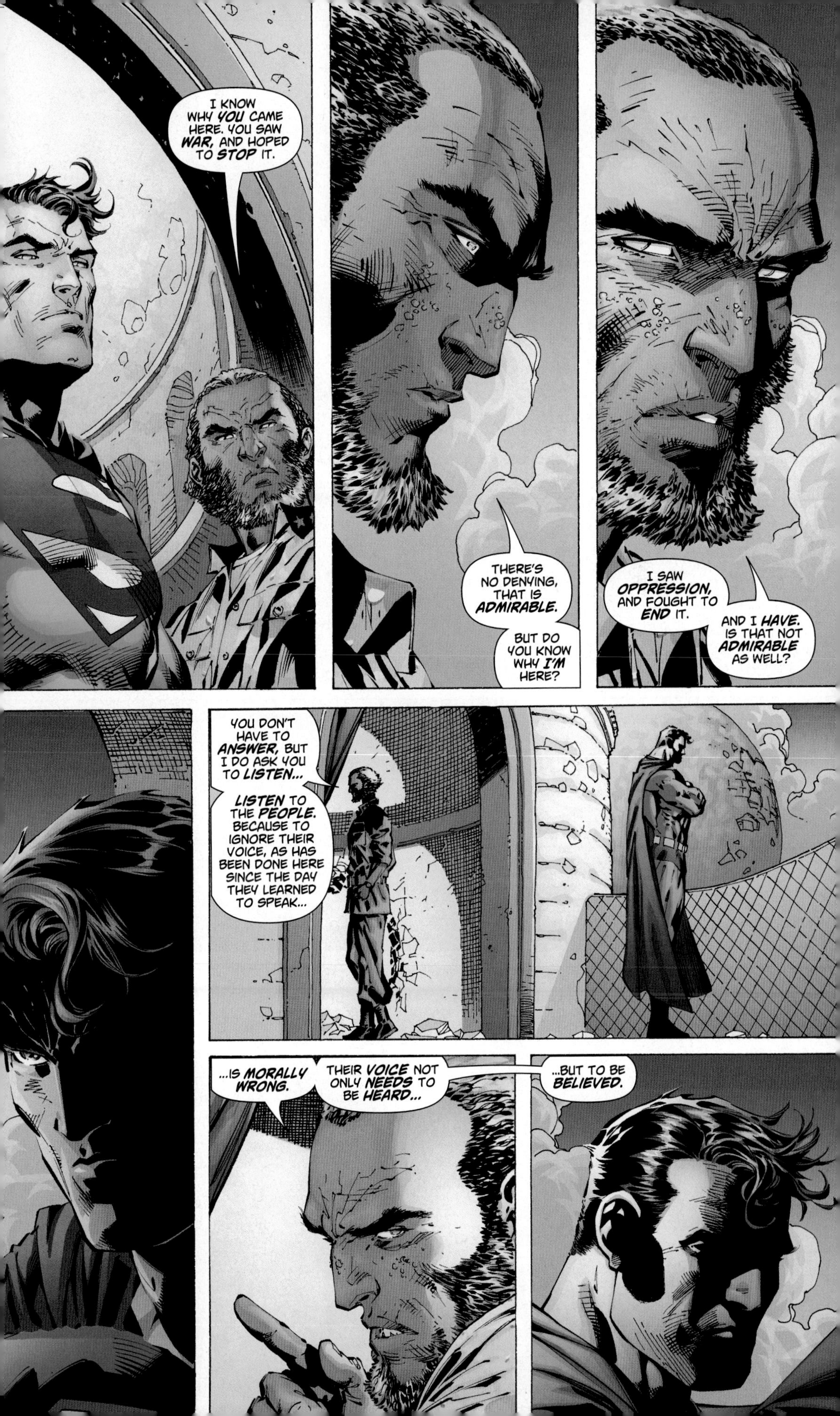
I KNOW WHY YOU CAME HERE. YOU SAW WAR, AND HOPED TO STOP IT.
THERE'S NO DENYING, THAT IS ADMIRABLE.
BUT DO YOU KNOW WHY I'M HERE?
I SAW OPPRESSION, AND FOUGHT TO END IT.
AND I HAVE. IS THAT NOT ADMIRABLE AS WELL?
YOU DON'T HAVE TO ANSWER, BUT I DO ASK YOU TO LISTEN...
LISTEN TO THE PEOPLE. BECAUSE TO IGNORE THEIR VOICE, AS HAS BEEN DONE HERE SINCE THE DAY THEY LEARNED TO SPEAK...
...IS MORALLY WRONG.
THEIR VOICE NOT ONLY NEEDS TO BE HEARD...
...BUT TO BE BELIEVED.

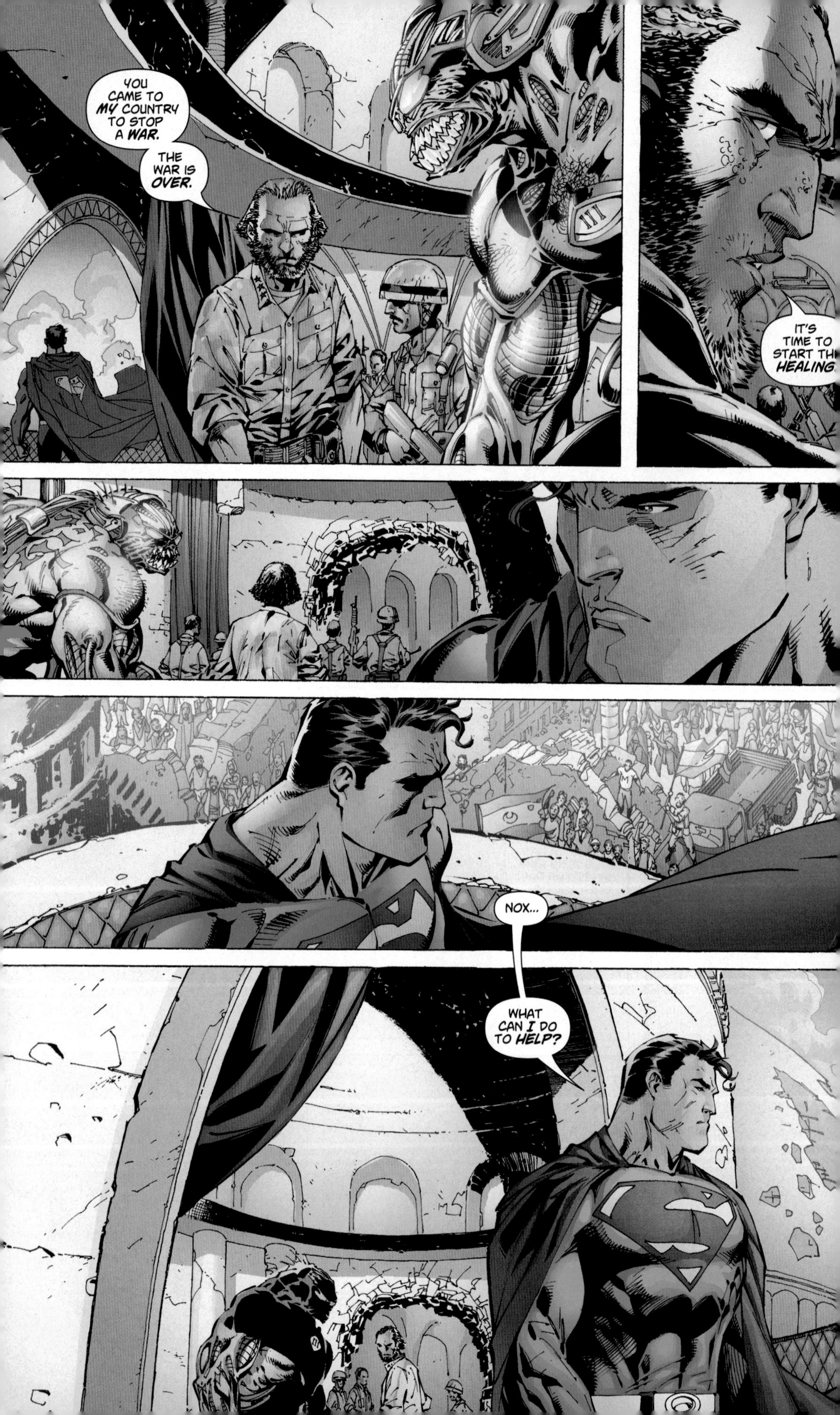
YOU CAME TO MY COUNTRY TO STOP A WAR.
THE WAR IS OVER.
IT'S TIME TO START TH HEALING.
NOX...
WHAT CAN I DO TO HELP?

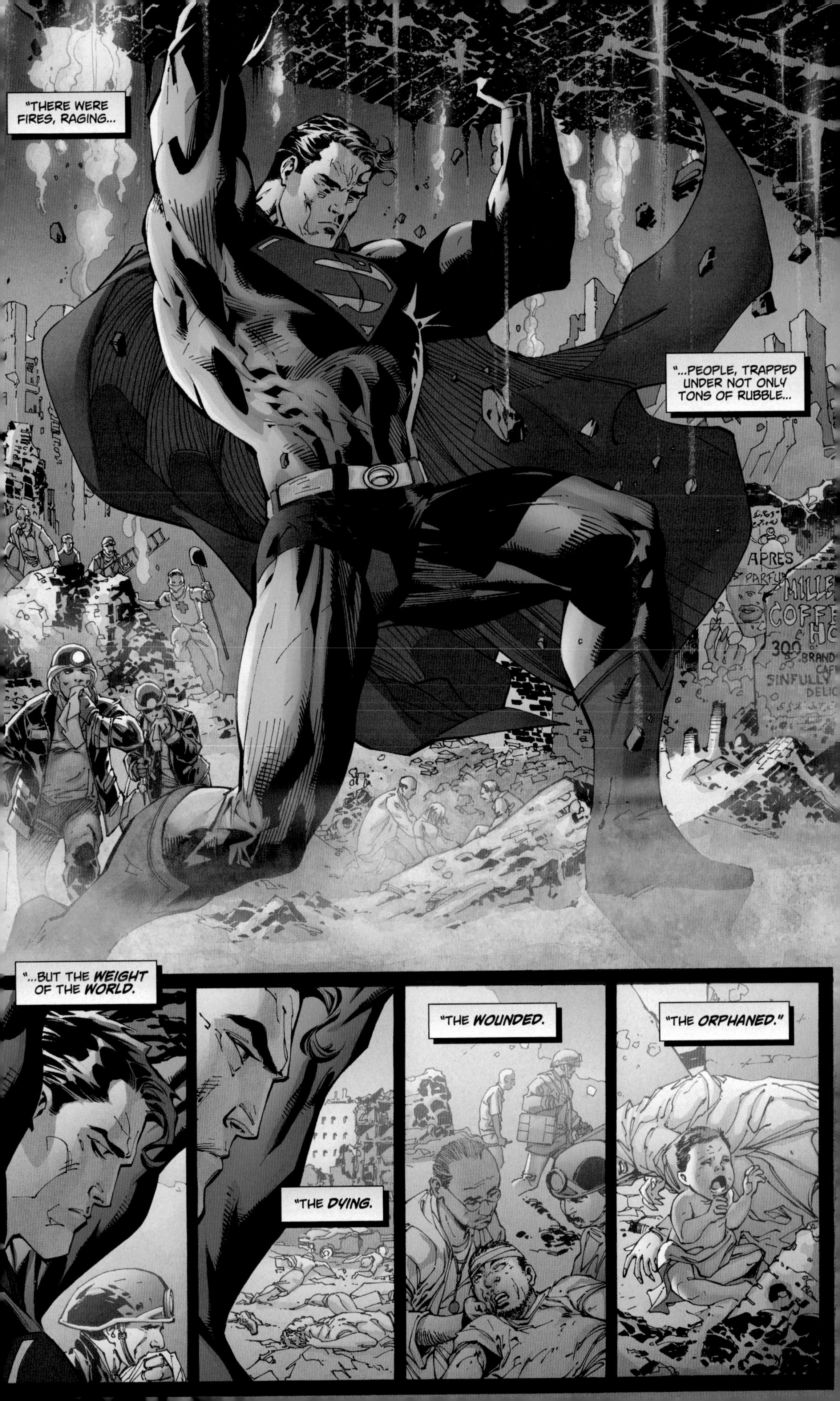
"THERE WERE FIRES, RAGING...
"...PEOPLE, TRAPPED UNDER NOT ONLY TONS OF RUBBLE...
APRES
SINFULLY
"...BUT THE *WEIGHT* OF THE *WORLD*.
"THE *DYING*.
"THE *WOUNDED*.
"THE *ORPHANED*."

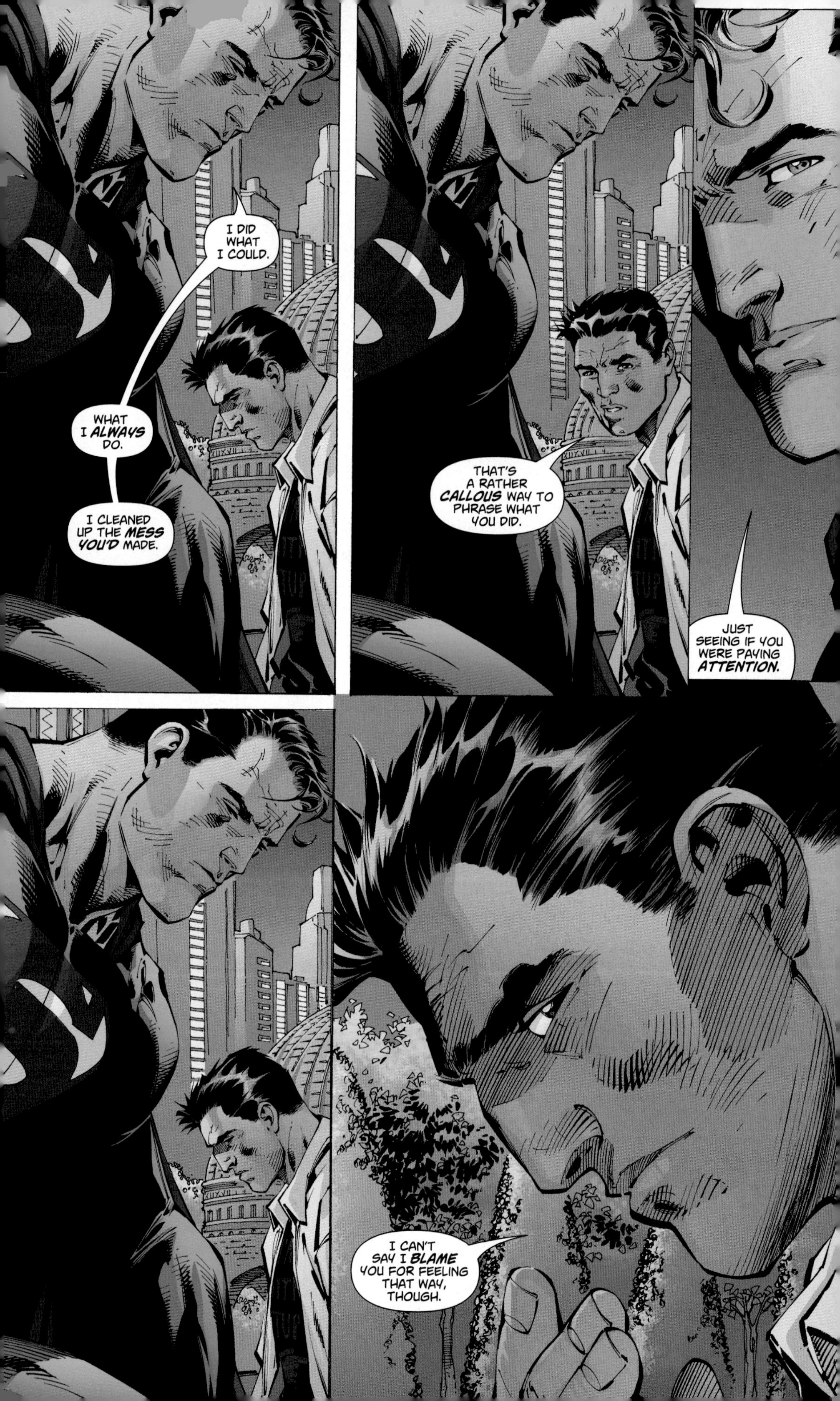
I DID WHAT I COULD.
WHAT I ALWAYS DO.
I CLEANED UP THE MESS YOU'D MADE.
THAT'S A RATHER CALLOUS WAY TO PHRASE WHAT YOU DID.
JUST SEEING IF YOU WERE PAYING ATTENTION.
I CAN'T SAY I BLAME YOU FOR FEELING THAT WAY, THOUGH.

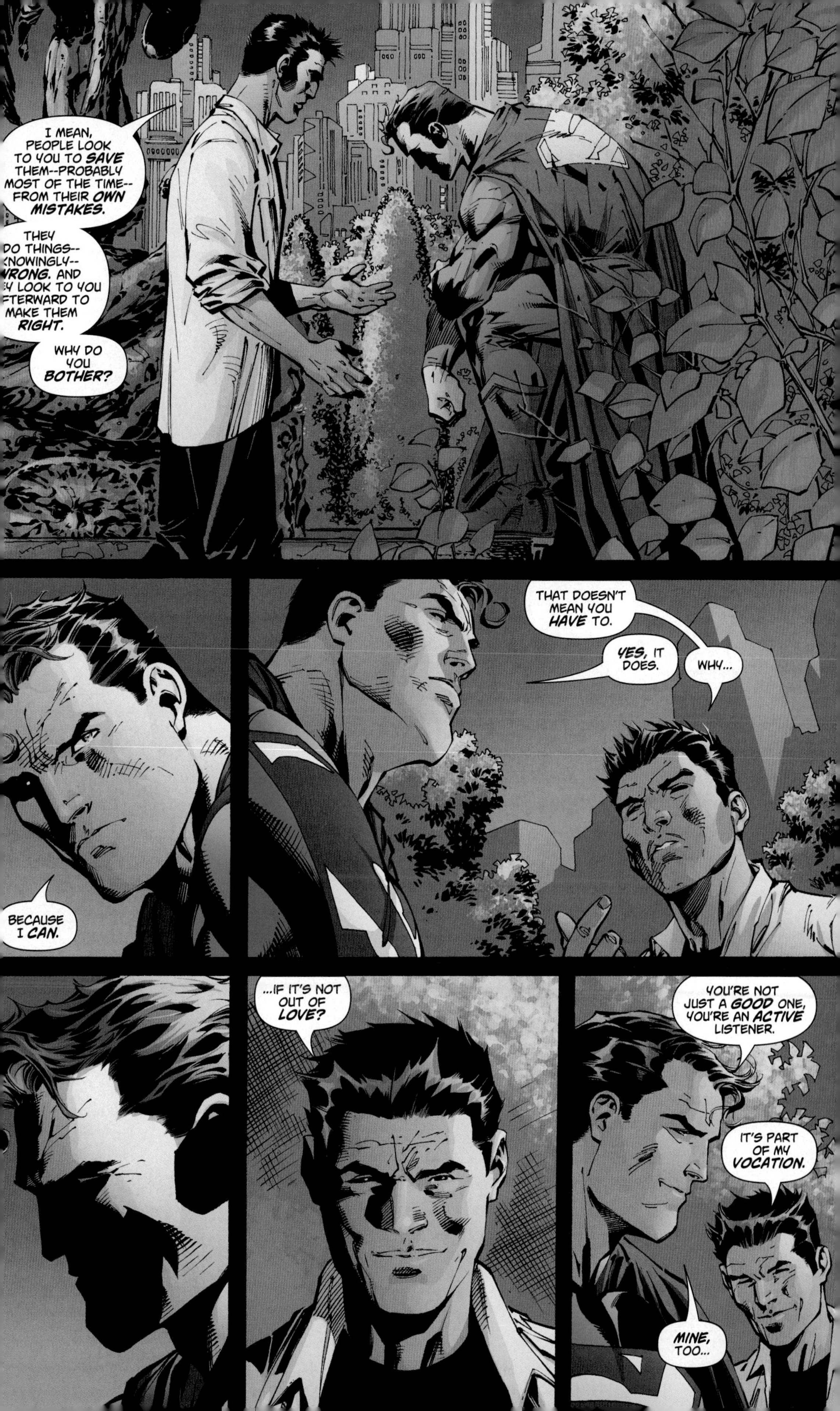
I MEAN, PEOPLE LOOK TO YOU TO SAVE THEM--PROBABLY MOST OF THE TIME--FROM THEIR OWN MISTAKES.
THEY DO THINGS--KNOWINGLY--WRONG. AND EY LOOK TO YOU FTERWARD TO MAKE THEM RIGHT.
WHY DO YOU BOTHER?
BECAUSE I CAN.
THAT DOESN'T MEAN YOU HAVE TO.
YES, IT DOES.
WHY...
...IF IT'S NOT OUT OF LOVE?
YOU'RE NOT JUST A GOOD ONE, YOU'RE AN ACTIVE LISTENER.
IT'S PART OF MY VOCATION.
MINE, TOO...

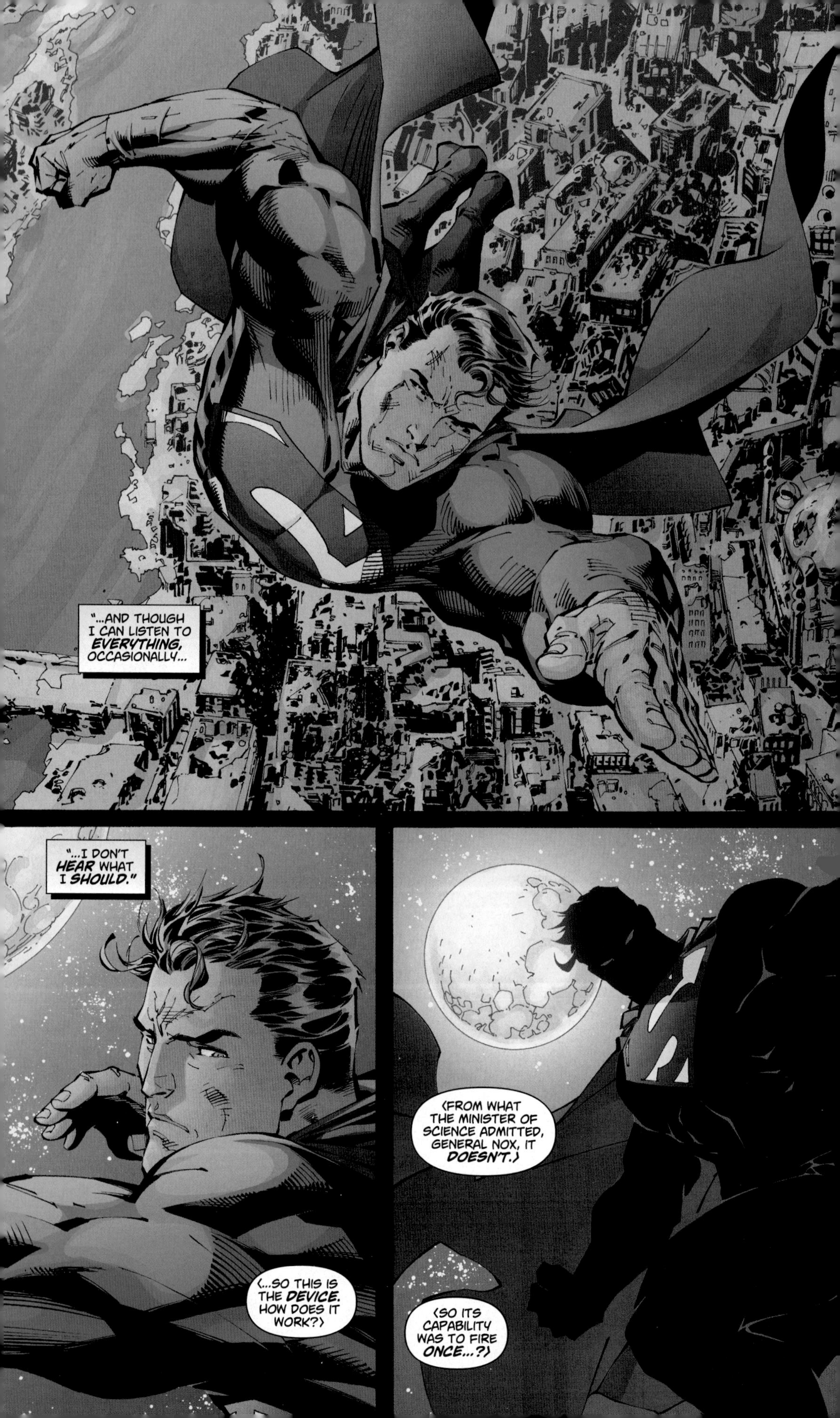
"...AND THOUGH I CAN LISTEN TO EVERYTHING, OCCASIONALLY...
"...I DON'T HEAR WHAT I SHOULD."
‹...SO THIS IS THE DEVICE. HOW DOES IT WORK?›
‹FROM WHAT THE MINISTER OF SCIENCE ADMITTED, GENERAL NOX, IT DOESN'T.›
‹SO ITS CAPABILITY WAS TO FIRE ONCE...?›

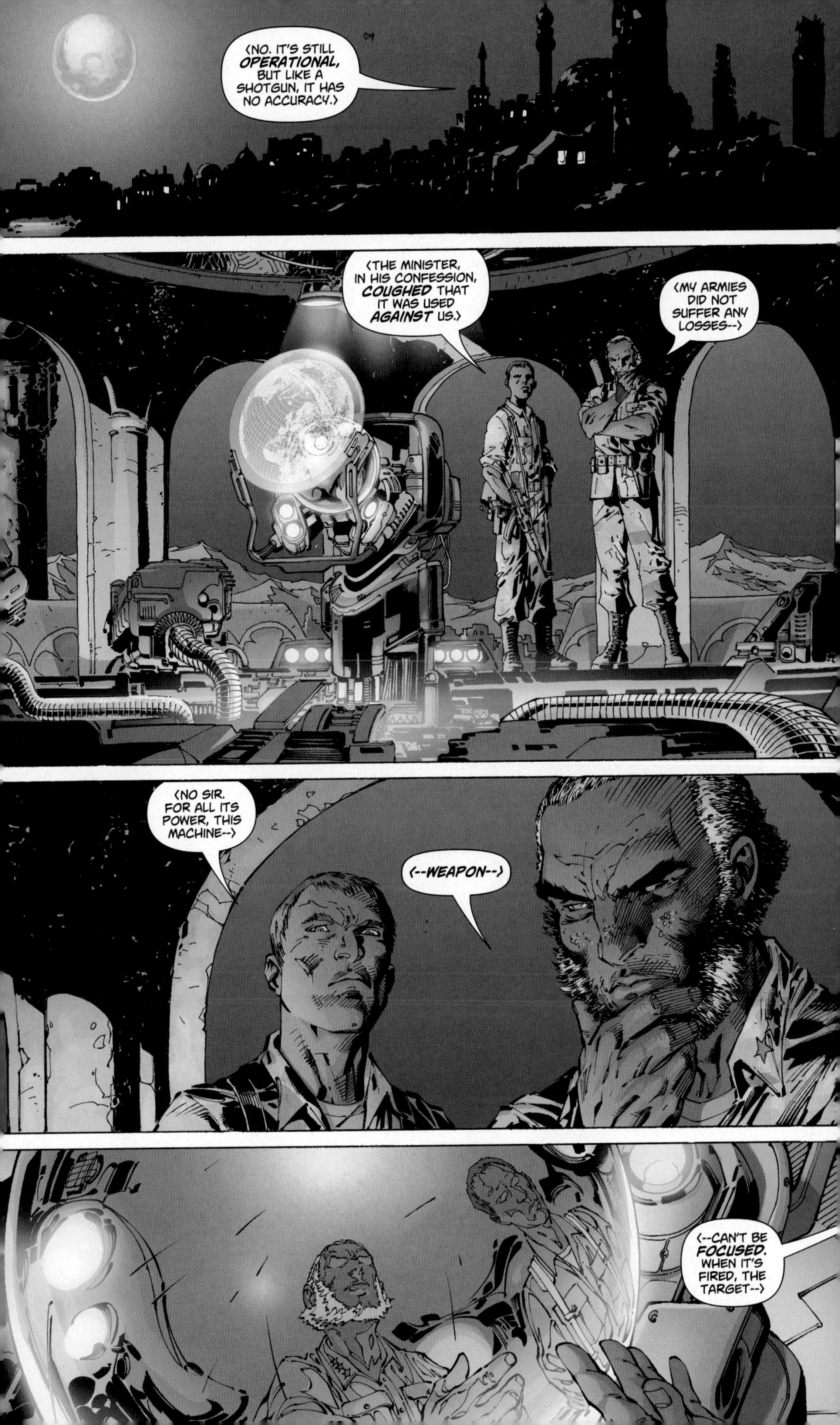
‹NO. IT'S STILL OPERATIONAL, BUT LIKE A SHOTGUN, IT HAS NO ACCURACY.›
‹THE MINISTER, IN HIS CONFESSION, COUGHED THAT IT WAS USED AGAINST US.›
‹MY ARMIES DID NOT SUFFER ANY LOSSES--›
‹NO SIR. FOR ALL ITS POWER, THIS MACHINE--›
‹--WEAPON--›
‹--CAN'T BE FOCUSED. WHEN IT'S FIRED, THE TARGET--›

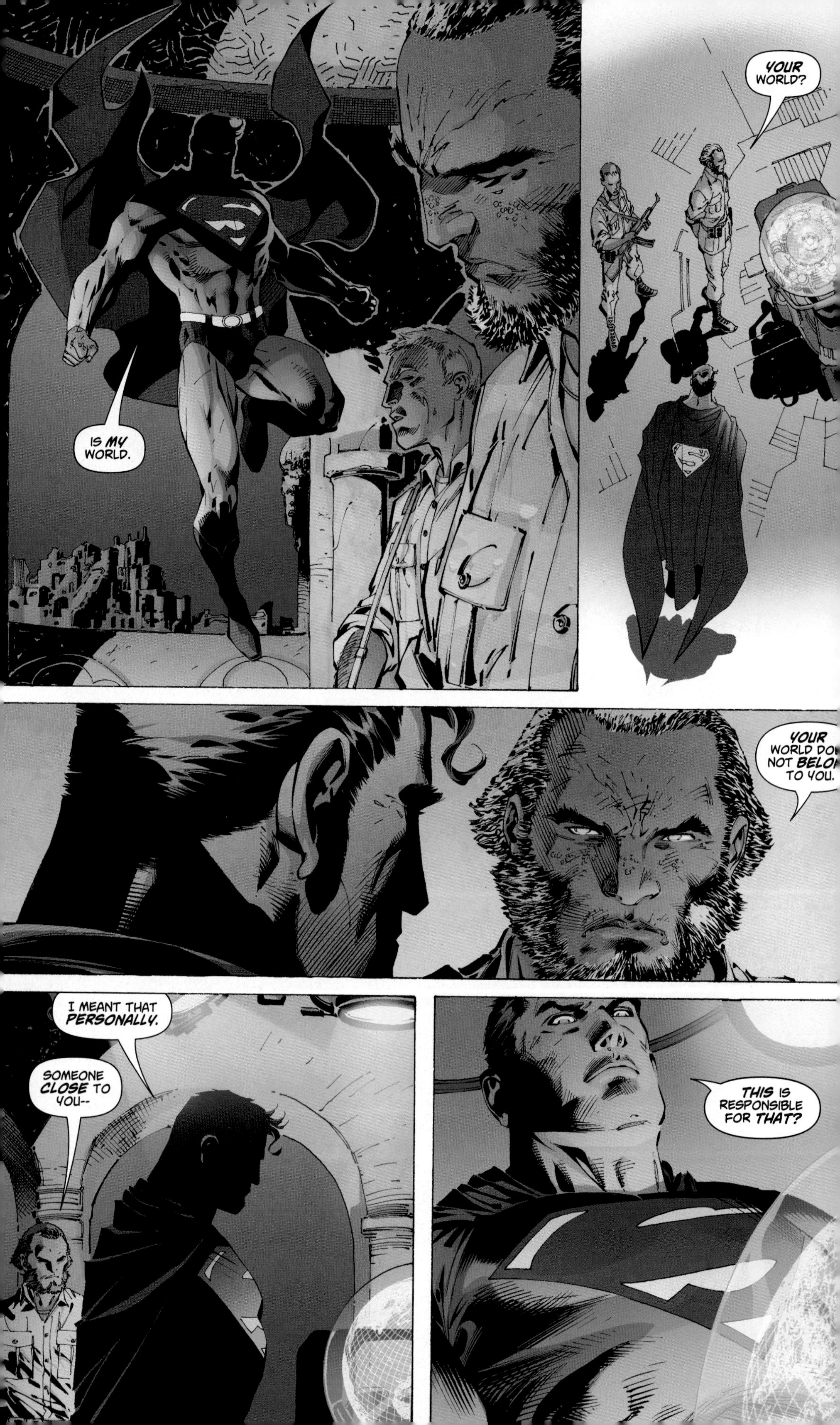
IS *MY* WORLD.
YOUR WORLD?
YOUR WORLD DO NOT *BELO* TO YOU.
I MEANT THAT *PERSONALLY*.
SOMEONE *CLOSE* TO YOU--
THIS IS RESPONSIBLE FOR *THAT*?

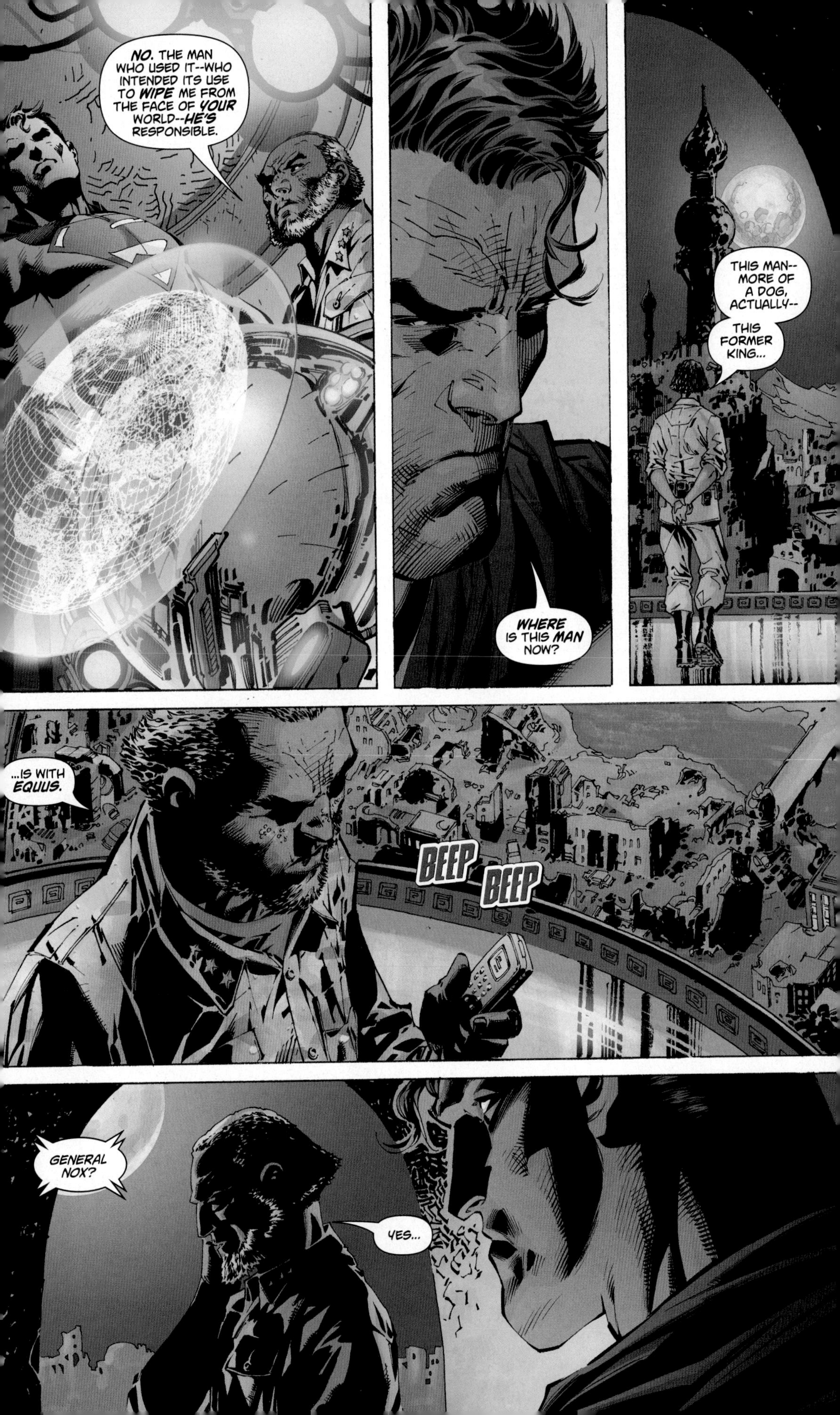
NO. THE MAN WHO USED IT--WHO INTENDED ITS USE TO WIPE ME FROM THE FACE OF YOUR WORLD--HE'S RESPONSIBLE.
WHERE IS THIS MAN NOW?
THIS MAN-- MORE OF A DOG, ACTUALLY--
THIS FORMER KING...
...IS WITH EQUUS.
BEEP
BEEP
GENERAL NOX?
YES...

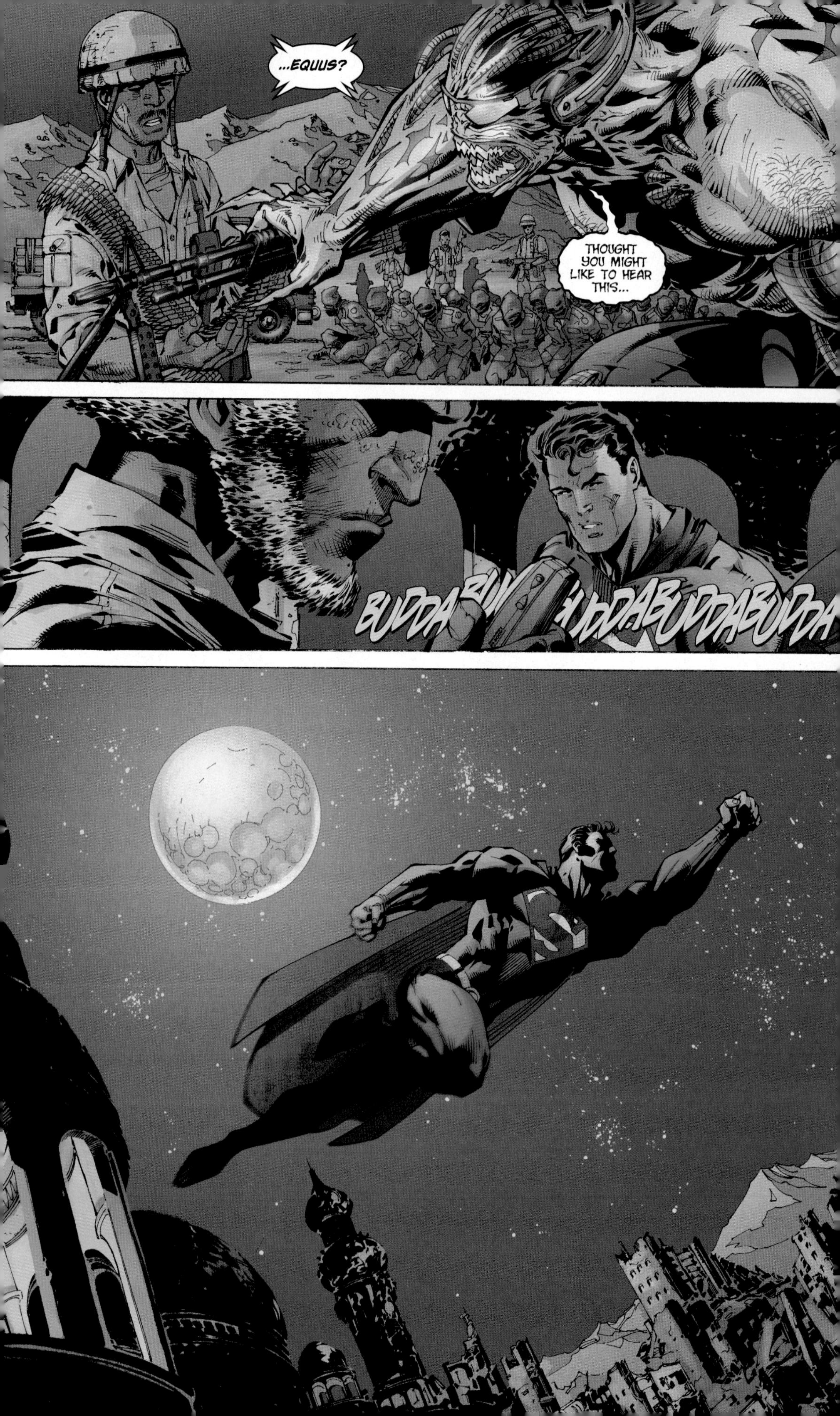
...EQUUS?
THOUGHT YOU MIGHT LIKE TO HEAR THIS...
BUDDA BUDDABUDDABUDDA

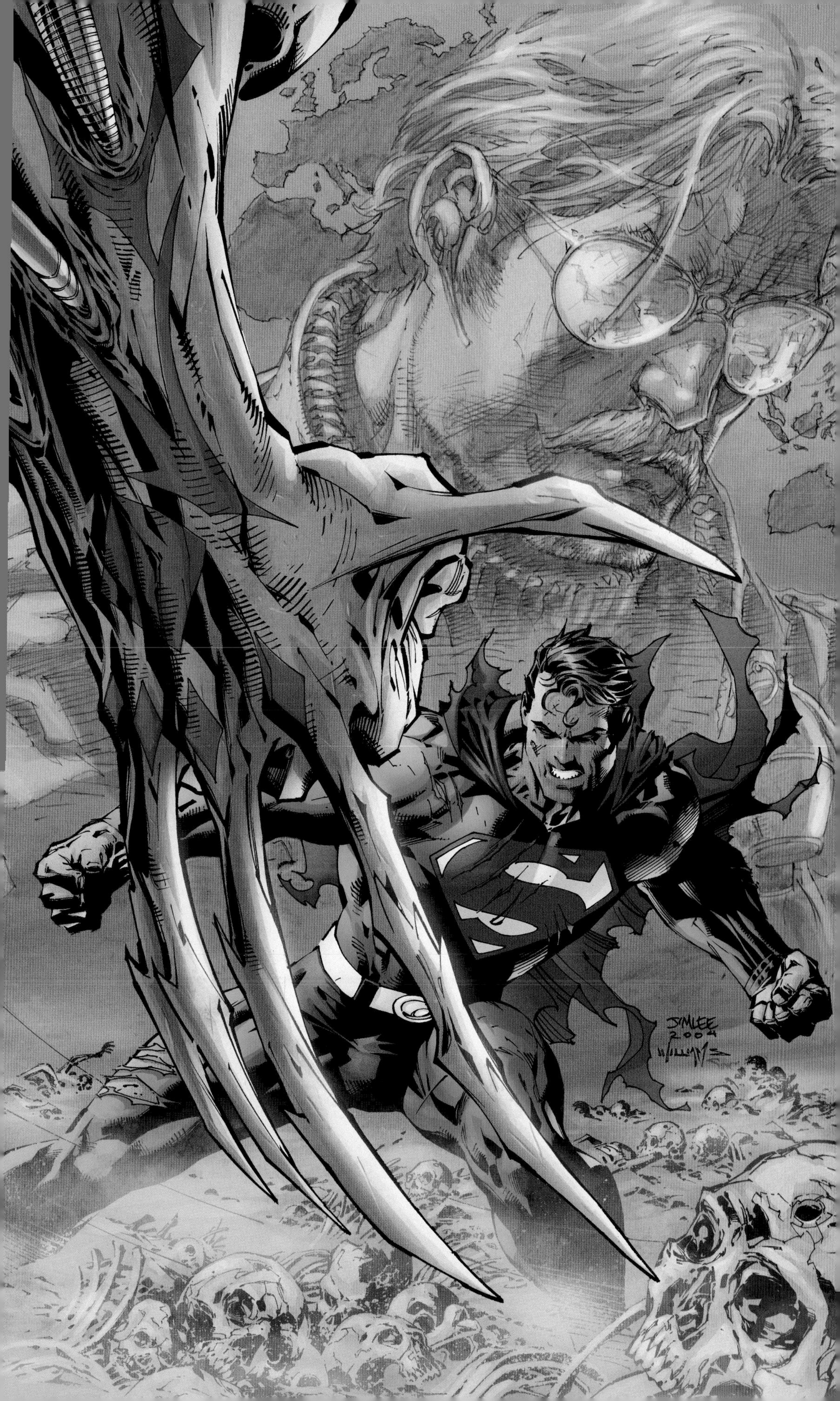
JIMLEE
2004

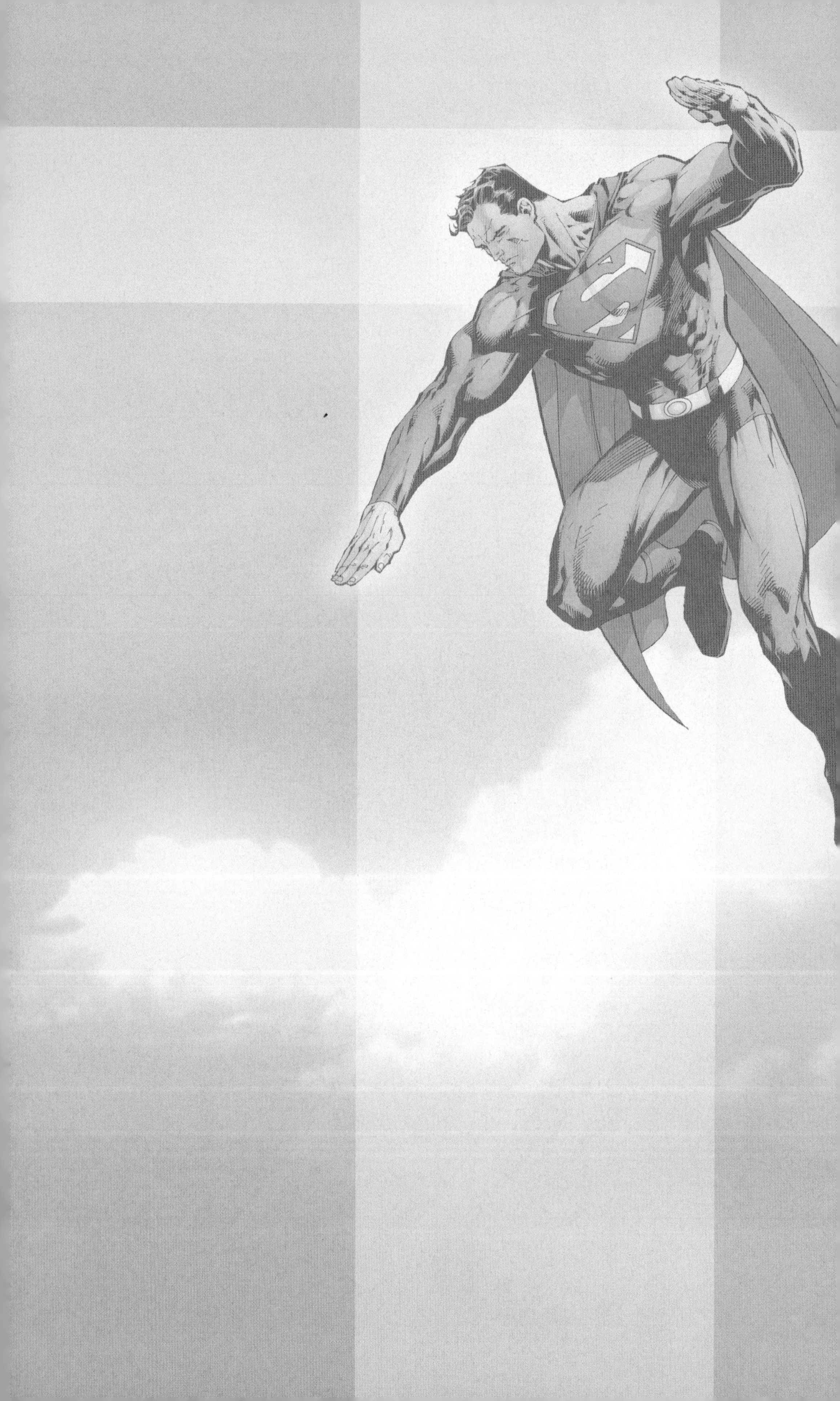

"SIX HUNDRED SEVENTY-TWO MILES PER HOUR.

"THAT'S THE SPEED OF A BULLET FIRED FROM AN M-60.

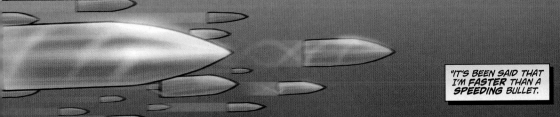

"IT'S BEEN SAID THAT I'M FASTER THAN A SPEEDING BULLET.

"AND I AM."

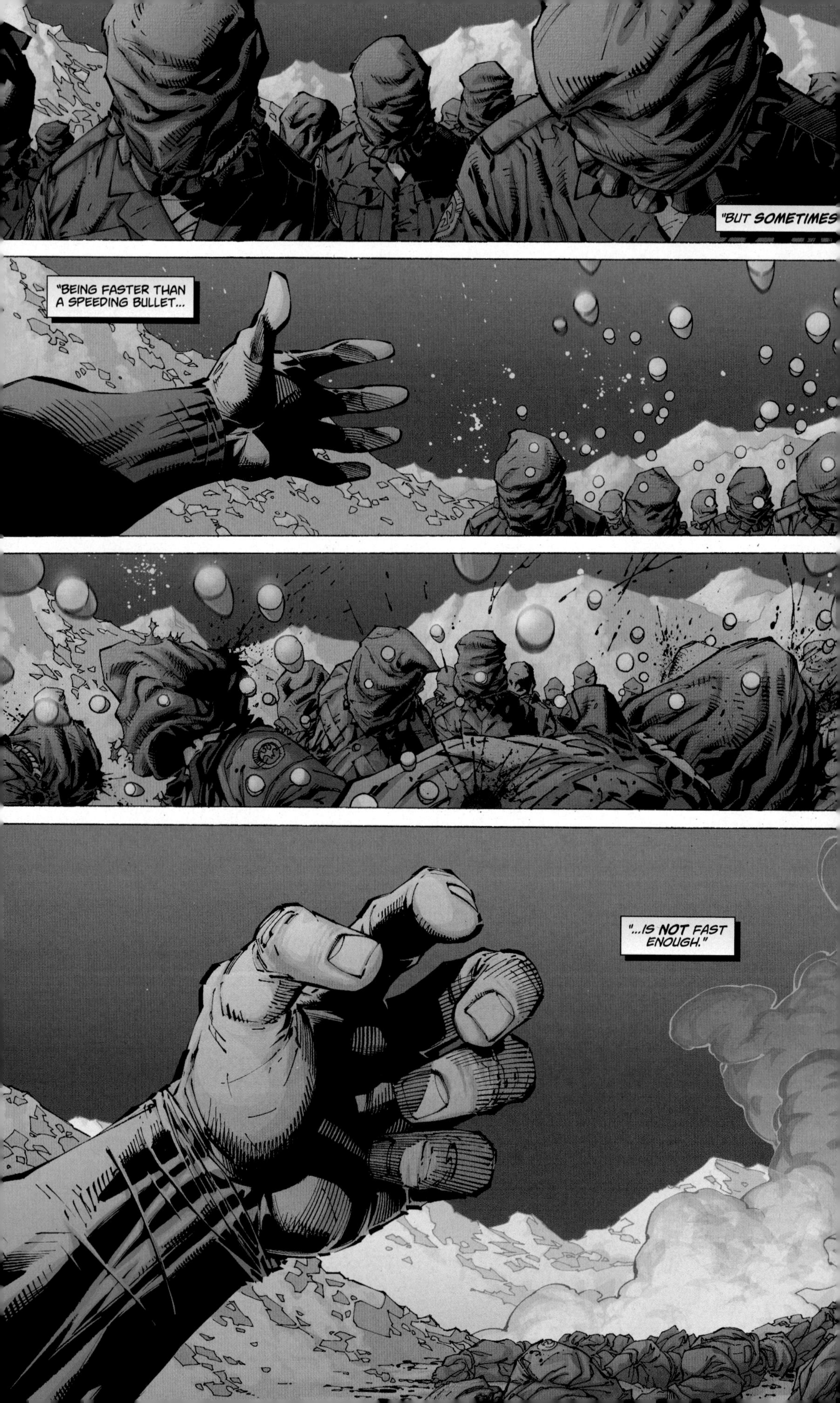
"BUT SOMETIMES
"BEING FASTER THAN A SPEEDING BULLET...
"...IS NOT FAST ENOUGH."

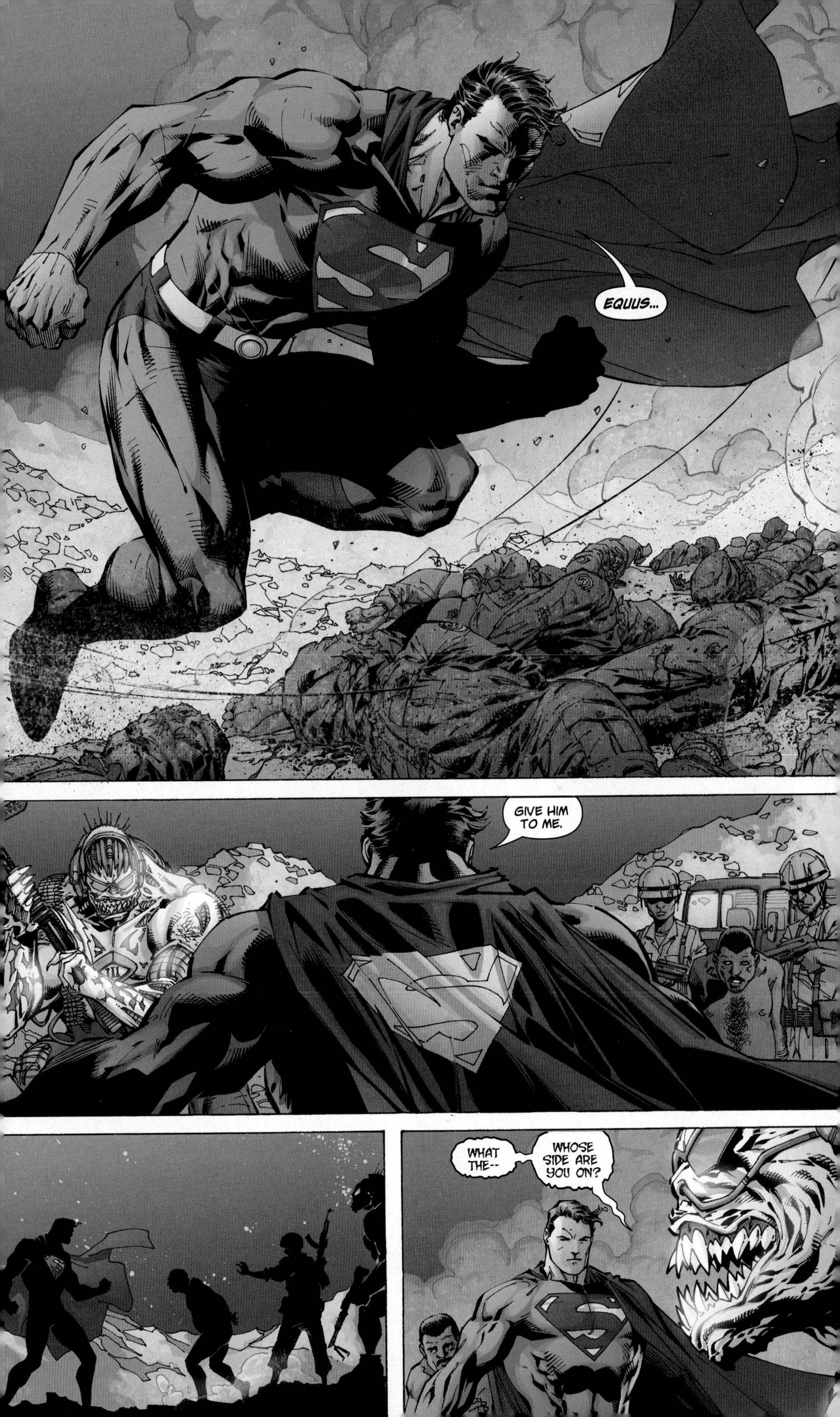
EQUUS...
GIVE HIM TO ME.
WHAT THE--
WHOSE SIDE ARE YOU ON?

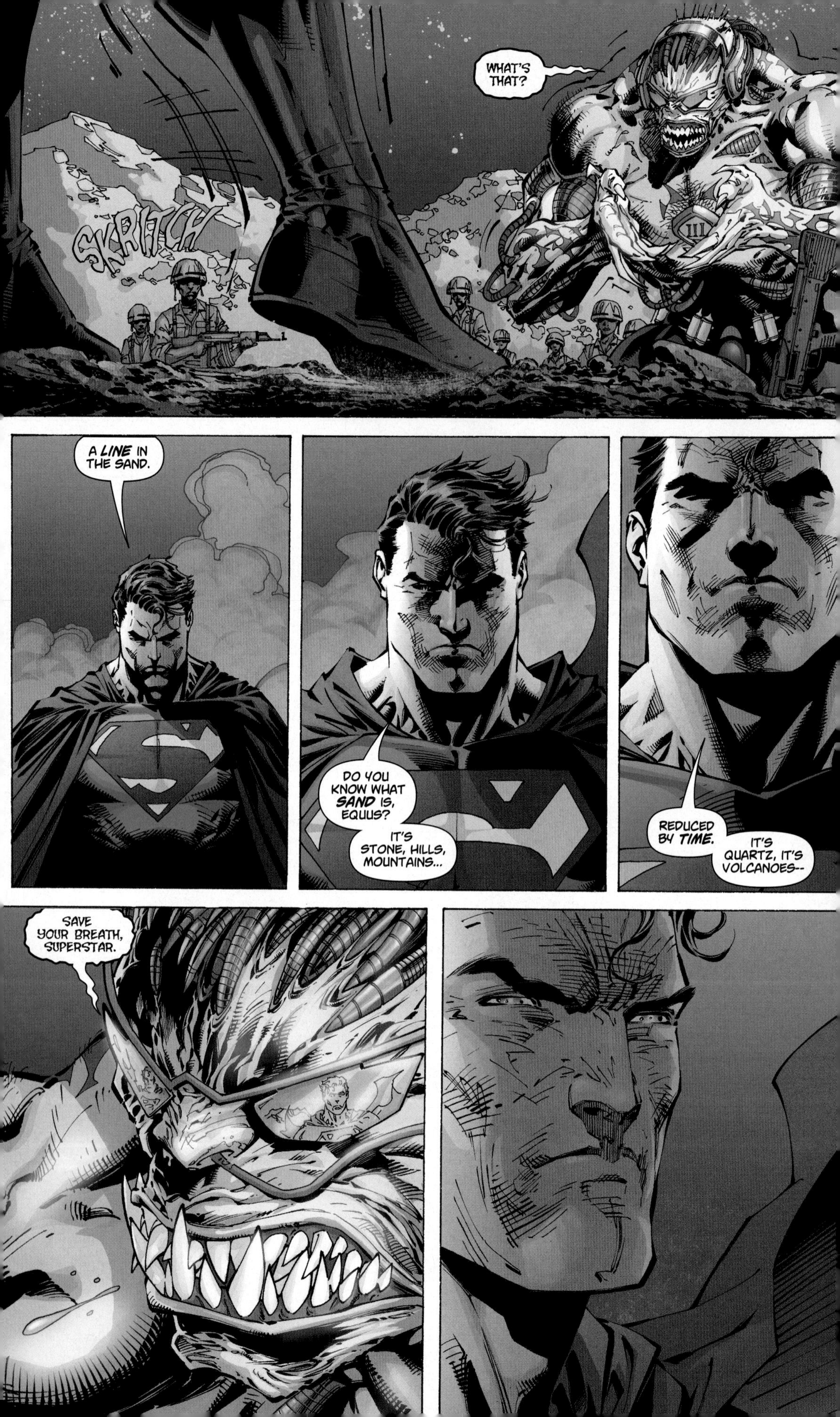
WHAT'S THAT?
SKRITCH
A LINE IN THE SAND.
DO YOU KNOW WHAT SAND IS, EQUUS?
IT'S STONE, HILLS, MOUNTAINS...
REDUCED BY TIME.
IT'S QUARTZ, IT'S VOLCANOES--
SAVE YOUR BREATH, SUPERSTAR.

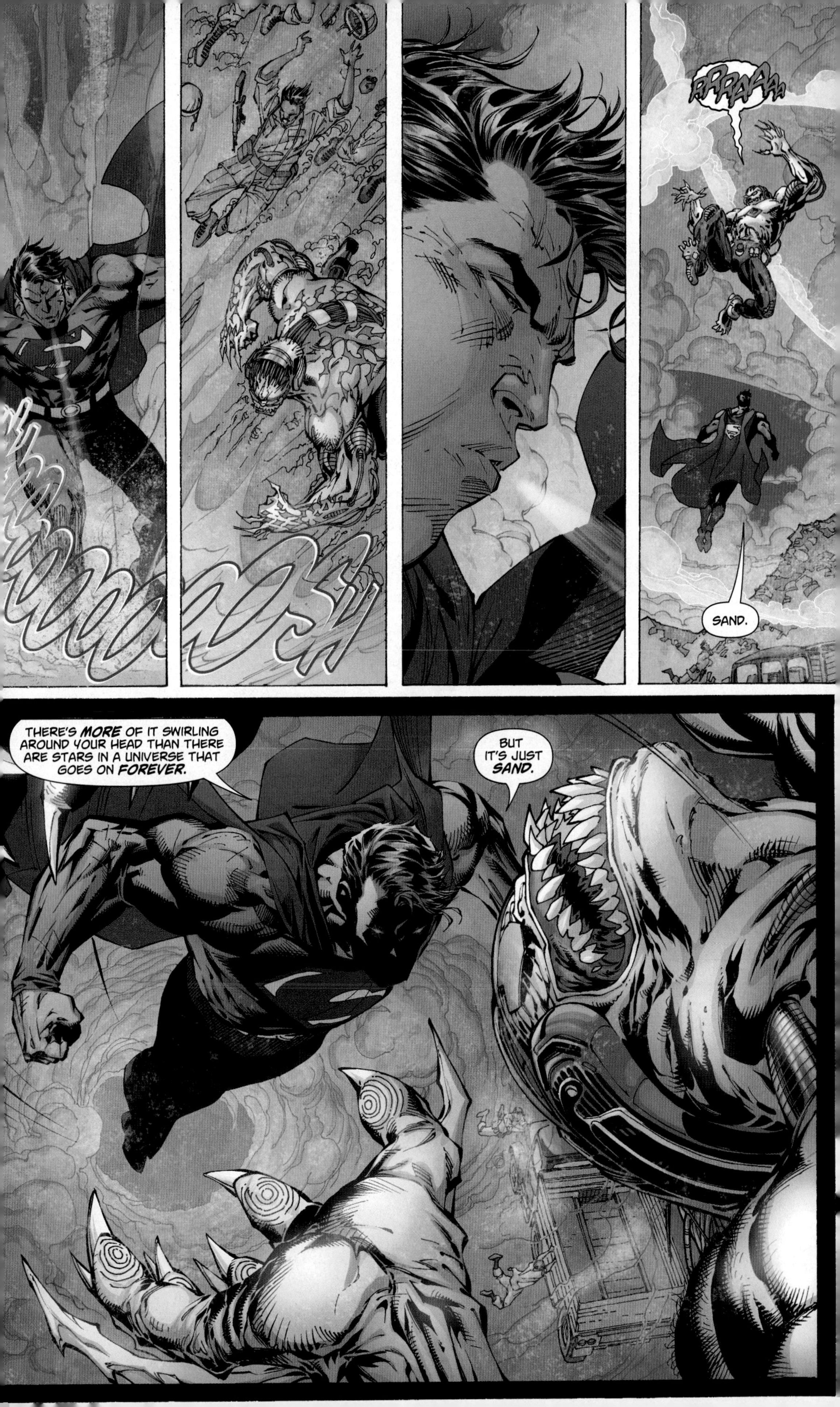
RRRAAAAA
SAND.
THERE'S MORE OF IT SWIRLING AROUND YOUR HEAD THAN THERE ARE STARS IN A UNIVERSE THAT GOES ON FOREVER.
BUT IT'S JUST SAND.

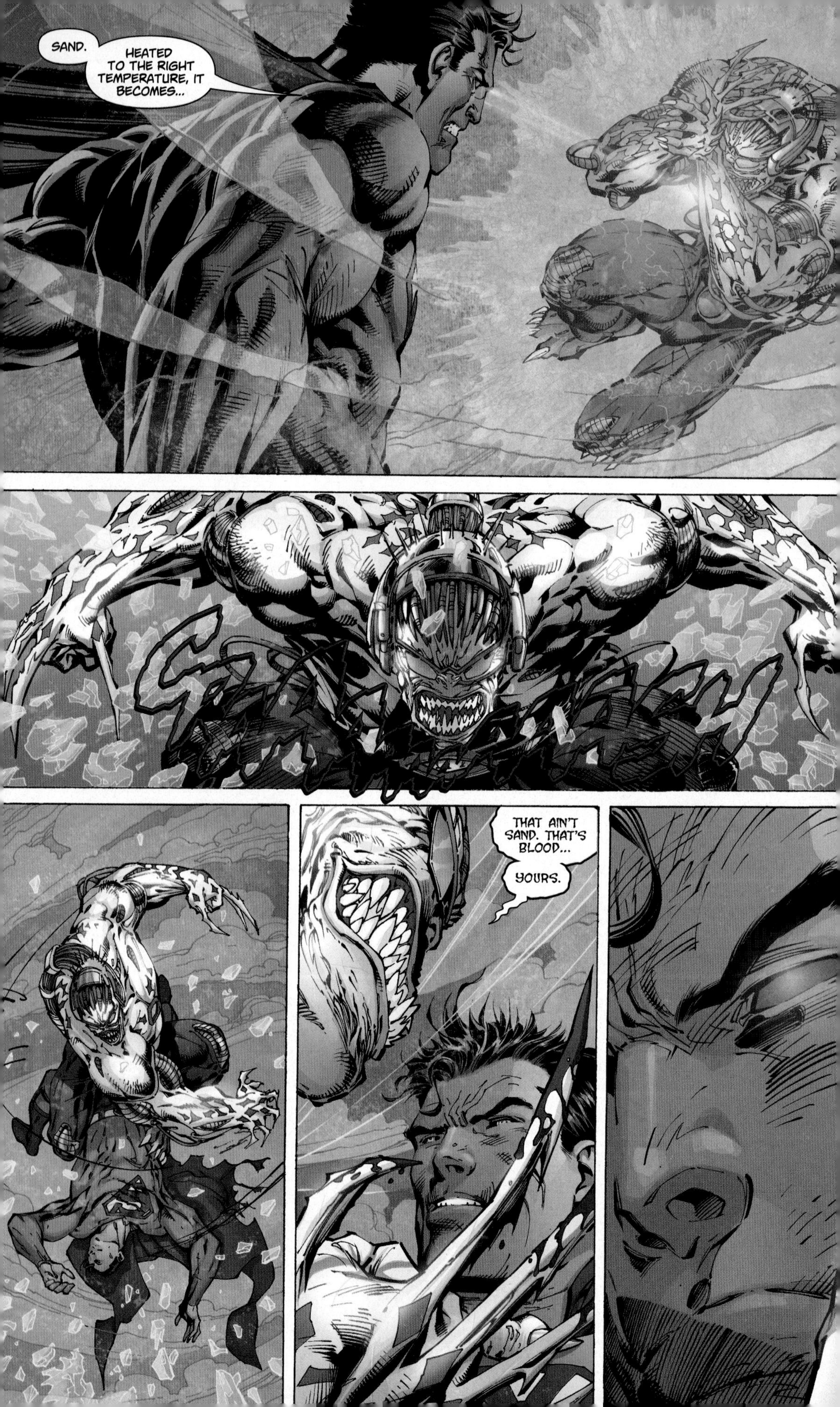
SAND.
HEATED TO THE RIGHT TEMPERATURE, IT BECOMES...
THAT AIN'T SAND. THAT'S BLOOD...
YOURS.

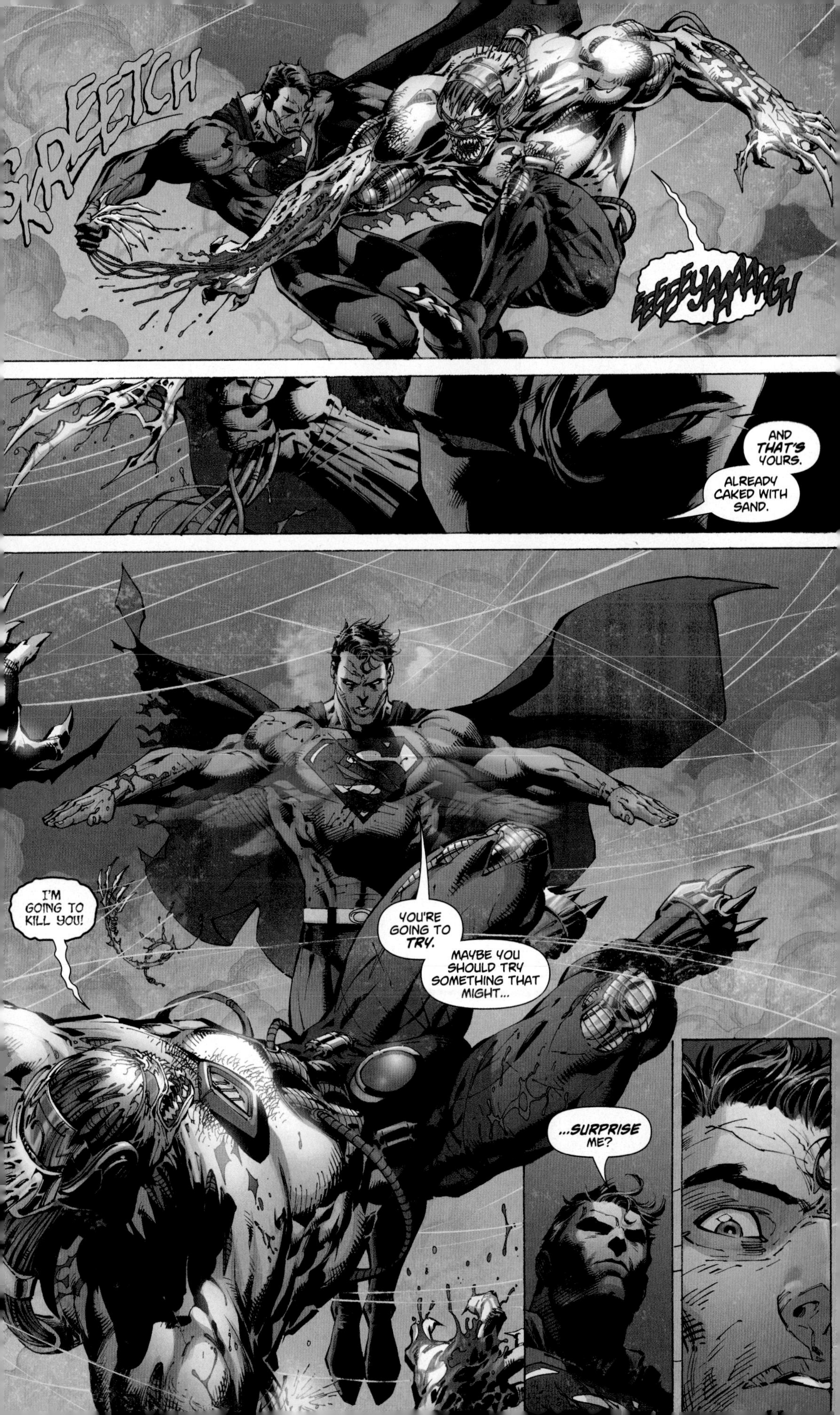
SKREEETCH
EEEEYAAAARGH
AND THAT'S YOURS.
ALREADY CAKED WITH SAND.
I'M GOING TO KILL YOU!
YOU'RE GOING TO TRY.
MAYBE YOU SHOULD TRY SOMETHING THAT MIGHT...
...SURPRISE ME?

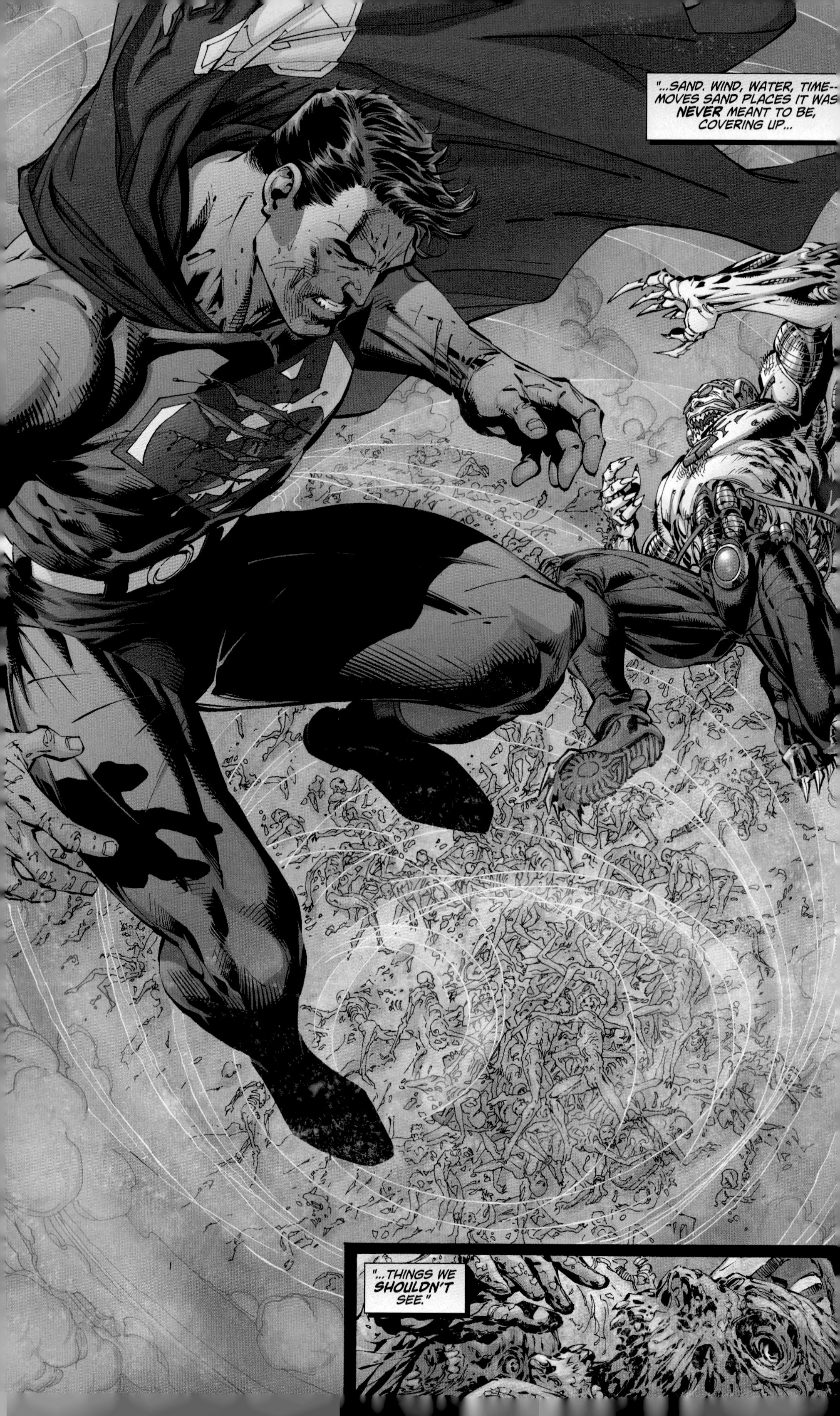
"...SAND. WIND, WATER, TIME--MOVES SAND PLACES IT WAS NEVER MEANT TO BE, COVERING UP...
"...THINGS WE SHOULDN'T SEE."

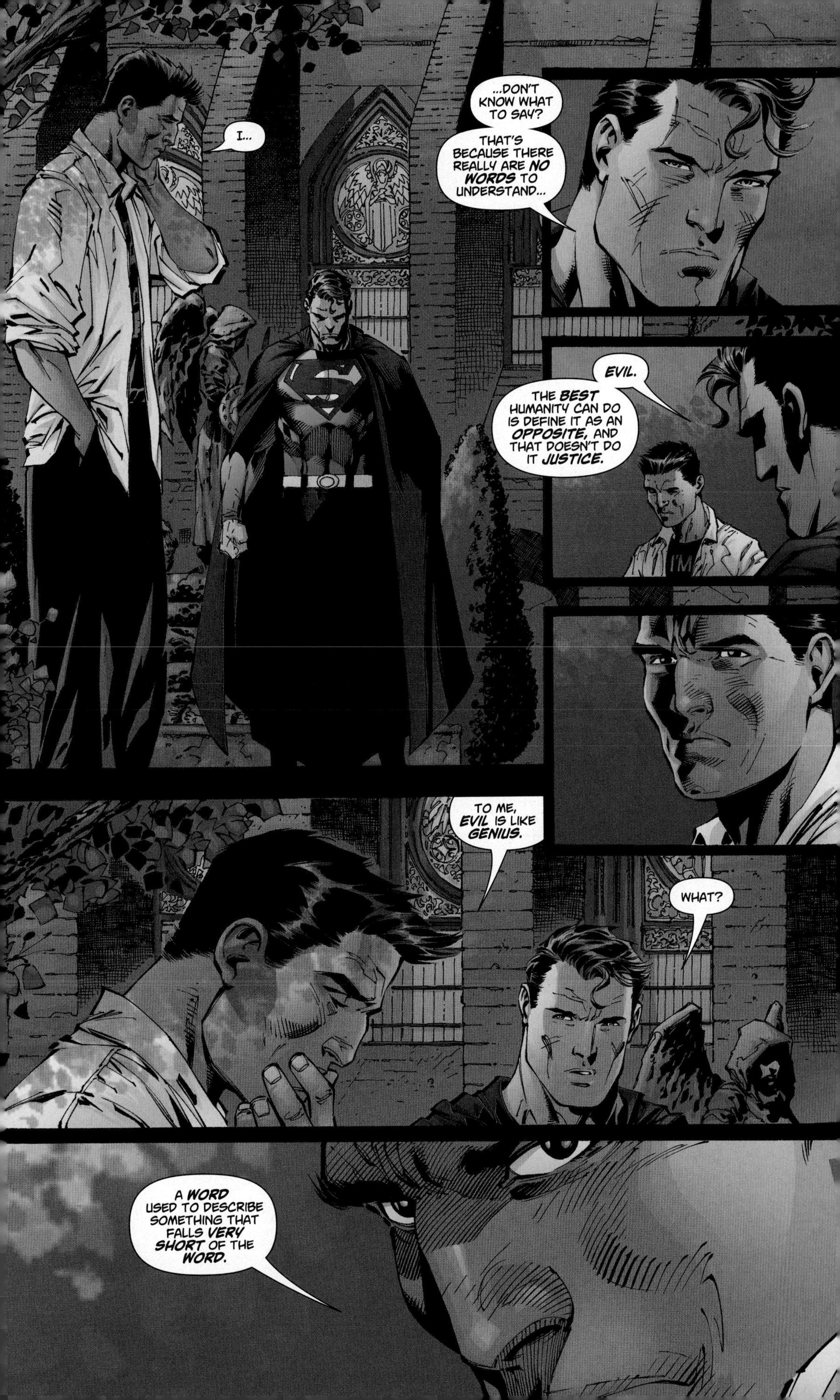

I...
...DON'T KNOW WHAT TO SAY?
THAT'S BECAUSE THERE REALLY ARE NO WORDS TO UNDERSTAND...
EVIL.
THE BEST HUMANITY CAN DO IS DEFINE IT AS AN OPPOSITE, AND THAT DOESN'T DO IT JUSTICE.
TO ME, EVIL IS LIKE GENIUS.
WHAT?
A WORD USED TO DESCRIBE SOMETHING THAT FALLS VERY SHORT OF THE WORD.

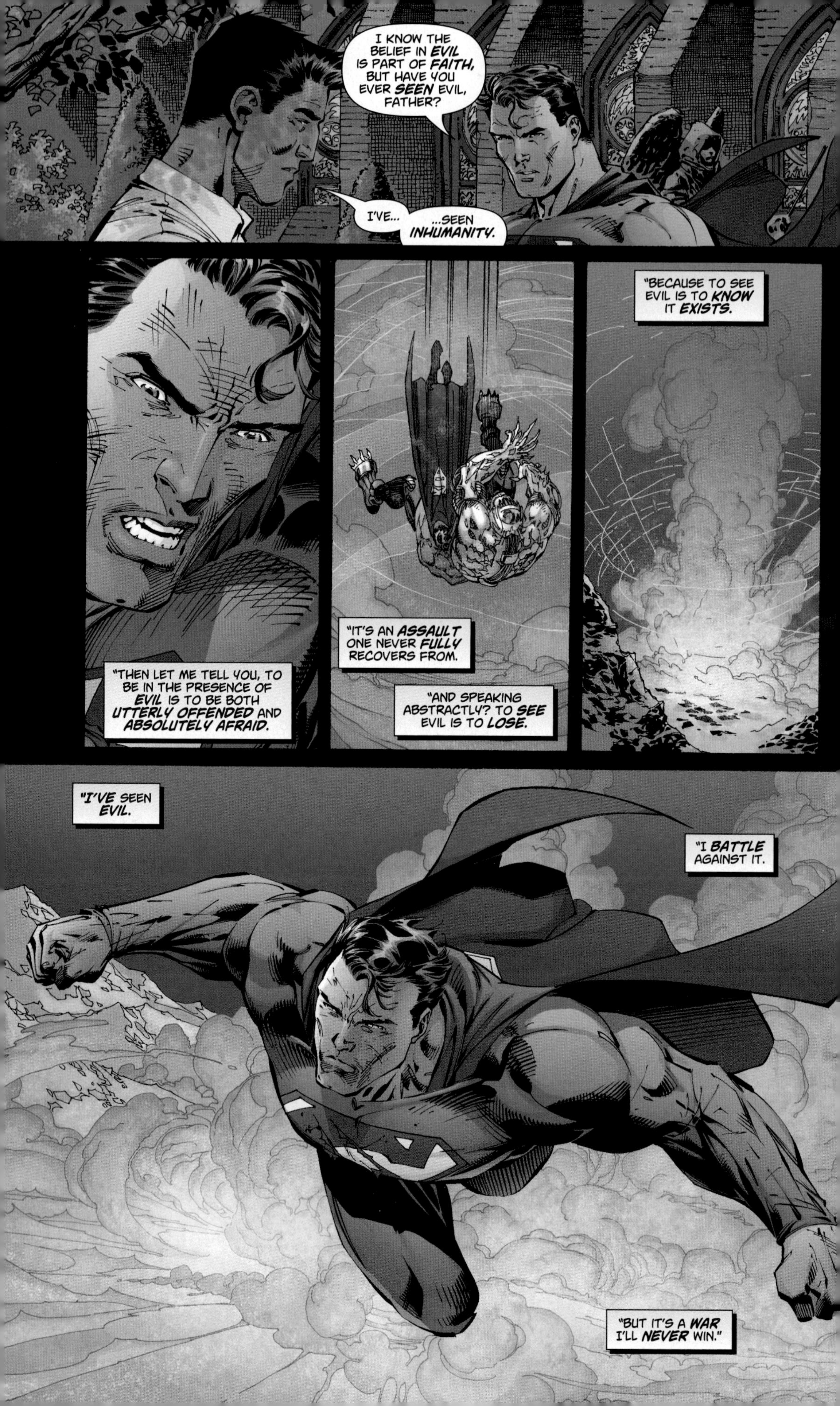
I KNOW THE BELIEF IN EVIL IS PART OF FAITH, BUT HAVE YOU EVER SEEN EVIL, FATHER?
I'VE...
...SEEN INHUMANITY.
"THEN LET ME TELL YOU, TO BE IN THE PRESENCE OF EVIL IS TO BE BOTH UTTERLY OFFENDED AND ABSOLUTELY AFRAID.
"IT'S AN ASSAULT ONE NEVER FULLY RECOVERS FROM.
"AND SPEAKING ABSTRACTLY? TO SEE EVIL IS TO LOSE.
"BECAUSE TO SEE EVIL IS TO KNOW IT EXISTS.
"I'VE SEEN EVIL.
"I BATTLE AGAINST IT.
"BUT IT'S A WAR I'LL NEVER WIN."

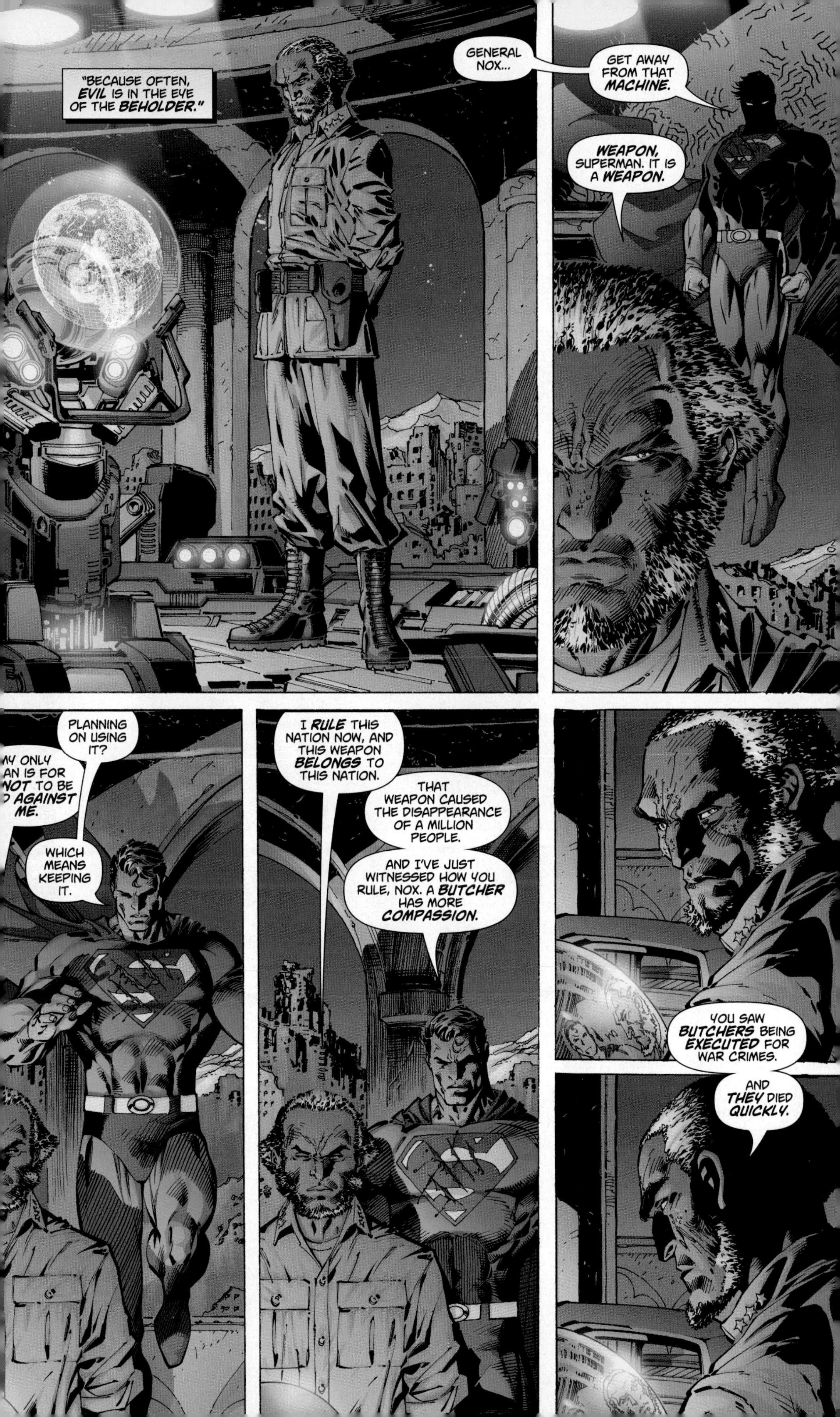
"BECAUSE OFTEN, EVIL IS IN THE EYE OF THE BEHOLDER."
GENERAL NOX...
GET AWAY FROM THAT MACHINE.
WEAPON, SUPERMAN. IT IS A WEAPON.
PLANNING ON USING IT?
MY ONLY
AN IS FOR
NOT TO BE
AGAINST
ME.
WHICH MEANS KEEPING IT.
I RULE THIS NATION NOW, AND THIS WEAPON BELONGS TO THIS NATION.
THAT WEAPON CAUSED THE DISAPPEARANCE OF A MILLION PEOPLE.
AND I'VE JUST WITNESSED HOW YOU RULE, NOX. A BUTCHER HAS MORE COMPASSION.
YOU SAW BUTCHERS BEING EXECUTED FOR WAR CRIMES.
AND THEY DIED QUICKLY.

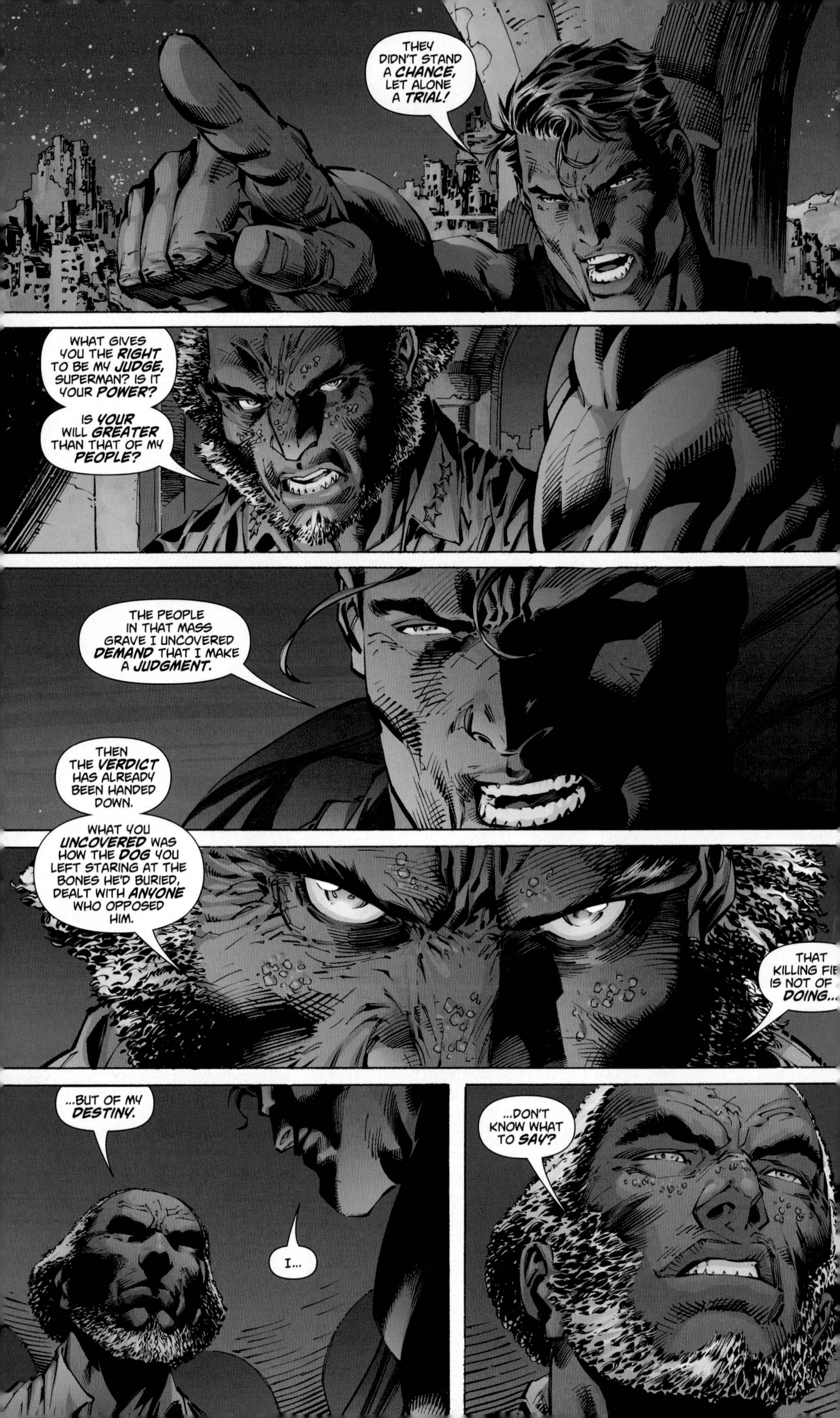

THEY DIDN'T STAND A CHANCE, LET ALONE A TRIAL!
WHAT GIVES YOU THE RIGHT TO BE MY JUDGE, SUPERMAN? IS IT YOUR POWER?
IS YOUR WILL GREATER THAN THAT OF MY PEOPLE?
THE PEOPLE IN THAT MASS GRAVE I UNCOVERED DEMAND THAT I MAKE A JUDGMENT.
THEN THE VERDICT HAS ALREADY BEEN HANDED DOWN.
WHAT YOU UNCOVERED WAS HOW THE DOG YOU LEFT STARING AT THE BONES HE'D BURIED, DEALT WITH ANYONE WHO OPPOSED HIM.
THAT KILLING FIE IS NOT OF DOING...
...BUT OF MY DESTINY.
I...
...DON'T KNOW WHAT TO SAY?

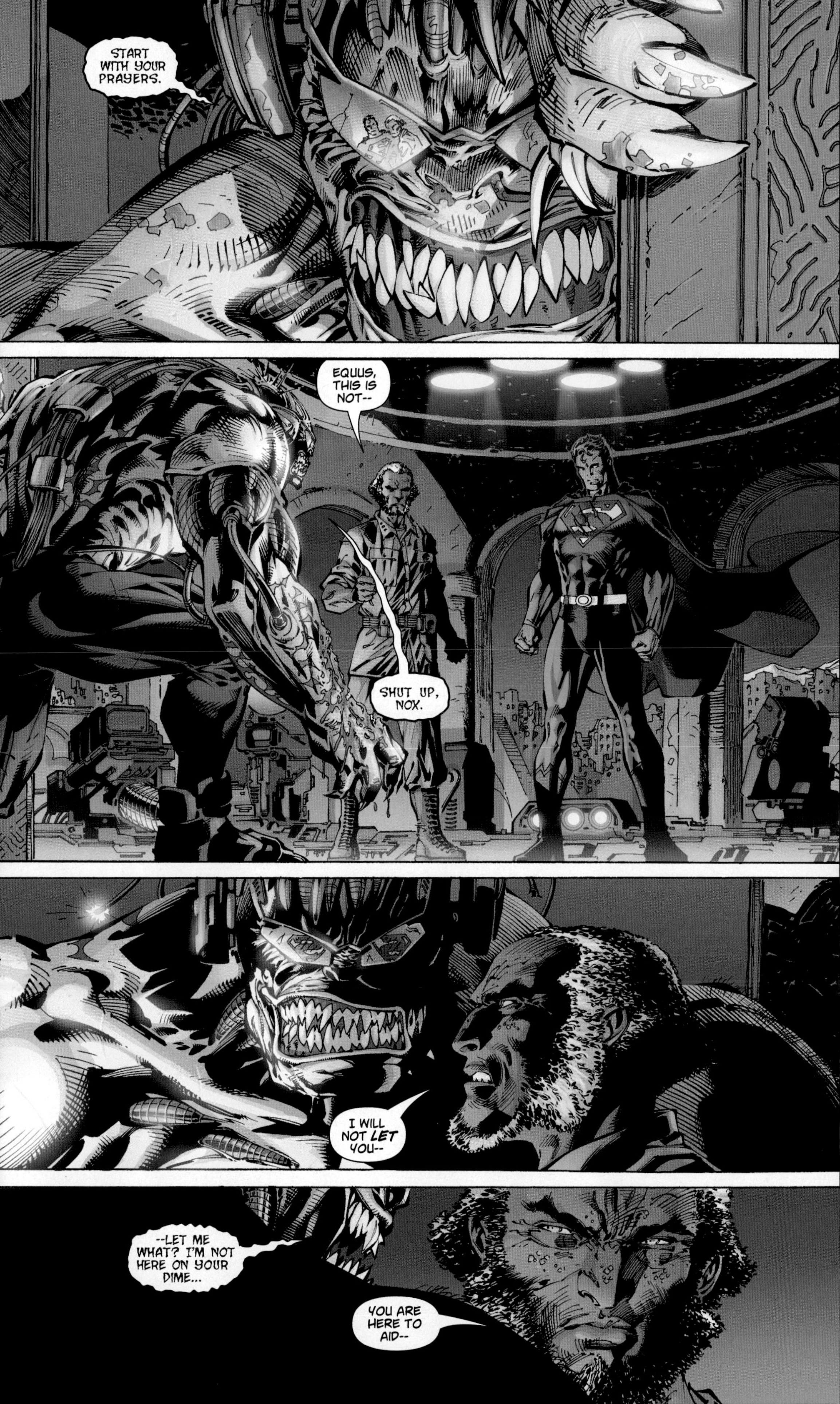

START WITH YOUR PRAYERS.
EQUUS, THIS IS NOT--
SHUT UP, NOX.
I WILL NOT LET YOU--
--LET ME WHAT? I'M NOT HERE ON YOUR DIME...
YOU ARE HERE TO AID--

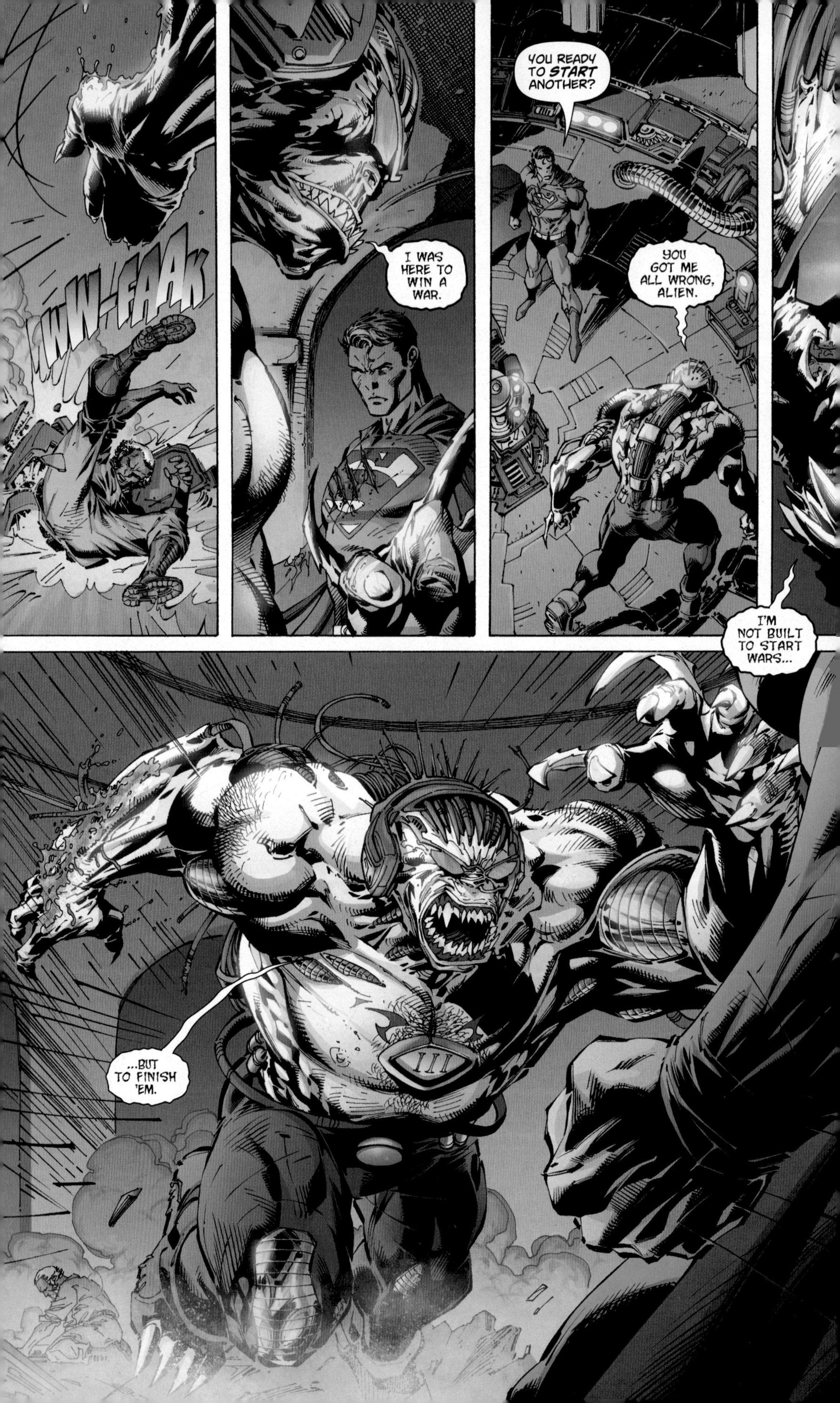
WW-FAAK
I WAS HERE TO WIN A WAR.
YOU READY TO START ANOTHER?
YOU GOT ME ALL WRONG, ALIEN.
I'M NOT BUILT TO START WARS...
...BUT TO FINISH 'EM.

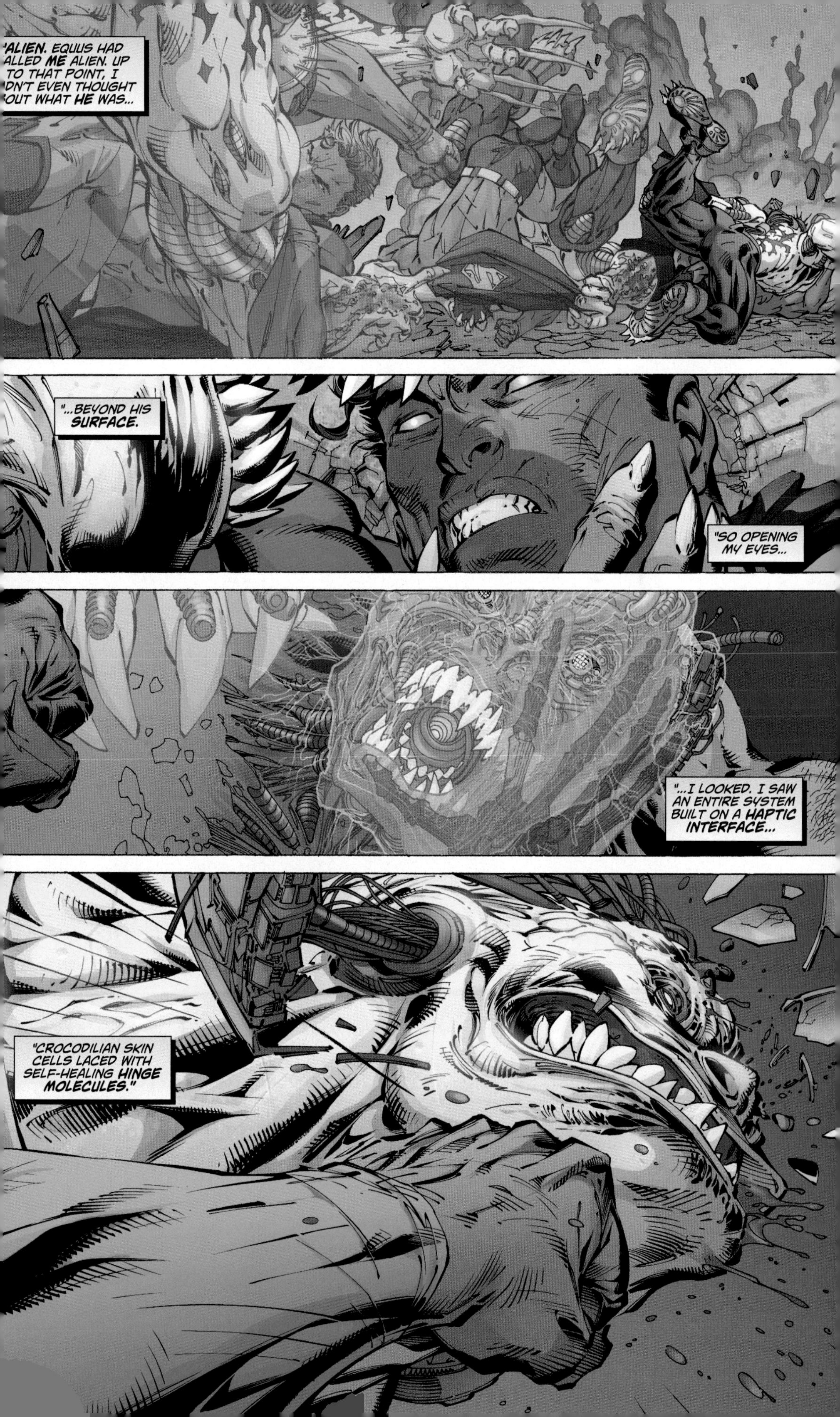
"ALIEN. EQUUS HAD CALLED ME ALIEN. UP TO THAT POINT, I DIDN'T EVEN THOUGHT ABOUT WHAT HE WAS...
"...BEYOND HIS SURFACE.
"SO OPENING MY EYES...
"...I LOOKED. I SAW AN ENTIRE SYSTEM BUILT ON A HAPTIC INTERFACE...
"CROCODILIAN SKIN CELLS LACED WITH SELF-HEALING HINGE MOLECULES."

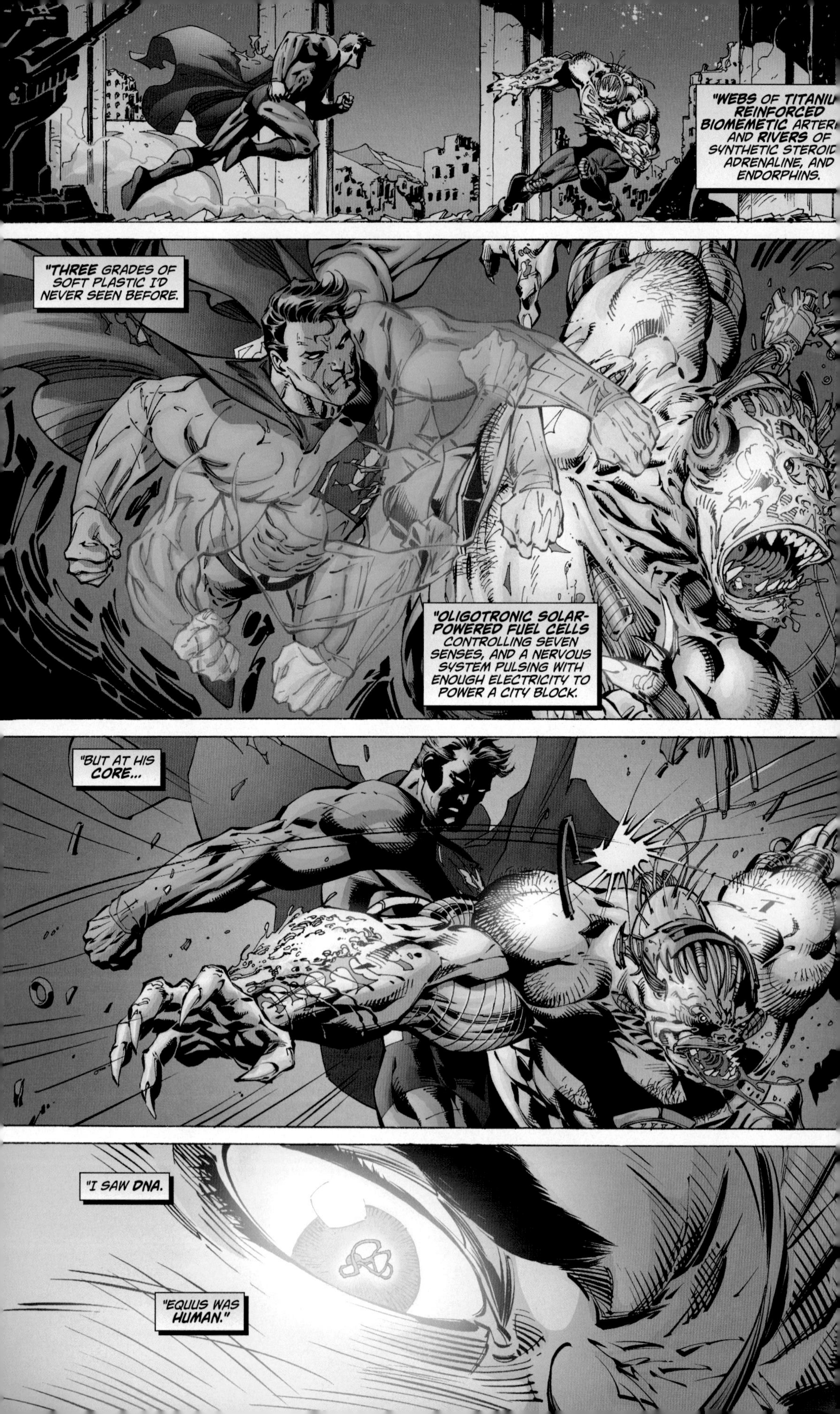
"WEBS OF TITANIU REINFORCED BIOMEMETIC ARTER AND RIVERS OF SYNTHETIC STEROID ADRENALINE, AND ENDORPHINS.
"THREE GRADES OF SOFT PLASTIC I'D NEVER SEEN BEFORE.
"OLIGOTRONIC SOLAR-POWERED FUEL CELLS CONTROLLING SEVEN SENSES, AND A NERVOUS SYSTEM PULSING WITH ENOUGH ELECTRICITY TO POWER A CITY BLOCK.
"BUT AT HIS CORE...
"I SAW DNA.
"EQUUS WAS HUMAN."

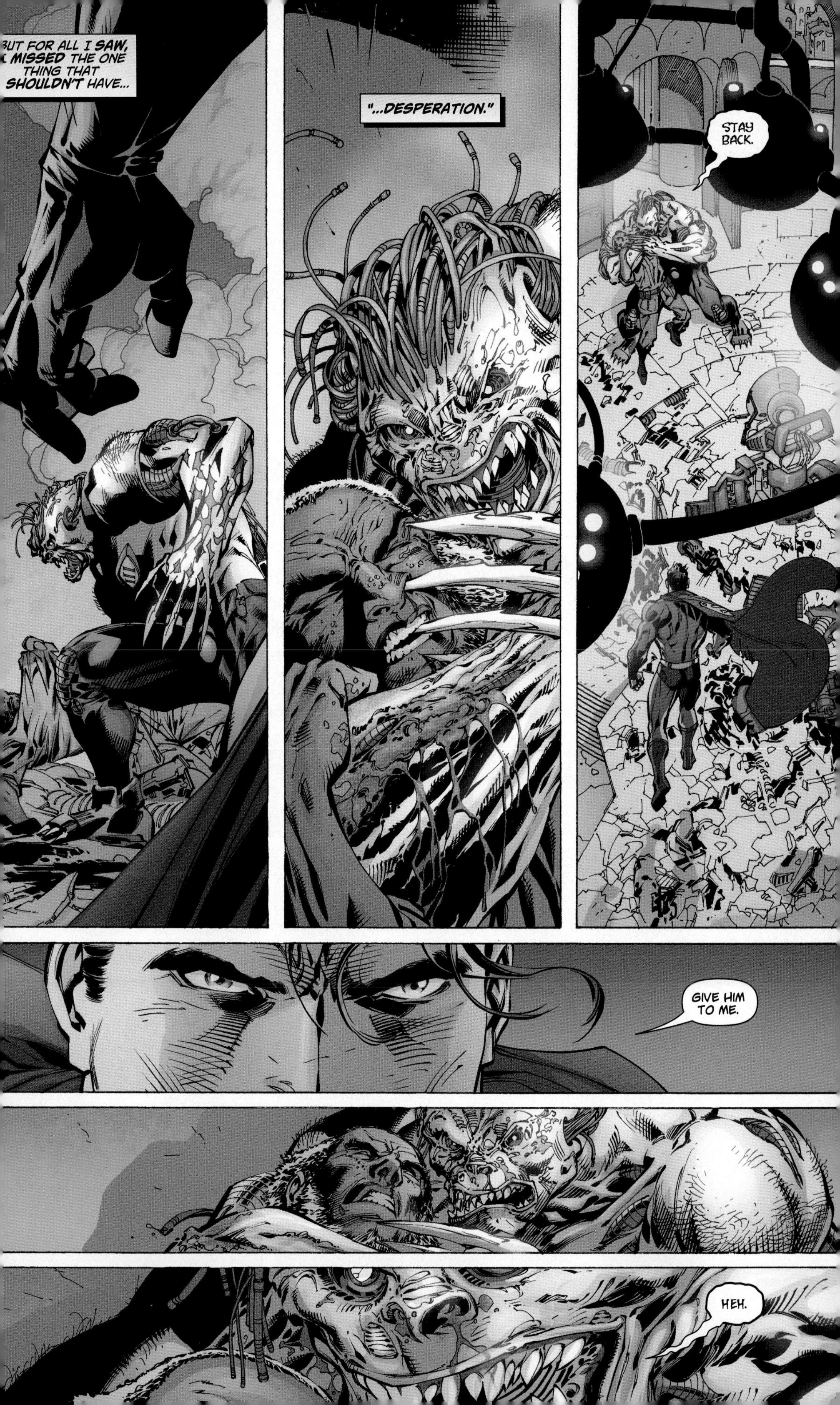
BUT FOR ALL I SAW, I MISSED THE ONE THING THAT I SHOULDN'T HAVE...
"...DESPERATION."
STAY BACK.
GIVE HIM TO ME.
HEH.

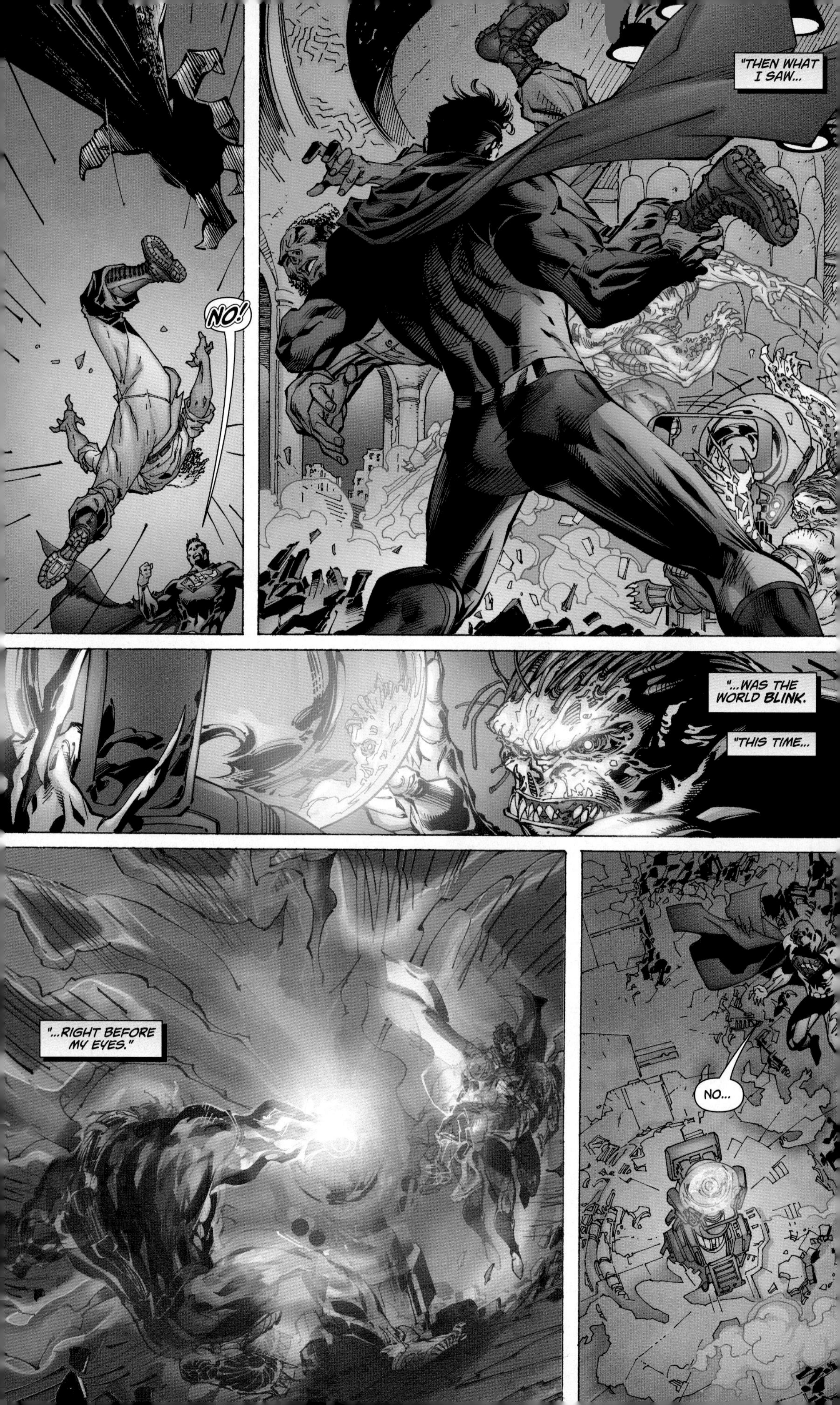
NO!
"THEN WHAT I SAW...
"...WAS THE WORLD BLINK.
"THIS TIME...
"...RIGHT BEFORE MY EYES."
NO...

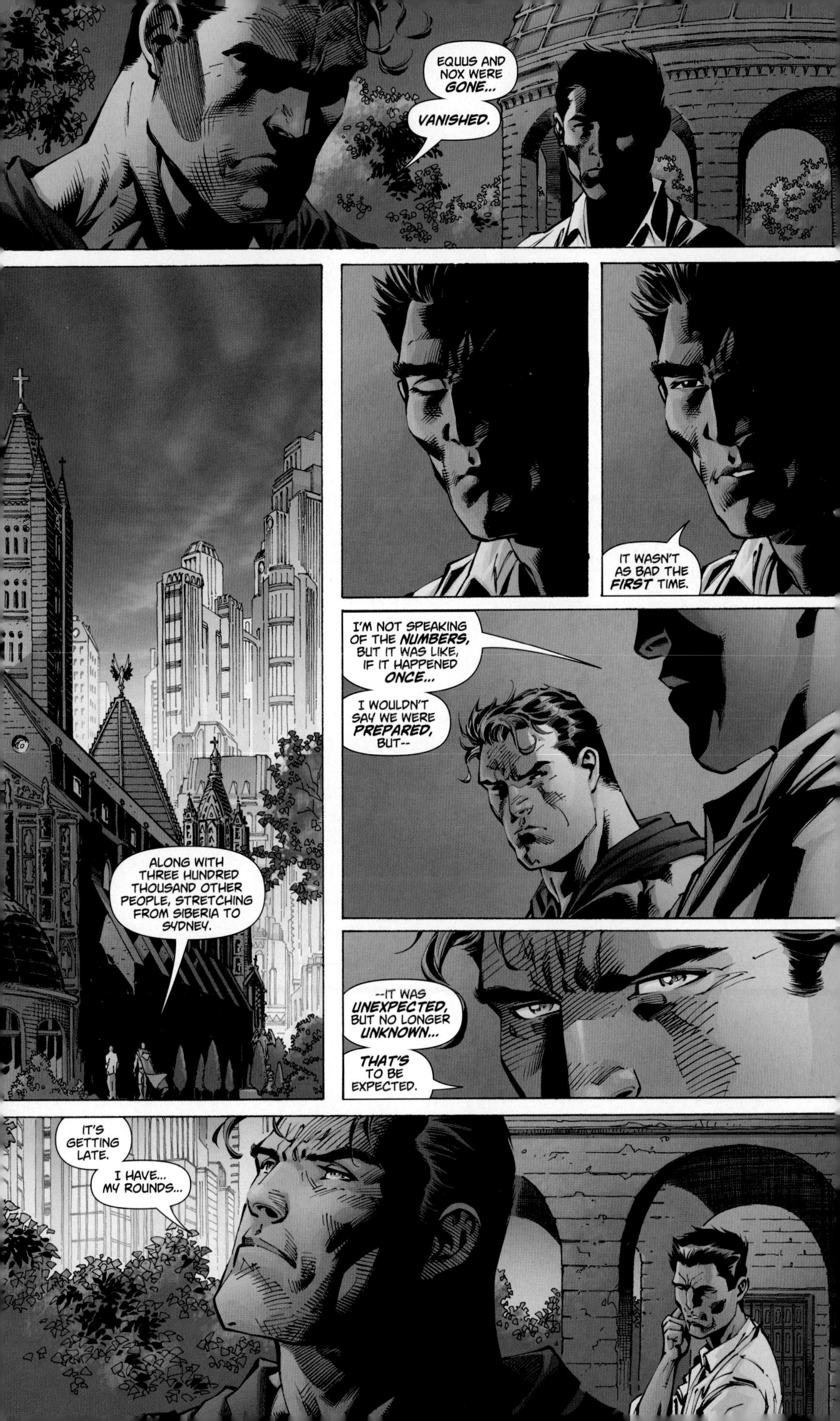
EQUUS AND NOX WERE GONE...
VANISHED.
ALONG WITH THREE HUNDRED THOUSAND OTHER PEOPLE, STRETCHING FROM SIBERIA TO SYDNEY.
IT WASN'T AS BAD THE FIRST TIME.
I'M NOT SPEAKING OF THE NUMBERS, BUT IT WAS LIKE, IF IT HAPPENED ONCE...
I WOULDN'T SAY WE WERE PREPARED, BUT--
--IT WAS UNEXPECTED, BUT NO LONGER UNKNOWN...
THAT'S TO BE EXPECTED.
IT'S GETTING LATE.
I HAVE... MY ROUNDS...

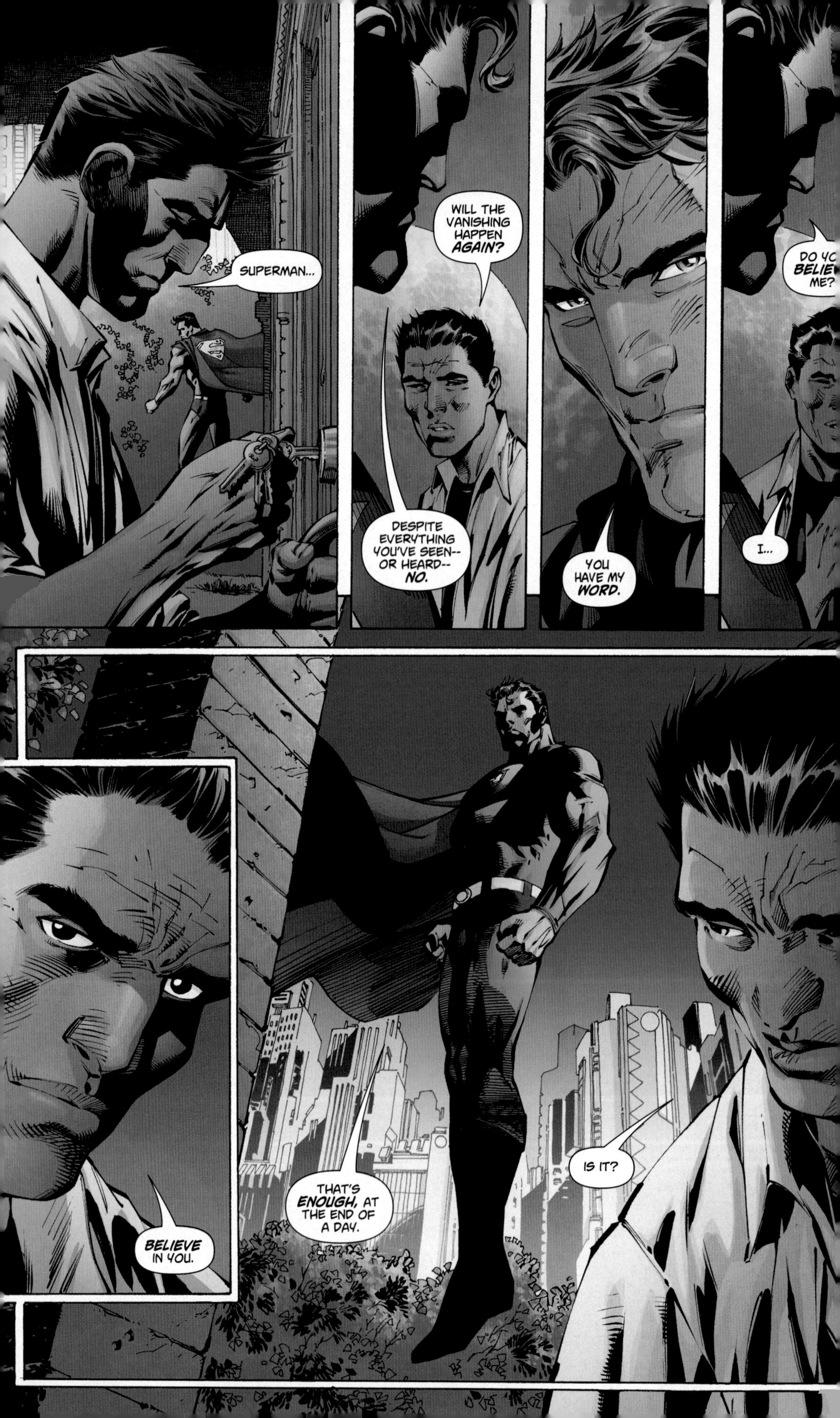
SUPERMAN...
WILL THE VANISHING HAPPEN AGAIN?
DESPITE EVERYTHING YOU'VE SEEN--OR HEARD--NO.
YOU HAVE MY WORD.
DO YO BELIE ME?
I...
BELIEVE IN YOU.
THAT'S ENOUGH, AT THE END OF A DAY.
IS IT?

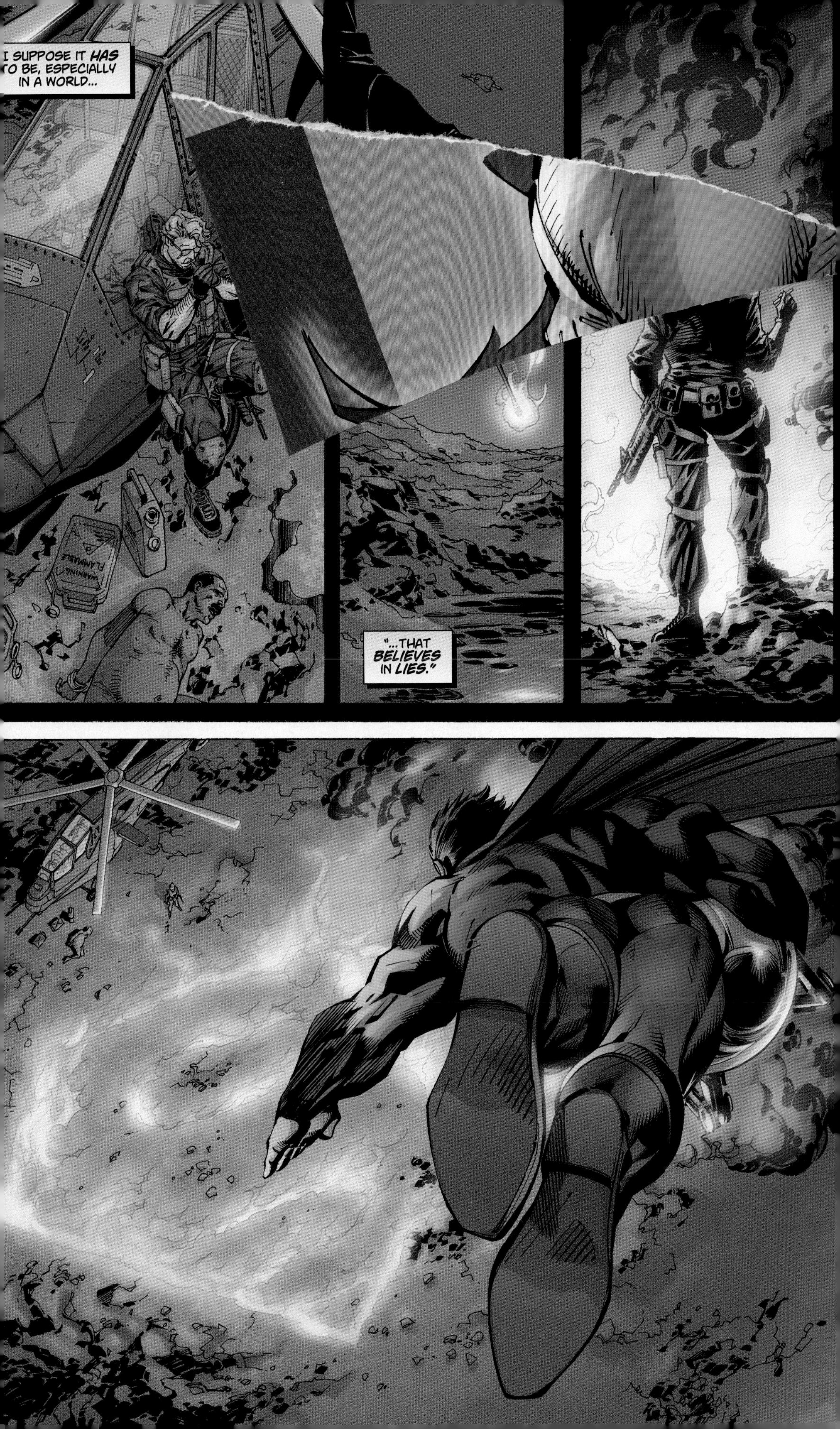
I SUPPOSE IT HAS TO BE, ESPECIALLY IN A WORLD...
WARNING FLAMMABLE
"...THAT BELIEVES IN LIES."

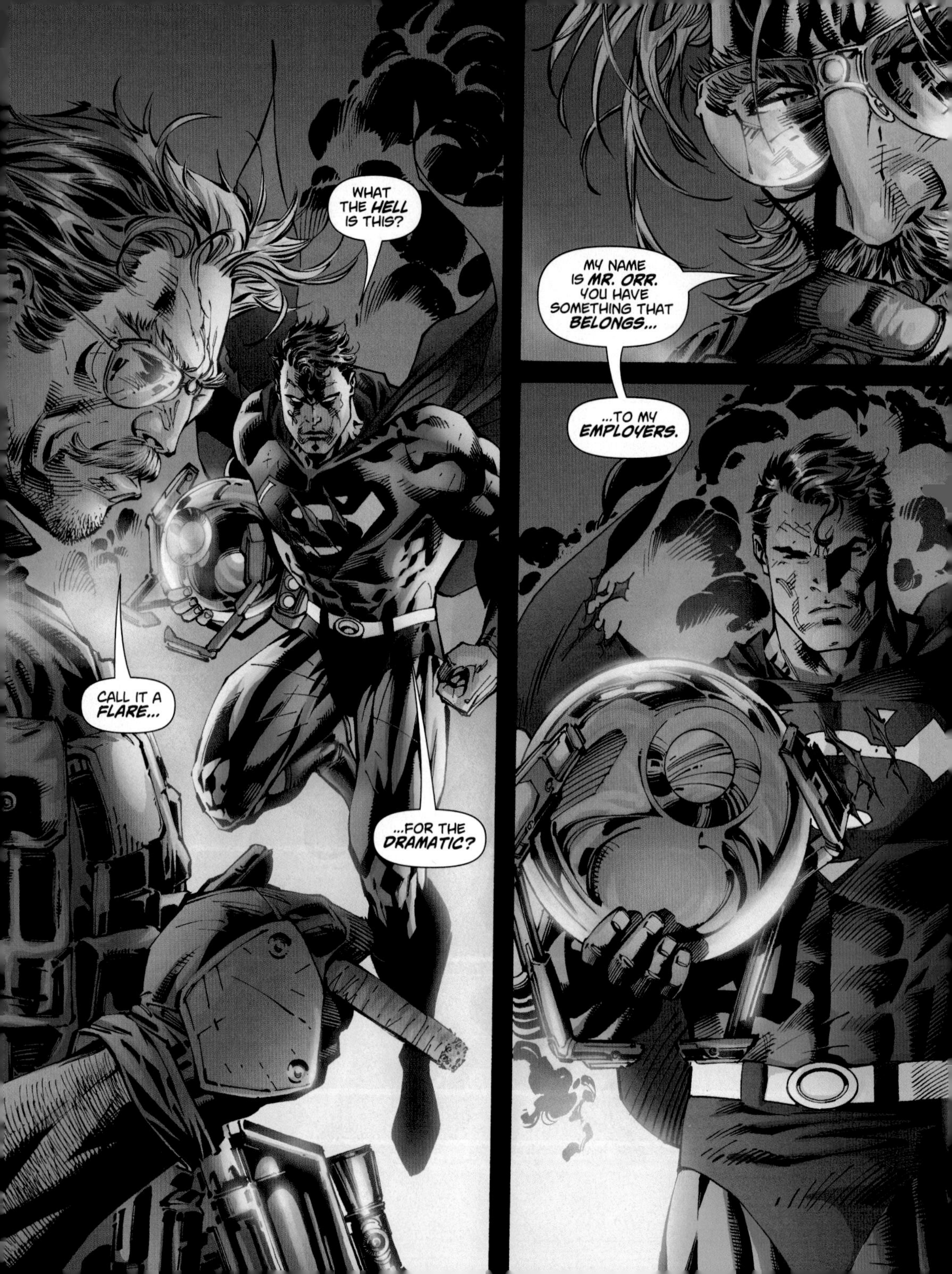
WHAT THE HELL IS THIS?
CALL IT A FLARE...
...FOR THE DRAMATIC?
MY NAME IS MR. ORR. YOU HAVE SOMETHING THAT BELONGS...
...TO MY EMPLOYERS.

DAILY PLANET
SUPERMAN WANTED

JIM LEE
WILLIAMS

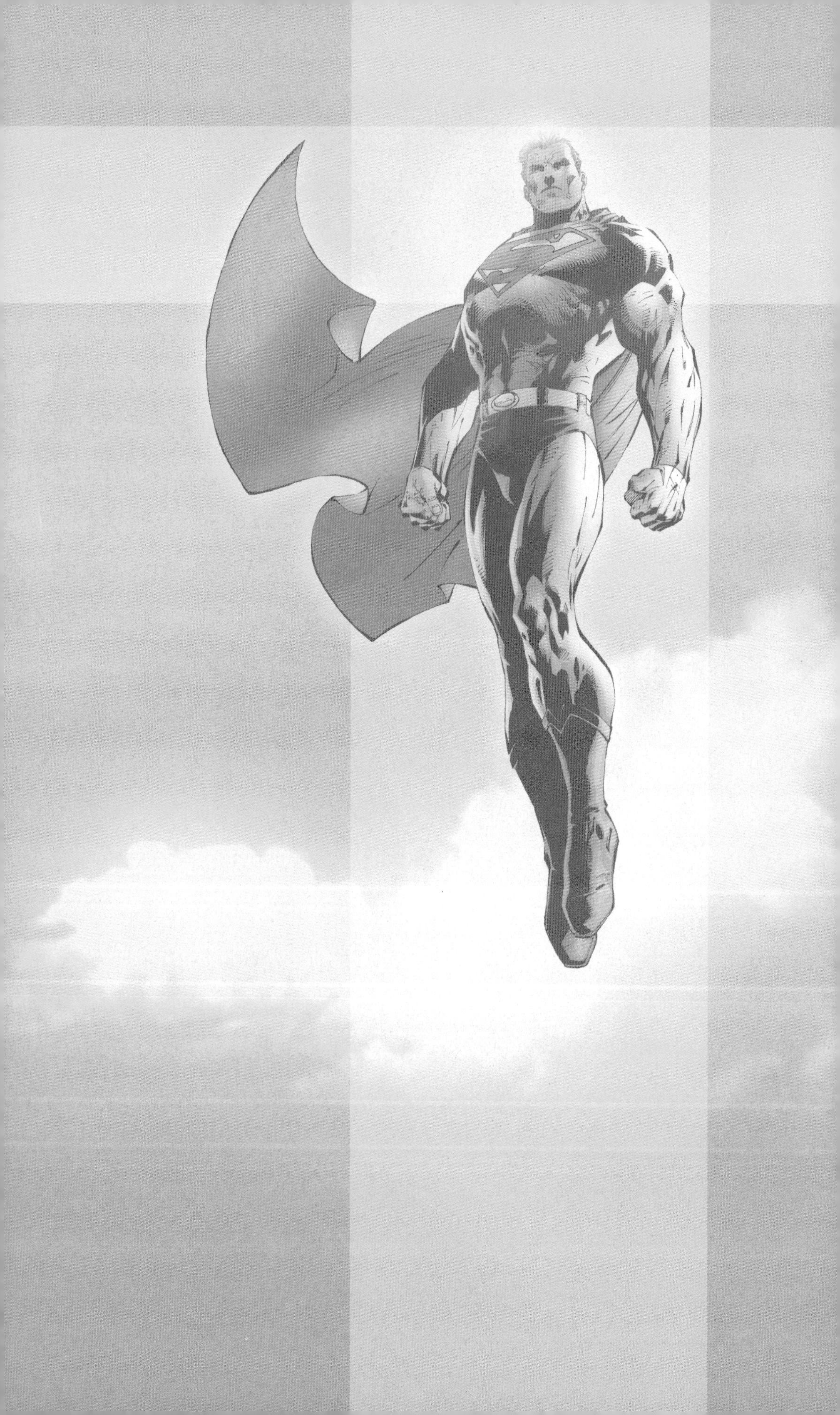

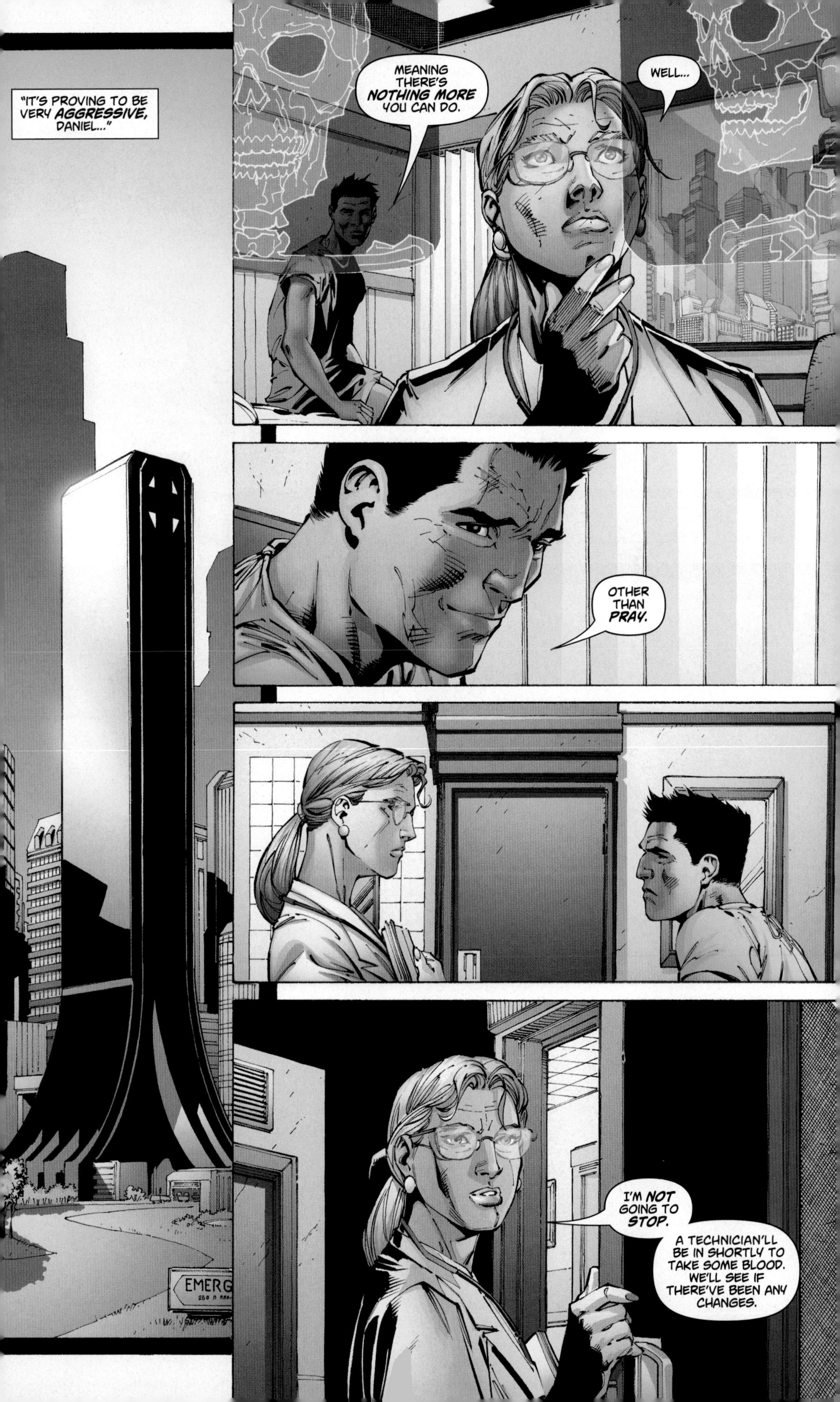
"IT'S PROVING TO BE VERY AGGRESSIVE, DANIEL..."
MEANING THERE'S NOTHING MORE YOU CAN DO.
WELL...
OTHER THAN PRAY.
I'M NOT GOING TO STOP.
A TECHNICIAN'LL BE IN SHORTLY TO TAKE SOME BLOOD. WE'LL SEE IF THERE'VE BEEN ANY CHANGES.
EMERG

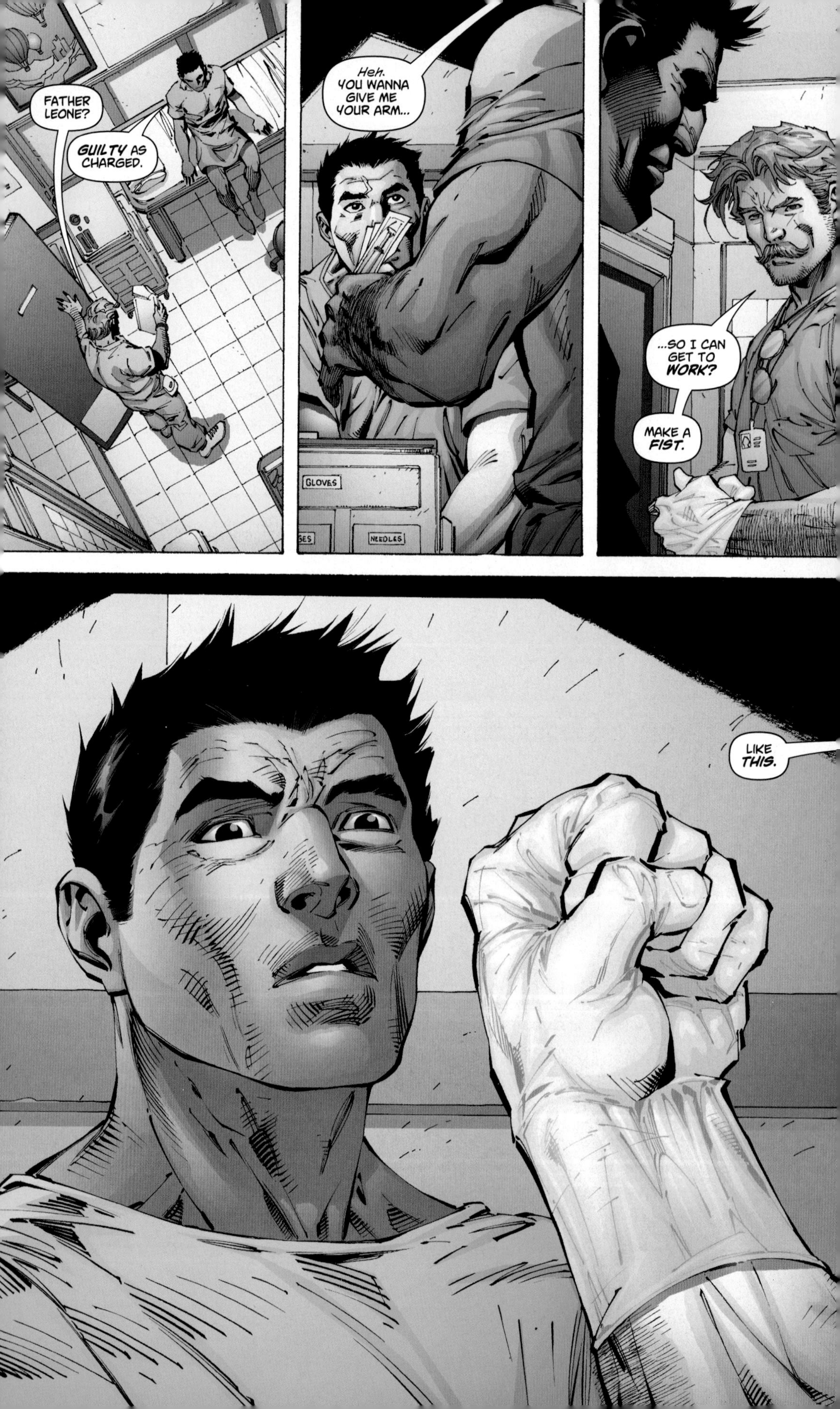
FATHER LEONE?
GUILTY AS CHARGED.
Heh. YOU WANNA GIVE ME YOUR ARM...
GLOVES
NEEDLES
...SO I CAN GET TO WORK?
MAKE A FIST.
LIKE THIS.

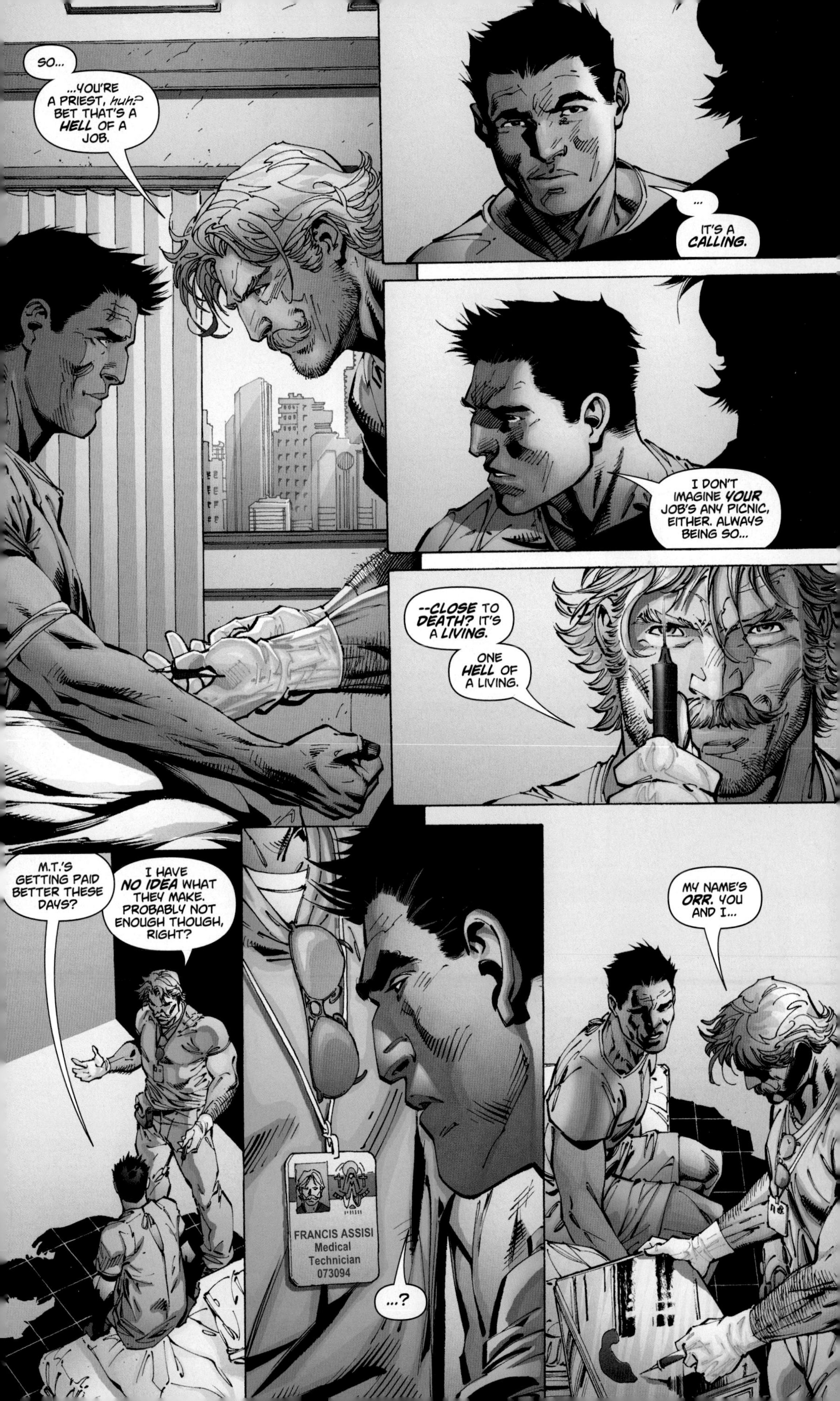
SO...
...YOU'RE A PRIEST, *huh?* BET THAT'S A **HELL** OF A JOB.
...
IT'S A **CALLING**.
I DON'T IMAGINE **YOUR** JOB'S ANY PICNIC, EITHER. ALWAYS BEING SO...
--CLOSE TO **DEATH?** IT'S A **LIVING**.
ONE **HELL** OF A LIVING.
M.T.'S GETTING PAID BETTER THESE DAYS?
I HAVE **NO IDEA** WHAT THEY MAKE. PROBABLY NOT ENOUGH THOUGH, RIGHT?
FRANCIS ASSISI
Medical Technician
073094
...?
MY NAME'S **ORR**. YOU AND I...

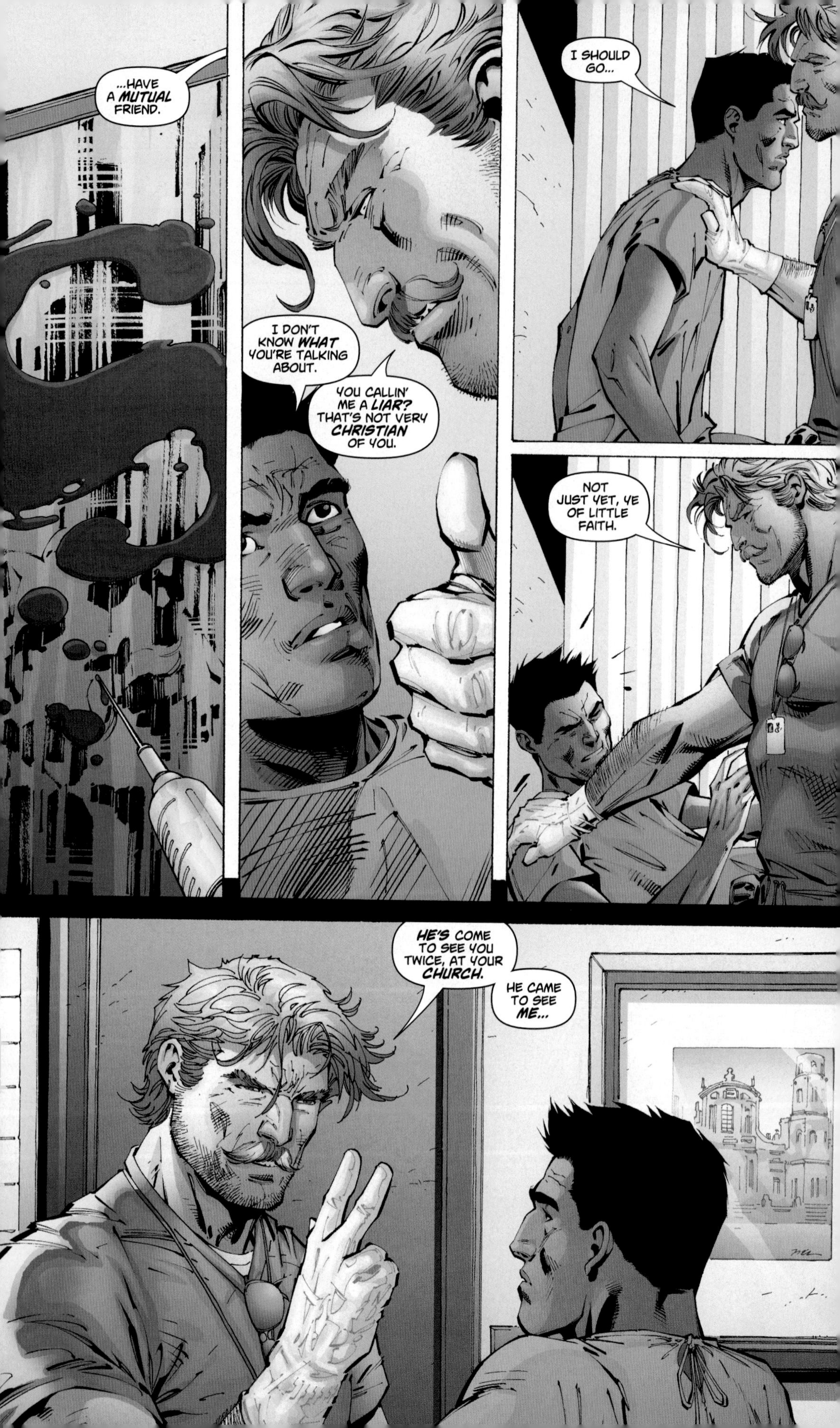
...HAVE A MUTUAL FRIEND.
I DON'T KNOW WHAT YOU'RE TALKING ABOUT.
YOU CALLIN' ME A LIAR? THAT'S NOT VERY CHRISTIAN OF YOU.
I SHOULD GO...
NOT JUST YET, YE OF LITTLE FAITH.
HE'S COME TO SEE YOU TWICE, AT YOUR CHURCH.
HE CAME TO SEE ME...

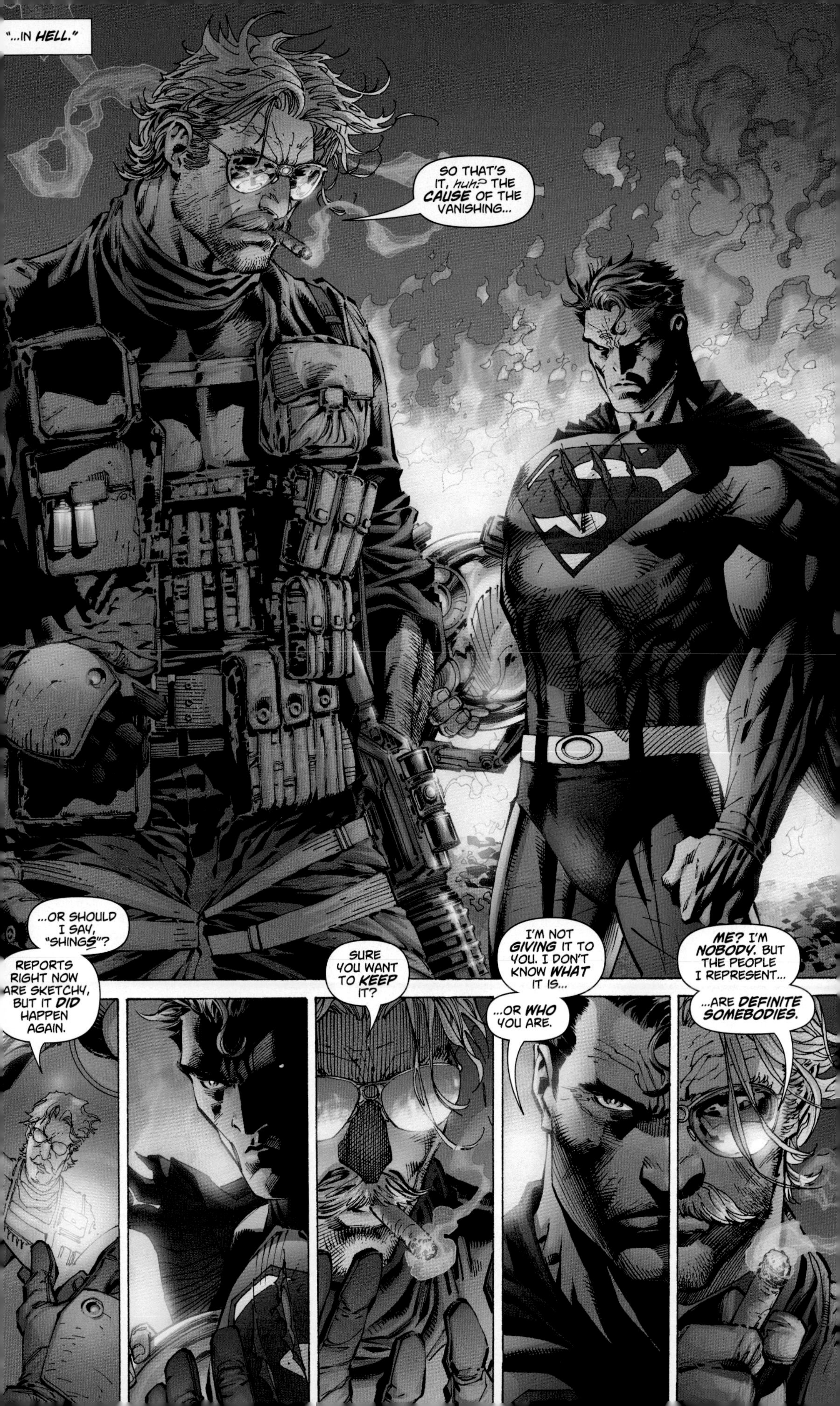
"...IN HELL."
SO THAT'S IT, huh? THE CAUSE OF THE VANISHING...
...OR SHOULD I SAY, "SHINGS"?
REPORTS RIGHT NOW ARE SKETCHY, BUT IT DID HAPPEN AGAIN.
SURE YOU WANT TO KEEP IT?
I'M NOT GIVING IT TO YOU. I DON'T KNOW WHAT IT IS...
...OR WHO YOU ARE.
ME? I'M NOBODY. BUT THE PEOPLE I REPRESENT...
...ARE DEFINITE SOMEBODIES.

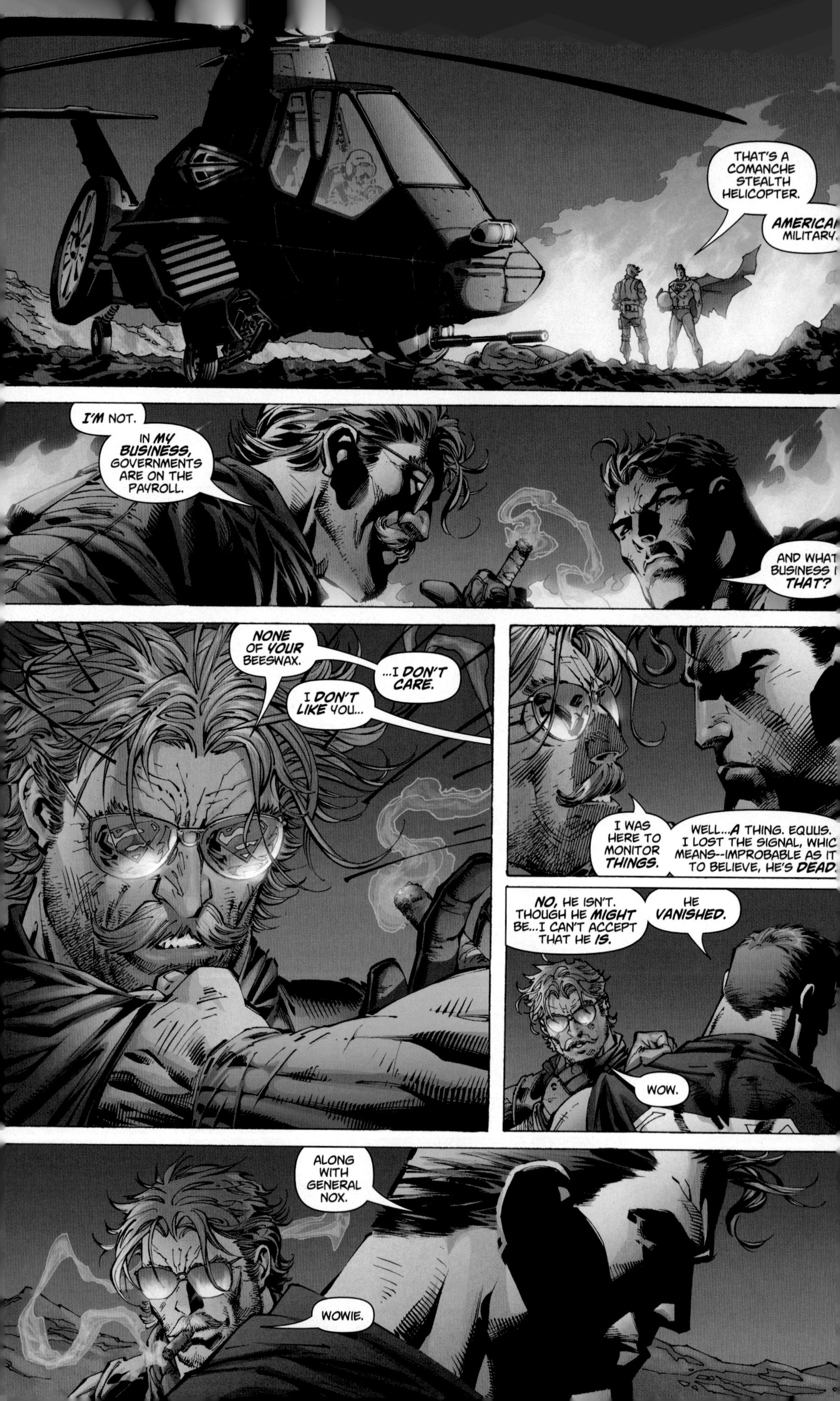
THAT'S A COMANCHE STEALTH HELICOPTER.
AMERICA MILITARY.
I'M NOT.
IN MY BUSINESS, GOVERNMENTS ARE ON THE PAYROLL.
AND WHAT BUSINESS I THAT?
NONE OF YOUR BEESWAX.
I DON'T LIKE YOU...
...I DON'T CARE.
I WAS HERE TO MONITOR THINGS.
WELL...A THING. EQUUS. I LOST THE SIGNAL, WHIC MEANS--IMPROBABLE AS IT TO BELIEVE, HE'S DEAD.
NO, HE ISN'T. THOUGH HE MIGHT BE...I CAN'T ACCEPT THAT HE IS.
HE VANISHED.
WOW.
ALONG WITH GENERAL NOX.
WOWIE.

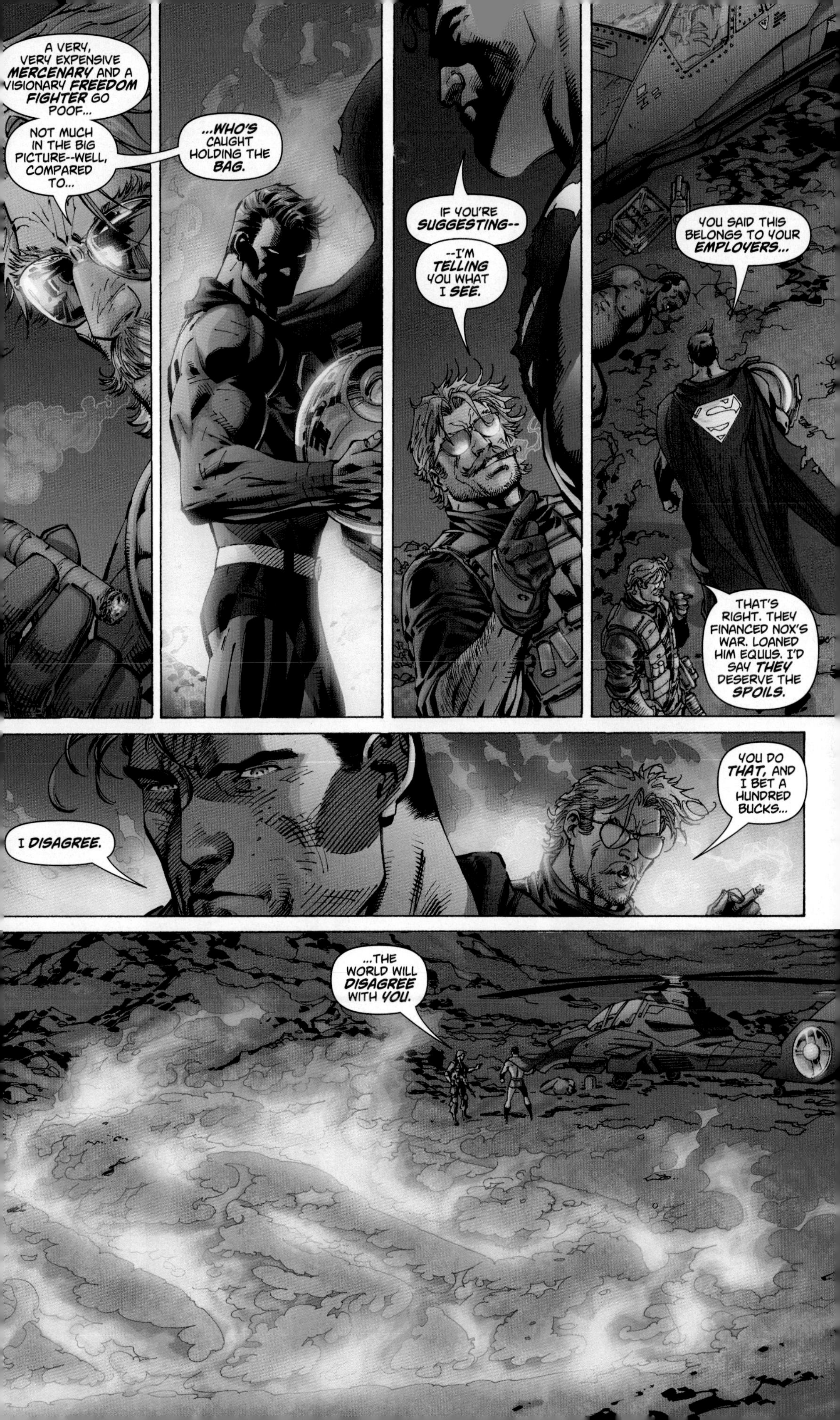

A VERY, VERY EXPENSIVE MERCENARY AND A VISIONARY FREEDOM FIGHTER GO POOF...
NOT MUCH IN THE BIG PICTURE--WELL, COMPARED TO...
...WHO'S CAUGHT HOLDING THE BAG.
IF YOU'RE SUGGESTING--
--I'M TELLING YOU WHAT I SEE.
YOU SAID THIS BELONGS TO YOUR EMPLOYERS...
THAT'S RIGHT. THEY FINANCED NOX'S WAR. LOANED HIM EQUUS. I'D SAY THEY DESERVE THE SPOILS.
I DISAGREE.
YOU DO THAT, AND I BET A HUNDRED BUCKS...
...THE WORLD WILL DISAGREE WITH YOU.

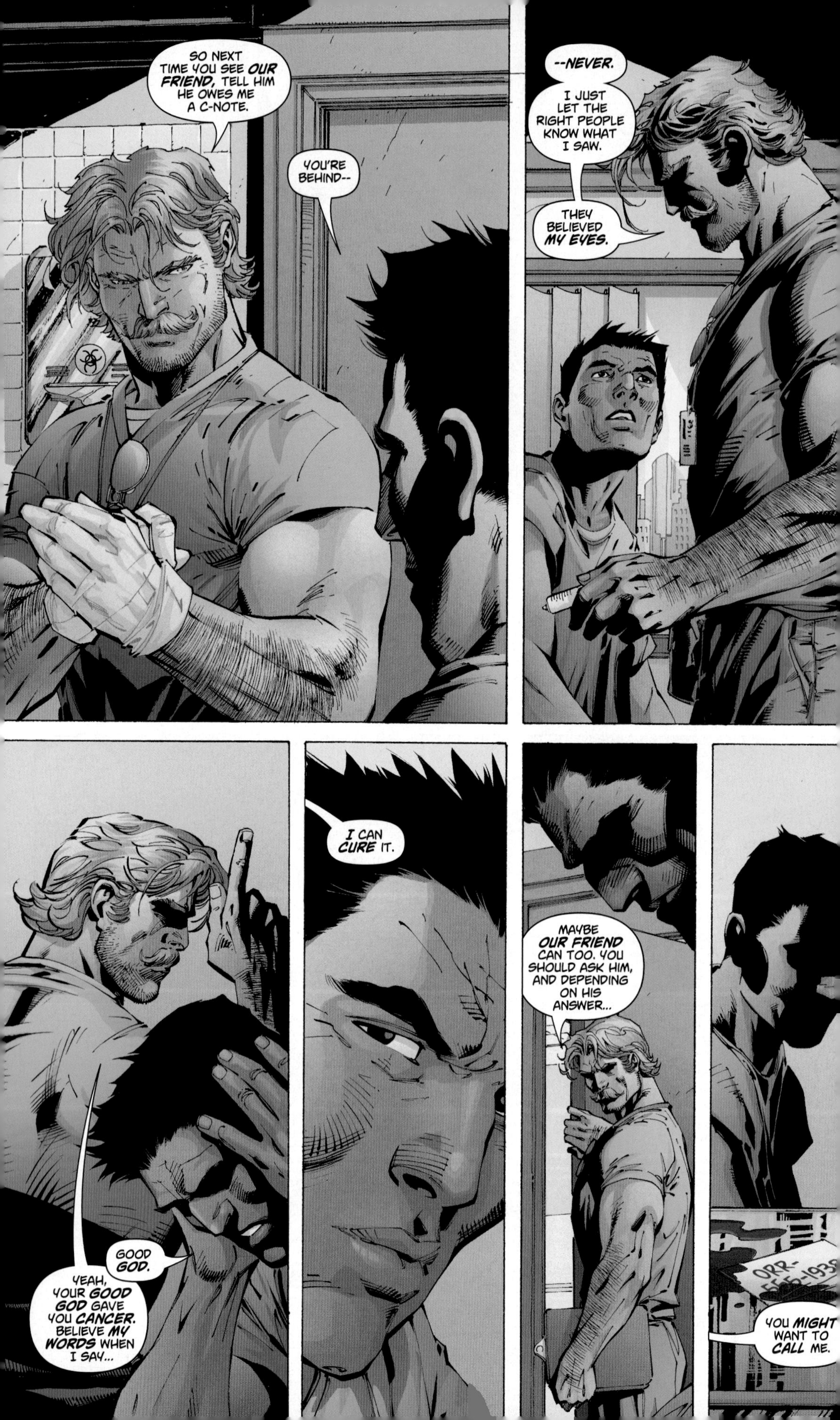
SO NEXT TIME YOU SEE OUR FRIEND, TELL HIM HE OWES ME A C-NOTE.
YOU'RE BEHIND--
--NEVER.
I JUST LET THE RIGHT PEOPLE KNOW WHAT I SAW.
THEY BELIEVED MY EYES.
GOOD GOD.
YEAH, YOUR GOOD GOD GAVE YOU CANCER. BELIEVE MY WORDS WHEN I SAY...
I CAN CURE IT.
MAYBE OUR FRIEND CAN TOO. YOU SHOULD ASK HIM, AND DEPENDING ON HIS ANSWER...
ORR-555-1939
YOU MIGHT WANT TO CALL ME.

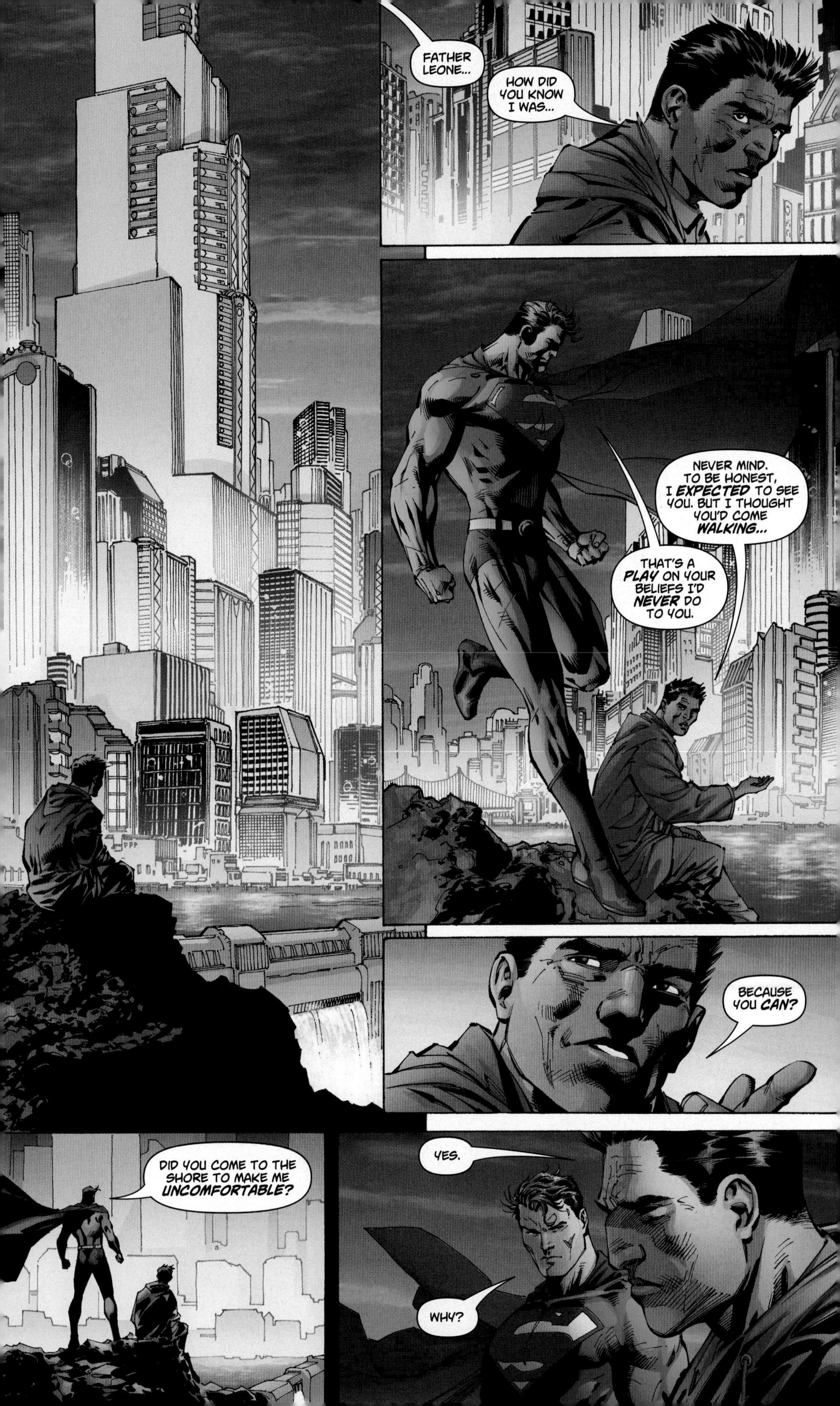
FATHER LEONE...
HOW DID YOU KNOW I WAS...
NEVER MIND. TO BE HONEST, I EXPECTED TO SEE YOU. BUT I THOUGHT YOU'D COME WALKING...
THAT'S A PLAY ON YOUR BELIEFS I'D NEVER DO TO YOU.
BECAUSE YOU CAN?
DID YOU COME TO THE SHORE TO MAKE ME UNCOMFORTABLE?
YES.
WHY?

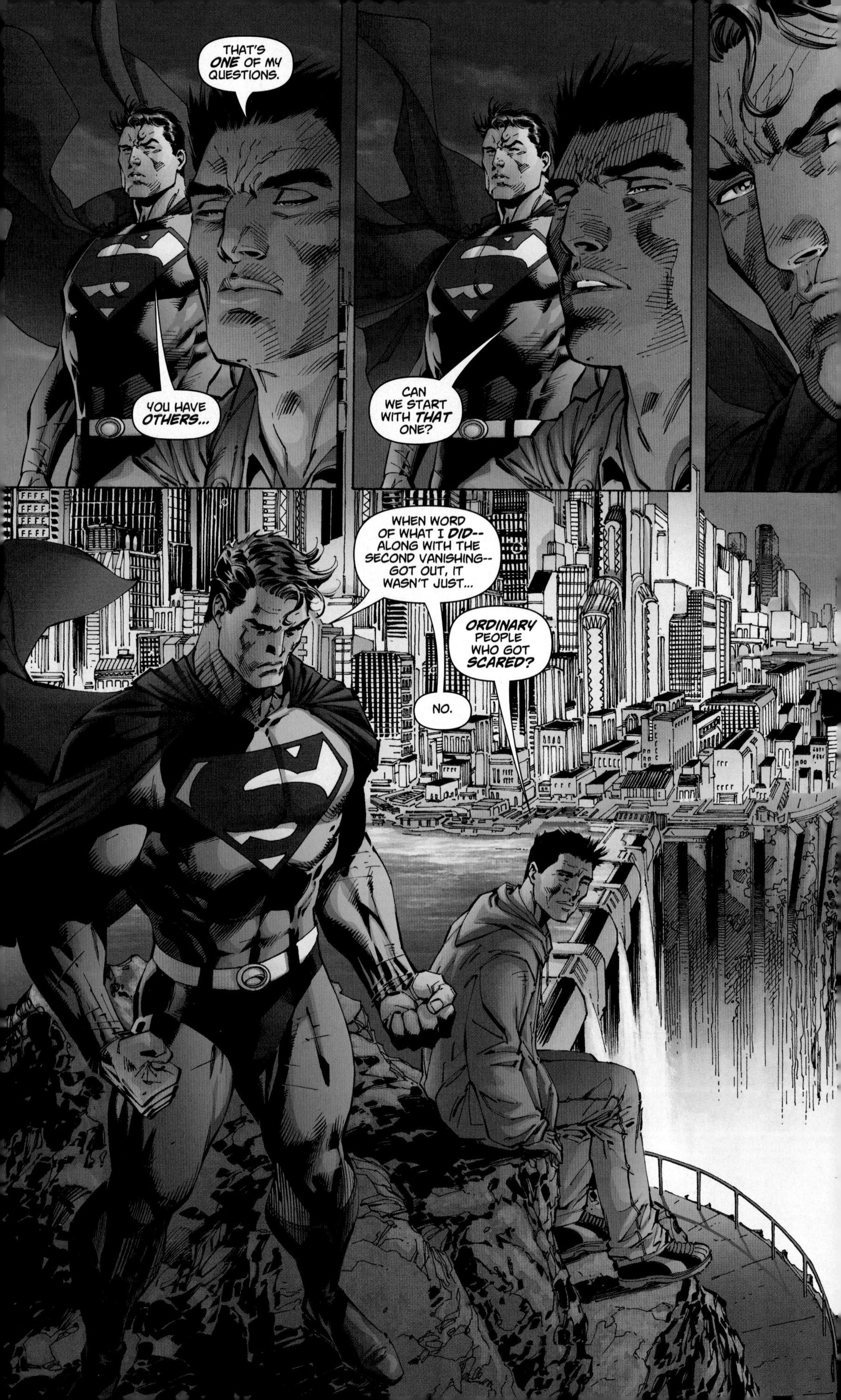

THAT'S ONE OF MY QUESTIONS.
YOU HAVE OTHERS...
CAN WE START WITH THAT ONE?
WHEN WORD OF WHAT I DID-- ALONG WITH THE SECOND VANISHING-- GOT OUT, IT WASN'T JUST...
ORDINARY PEOPLE WHO GOT SCARED?
NO.

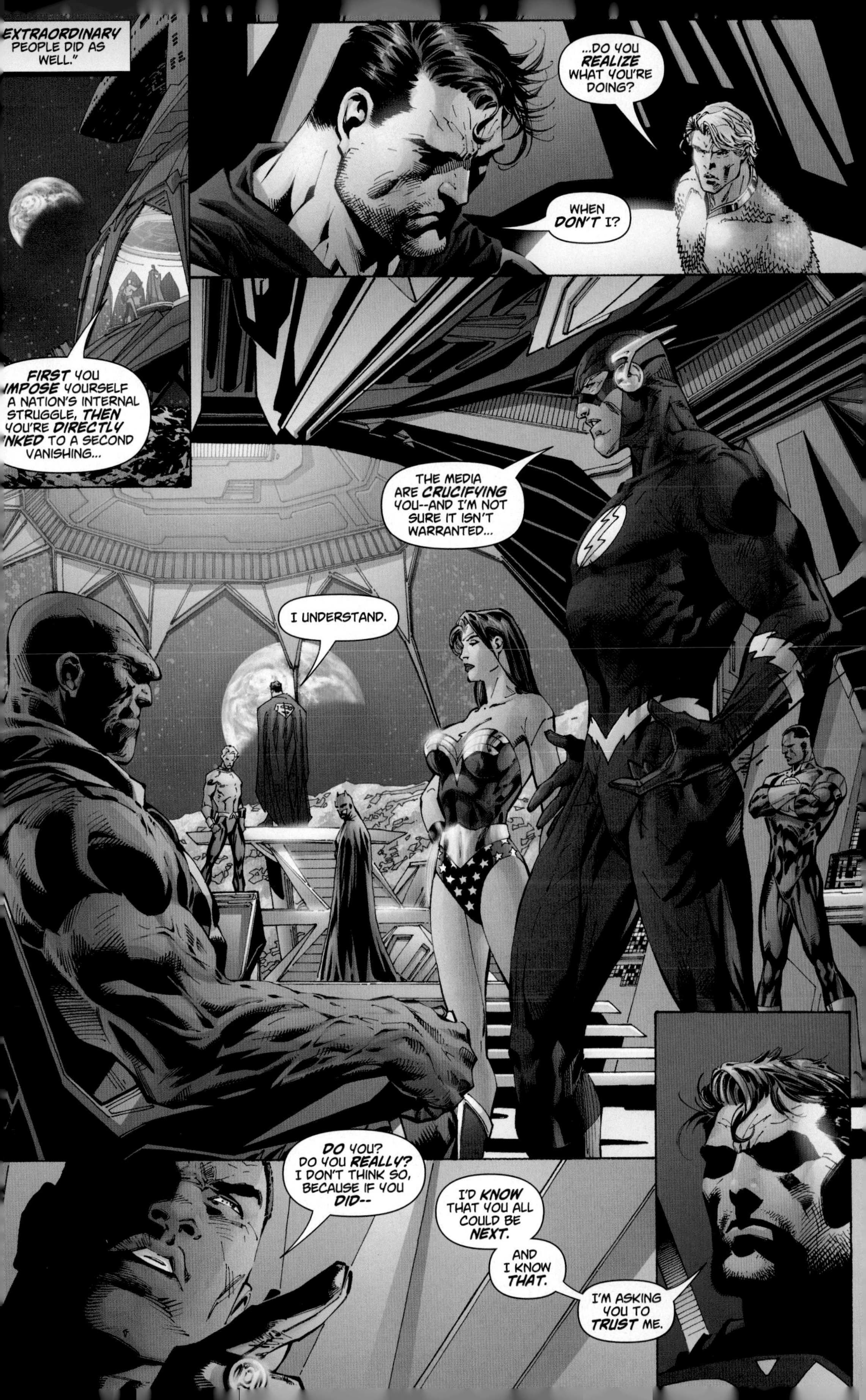
EXTRAORDINARY PEOPLE DID AS WELL."
...DO YOU REALIZE WHAT YOU'RE DOING?
WHEN DON'T I?
FIRST YOU IMPOSE YOURSELF A NATION'S INTERNAL STRUGGLE, THEN YOU'RE DIRECTLY NKED TO A SECOND VANISHING...
THE MEDIA ARE CRUCIFYING YOU--AND I'M NOT SURE IT ISN'T WARRANTED...
I UNDERSTAND.
DO YOU? DO YOU REALLY? I DON'T THINK SO, BECAUSE IF YOU DID--
I'D KNOW THAT YOU ALL COULD BE NEXT.
AND I KNOW THAT.
I'M ASKING YOU TO TRUST ME.

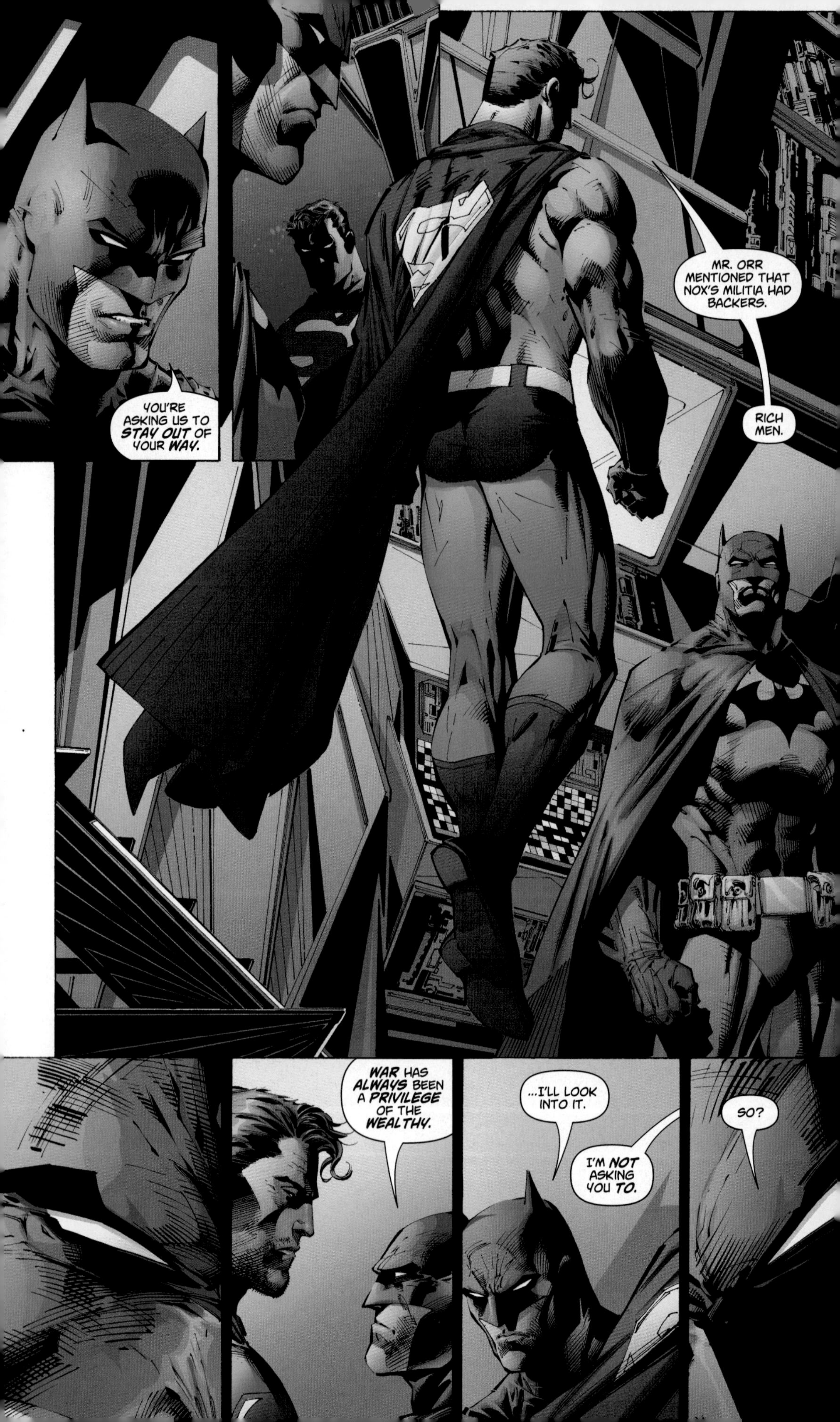
YOU'RE ASKING US TO STAY OUT OF YOUR WAY.
MR. ORR MENTIONED THAT NOX'S MILITIA HAD BACKERS.
RICH MEN.
WAR HAS ALWAYS BEEN A PRIVILEGE OF THE WEALTHY.
...I'LL LOOK INTO IT.
I'M NOT ASKING YOU TO.
SO?

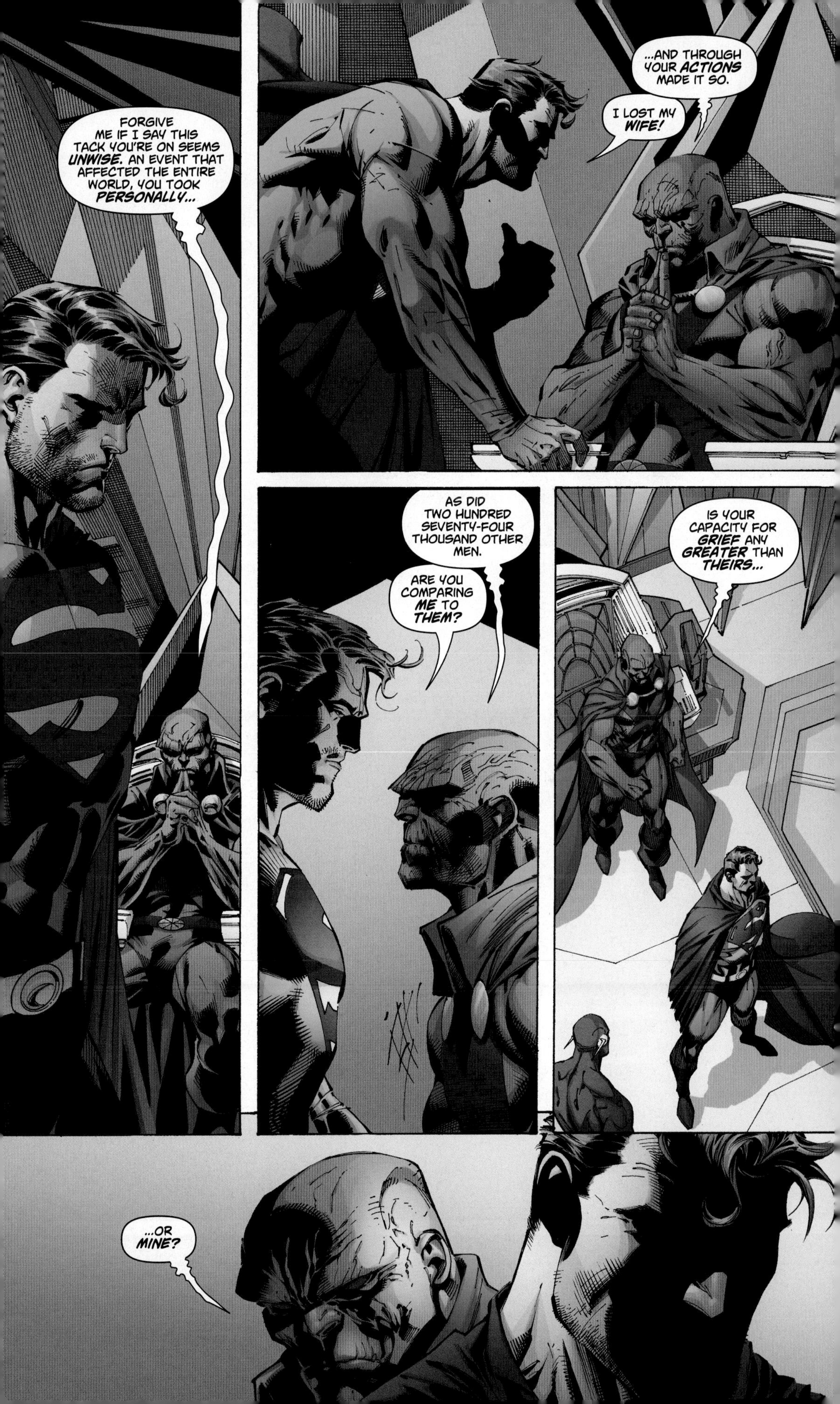
FORGIVE ME IF I SAY THIS TACK YOU'RE ON SEEMS UNWISE. AN EVENT THAT AFFECTED THE ENTIRE WORLD, YOU TOOK PERSONALLY...
I LOST MY WIFE!
...AND THROUGH YOUR ACTIONS MADE IT SO.
AS DID TWO HUNDRED SEVENTY-FOUR THOUSAND OTHER MEN.
ARE YOU COMPARING ME TO THEM?
IS YOUR CAPACITY FOR GRIEF ANY GREATER THAN THEIRS...
...OR MINE?

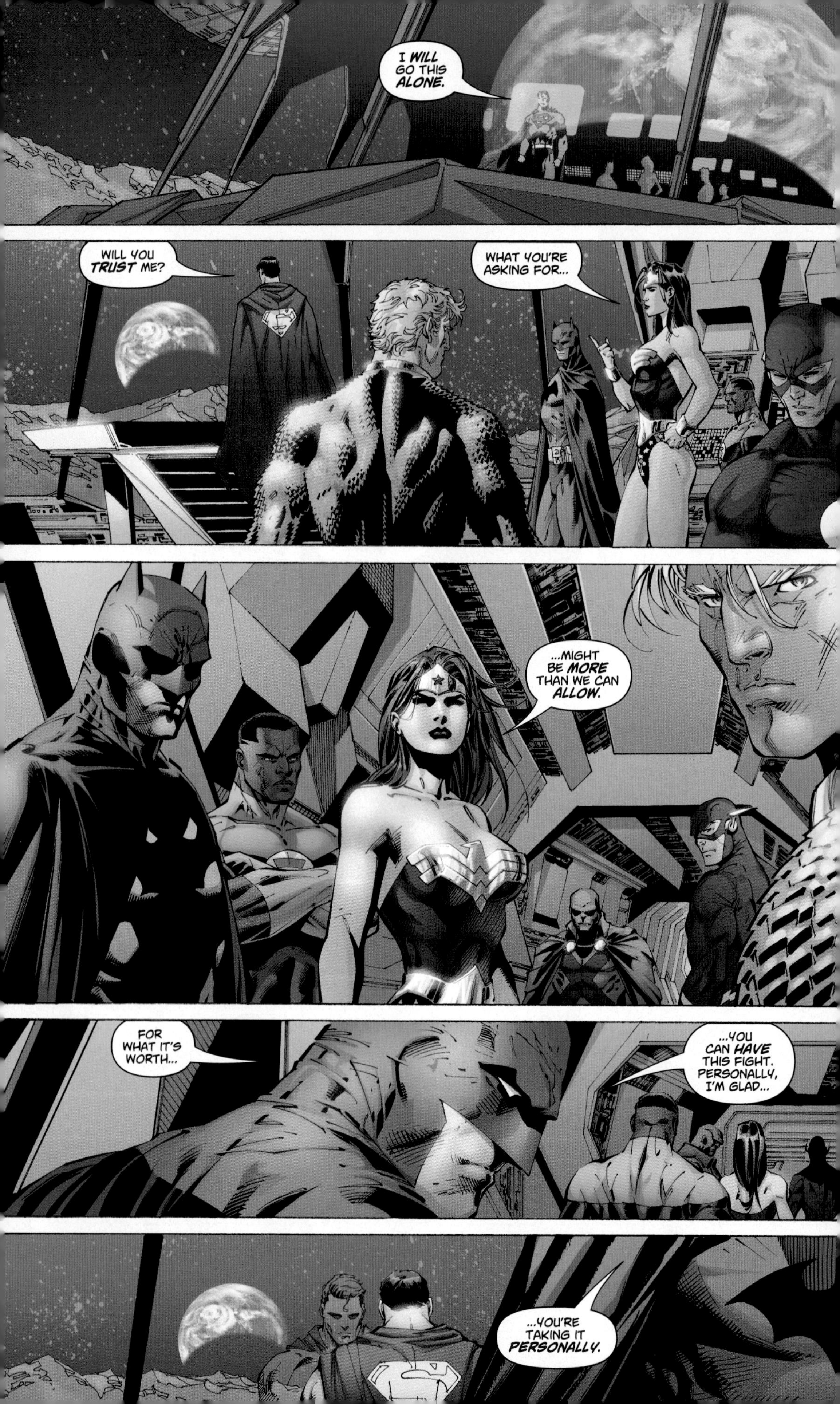
I WILL GO THIS ALONE.
WILL YOU TRUST ME?
WHAT YOU'RE ASKING FOR...
...MIGHT BE MORE THAN WE CAN ALLOW.
FOR WHAT IT'S WORTH...
...YOU CAN HAVE THIS FIGHT. PERSONALLY, I'M GLAD...
...YOU'RE TAKING IT PERSONALLY.

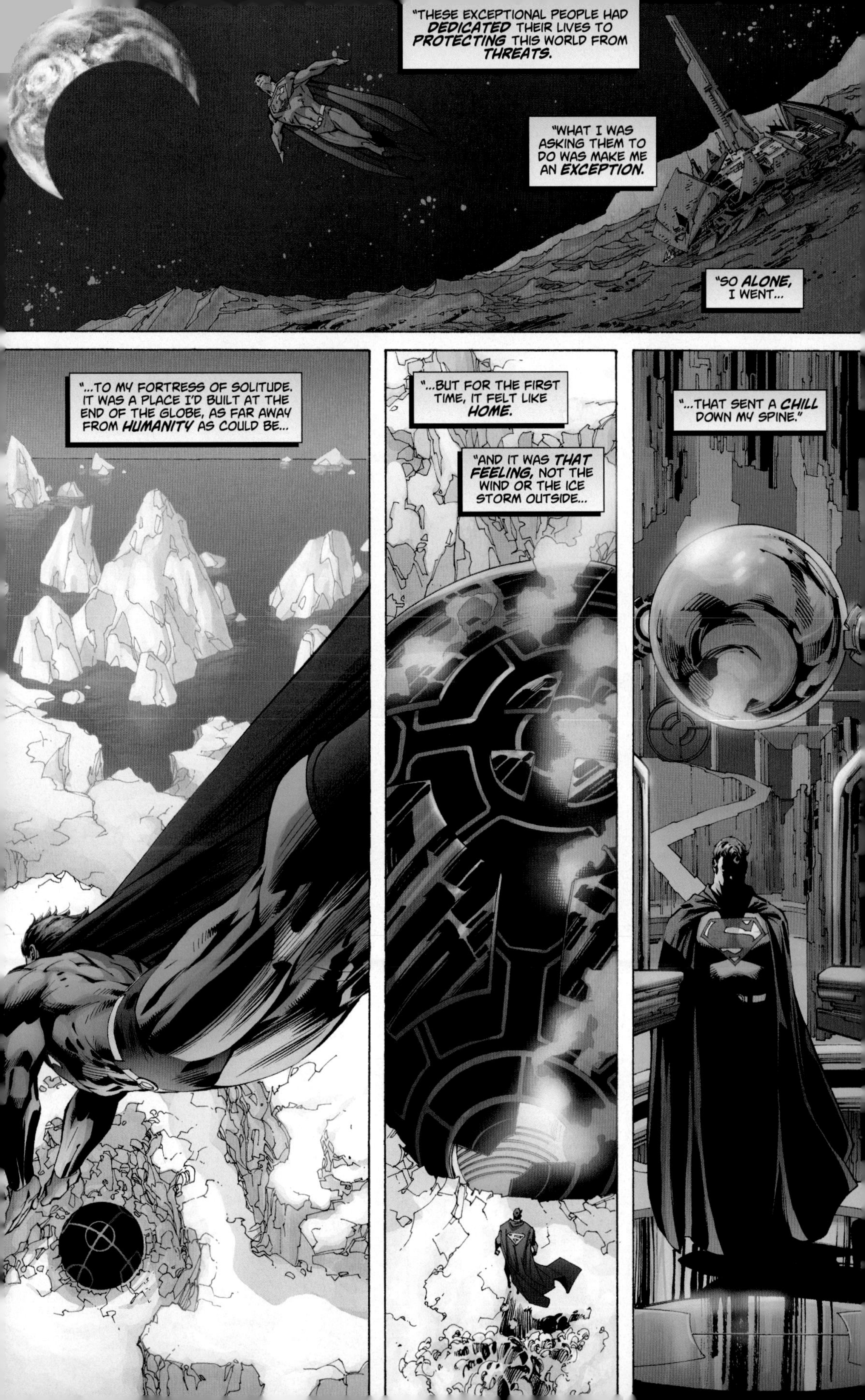
"THESE EXCEPTIONAL PEOPLE HAD DEDICATED THEIR LIVES TO PROTECTING THIS WORLD FROM THREATS.
"WHAT I WAS ASKING THEM TO DO WAS MAKE ME AN EXCEPTION.
"SO ALONE, I WENT...
"...TO MY FORTRESS OF SOLITUDE. IT WAS A PLACE I'D BUILT AT THE END OF THE GLOBE, AS FAR AWAY FROM HUMANITY AS COULD BE...
"...BUT FOR THE FIRST TIME, IT FELT LIKE HOME.
"AND IT WAS THAT FEELING, NOT THE WIND OR THE ICE STORM OUTSIDE...
"...THAT SENT A CHILL DOWN MY SPINE."

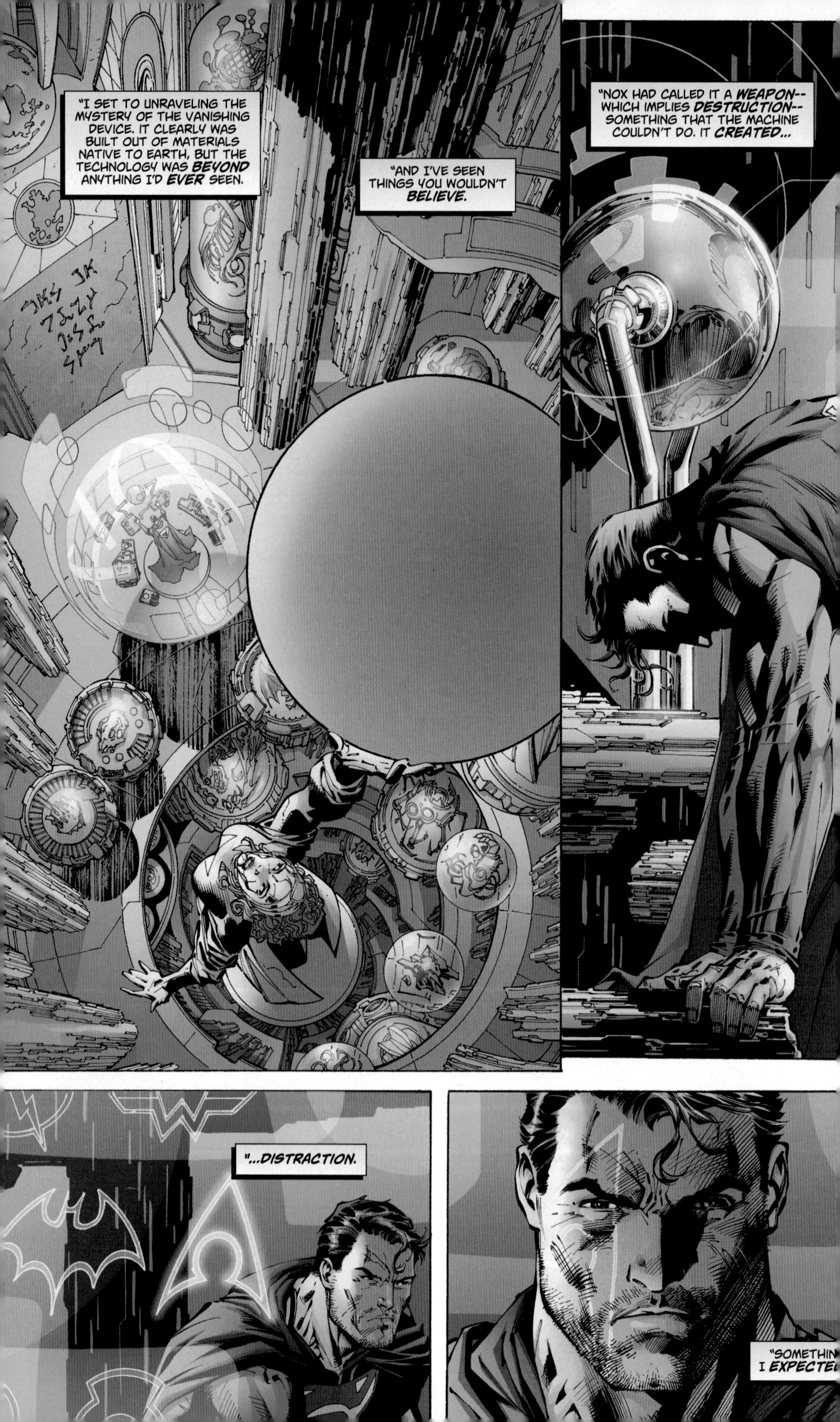
"I SET TO UNRAVELING THE MYSTERY OF THE VANISHING DEVICE. IT CLEARLY WAS BUILT OUT OF MATERIALS NATIVE TO EARTH, BUT THE TECHNOLOGY WAS **BEYOND** ANYTHING I'D **EVER** SEEN.
"AND I'VE SEEN THINGS YOU WOULDN'T **BELIEVE**.
"NOX HAD CALLED IT A **WEAPON**-- WHICH IMPLIES **DESTRUCTION**-- SOMETHING THAT THE MACHINE COULDN'T DO. IT **CREATED**...
"...**DISTRACTION**.

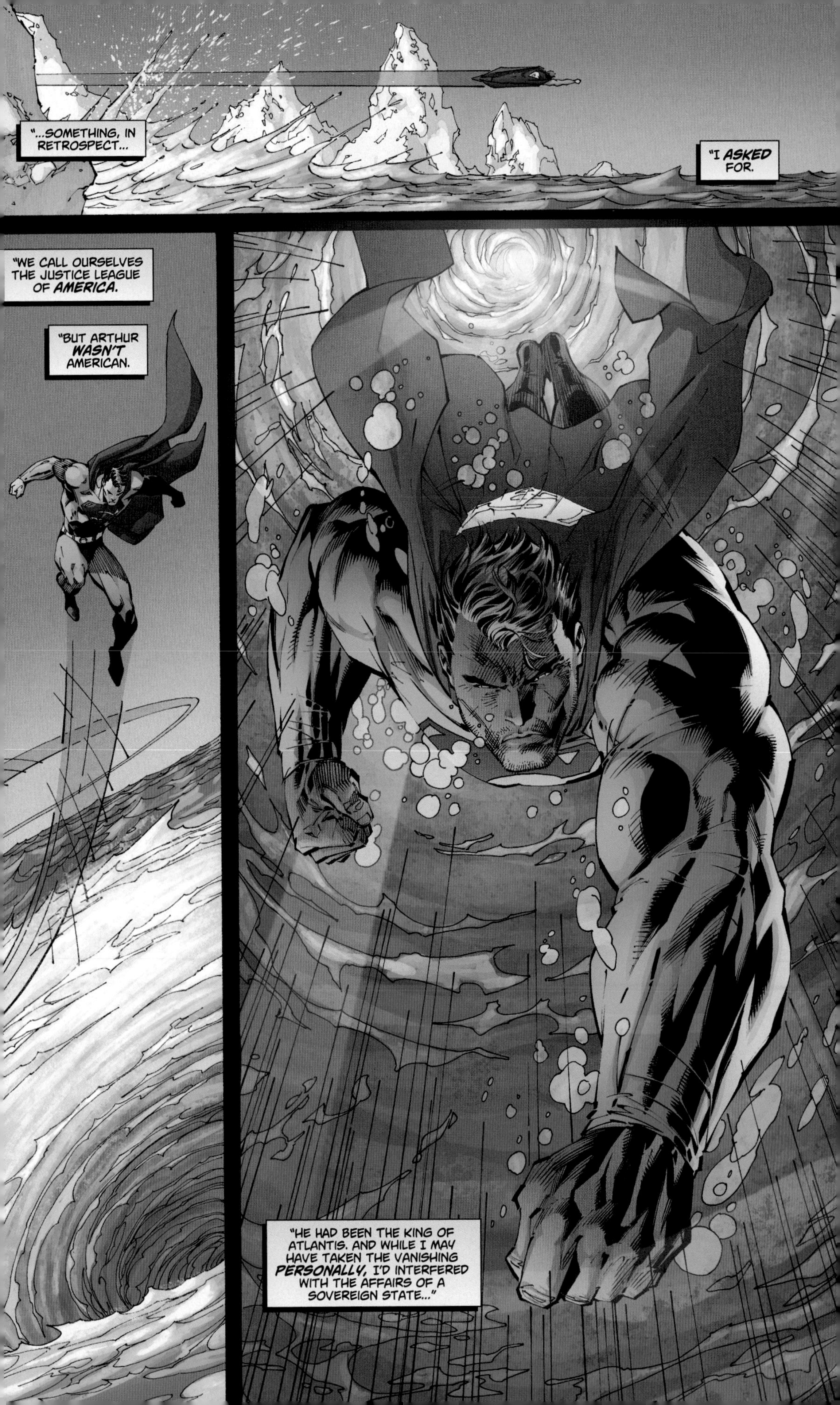
"...SOMETHING, IN RETROSPECT...
"I ASKED FOR.
"WE CALL OURSELVES THE JUSTICE LEAGUE OF AMERICA.
"BUT ARTHUR WASN'T AMERICAN.
"HE HAD BEEN THE KING OF ATLANTIS. AND WHILE I MAY HAVE TAKEN THE VANISHING PERSONALLY, I'D INTERFERED WITH THE AFFAIRS OF A SOVEREIGN STATE..."

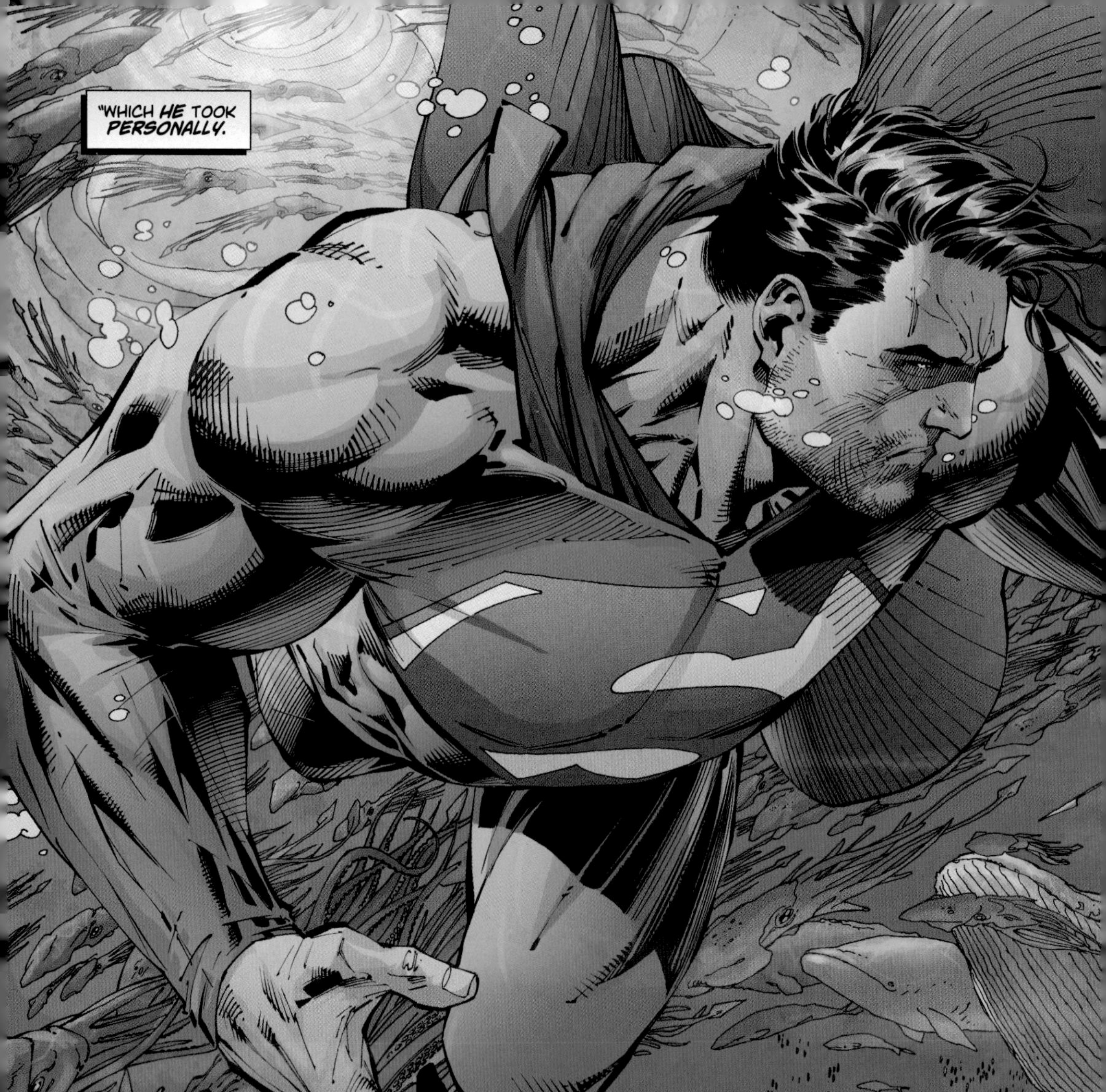
"WHICH HE TOOK PERSONALLY.

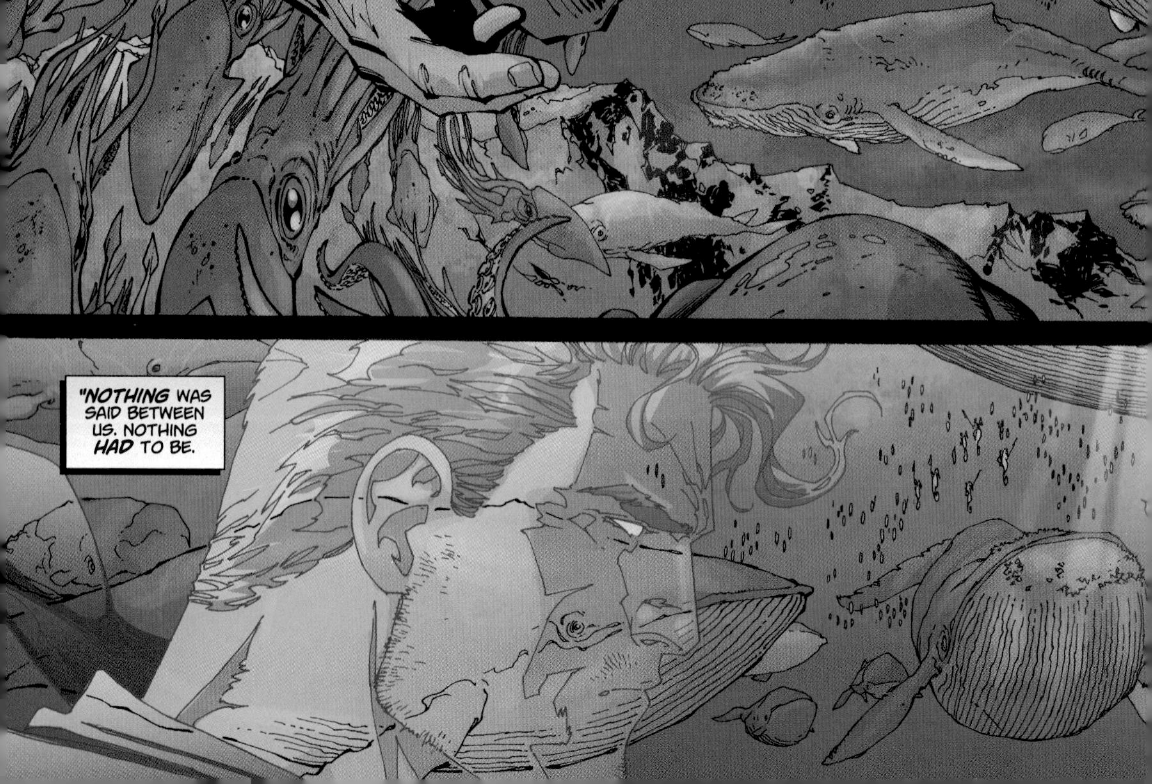
"NOTHING WAS SAID BETWEEN US. NOTHING HAD TO BE.

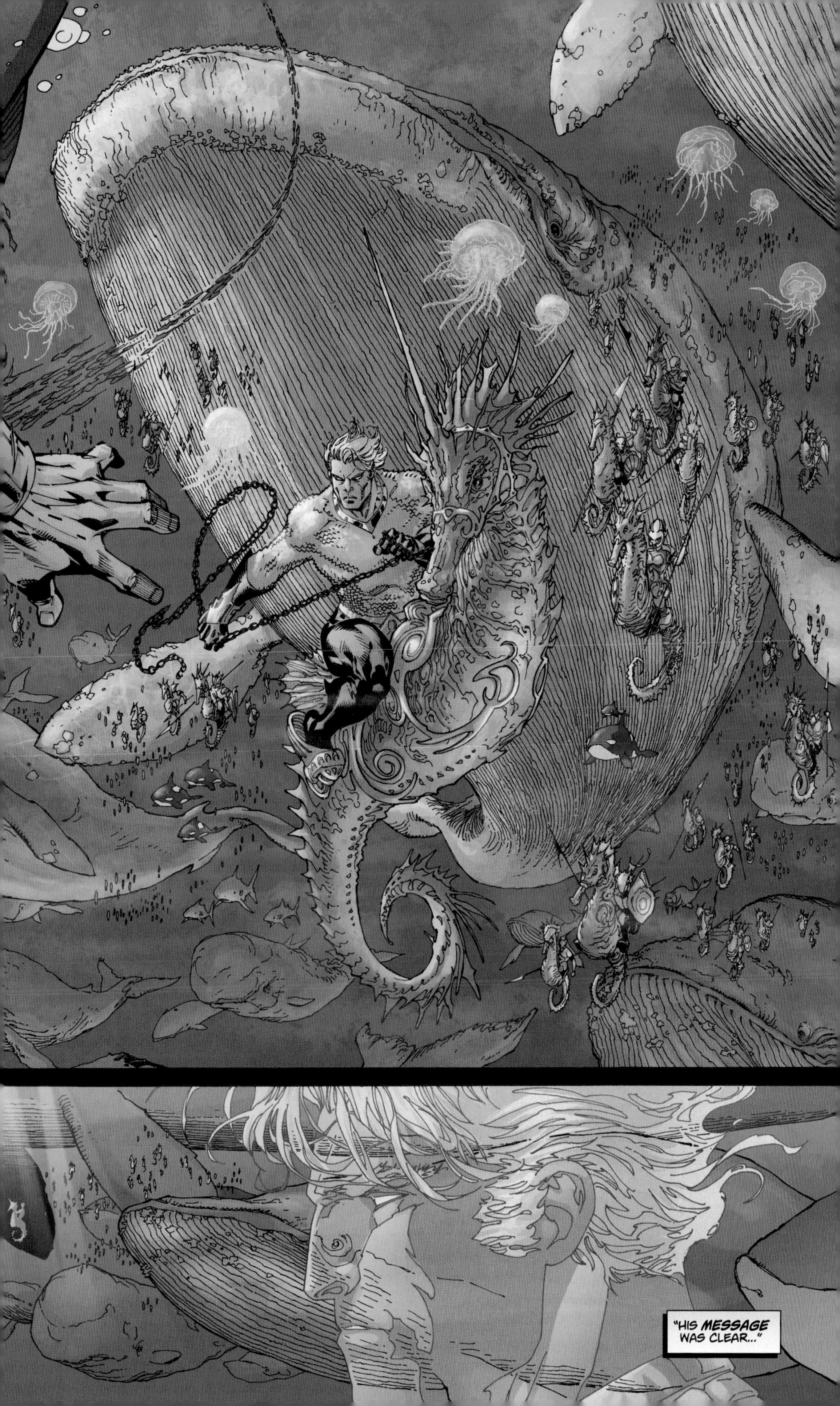
"HIS MESSAGE WAS CLEAR..."

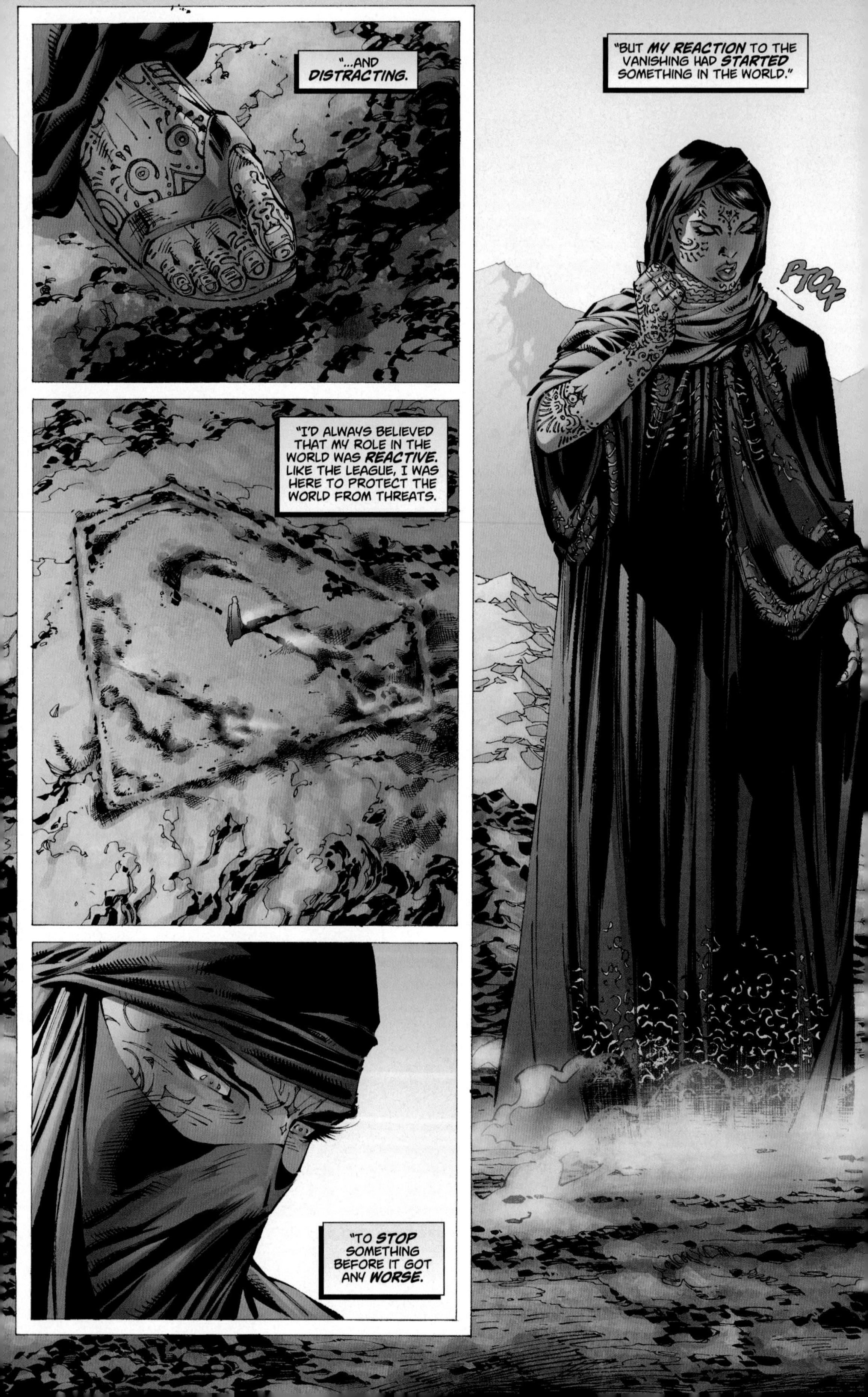
"...AND DISTRACTING.
"I'D ALWAYS BELIEVED THAT MY ROLE IN THE WORLD WAS REACTIVE. LIKE THE LEAGUE, I WAS HERE TO PROTECT THE WORLD FROM THREATS.
"TO STOP SOMETHING BEFORE IT GOT ANY WORSE.
"BUT MY REACTION TO THE VANISHING HAD STARTED SOMETHING IN THE WORLD."
PTOCK

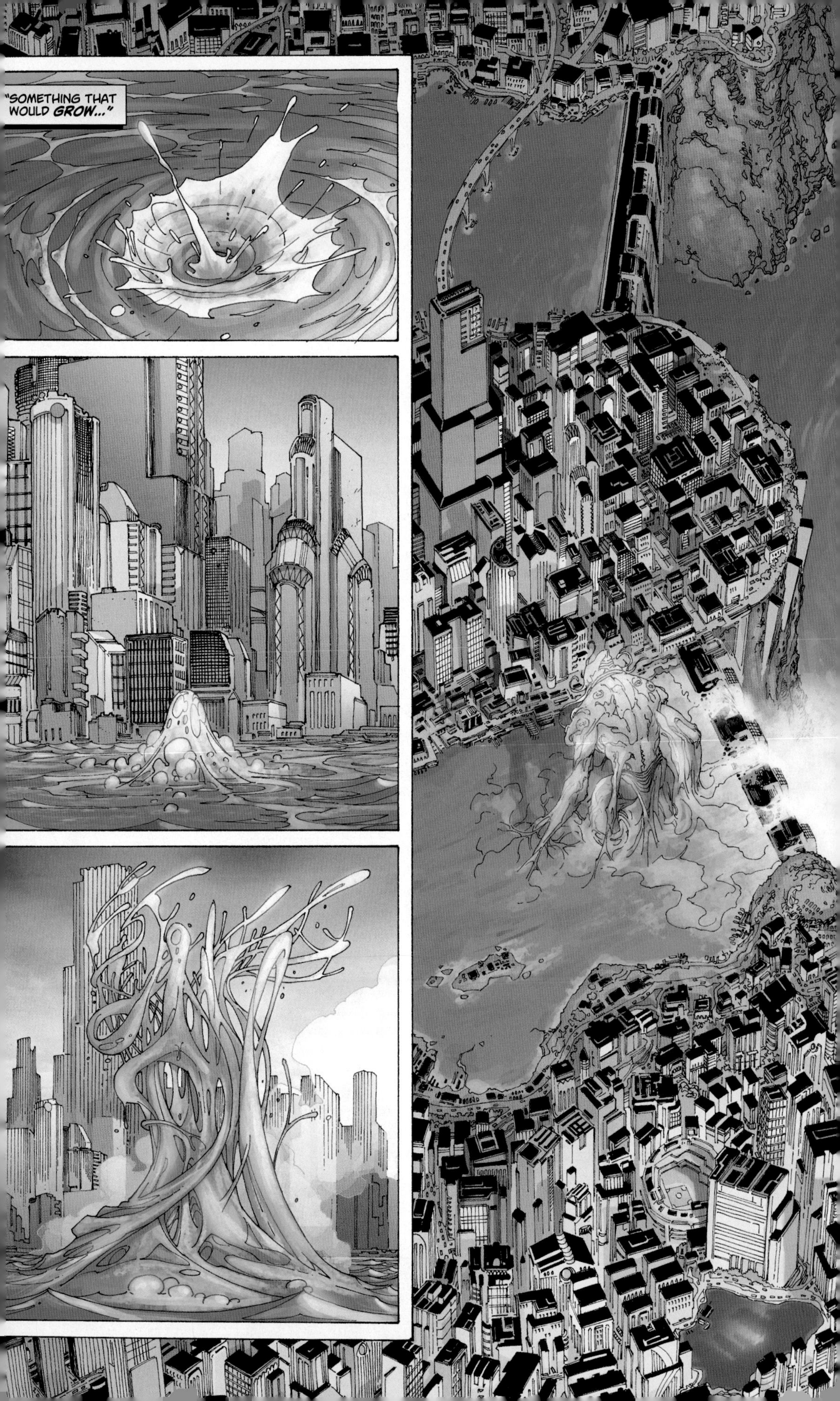
"SOMETHING THAT WOULD GROW..."

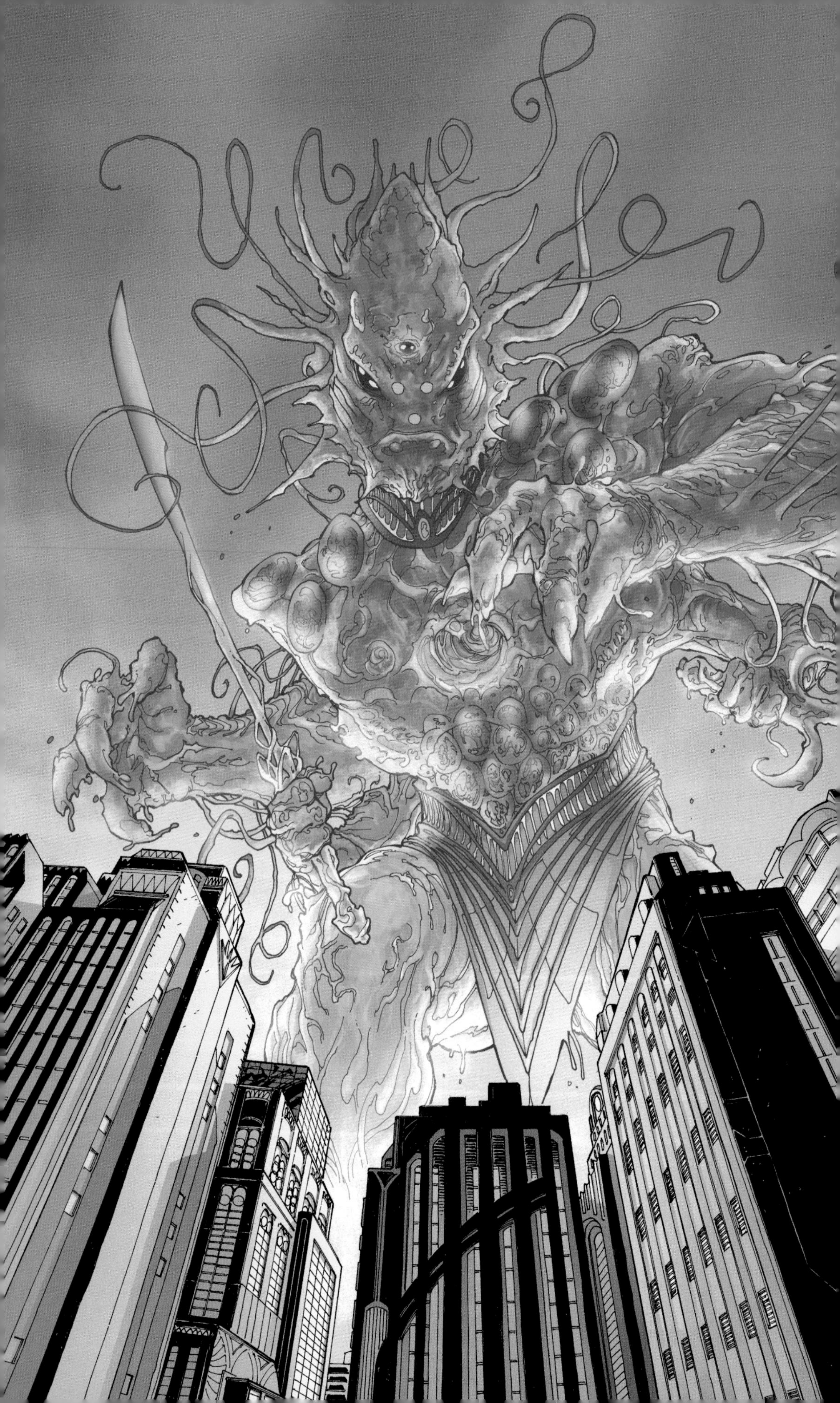

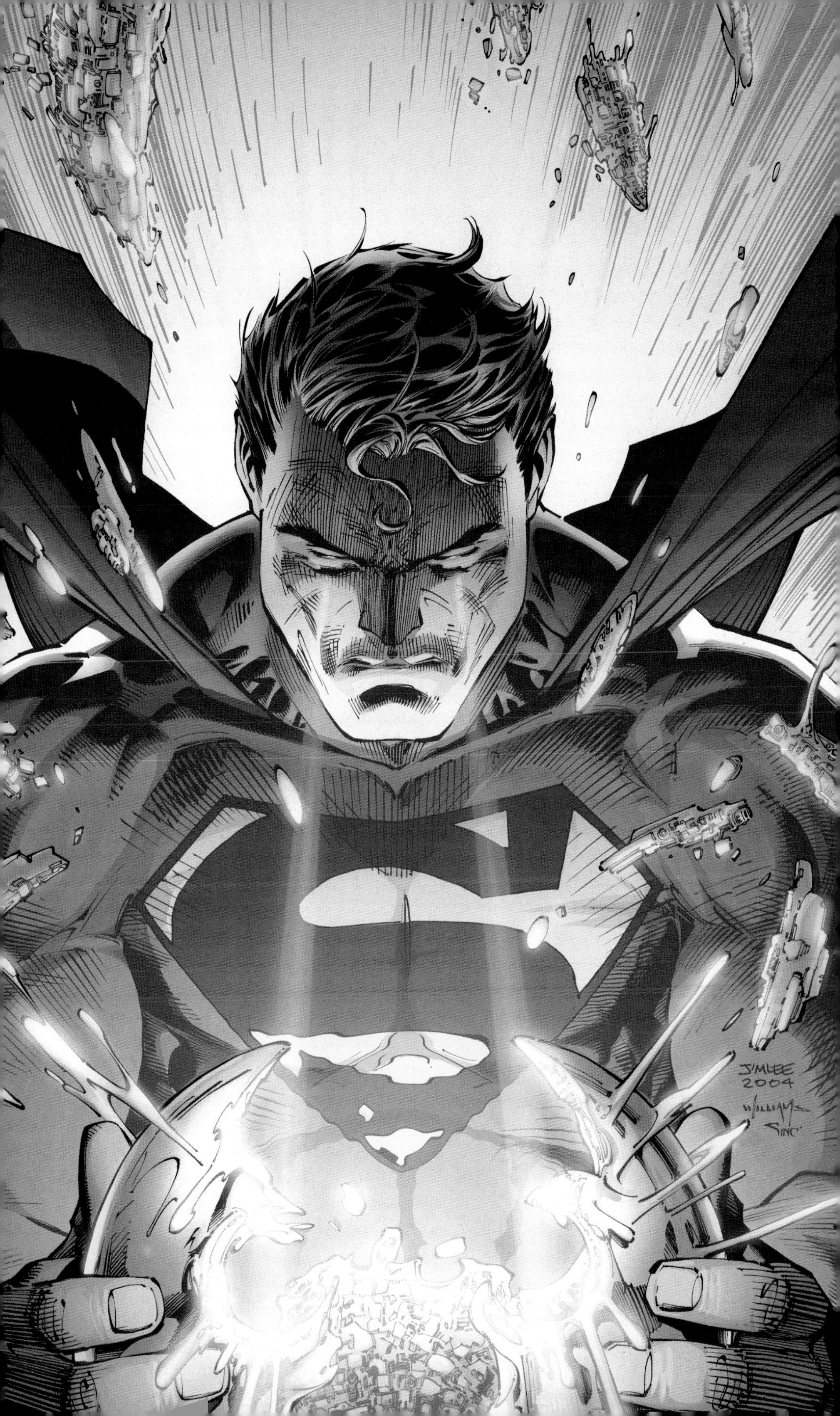
JIMLEE 2004
WILLIAMS SINC

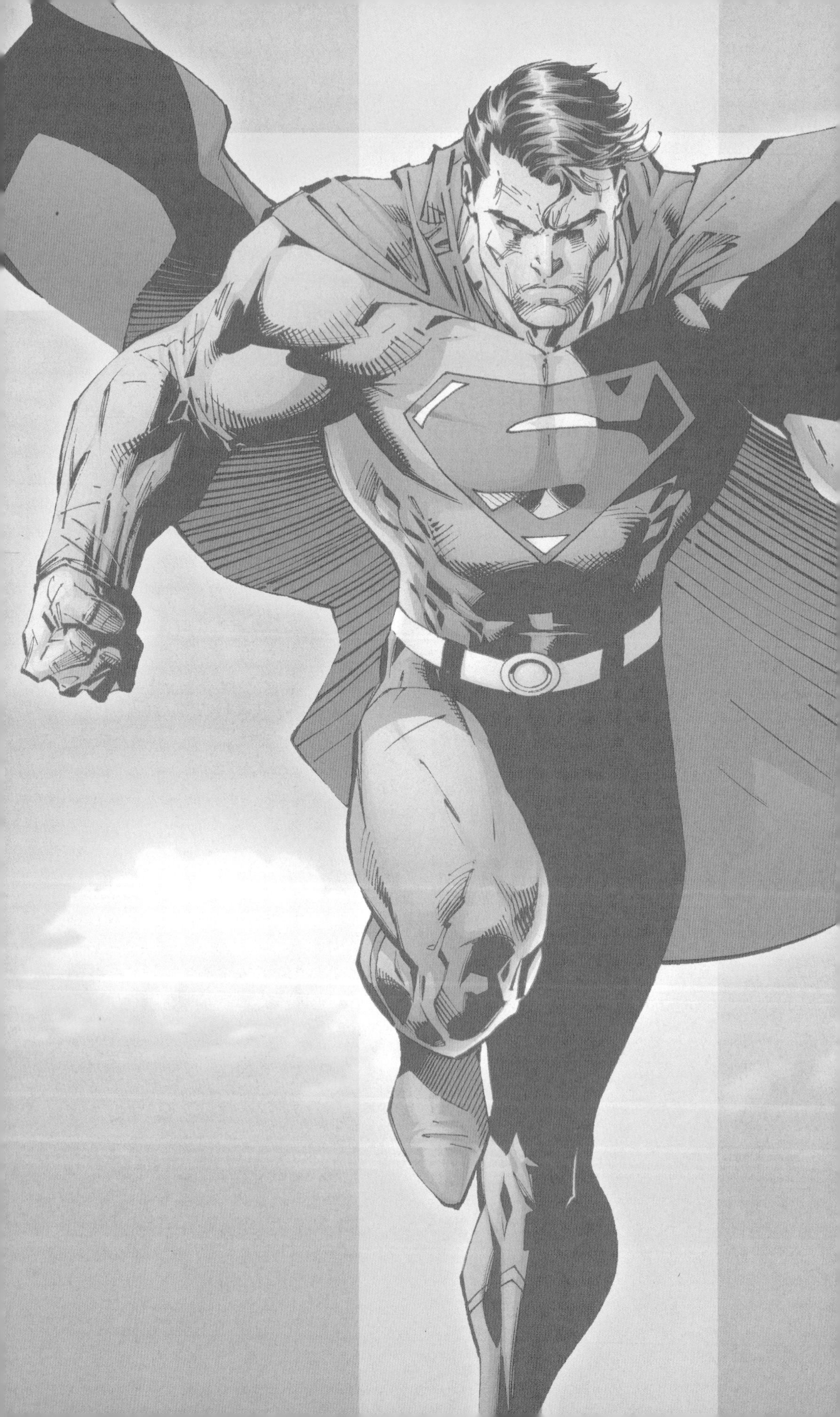

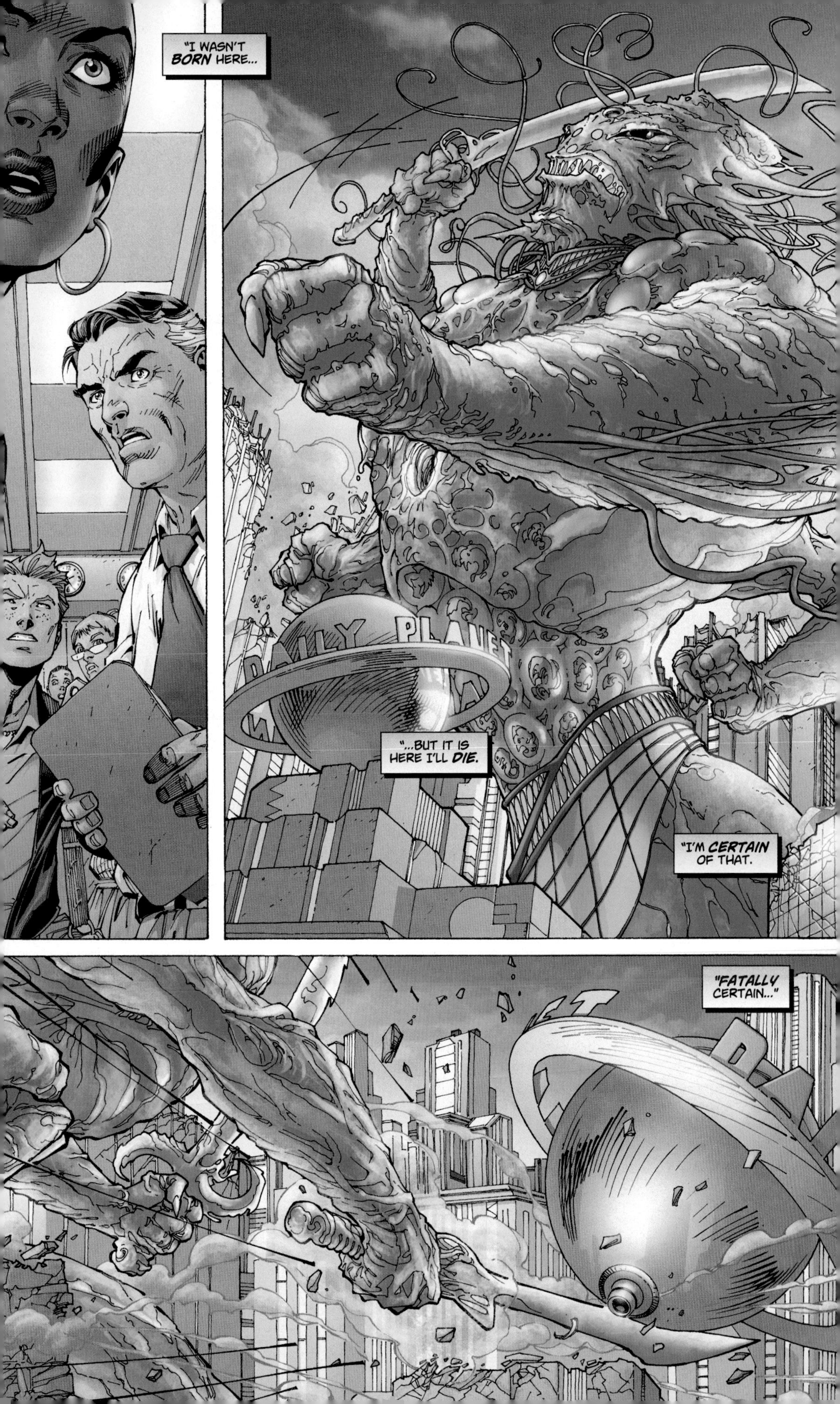
"I WASN'T BORN HERE...
"...BUT IT IS HERE I'LL DIE.
"I'M CERTAIN OF THAT.
"FATALLY CERTAIN..."

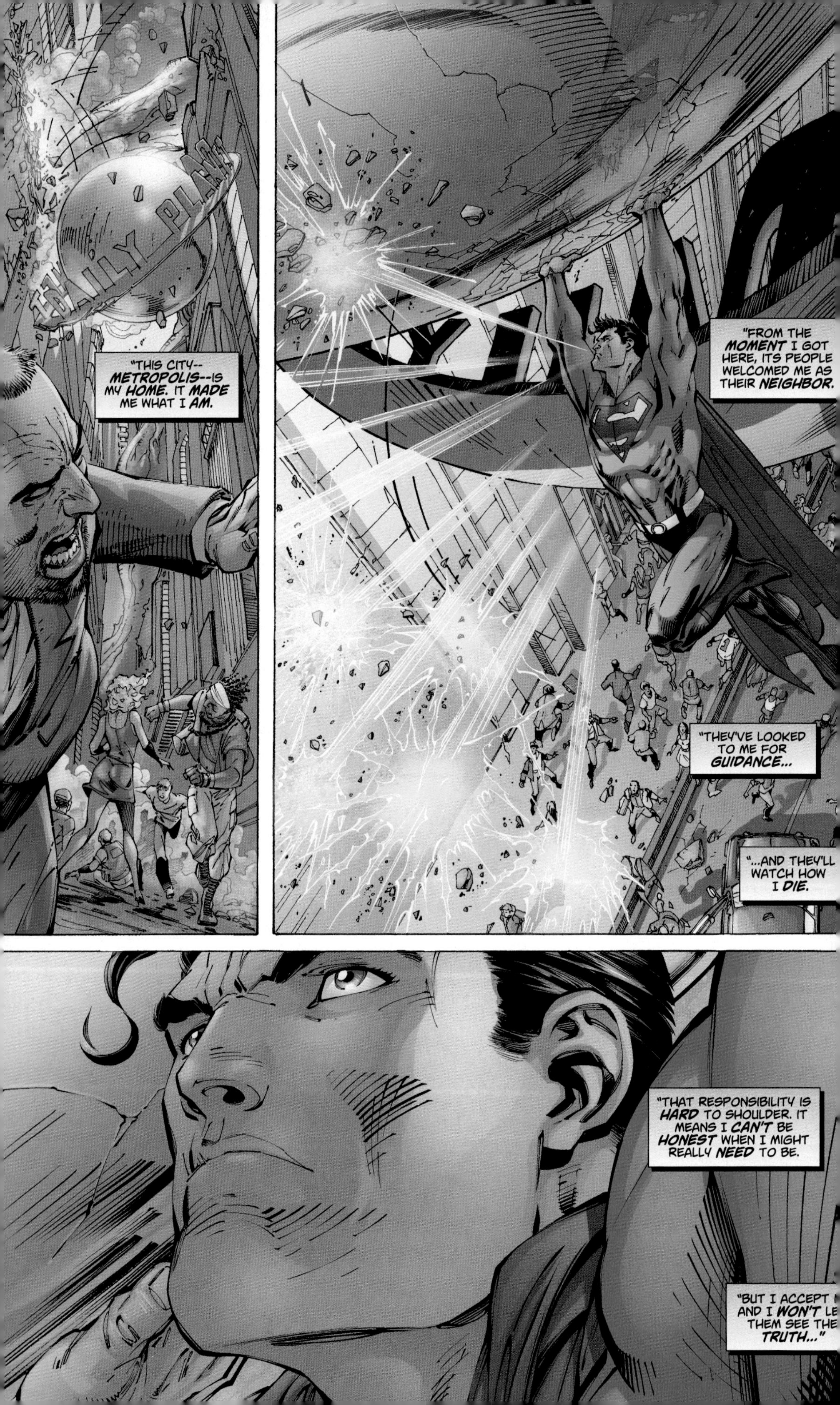
DAILY PLANET
"THIS CITY-- METROPOLIS--IS MY HOME. IT MADE ME WHAT I AM.
"FROM THE MOMENT I GOT HERE, ITS PEOPLE WELCOMED ME AS THEIR NEIGHBOR.
"THEY'VE LOOKED TO ME FOR GUIDANCE...
"...AND THEY'LL WATCH HOW I DIE.
"THAT RESPONSIBILITY IS HARD TO SHOULDER. IT MEANS I CAN'T BE HONEST WHEN I MIGHT REALLY NEED TO BE.
"BUT I ACCEPT AND I WON'T LE THEM SEE THE TRUTH..."

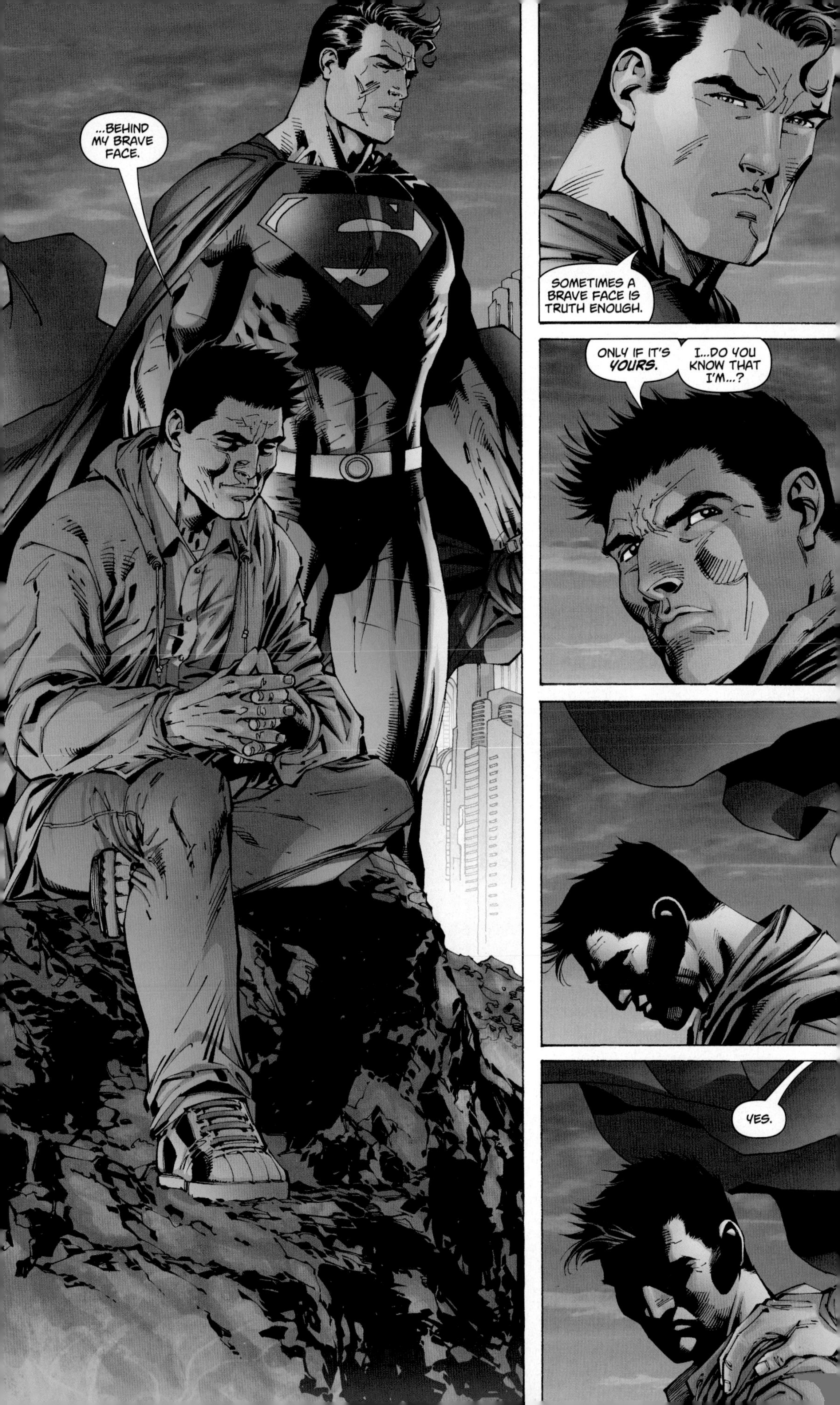
...BEHIND MY BRAVE FACE.
SOMETIMES A BRAVE FACE IS TRUTH ENOUGH.
ONLY IF IT'S *YOURS*.
I...DO YOU KNOW THAT I'M...?
YES.

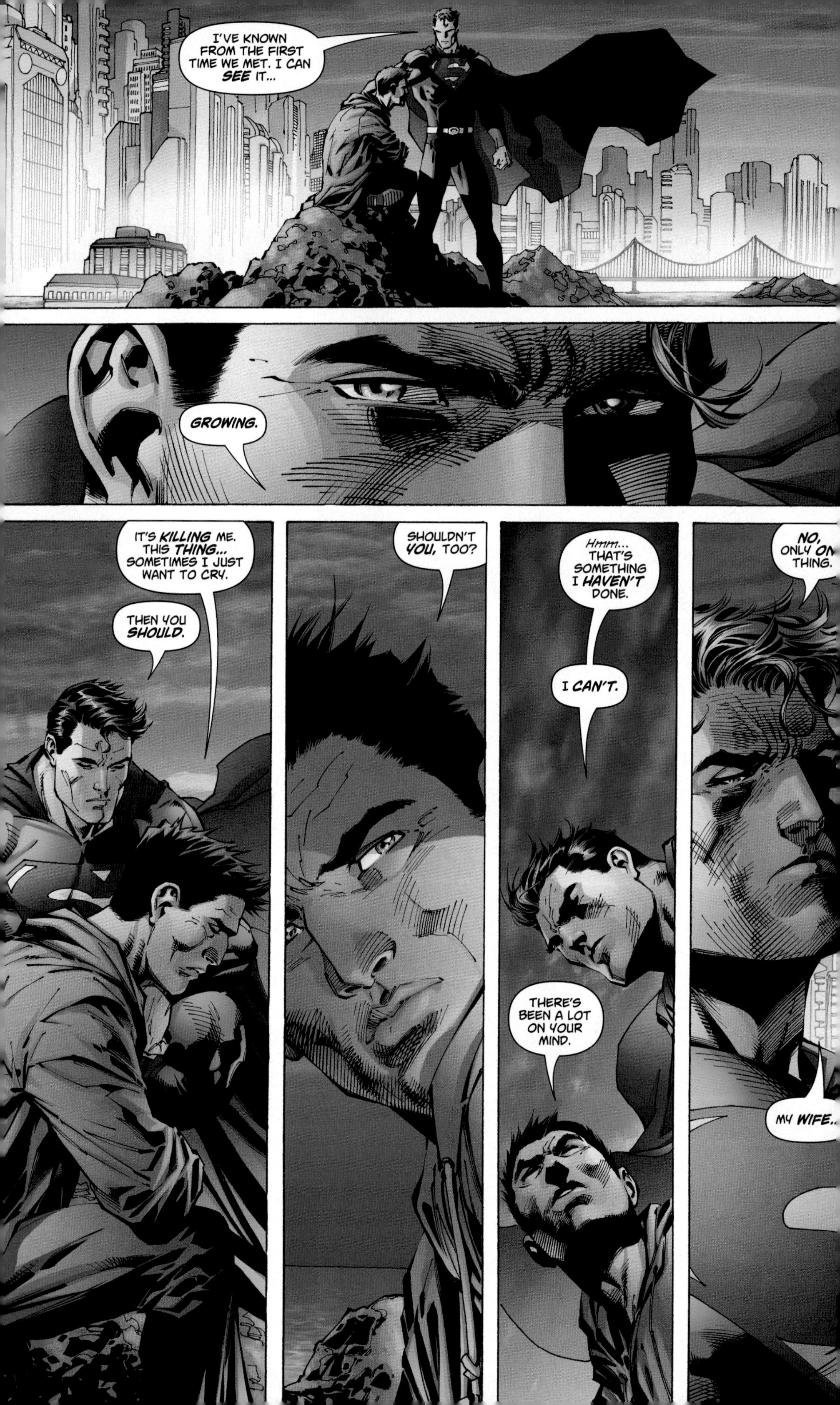
I'VE KNOWN FROM THE FIRST TIME WE MET. I CAN SEE IT...
GROWING.
IT'S KILLING ME. THIS THING... SOMETIMES I JUST WANT TO CRY.
THEN YOU SHOULD.
SHOULDN'T YOU, TOO?
Hmm... THAT'S SOMETHING I HAVEN'T DONE.
I CAN'T.
THERE'S BEEN A LOT ON YOUR MIND.
NO, ONLY ON THING.
MY WIFE..

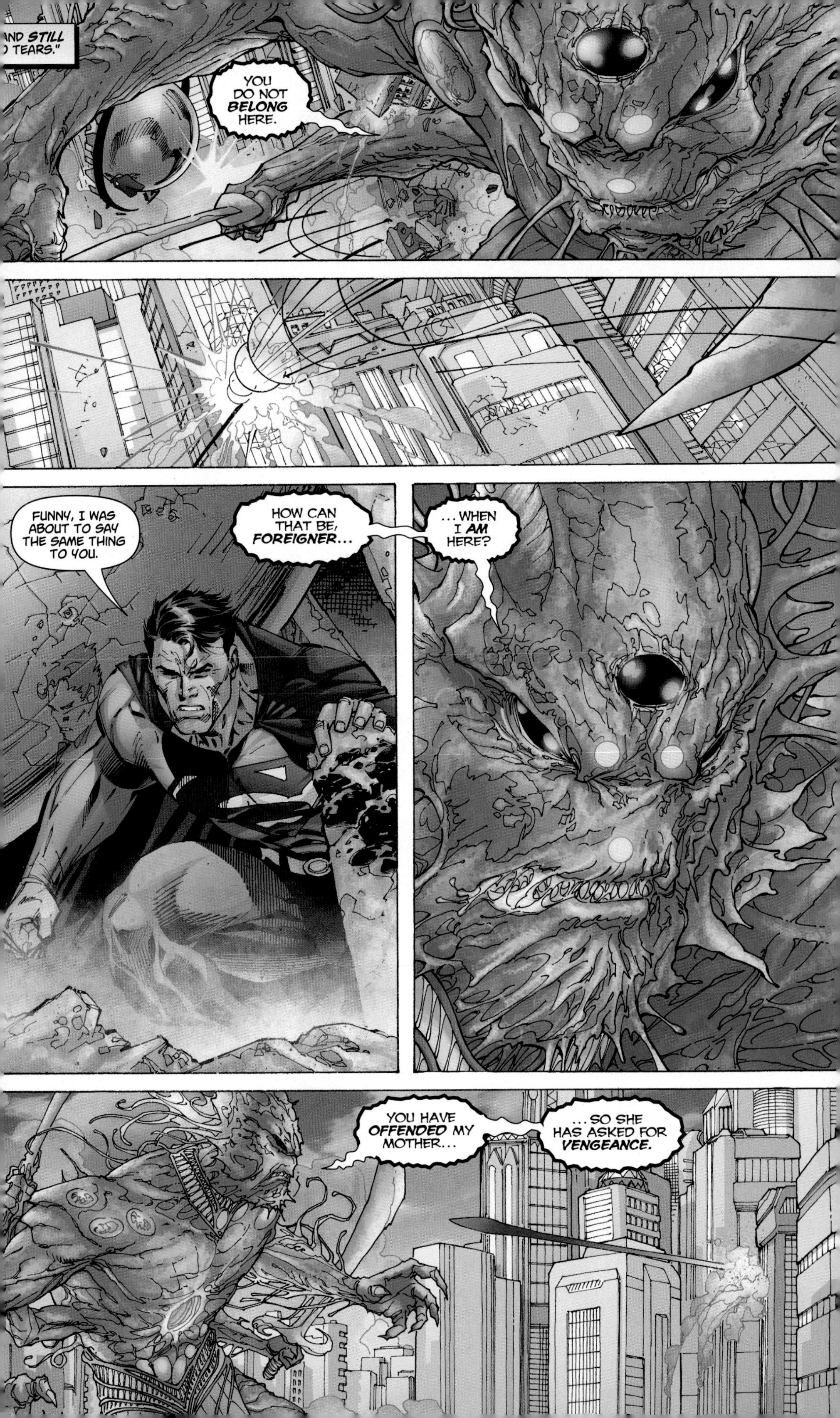
...AND STILL ...TEARS."
YOU DO NOT BELONG HERE.
FUNNY, I WAS ABOUT TO SAY THE SAME THING TO YOU.
HOW CAN THAT BE, FOREIGNER...
...WHEN I AM HERE?
YOU HAVE OFFENDED MY MOTHER...
...SO SHE HAS ASKED FOR VENGEANCE.

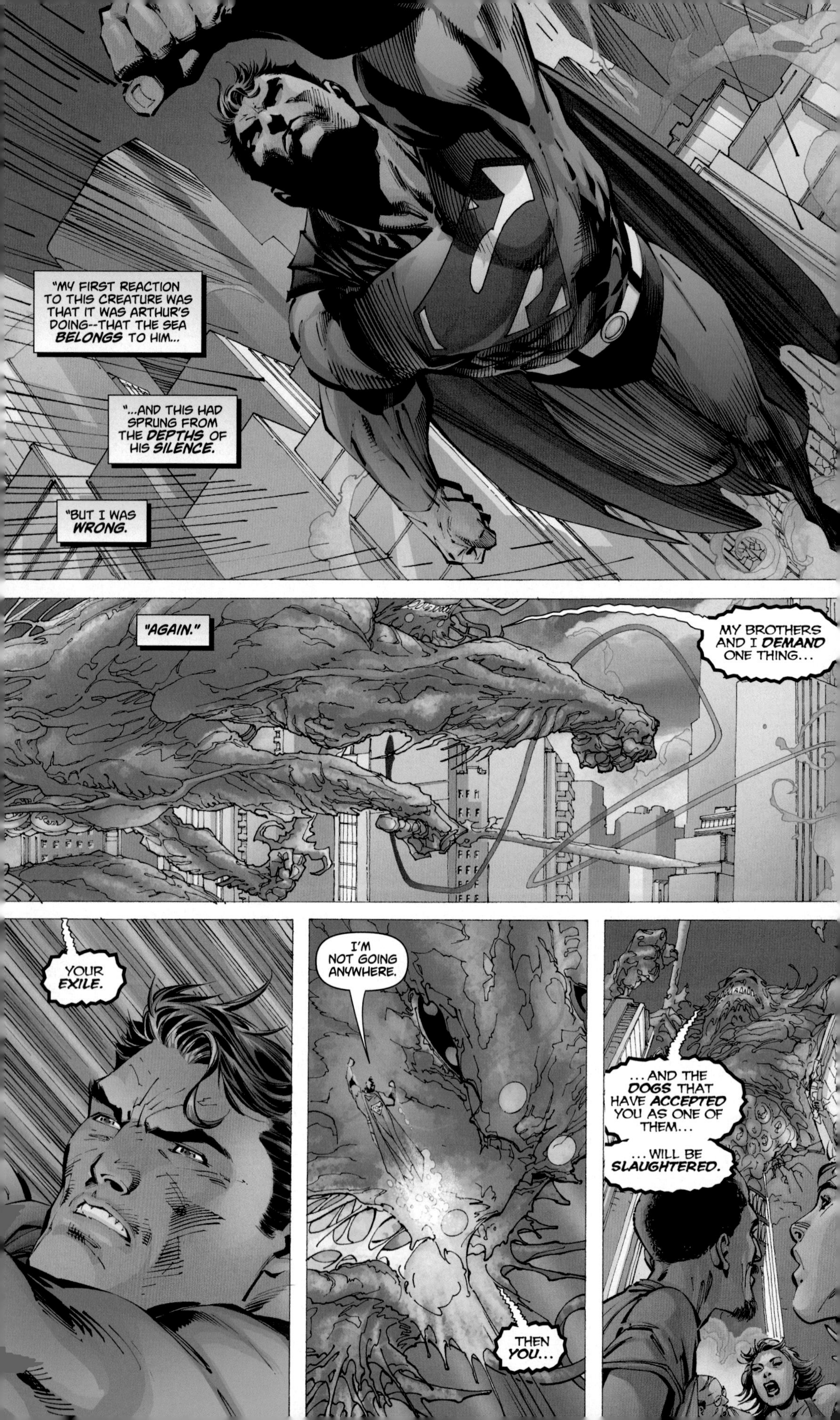
"MY FIRST REACTION TO THIS CREATURE WAS THAT IT WAS ARTHUR'S DOING--THAT THE SEA BELONGS TO HIM...
"...AND THIS HAD SPRUNG FROM THE DEPTHS OF HIS SILENCE.
"BUT I WAS WRONG.
"AGAIN."
MY BROTHERS AND I DEMAND ONE THING...
YOUR EXILE.
I'M NOT GOING ANYWHERE.
THEN YOU...
...AND THE DOGS THAT HAVE ACCEPTED YOU AS ONE OF THEM...
...WILL BE SLAUGHTERED.

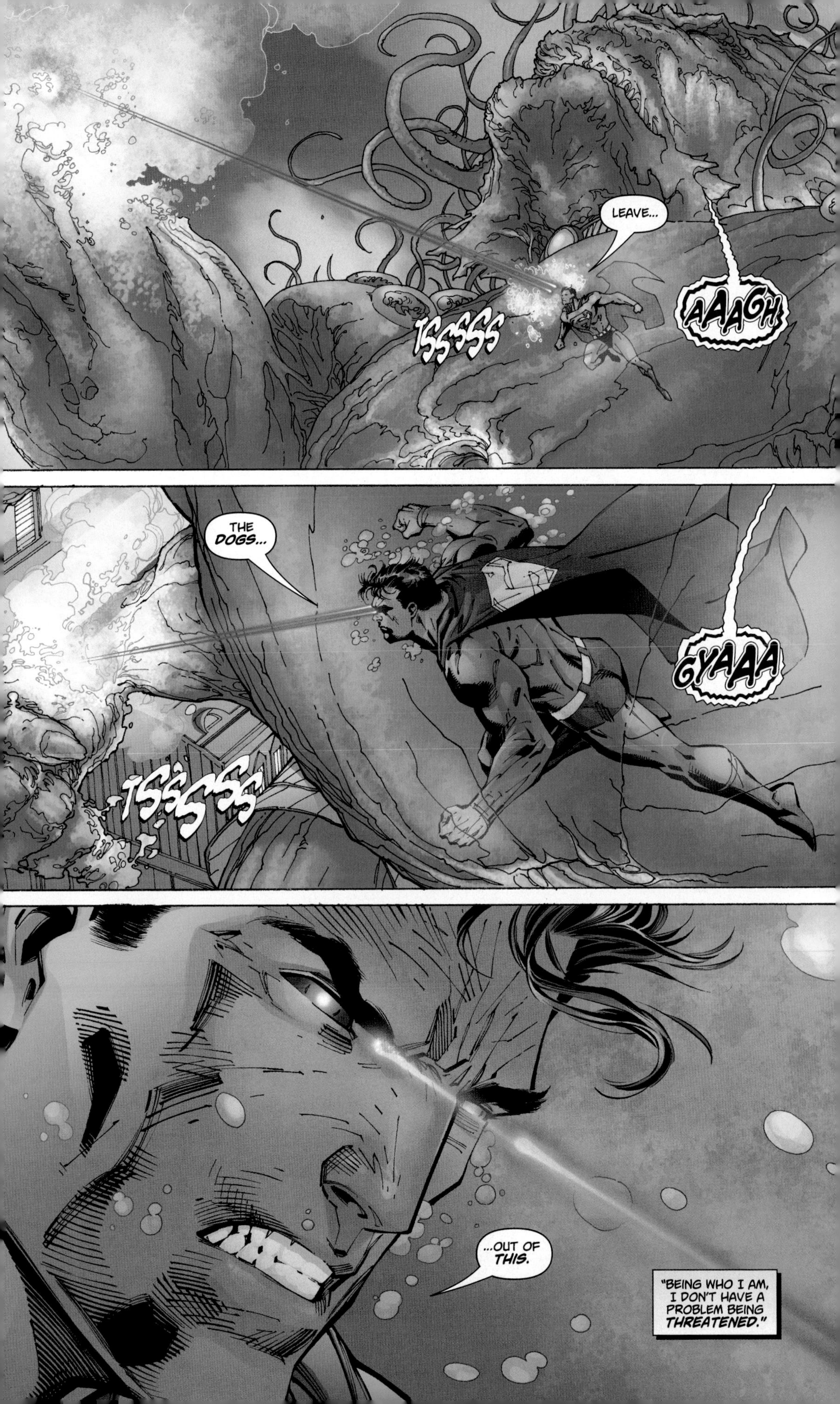
LEAVE...
AAAGH
TSSSSS
THE DOGS...
GYAAA
TSSSSS
...OUT OF THIS.
"BEING WHO I AM, I DON'T HAVE A PROBLEM BEING THREATENED."

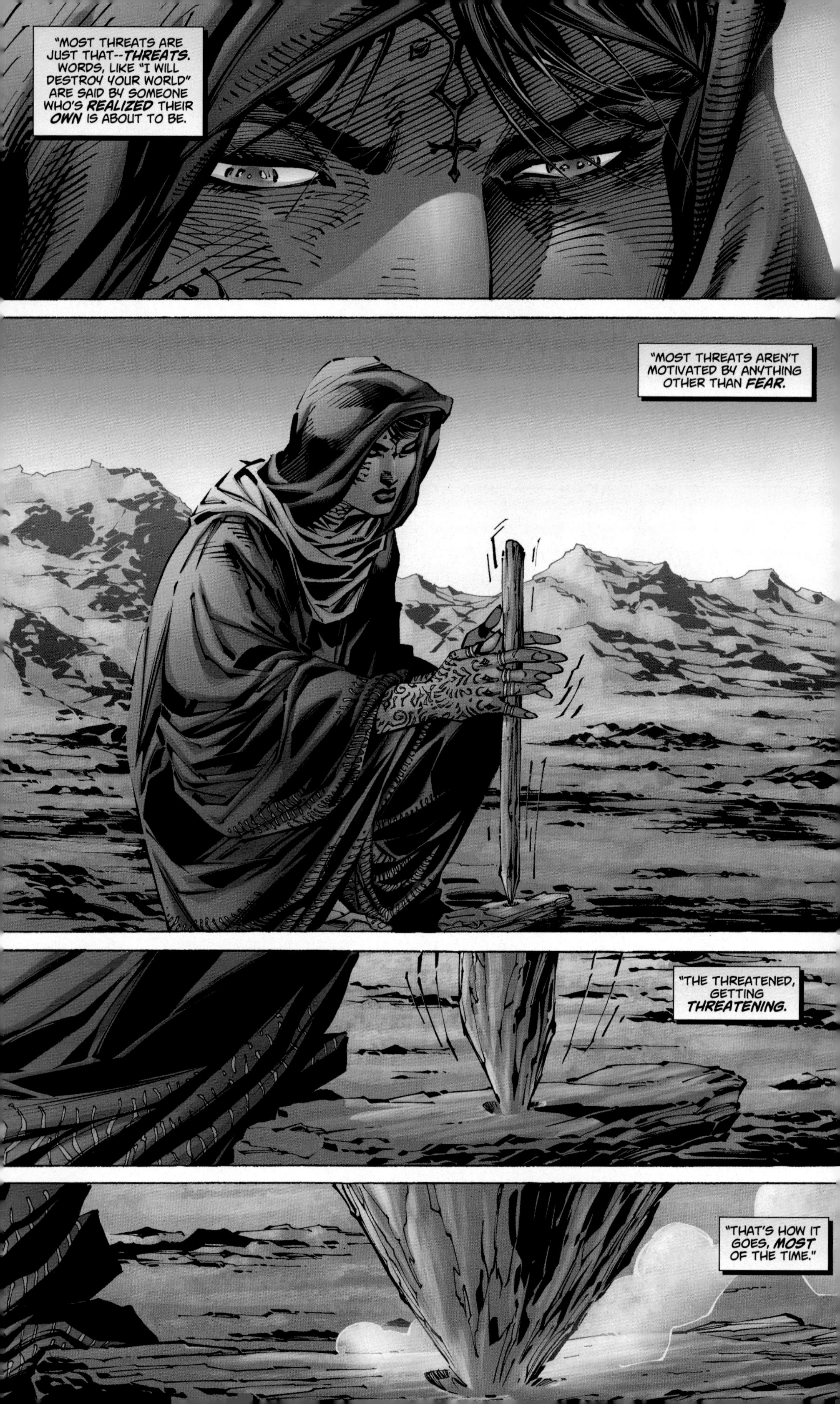
"MOST THREATS ARE JUST THAT--THREATS. WORDS, LIKE "I WILL DESTROY YOUR WORLD" ARE SAID BY SOMEONE WHO'S REALIZED THEIR OWN IS ABOUT TO BE.
"MOST THREATS AREN'T MOTIVATED BY ANYTHING OTHER THAN FEAR.
"THE THREATENED, GETTING THREATENING.
"THAT'S HOW IT GOES, MOST OF THE TIME."

"BUT NOT ALL."

SSSSSS

AAAHH

FFFF...

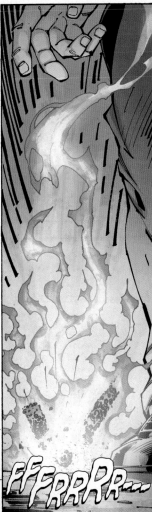

FFFRRRR...

FWHWRA

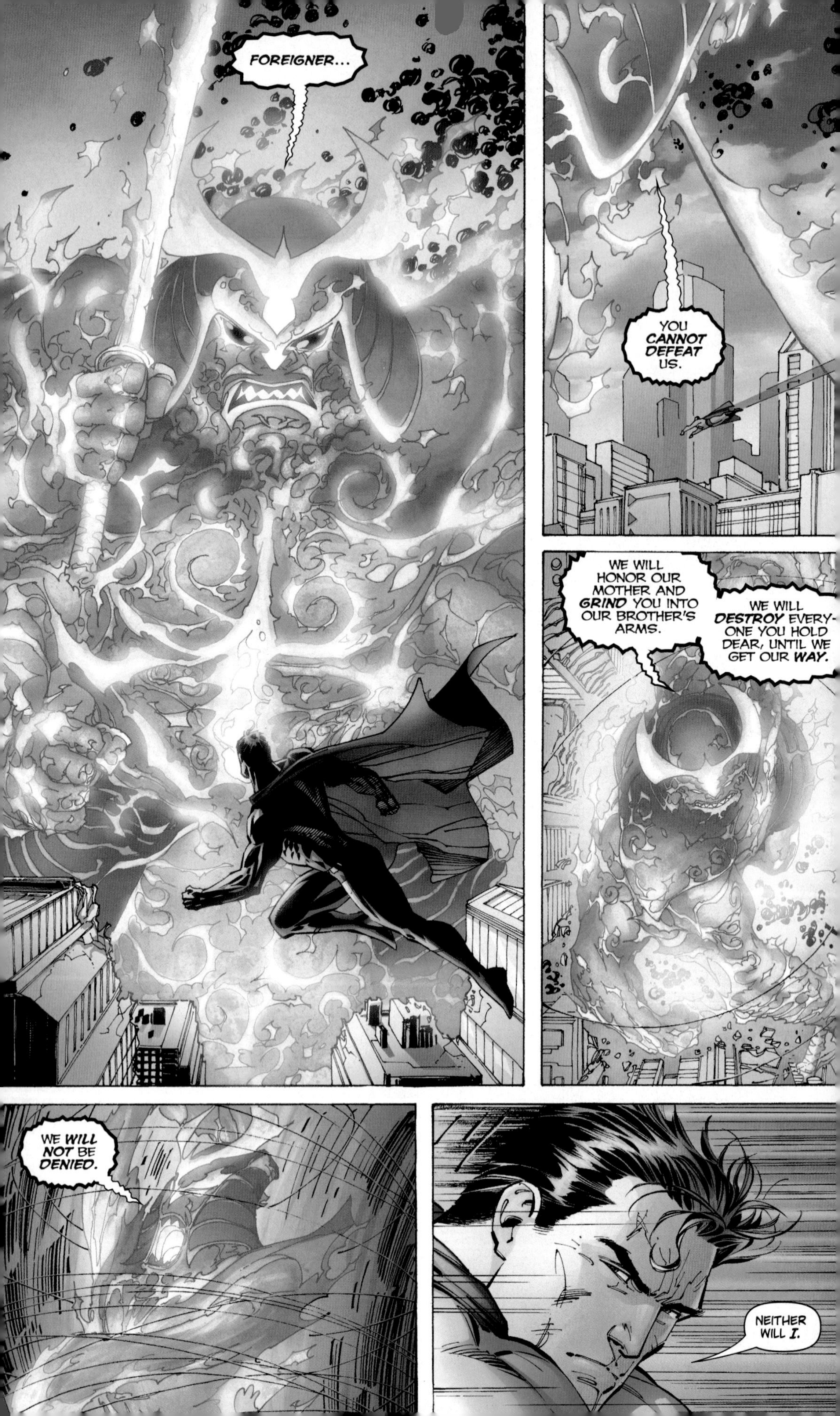
FOREIGNER...
YOU CANNOT DEFEAT US.
WE WILL HONOR OUR MOTHER AND GRIND YOU INTO OUR BROTHER'S ARMS.
WE WILL DESTROY EVERY-ONE YOU HOLD DEAR, UNTIL WE GET OUR WAY.
WE WILL NOT BE DENIED.
NEITHER WILL I.

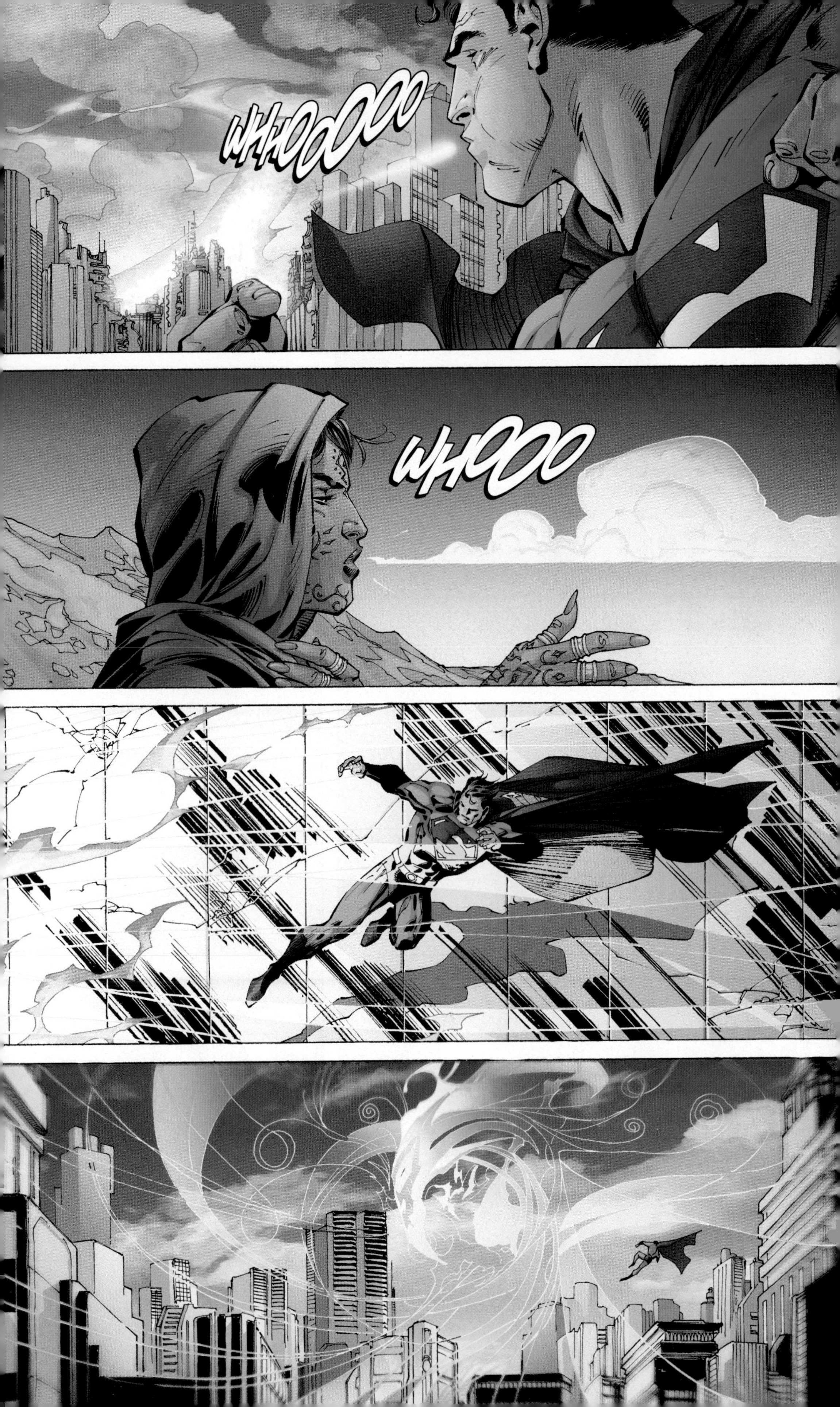
WHHOOOOOO
WHOOO

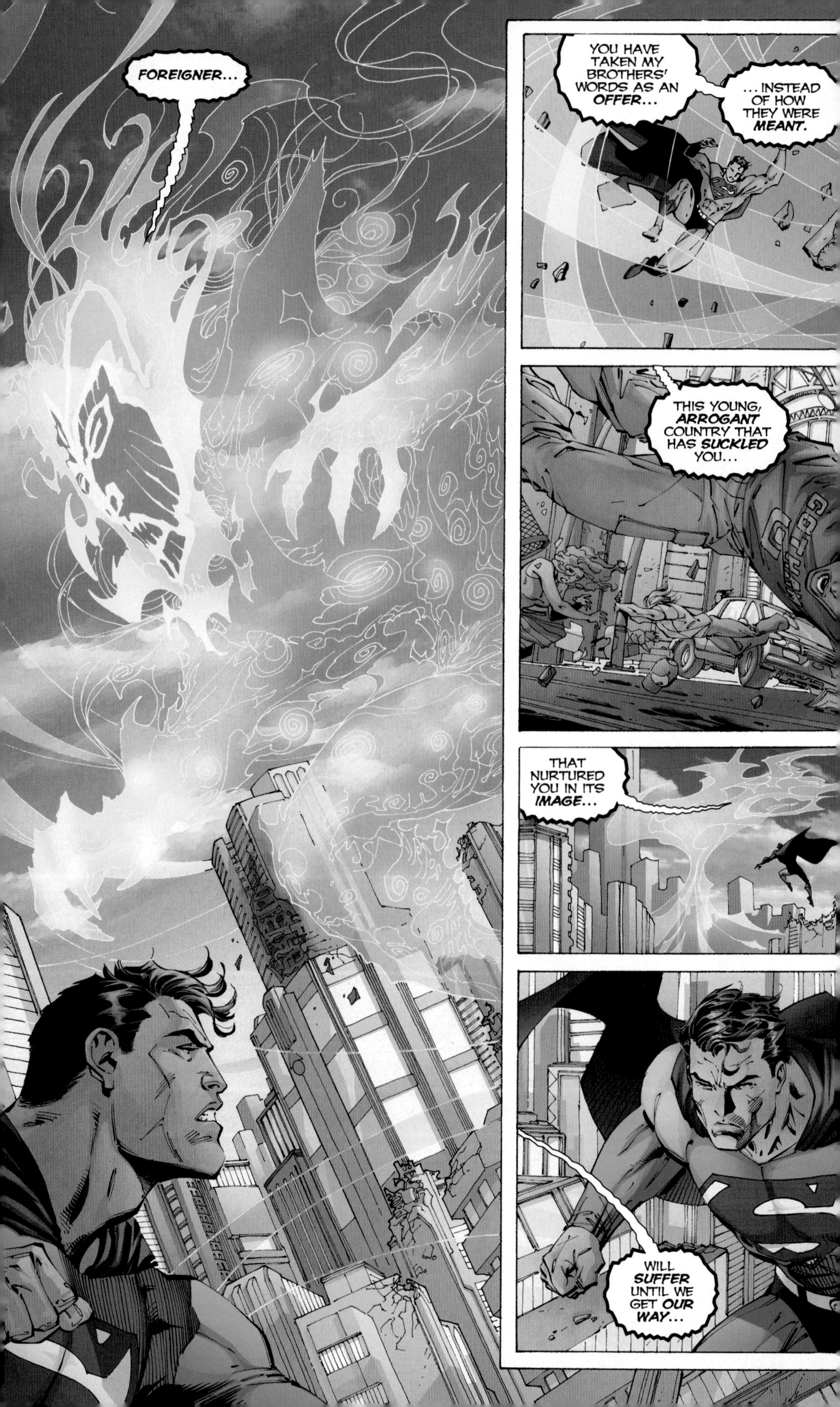
FOREIGNER...
YOU HAVE TAKEN MY BROTHERS' WORDS AS AN OFFER...
...INSTEAD OF HOW THEY WERE MEANT.
THIS YOUNG, ARROGANT COUNTRY THAT HAS SUCKLED YOU...
THAT NURTURED YOU IN ITS IMAGE...
WILL SUFFER UNTIL WE GET OUR WAY...

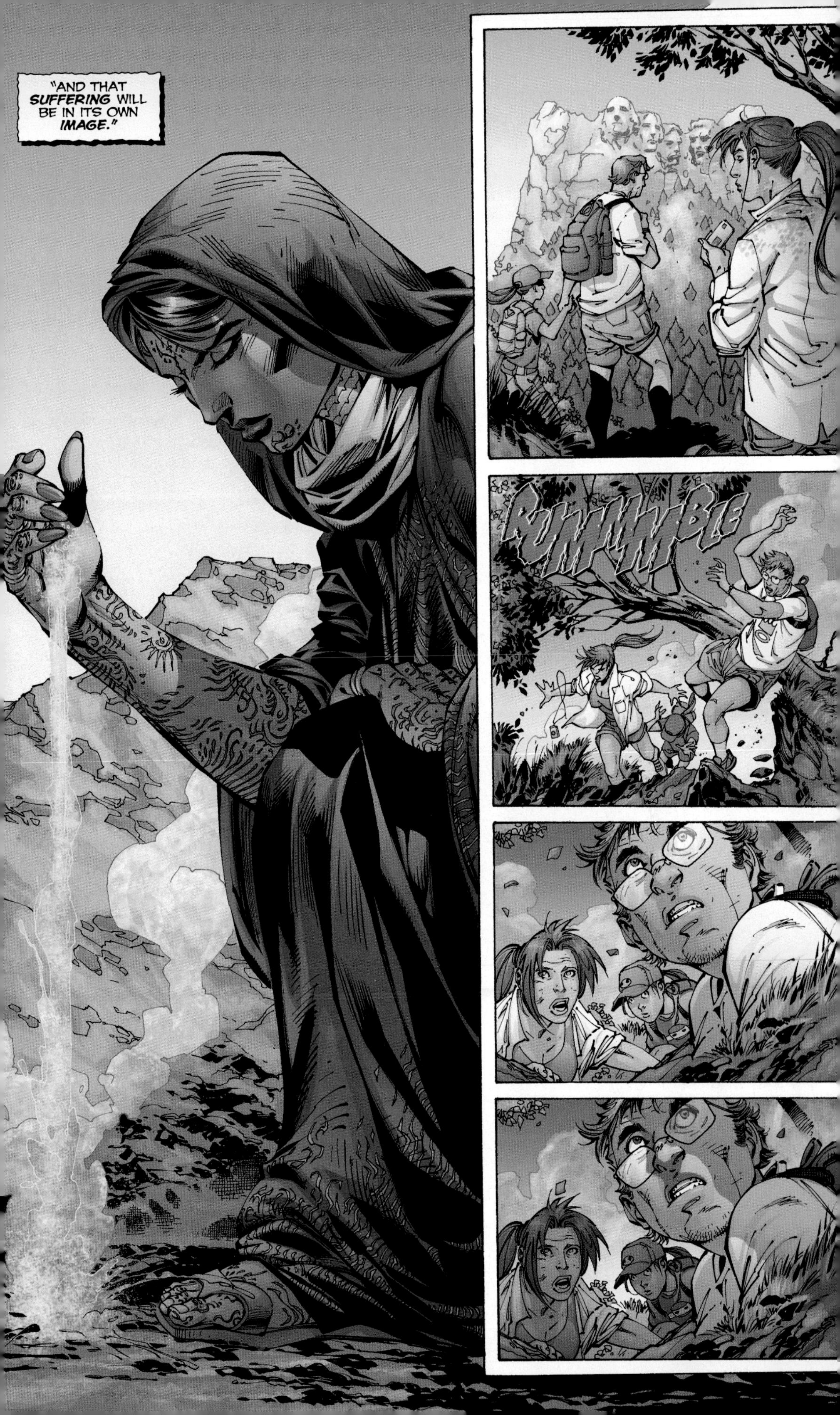
"AND THAT SUFFERING WILL BE IN ITS OWN IMAGE."
RUMMMMBLE

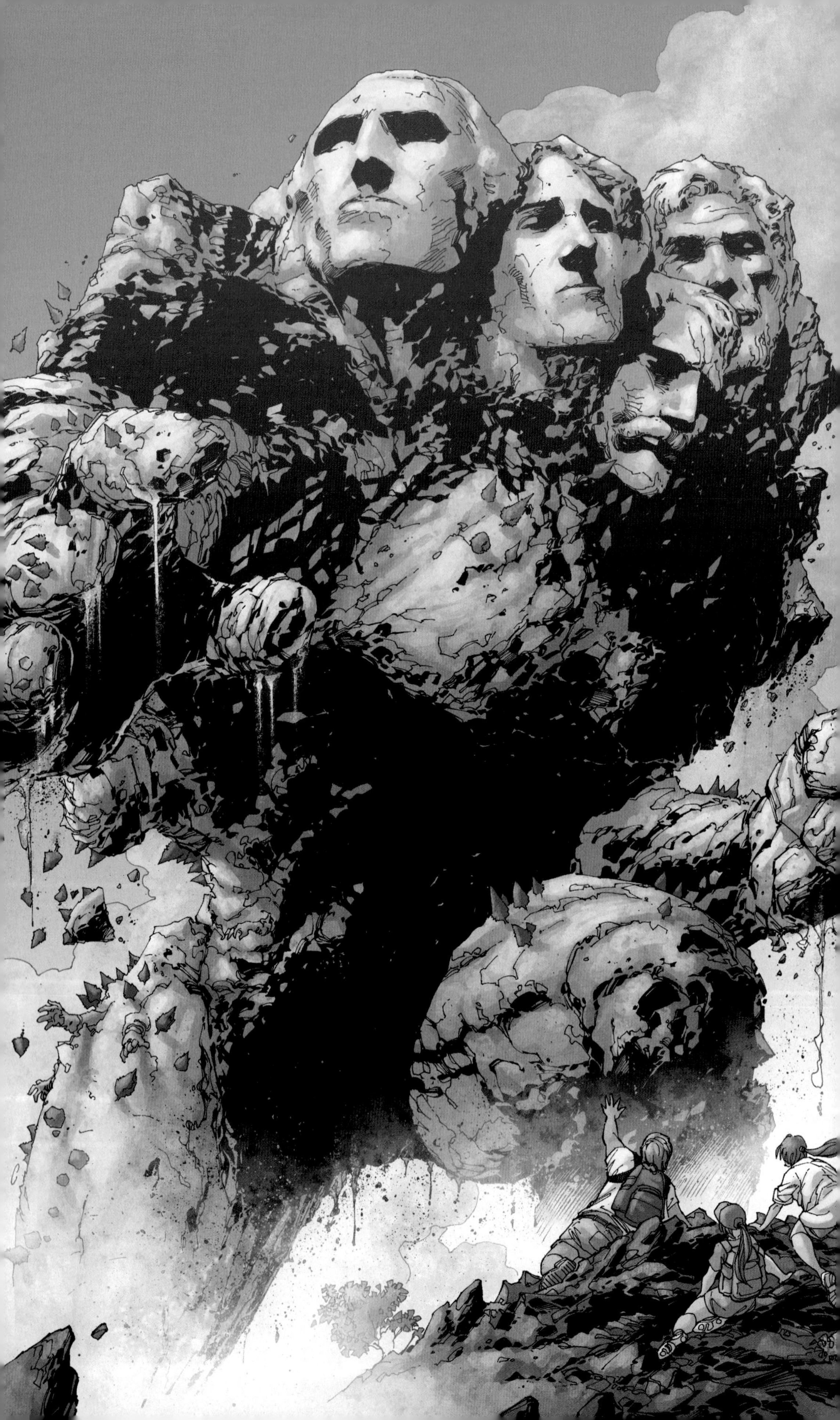

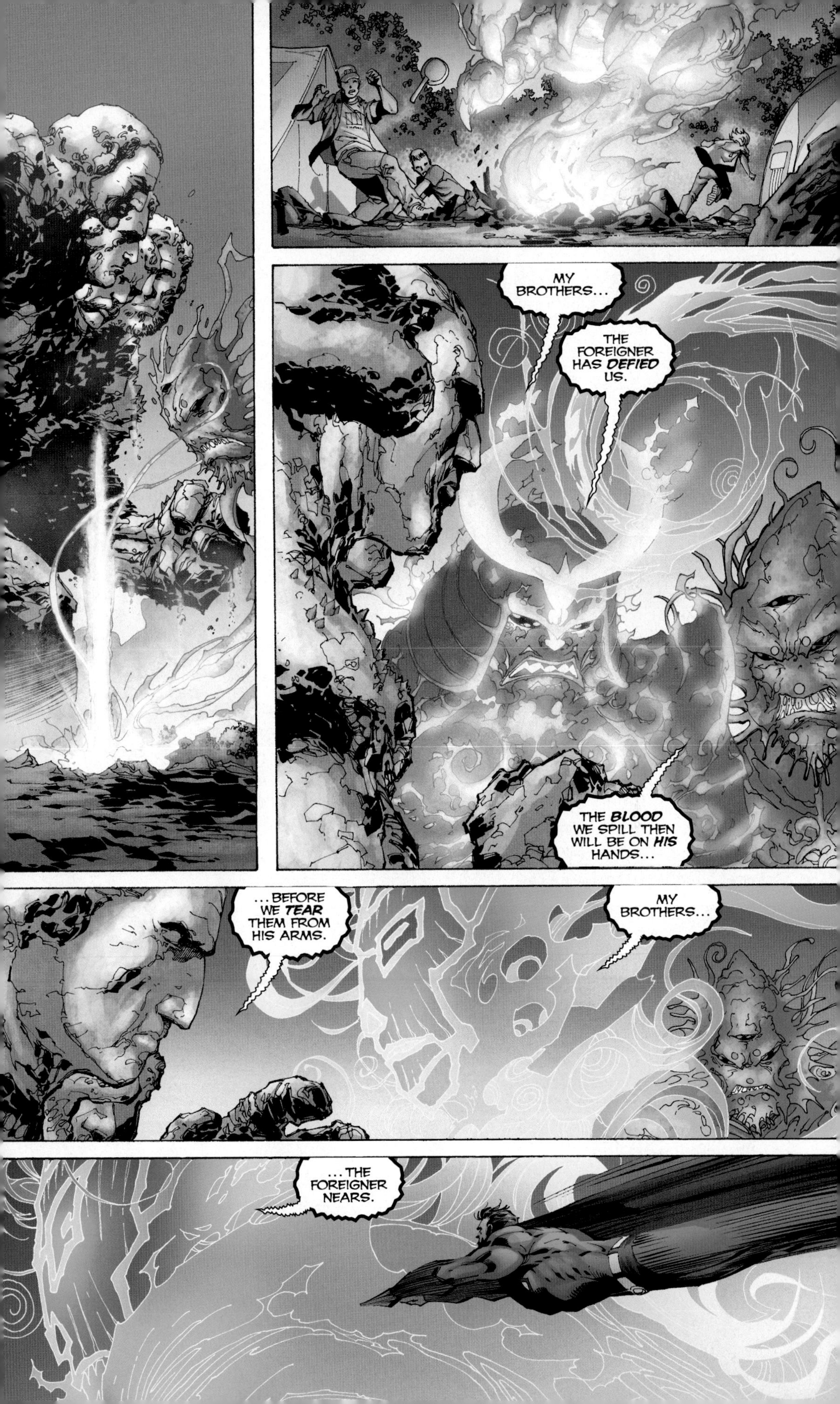
MY BROTHERS...
THE FOREIGNER HAS DEFIED US.
THE BLOOD WE SPILL THEN WILL BE ON HIS HANDS...
...BEFORE WE TEAR THEM FROM HIS ARMS.
MY BROTHERS...
...THE FOREIGNER NEARS.

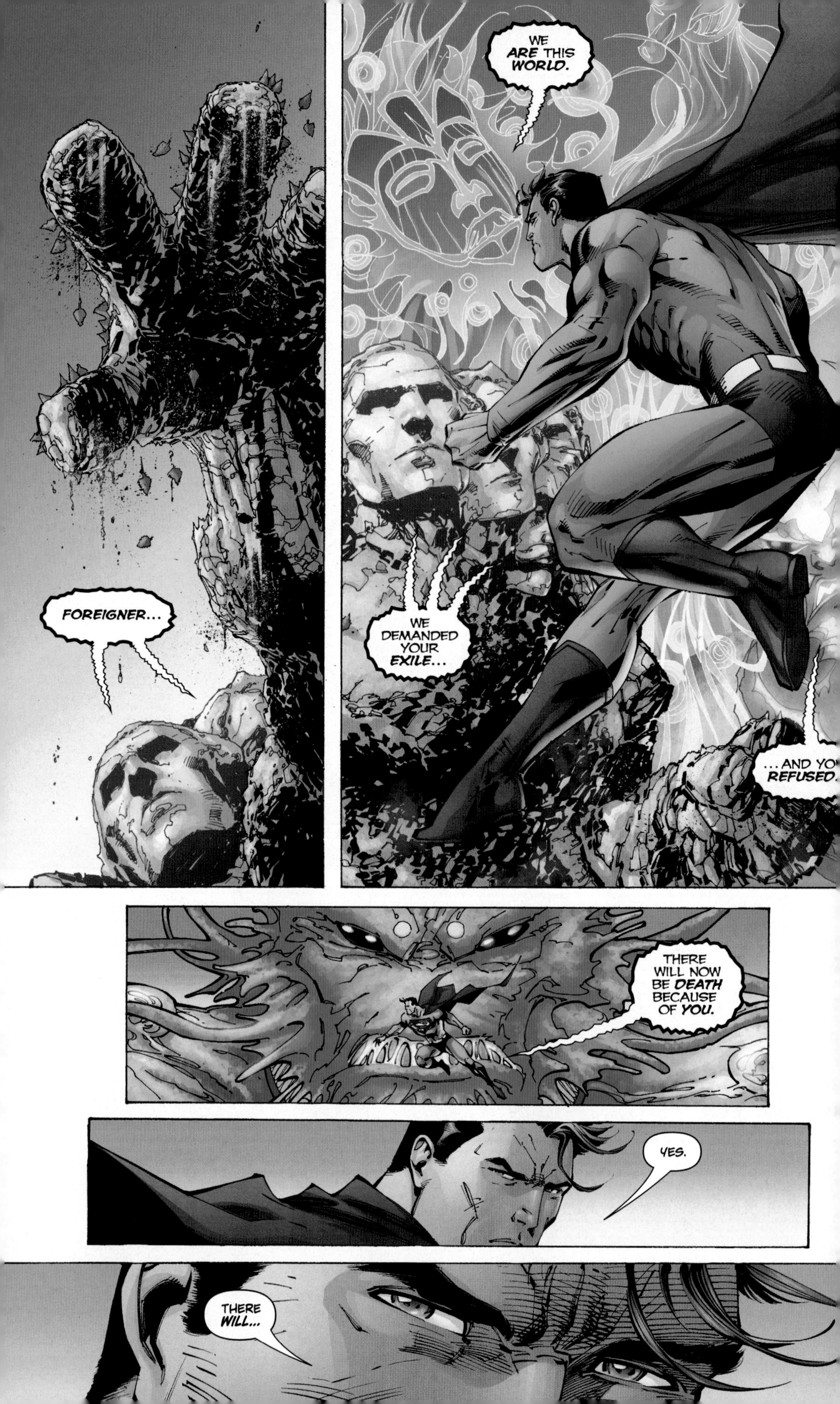
FOREIGNER...
WE ARE THIS WORLD.
WE DEMANDED YOUR EXILE...
...AND YO REFUSED.
THERE WILL NOW BE DEATH BECAUSE OF YOU.
YES.
THERE WILL...

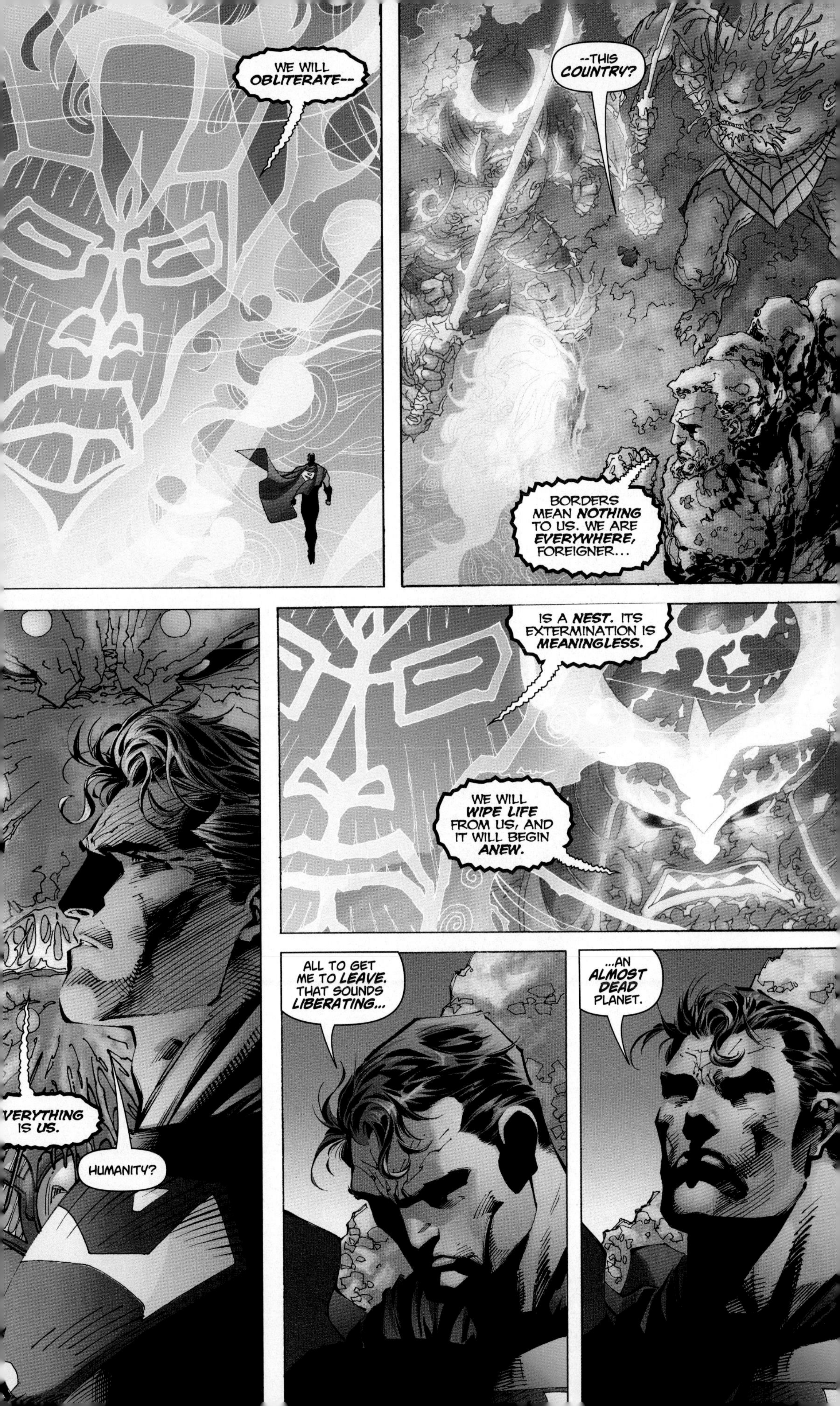

WE WILL OBLITERATE--
--THIS COUNTRY?
BORDERS MEAN NOTHING TO US. WE ARE EVERYWHERE, FOREIGNER...
VERYTHING IS US.
HUMANITY?
IS A NEST. ITS EXTERMINATION IS MEANINGLESS.
WE WILL WIPE LIFE FROM US, AND IT WILL BEGIN ANEW.
ALL TO GET ME TO LEAVE. THAT SOUNDS LIBERATING...
...AN ALMOST DEAD PLANET.

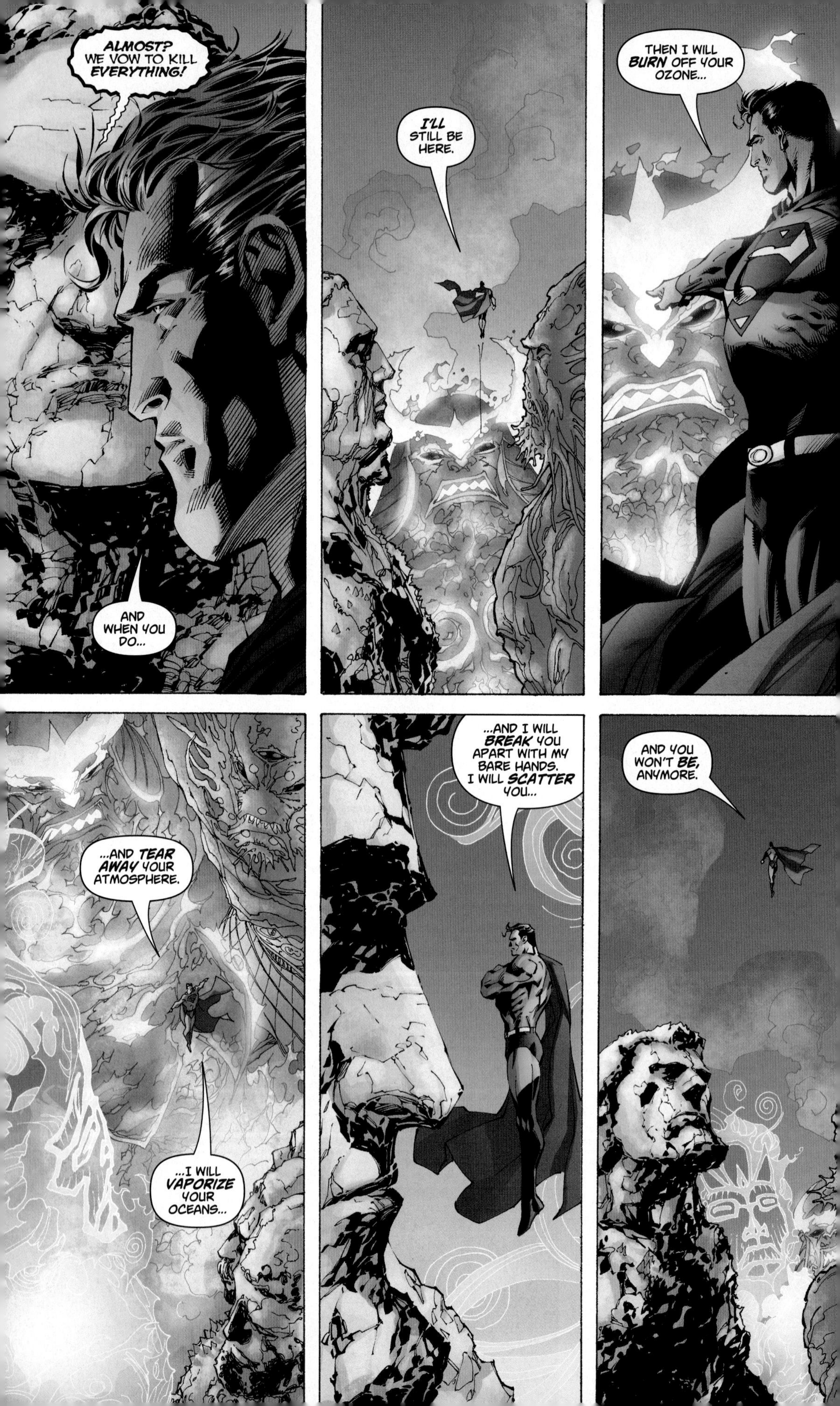
ALMOST? WE VOW TO KILL EVERYTHING!
AND WHEN YOU DO...
I'LL STILL BE HERE.
THEN I WILL BURN OFF YOUR OZONE...
...AND TEAR AWAY YOUR ATMOSPHERE.
...I WILL VAPORIZE YOUR OCEANS...
...AND I WILL BREAK YOU APART WITH MY BARE HANDS. I WILL SCATTER YOU...
AND YOU WON'T BE, ANYMORE.

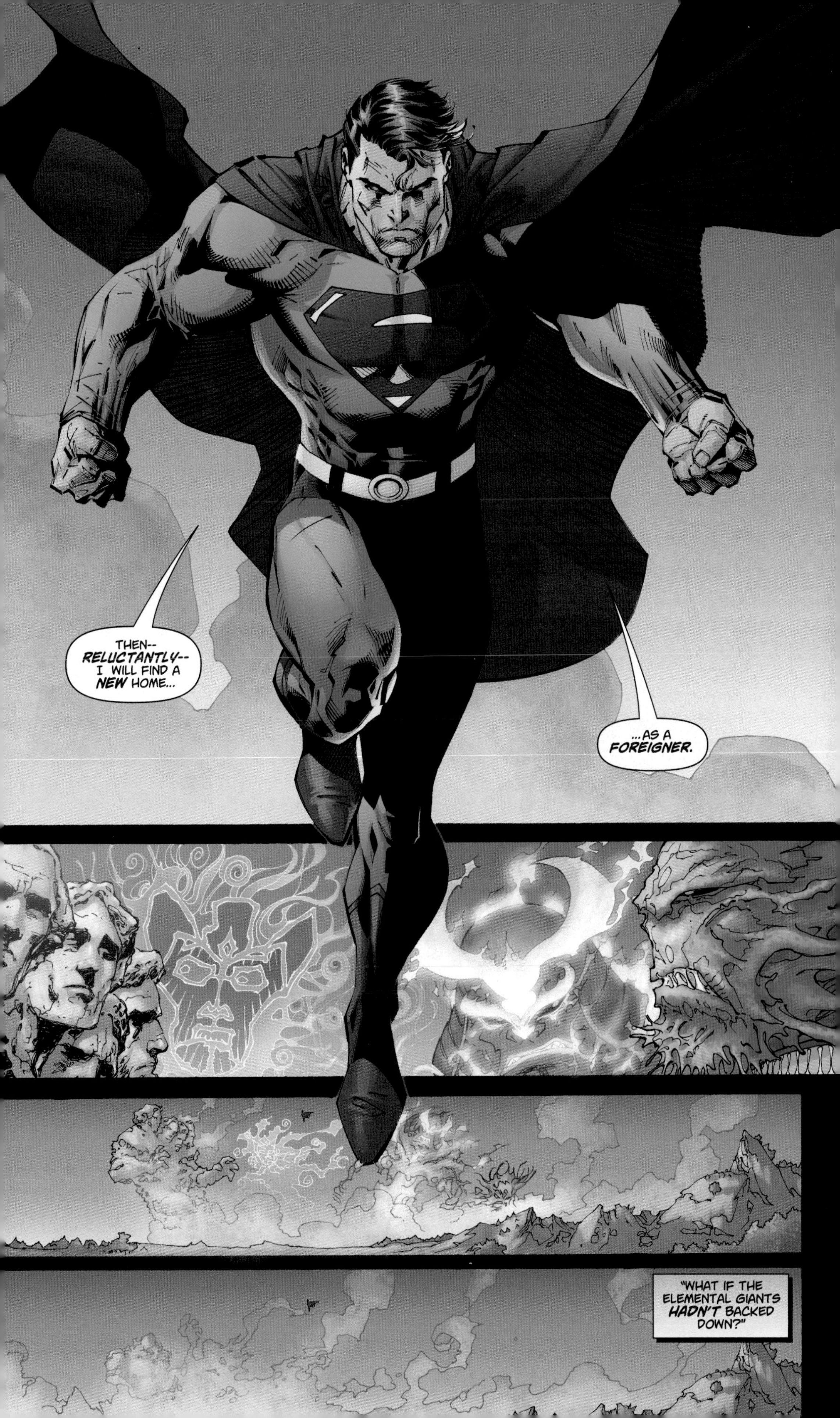
THEN-- RELUCTANTLY-- I WILL FIND A NEW HOME...
...AS A FOREIGNER.
"WHAT IF THE ELEMENTAL GIANTS HADN'T BACKED DOWN?"

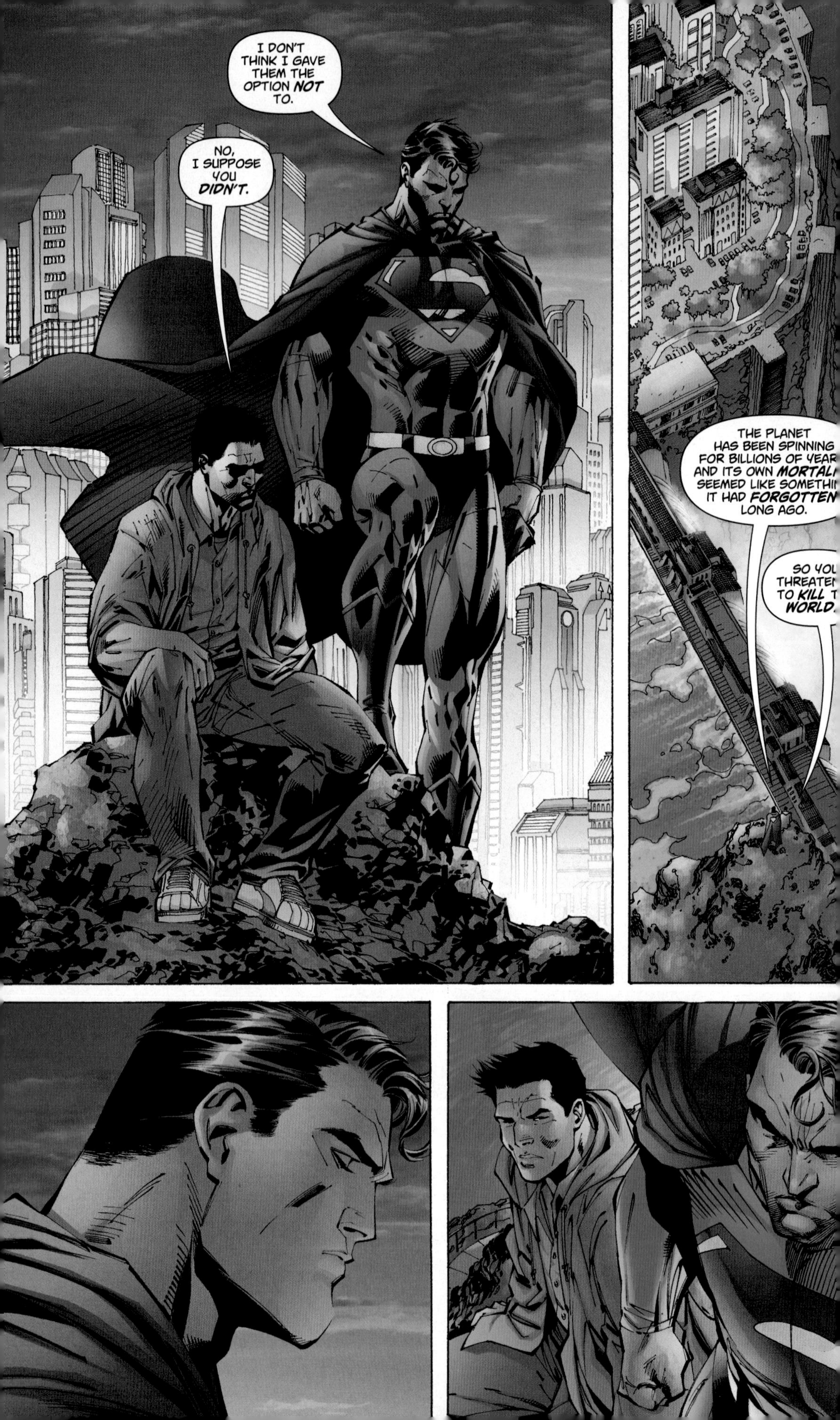
I DON'T THINK I GAVE THEM THE OPTION NOT TO.
NO, I SUPPOSE YOU DIDN'T.
THE PLANET HAS BEEN SPINNING FOR BILLIONS OF YEAR AND ITS OWN MORTALI SEEMED LIKE SOMETHI IT HAD FORGOTTEN LONG AGO.
SO YOU THREATEN TO KILL T WORLD.

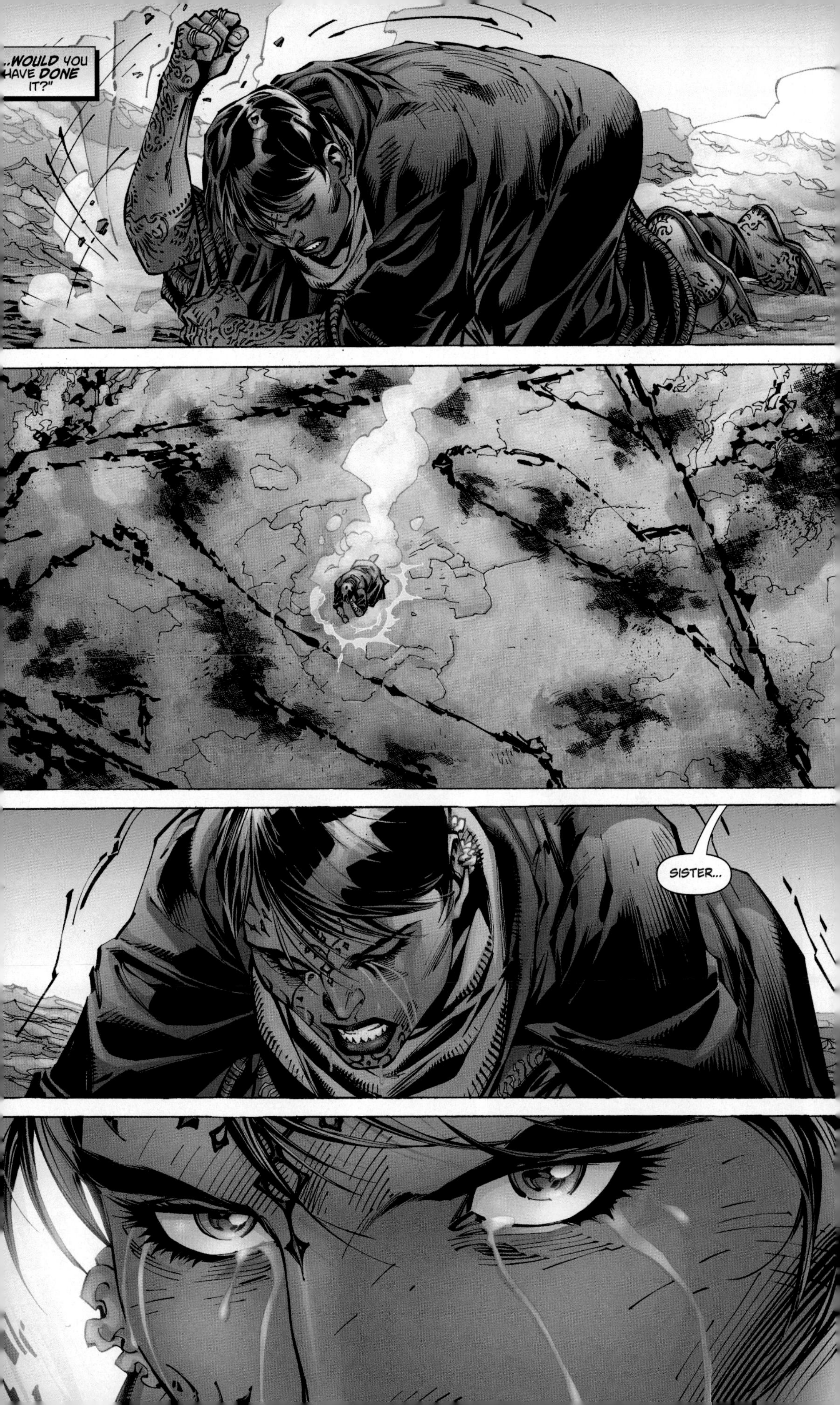
..WOULD YOU HAVE DONE IT?"
SISTER...

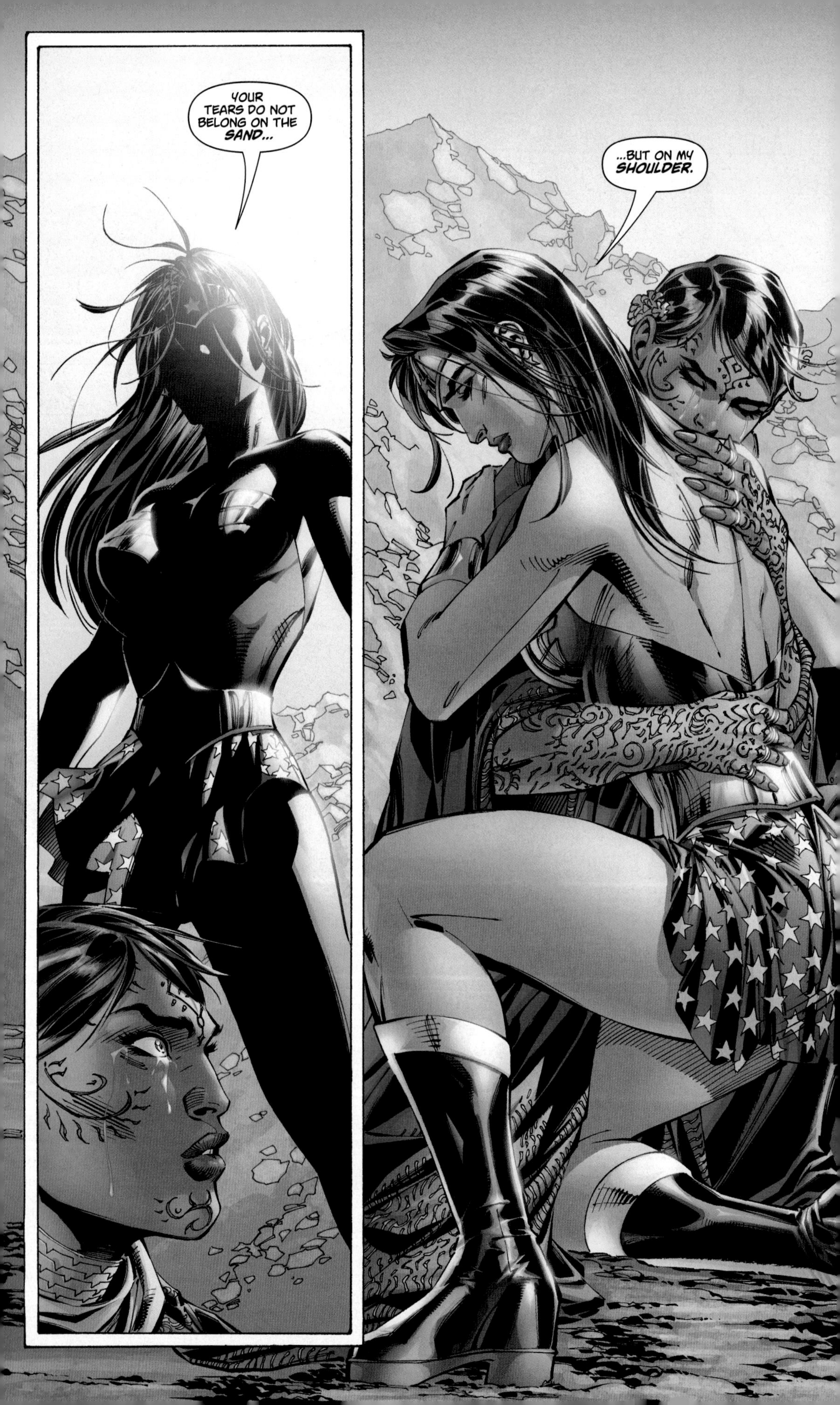
YOUR TEARS DO NOT BELONG ON THE SAND...
...BUT ON MY SHOULDER.

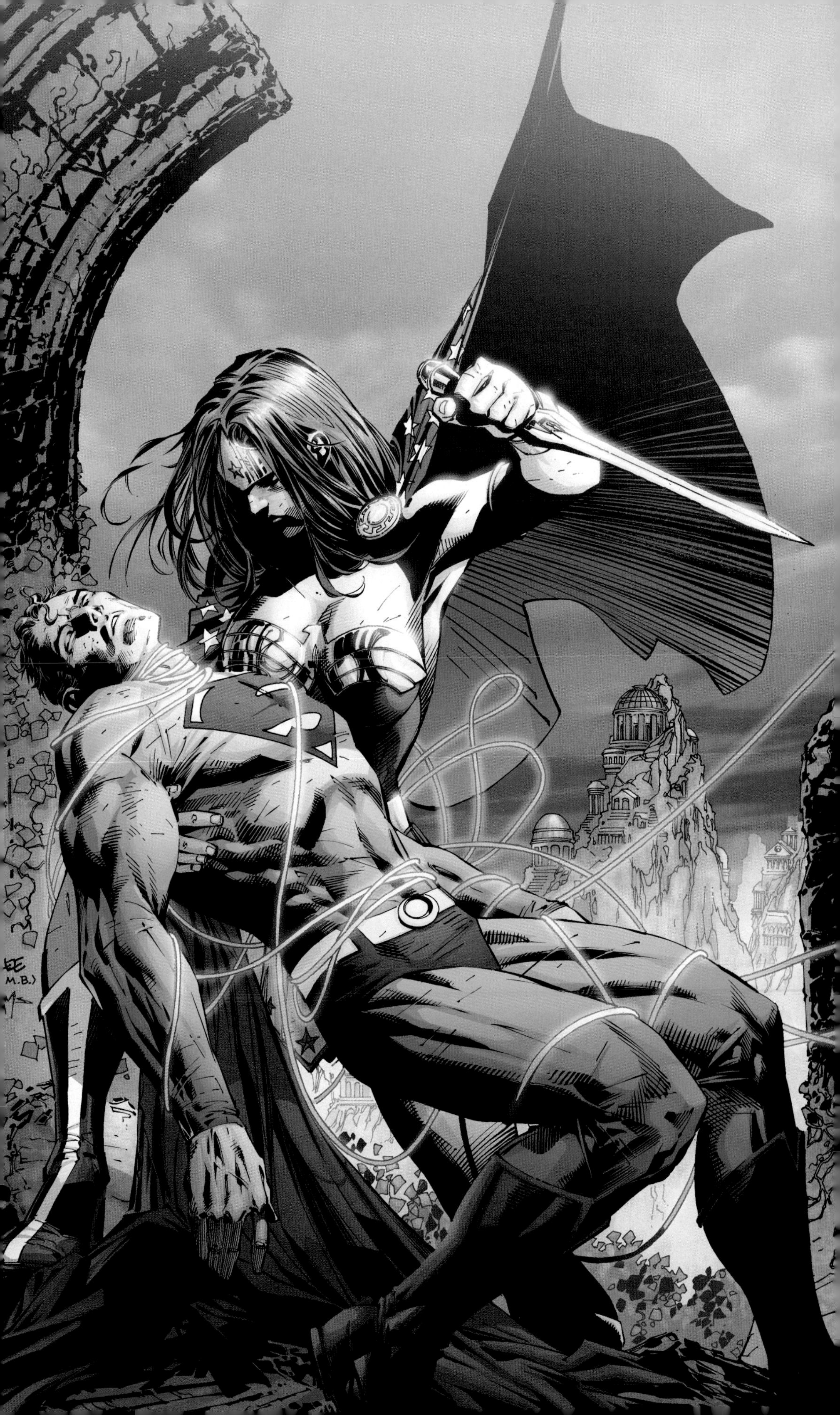

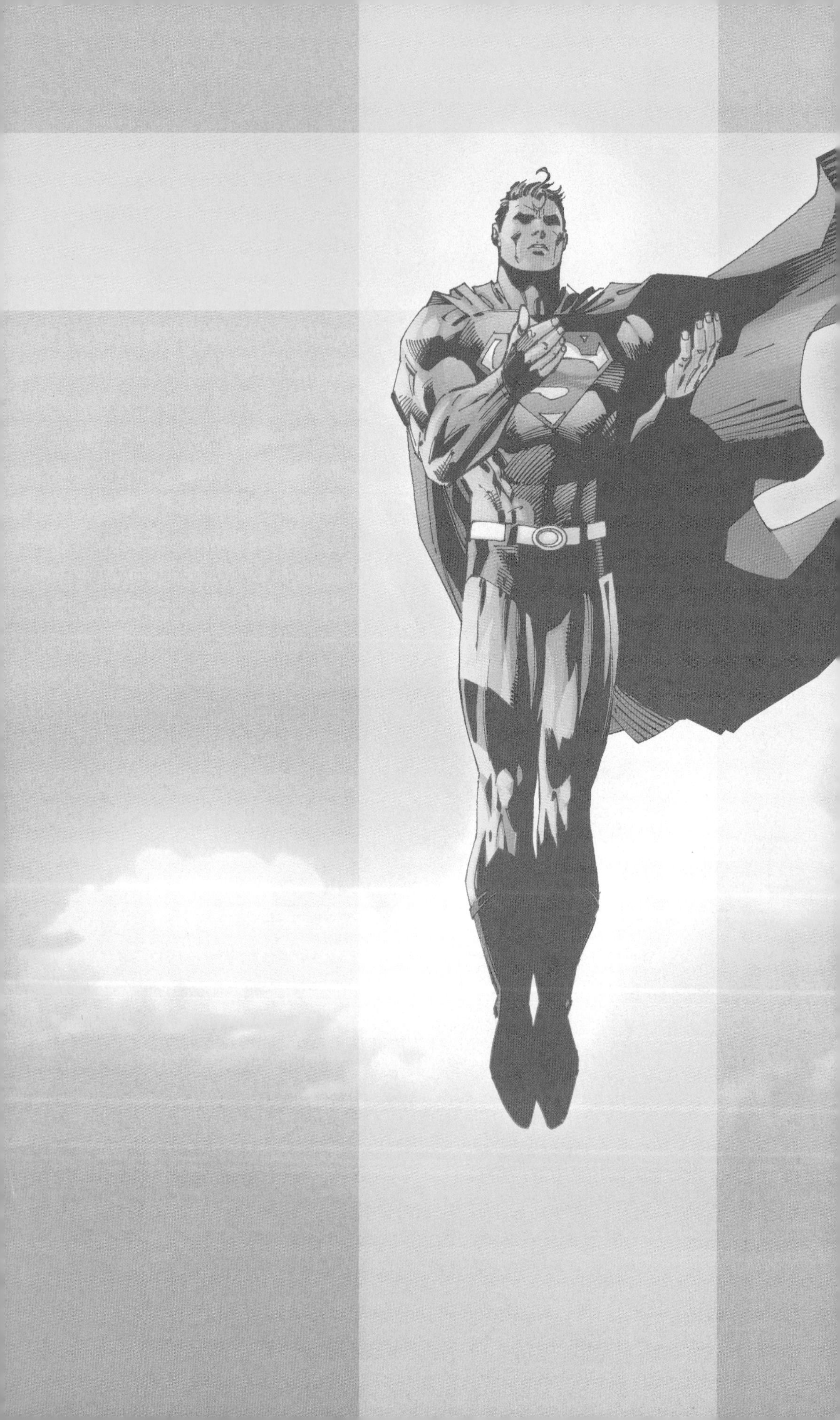

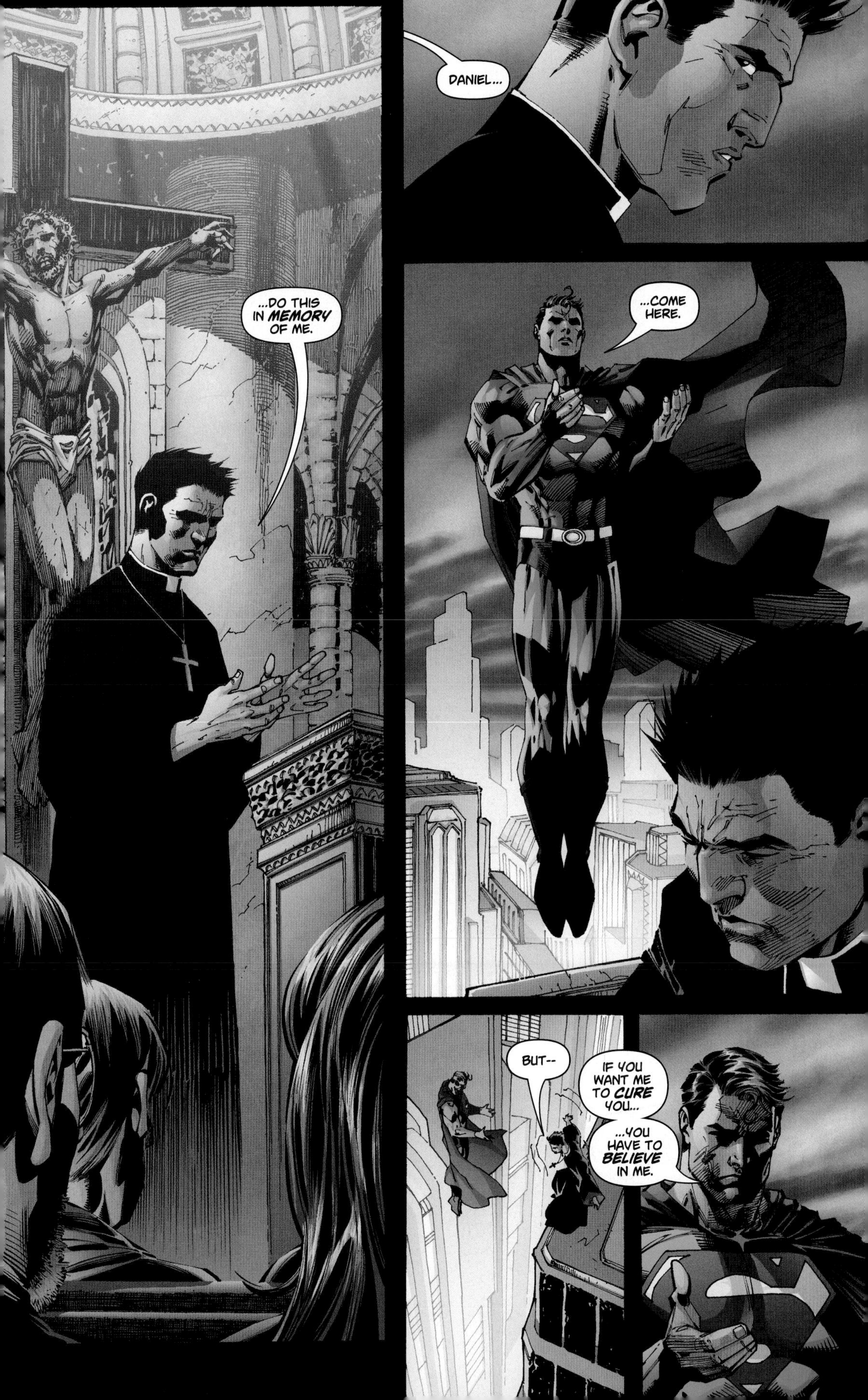
...DO THIS IN MEMORY OF ME.
DANIEL...
...COME HERE.
BUT--
IF YOU WANT ME TO CURE YOU...
...YOU HAVE TO BELIEVE IN ME.

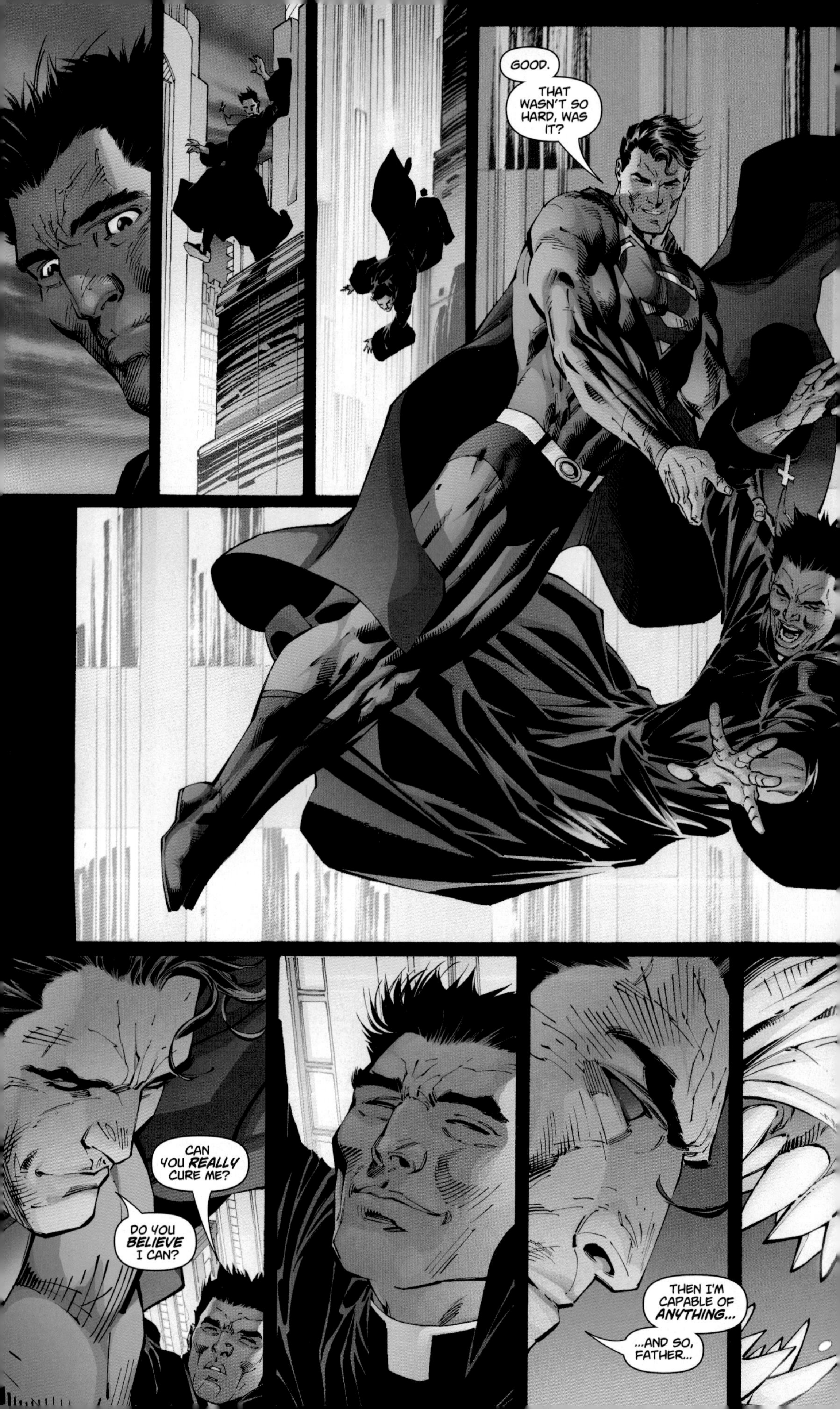
GOOD.
THAT WASN'T SO HARD, WAS IT?
CAN YOU REALLY CURE ME?
DO YOU BELIEVE I CAN?
THEN I'M CAPABLE OF ANYTHING...
...AND SO, FATHER...

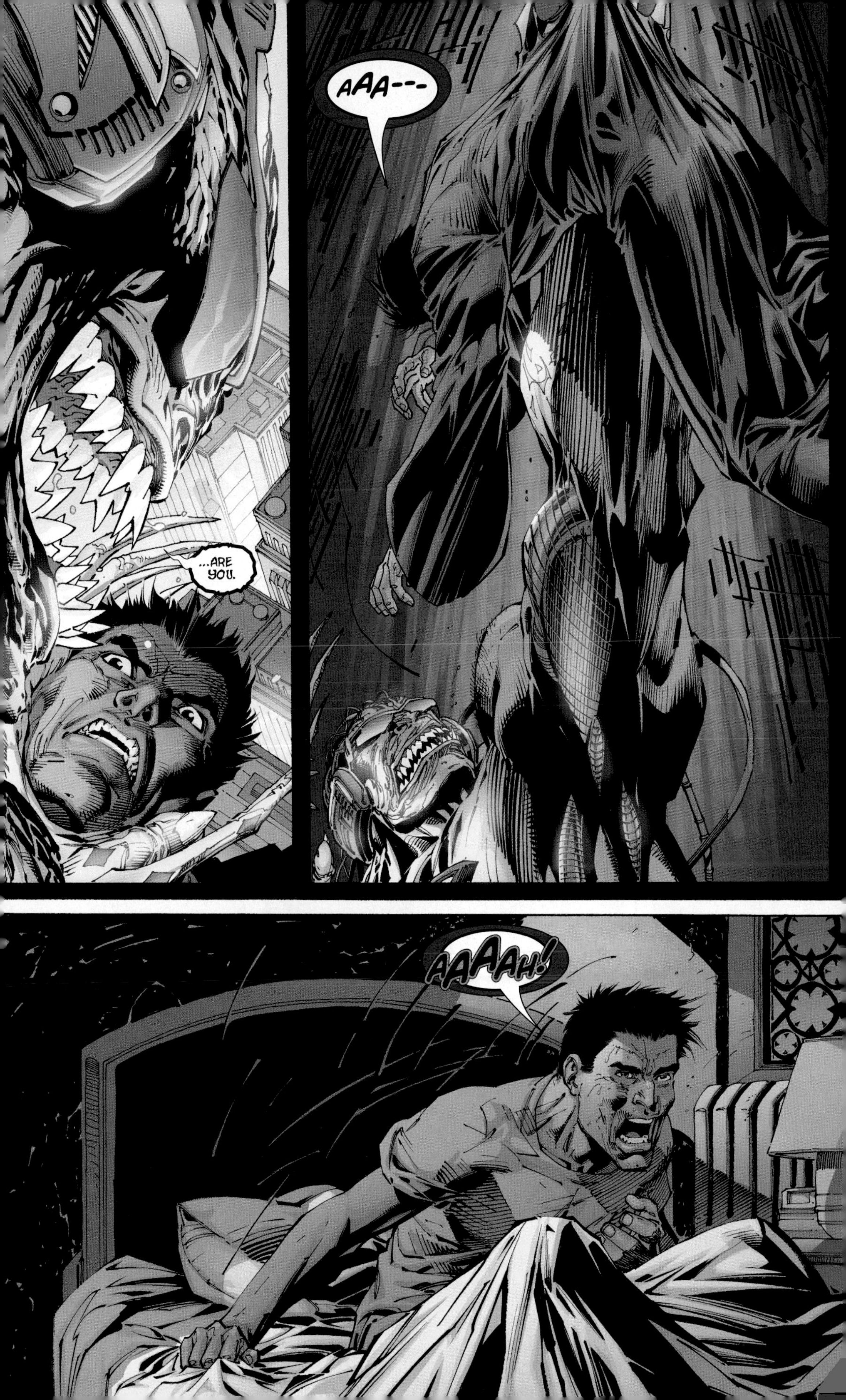
...ARE YOU.
AAA---
AAAAH!

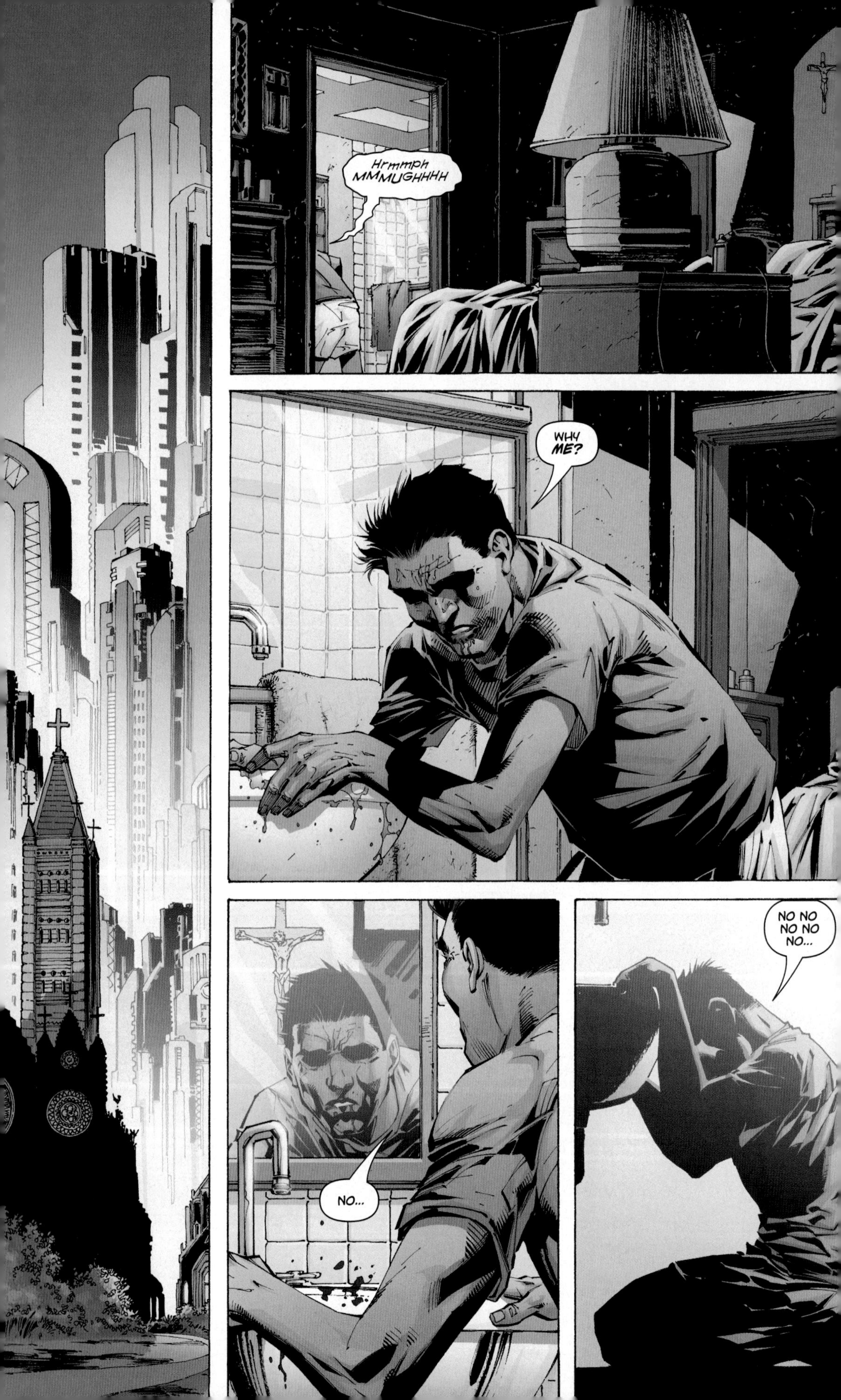
Hrmmph MMMUGHHHH
WHY ME?
NO...
NO NO NO NO NO...

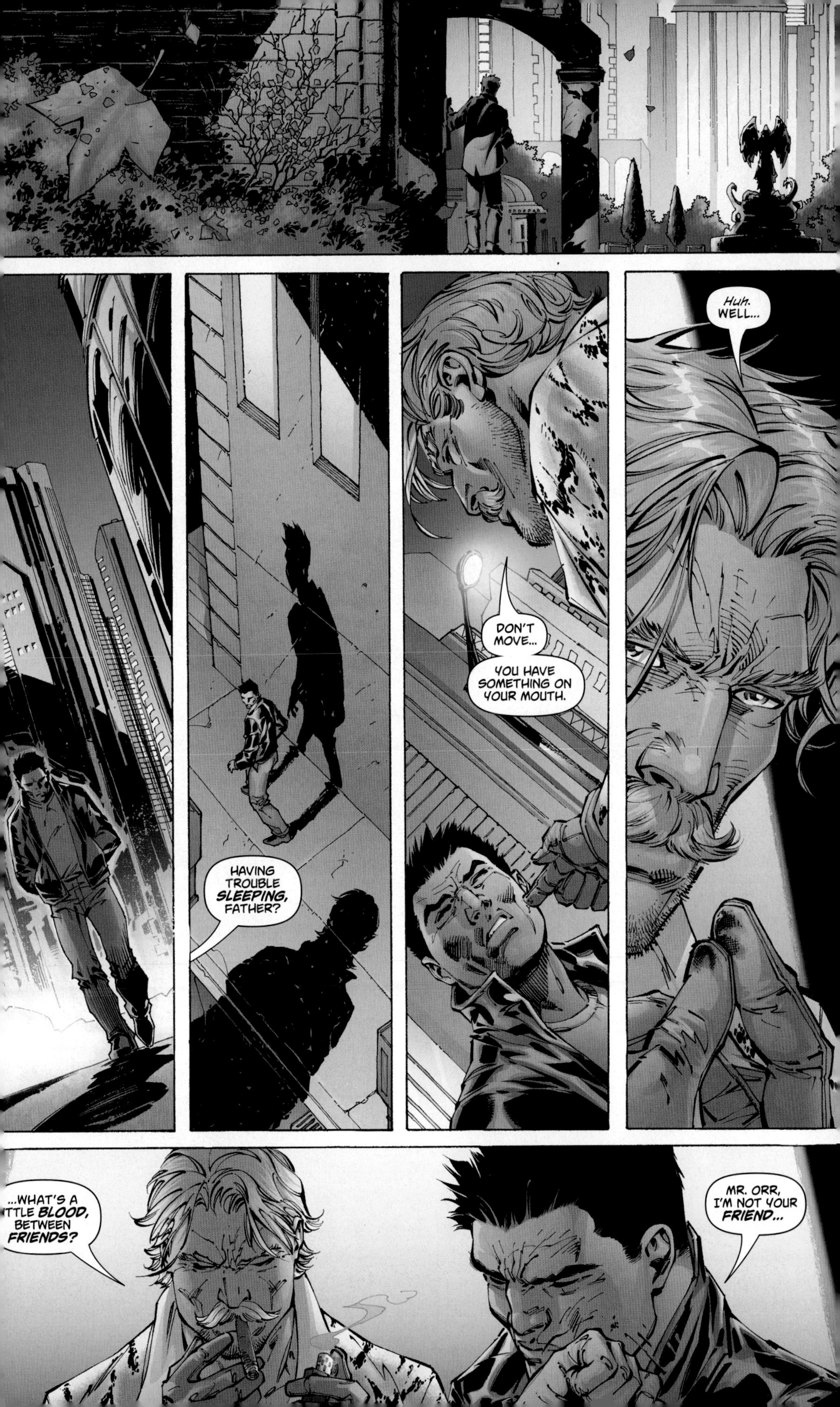
HAVING TROUBLE SLEEPING, FATHER?
DON'T MOVE...
YOU HAVE SOMETHING ON YOUR MOUTH.
Huh. WELL...
...WHAT'S A TTLE BLOOD, BETWEEN FRIENDS?
MR. ORR, I'M NOT YOUR FRIEND...

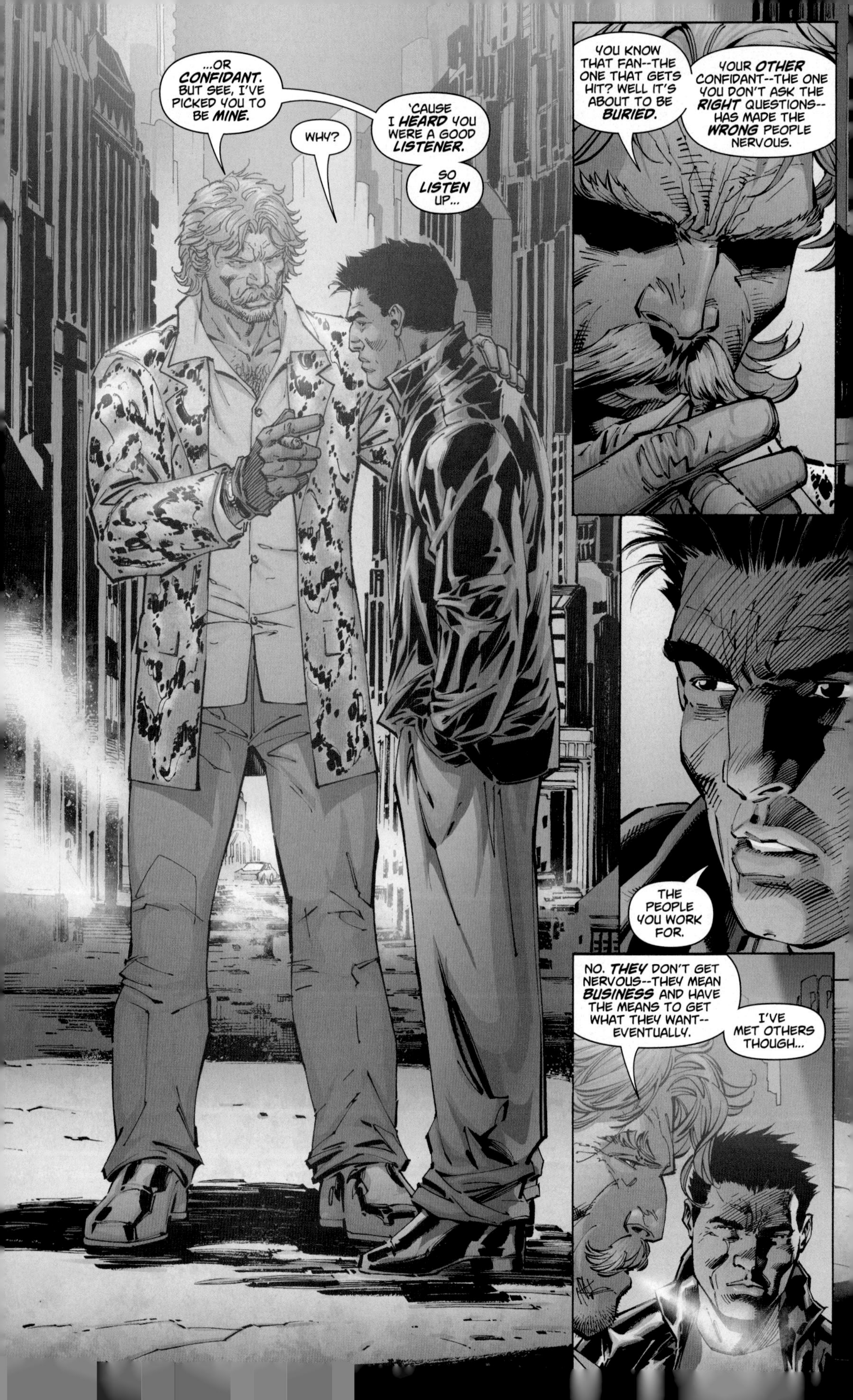

...OR CONFIDANT. BUT SEE, I'VE PICKED YOU TO BE MINE.
WHY?
'CAUSE I HEARD YOU WERE A GOOD LISTENER.
SO LISTEN UP...
YOU KNOW THAT FAN--THE ONE THAT GETS HIT? WELL IT'S ABOUT TO BE BURIED.
YOUR OTHER CONFIDANT--THE ONE YOU DON'T ASK THE RIGHT QUESTIONS--HAS MADE THE WRONG PEOPLE NERVOUS.
THE PEOPLE YOU WORK FOR.
NO. THEY DON'T GET NERVOUS--THEY MEAN BUSINESS AND HAVE THE MEANS TO GET WHAT THEY WANT--EVENTUALLY.
I'VE MET OTHERS THOUGH...

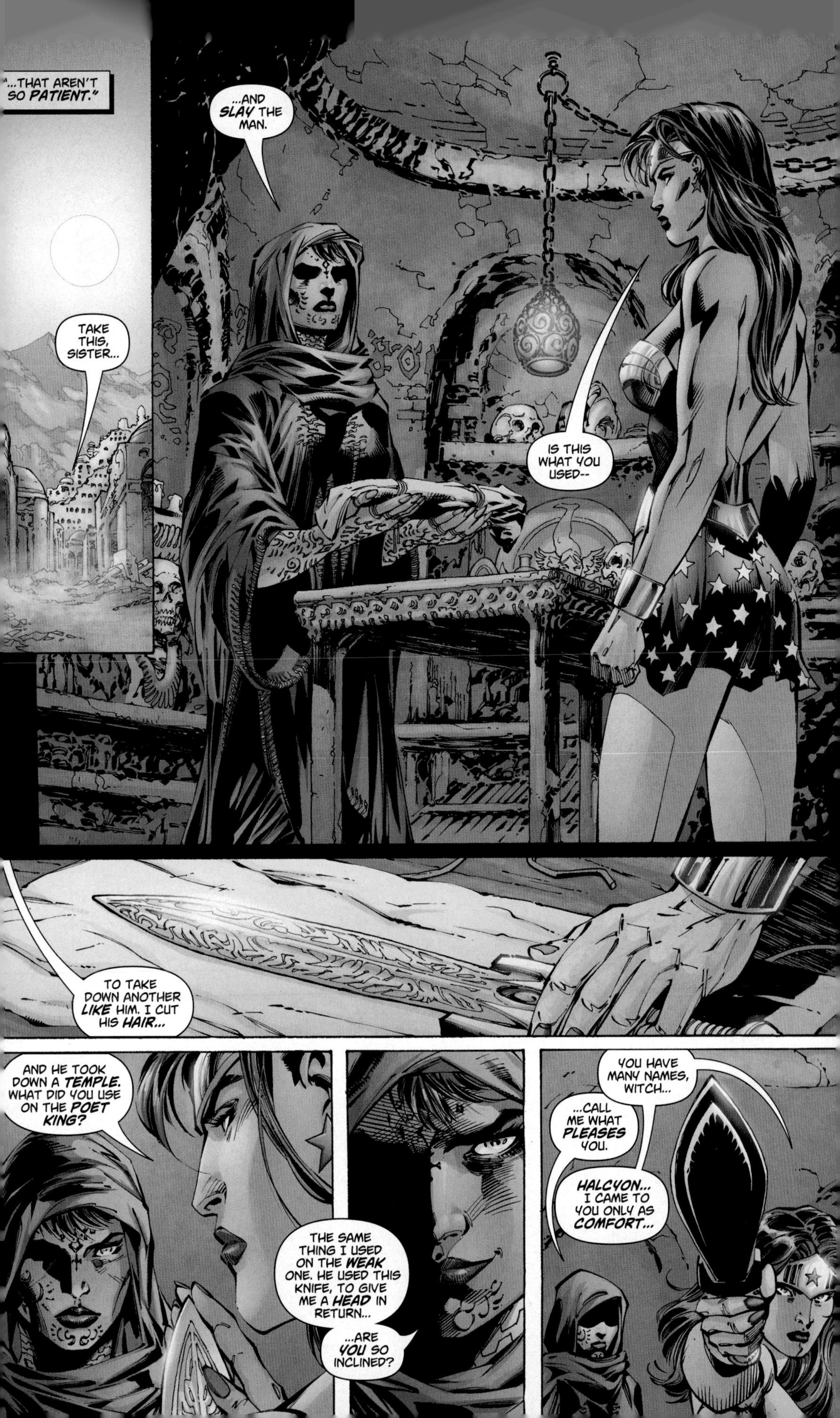

"...THAT AREN'T SO PATIENT."
...AND SLAY THE MAN.
TAKE THIS, SISTER...
IS THIS WHAT YOU USED--
TO TAKE DOWN ANOTHER LIKE HIM. I CUT HIS HAIR...
AND HE TOOK DOWN A TEMPLE. WHAT DID YOU USE ON THE POET KING?
THE SAME THING I USED ON THE WEAK ONE. HE USED THIS KNIFE, TO GIVE ME A HEAD IN RETURN...
...ARE YOU SO INCLINED?
YOU HAVE MANY NAMES, WITCH...
...CALL ME WHAT PLEASES YOU.
HALCYON... I CAME TO YOU ONLY AS COMFORT...

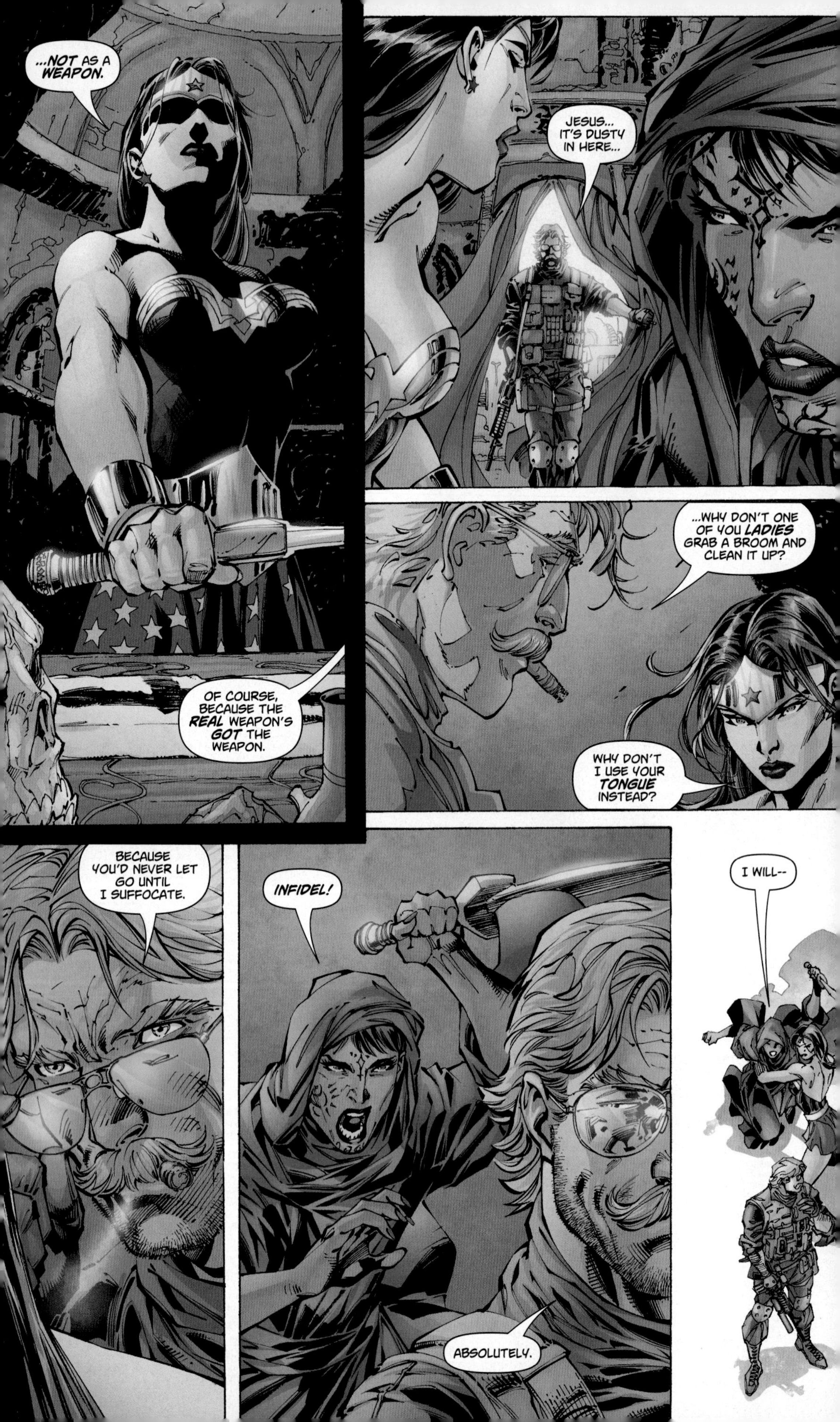

...NOT AS A WEAPON.
OF COURSE, BECAUSE THE REAL WEAPON'S GOT THE WEAPON.
JESUS... IT'S DUSTY IN HERE...
...WHY DON'T ONE OF YOU LADIES GRAB A BROOM AND CLEAN IT UP?
WHY DON'T I USE YOUR TONGUE INSTEAD?
BECAUSE YOU'D NEVER LET GO UNTIL I SUFFOCATE.
INFIDEL!
ABSOLUTELY.
I WILL--

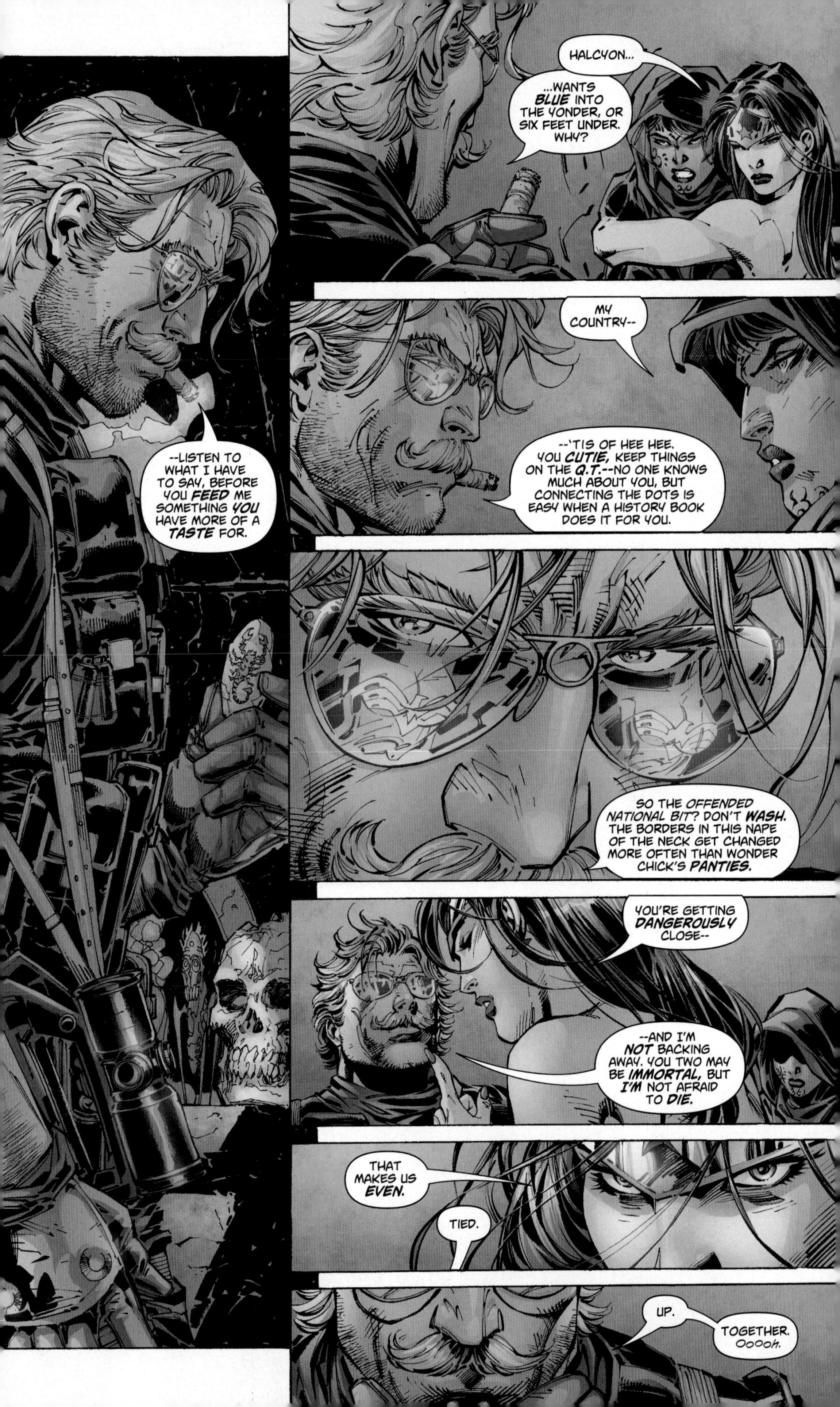

HALCYON...
...WANTS BLUE INTO THE YONDER, OR SIX FEET UNDER. WHY?
--LISTEN TO WHAT I HAVE TO SAY, BEFORE YOU FEED ME SOMETHING YOU HAVE MORE OF A TASTE FOR.
MY COUNTRY--
--'TIS OF HEE HEE. YOU CUTIE, KEEP THINGS ON THE Q.T.--NO ONE KNOWS MUCH ABOUT YOU, BUT CONNECTING THE DOTS IS EASY WHEN A HISTORY BOOK DOES IT FOR YOU.
SO THE OFFENDED NATIONAL BIT? DON'T WASH. THE BORDERS IN THIS NAPE OF THE NECK GET CHANGED MORE OFTEN THAN WONDER CHICK'S PANTIES.
YOU'RE GETTING DANGEROUSLY CLOSE--
--AND I'M NOT BACKING AWAY. YOU TWO MAY BE IMMORTAL, BUT I'M NOT AFRAID TO DIE.
THAT MAKES US EVEN.
TIED.
UP.
TOGETHER. Ooooh.

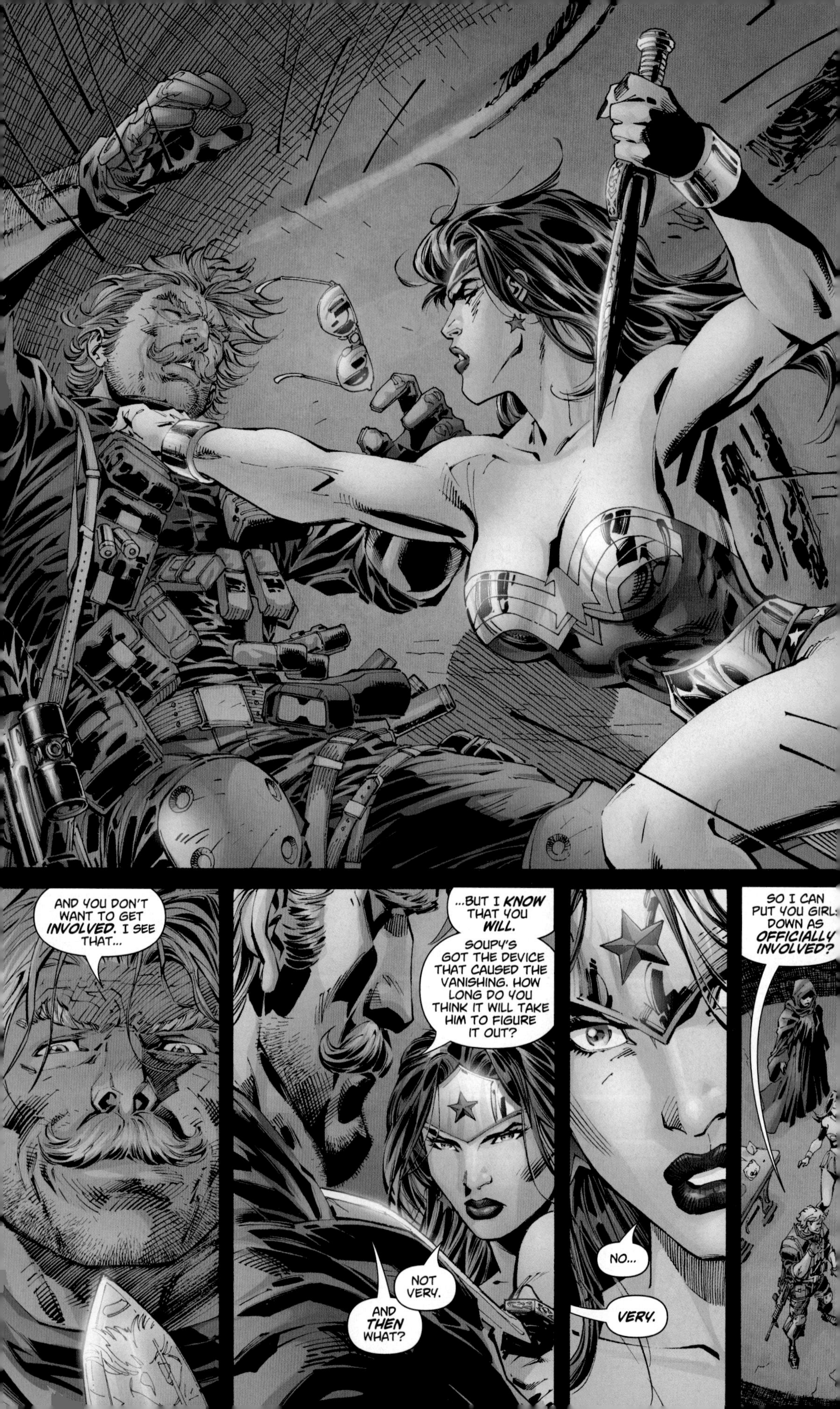
AND YOU DON'T WANT TO GET INVOLVED. I SEE THAT...
...BUT I KNOW THAT YOU WILL.
SOUPY'S GOT THE DEVICE THAT CAUSED THE VANISHING. HOW LONG DO YOU THINK IT WILL TAKE HIM TO FIGURE IT OUT?
NOT VERY.
AND THEN WHAT?
NO...
VERY.
SO I CAN PUT YOU GIRL DOWN AS OFFICIALLY INVOLVED?

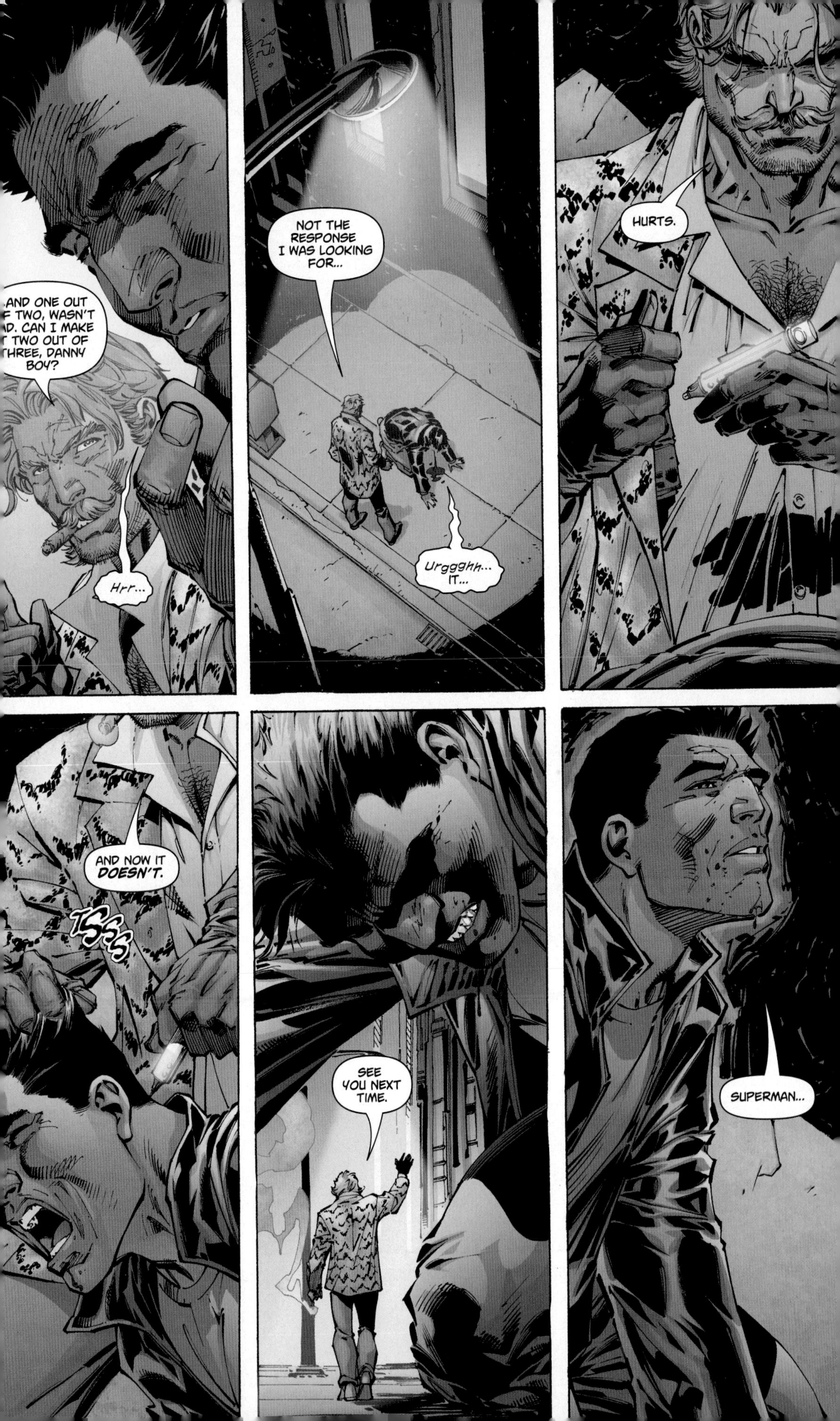
...AND ONE OUT OF TWO, WASN'T BAD. CAN I MAKE IT TWO OUT OF THREE, DANNY BOY?
Hrr...
NOT THE RESPONSE I WAS LOOKING FOR...
Urggghh... IT...
HURTS.
AND NOW IT DOESN'T.
TSSS
SEE YOU NEXT TIME.
SUPERMAN...

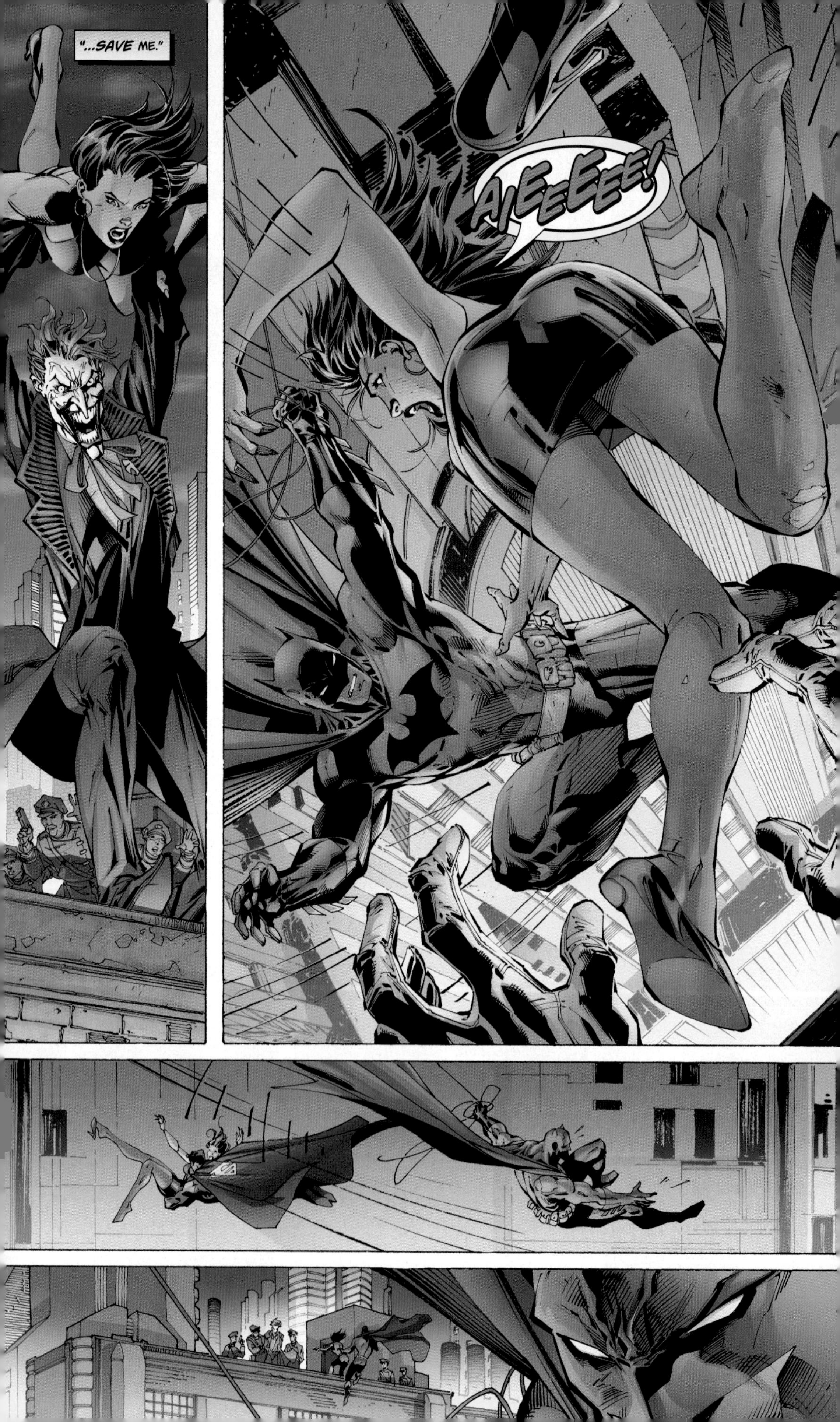
"...SAVE ME."
AIEEEEEE!

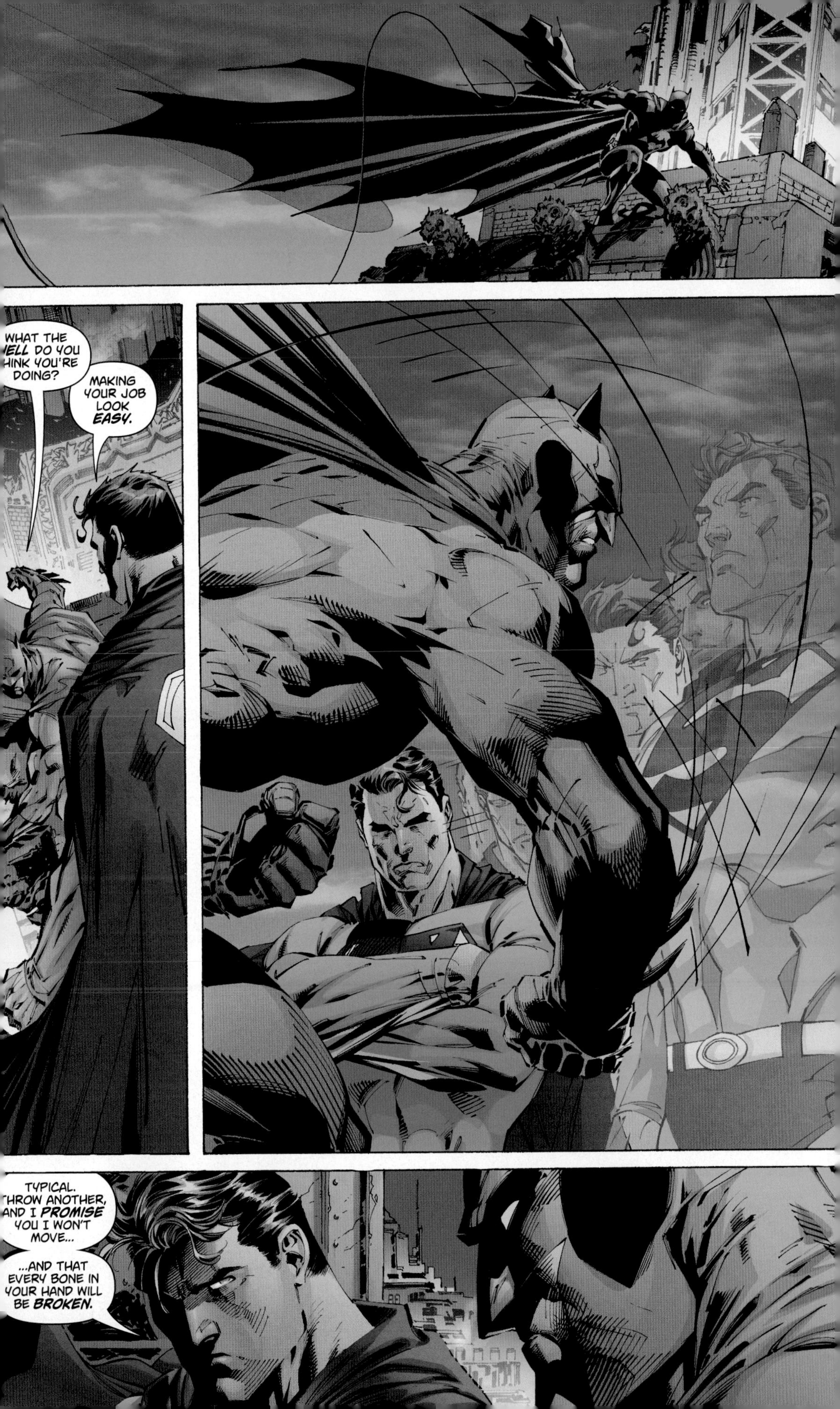

WHAT THE HELL DO YOU THINK YOU'RE DOING?
MAKING YOUR JOB LOOK EASY.
TYPICAL. THROW ANOTHER, AND I PROMISE YOU I WON'T MOVE...
...AND THAT EVERY BONE IN YOUR HAND WILL BE BROKEN.

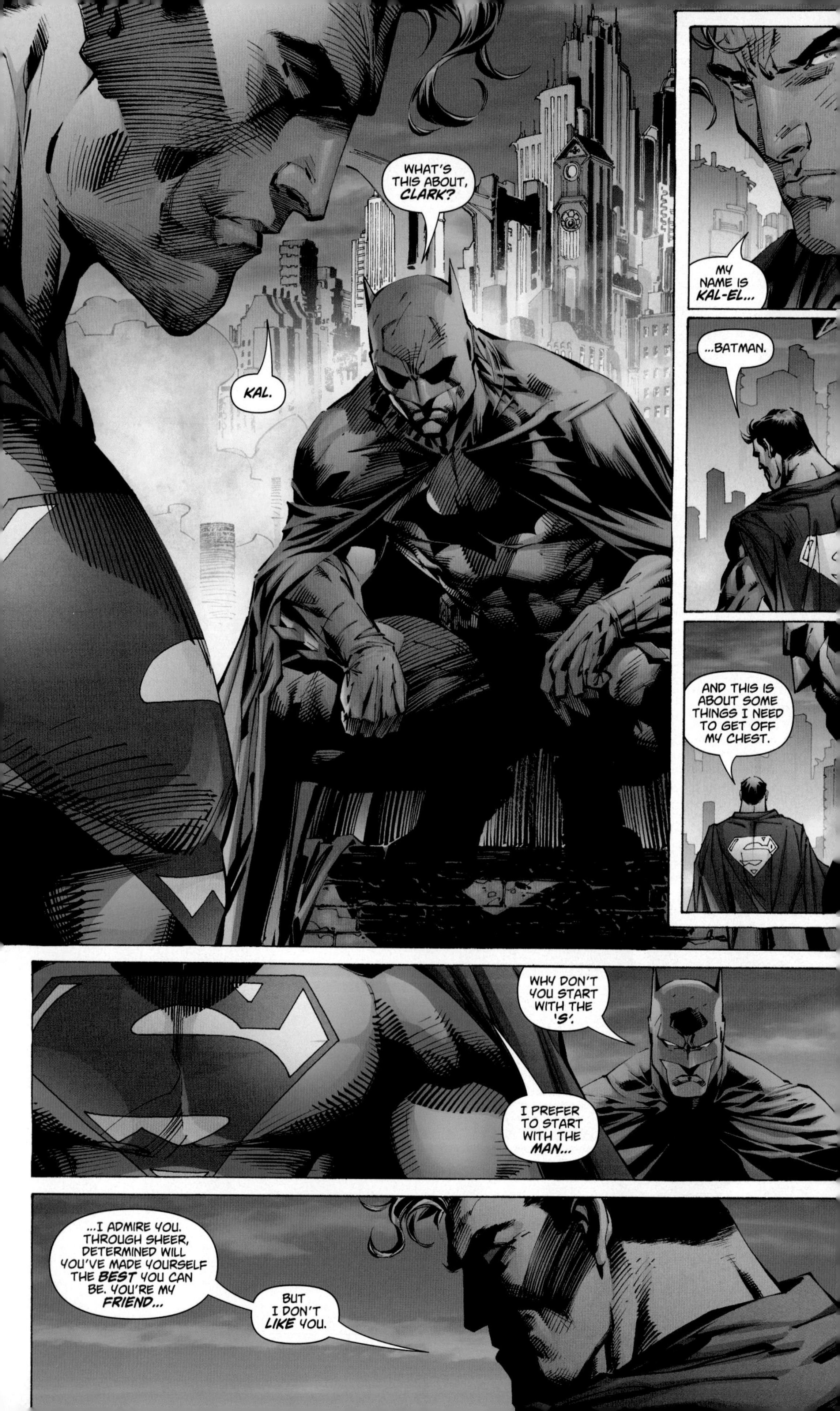

WHAT'S THIS ABOUT, CLARK?
KAL.
MY NAME IS KAL-EL...
...BATMAN.
AND THIS IS ABOUT SOME THINGS I NEED TO GET OFF MY CHEST.
WHY DON'T YOU START WITH THE 'S'.
I PREFER TO START WITH THE MAN...
...I ADMIRE YOU. THROUGH SHEER, DETERMINED WILL YOU'VE MADE YOURSELF THE BEST YOU CAN BE. YOU'RE MY FRIEND...
BUT I DON'T LIKE YOU.

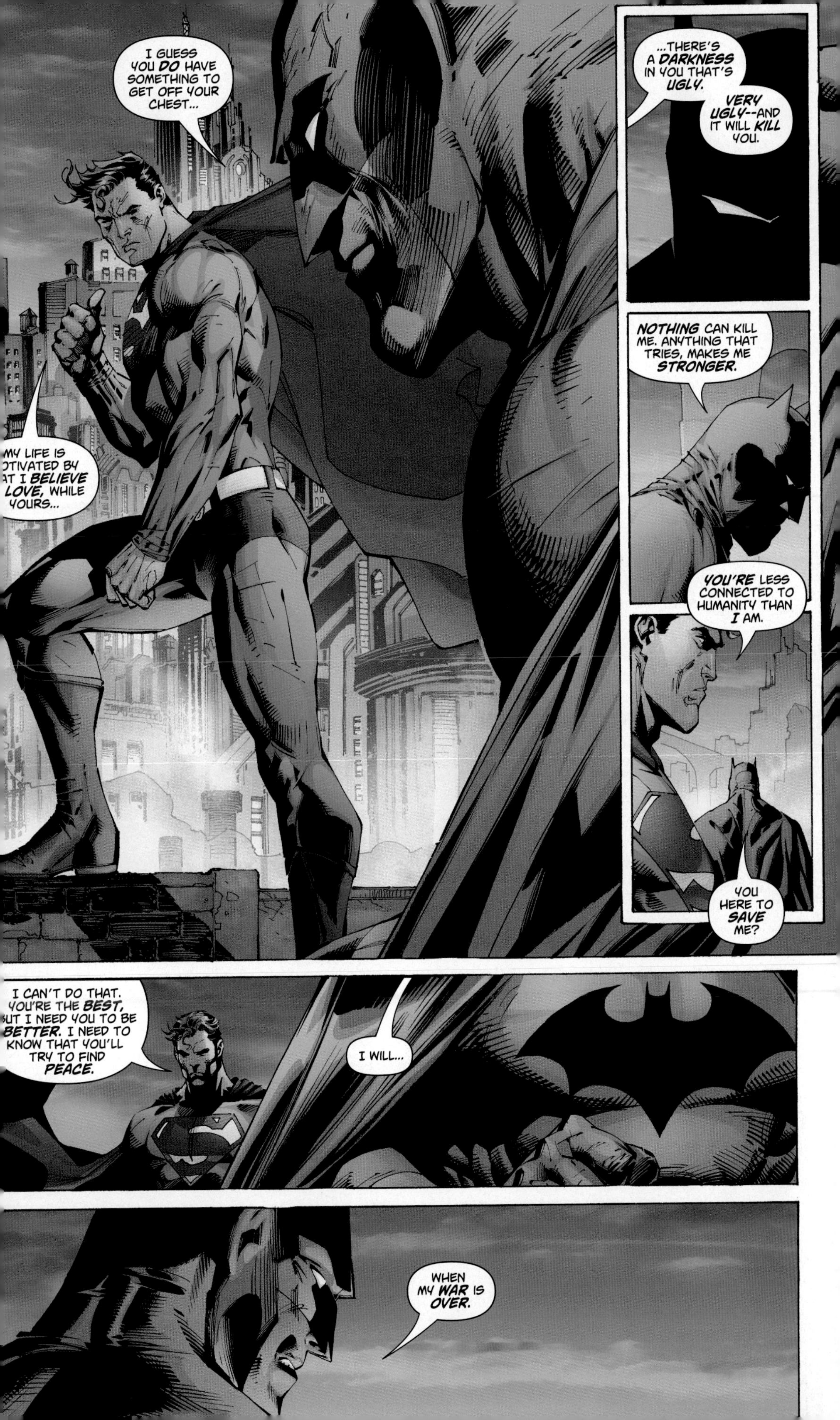

I GUESS YOU DO HAVE SOMETHING TO GET OFF YOUR CHEST...
MY LIFE IS OTIVATED BY AT I BELIEVE LOVE, WHILE YOURS...
...THERE'S A DARKNESS IN YOU THAT'S UGLY.
VERY UGLY--AND IT WILL KILL YOU.
NOTHING CAN KILL ME. ANYTHING THAT TRIES, MAKES ME STRONGER.
YOU'RE LESS CONNECTED TO HUMANITY THAN I AM.
YOU HERE TO SAVE ME?
I CAN'T DO THAT. YOU'RE THE BEST, UT I NEED YOU TO BE BETTER. I NEED TO KNOW THAT YOU'LL TRY TO FIND PEACE.
I WILL...
WHEN MY WAR IS OVER.

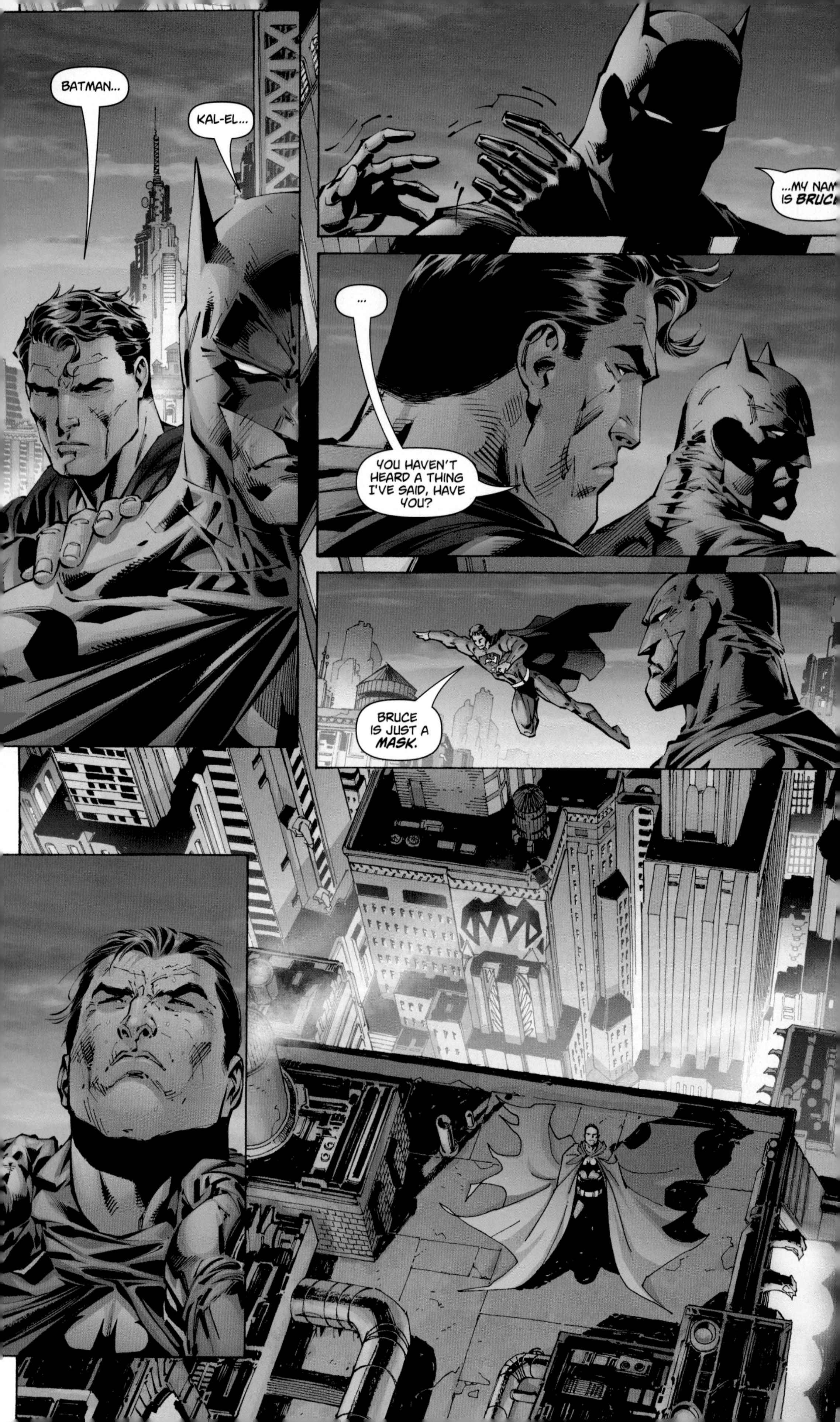
BATMAN...
KAL-EL...
...MY NAM IS BRUC
...
YOU HAVEN'T HEARD A THING I'VE SAID, HAVE YOU?
BRUCE IS JUST A MASK.

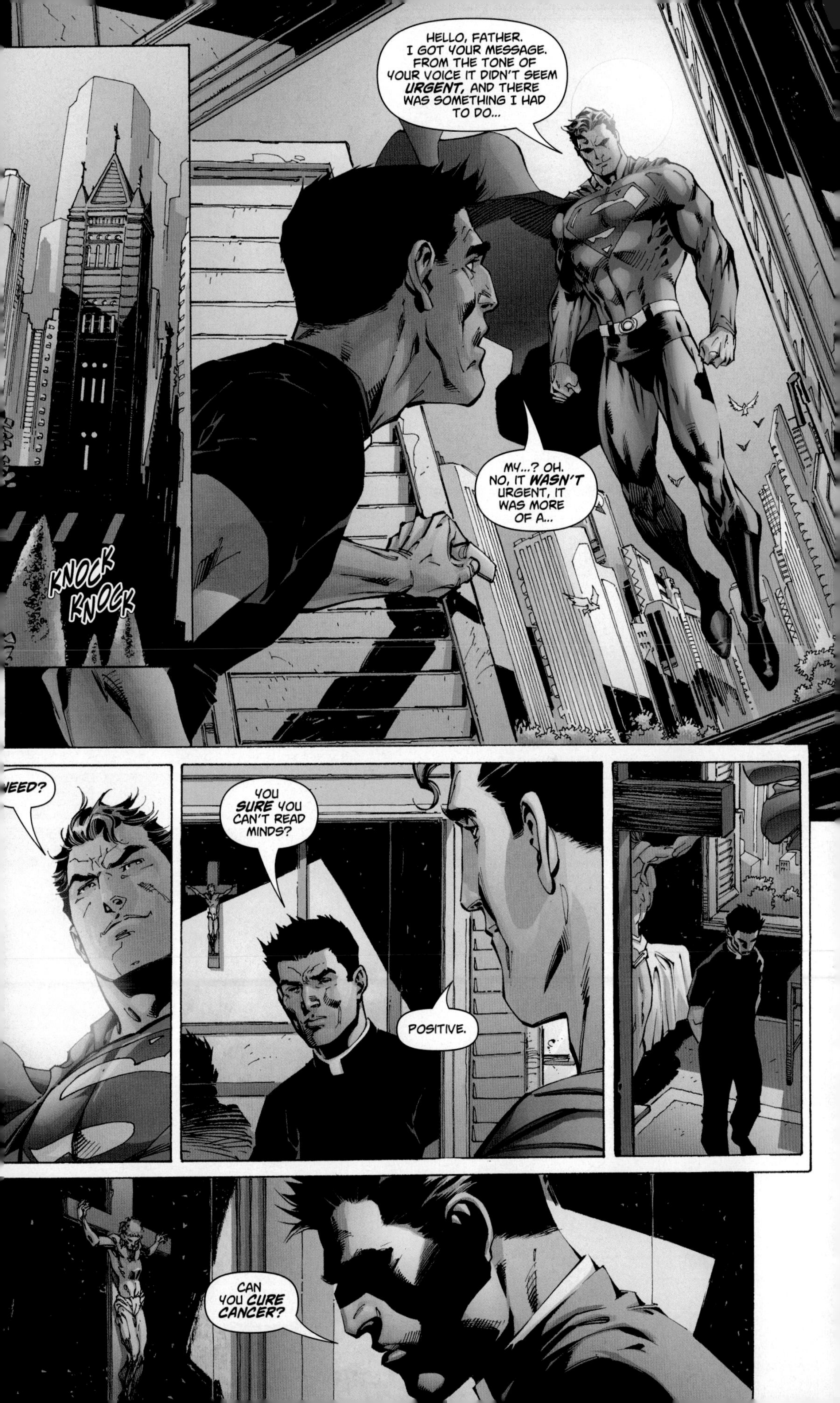
KNOCK KNOCK
HELLO, FATHER. I GOT YOUR MESSAGE. FROM THE TONE OF YOUR VOICE IT DIDN'T SEEM URGENT, AND THERE WAS SOMETHING I HAD TO DO...
MY...? OH. NO, IT WASN'T URGENT, IT WAS MORE OF A...
NEED?
YOU SURE YOU CAN'T READ MINDS?
POSITIVE.
CAN YOU CURE CANCER?

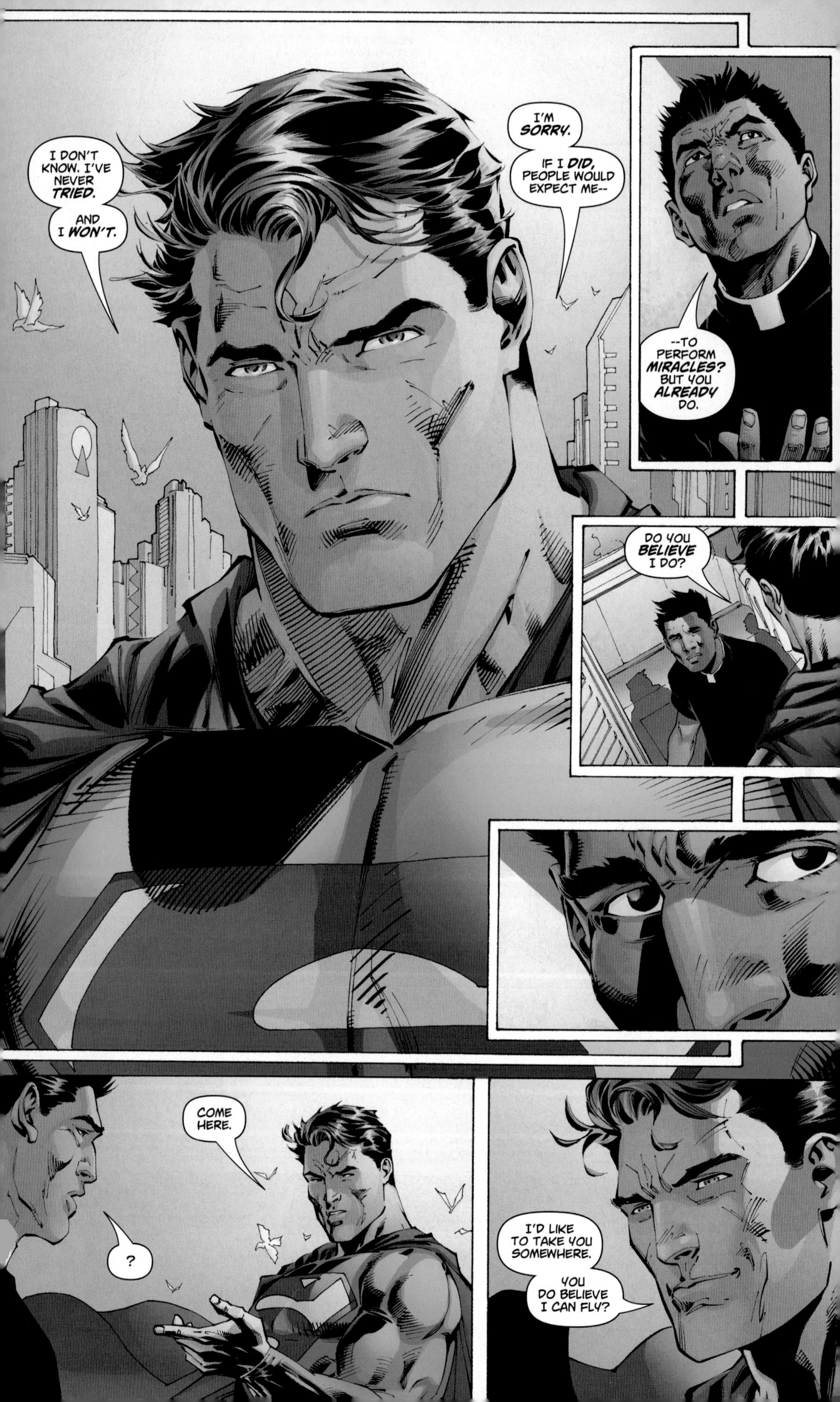
I DON'T KNOW. I'VE NEVER TRIED.
AND I WON'T.
I'M SORRY.
IF I DID, PEOPLE WOULD EXPECT ME--
--TO PERFORM MIRACLES? BUT YOU ALREADY DO.
DO YOU BELIEVE I DO?
COME HERE.
?
I'D LIKE TO TAKE YOU SOMEWHERE.
YOU DO BELIEVE I CAN FLY?

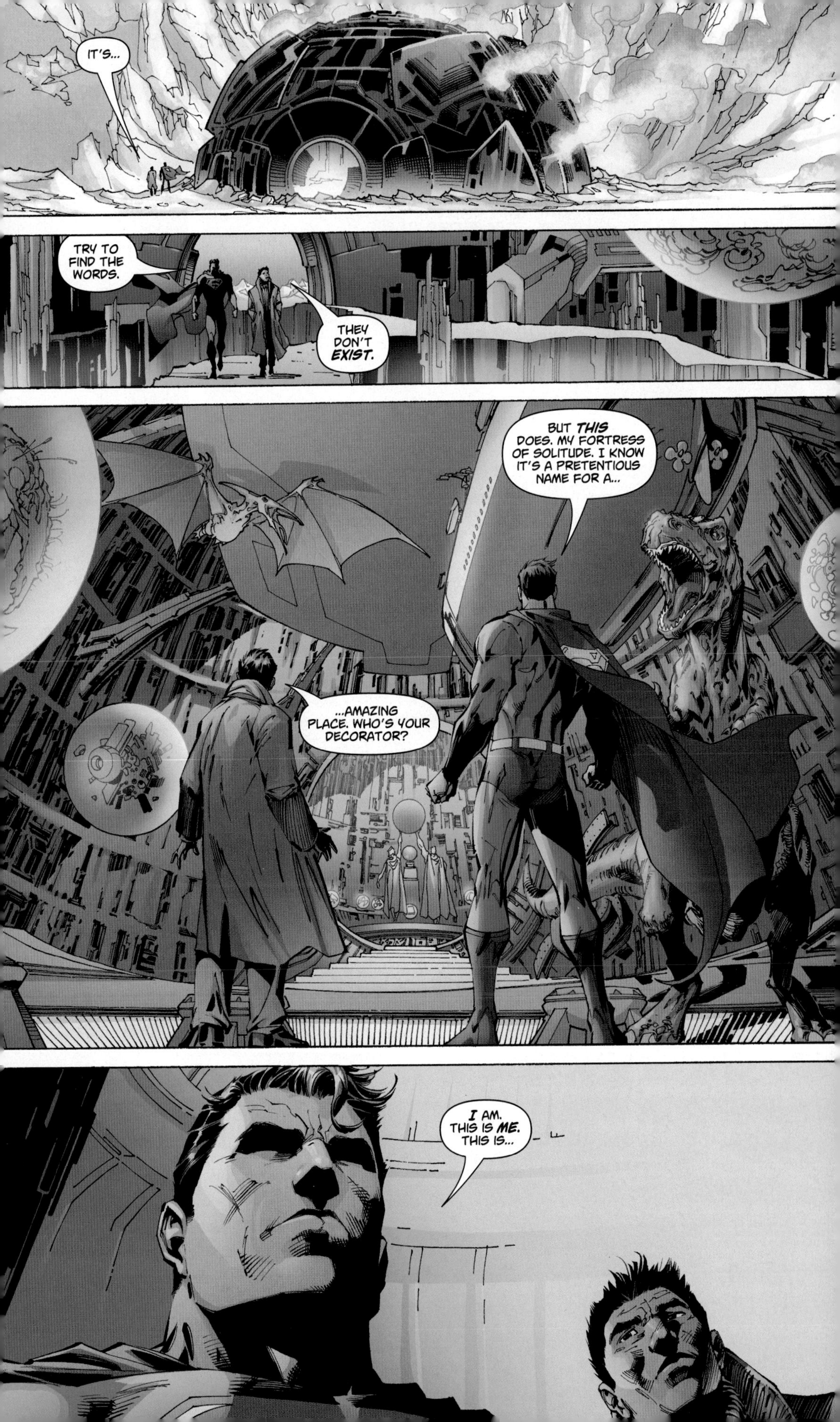
IT'S...
TRY TO FIND THE WORDS.
THEY DON'T *EXIST*.
BUT *THIS* DOES. MY FORTRESS OF SOLITUDE. I KNOW IT'S A PRETENTIOUS NAME FOR A...
...AMAZING PLACE. WHO'S YOUR DECORATOR?
I AM. THIS IS *ME*. THIS IS...

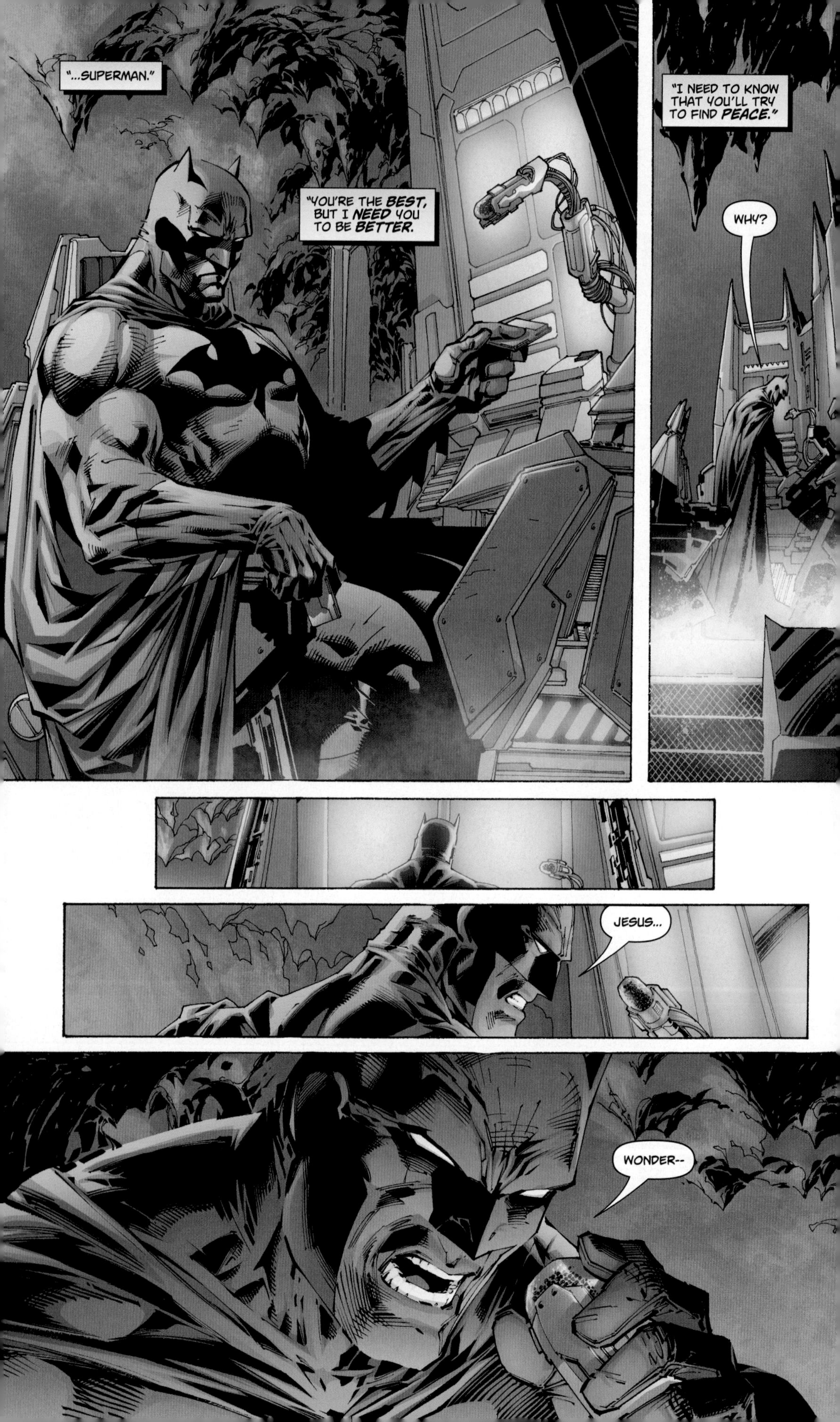
"...SUPERMAN."
"YOU'RE THE BEST, BUT I NEED YOU TO BE BETTER.
"I NEED TO KNOW THAT YOU'LL TRY TO FIND PEACE."
WHY?
JESUS...
WONDER--

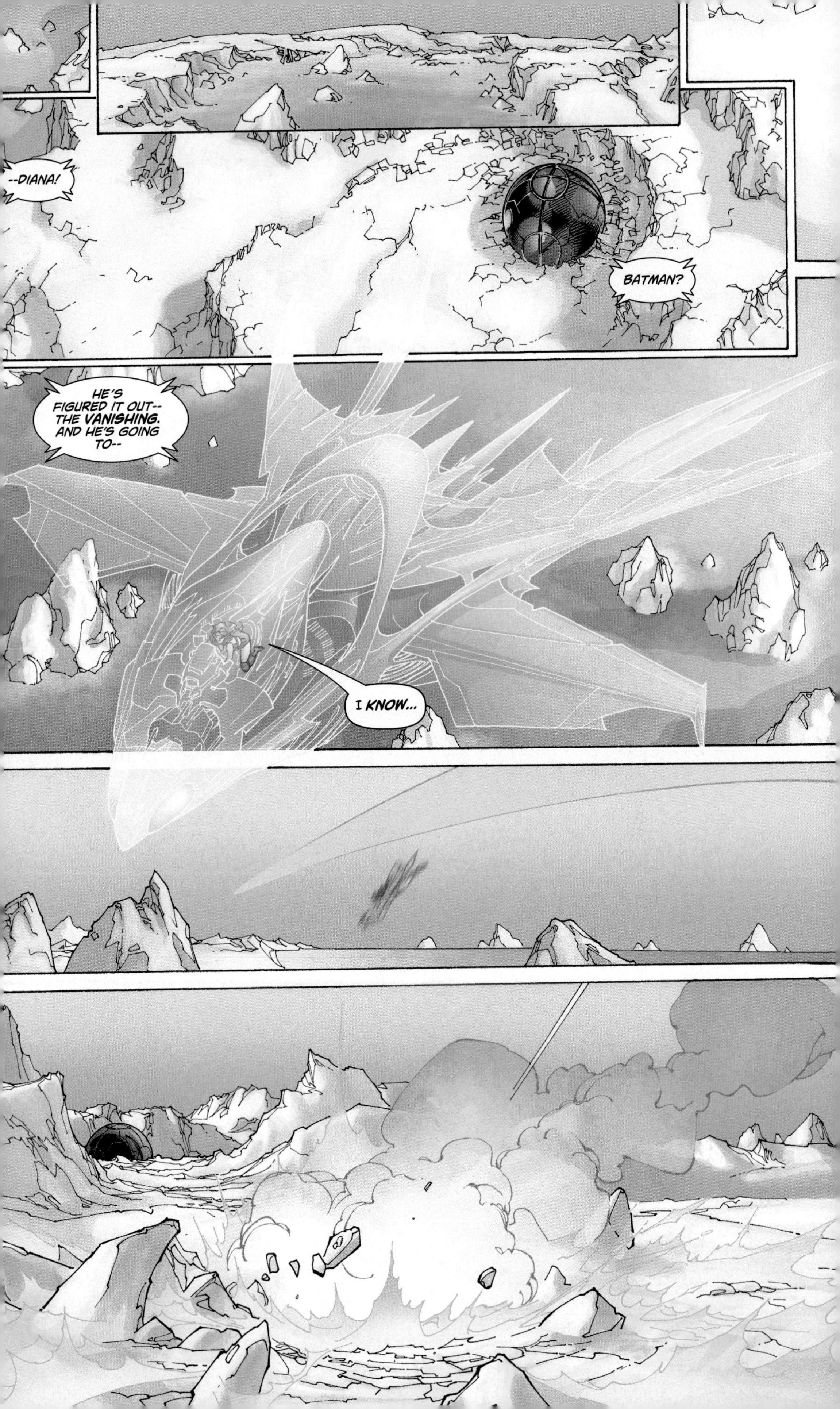
--DIANA!
BATMAN?
HE'S FIGURED IT OUT-- THE VANISHING. AND HE'S GOING TO--
I KNOW...

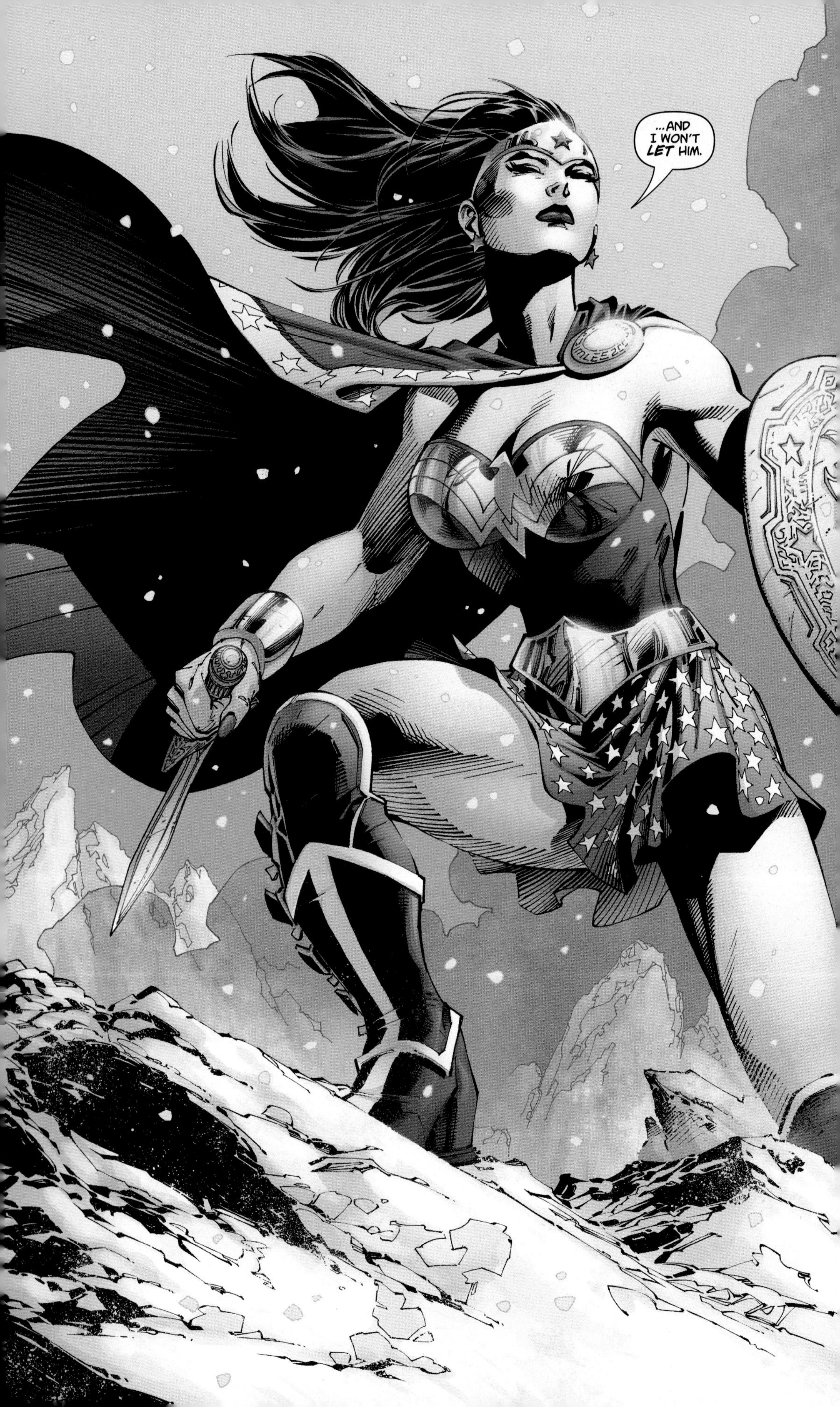
...AND I WON'T LET HIM.

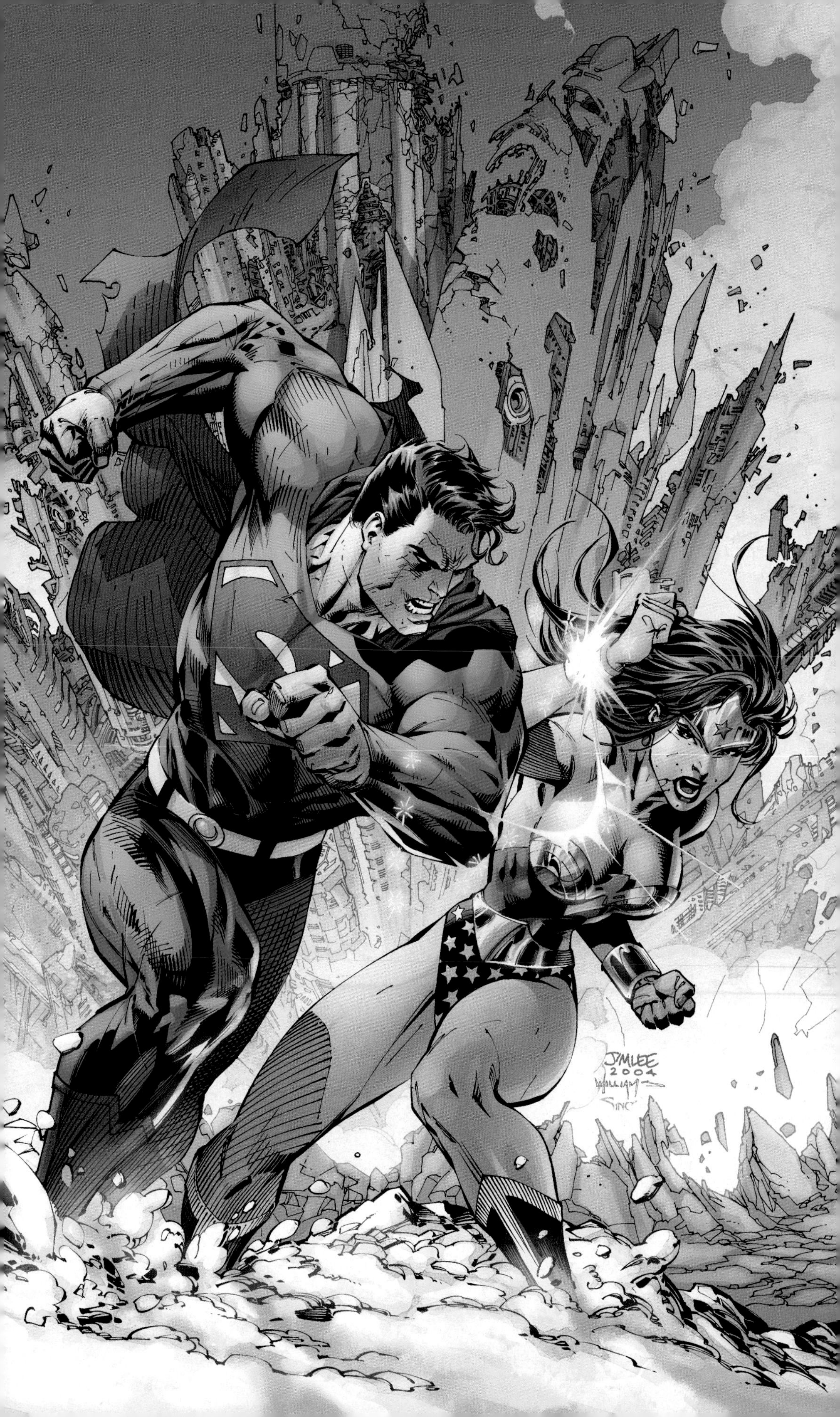
JIMLEE
2004

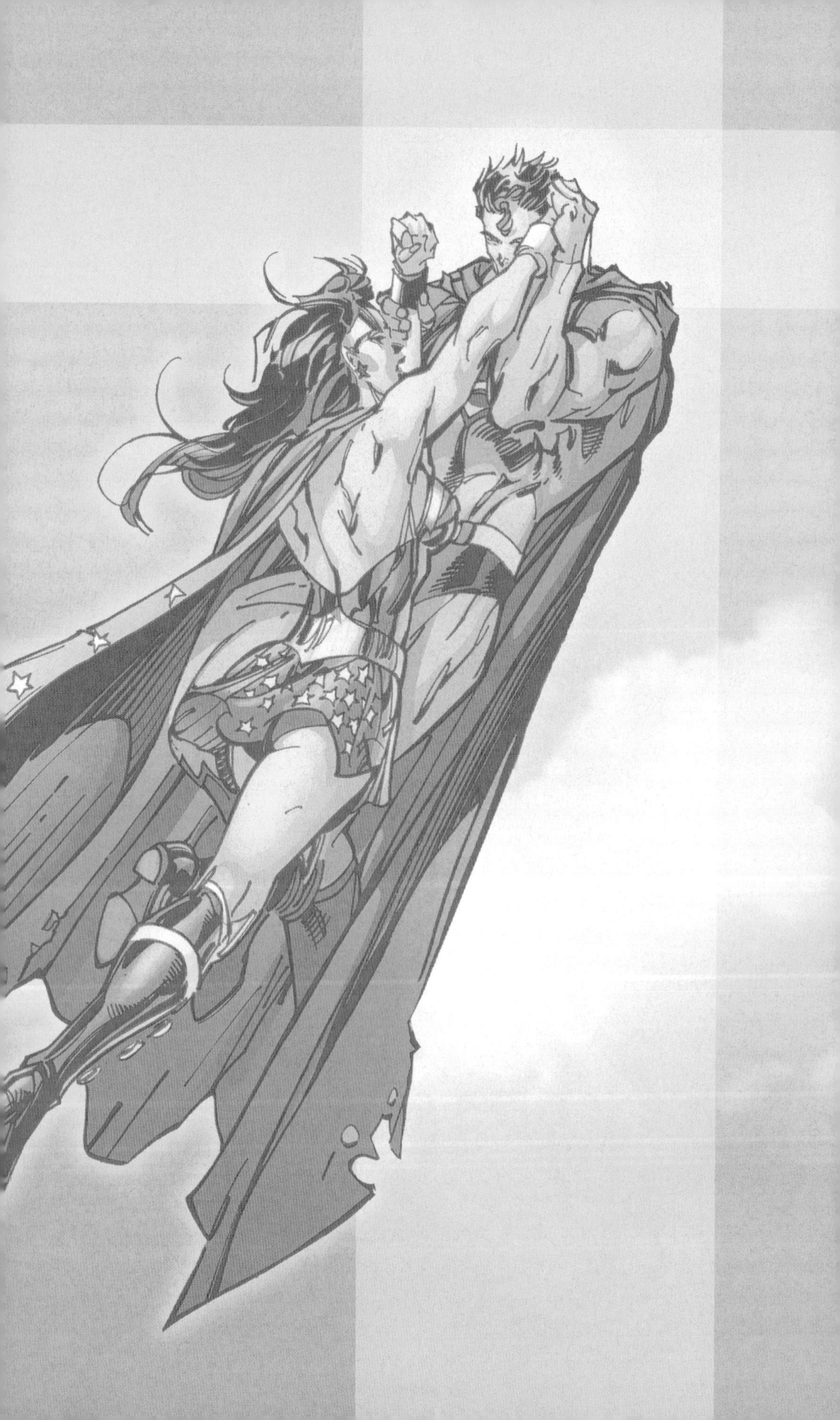

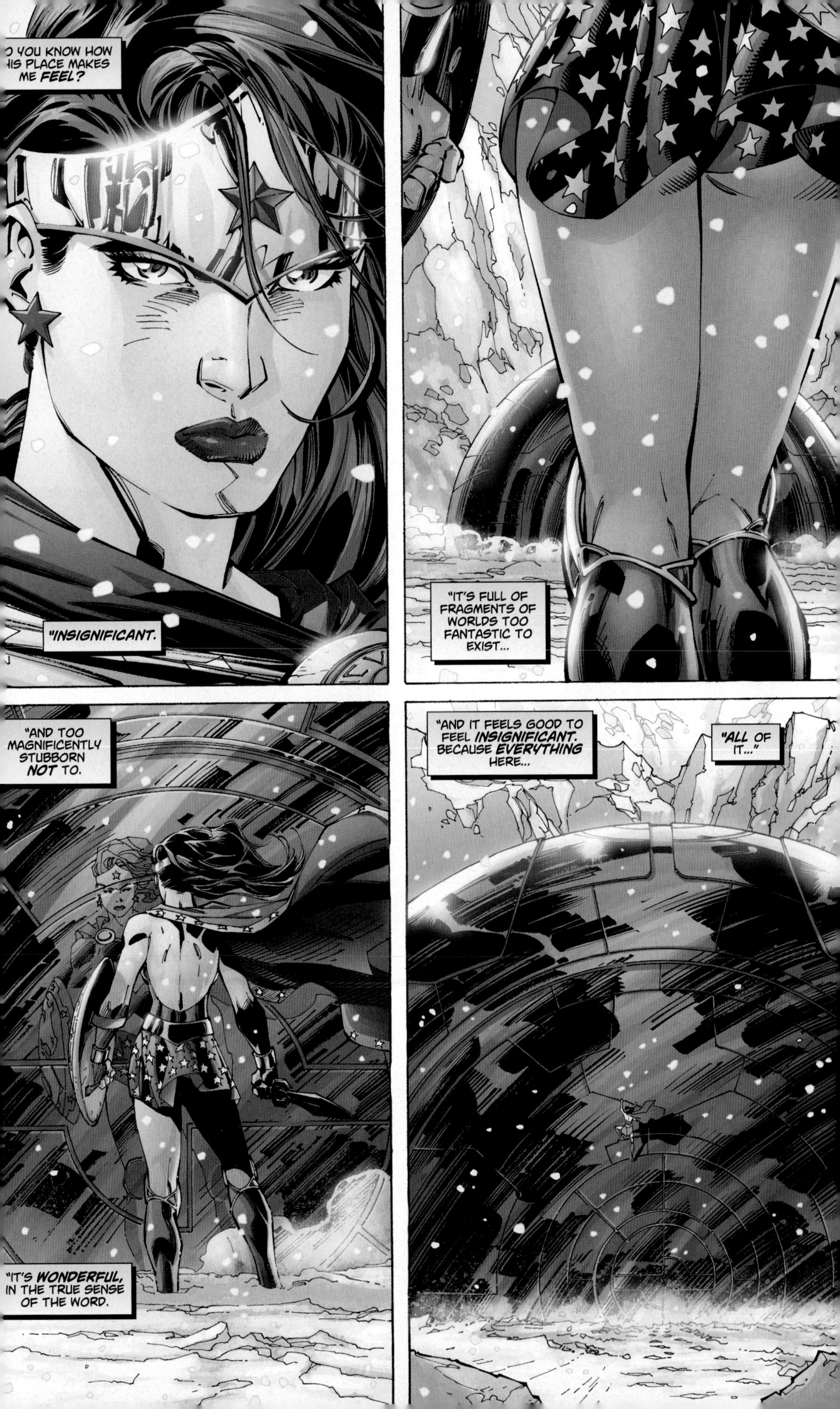
O YOU KNOW HOW
IS PLACE MAKES
ME FEEL?
"INSIGNIFICANT.
"IT'S FULL OF FRAGMENTS OF WORLDS TOO FANTASTIC TO EXIST...
"AND TOO MAGNIFICENTLY STUBBORN NOT TO.
"IT'S WONDERFUL, IN THE TRUE SENSE OF THE WORD.
"AND IT FEELS GOOD TO FEEL INSIGNIFICANT. BECAUSE EVERYTHING HERE...
"ALL OF IT..."

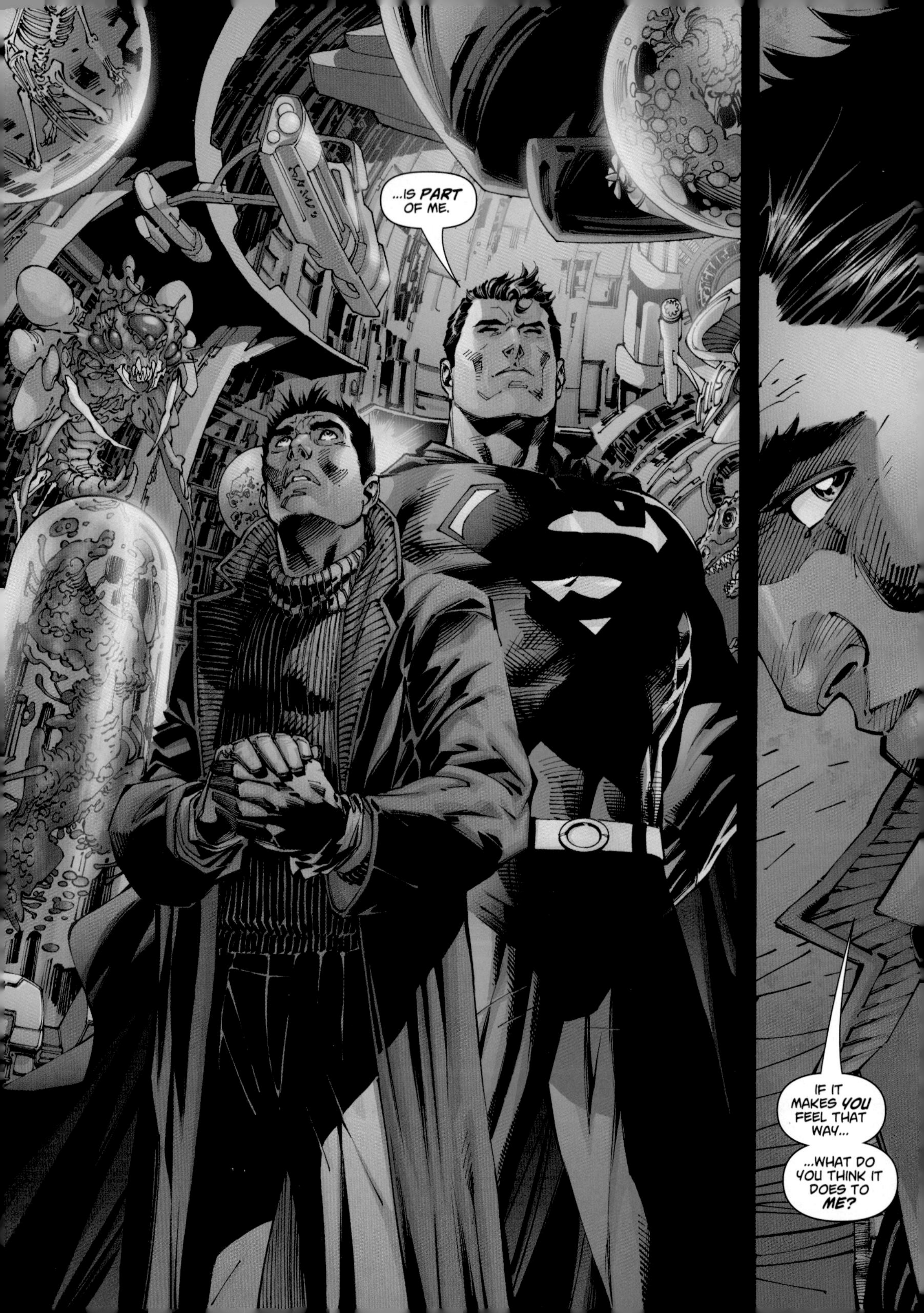
...IS PART OF ME.
IF IT MAKES YOU FEEL THAT WAY...
...WHAT DO YOU THINK IT DOES TO ME?

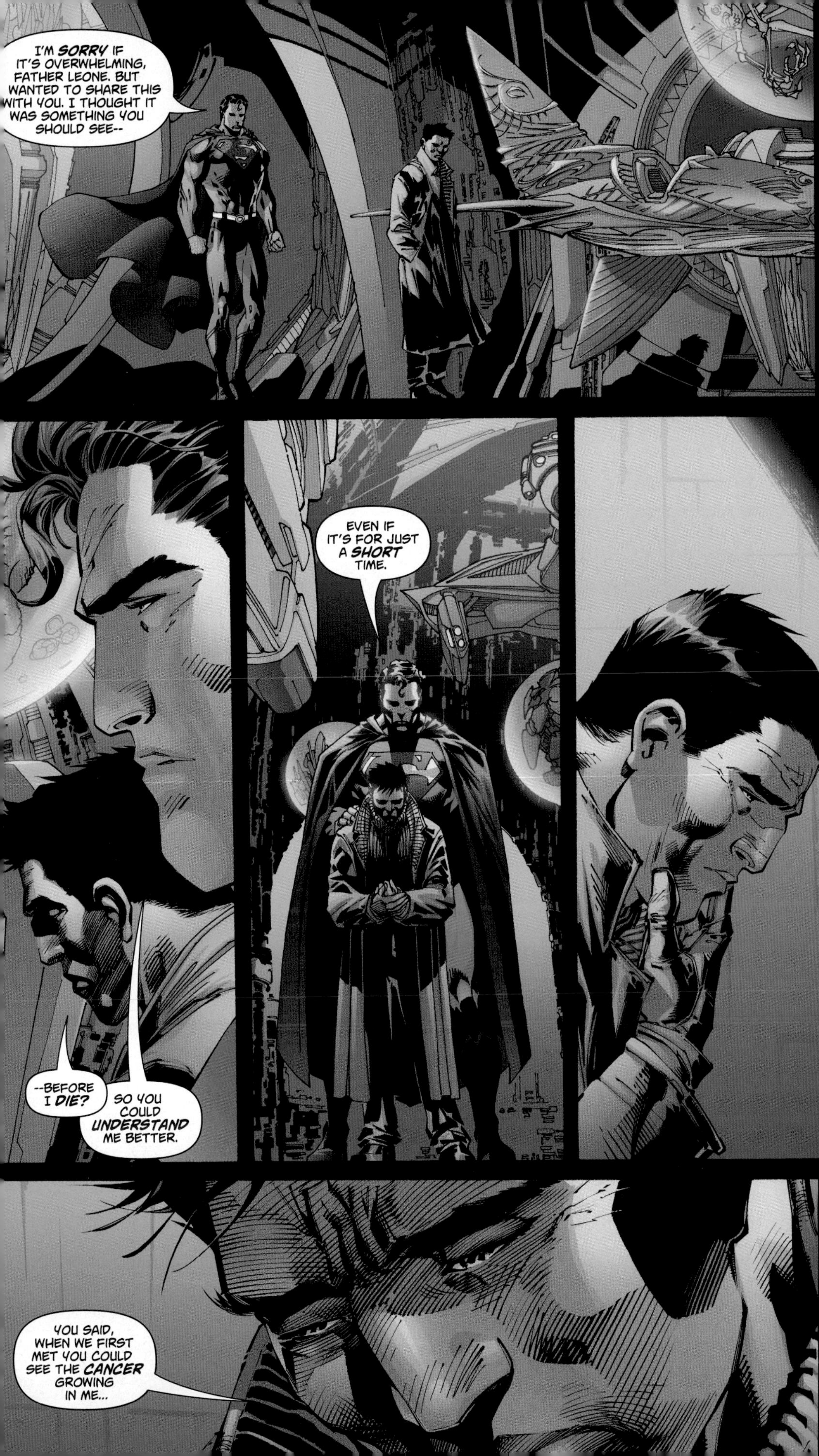
I'M SORRY IF IT'S OVERWHELMING, FATHER LEONE. BUT WANTED TO SHARE THIS WITH YOU. I THOUGHT IT WAS SOMETHING YOU SHOULD SEE--
EVEN IF IT'S FOR JUST A SHORT TIME.
--BEFORE I DIE?
SO YOU COULD UNDERSTAND ME BETTER.
YOU SAID, WHEN WE FIRST MET YOU COULD SEE THE CANCER GROWING IN ME...

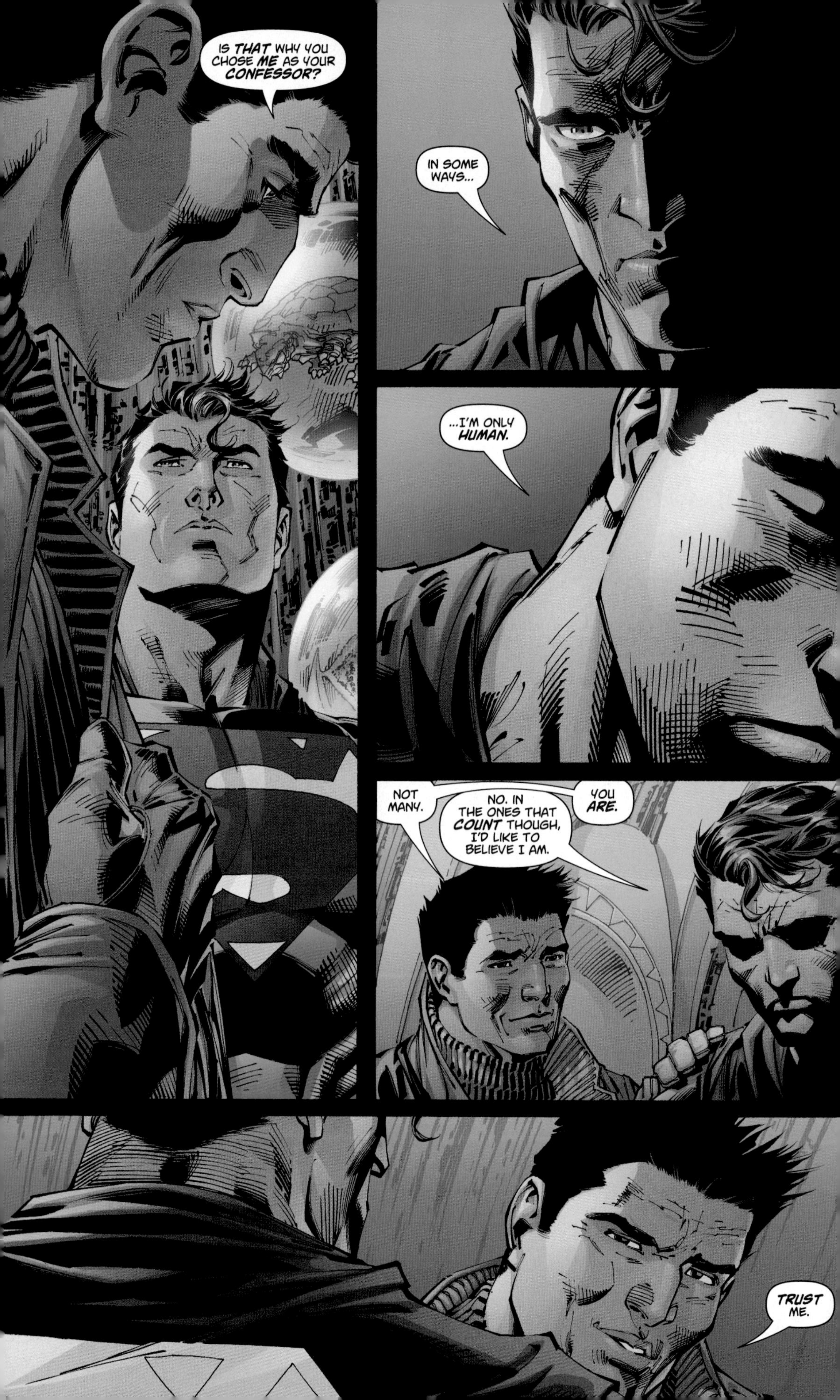
IS THAT WHY YOU CHOSE ME AS YOUR CONFESSOR?
IN SOME WAYS...
...I'M ONLY HUMAN.
NOT MANY.
YOU ARE.
NO. IN THE ONES THAT COUNT THOUGH, I'D LIKE TO BELIEVE I AM.
TRUST ME.

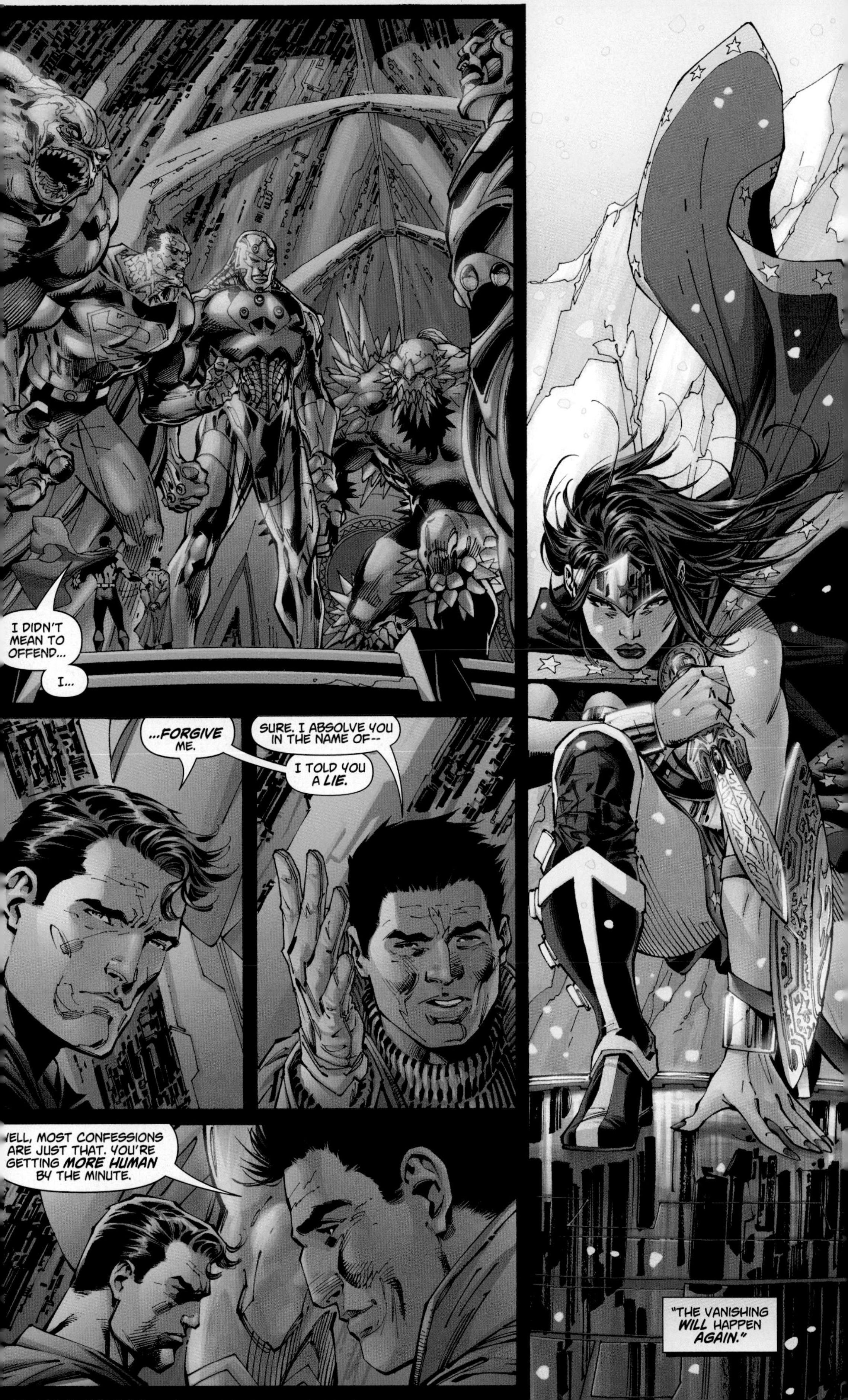
I DIDN'T MEAN TO OFFEND...
I...
...FORGIVE ME.
SURE. I ABSOLVE YOU IN THE NAME OF--
I TOLD YOU A LIE.
ELL, MOST CONFESSIONS ARE JUST THAT. YOU'RE GETTING MORE HUMAN BY THE MINUTE.
"THE VANISHING WILL HAPPEN AGAIN."

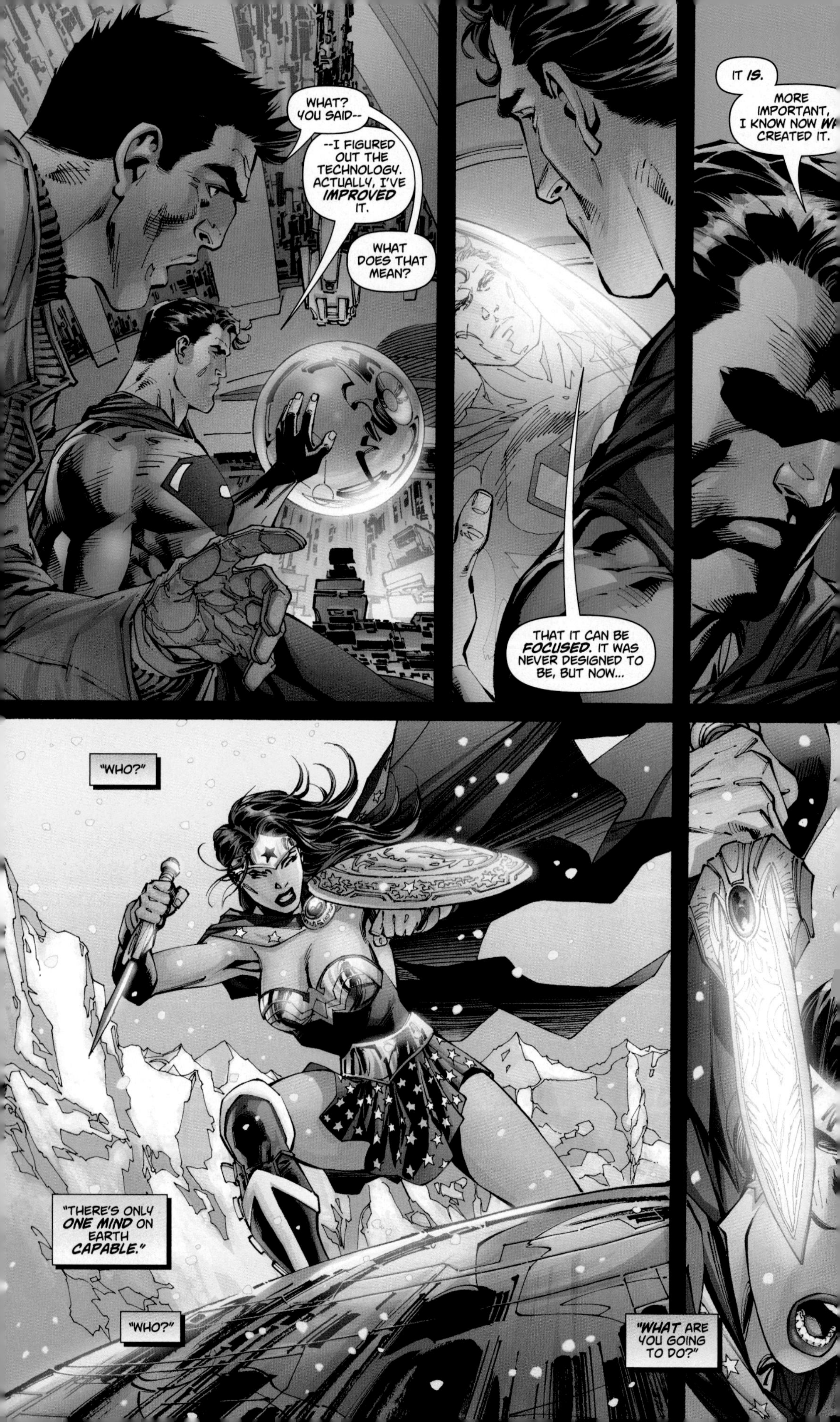
WHAT? YOU SAID--
--I FIGURED OUT THE TECHNOLOGY. ACTUALLY, I'VE *IMPROVED* IT.
WHAT DOES THAT MEAN?
THAT IT CAN BE *FOCUSED*. IT WAS NEVER DESIGNED TO BE, BUT NOW...
IT *IS*.
MORE IMPORTANT, I KNOW NOW
CREATED IT.
"WHO?"
"THERE'S ONLY *ONE MIND* ON EARTH *CAPABLE*."
"WHO?"
"*WHAT* ARE YOU GOING TO DO?"

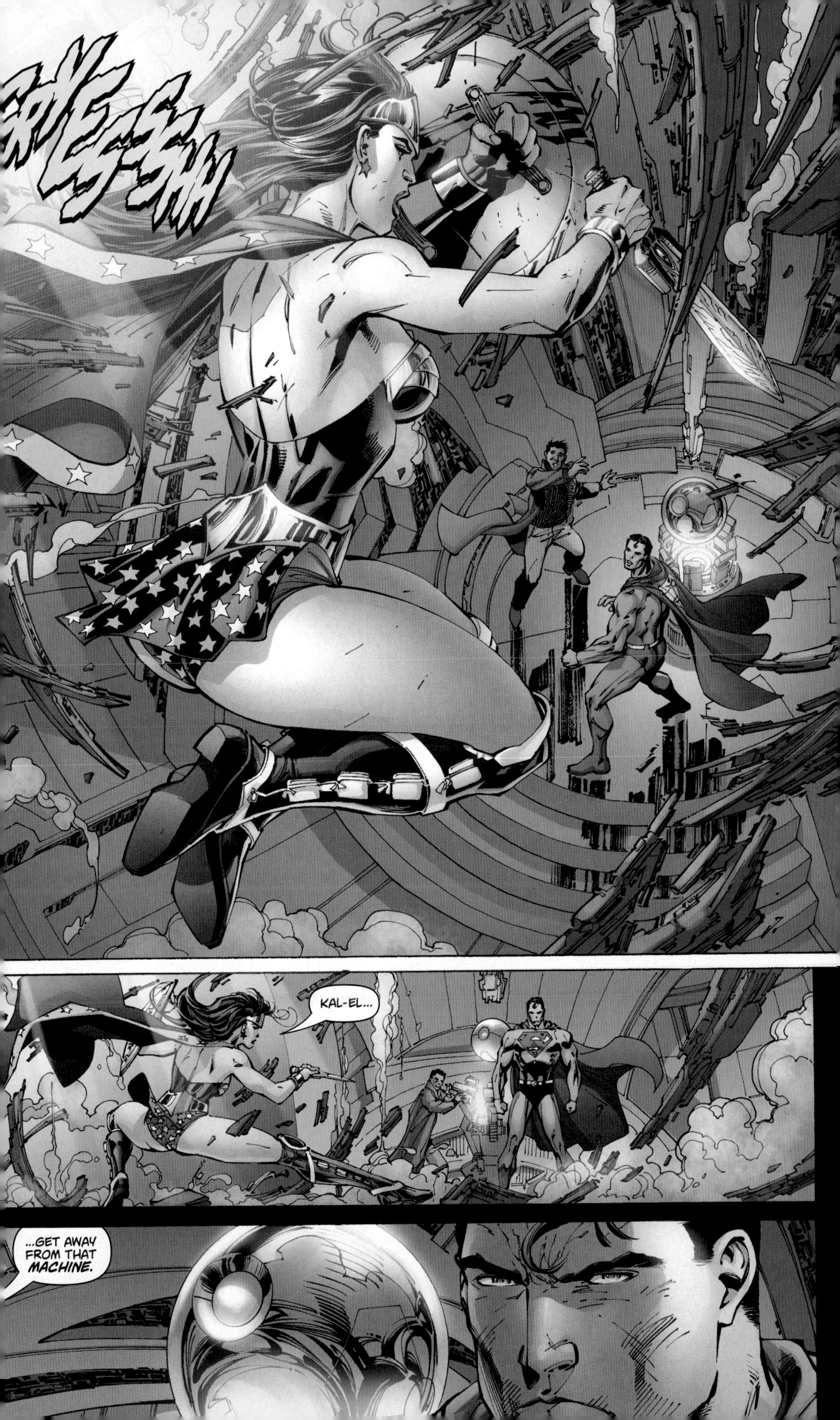
KAL-EL...
...GET AWAY FROM THAT MACHINE.

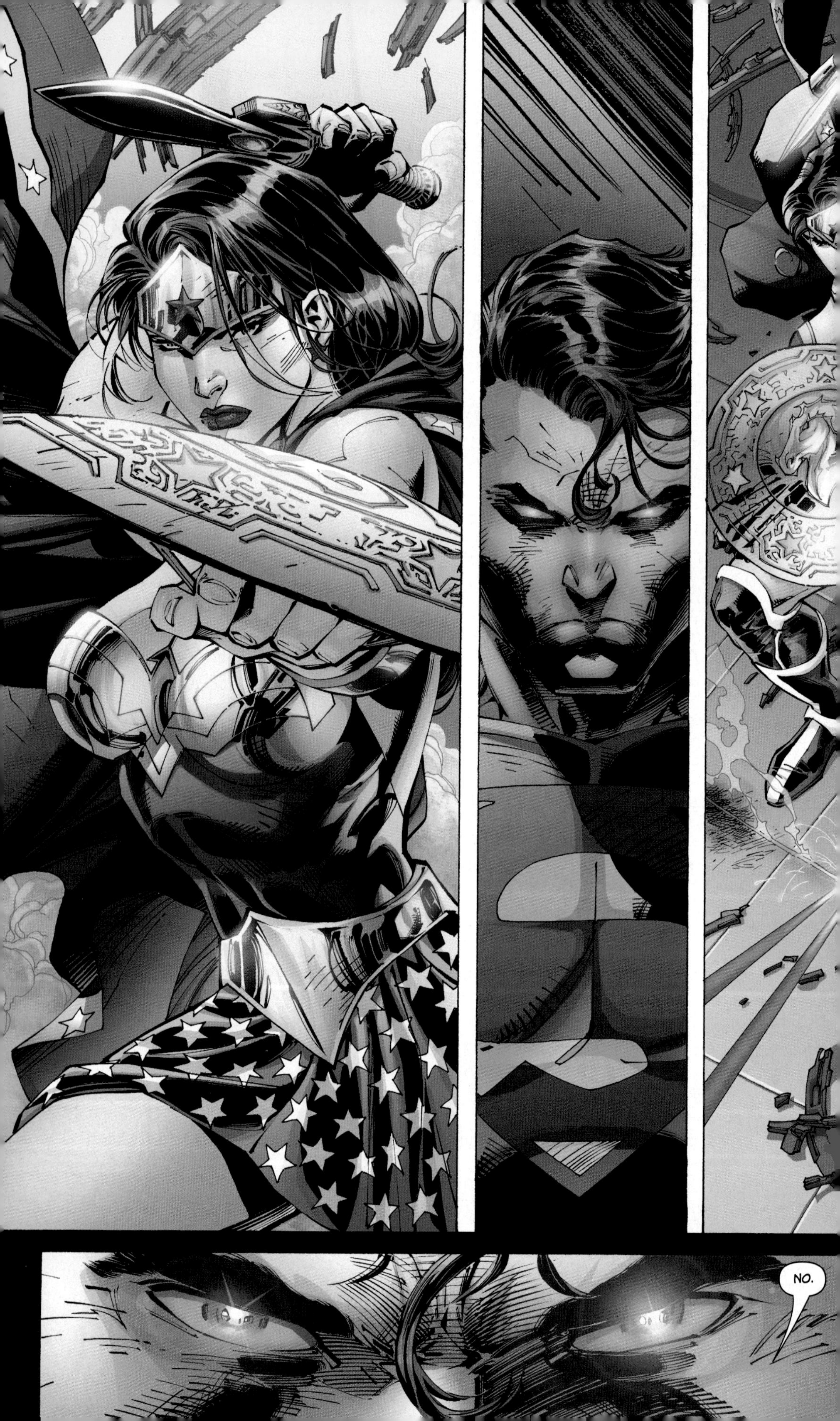
NO.

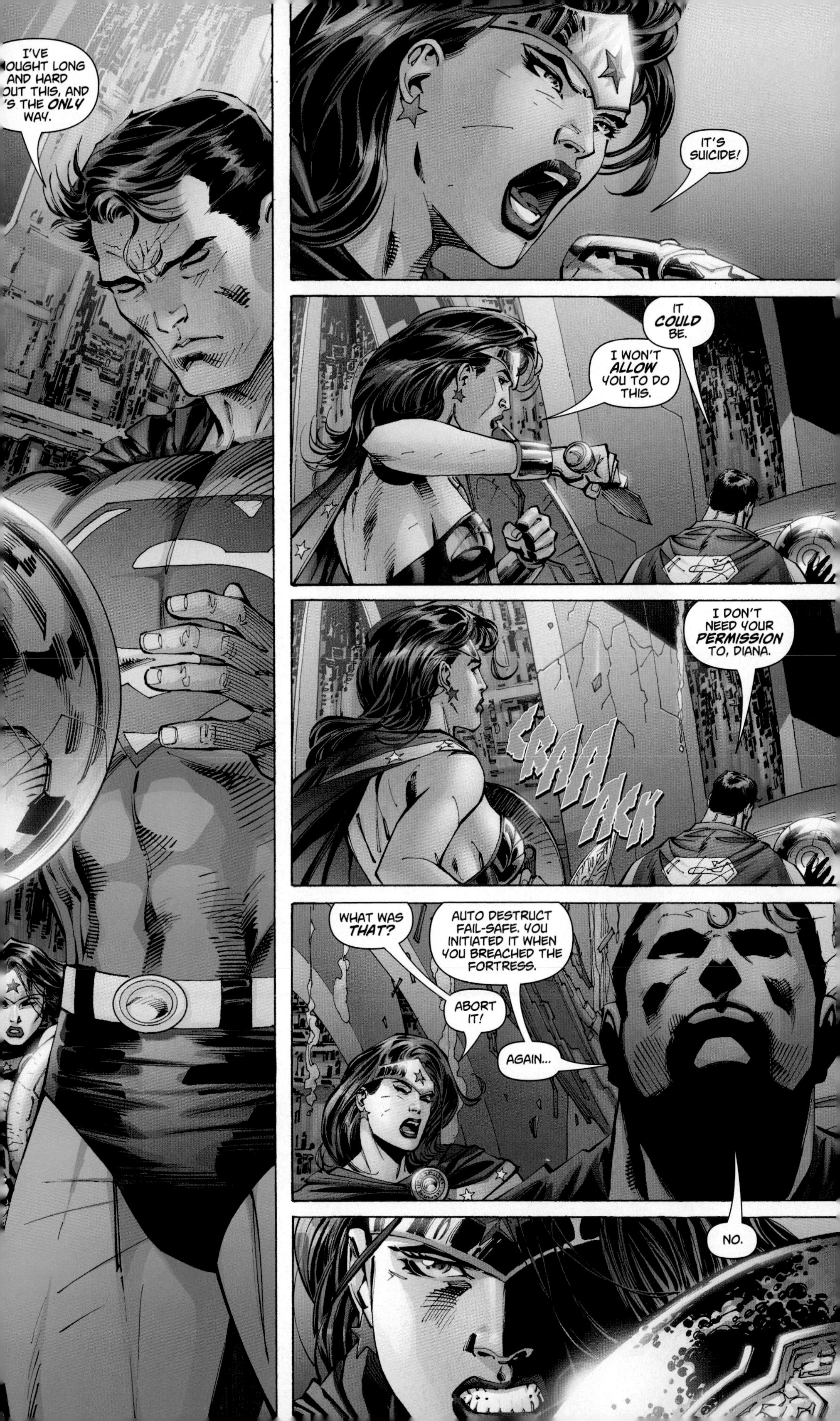

I'VE
OUGHT LONG
AND HARD
OUT THIS, AND
'S THE ONLY
WAY.
IT'S SUICIDE!
IT COULD BE.
I WON'T ALLOW YOU TO DO THIS.
I DON'T NEED YOUR PERMISSION TO, DIANA.
CRAAACK
WHAT WAS THAT?
AUTO DESTRUCT FAIL-SAFE. YOU INITIATED IT WHEN YOU BREACHED THE FORTRESS.
ABORT IT!
AGAIN...
NO.

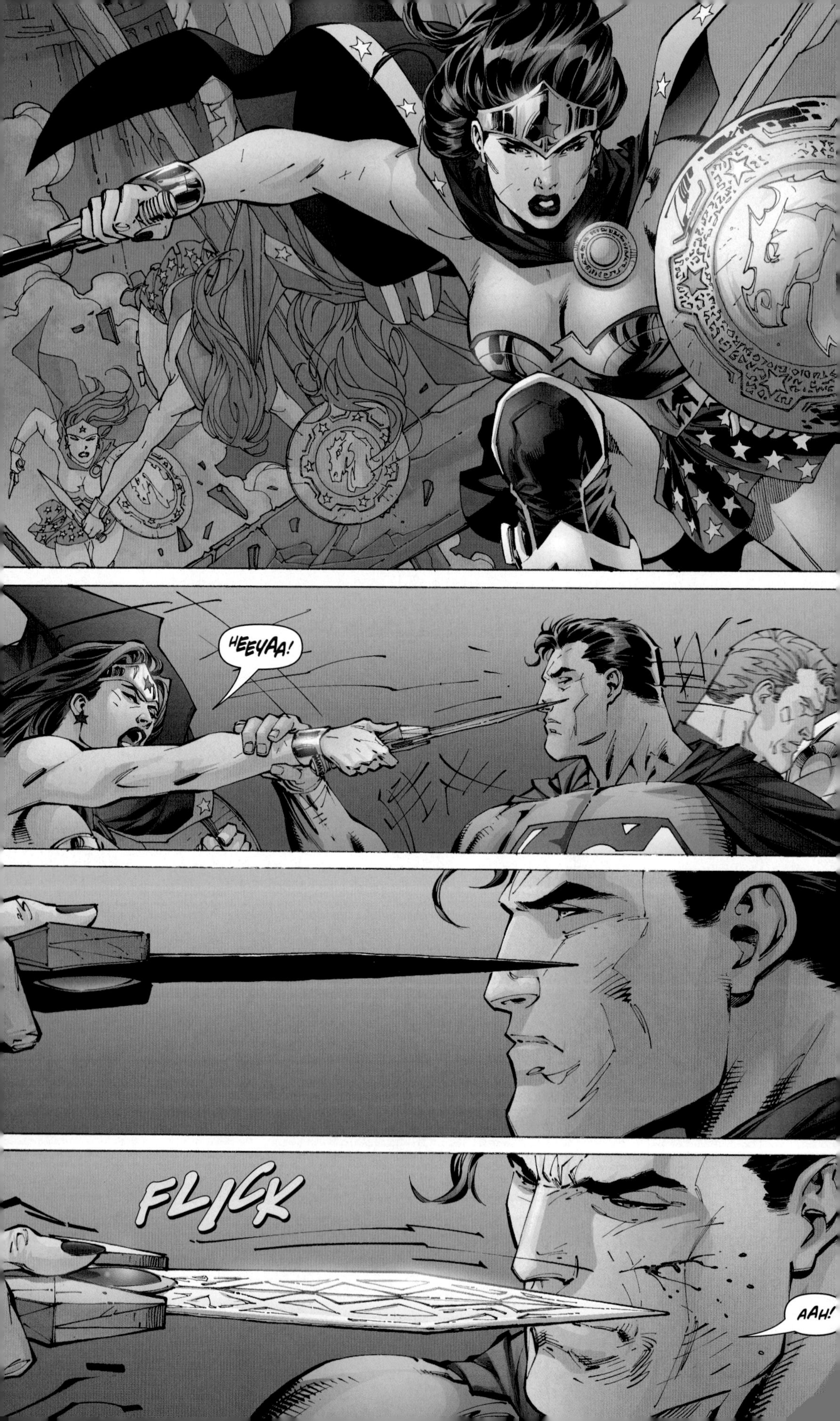
HEEYAA!
FLICK
AAH!

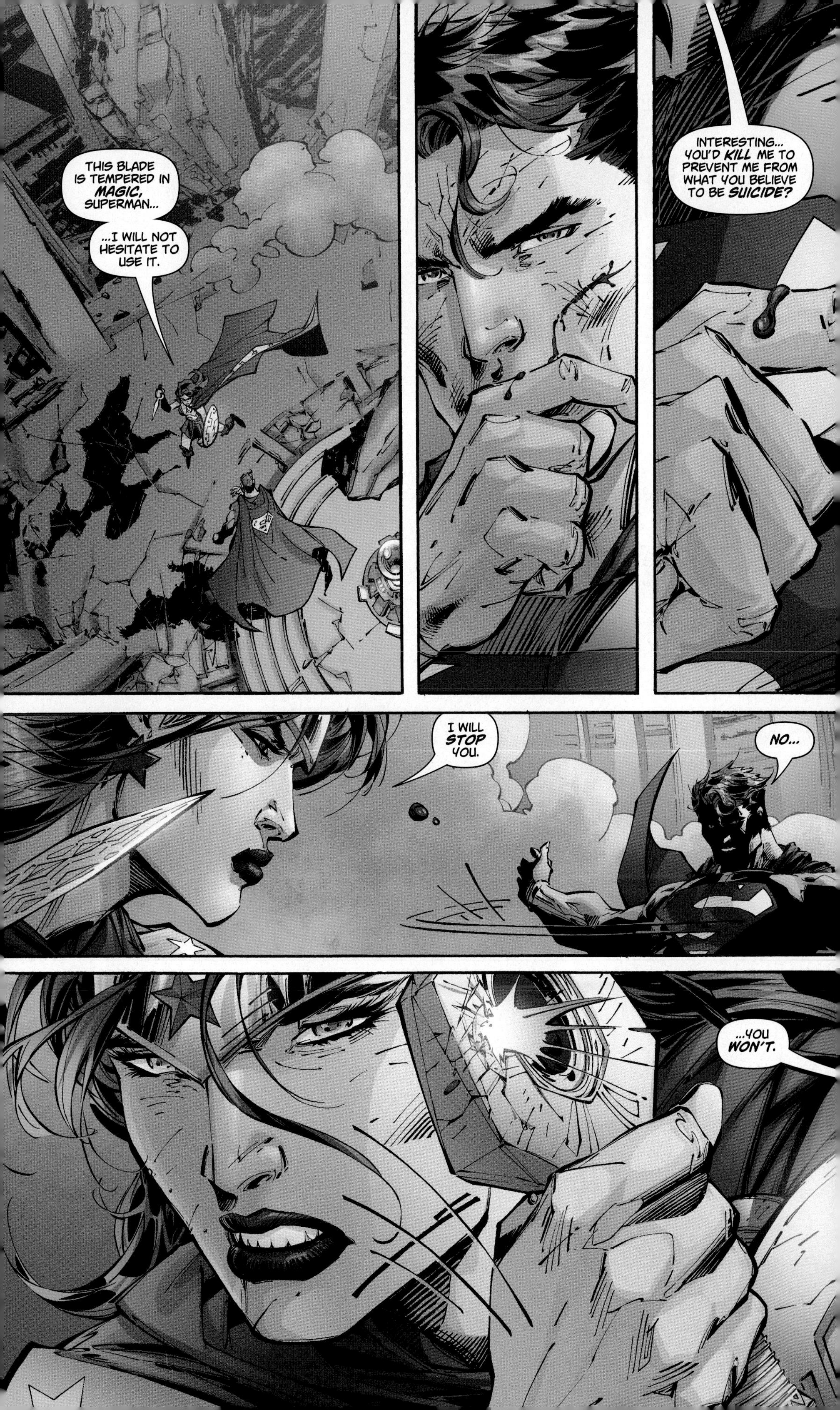
THIS BLADE IS TEMPERED IN MAGIC, SUPERMAN...
...I WILL NOT HESITATE TO USE IT.
INTERESTING... YOU'D KILL ME TO PREVENT ME FROM WHAT YOU BELIEVE TO BE SUICIDE?
I WILL STOP YOU.
NO...
...YOU WON'T.

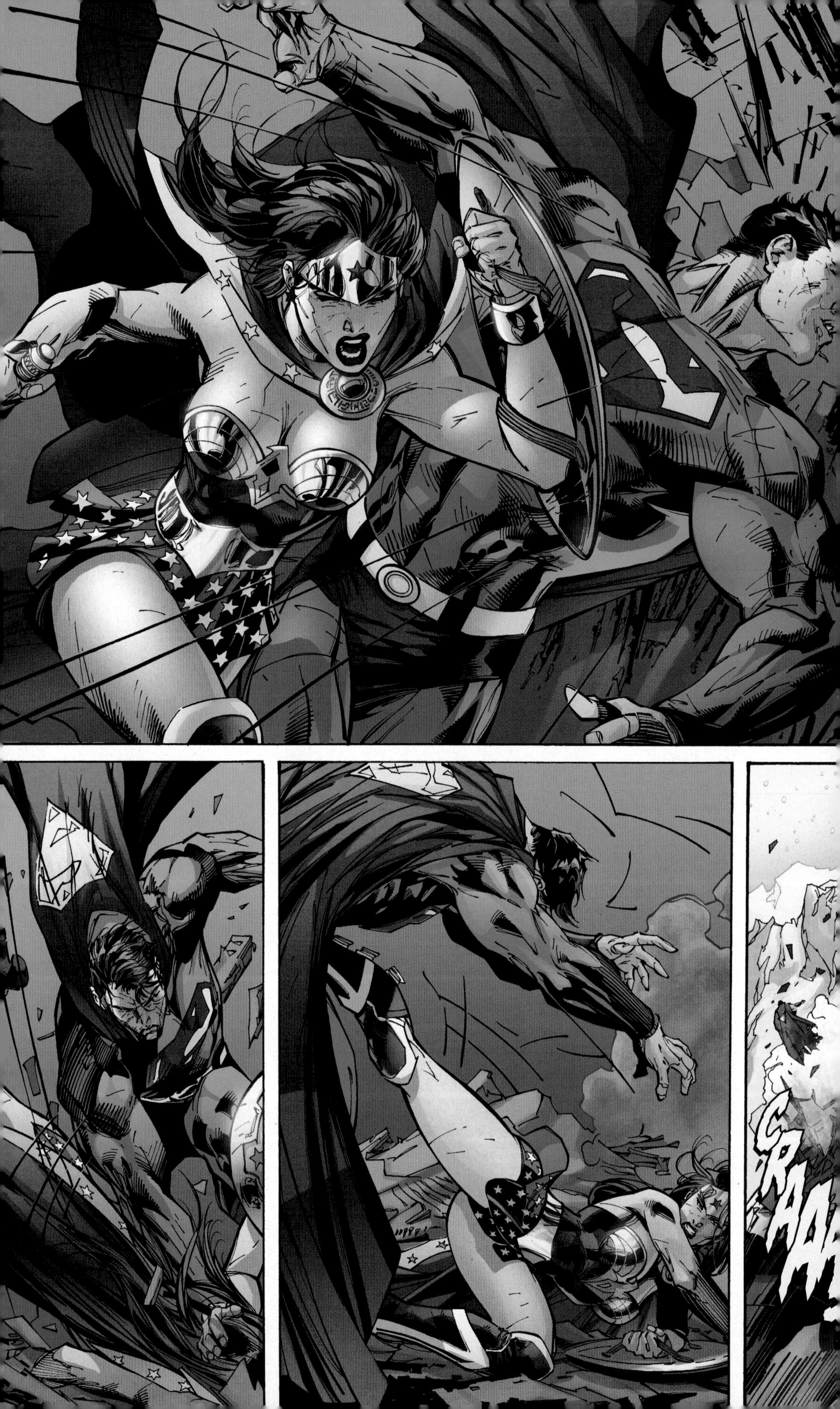
CRAA

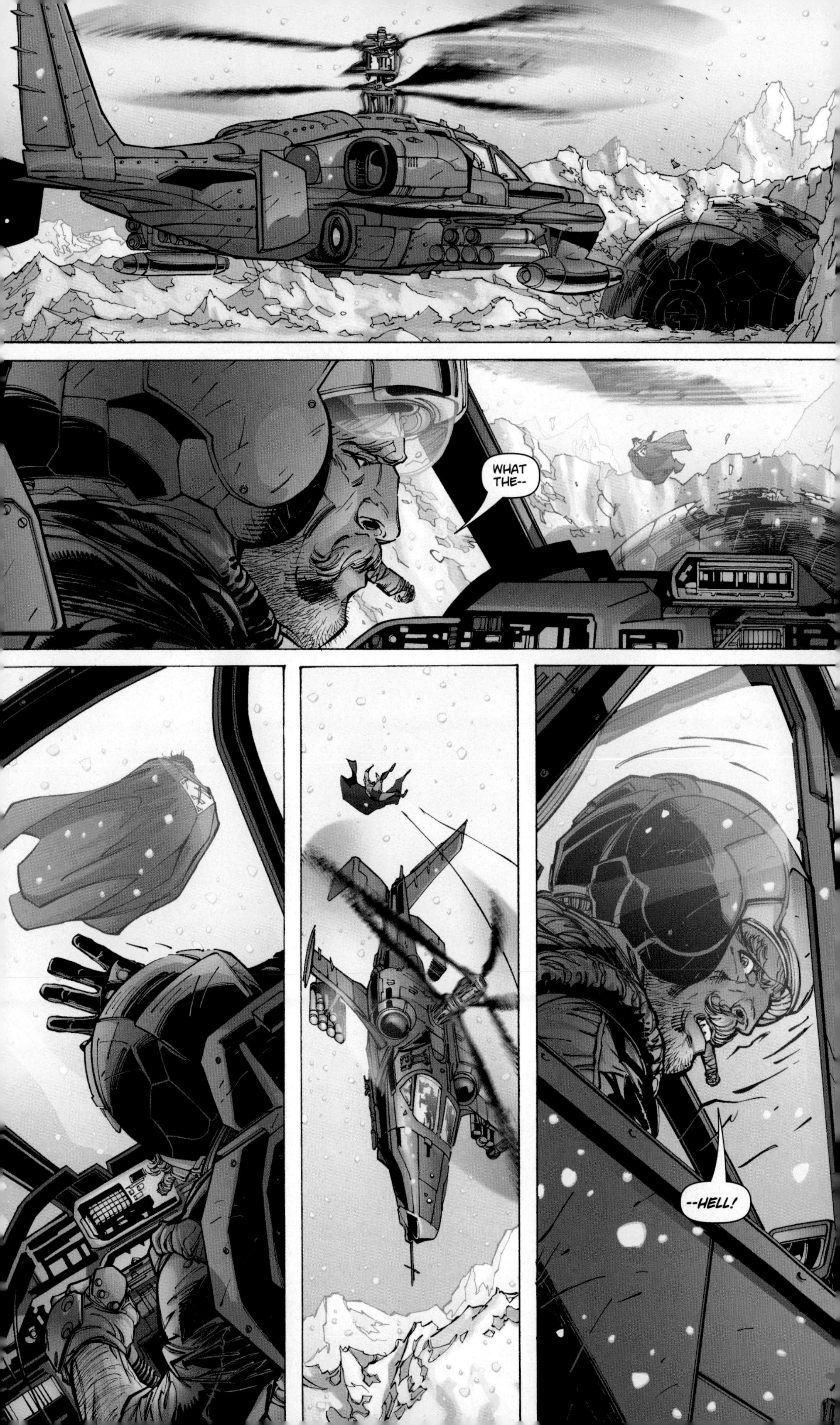
WHAT THE--
--HELL!

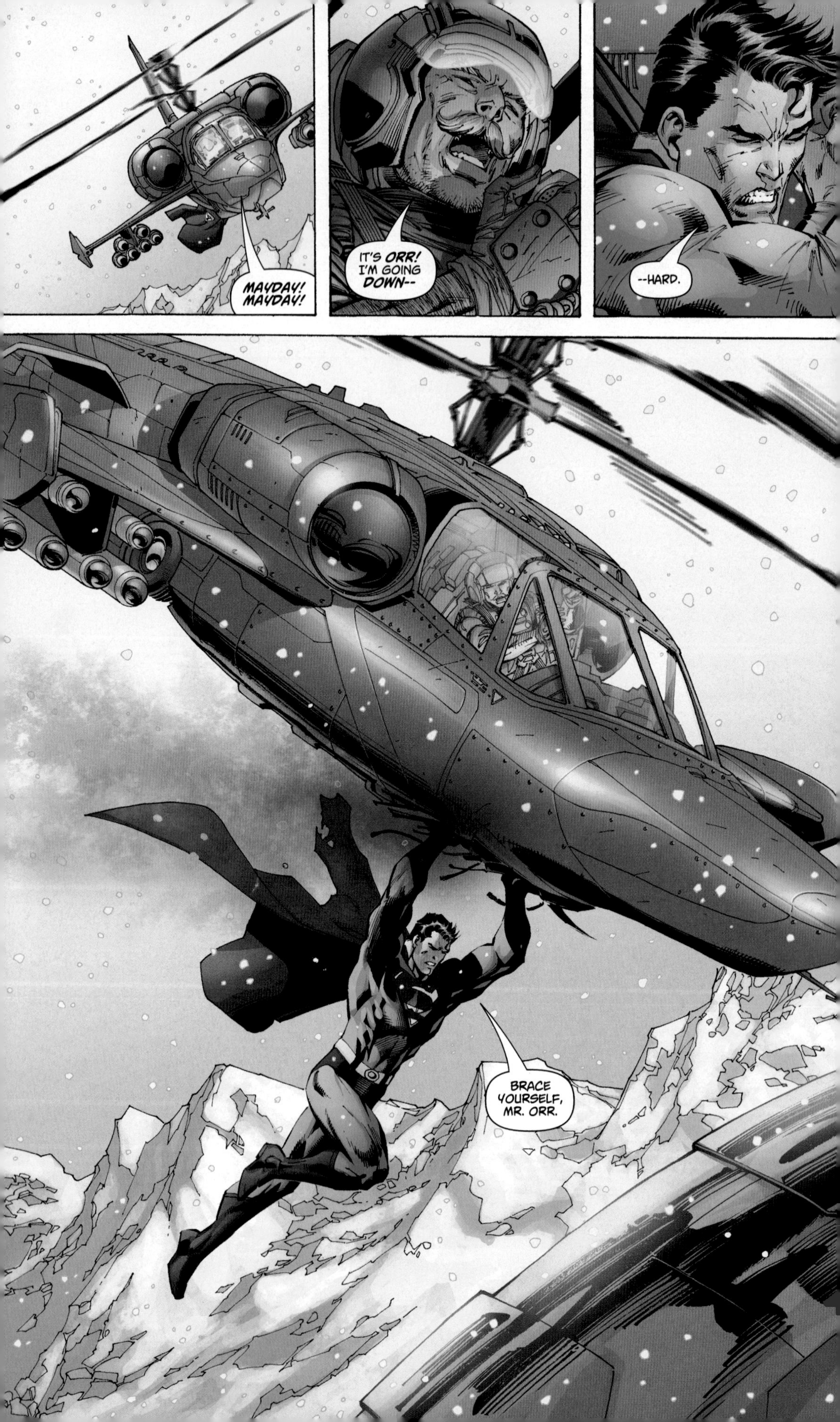
MAYDAY! MAYDAY!
IT'S ORR! I'M GOING DOWN--
--HARD.
BRACE YOURSELF, MR. ORR.

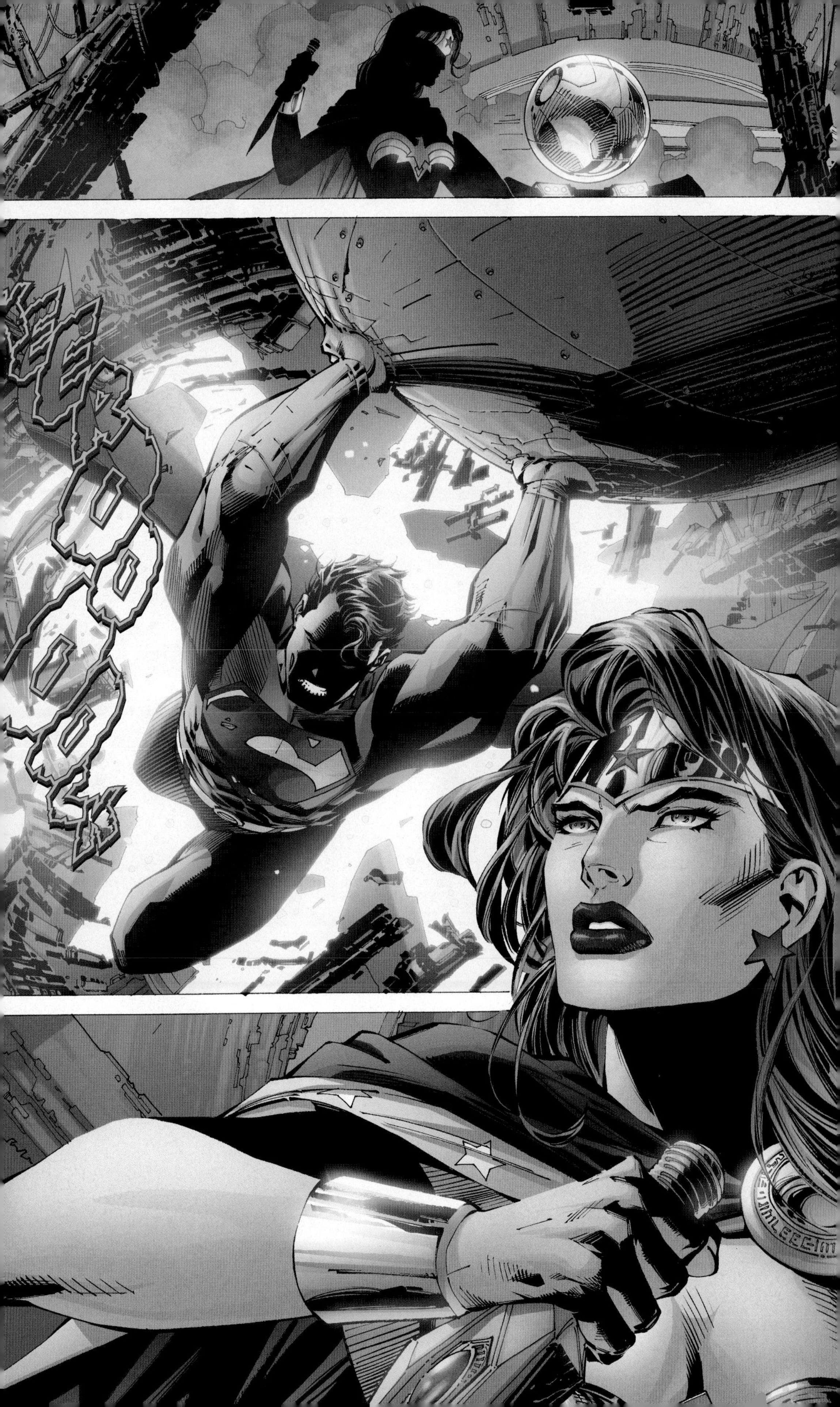

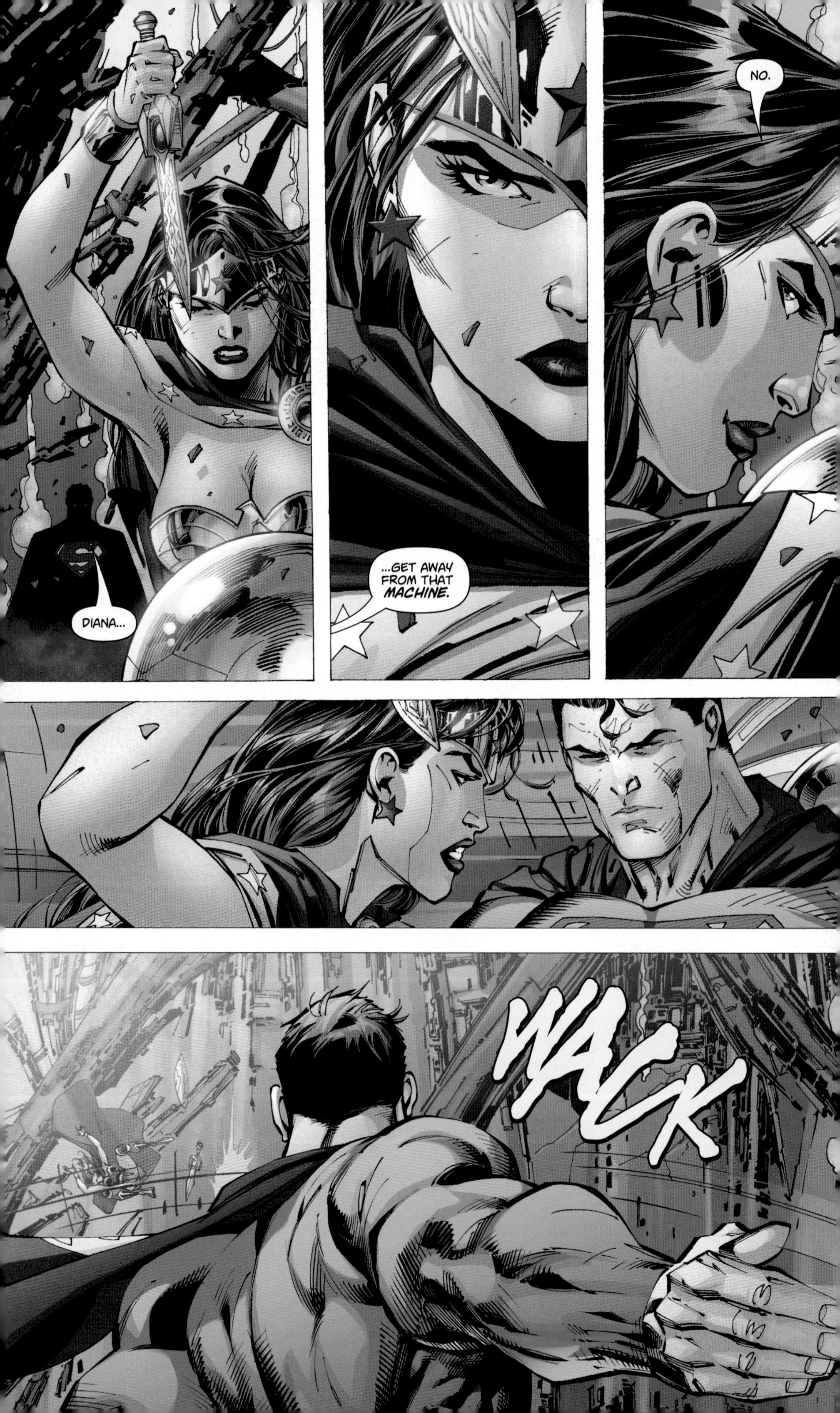
DIANA...
...GET AWAY FROM THAT MACHINE.
NO.
WACK

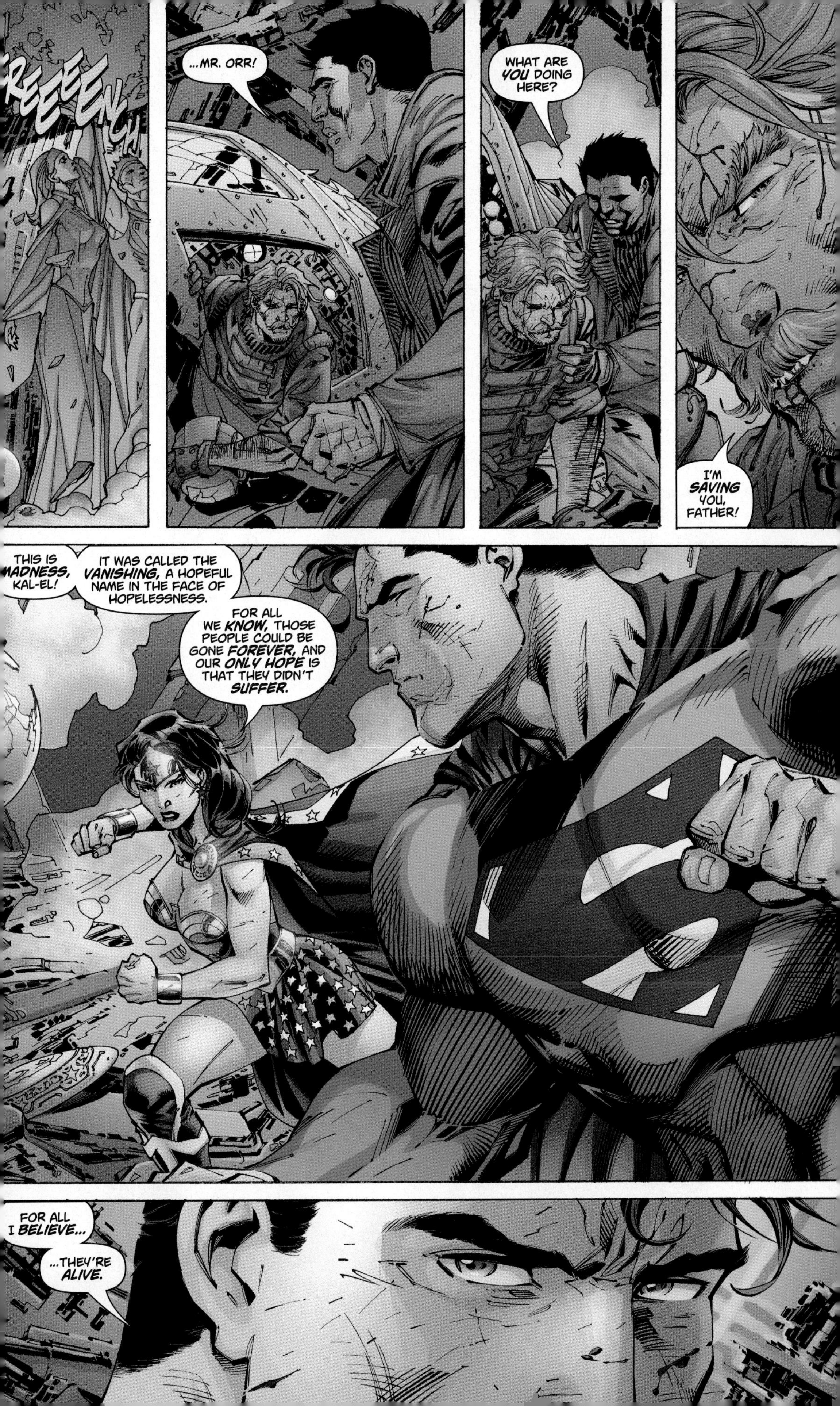

REEEEENCH
...MR. ORR!
WHAT ARE YOU DOING HERE?
I'M SAVING YOU, FATHER!
THIS IS MADNESS, KAL-EL!
IT WAS CALLED THE VANISHING, A HOPEFUL NAME IN THE FACE OF HOPELESSNESS.
FOR ALL WE KNOW, THOSE PEOPLE COULD BE GONE FOREVER, AND OUR ONLY HOPE IS THAT THEY DIDN'T SUFFER.
FOR ALL I BELIEVE...
...THEY'RE ALIVE.

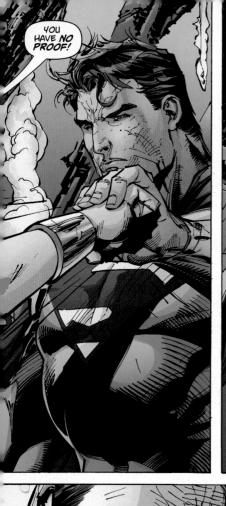

YOU HAVE **NO** PROOF!

DIANA... I DON'T NEED **PROOF.**

I HAVE SOMETHING **STRONGER.**

I HAVE **FAITH.**

SUPERMAN!

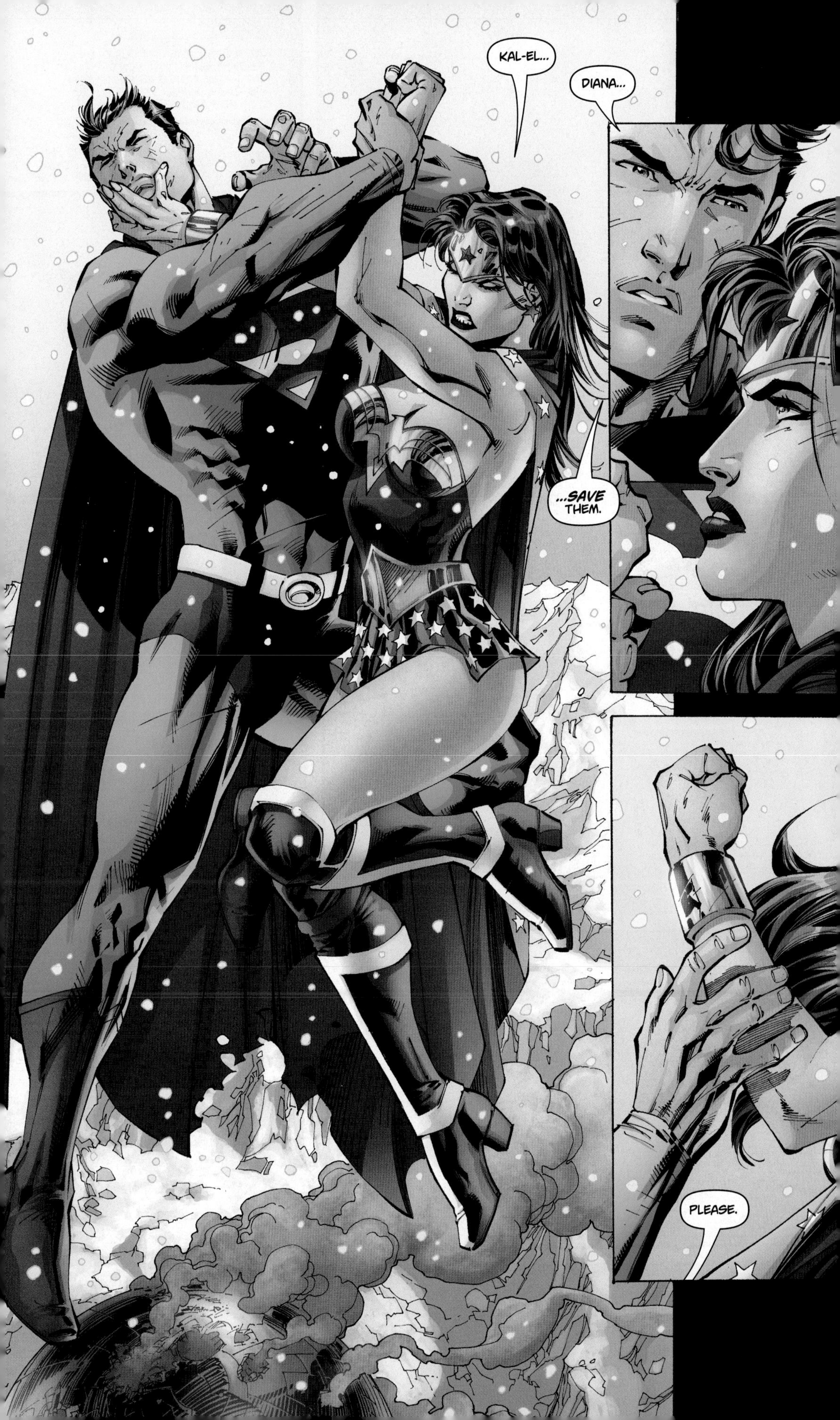
KAL-EL...
DIANA...
...SAVE THEM.
PLEASE.

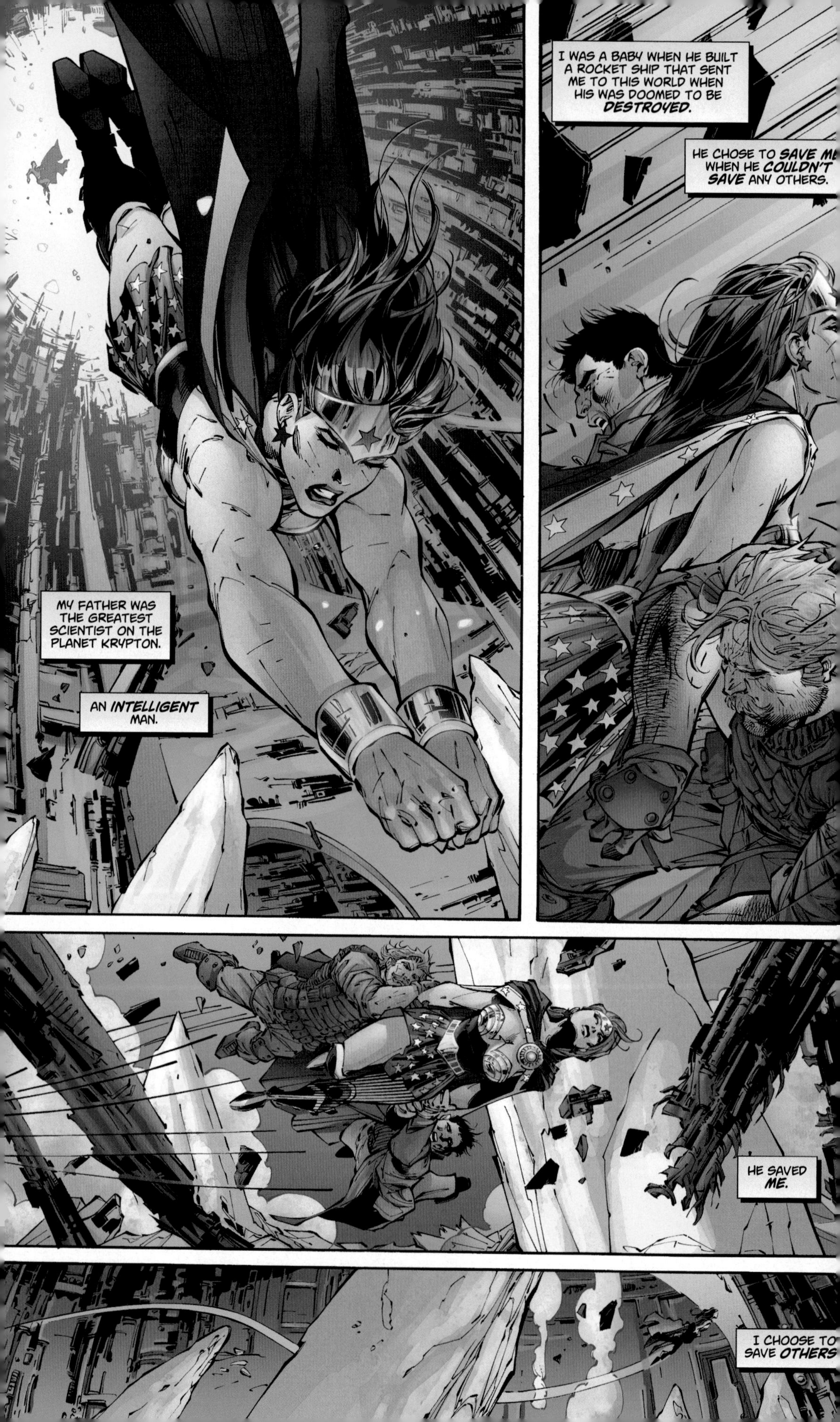
MY FATHER WAS THE GREATEST SCIENTIST ON THE PLANET KRYPTON.
AN INTELLIGENT MAN.
I WAS A BABY WHEN HE BUILT A ROCKET SHIP THAT SENT ME TO THIS WORLD WHEN HIS WAS DOOMED TO BE DESTROYED.
HE CHOSE TO SAVE M WHEN HE COULDN'T SAVE ANY OTHERS.
HE SAVED ME.
I CHOOSE TO SAVE OTHERS

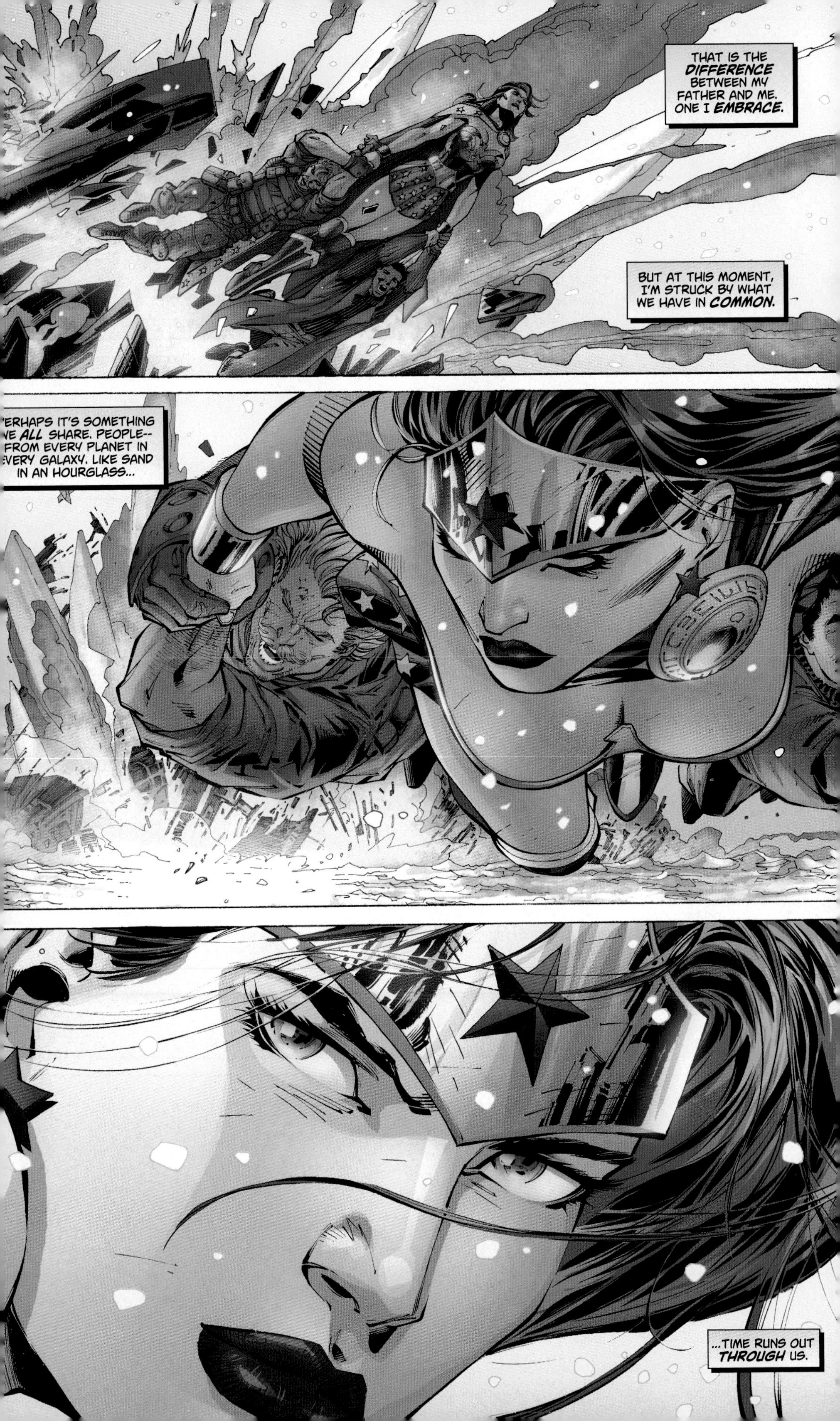
THAT IS THE DIFFERENCE BETWEEN MY FATHER AND ME. ONE I EMBRACE.
BUT AT THIS MOMENT, I'M STRUCK BY WHAT WE HAVE IN COMMON.
ERHAPS IT'S SOMETHING WE ALL SHARE. PEOPLE-- FROM EVERY PLANET IN EVERY GALAXY. LIKE SAND IN AN HOURGLASS...
...TIME RUNS OUT THROUGH US.

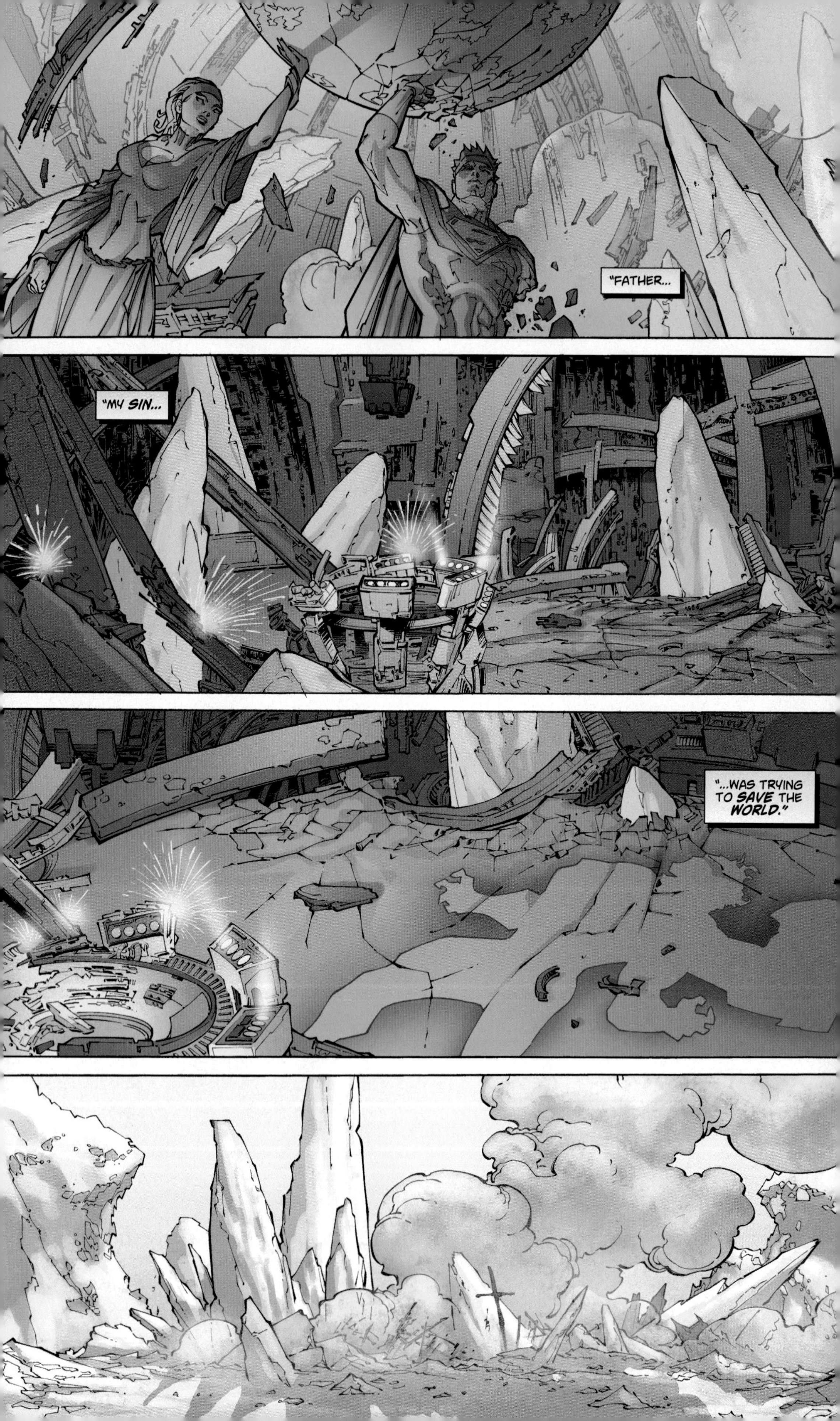
"FATHER...
"MY SIN...
"...WAS TRYING TO SAVE THE WORLD."

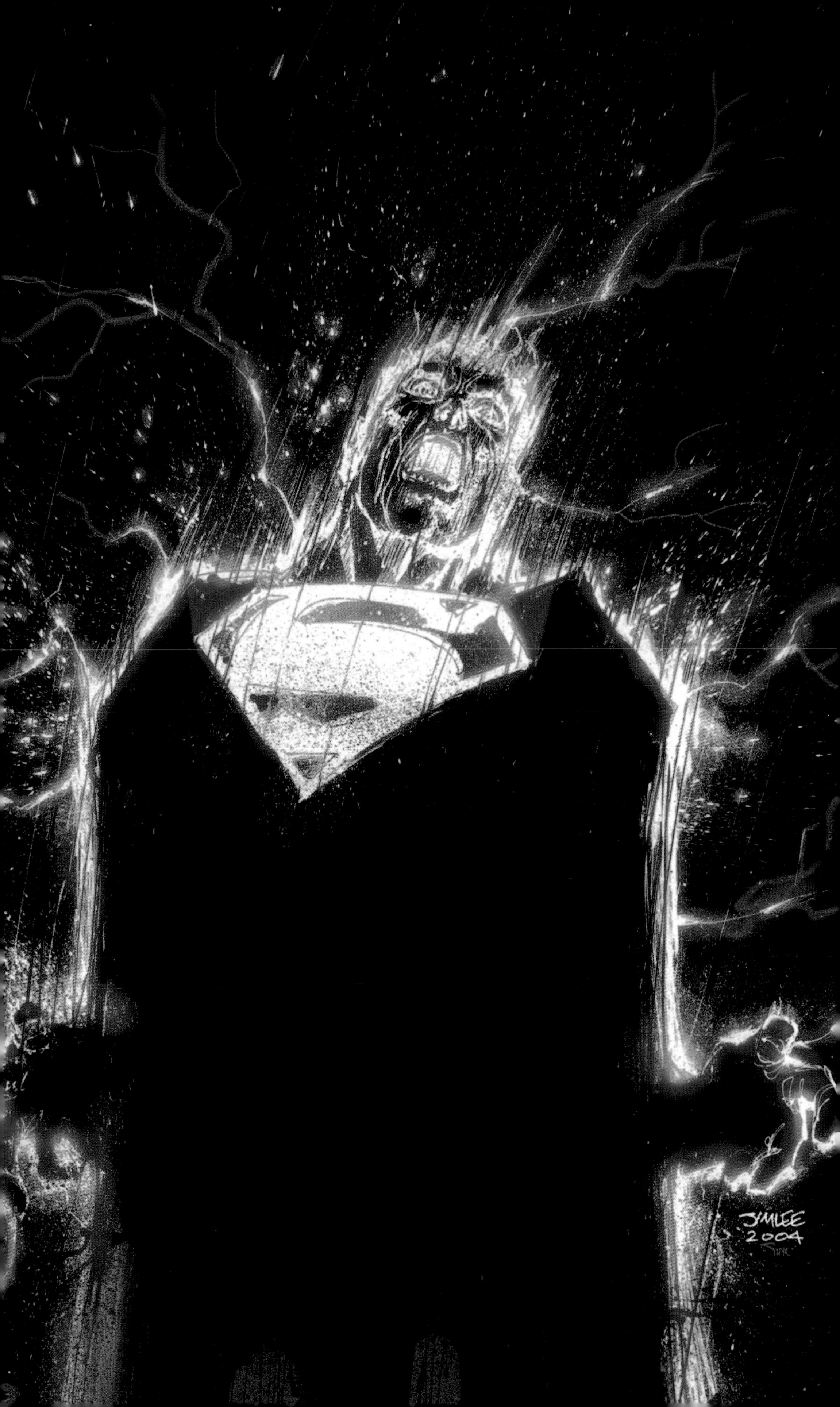
JIMLEE
2004

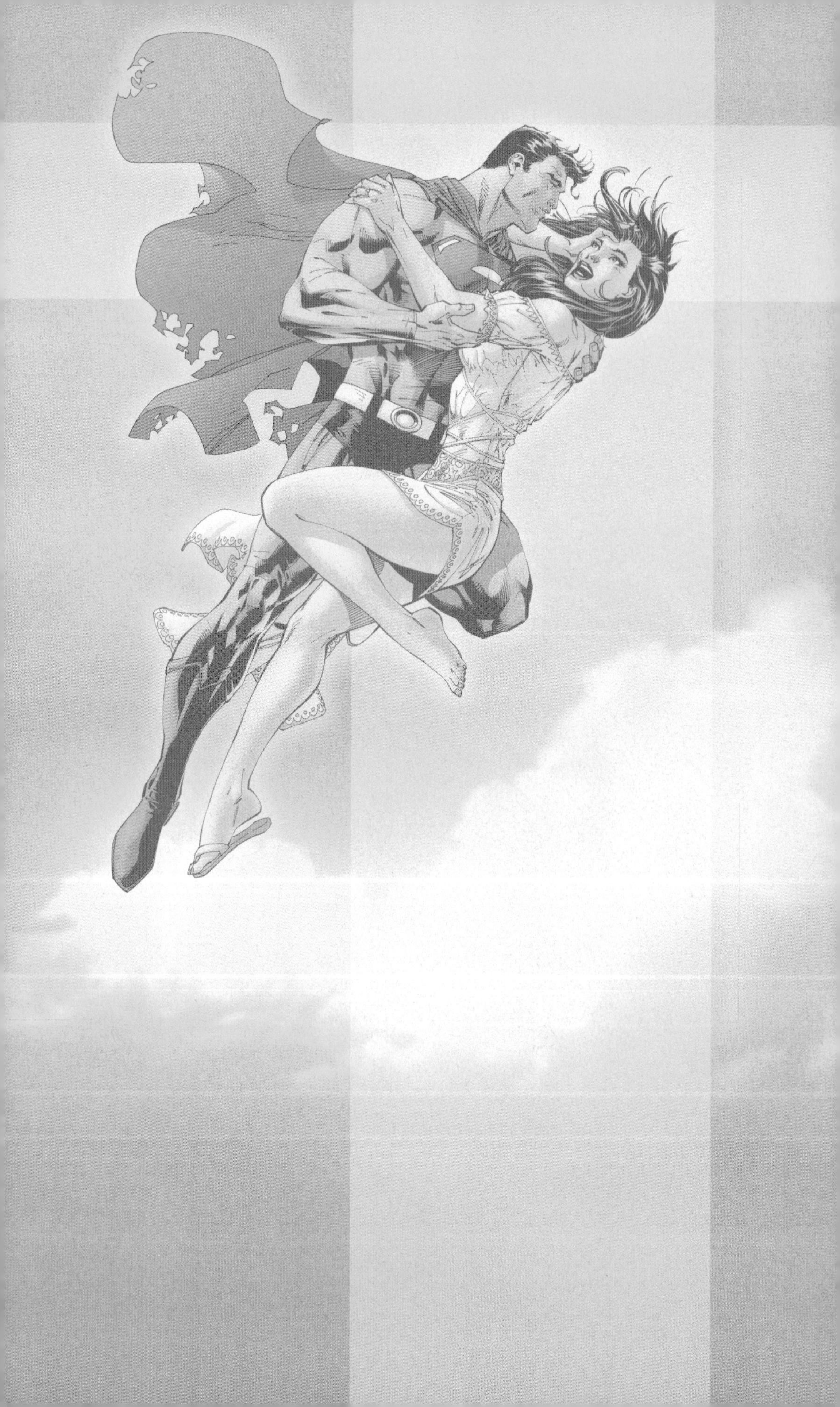

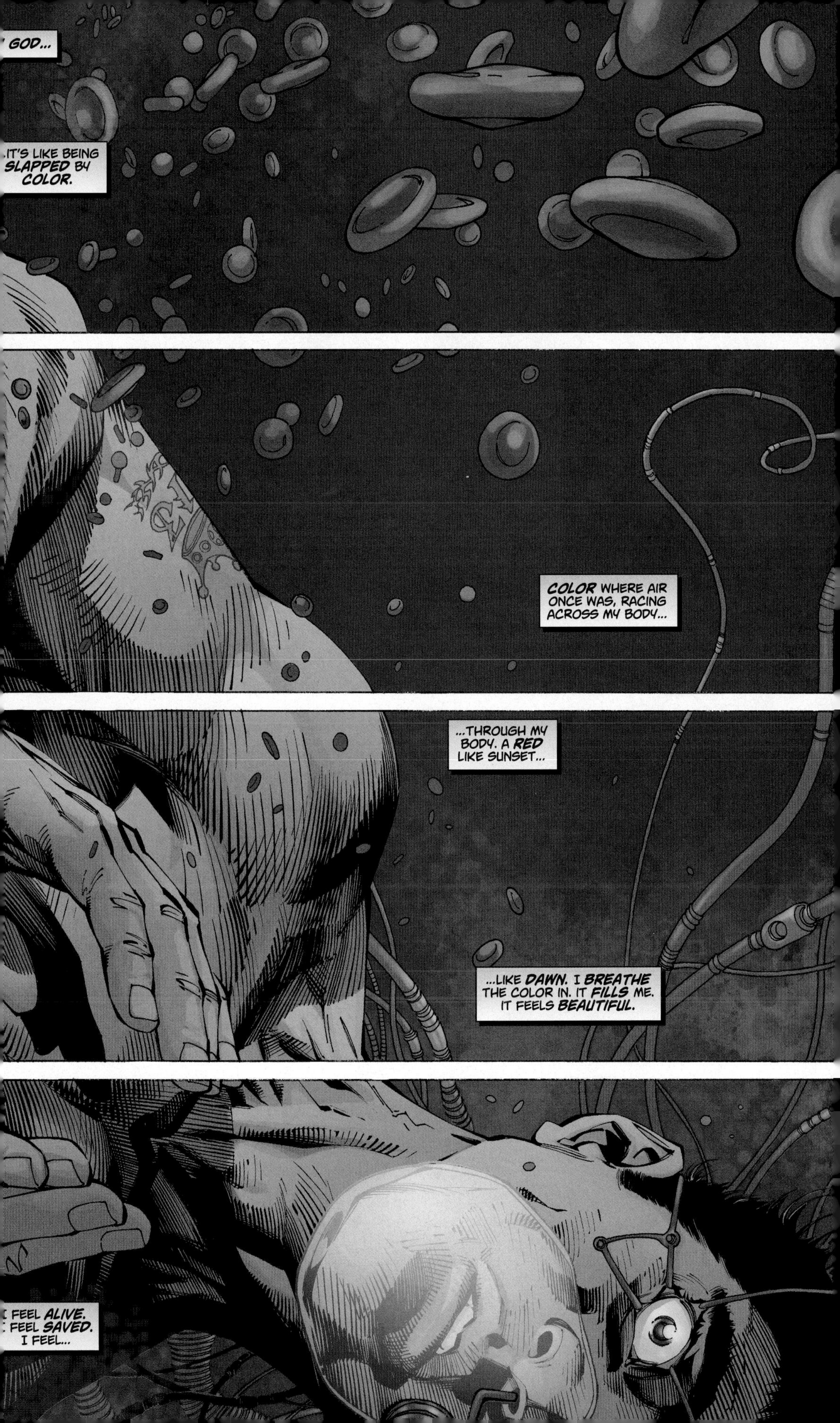

GOD...
IT'S LIKE BEING SLAPPED BY COLOR.
COLOR WHERE AIR ONCE WAS, RACING ACROSS MY BODY...
...THROUGH MY BODY. A RED LIKE SUNSET...
...LIKE DAWN. I BREATHE THE COLOR IN. IT FILLS ME. IT FEELS BEAUTIFUL.
FEEL ALIVE. FEEL SAVED. I FEEL...

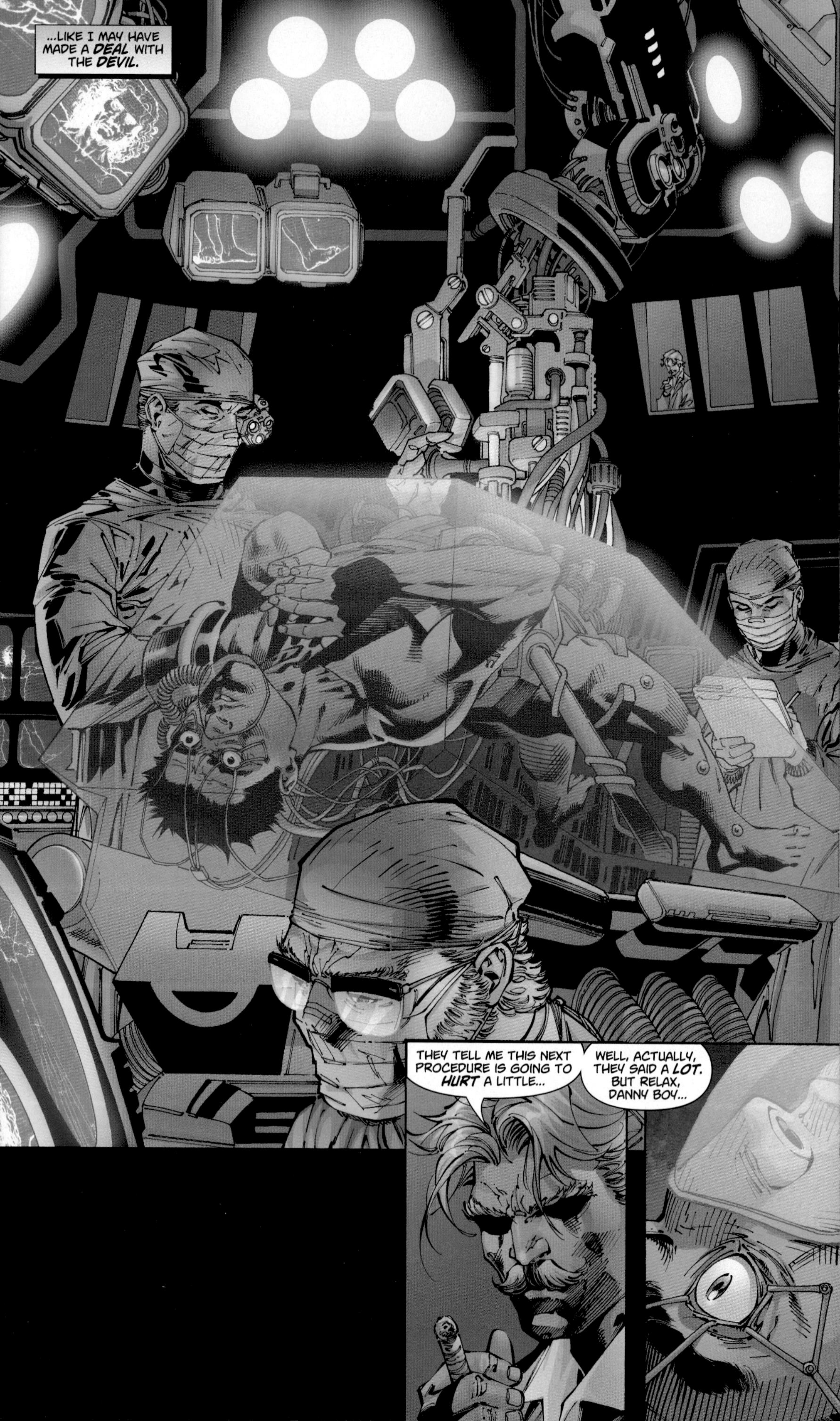
...LIKE I MAY HAVE MADE A DEAL WITH THE DEVIL.
THEY TELL ME THIS NEXT PROCEDURE IS GOING TO HURT A LITTLE...
WELL, ACTUALLY, THEY SAID A LOT. BUT RELAX, DANNY BOY...

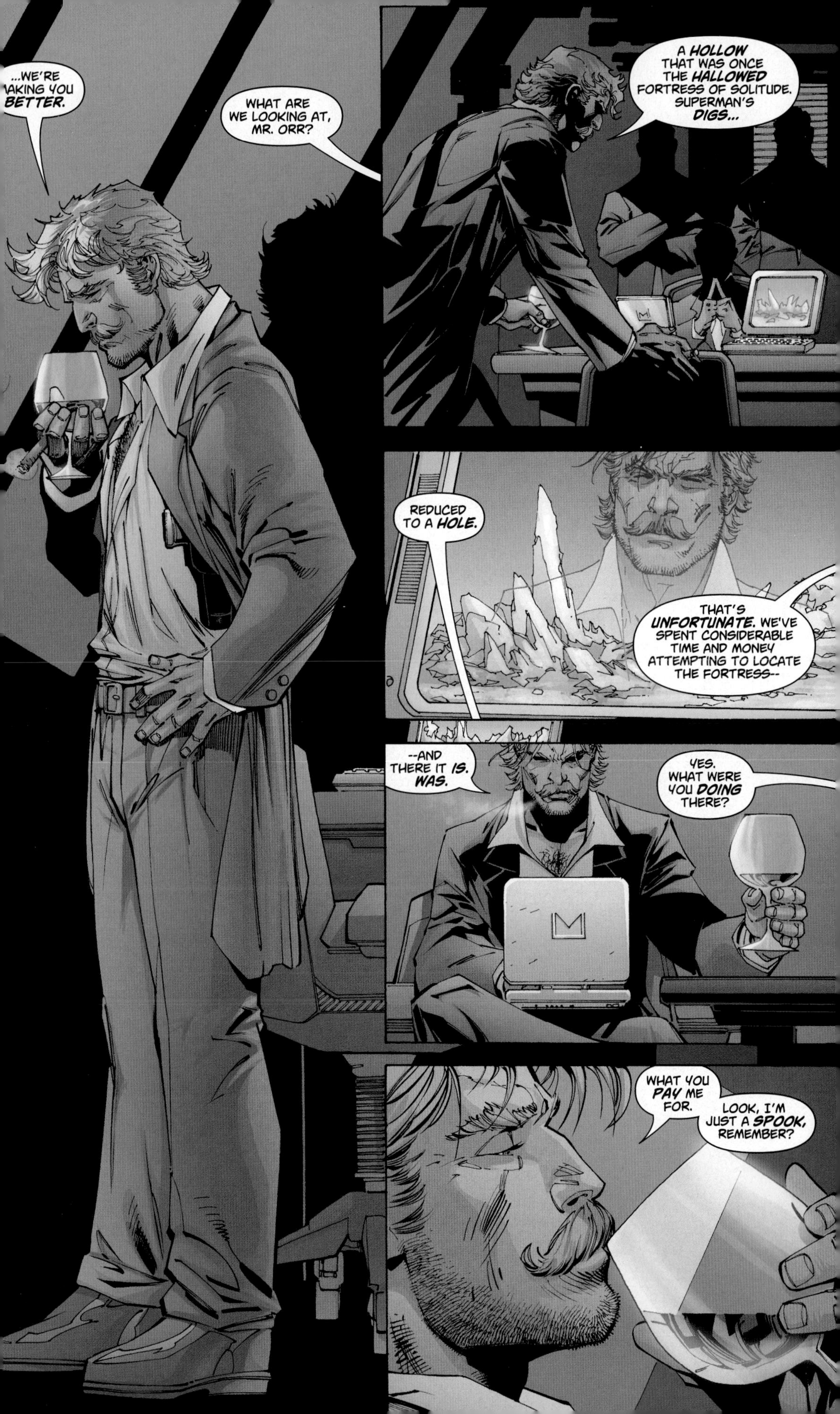

...WE'RE MAKING YOU BETTER.
WHAT ARE WE LOOKING AT, MR. ORR?
A HOLLOW THAT WAS ONCE THE HALLOWED FORTRESS OF SOLITUDE. SUPERMAN'S DIGS...
REDUCED TO A HOLE.
THAT'S UNFORTUNATE. WE'VE SPENT CONSIDERABLE TIME AND MONEY ATTEMPTING TO LOCATE THE FORTRESS--
--AND THERE IT IS. WAS.
YES. WHAT WERE YOU DOING THERE?
WHAT YOU PAY ME FOR.
LOOK, I'M JUST A SPOOK, REMEMBER?

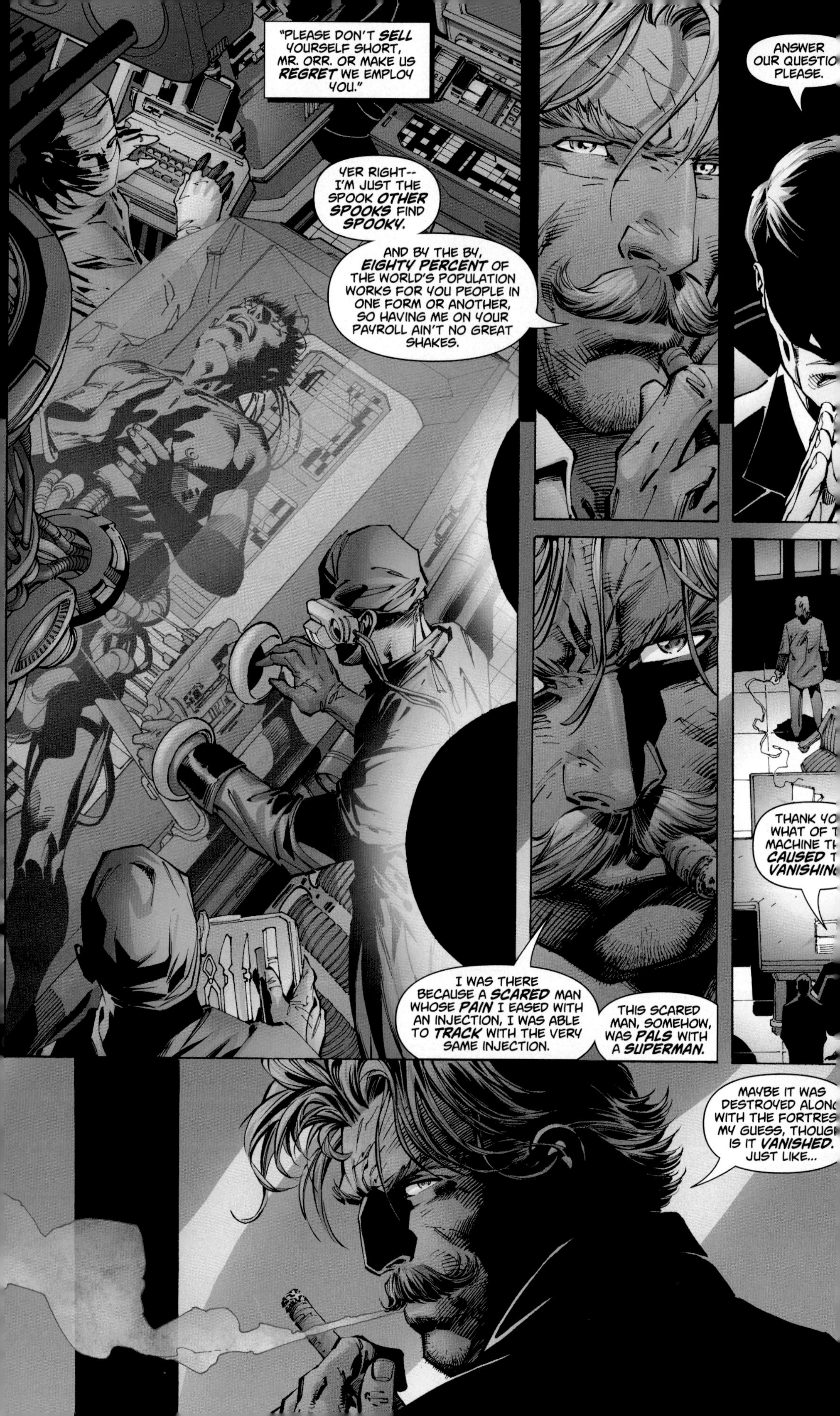
"PLEASE DON'T SELL YOURSELF SHORT, MR. ORR. OR MAKE US REGRET WE EMPLOY YOU."
YER RIGHT-- I'M JUST THE SPOOK OTHER SPOOKS FIND SPOOKY.
AND BY THE BY, EIGHTY PERCENT OF THE WORLD'S POPULATION WORKS FOR YOU PEOPLE IN ONE FORM OR ANOTHER, SO HAVING ME ON YOUR PAYROLL AIN'T NO GREAT SHAKES.
ANSWER OUR QUESTIO PLEASE.
I WAS THERE BECAUSE A SCARED MAN WHOSE PAIN I EASED WITH AN INJECTION, I WAS ABLE TO TRACK WITH THE VERY SAME INJECTION.
THIS SCARED MAN, SOMEHOW, WAS PALS WITH A SUPERMAN.
THANK YO WHAT OF T MACHINE T CAUSED T VANISHIN
MAYBE IT WAS DESTROYED ALON WITH THE FORTRES MY GUESS, THOUG IS IT VANISHED. JUST LIKE...

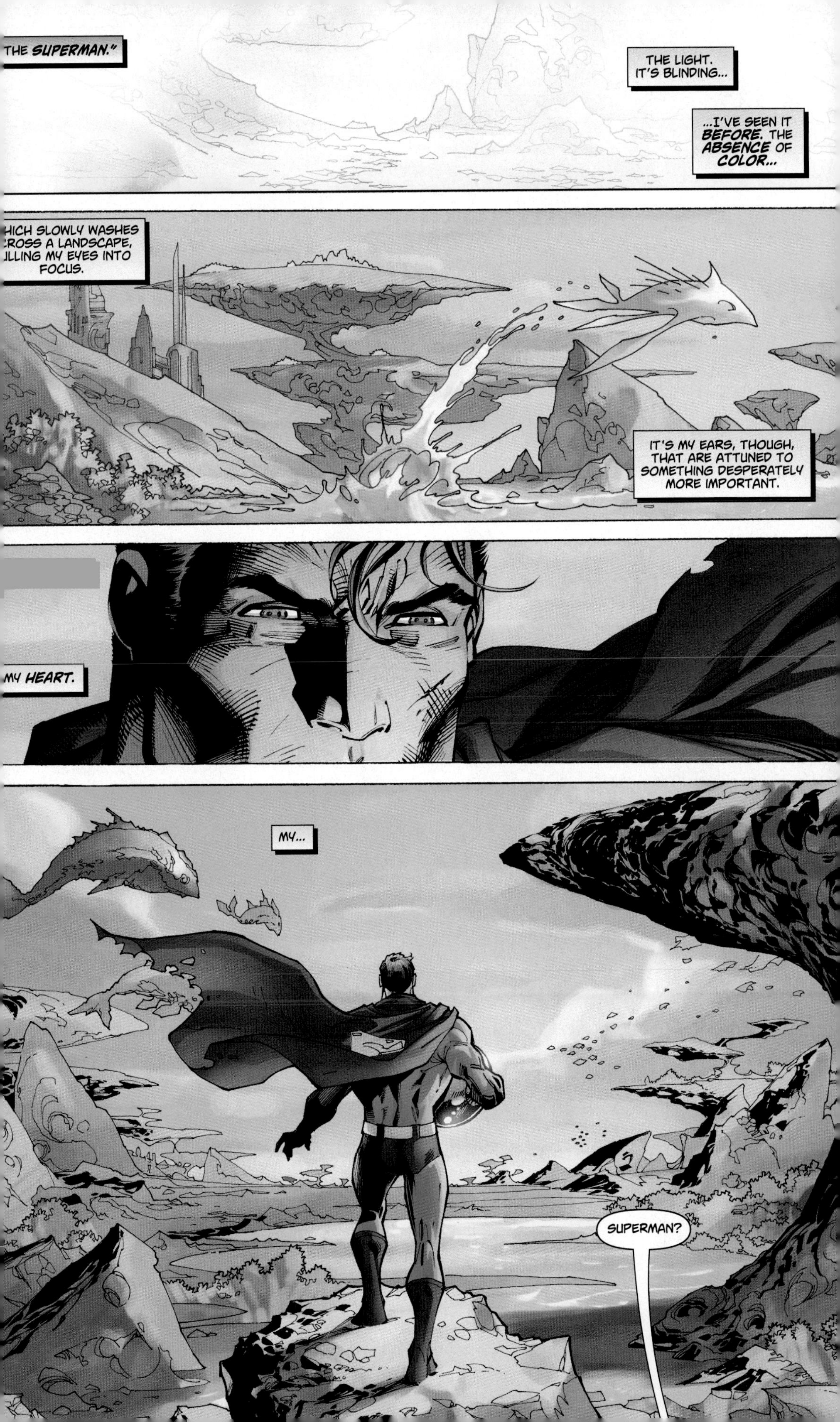
THE SUPERMAN."
THE LIGHT. IT'S BLINDING...
...I'VE SEEN IT BEFORE. THE ABSENCE OF COLOR...
HICH SLOWLY WASHES CROSS A LANDSCAPE, ULLING MY EYES INTO FOCUS.
IT'S MY EARS, THOUGH, THAT ARE ATTUNED TO SOMETHING DESPERATELY MORE IMPORTANT.
MY HEART.
MY...
SUPERMAN?

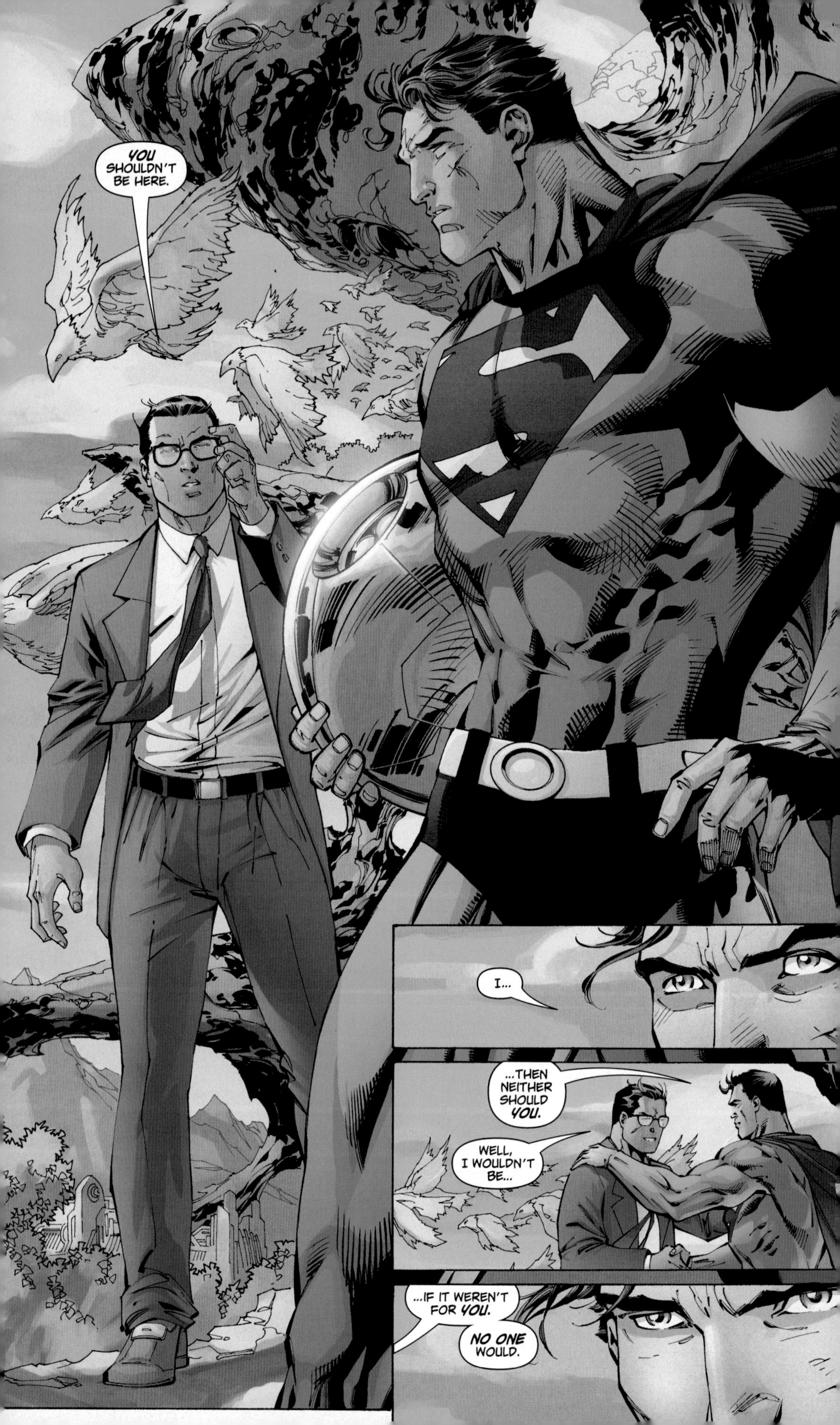
YOU SHOULDN'T BE HERE.
I...
...THEN NEITHER SHOULD YOU.
WELL, I WOULDN'T BE...
...IF IT WEREN'T FOR YOU.
NO ONE WOULD.

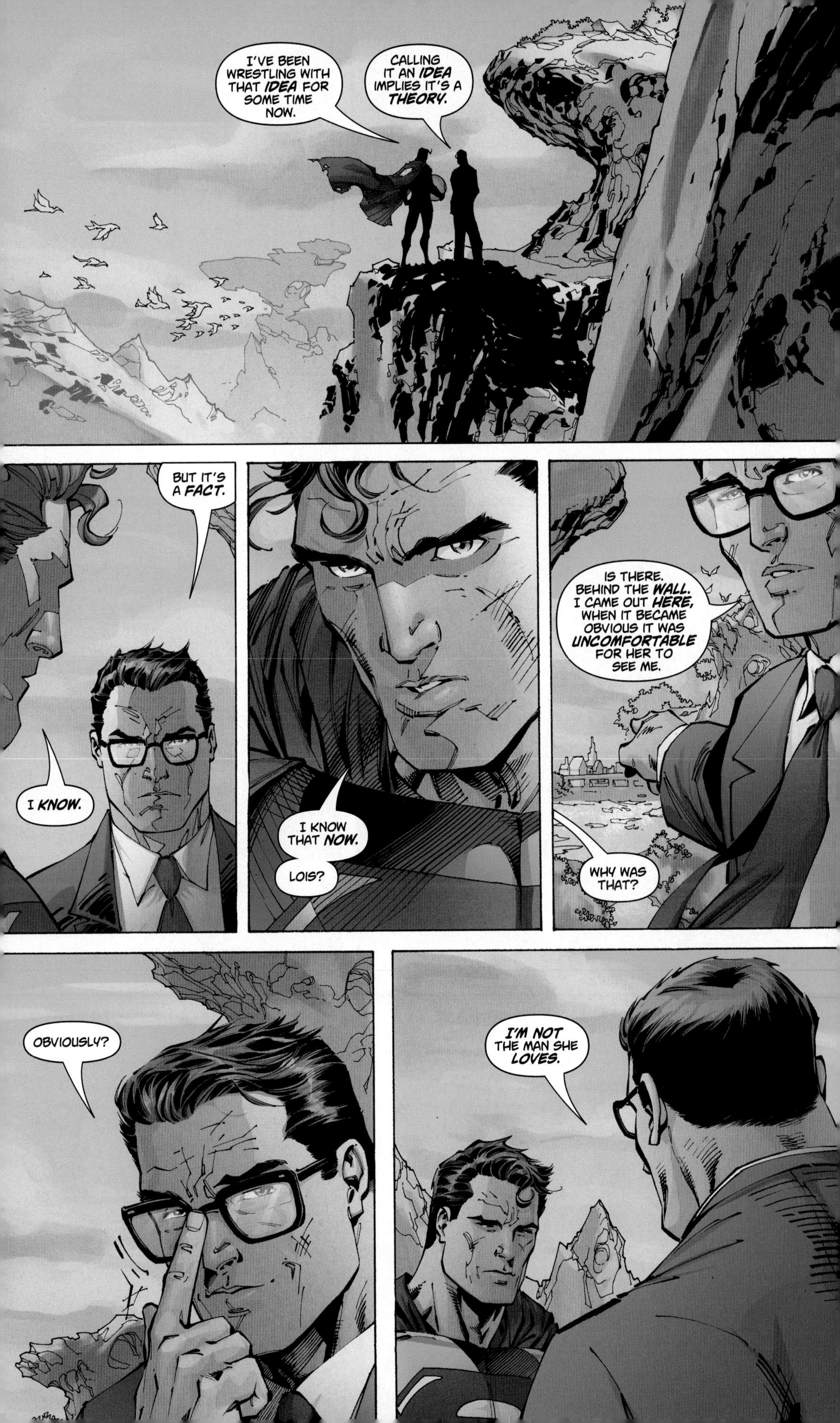
I'VE BEEN WRESTLING WITH THAT *IDEA* FOR SOME TIME NOW.
CALLING IT AN *IDEA* IMPLIES IT'S A *THEORY*.
BUT IT'S A *FACT*.
I *KNOW*.
I KNOW THAT *NOW*.
LOIS?
IS THERE. BEHIND THE *WALL*. I CAME OUT *HERE*, WHEN IT BECAME OBVIOUS IT WAS *UNCOMFORTABLE* FOR HER TO SEE ME.
WHY WAS THAT?
OBVIOUSLY?
I'M NOT THE MAN SHE *LOVES*.

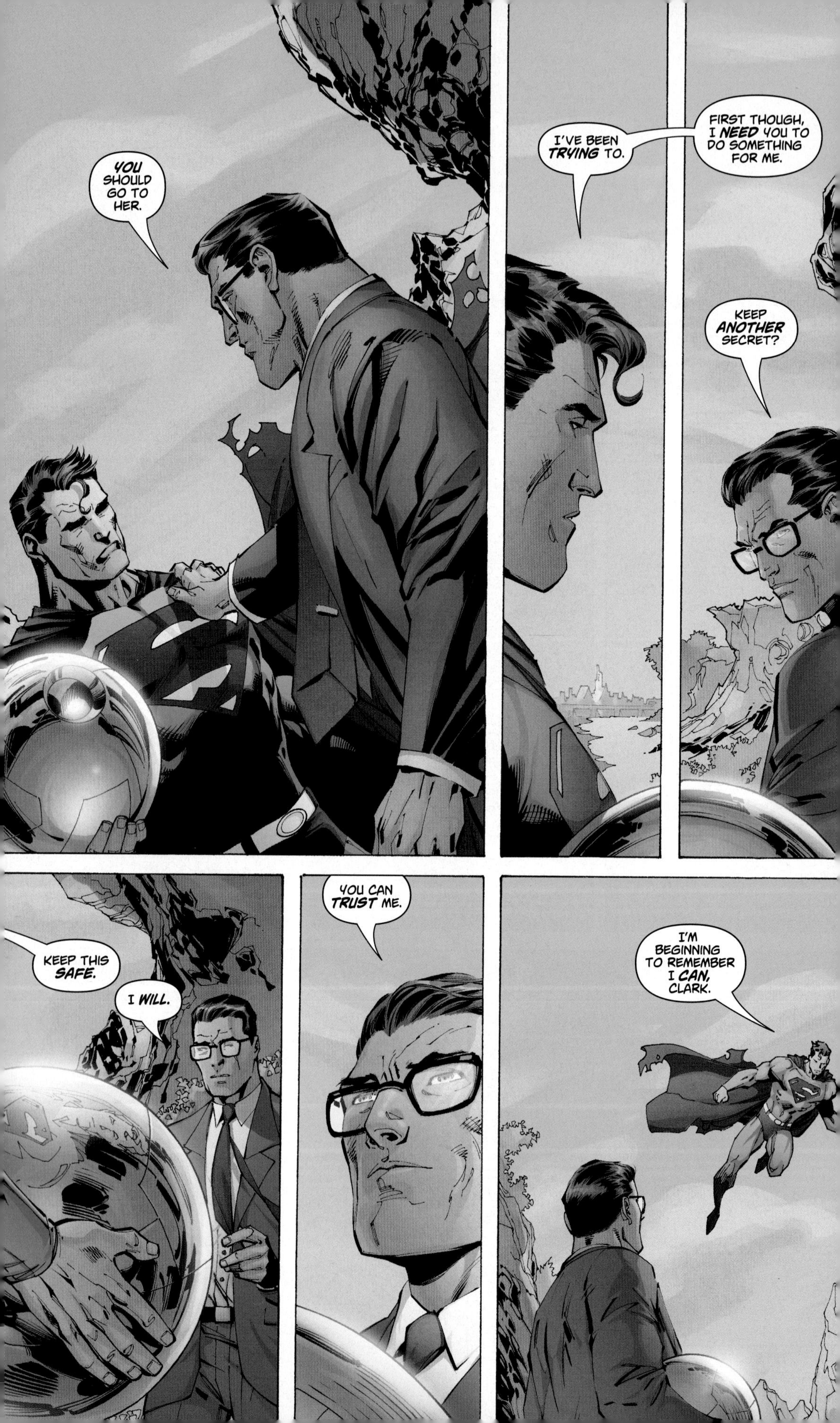
YOU SHOULD GO TO HER.
I'VE BEEN TRYING TO.
FIRST THOUGH, I NEED YOU TO DO SOMETHING FOR ME.
KEEP ANOTHER SECRET?
KEEP THIS SAFE.
I WILL.
YOU CAN TRUST ME.
I'M BEGINNING TO REMEMBER I CAN, CLARK.

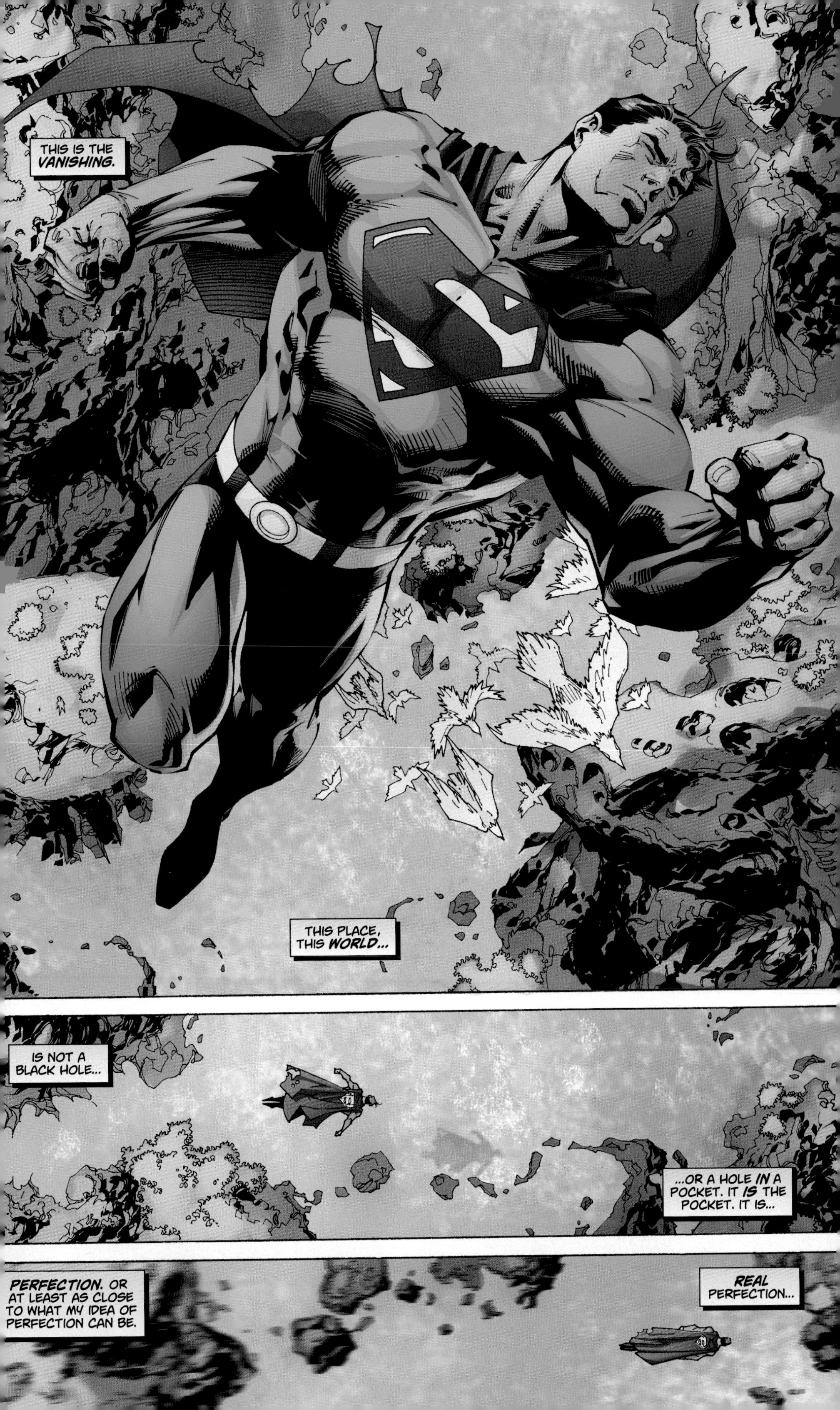
THIS IS THE VANISHING.
THIS PLACE, THIS WORLD...
IS NOT A BLACK HOLE...
...OR A HOLE IN A POCKET. IT IS THE POCKET. IT IS...
PERFECTION. OR AT LEAST AS CLOSE TO WHAT MY IDEA OF PERFECTION CAN BE.
REAL PERFECTION...

...I SPEED *TOWARDS.*

WHAT DO YOU THINK, ALBA? ARE THE FRUITS OF OUR *LABOR* READY TO BE *PICKED?*

JA, LOIS.

THOUGH I SAY, *WE* HAD LITTLE TO DO WITH THIS *HARVEST.* THIS PLACE GIVES US *EVERYTHING* WE NEED.

I *REFUSE* TO *BELIEVE* THAT. SURE, THESE PEACHES WOULD HAVE GROWN WITHOUT US...

...BUT THEY'LL TASTE BETTER BECAUSE WE HAD OUR HANDS IN THE SOIL.

WE MADE *DIFFEREN*

THAT COUNTS F *SOMETHI*

SHE HAS HER *FAULTS,* OF COURSE, BUT THEY ONLY PROVE TO MAKE HER *PERFECT...*

ECAUSE WHEN 'M WITH HER, *FORGET* MY OWN.

I *LOVE* HER.

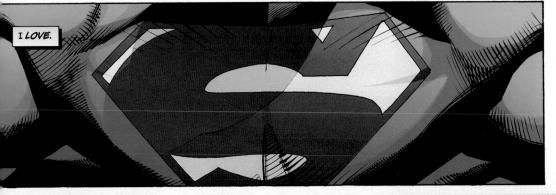

I *LOVE.*

SHE MAKES ME...

HUMAN? NO. I *CAN'T* BE THAT.

BUT SHE DOES MAKE ME...

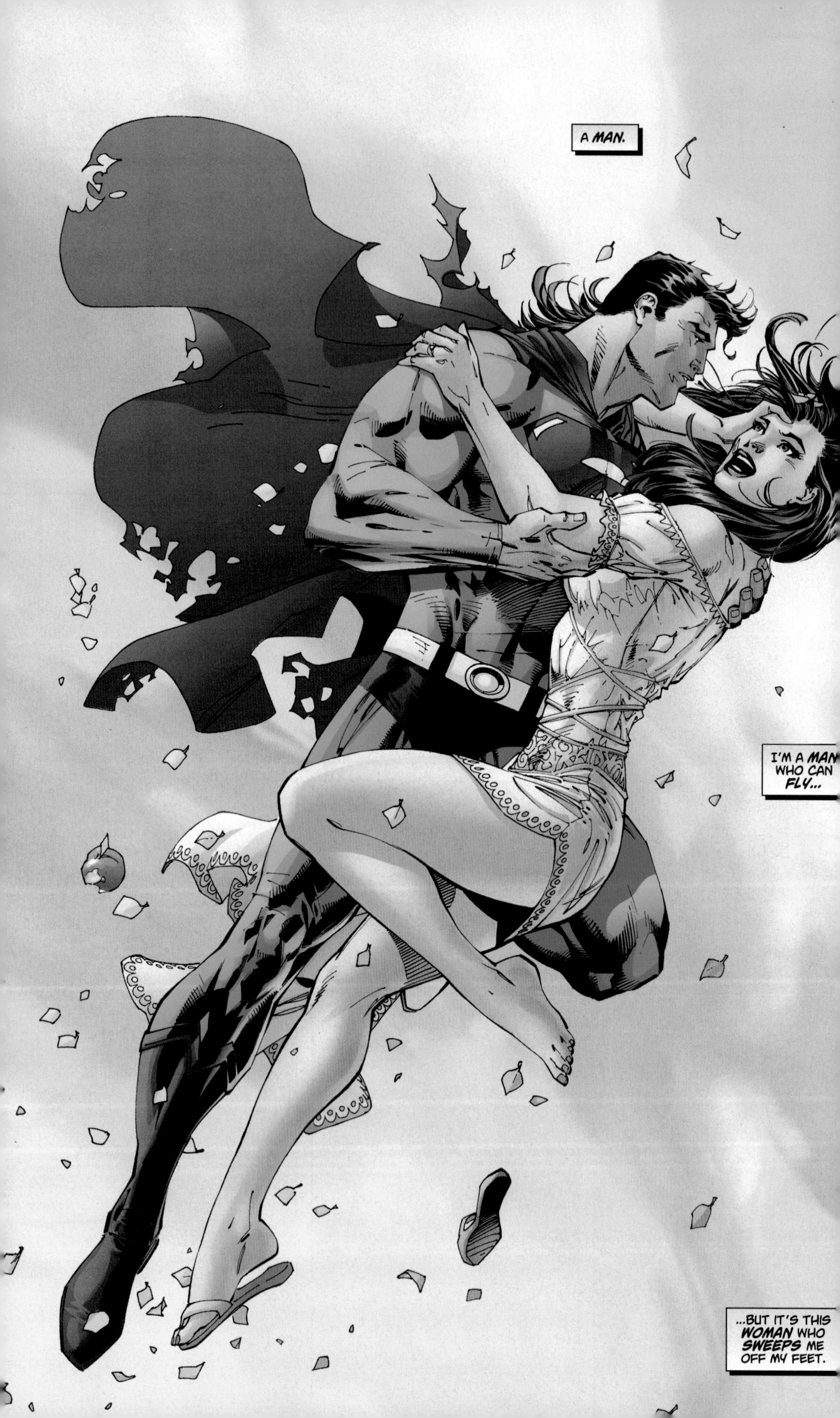
A MAN.
I'M A MAN WHO CAN FLY...
...BUT IT'S THIS WOMAN WHO SWEEPS ME OFF MY FEET.

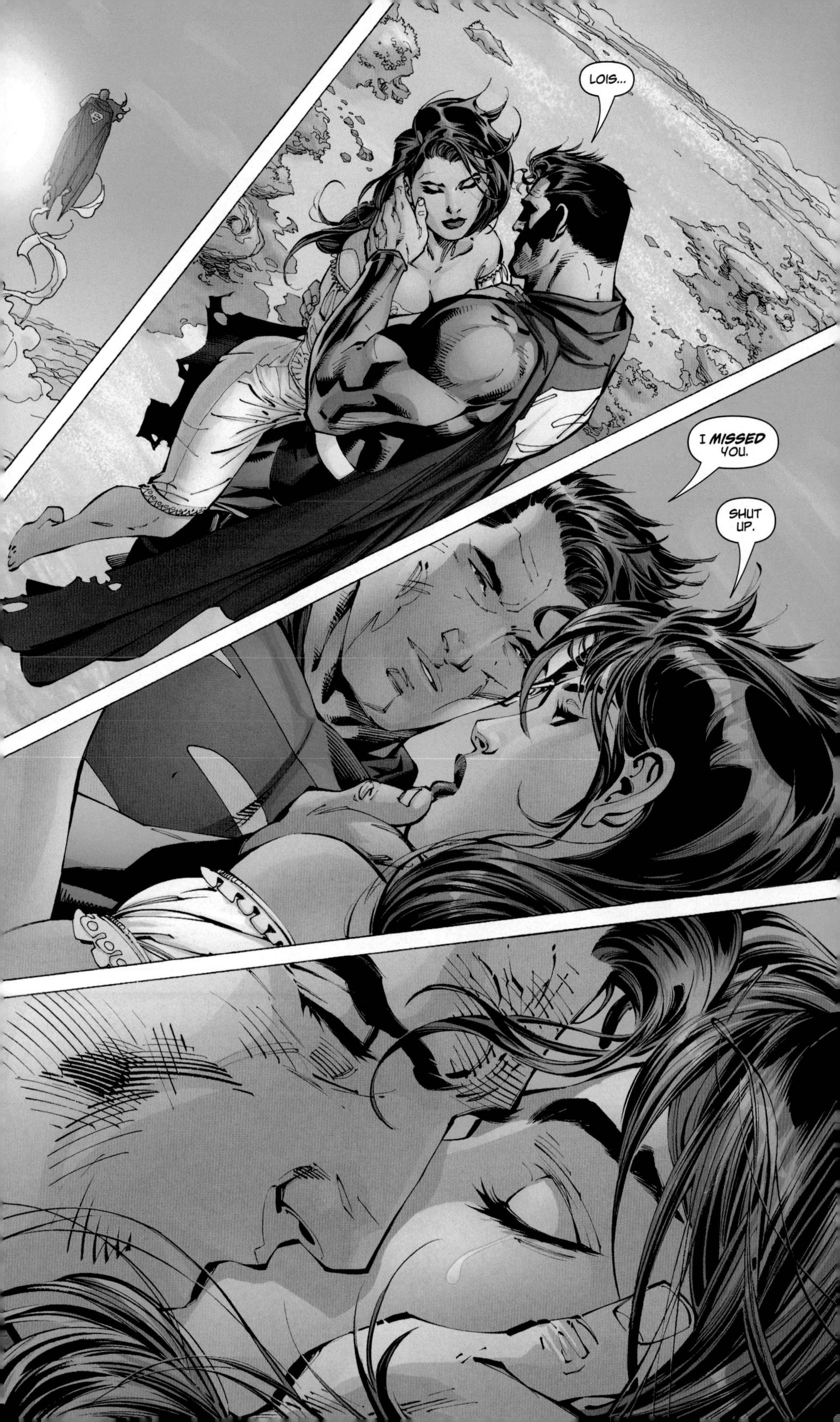
LOIS...
I *MISSED* YOU.
SHUT UP.

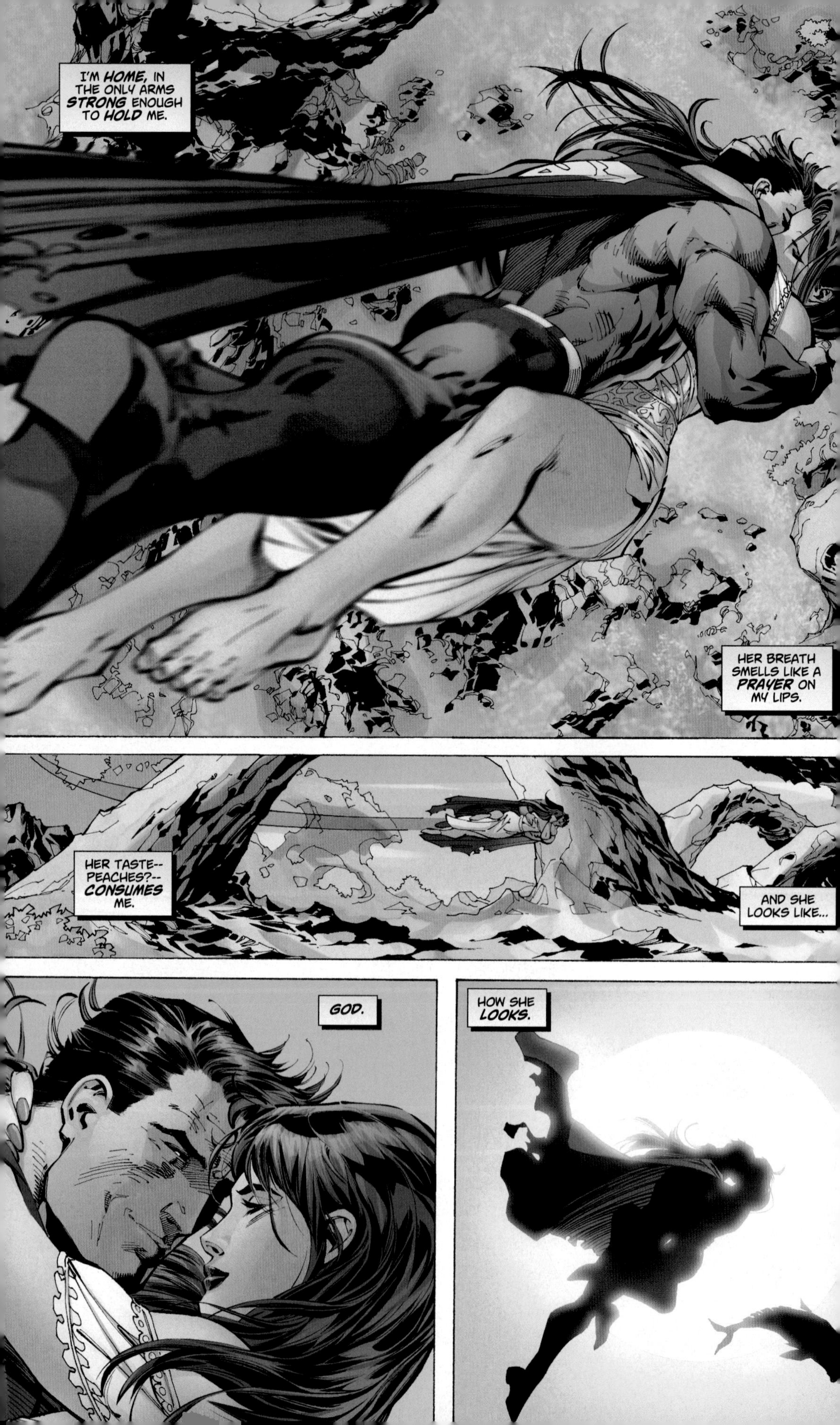
I'M HOME, IN THE ONLY ARMS STRONG ENOUGH TO HOLD ME.
HER BREATH SMELLS LIKE A PRAYER ON MY LIPS.
HER TASTE--PEACHES?--CONSUMES ME.
AND SHE LOOKS LIKE...
GOD.
HOW SHE LOOKS.

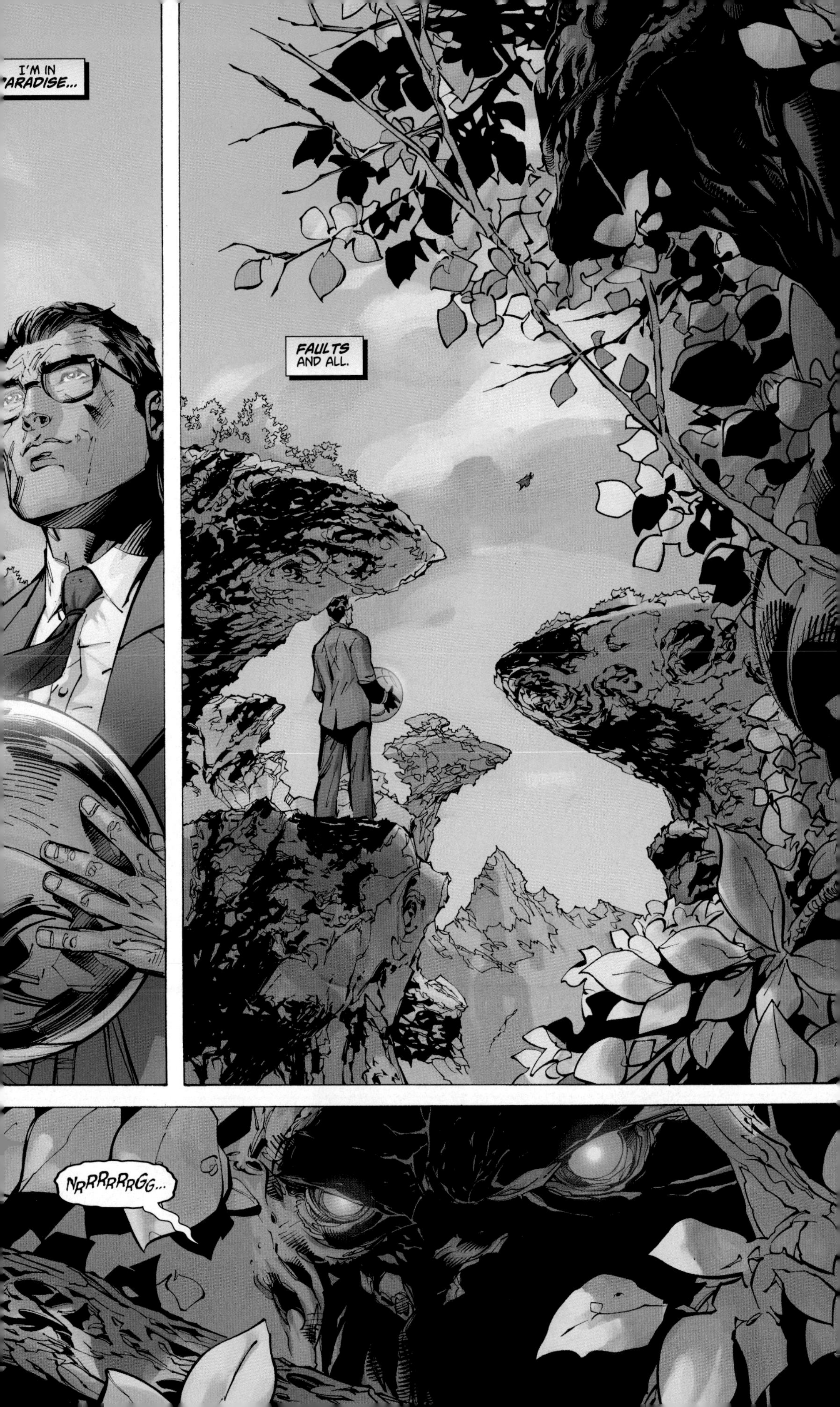
I'M IN
ARADISE...
FAULTS
AND ALL.
NRRRRRRGG...

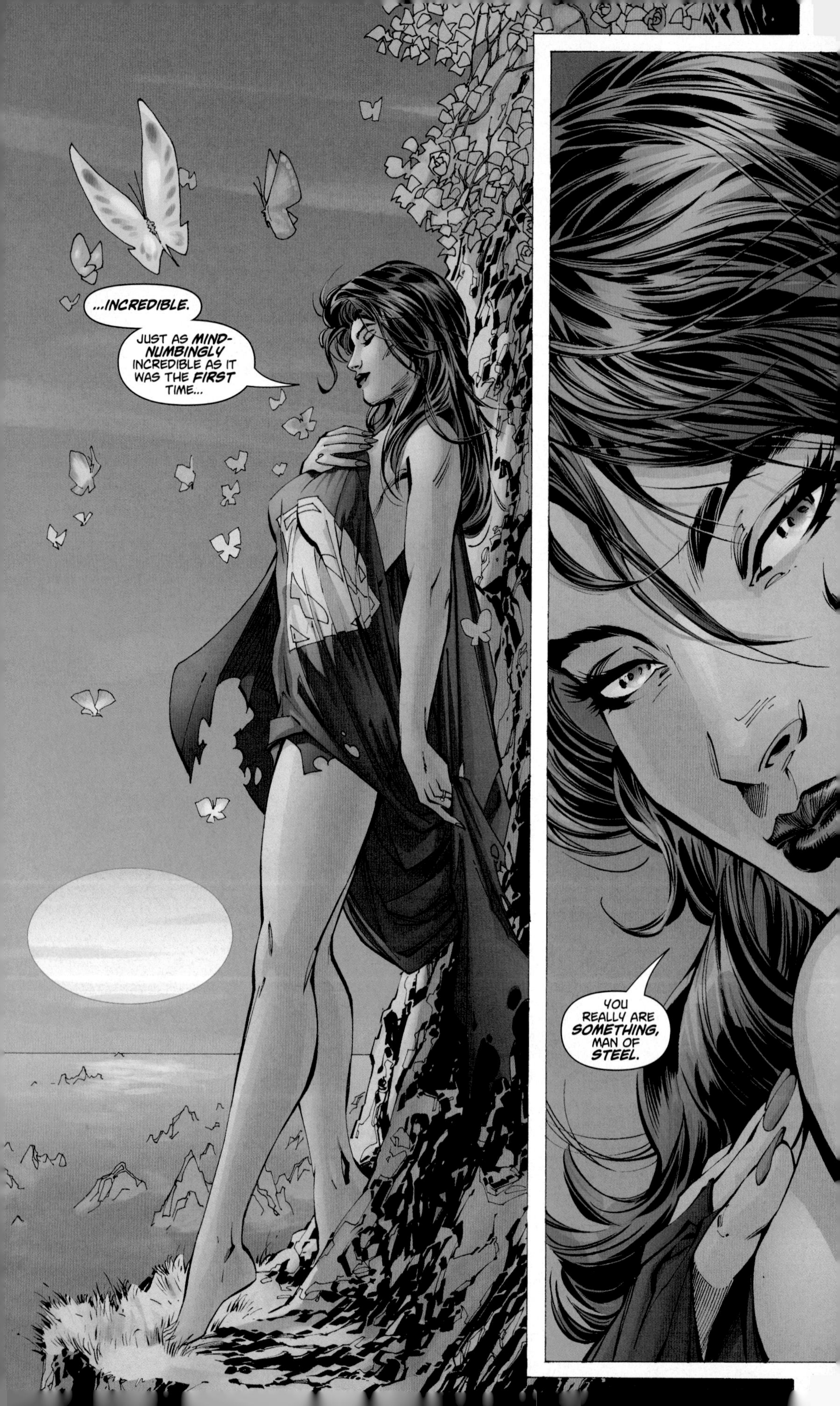
...INCREDIBLE.
JUST AS MIND-NUMBINGLY INCREDIBLE AS IT WAS THE FIRST TIME...
YOU REALLY ARE SOMETHING, MAN OF STEEL.

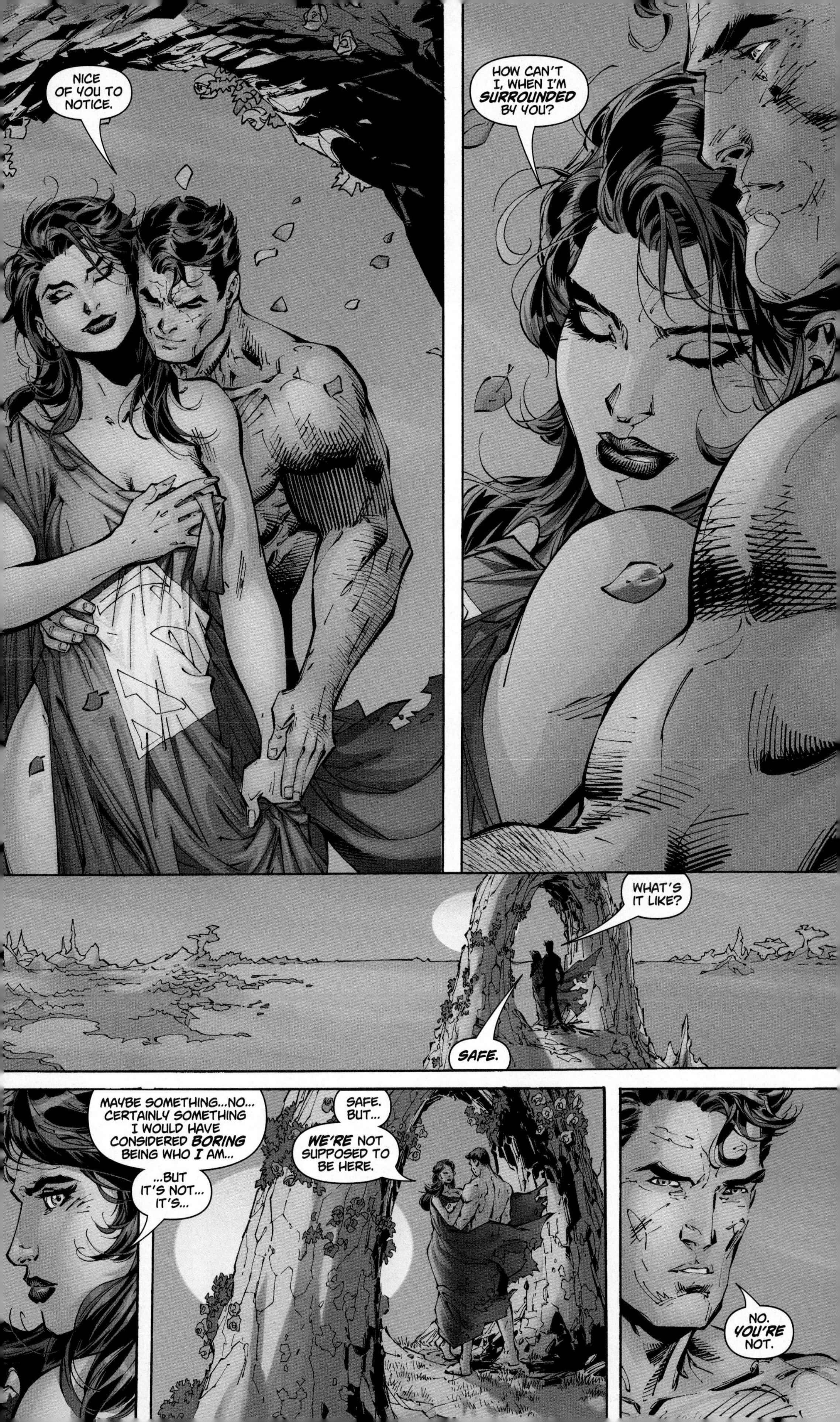
NICE OF YOU TO NOTICE.
HOW CAN'T I, WHEN I'M SURROUNDED BY YOU?
WHAT'S IT LIKE?
SAFE.
MAYBE SOMETHING...NO... CERTAINLY SOMETHING I WOULD HAVE CONSIDERED BORING BEING WHO I AM...
...BUT IT'S NOT... IT'S...
SAFE. BUT...
WE'RE NOT SUPPOSED TO BE HERE.
NO. YOU'RE NOT.

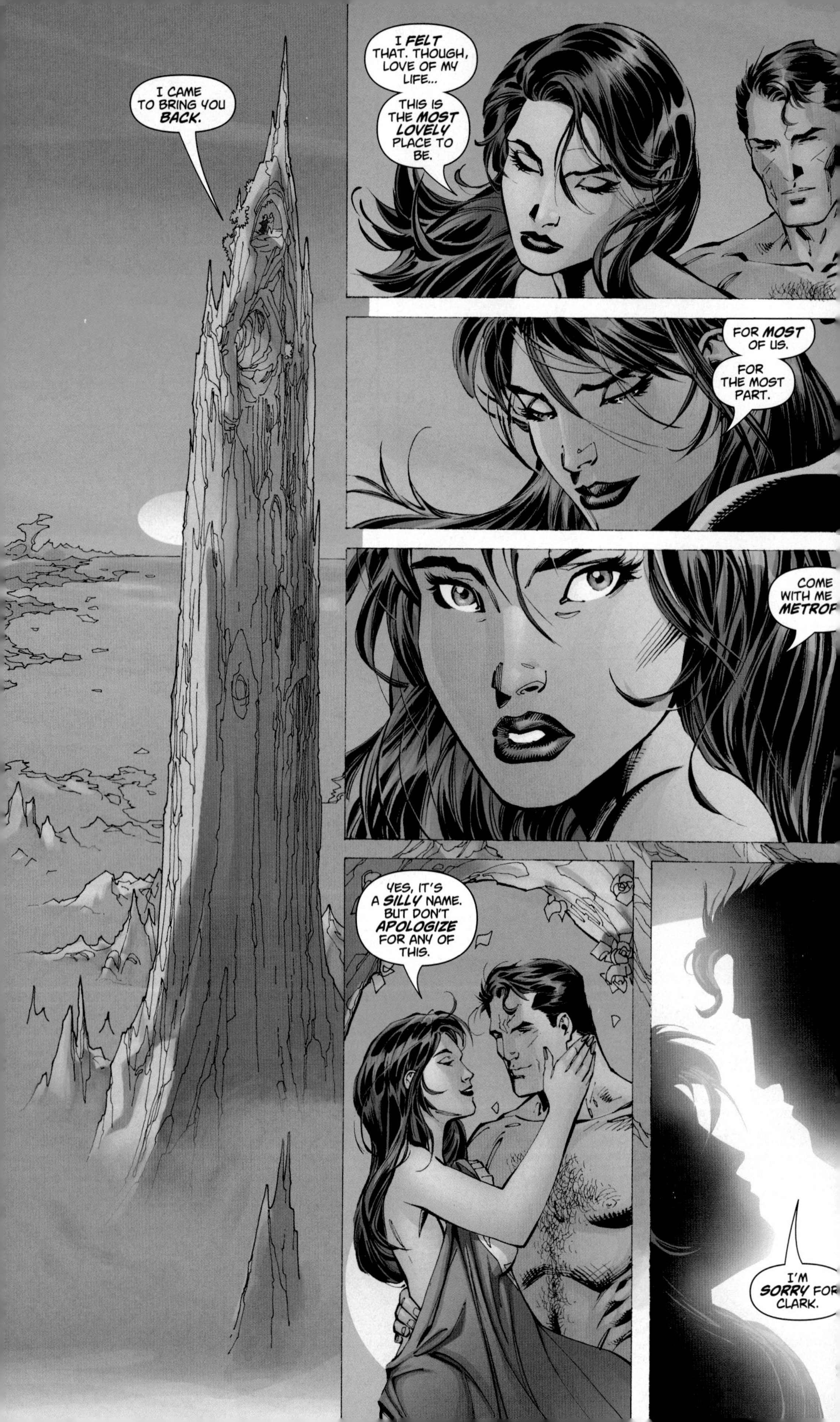
I CAME TO BRING YOU BACK.
I FELT THAT. THOUGH, LOVE OF MY LIFE...
THIS IS THE MOST LOVELY PLACE TO BE.
FOR MOST OF US.
FOR THE MOST PART.
COME WITH ME
YES, IT'S A SILLY NAME. BUT DON'T APOLOGIZE FOR ANY OF THIS.
I'M SORRY
CLARK.

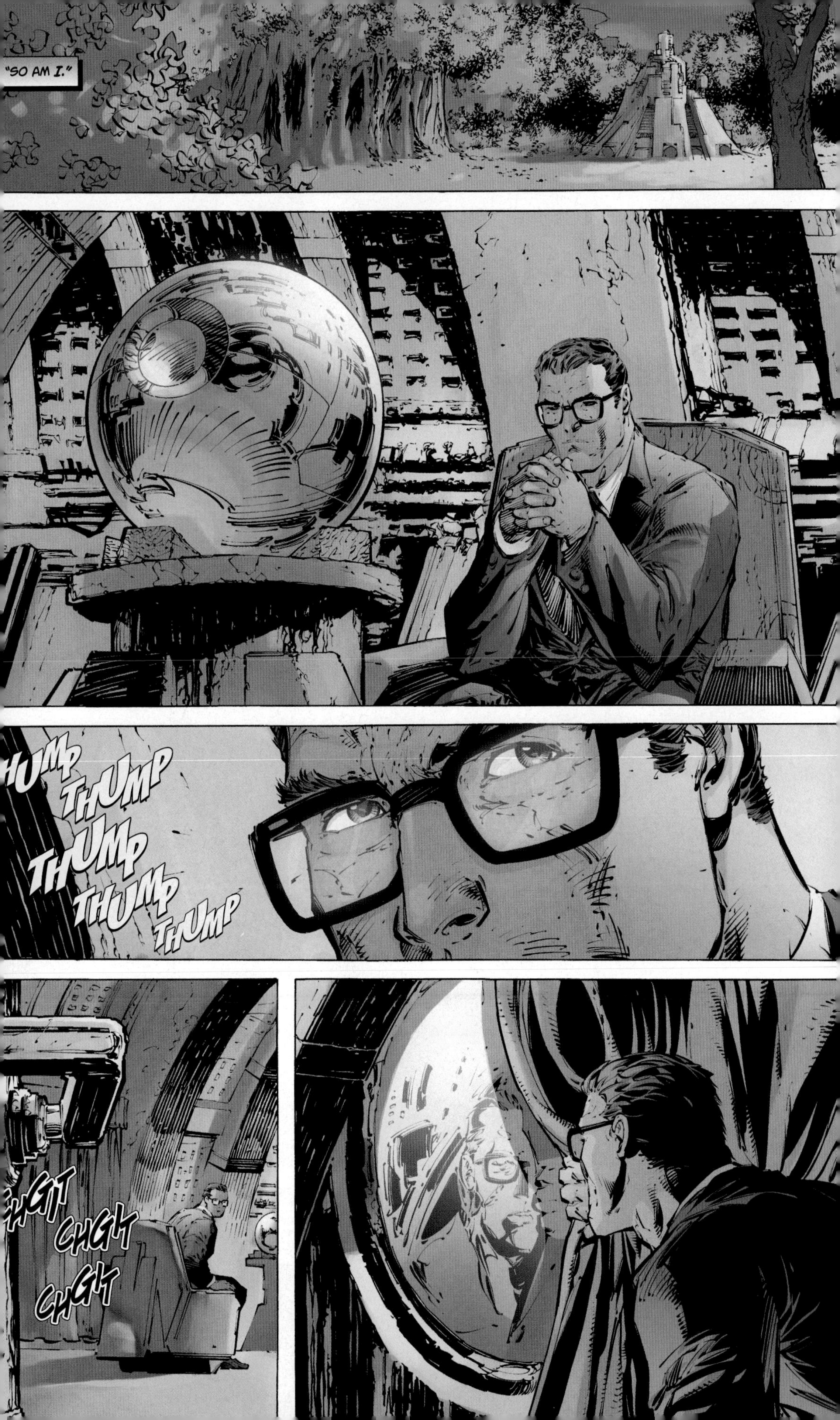
"SO AM I."
THUMP THUMP
THUMP
THUMP
THUMP
THUMP
CHGIT
CHGIT
CHGIT

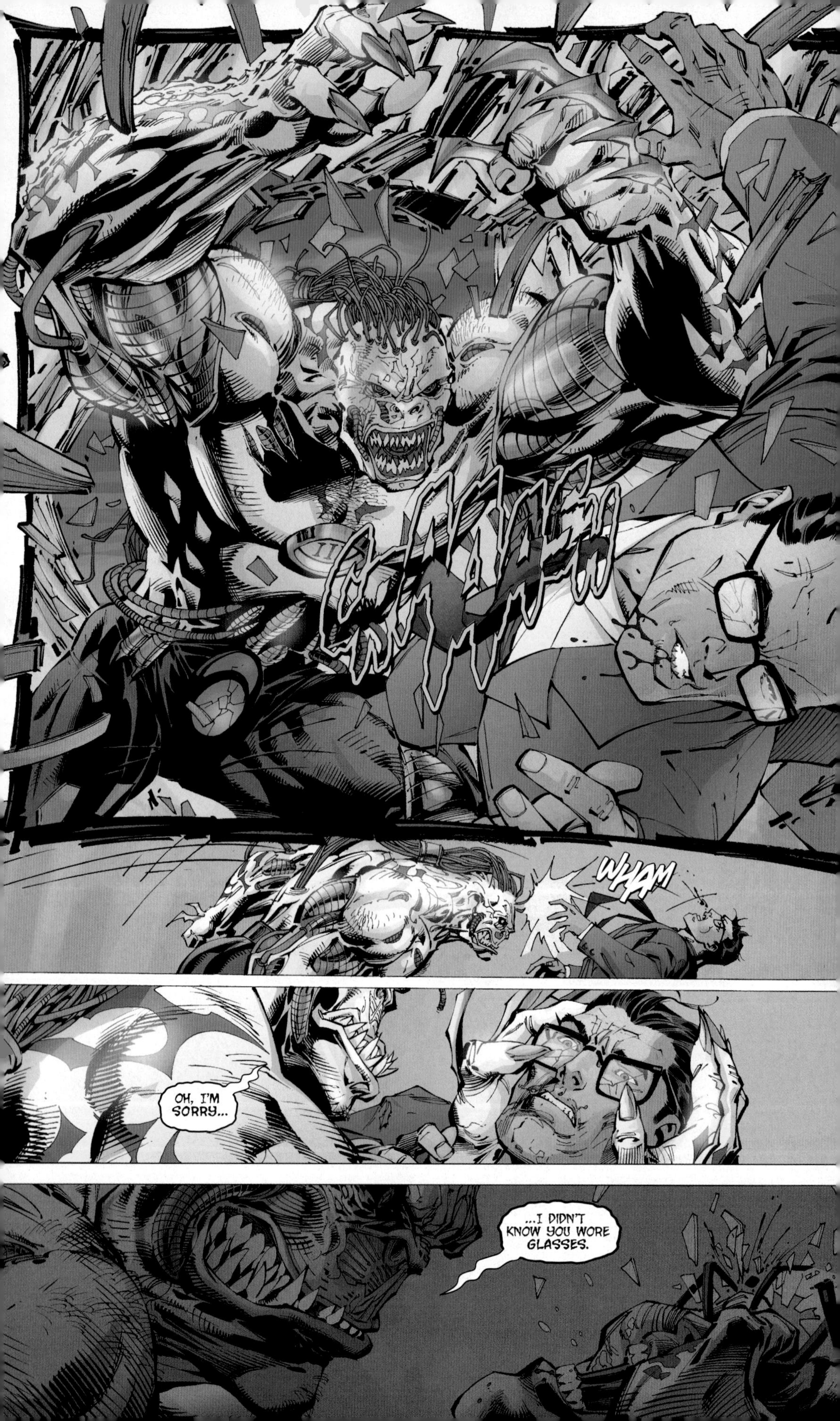
WHAM
OH, I'M SORRY...
...I DIDN'T KNOW YOU WORE GLASSES.

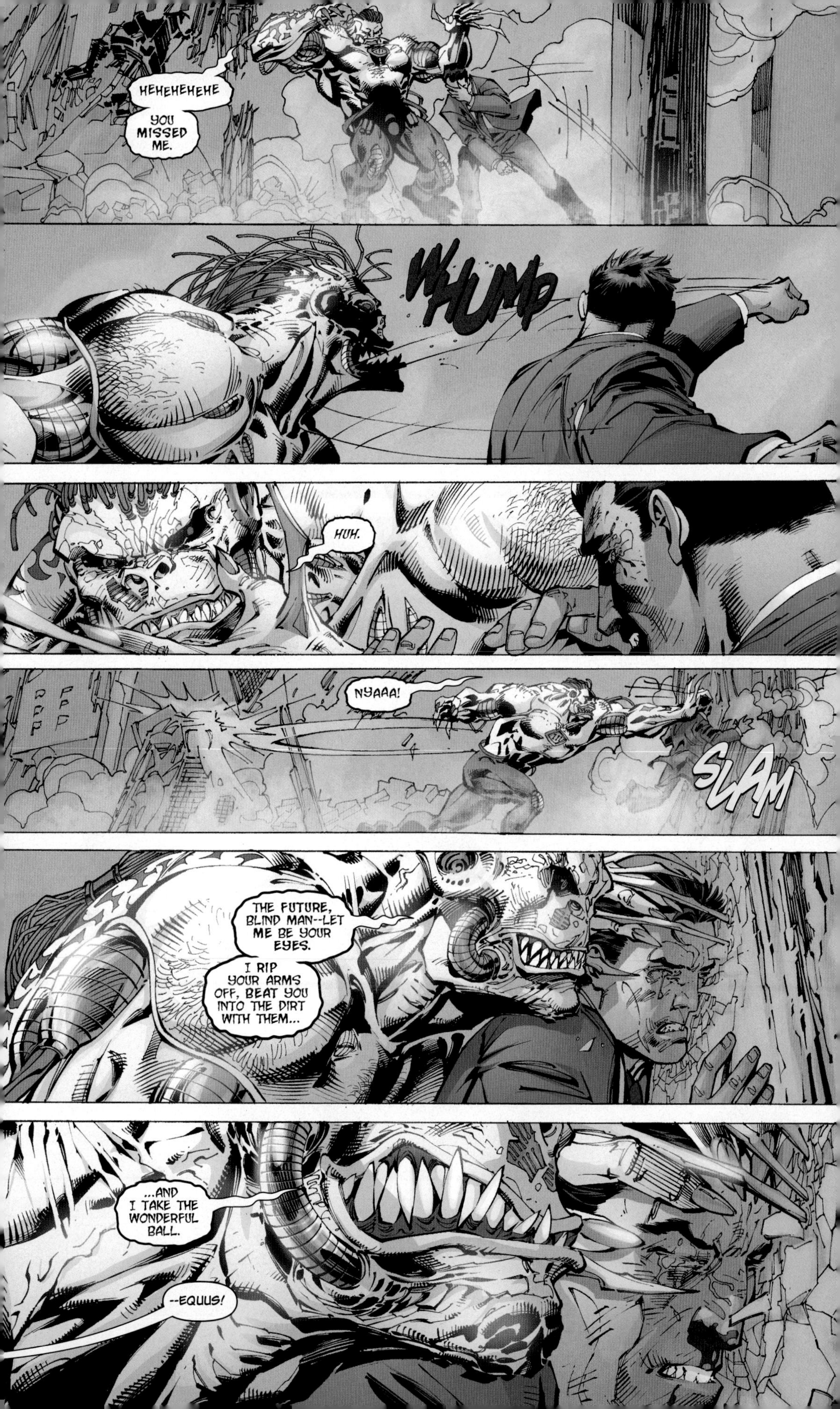
HEHEHEHEHE
YOU MISSED ME.
WHUMP
HUH.
NYAAA!
SLAM
THE FUTURE, BLIND MAN--LET ME BE YOUR EYES.
I RIP YOUR ARMS OFF, BEAT YOU INTO THE DIRT WITH THEM...
...AND I TAKE THE WONDERFUL BALL.
--EQUUS!

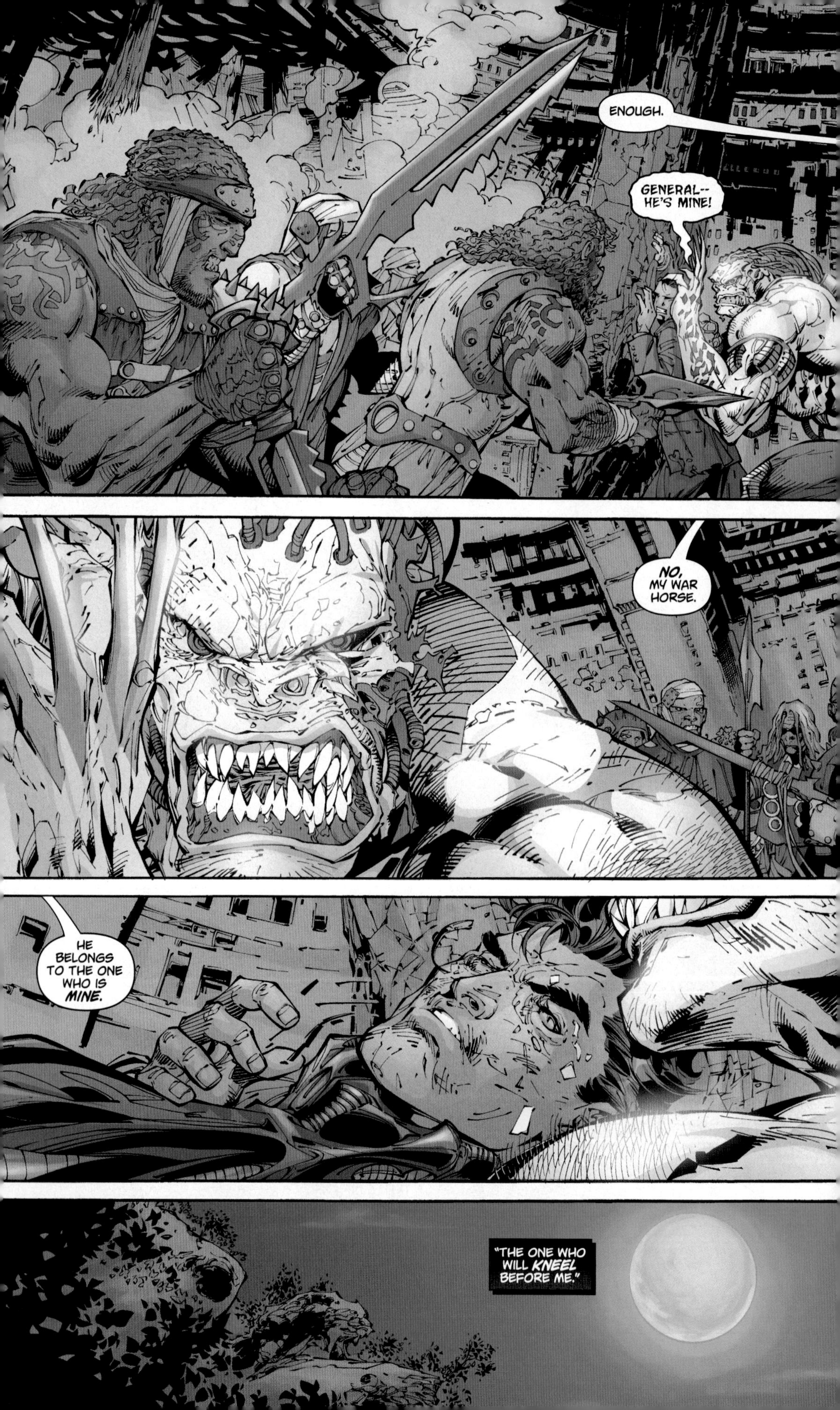
ENOUGH.
GENERAL-- HE'S MINE!
NO, MY WAR HORSE.
HE BELONGS TO THE ONE WHO IS MINE.
"THE ONE WHO WILL KNEEL BEFORE ME."

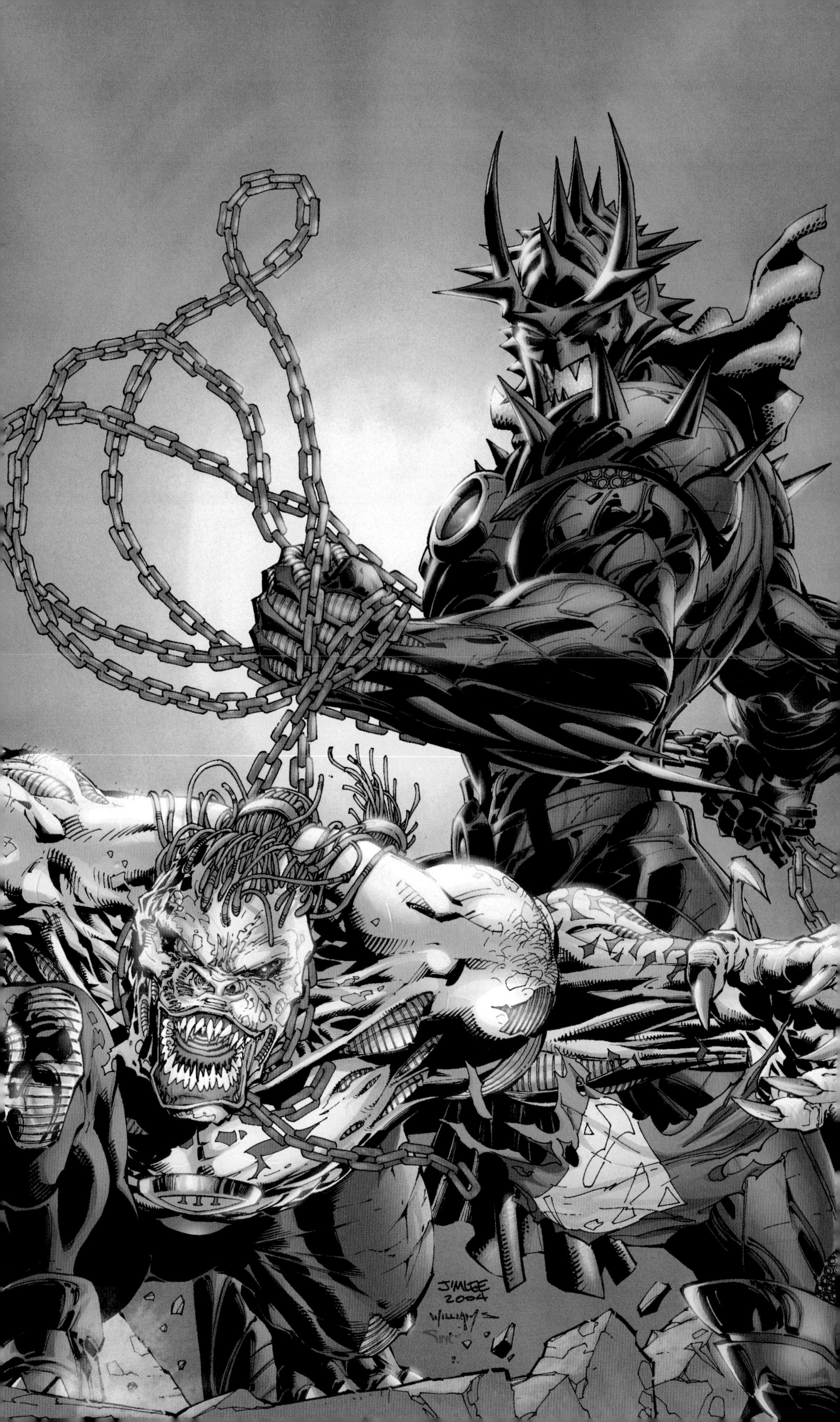
JIMLEE
2004
WILLIAMS

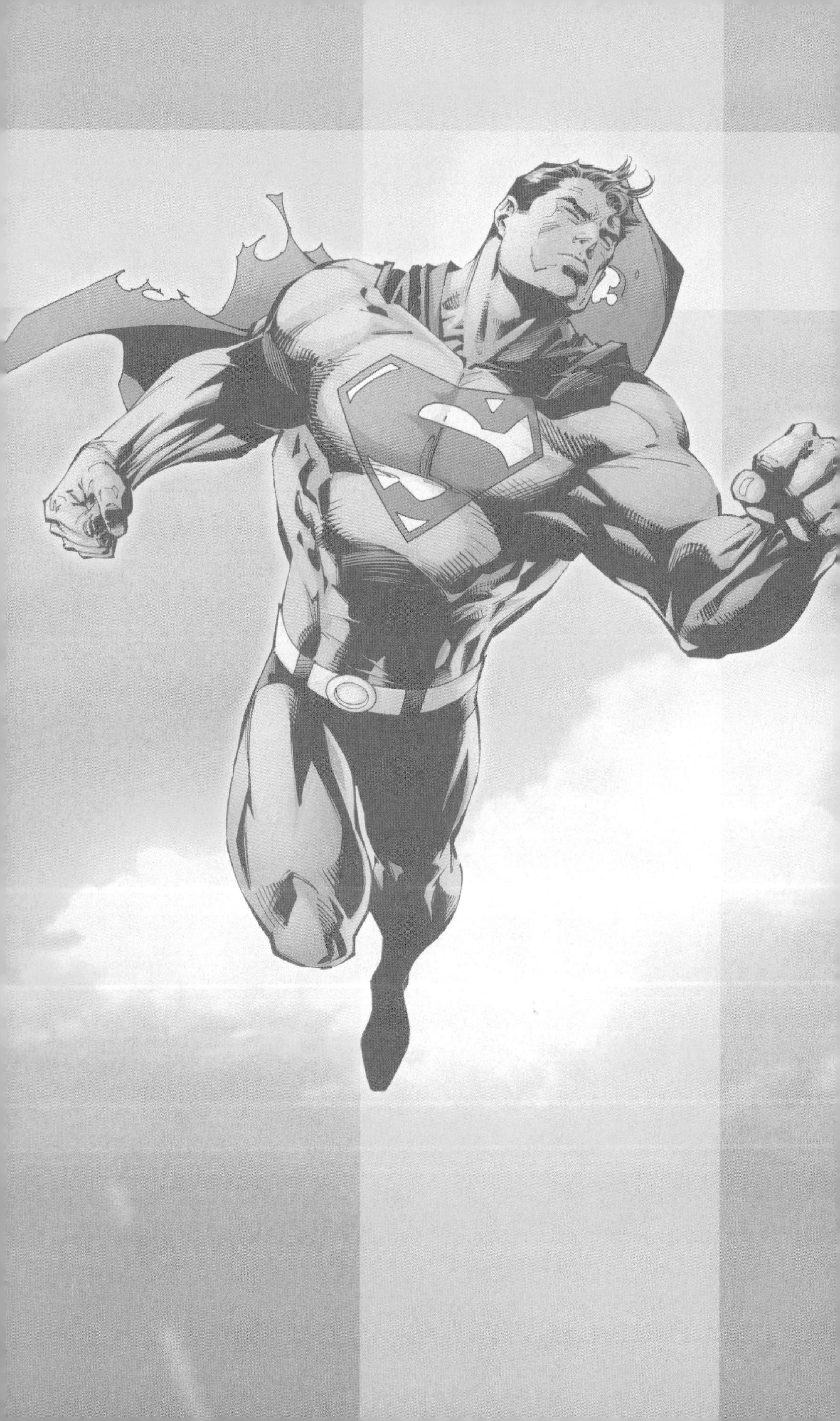

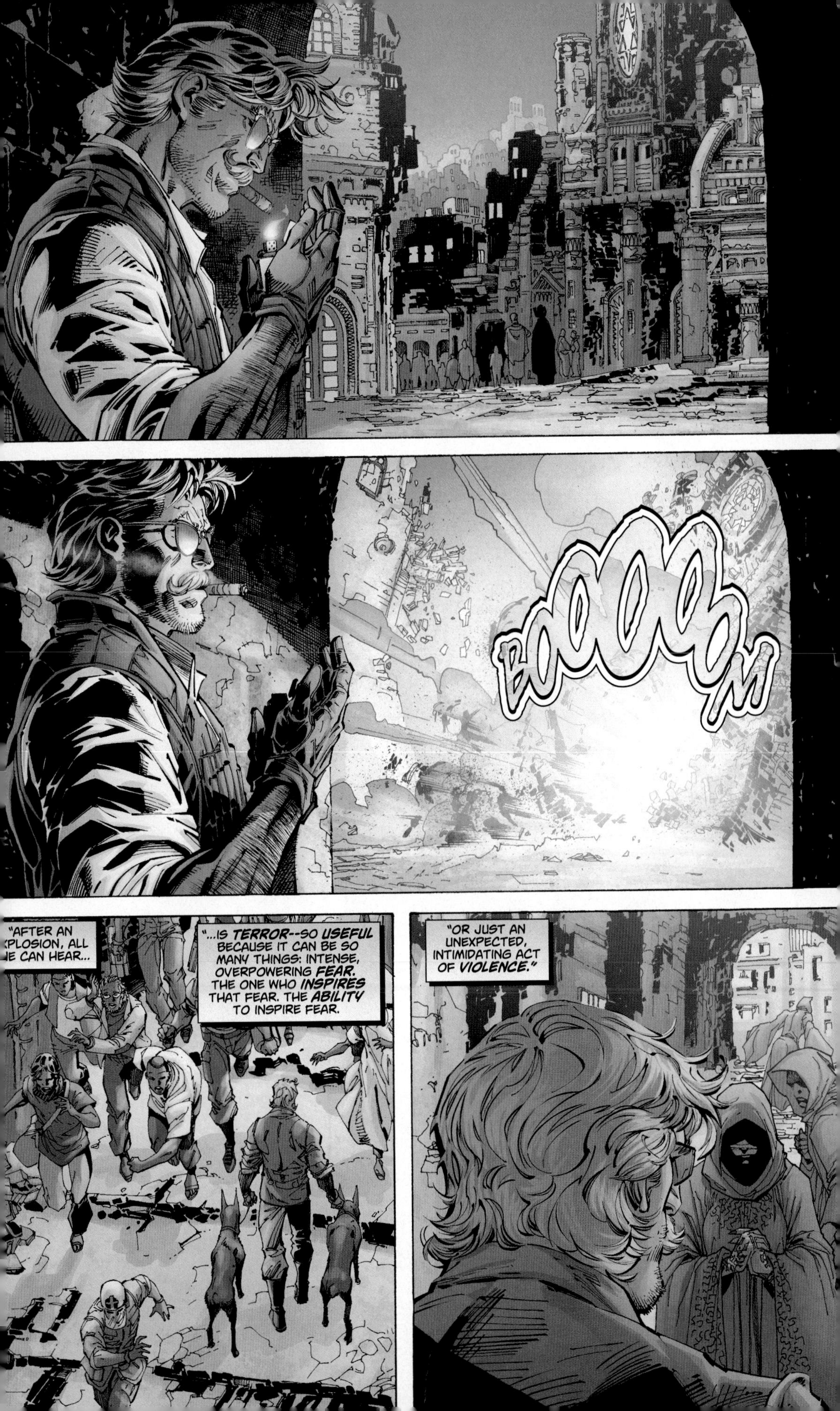
BOOOOM
"AFTER AN
XPLOSION, ALL
E CAN HEAR...
"...IS TERROR--SO USEFUL BECAUSE IT CAN BE SO MANY THINGS: INTENSE, OVERPOWERING FEAR. THE ONE WHO INSPIRES THAT FEAR. THE ABILITY TO INSPIRE FEAR.
"OR JUST AN UNEXPECTED, INTIMIDATING ACT OF VIOLENCE."

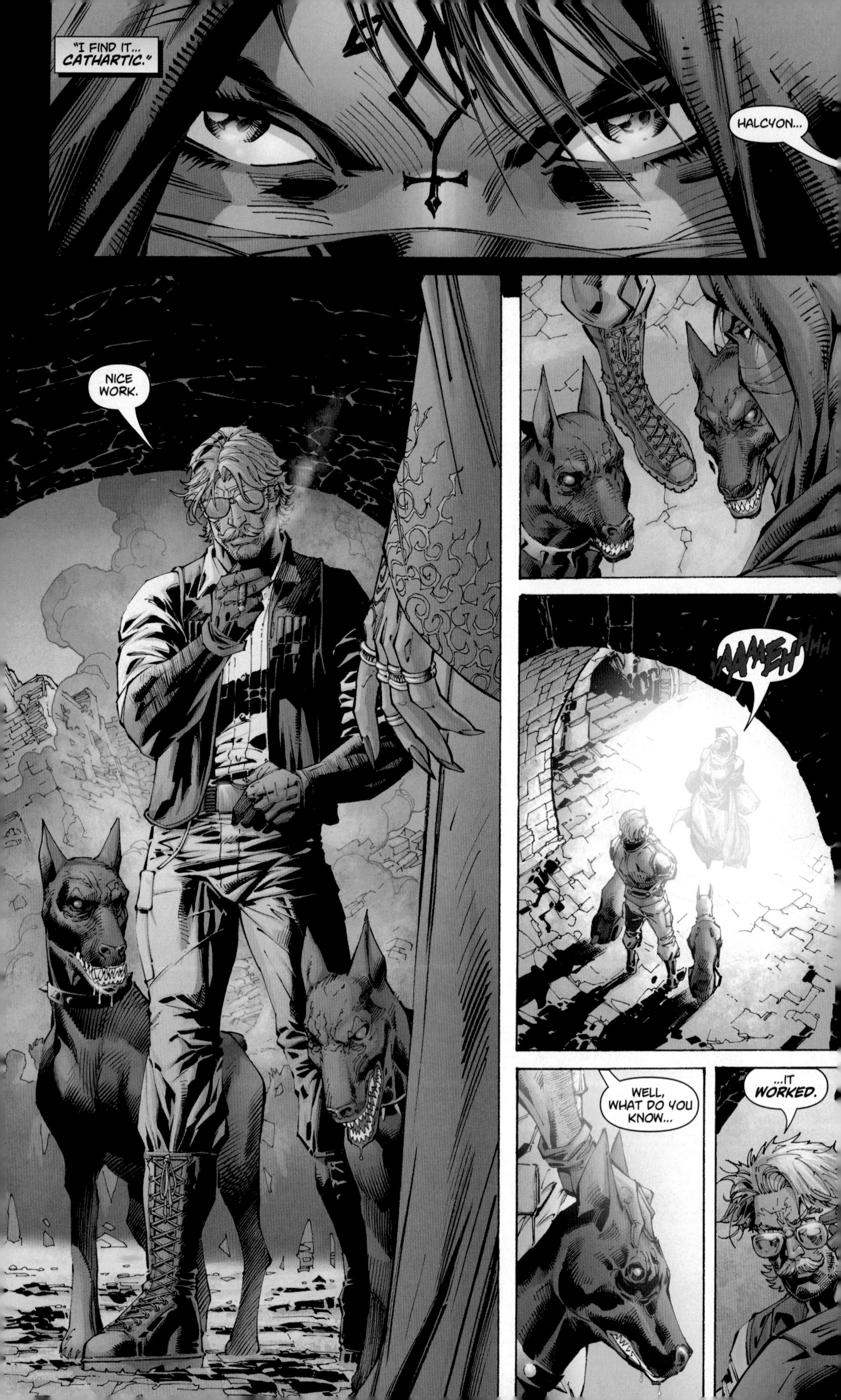
"I FIND IT... CATHARTIC."
HALCYON...
NICE WORK.
YAAAAEHHHH
WELL, WHAT DO YOU KNOW...
...IT WORKED.

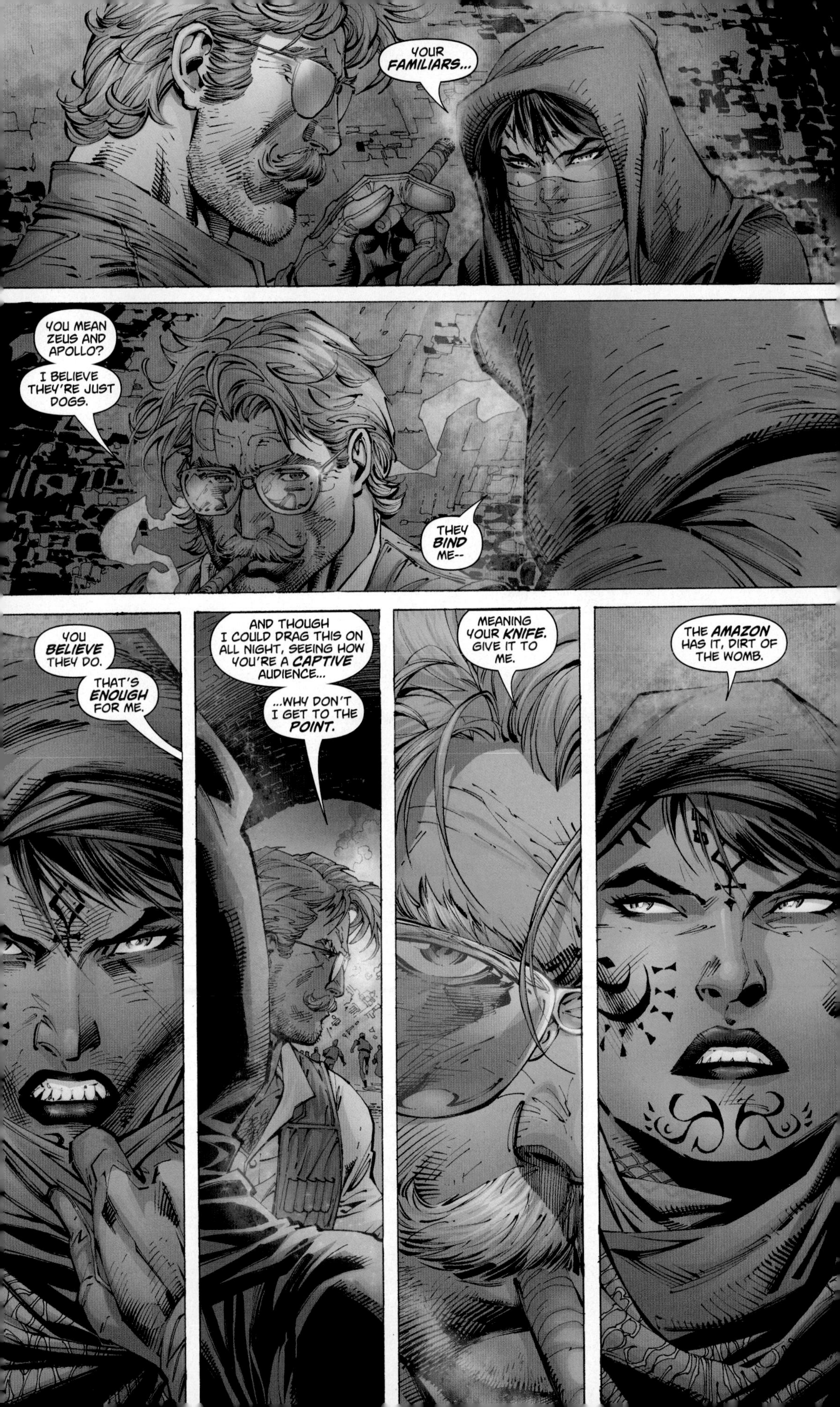

YOUR FAMILIARS...
YOU MEAN ZEUS AND APOLLO?
I BELIEVE THEY'RE JUST DOGS.
THEY BIND ME--
YOU BELIEVE THEY DO.
THAT'S ENOUGH FOR ME.
AND THOUGH I COULD DRAG THIS ON ALL NIGHT, SEEING HOW YOU'RE A CAPTIVE AUDIENCE...
...WHY DON'T I GET TO THE POINT.
MEANING YOUR KNIFE. GIVE IT TO ME.
THE AMAZON HAS IT, DIRT OF THE WOMB.

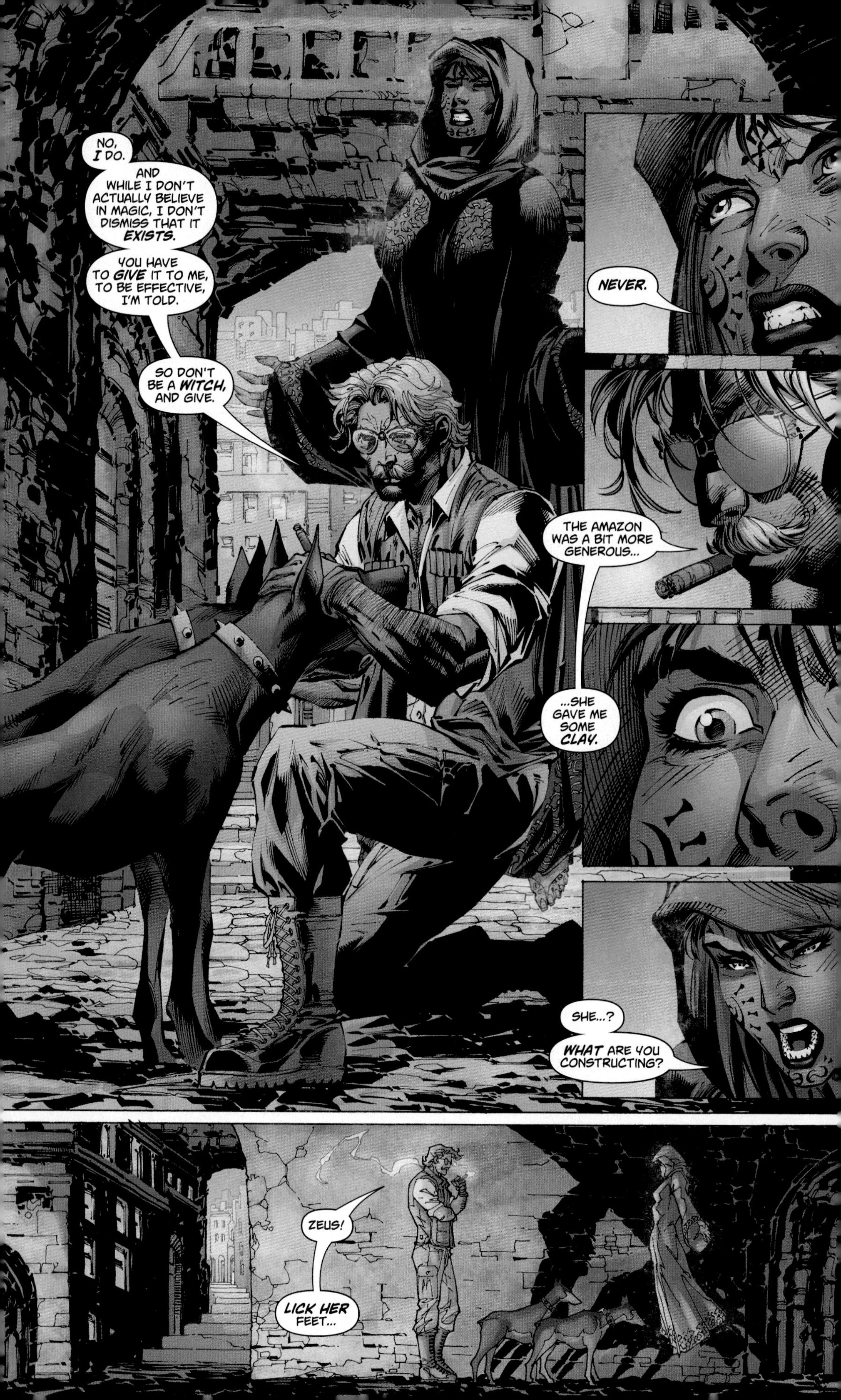
NO, I DO.
AND WHILE I DON'T ACTUALLY BELIEVE IN MAGIC, I DON'T DISMISS THAT IT EXISTS.
YOU HAVE TO GIVE IT TO ME, TO BE EFFECTIVE, I'M TOLD.
SO DON'T BE A WITCH, AND GIVE.
NEVER.
THE AMAZON WAS A BIT MORE GENEROUS...
...SHE GAVE ME SOME CLAY.
SHE...?
WHAT ARE YOU CONSTRUCTING?
ZEUS!
LICK HER FEET...

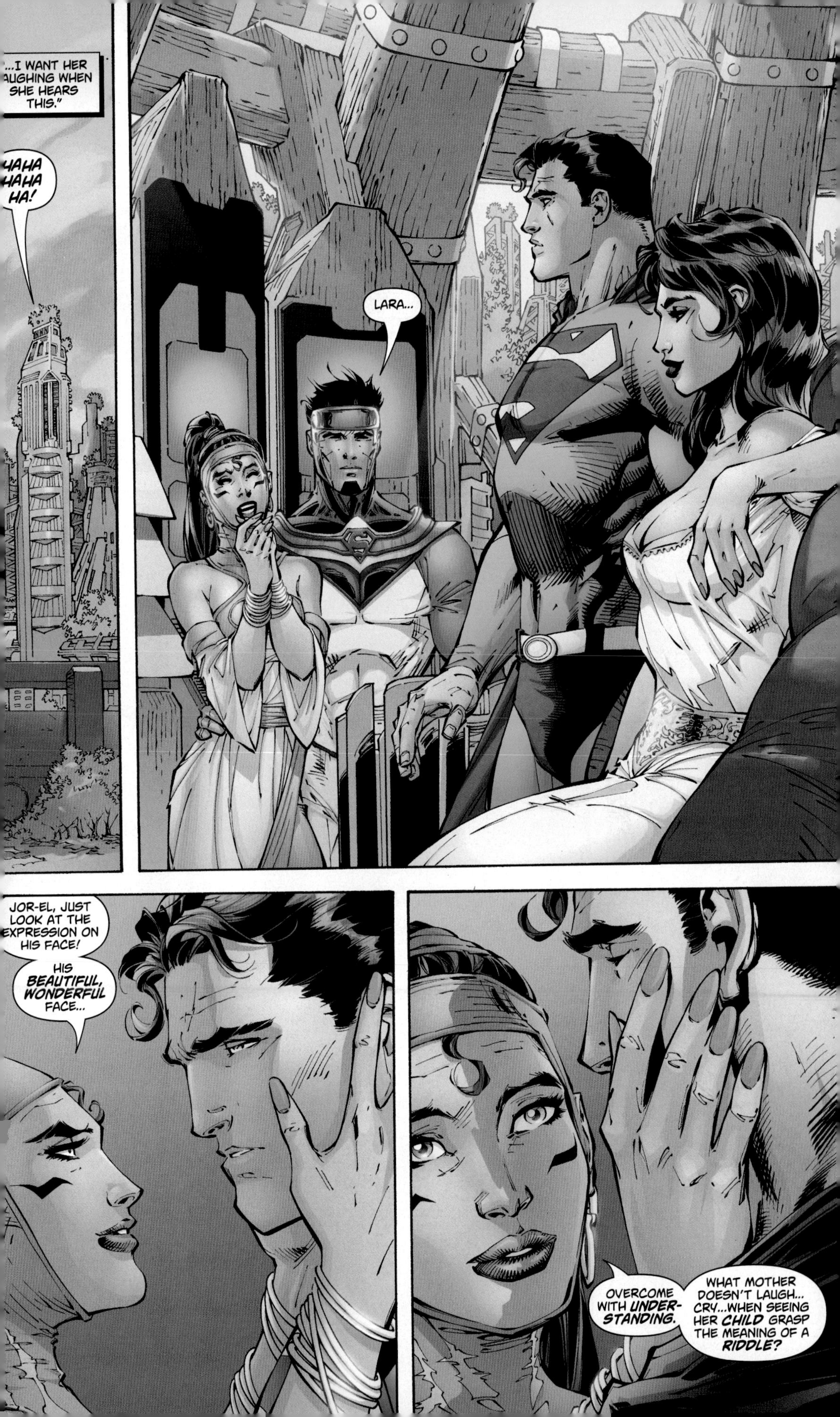
...I WANT HER LAUGHING WHEN SHE HEARS THIS."
HAHA HAHA HA!
LARA...
JOR-EL, JUST LOOK AT THE EXPRESSION ON HIS FACE!
HIS BEAUTIFUL, WONDERFUL FACE...
OVERCOME WITH UNDER-STANDING.
WHAT MOTHER DOESN'T LAUGH... CRY...WHEN SEEING HER CHILD GRASP THE MEANING OF A RIDDLE?

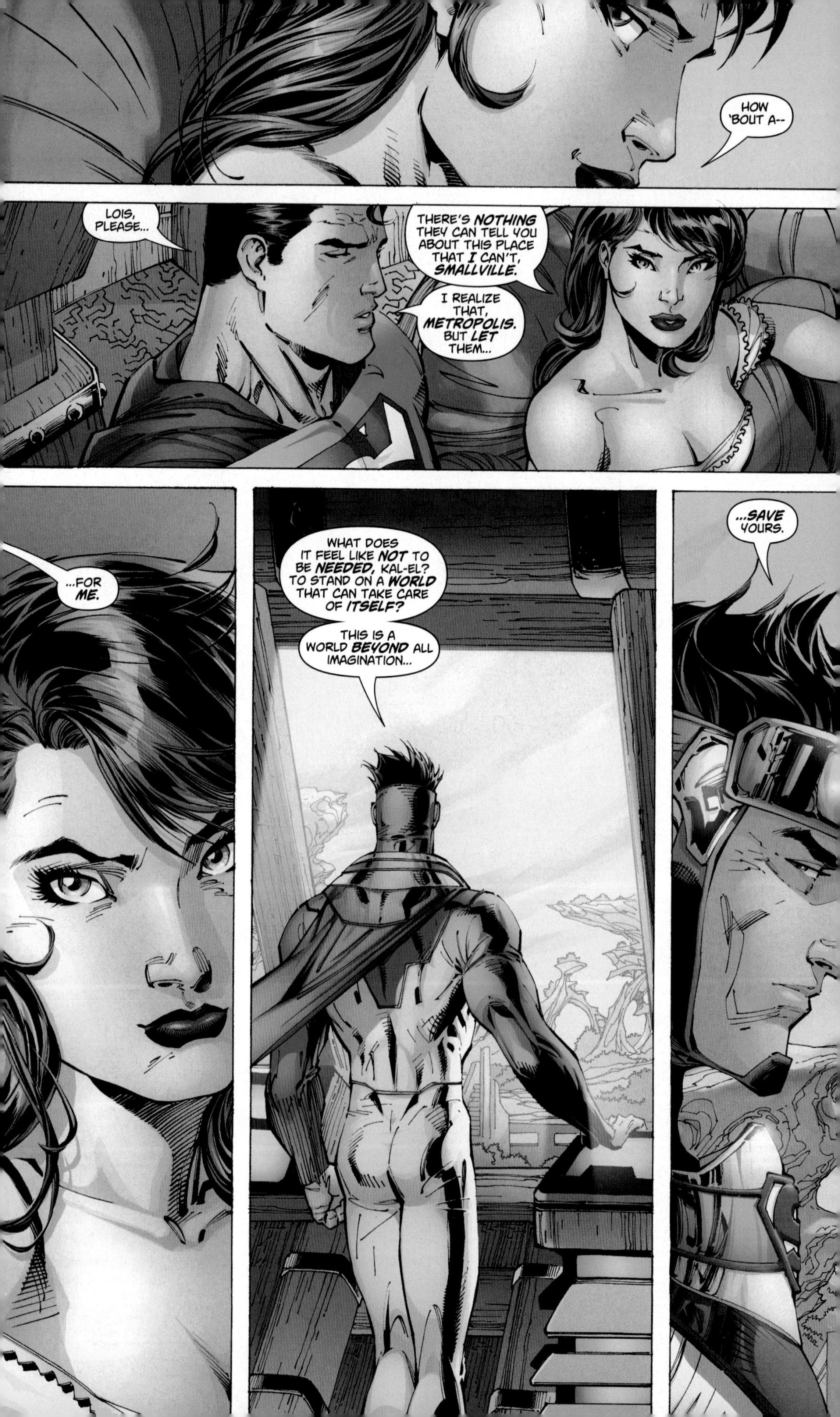
HOW 'BOUT A--
LOIS, PLEASE...
THERE'S NOTHING THEY CAN TELL YOU ABOUT THIS PLACE THAT I CAN'T, SMALLVILLE.
I REALIZE THAT, METROPOLIS. BUT LET THEM...
...FOR ME.
WHAT DOES IT FEEL LIKE NOT TO BE NEEDED, KAL-EL? TO STAND ON A WORLD THAT CAN TAKE CARE OF ITSELF?
THIS IS A WORLD BEYOND ALL IMAGINATION...
...SAVE YOURS.

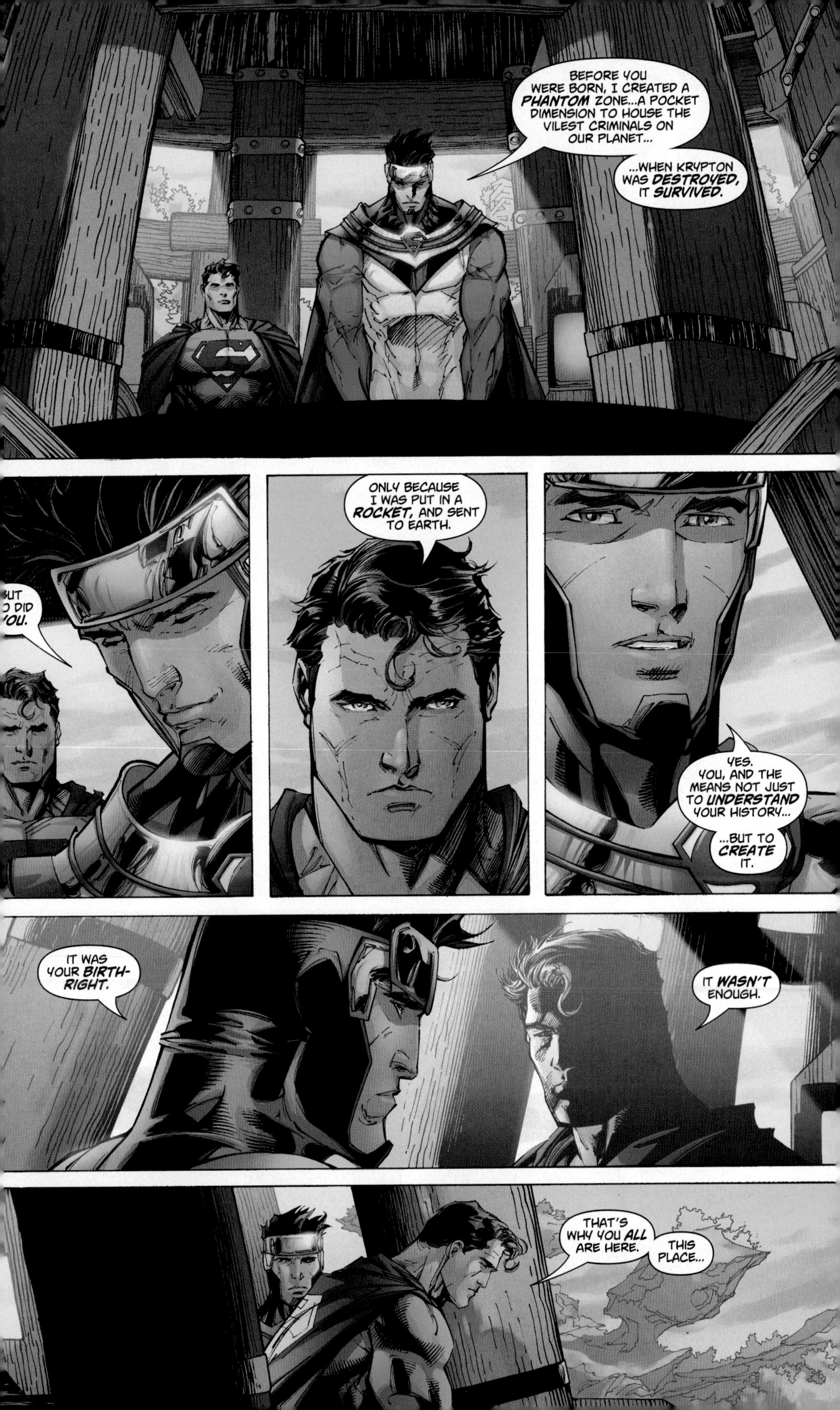
BEFORE YOU WERE BORN, I CREATED A PHANTOM ZONE...A POCKET DIMENSION TO HOUSE THE VILEST CRIMINALS ON OUR PLANET...
...WHEN KRYPTON WAS DESTROYED, IT SURVIVED.
ONLY BECAUSE I WAS PUT IN A ROCKET, AND SENT TO EARTH.
YES. YOU, AND THE MEANS NOT JUST TO UNDERSTAND YOUR HISTORY...
...BUT TO CREATE IT.
IT WAS YOUR BIRTH-RIGHT.
IT WASN'T ENOUGH.
THAT'S WHY YOU ALL ARE HERE.
THIS PLACE...

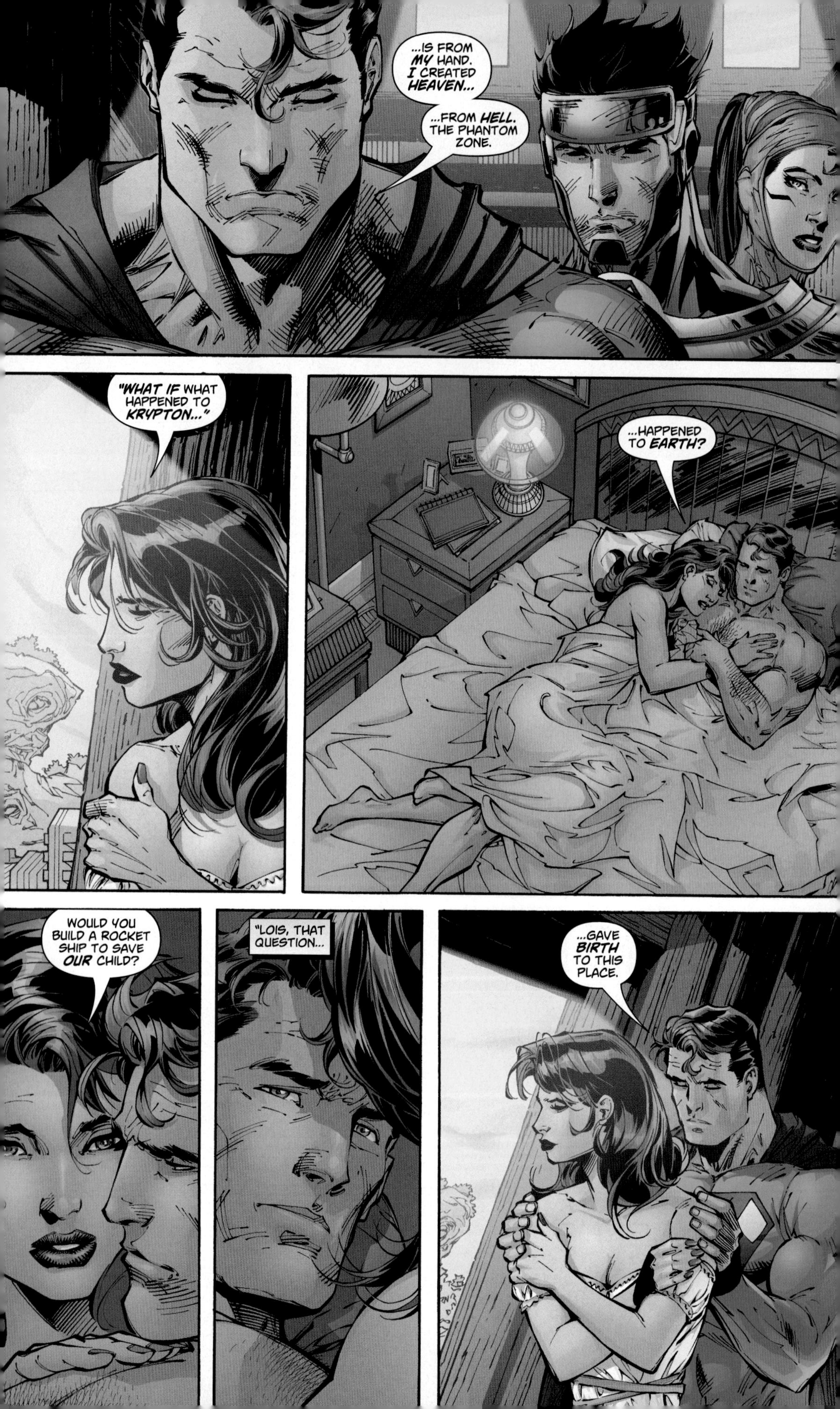
...IS FROM MY HAND. I CREATED HEAVEN...
...FROM HELL. THE PHANTOM ZONE.
"WHAT IF WHAT HAPPENED TO KRYPTON..."
...HAPPENED TO EARTH?
WOULD YOU BUILD A ROCKET SHIP TO SAVE OUR CHILD?
"LOIS, THAT QUESTION...
...GAVE BIRTH TO THIS PLACE.

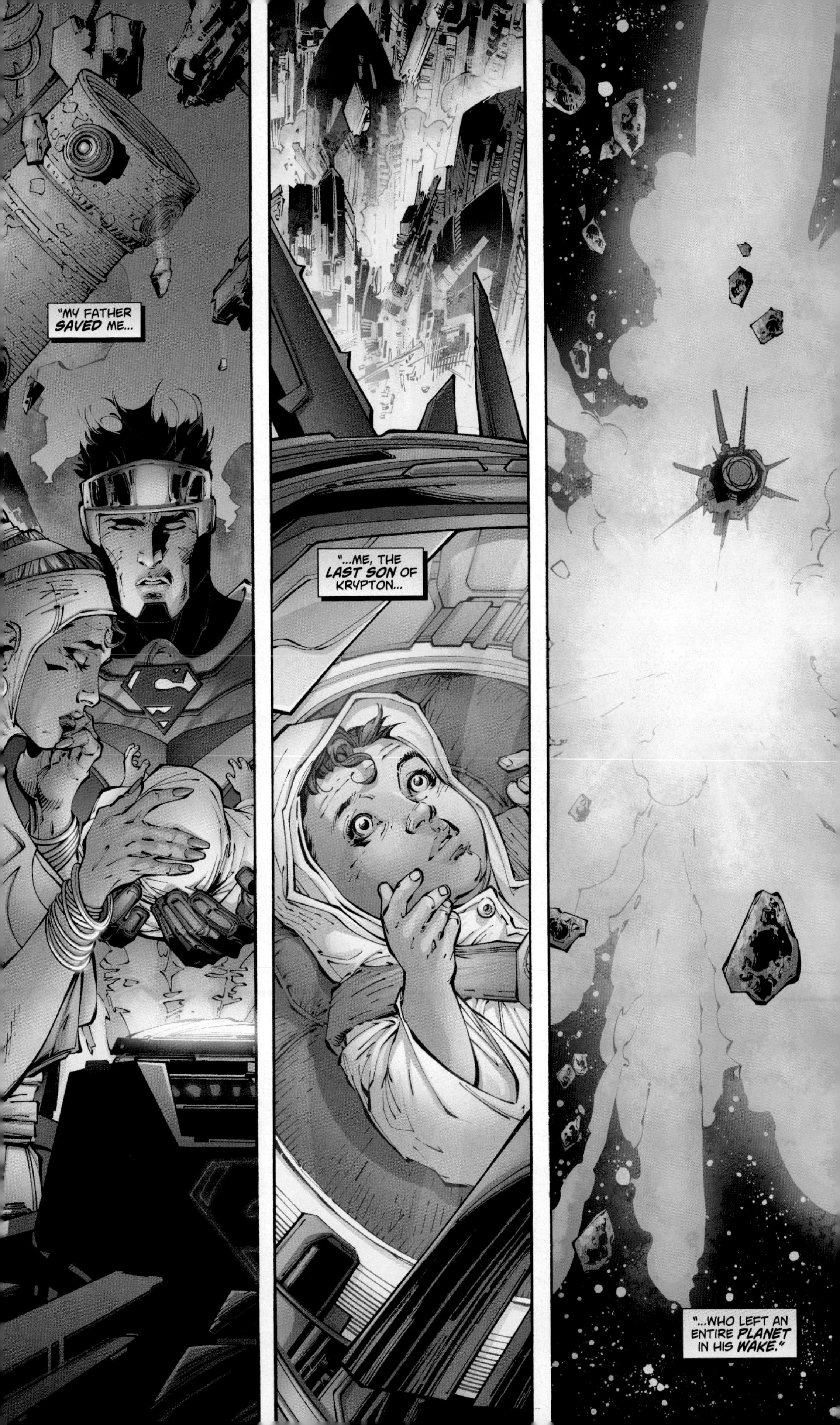
"MY FATHER SAVED ME...
"...ME, THE LAST SON OF KRYPTON...
"...WHO LEFT AN ENTIRE PLANET IN HIS WAKE."

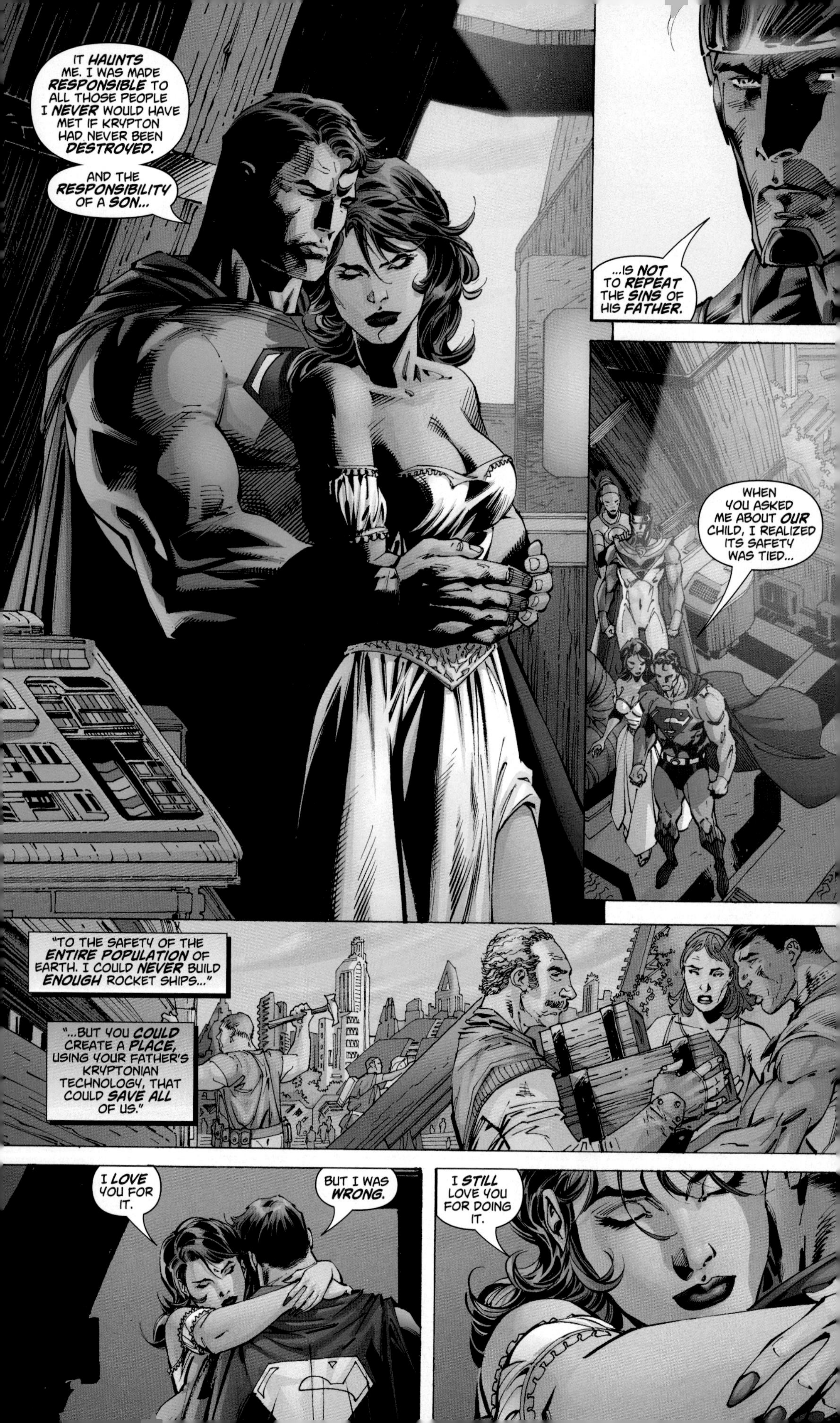

IT HAUNTS ME. I WAS MADE RESPONSIBLE TO ALL THOSE PEOPLE I NEVER WOULD HAVE MET IF KRYPTON HAD NEVER BEEN DESTROYED.
AND THE RESPONSIBILITY OF A SON...
...IS NOT TO REPEAT THE SINS OF HIS FATHER.
WHEN YOU ASKED ME ABOUT OUR CHILD, I REALIZED ITS SAFETY WAS TIED...
"TO THE SAFETY OF THE ENTIRE POPULATION OF EARTH. I COULD NEVER BUILD ENOUGH ROCKET SHIPS..."
"...BUT YOU COULD CREATE A PLACE, USING YOUR FATHER'S KRYPTONIAN TECHNOLOGY, THAT COULD SAVE ALL OF US."
I LOVE YOU FOR IT.
BUT I WAS WRONG.
I STILL LOVE YOU FOR DOING IT.

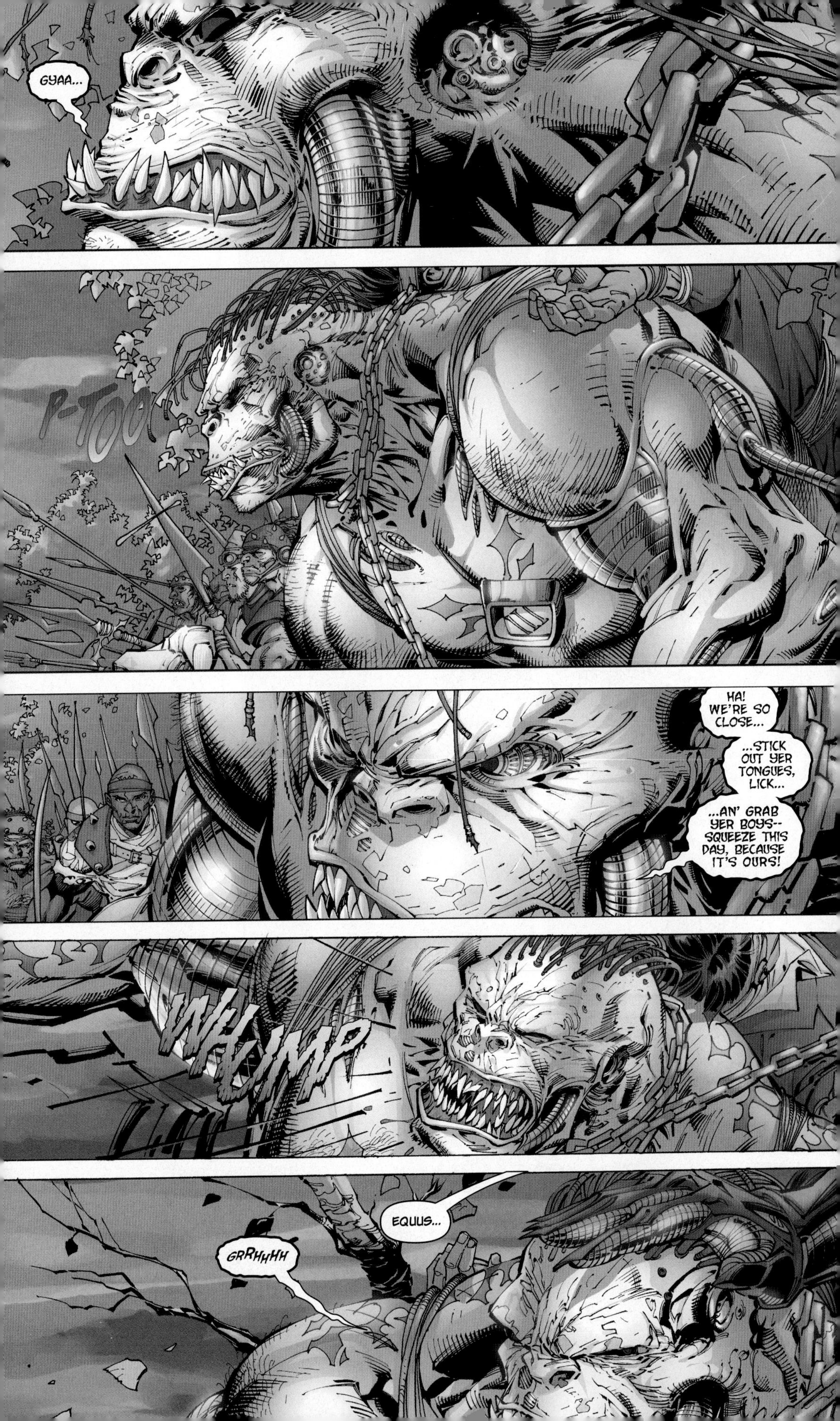
GYAA...
P-TOOO
HA! WE'RE SO CLOSE...
...STICK OUT YER TONGUES, LICK...
...AN' GRAB YER BOYS-- SQUEEZE THIS DAY, BECAUSE IT'S OURS!
WHUMP
EQUUS...
GRRHHHH

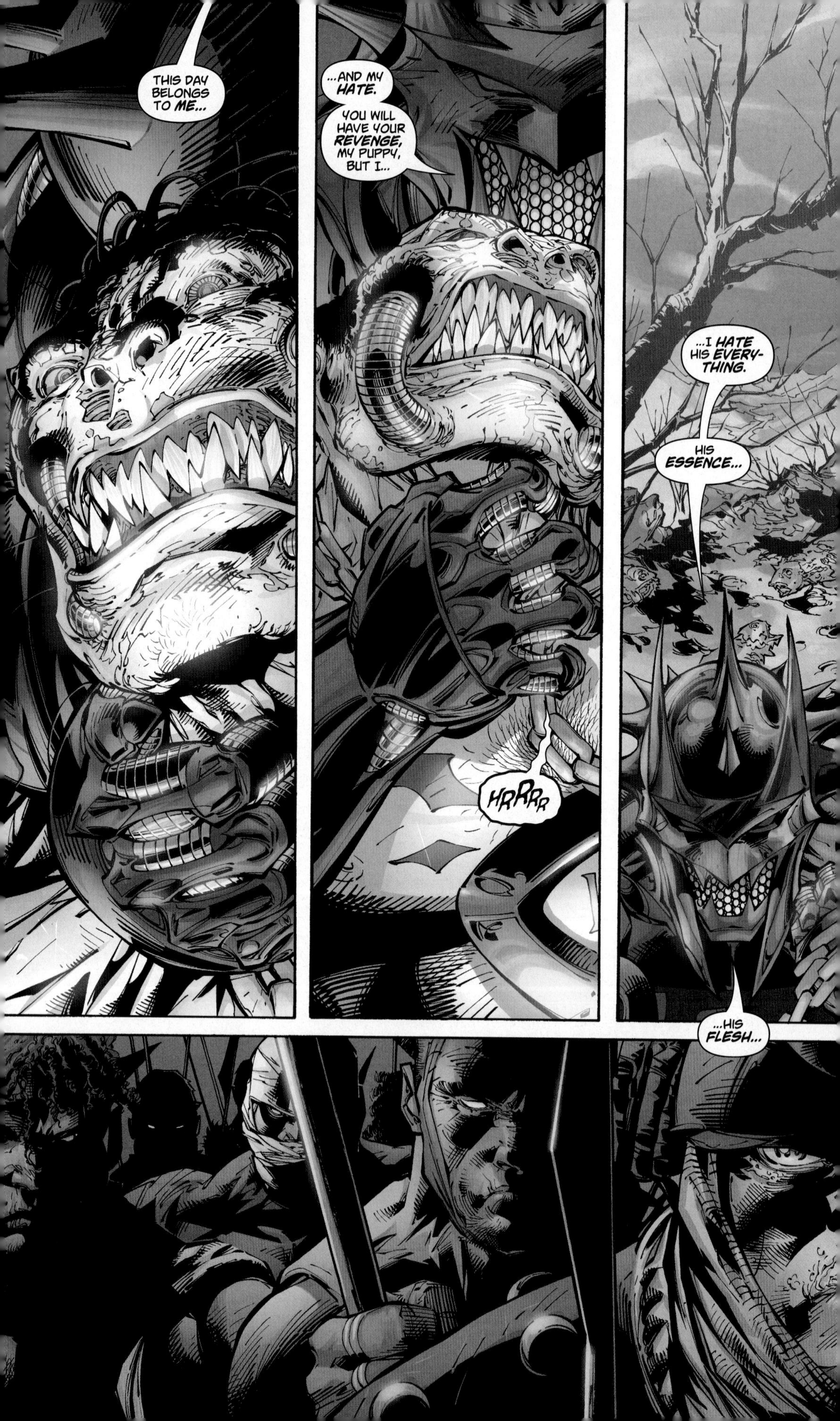
THIS DAY BELONGS TO ME...
...AND MY HATE.
YOU WILL HAVE YOUR REVENGE, MY PUPPY, BUT I...
HRRRR
...I HATE HIS EVERY-THING.
HIS ESSENCE...
...HIS FLESH...

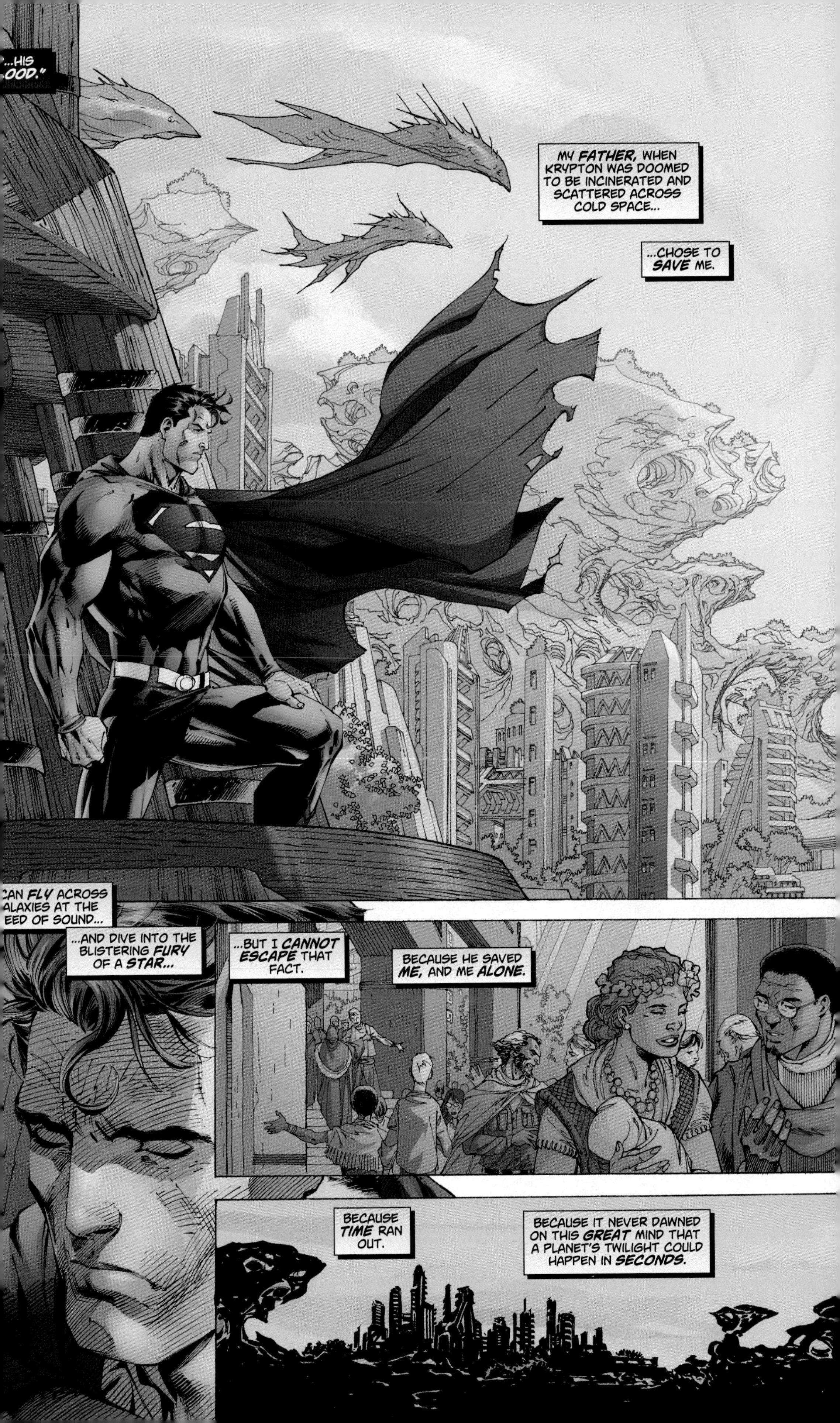

"...HIS
...OOD."
MY FATHER, WHEN KRYPTON WAS DOOMED TO BE INCINERATED AND SCATTERED ACROSS COLD SPACE...
...CHOSE TO SAVE ME.
CAN FLY ACROSS ALAXIES AT THE EED OF SOUND...
...AND DIVE INTO THE BLISTERING FURY OF A STAR...
...BUT I CANNOT ESCAPE THAT FACT.
BECAUSE HE SAVED ME, AND ME ALONE.
BECAUSE TIME RAN OUT.
BECAUSE IT NEVER DAWNED ON THIS GREAT MIND THAT A PLANET'S TWILIGHT COULD HAPPEN IN SECONDS.

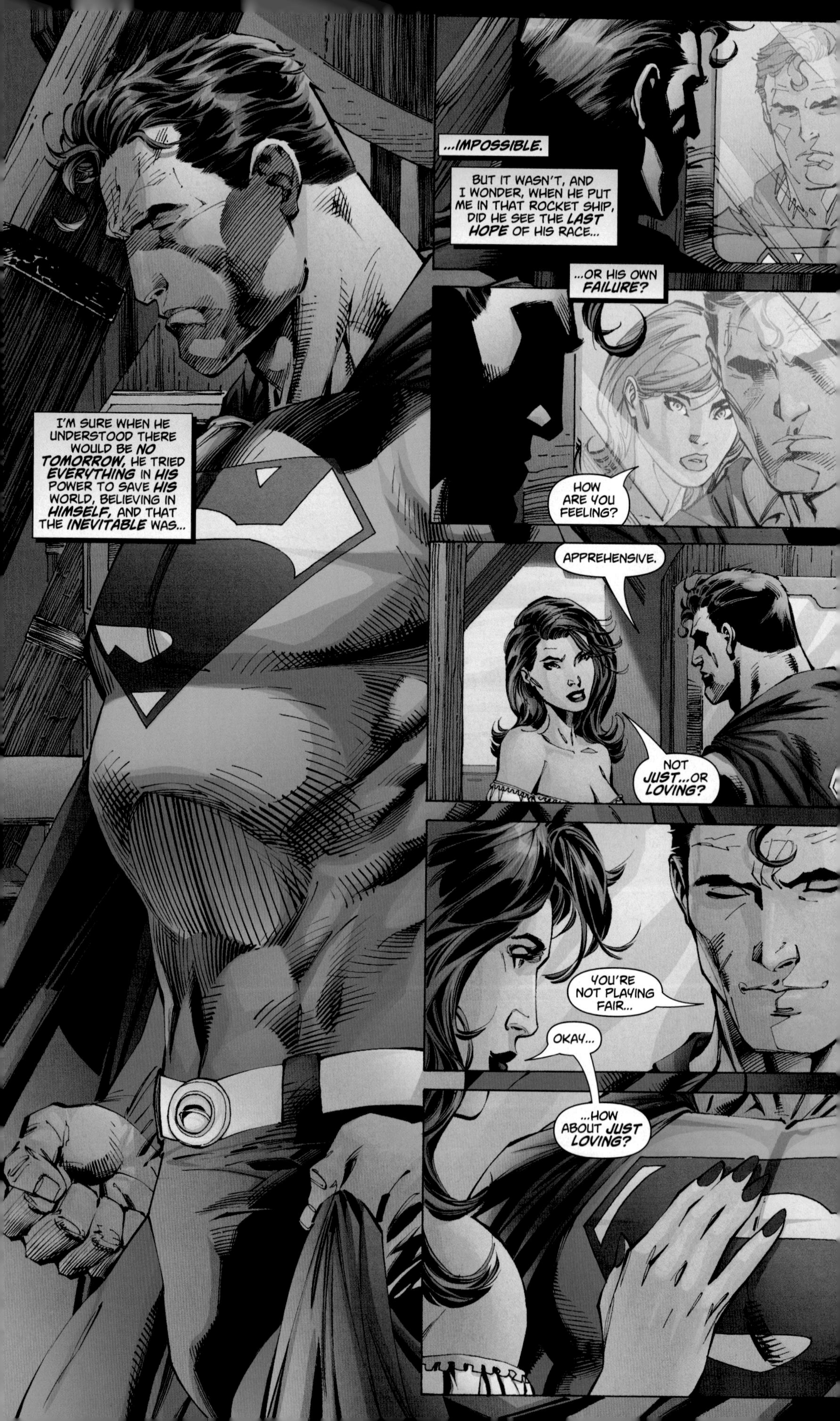
I'M SURE WHEN HE UNDERSTOOD THERE WOULD BE NO TOMORROW, HE TRIED EVERYTHING IN HIS POWER TO SAVE HIS WORLD, BELIEVING IN HIMSELF, AND THAT THE INEVITABLE WAS...
...IMPOSSIBLE.
BUT IT WASN'T, AND I WONDER, WHEN HE PUT ME IN THAT ROCKET SHIP, DID HE SEE THE LAST HOPE OF HIS RACE...
...OR HIS OWN FAILURE?
HOW ARE YOU FEELING?
APPREHENSIVE.
NOT JUST...OR LOVING?
YOU'RE NOT PLAYING FAIR...
OKAY...
...HOW ABOUT JUST LOVING?

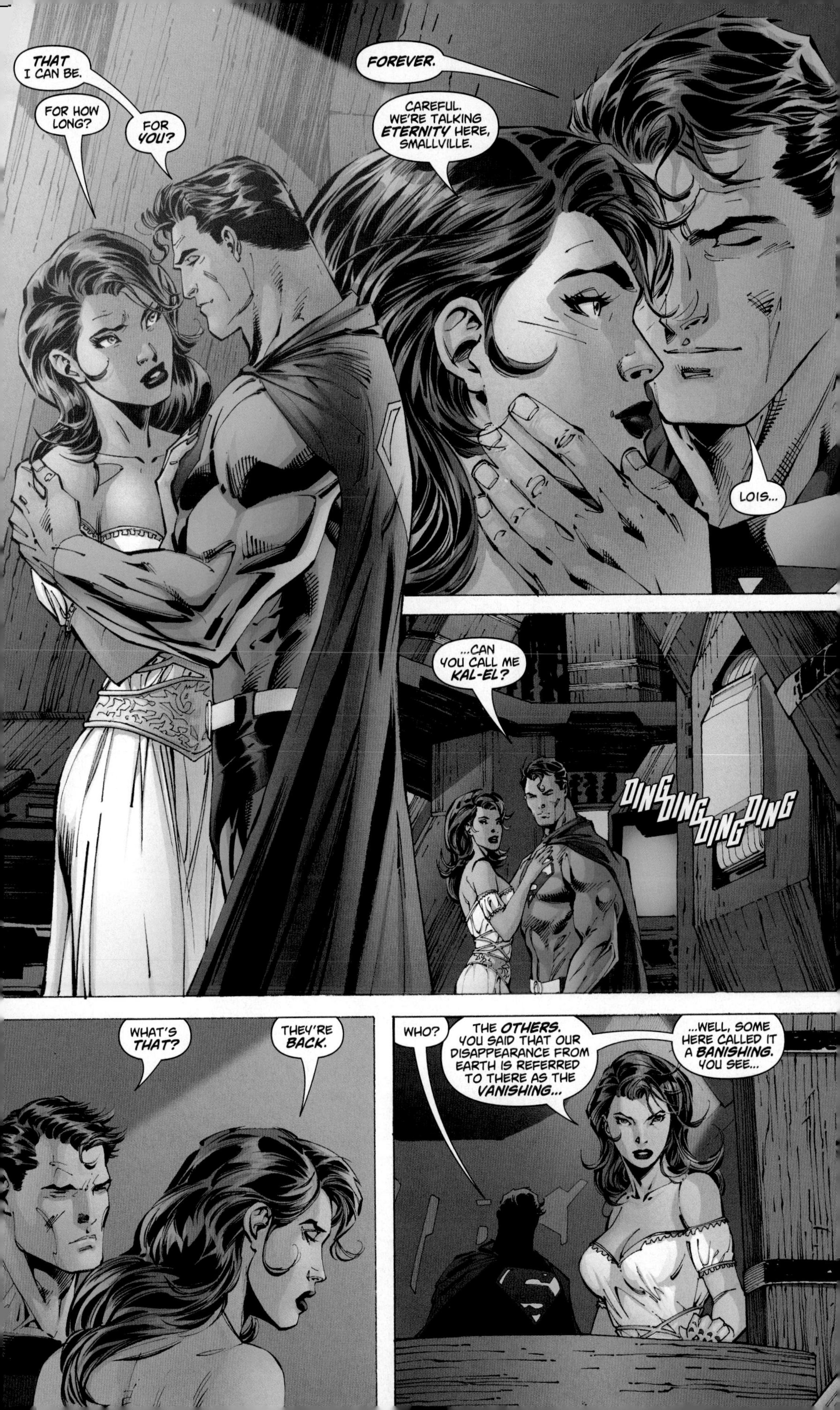
THAT I CAN BE.
FOR HOW LONG?
FOR YOU?
FOREVER.
CAREFUL. WE'RE TALKING ETERNITY HERE, SMALLVILLE.
LOIS...
...CAN YOU CALL ME KAL-EL?
DING DING DING DING
WHAT'S THAT?
THEY'RE BACK.
WHO?
THE OTHERS. YOU SAID THAT OUR DISAPPEARANCE FROM EARTH IS REFERRED TO THERE AS THE VANISHING...
...WELL, SOME HERE CALLED IT A BANISHING. YOU SEE...

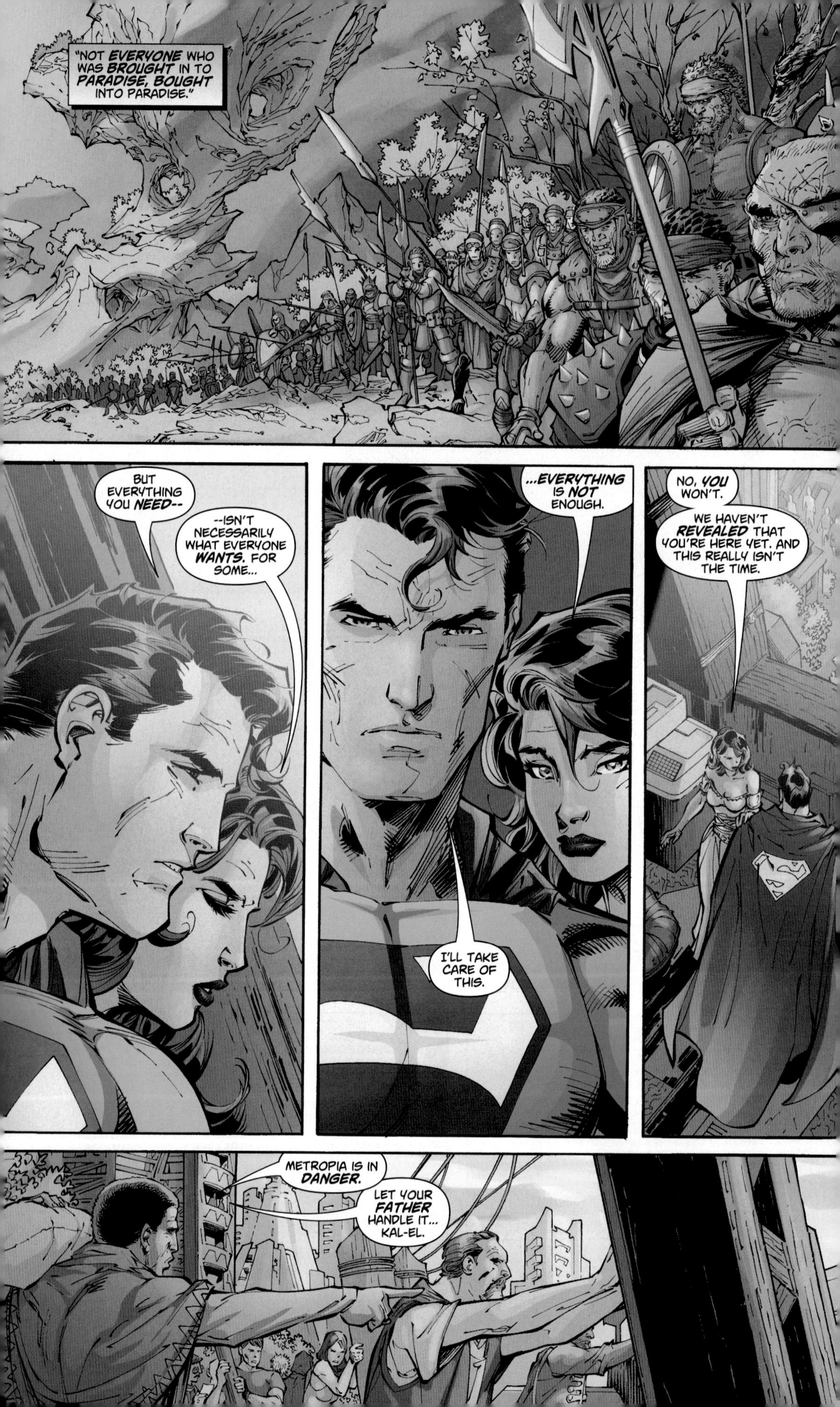
"NOT EVERYONE WHO WAS BROUGHT IN TO PARADISE, BOUGHT INTO PARADISE."
BUT EVERYTHING YOU NEED--
--ISN'T NECESSARILY WHAT EVERYONE WANTS. FOR SOME...
...EVERYTHING IS NOT ENOUGH.
I'LL TAKE CARE OF THIS.
NO, YOU WON'T.
WE HAVEN'T REVEALED THAT YOU'RE HERE YET. AND THIS REALLY ISN'T THE TIME.
METROPIA IS IN DANGER.
LET YOUR FATHER HANDLE IT... KAL-EL.

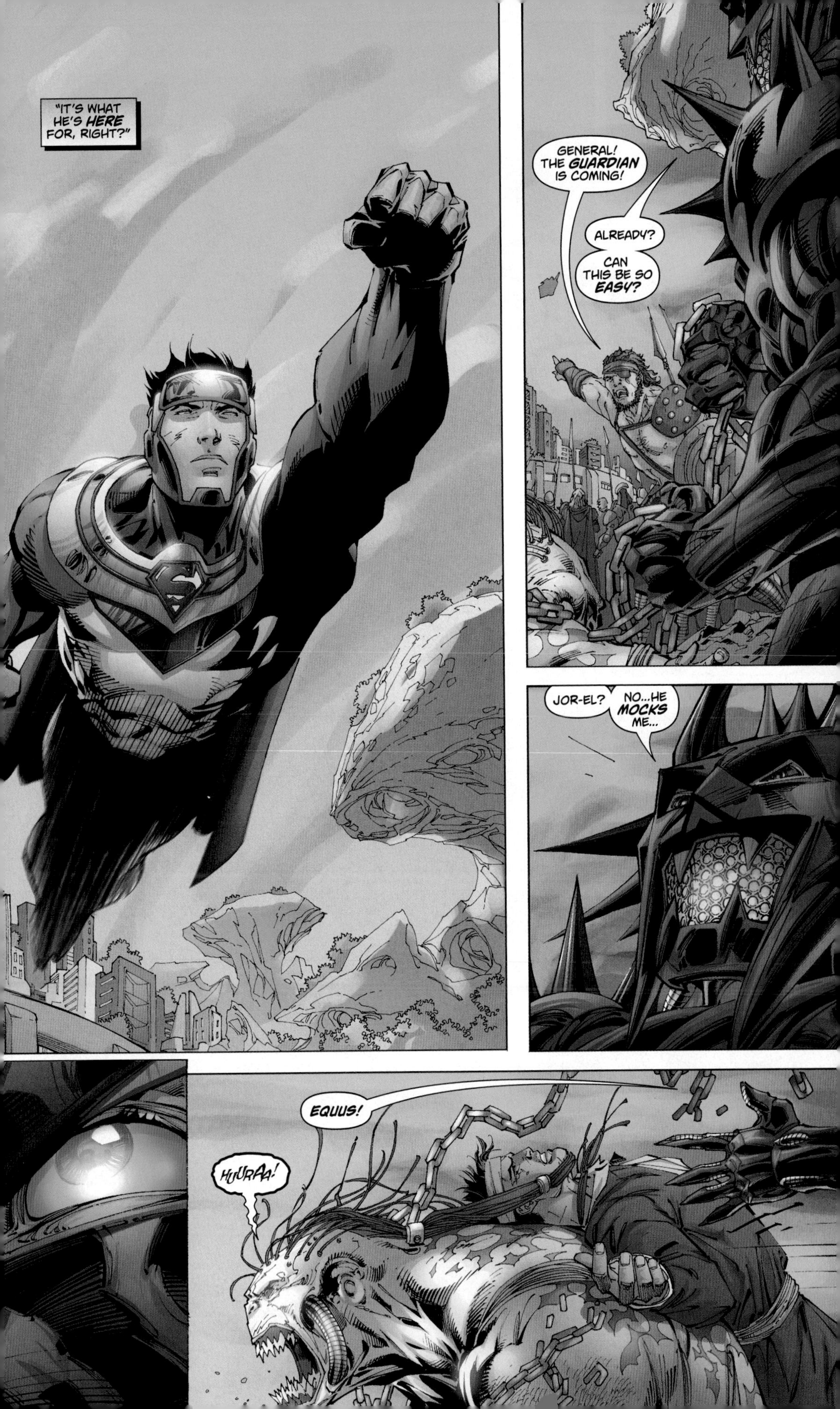
"IT'S WHAT HE'S HERE FOR, RIGHT?"
GENERAL! THE GUARDIAN IS COMING!
ALREADY?
CAN THIS BE SO EASY?
JOR-EL?
NO...HE MOCKS ME...
EQUUS!
HUURAA!

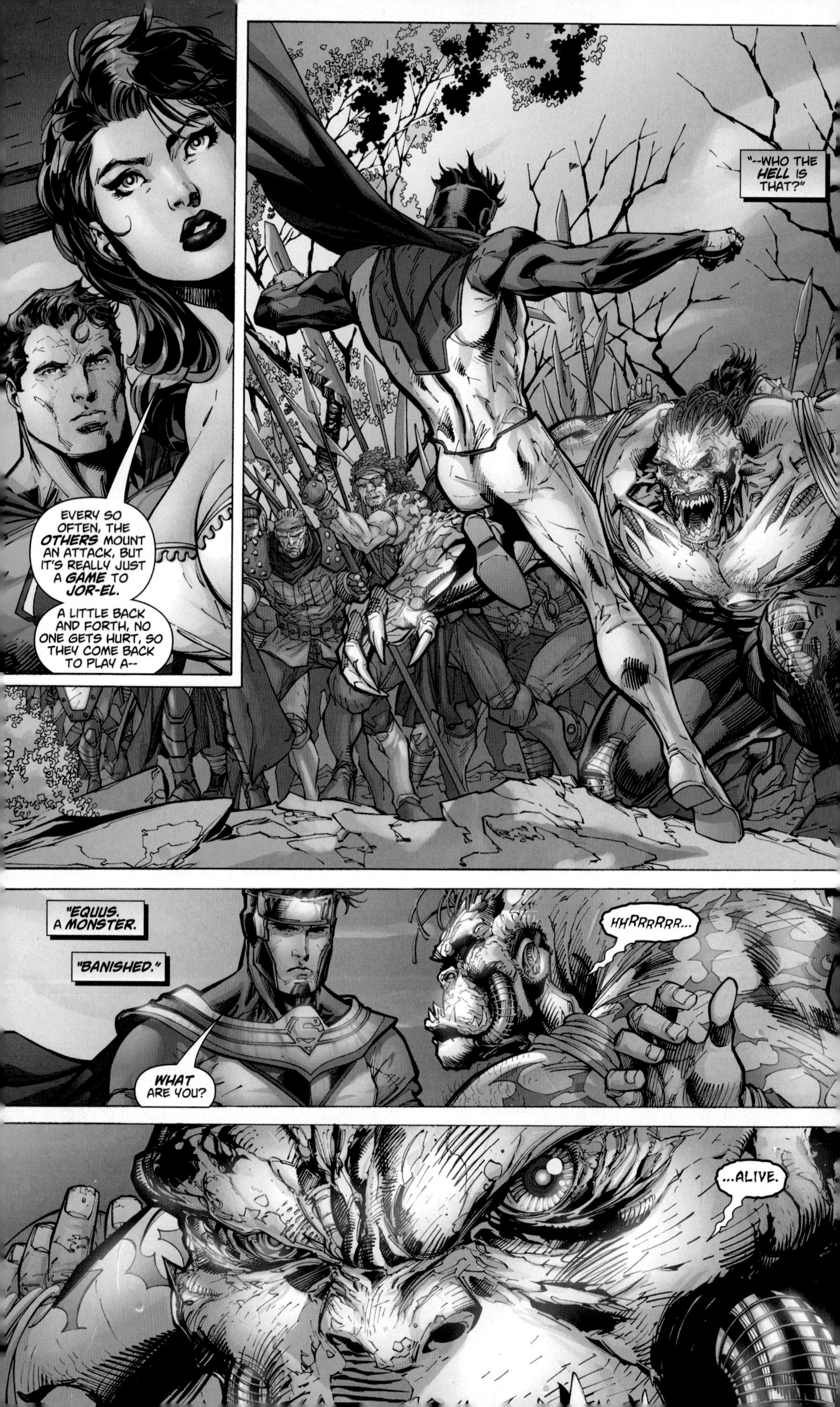
EVERY SO OFTEN, THE OTHERS MOUNT AN ATTACK, BUT IT'S REALLY JUST A GAME TO JOR-EL.
A LITTLE BACK AND FORTH, NO ONE GETS HURT, SO THEY COME BACK TO PLAY A--
"--WHO THE HELL IS THAT?"
"EQUUS. A MONSTER.
"BANISHED."
WHAT ARE YOU?
HHRRRRRR...
...ALIVE.

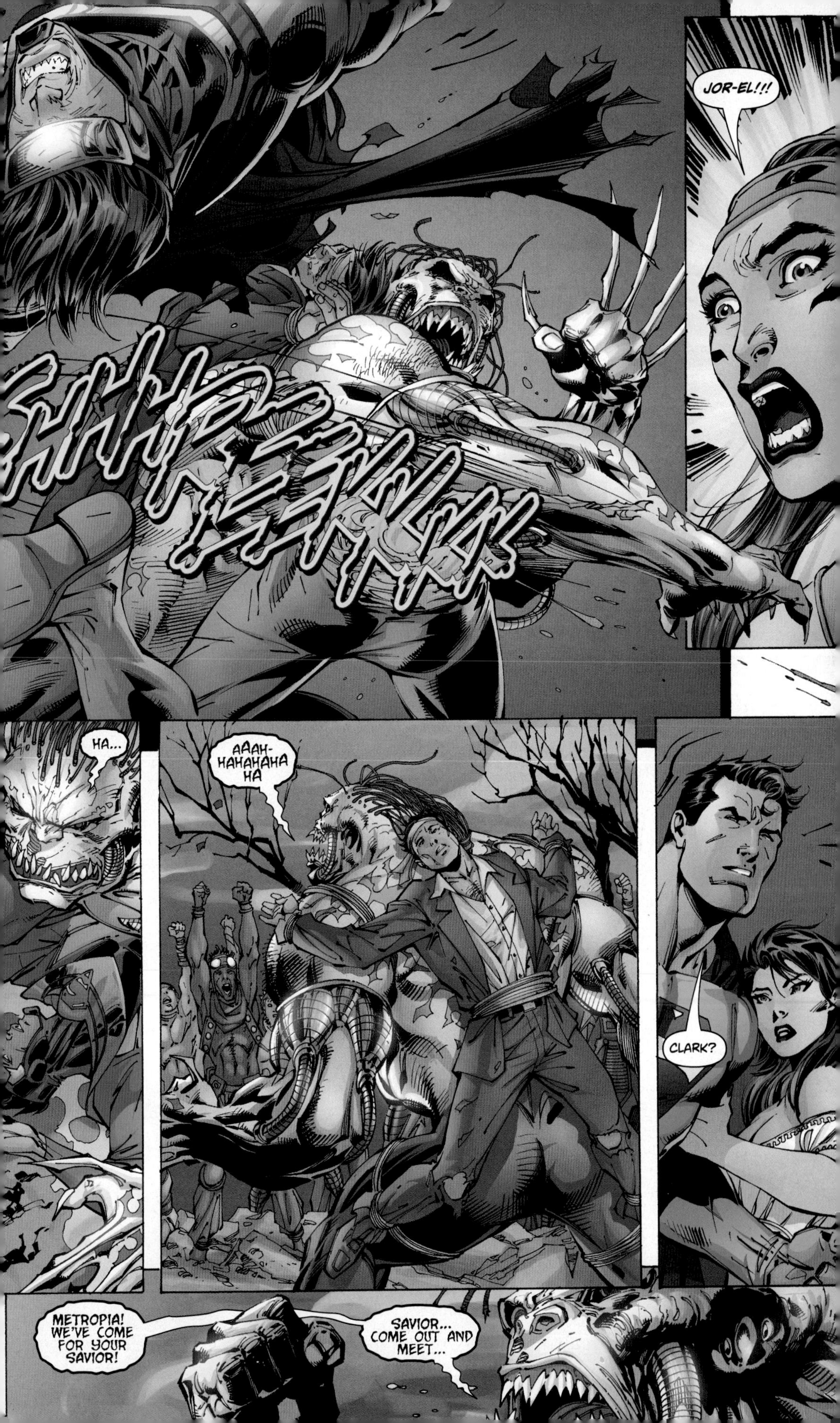
JOR-EL!!!
HA...
AAAH-HAHAHAHA HA
CLARK?
METROPIA! WE'VE COME FOR YOUR SAVIOR!
SAVIOR... COME OUT AND MEET...

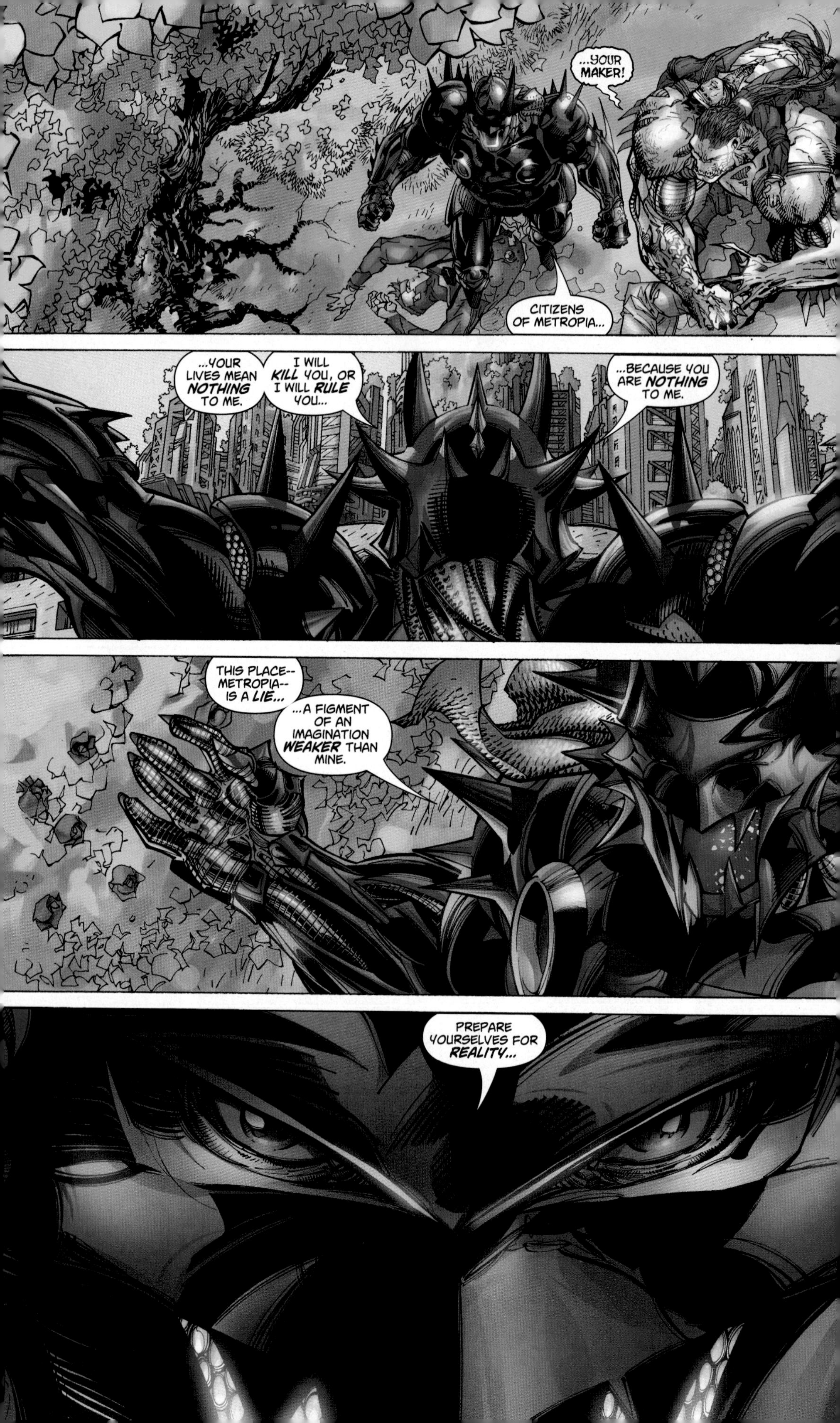

...YOUR MAKER!
CITIZENS OF METROPIA...
...YOUR LIVES MEAN NOTHING TO ME.
I WILL KILL YOU, OR I WILL RULE YOU...
...BECAUSE YOU ARE NOTHING TO ME.
THIS PLACE-- METROPIA-- IS A LIE...
...A FIGMENT OF AN IMAGINATION WEAKER THAN MINE.
PREPARE YOURSELVES FOR REALITY...

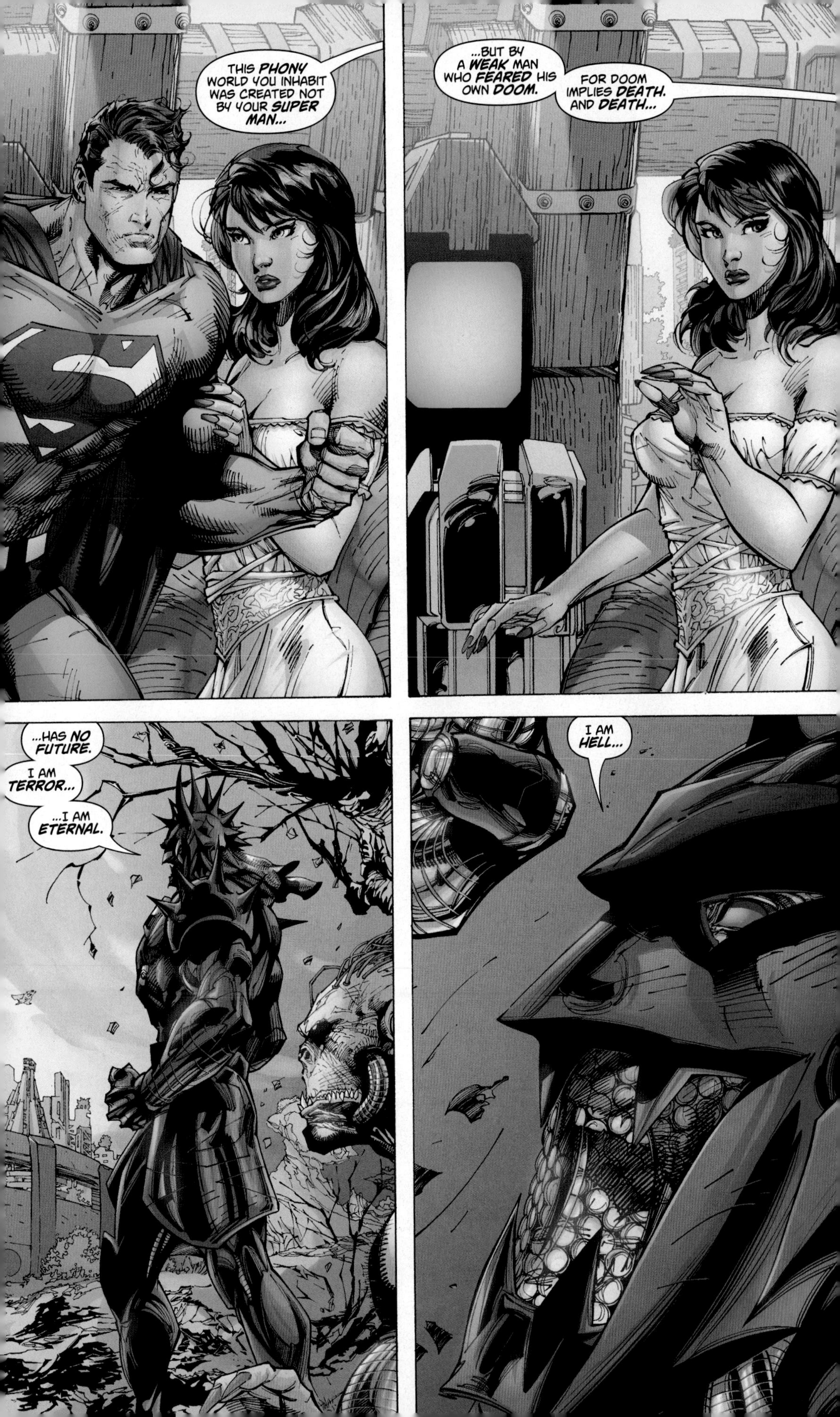
THIS PHONY WORLD YOU INHABIT WAS CREATED NOT BY YOUR SUPER MAN...
...BUT BY A WEAK MAN WHO FEARED HIS OWN DOOM.
FOR DOOM IMPLIES DEATH. AND DEATH...
...HAS NO FUTURE.
I AM TERROR...
...I AM ETERNAL.
I AM HELL...

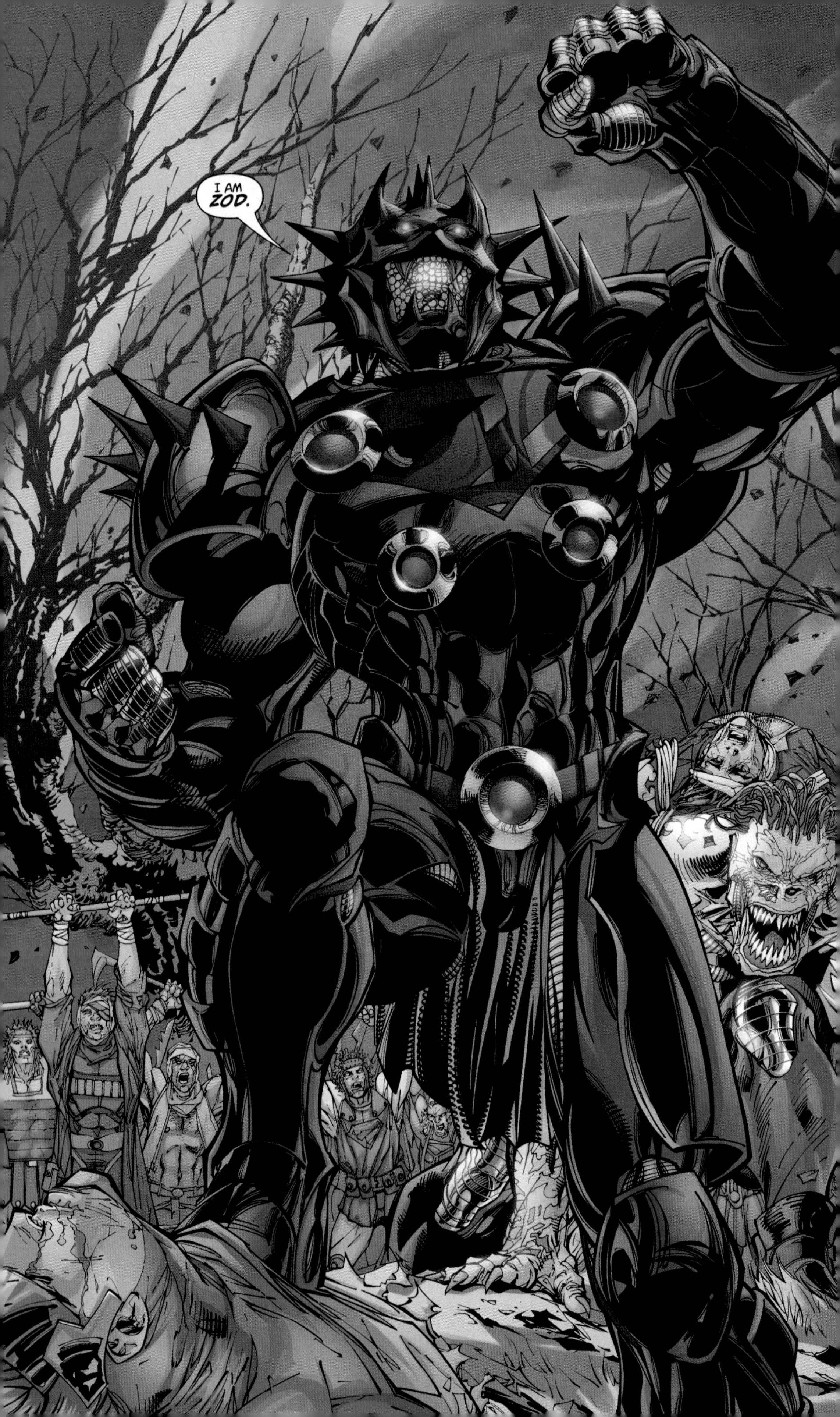
I AM ZOD.

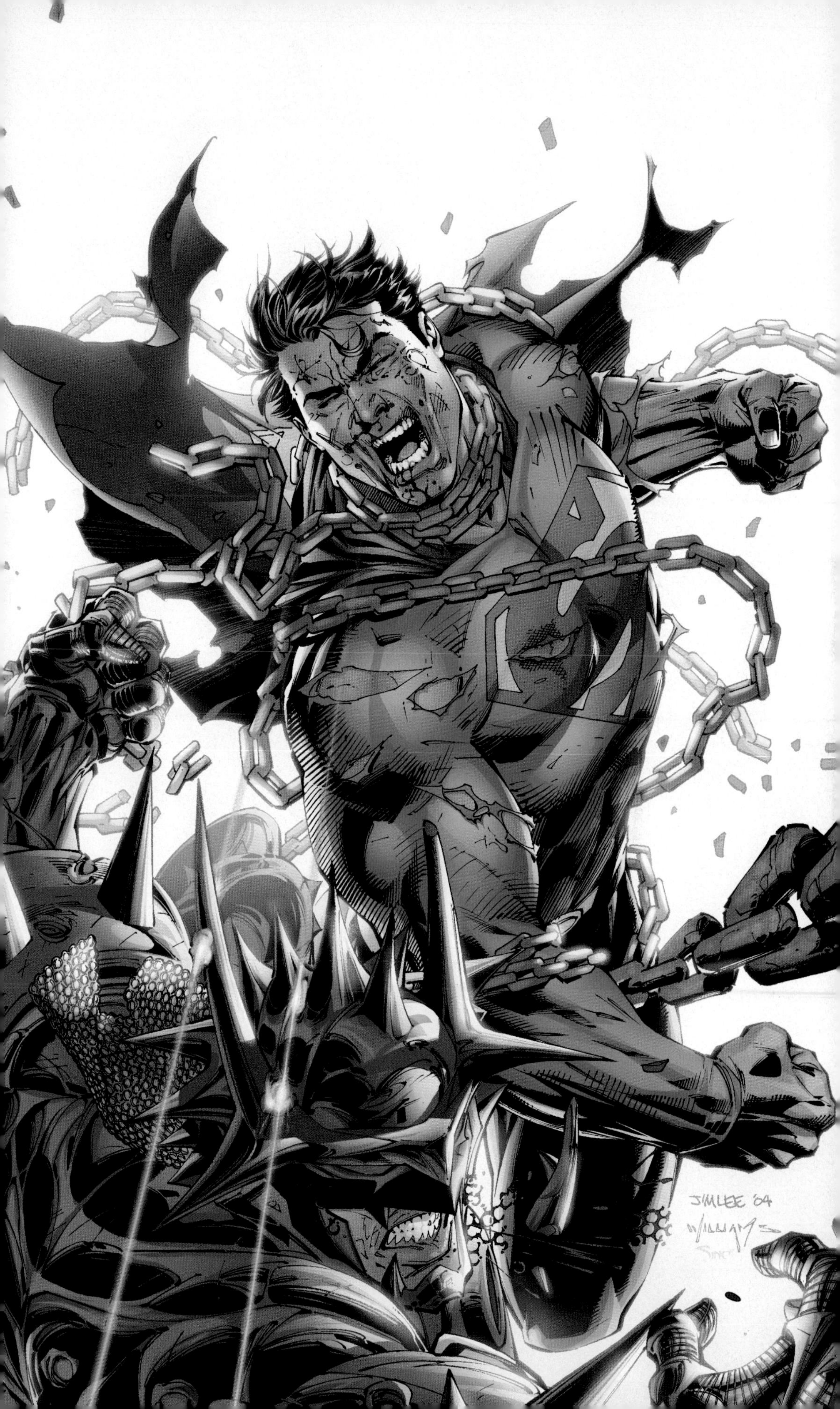

JIM LEE '04

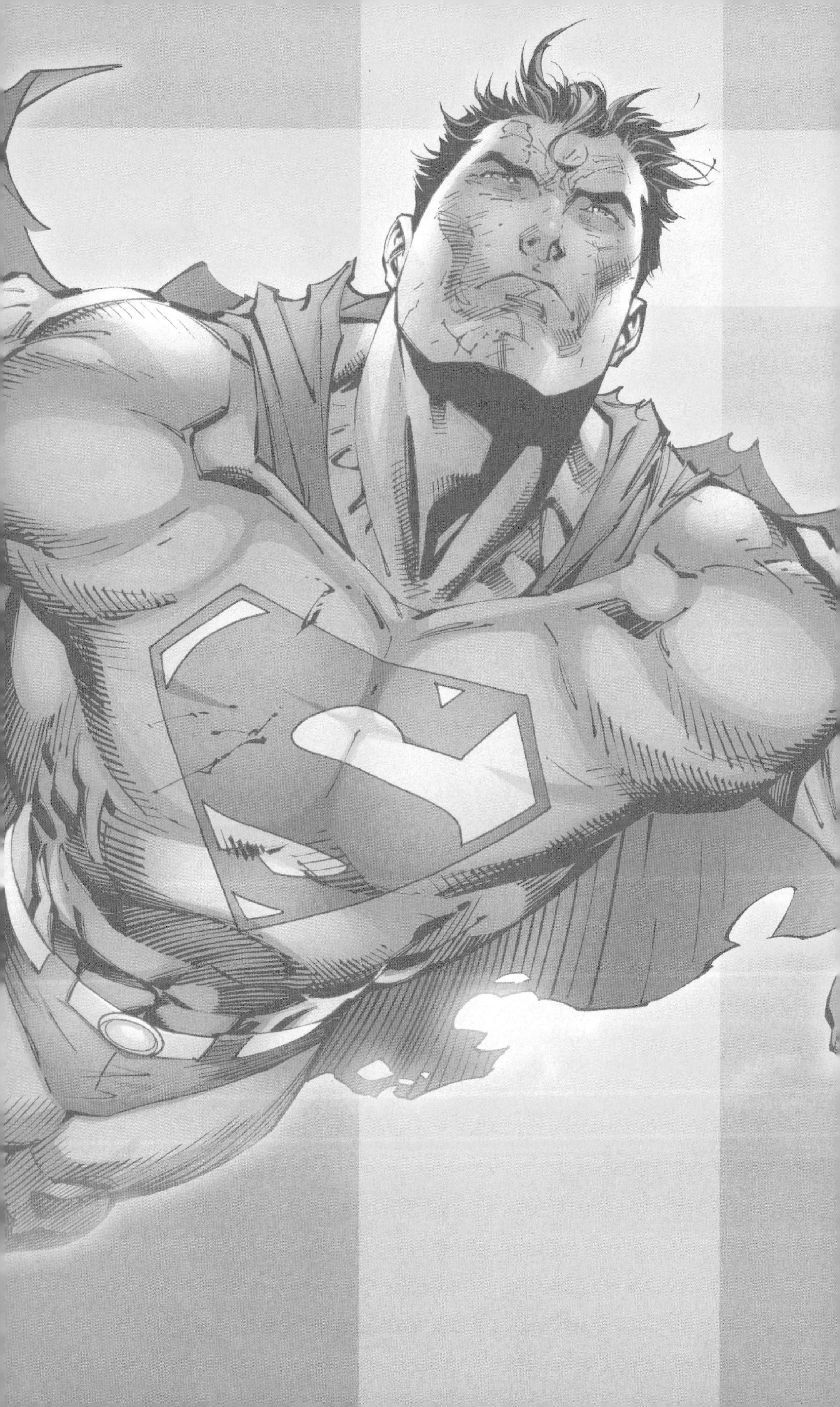

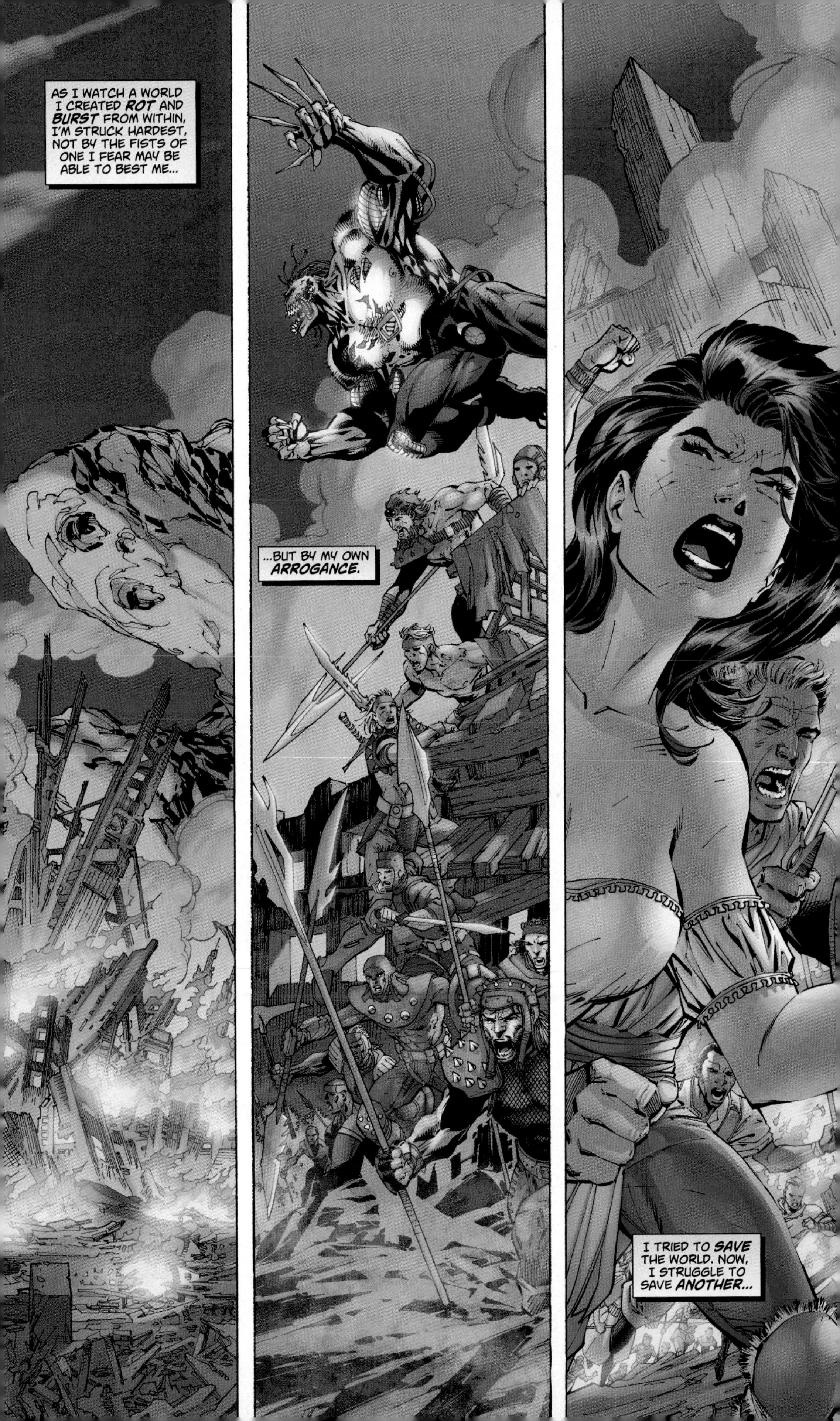

AS I WATCH A WORLD I CREATED ROT AND BURST FROM WITHIN, I'M STRUCK HARDEST, NOT BY THE FISTS OF ONE I FEAR MAY BE ABLE TO BEST ME...
...BUT BY MY OWN ARROGANCE.
I TRIED TO SAVE THE WORLD. NOW, I STRUGGLE TO SAVE ANOTHER...

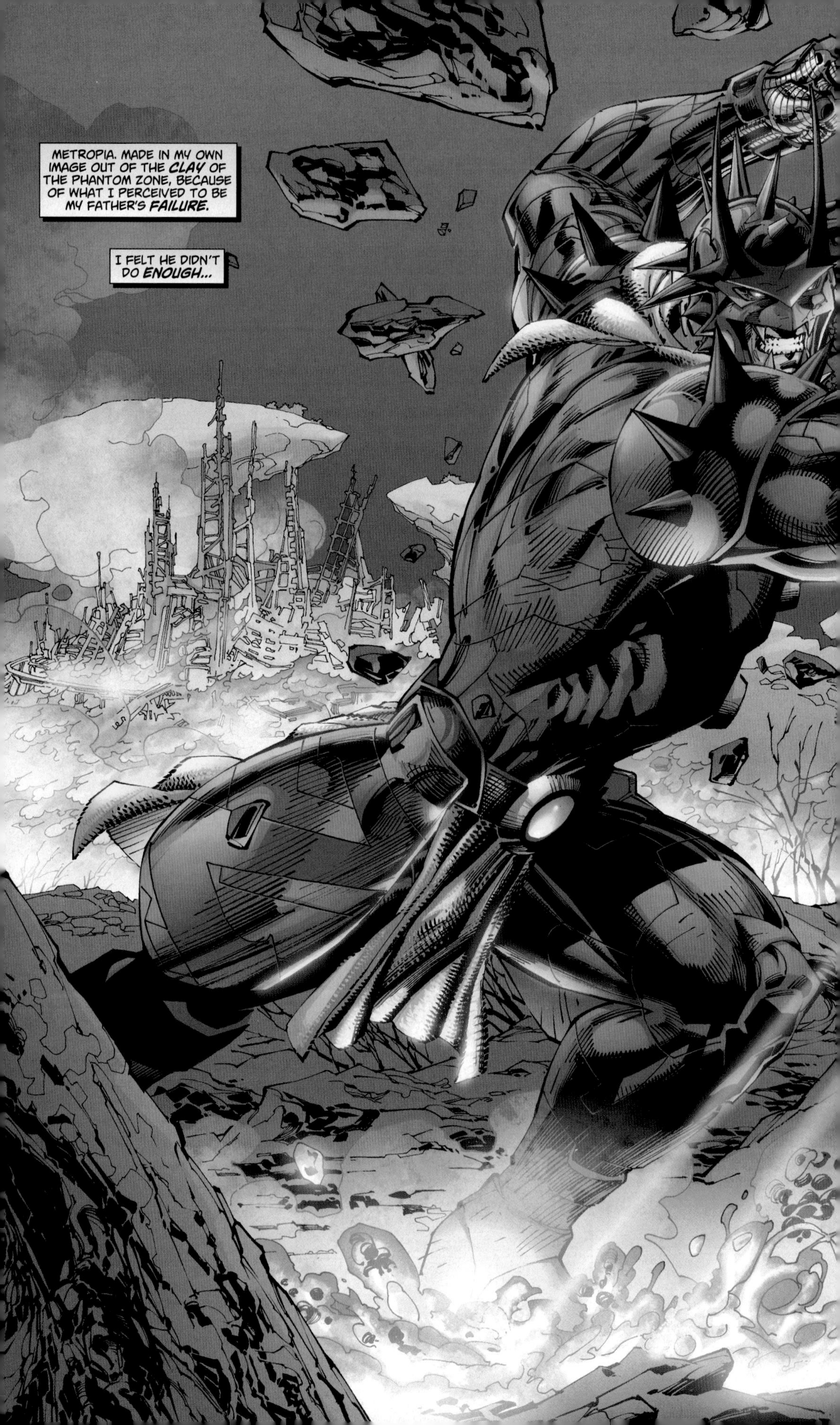
METROPIA. MADE IN MY OWN IMAGE OUT OF THE CLAY OF THE PHANTOM ZONE, BECAUSE OF WHAT I PERCEIVED TO BE MY FATHER'S FAILURE.
I FELT HE DIDN'T DO ENOUGH...

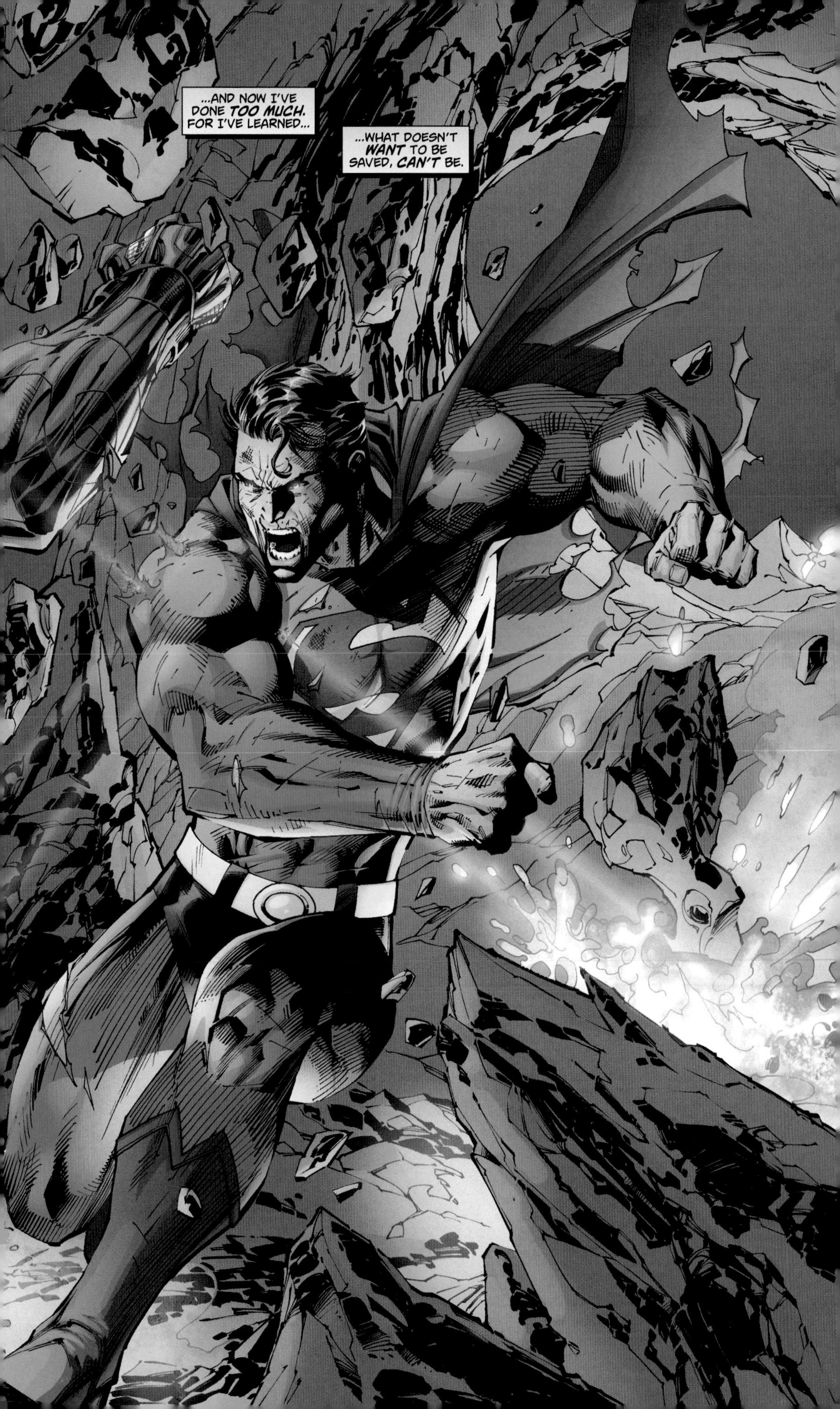
...AND NOW I'VE DONE TOO MUCH. FOR I'VE LEARNED...
...WHAT DOESN'T WANT TO BE SAVED, CAN'T BE.

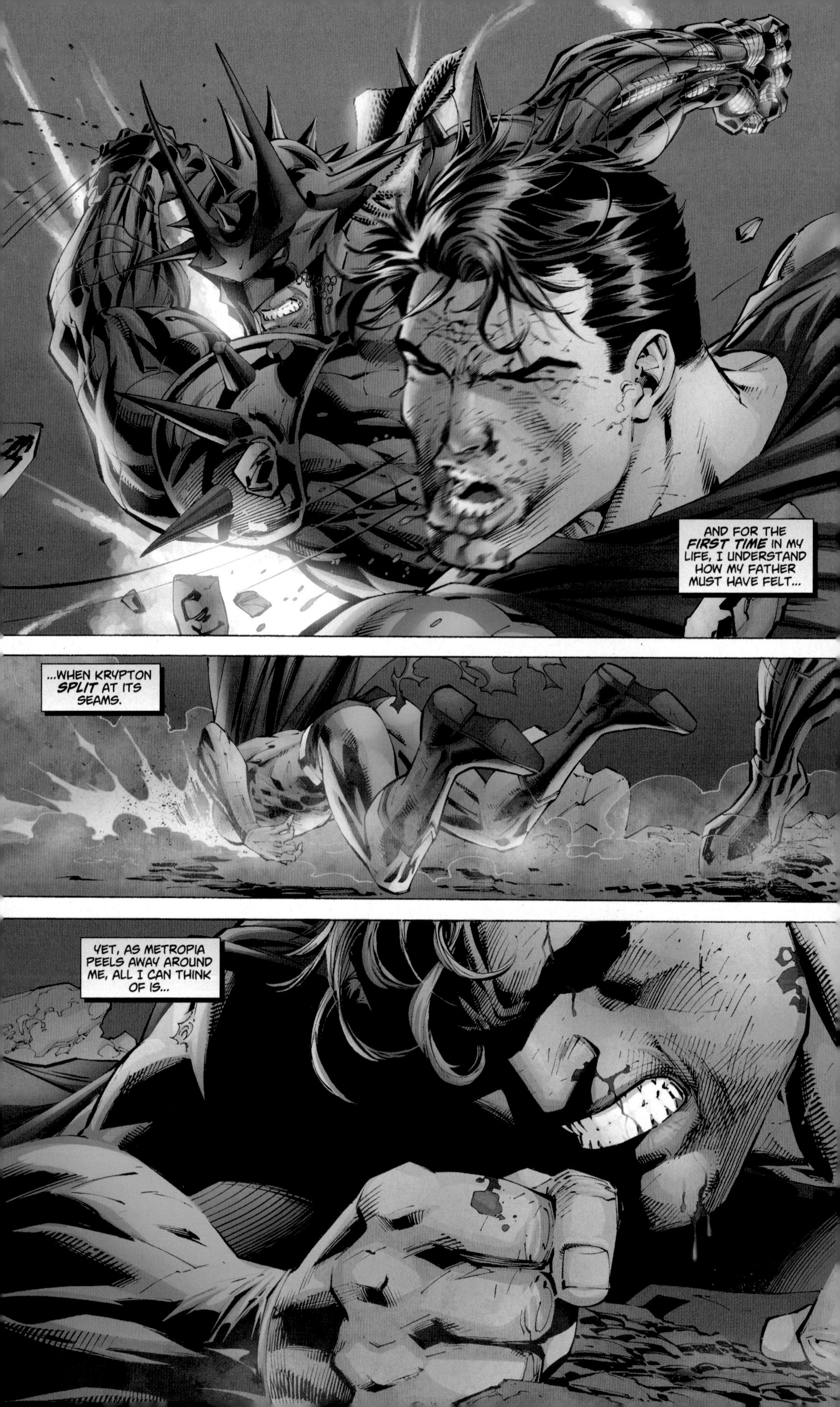
AND FOR THE FIRST TIME IN MY LIFE, I UNDERSTAND HOW MY FATHER MUST HAVE FELT...
...WHEN KRYPTON SPLIT AT ITS SEAMS.
YET, AS METROPIA PEELS AWAY AROUND ME, ALL I CAN THINK OF IS...

THE WORLD I LEFT BEHIND.

ONE MAN ARMY CORPS, VERSION FOUR.

I THINK YOU'LL LIKE THE INNOVATIONS.

SUCH AS...?

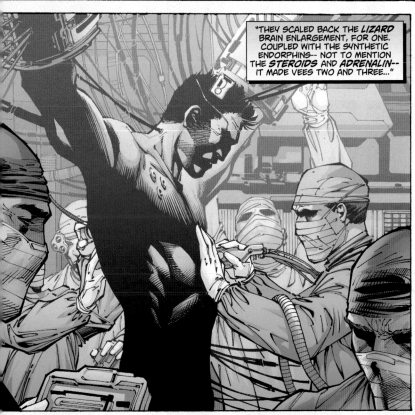

"THEY SCALED BACK THE LIZARD BRAIN ENLARGEMENT, FOR ONE. COUPLED WITH THE SYNTHETIC ENDORPHINS-- NOT TO MENTION THE STEROIDS AND ADRENALIN-- IT MADE VEES TWO AND THREE..."

UNRULY?

WHAT A QUAINT WAY OF PUTTING PSYCHOTIC.

THE HAPTIC, OLIGOTRONIC, AND HINGE TECH HAVE ALL BEEN RETAINED, BUT--WITH A *BONUS*...

...NANOPARTICLE MAGNETO-RHEOLOGICAL FLUIDS, HOUSED IN A CARBON NANOTUBULAR VASCULATURE SYSTEM. YOU COULD *KILL* HIM...

...AND HE *WOULDN'T DIE.*

AS PER ONE OF YOUR REQUESTS, THE *VOODOO* ENHANCEMENTS HAVE BEEN *INCREASED.*

IT'S NOT *VOODOO,* MR. ORR.

RIGHT.

WHERE VEE-THREE HAD-- THIS IS REALLY HARD FOR ME TO SAY--THE SKELETAL WINGS OF A *FALLEN ANGEL* EMBEDDED IN ITS FOREARMS...

WHERE'D YOU GET *THAT,* ANYWAY?

PLEASE CONTINUE, MR. ORR.

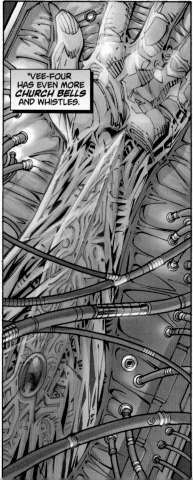

"VEE-FOUR HAS EVEN MORE *CHURCH BELLS* AND WHISTLES.

"AND A *CRICKET.*"

"EXCUSE ME?"

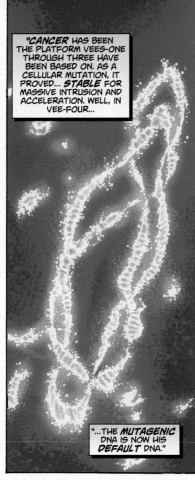

"CANCER HAS BEEN THE PLATFORM VEES-ONE THROUGH THREE HAVE BEEN BASED ON. AS A CELLULAR MUTATION, IT PROVED... STABLE FOR MASSIVE INTRUSION AND ACCELERATION. WELL, IN VEE-FOUR...

"...THE MUTAGENIC DNA IS NOW HIS DEFAULT DNA."

"WE'VE CURED CANCER?"

"THAT'S ONE WAY OF PUTTING IT. ANOTHER IS...

"...YOU'VE HARNESSED IT."

WELL, IT ALL LOOKS PROMISING, BUT UNFORTUNATELY...

...WE'VE DECIDED TO GO IN ANOTHER DIRECTION.

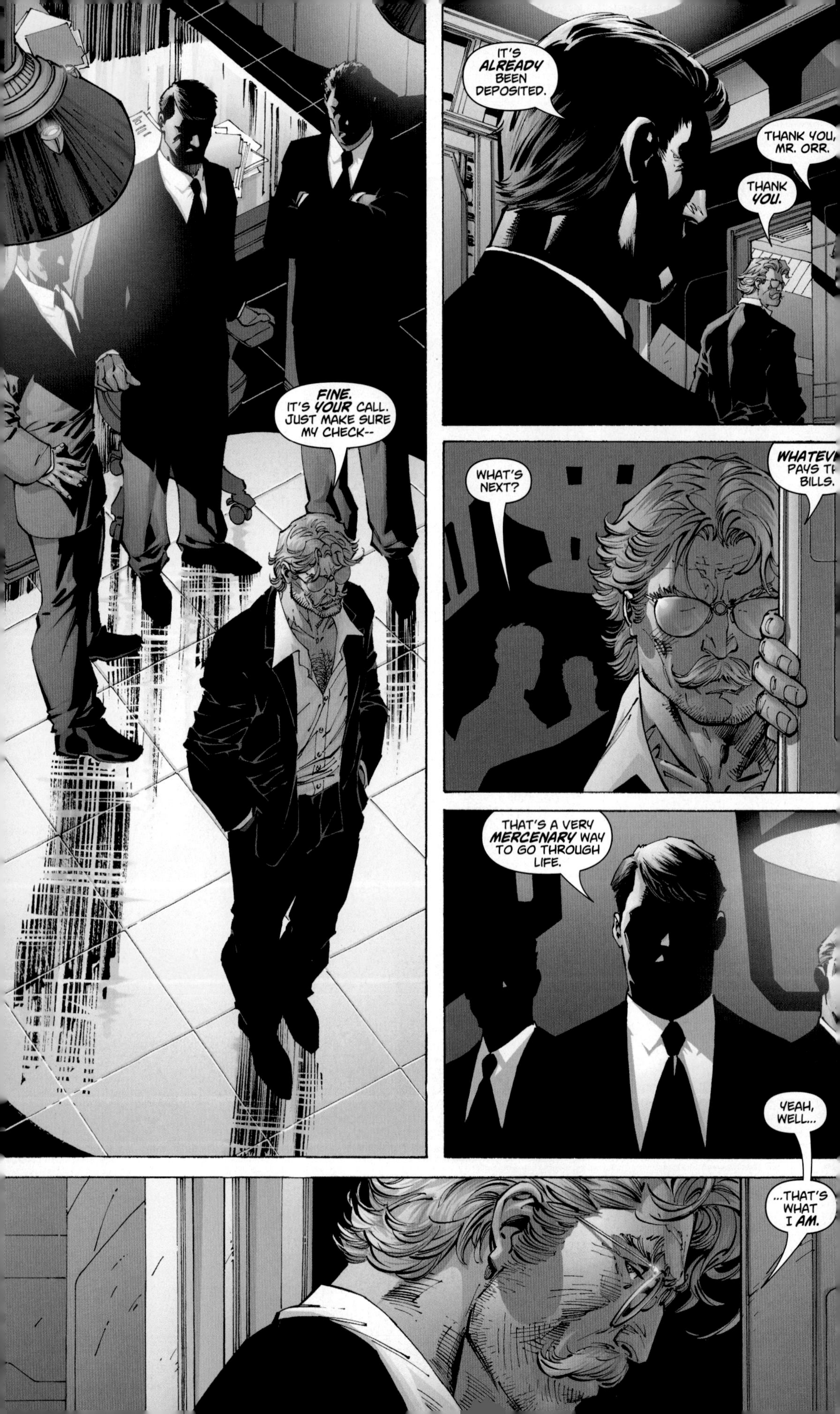
FINE. IT'S YOUR CALL. JUST MAKE SURE MY CHECK--
IT'S ALREADY BEEN DEPOSITED.
THANK YOU, MR. ORR.
THANK YOU.
WHAT'S NEXT?
WHATEV PAYS T BILLS.
THAT'S A VERY MERCENARY WAY TO GO THROUGH LIFE.
YEAH, WELL...
...THAT'S WHAT I AM.

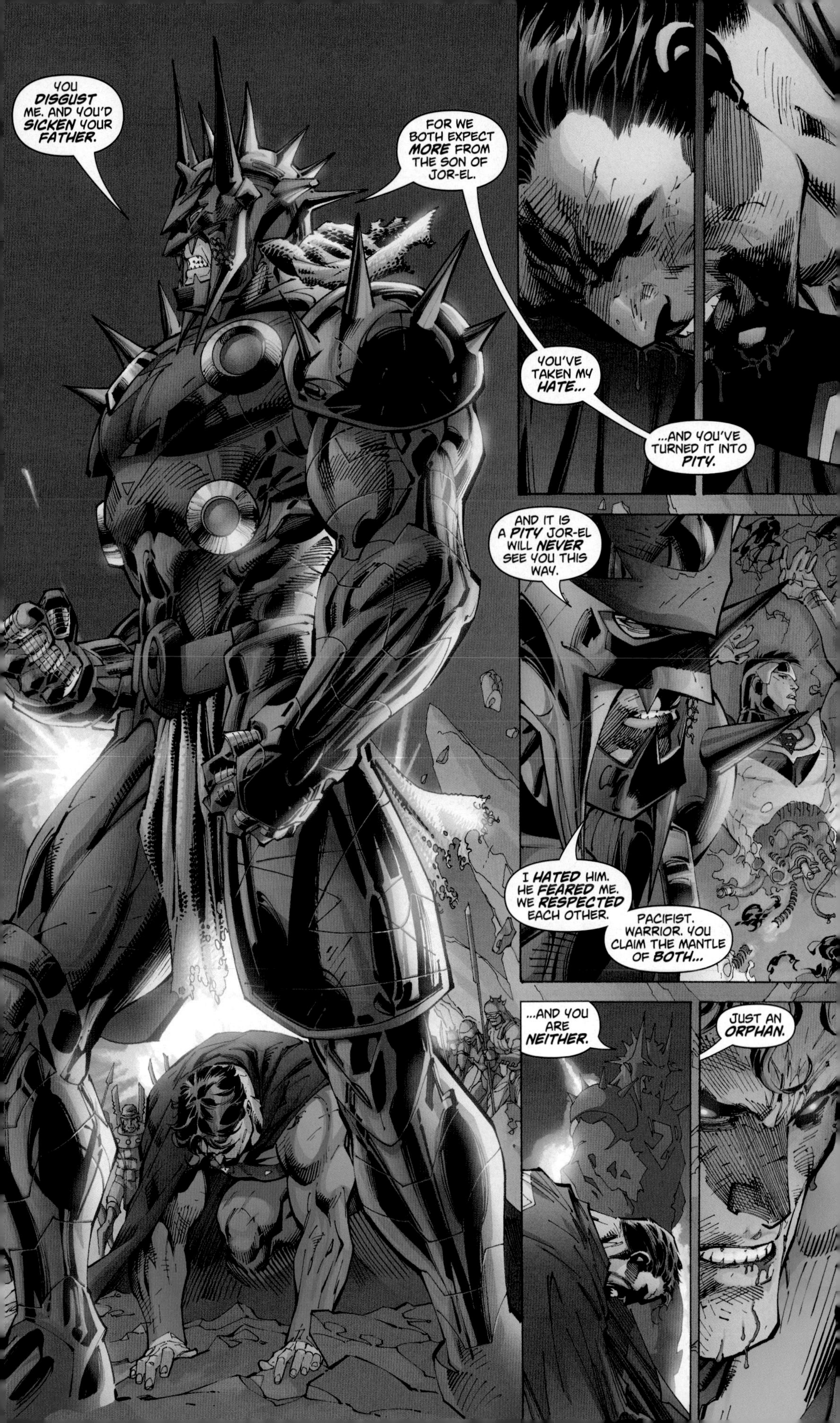
YOU DISGUST ME. AND YOU'D SICKEN YOUR FATHER.
FOR WE BOTH EXPECT MORE FROM THE SON OF JOR-EL.
YOU'VE TAKEN MY HATE...
...AND YOU'VE TURNED IT INTO PITY.
AND IT IS A PITY JOR-EL WILL NEVER SEE YOU THIS WAY.
I HATED HIM. HE FEARED ME. WE RESPECTED EACH OTHER.
PACIFIST. WARRIOR. YOU CLAIM THE MANTLE OF BOTH...
...AND YOU ARE NEITHER.
JUST AN ORPHAN.

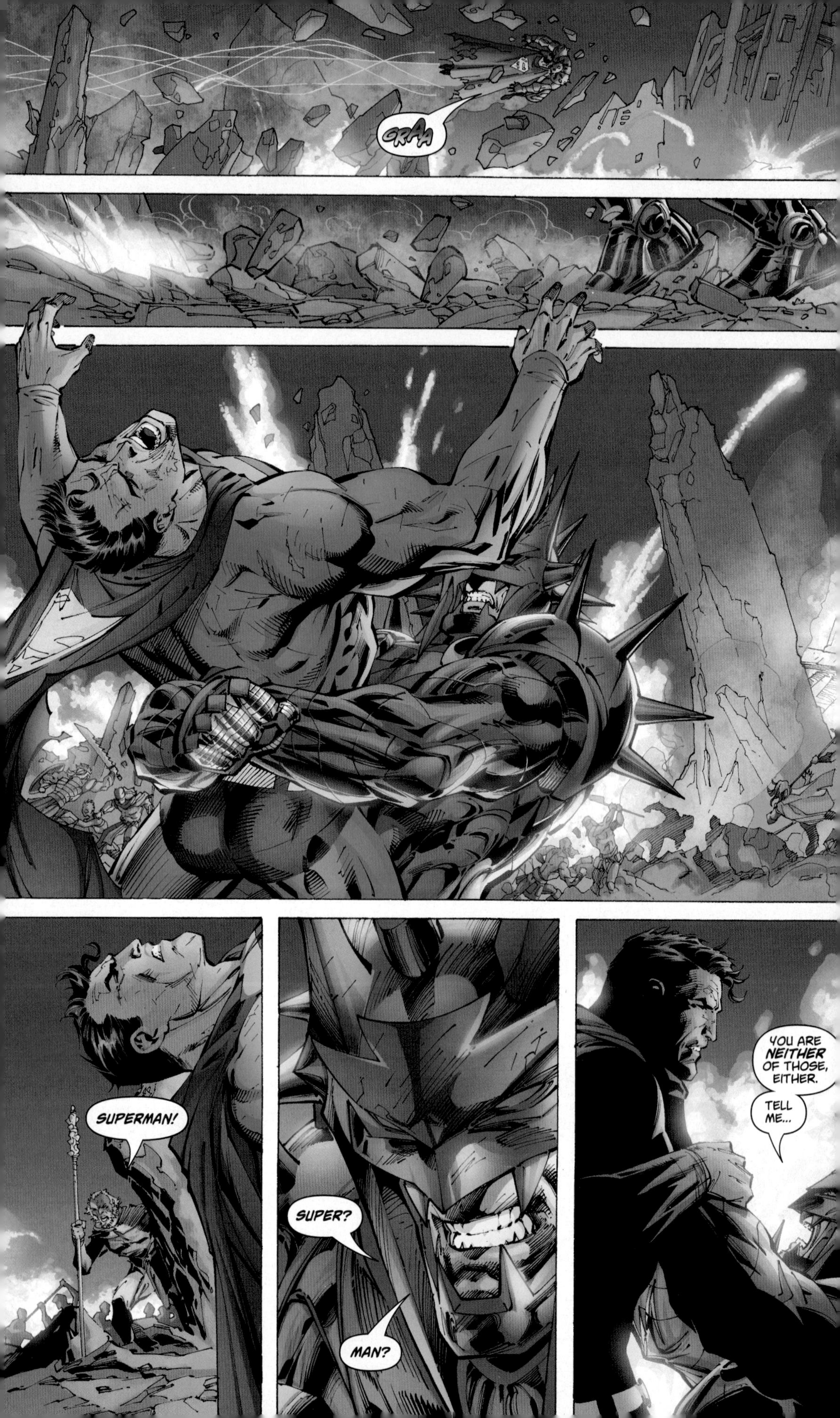
GRAA
SUPERMAN!
SUPER?
MAN?
YOU ARE NEITHER OF THOSE, EITHER.
TELL ME...

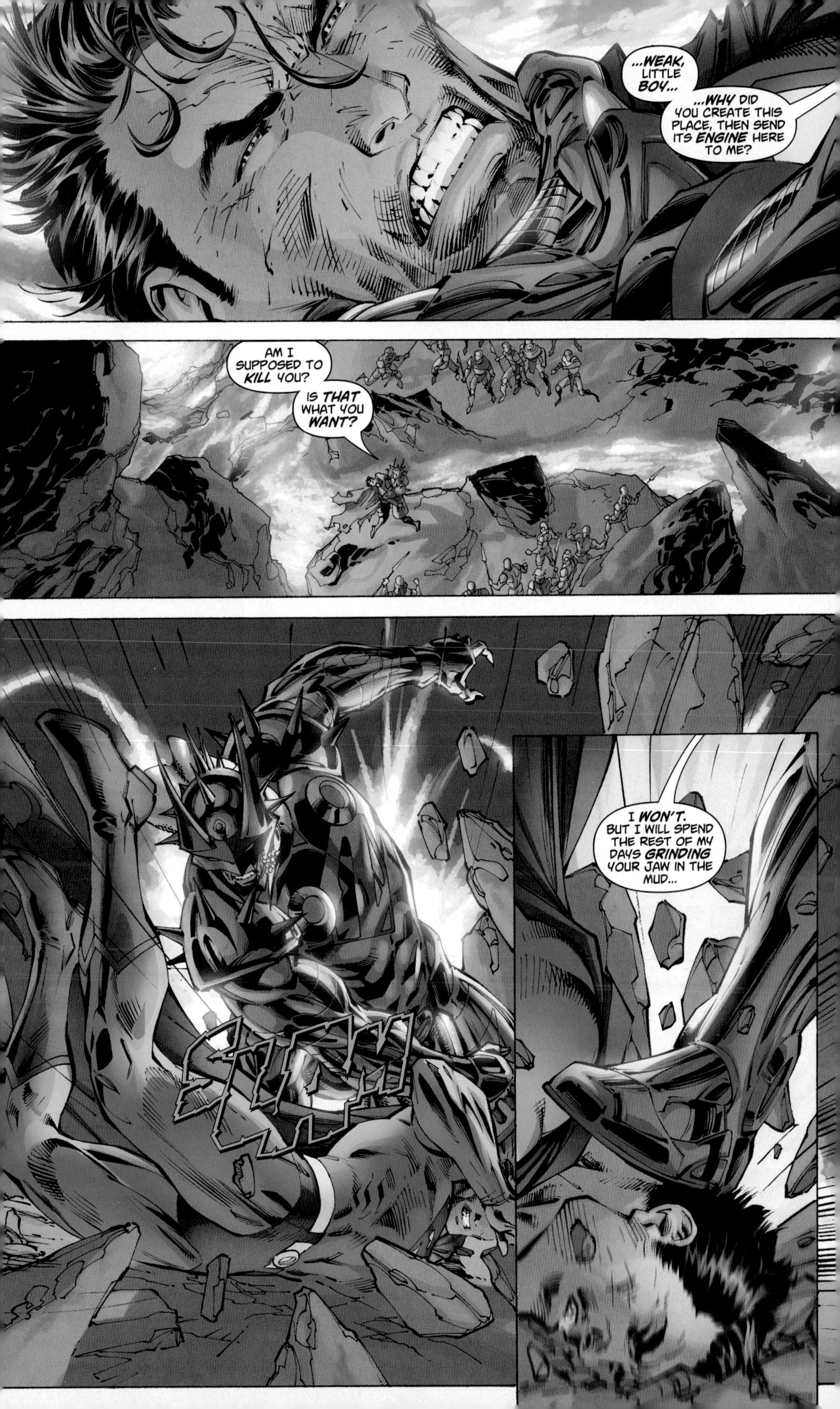
...WEAK, LITTLE BOY...
...WHY DID YOU CREATE THIS PLACE, THEN SEND ITS ENGINE HERE TO ME?
AM I SUPPOSED TO KILL YOU?
IS THAT WHAT YOU WANT?
I WON'T. BUT I WILL SPEND THE REST OF MY DAYS GRINDING YOUR JAW IN THE MUD...

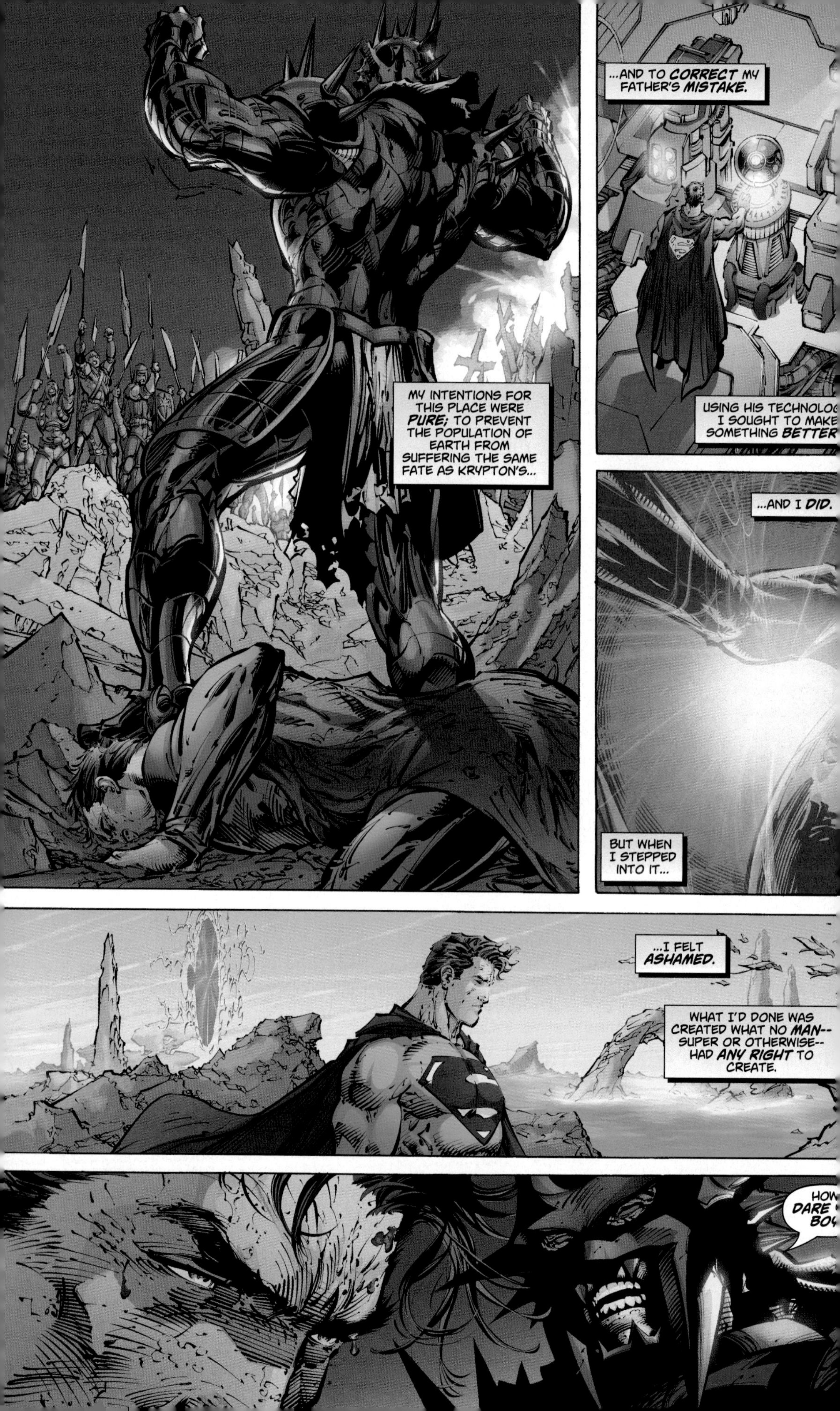
MY INTENTIONS FOR THIS PLACE WERE PURE; TO PREVENT THE POPULATION OF EARTH FROM SUFFERING THE SAME FATE AS KRYPTON'S...
...AND TO CORRECT MY FATHER'S MISTAKE.
USING HIS TECHNOLOG I SOUGHT TO MAKE SOMETHING BETTER
...AND I DID.
BUT WHEN I STEPPED INTO IT...
...I FELT ASHAMED.
WHAT I'D DONE WAS CREATED WHAT NO MAN-- SUPER OR OTHERWISE-- HAD ANY RIGHT TO CREATE.
HOW DARE BOY

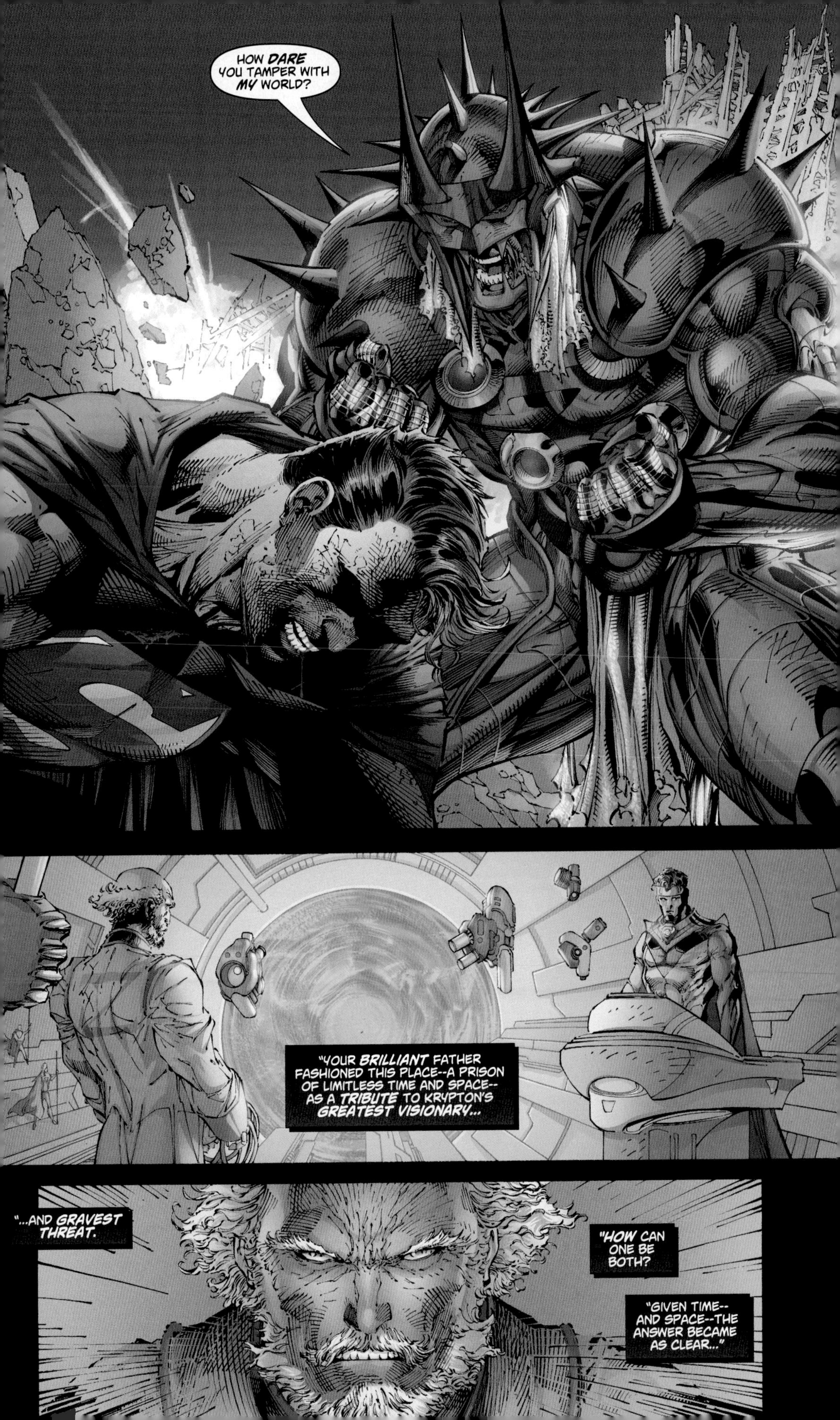
HOW DARE YOU TAMPER WITH MY WORLD?
"YOUR BRILLIANT FATHER FASHIONED THIS PLACE--A PRISON OF LIMITLESS TIME AND SPACE--AS A TRIBUTE TO KRYPTON'S GREATEST VISIONARY...
"...AND GRAVEST THREAT.
"HOW CAN ONE BE BOTH?
"GIVEN TIME--AND SPACE--THE ANSWER BECAME AS CLEAR..."

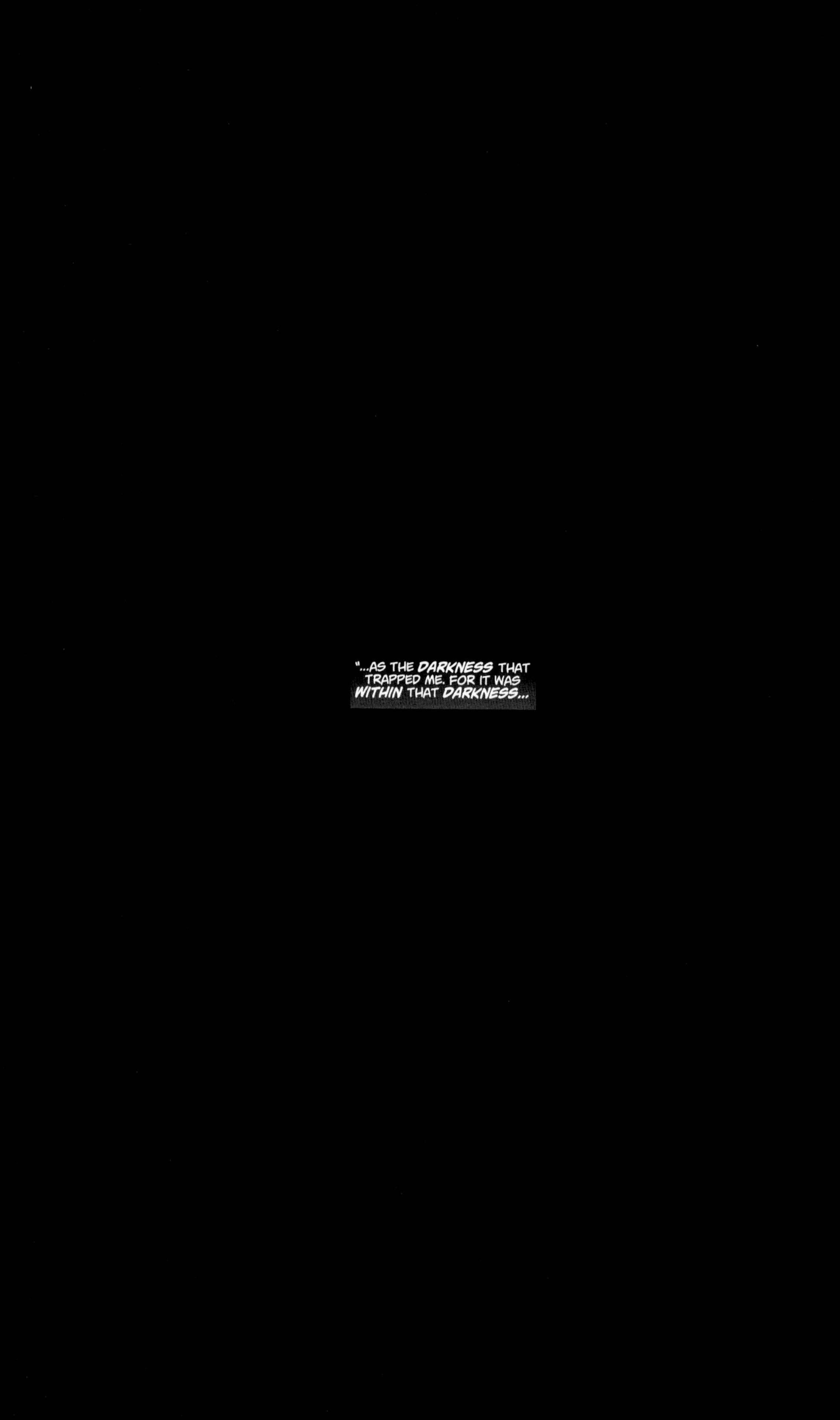
"...AS THE DARKNESS THAT TRAPPED ME. FOR IT WAS WITHIN THAT DARKNESS...

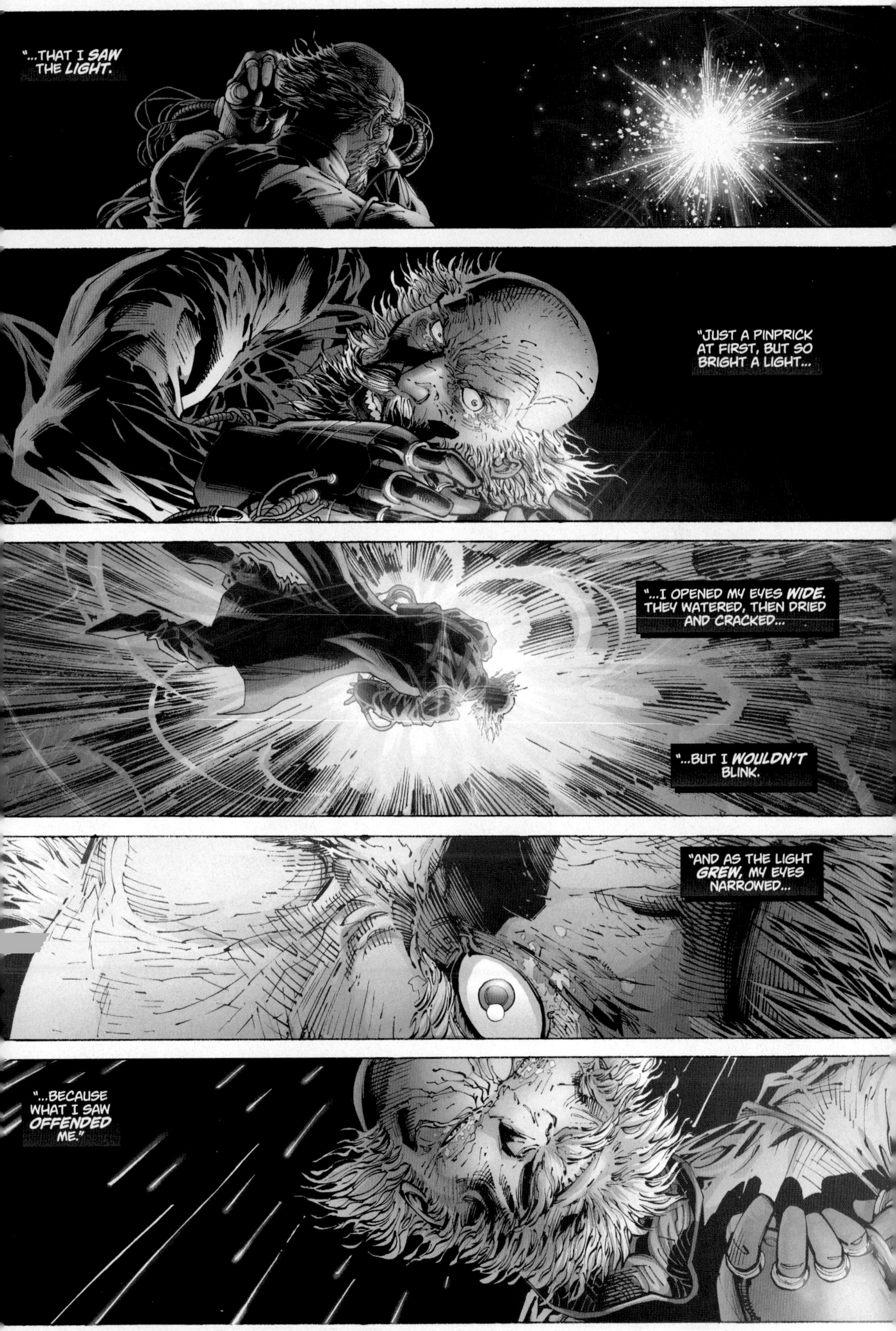
"...THAT I SAW THE LIGHT.
"JUST A PINPRICK AT FIRST, BUT SO BRIGHT A LIGHT...
"...I OPENED MY EYES WIDE. THEY WATERED, THEN DRIED AND CRACKED...
"...BUT I WOULDN'T BLINK.
"AND AS THE LIGHT GREW, MY EYES NARROWED...
"...BECAUSE WHAT I SAW OFFENDED ME."

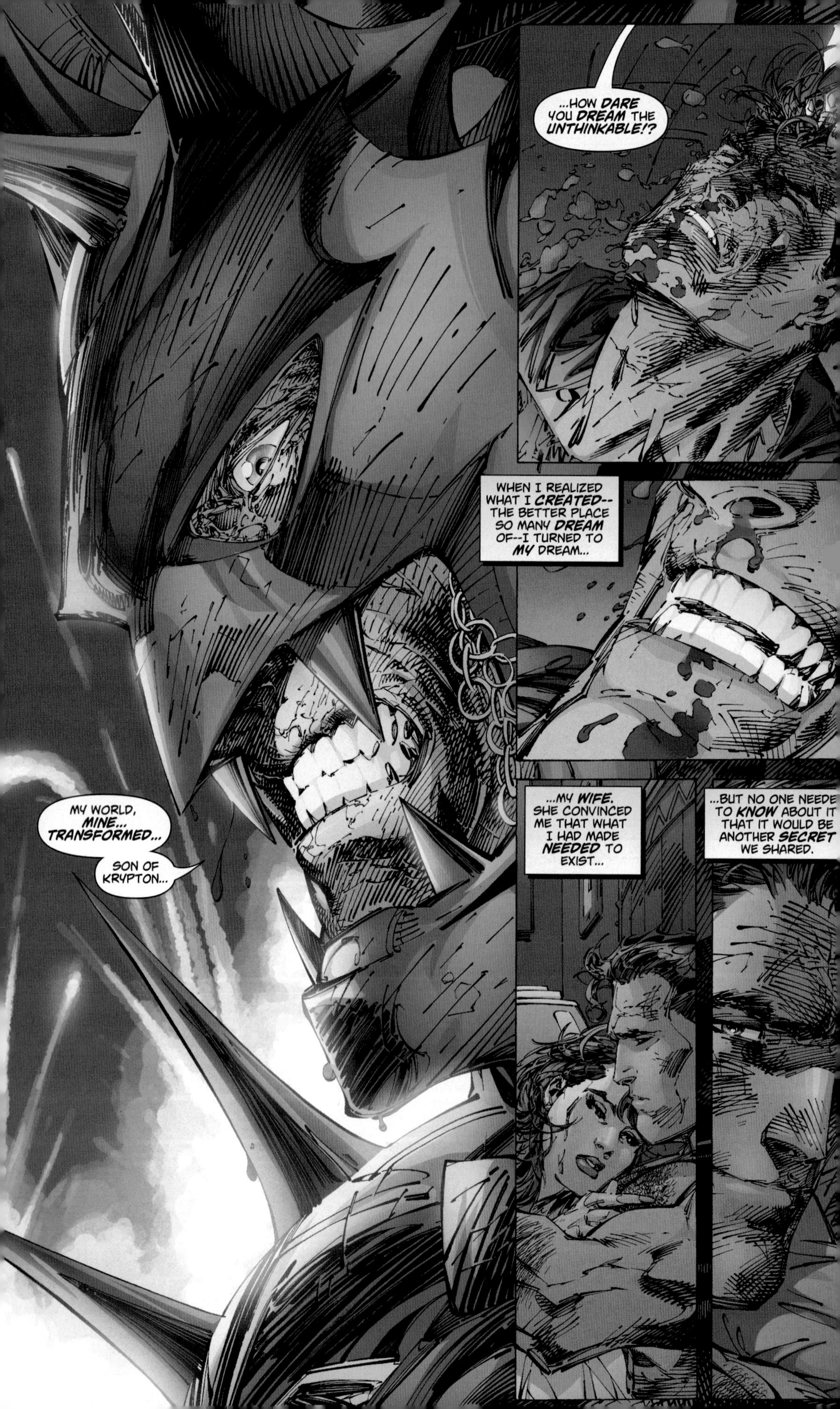
...HOW DARE YOU DREAM THE UNTHINKABLE!?
MY WORLD, MINE... TRANSFORMED...
SON OF KRYPTON...
WHEN I REALIZED WHAT I CREATED-- THE BETTER PLACE SO MANY DREAM OF--I TURNED TO MY DREAM...
...MY WIFE. SHE CONVINCED ME THAT WHAT I HAD MADE NEEDED TO EXIST...
...BUT NO ONE NEEDE TO KNOW ABOUT IT THAT IT WOULD BE ANOTHER SECRET WE SHARED.

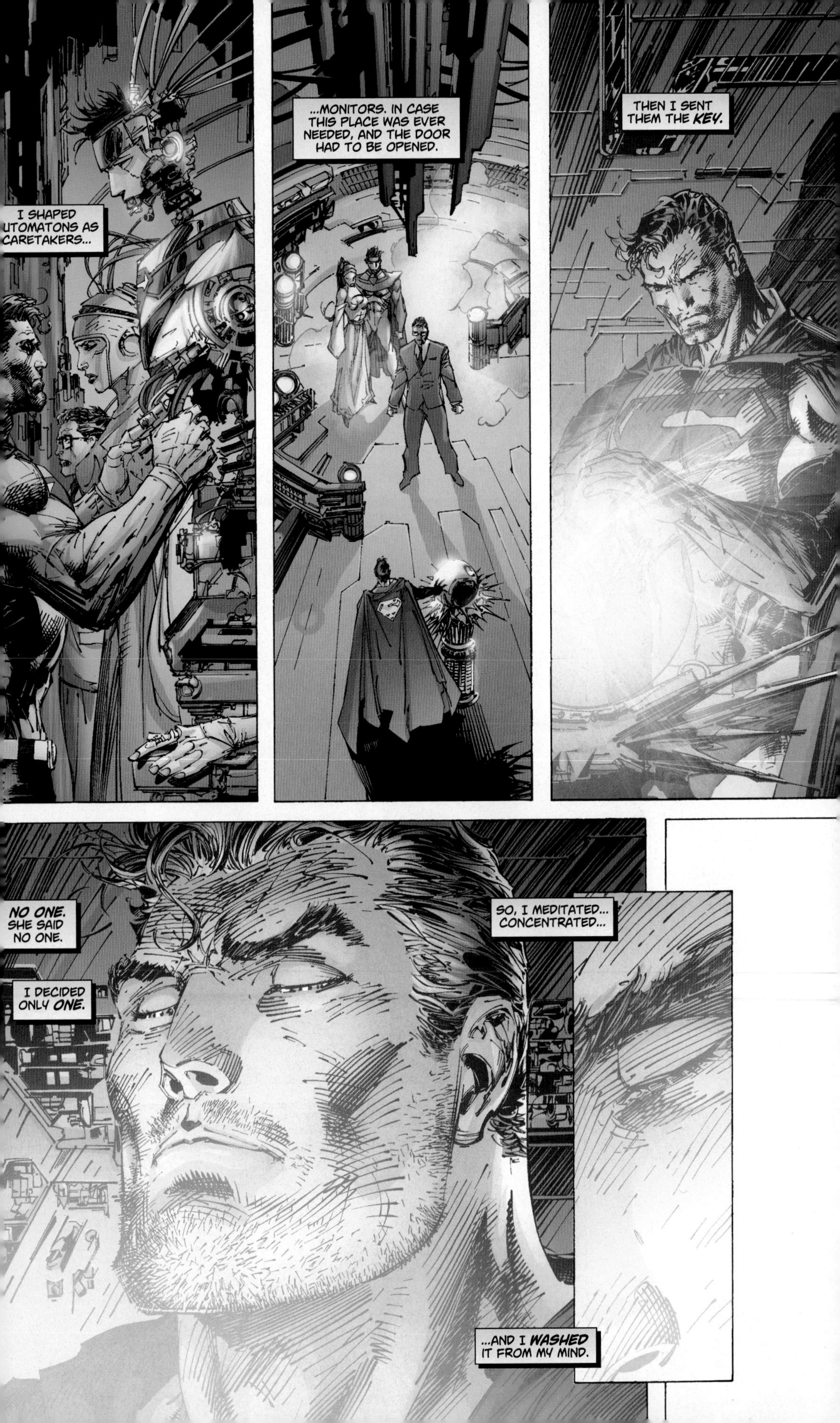
I SHAPED
UTOMATONS AS
CARETAKERS...
...MONITORS. IN CASE THIS PLACE WAS EVER NEEDED, AND THE DOOR HAD TO BE OPENED.
THEN I SENT THEM THE KEY.
NO ONE. SHE SAID NO ONE.
I DECIDED ONLY ONE.
SO, I MEDITATED... CONCENTRATED...
...AND I WASHED IT FROM MY MIND.

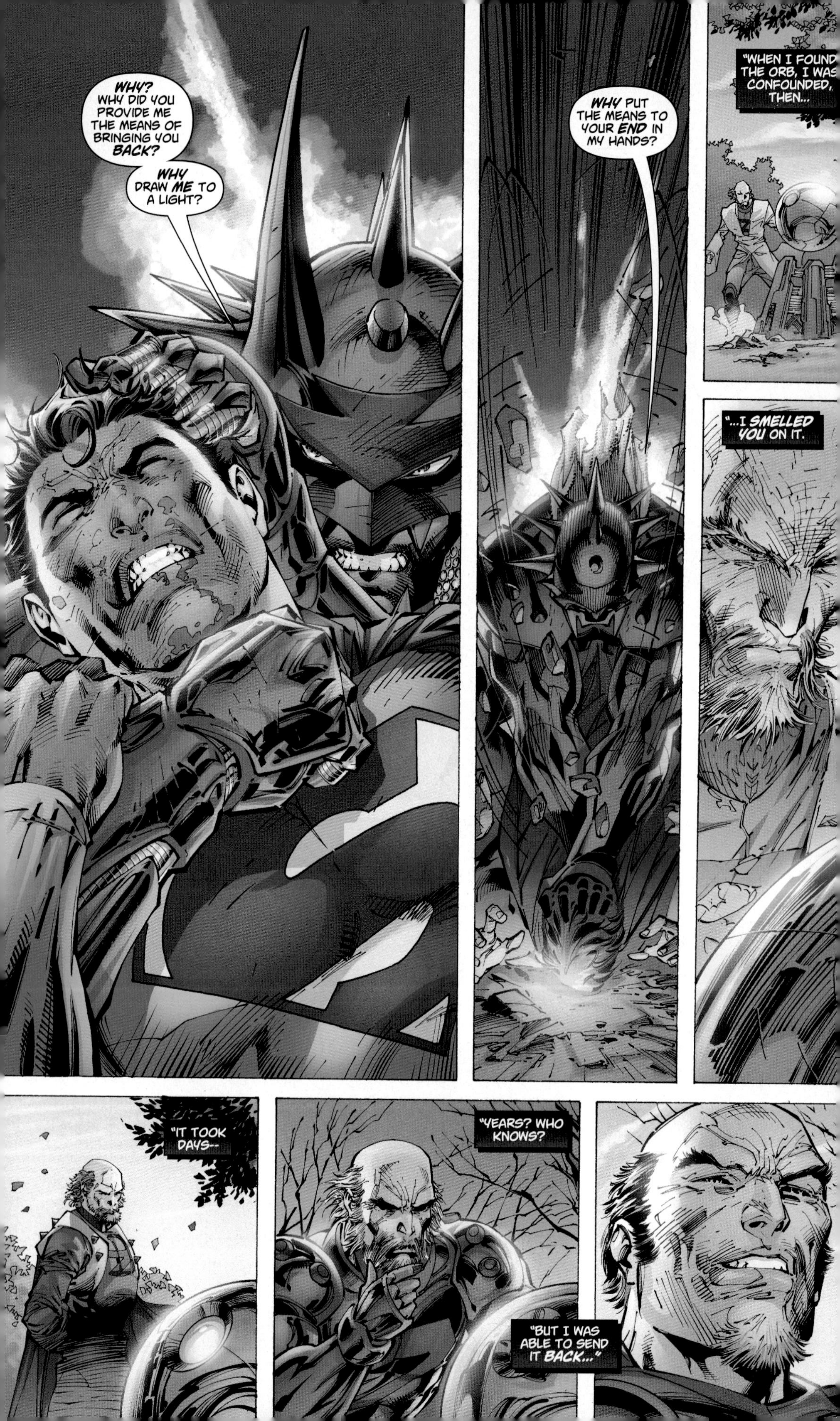
WHY? WHY DID YOU PROVIDE ME THE MEANS OF BRINGING YOU BACK?
WHY DRAW ME TO A LIGHT?
WHY PUT THE MEANS TO YOUR END IN MY HANDS?
"WHEN I FOUND THE ORB, I WAS CONFOUNDED, THEN...
"...I SMELLED YOU ON IT.
"IT TOOK DAYS--
"YEARS? WHO KNOWS?
"BUT I WAS ABLE TO SEND IT BACK..."

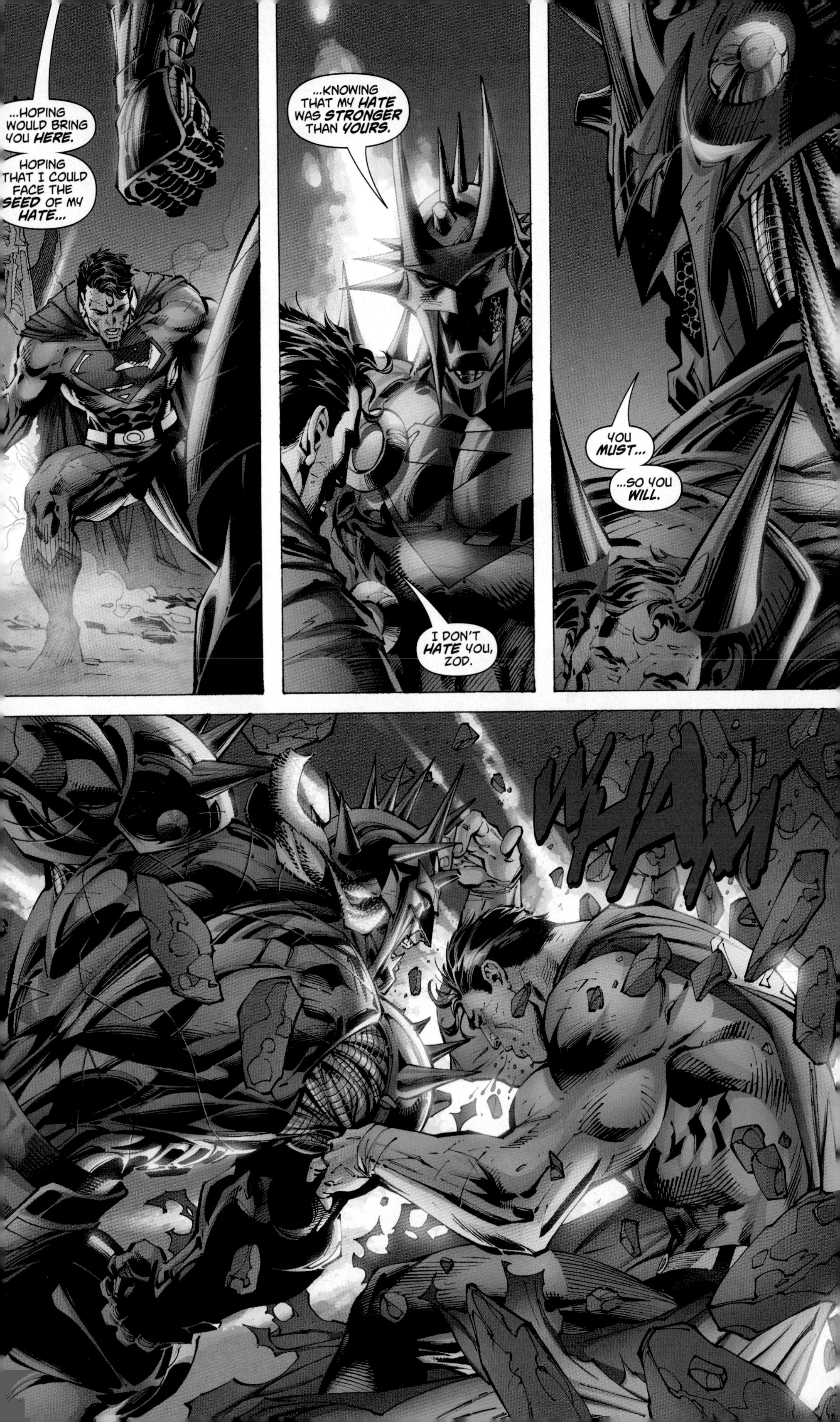
...HOPING WOULD BRING YOU HERE.
HOPING THAT I COULD FACE THE SEED OF MY HATE...
...KNOWING THAT MY HATE WAS STRONGER THAN YOURS.
I DON'T HATE YOU, ZOD.
YOU MUST...
...SO YOU WILL.
WHAM

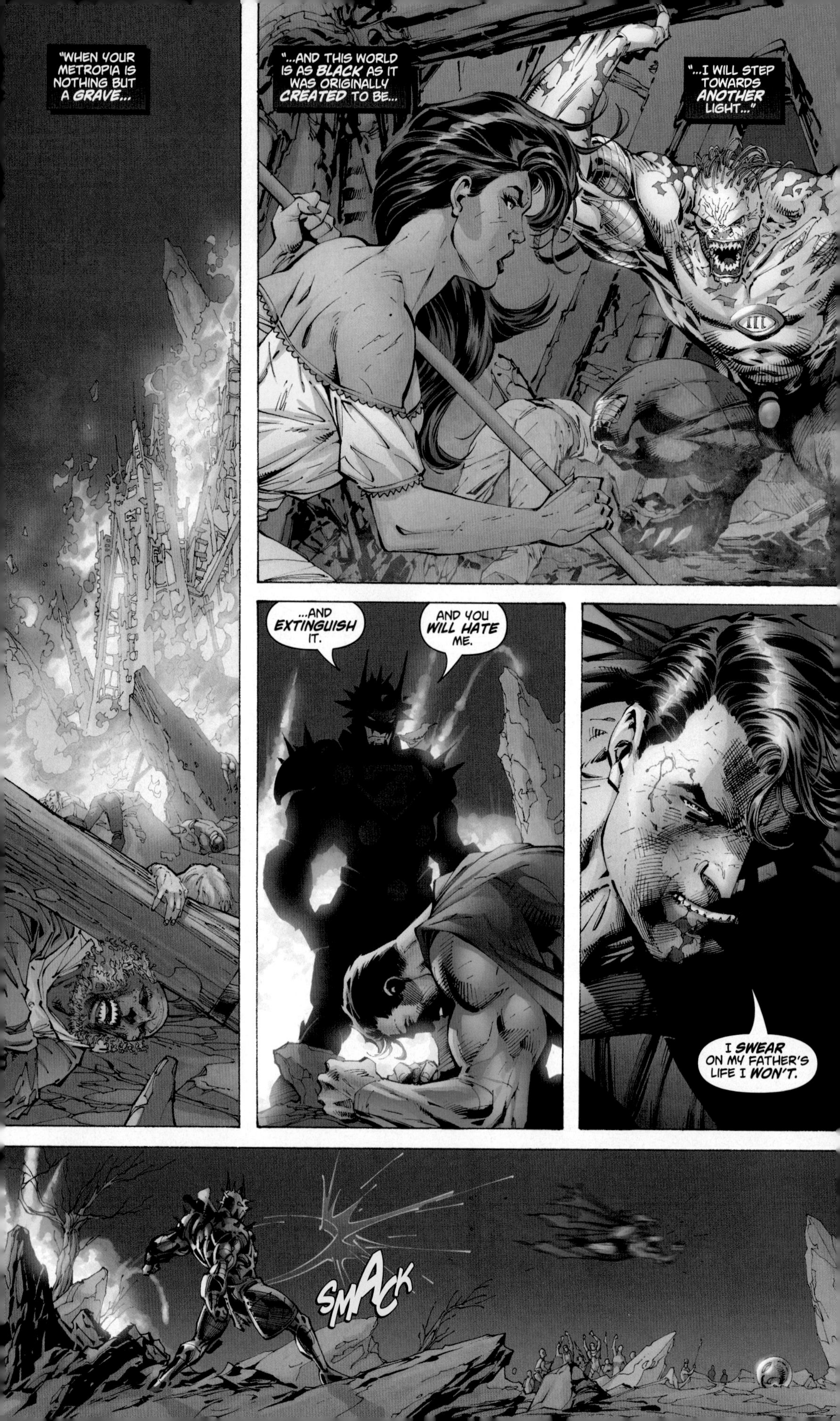
"WHEN YOUR METROPIA IS NOTHING BUT A GRAVE...
"...AND THIS WORLD IS AS BLACK AS IT WAS ORIGINALLY CREATED TO BE...
"...I WILL STEP TOWARDS ANOTHER LIGHT..."
...AND EXTINGUISH IT.
AND YOU WILL HATE ME.
I SWEAR ON MY FATHER'S LIFE I WON'T.
SMACK

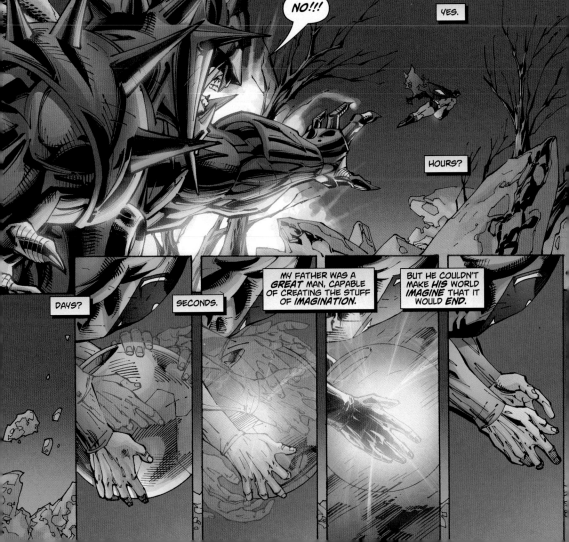

NO!!!

YES.

HOURS?

DAYS?

SECONDS.

MY FATHER WAS A *GREAT* MAN, CAPABLE OF CREATING THE STUFF OF *IMAGINATION*.

BUT HE COULDN'T MAKE *HIS* WORLD *IMAGINE* THAT IT WOULD *END*.

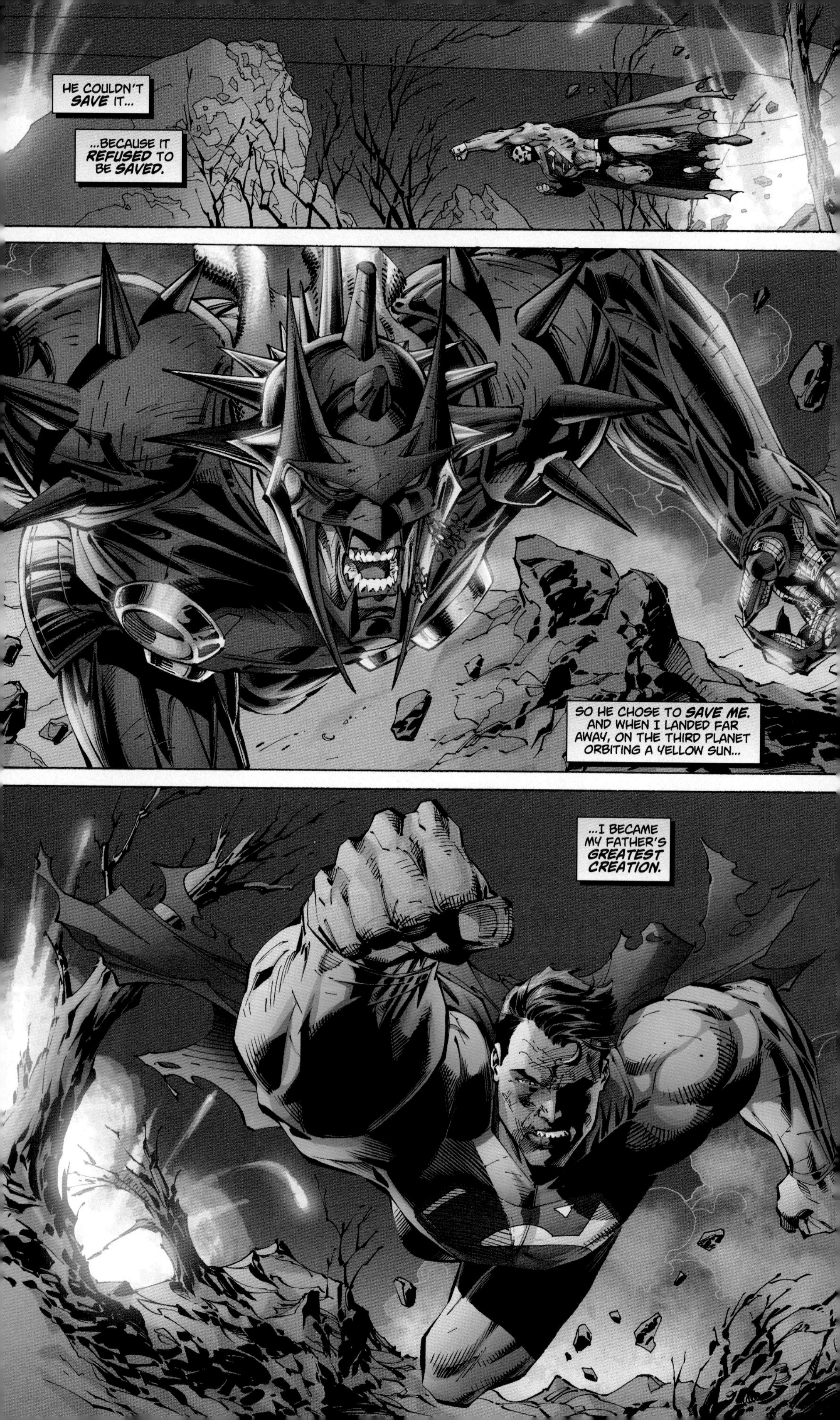
HE COULDN'T SAVE IT...
...BECAUSE IT REFUSED TO BE SAVED.
SO HE CHOSE TO SAVE ME. AND WHEN I LANDED FAR AWAY, ON THE THIRD PLANET ORBITING A YELLOW SUN...
...I BECAME MY FATHER'S GREATEST CREATION.

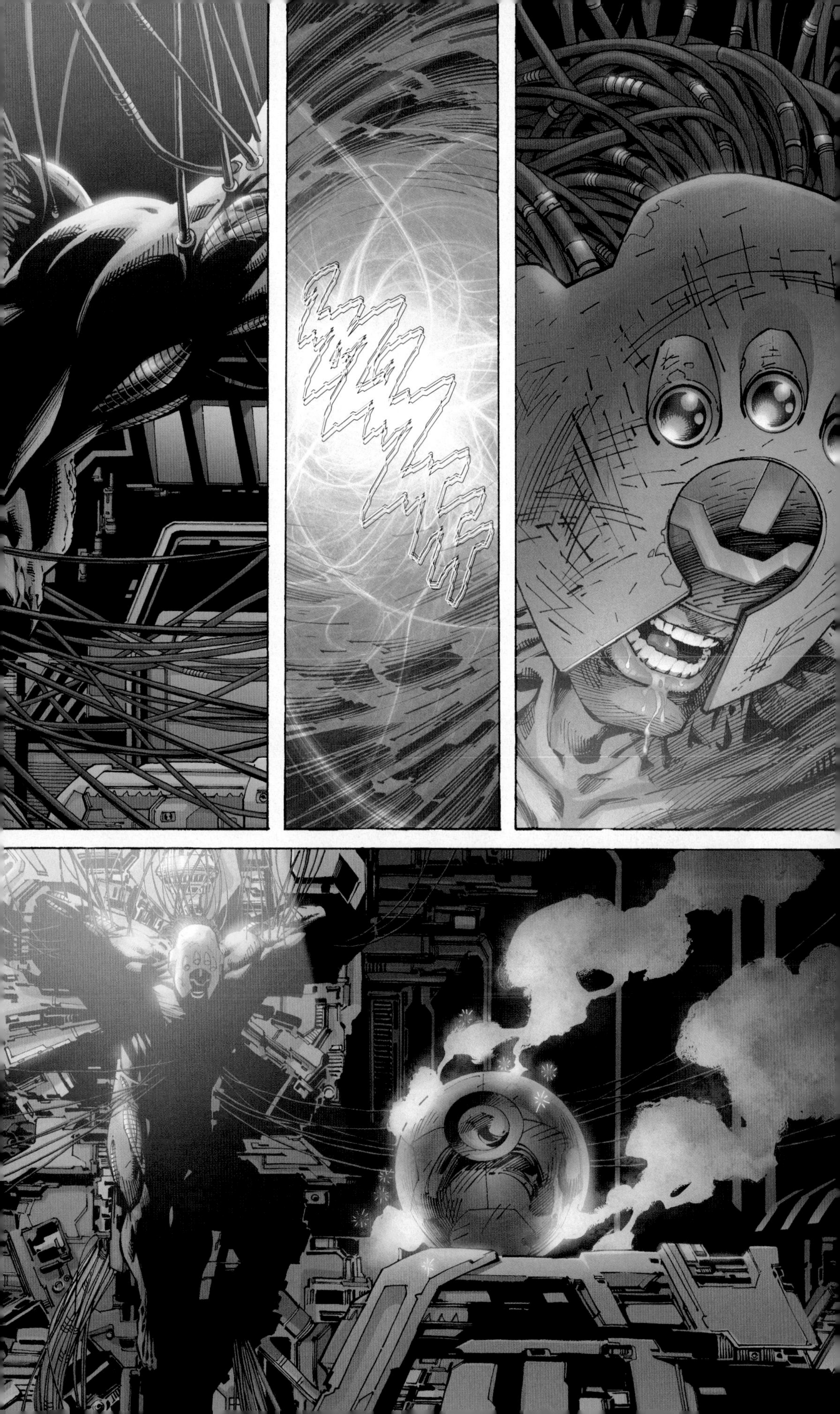

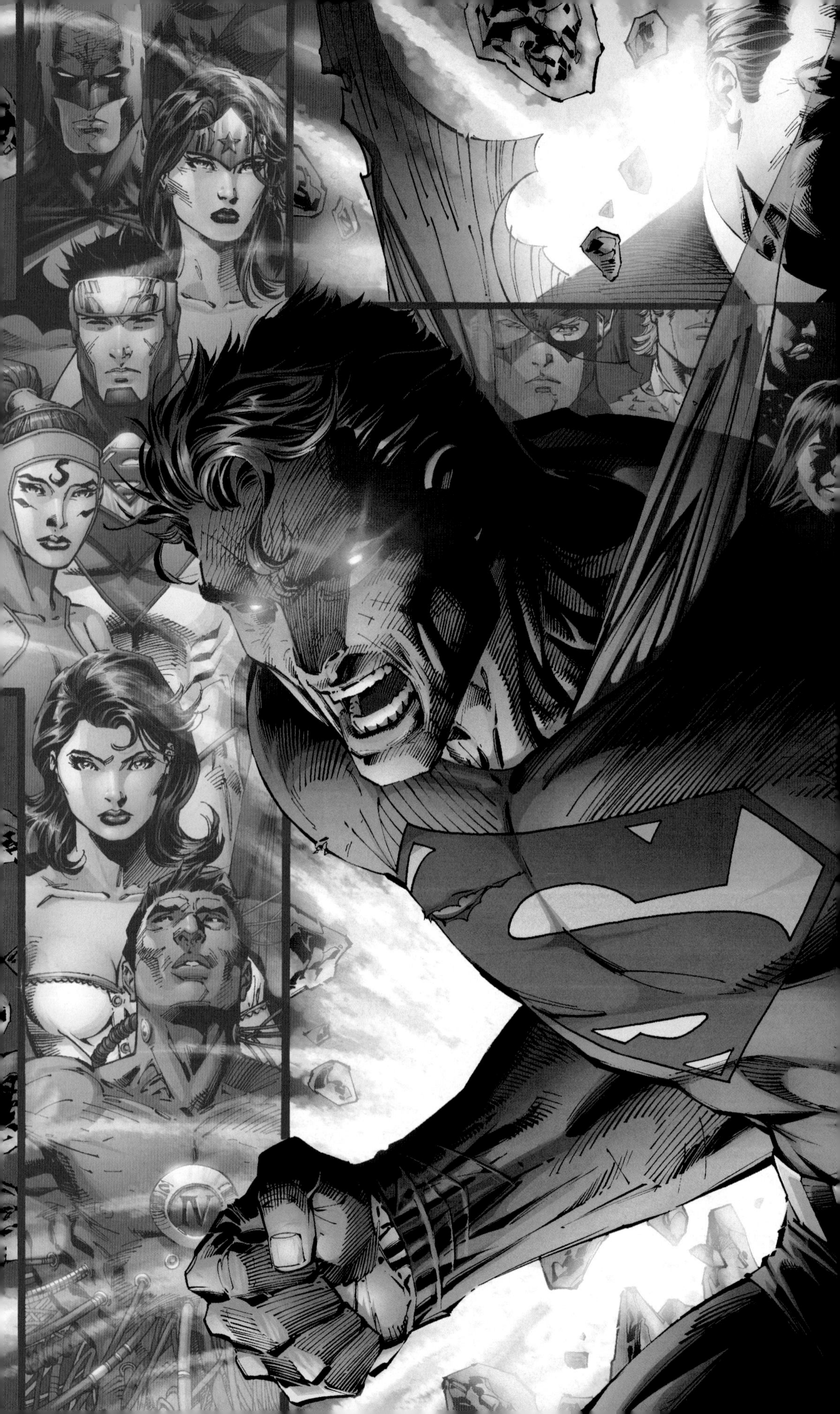

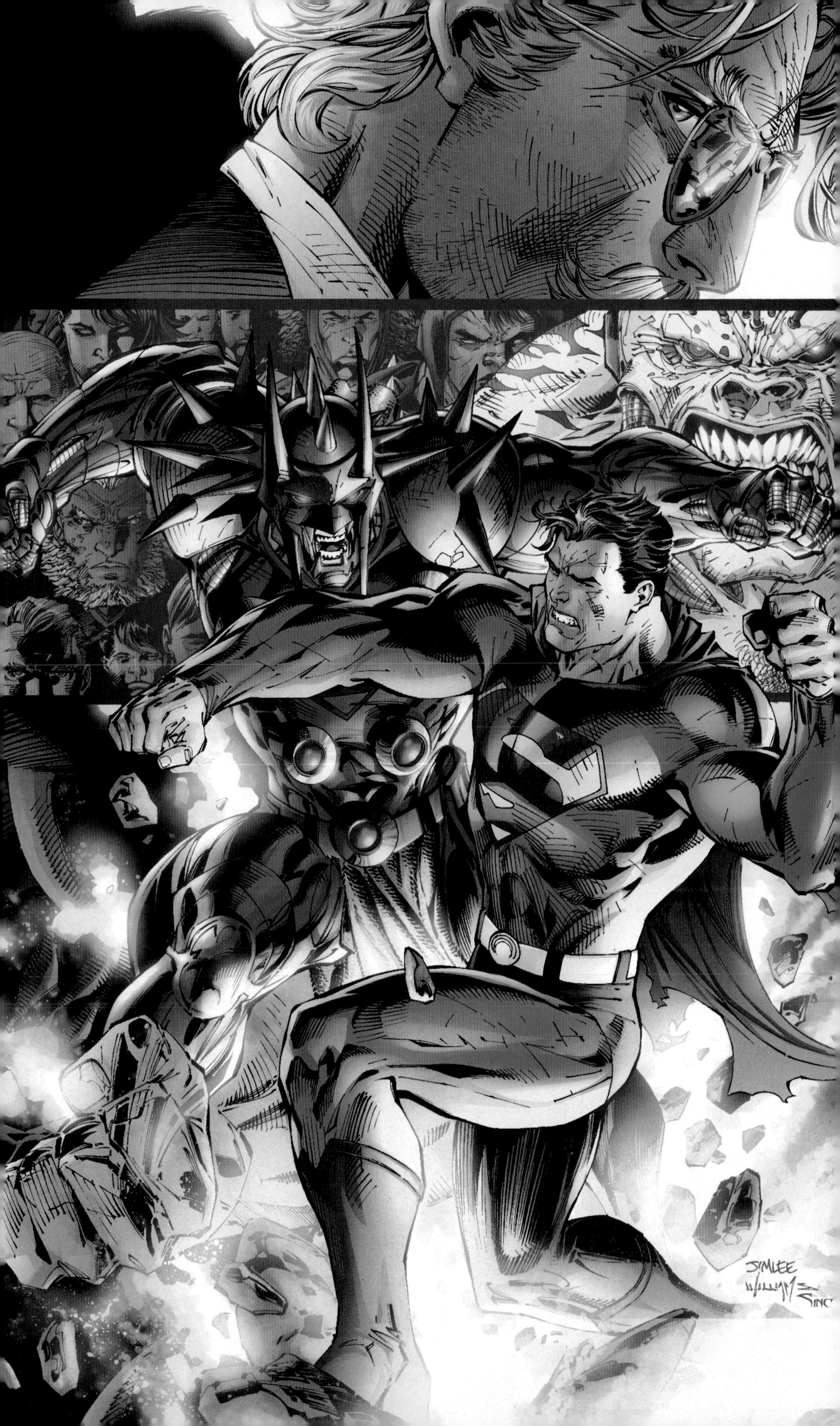

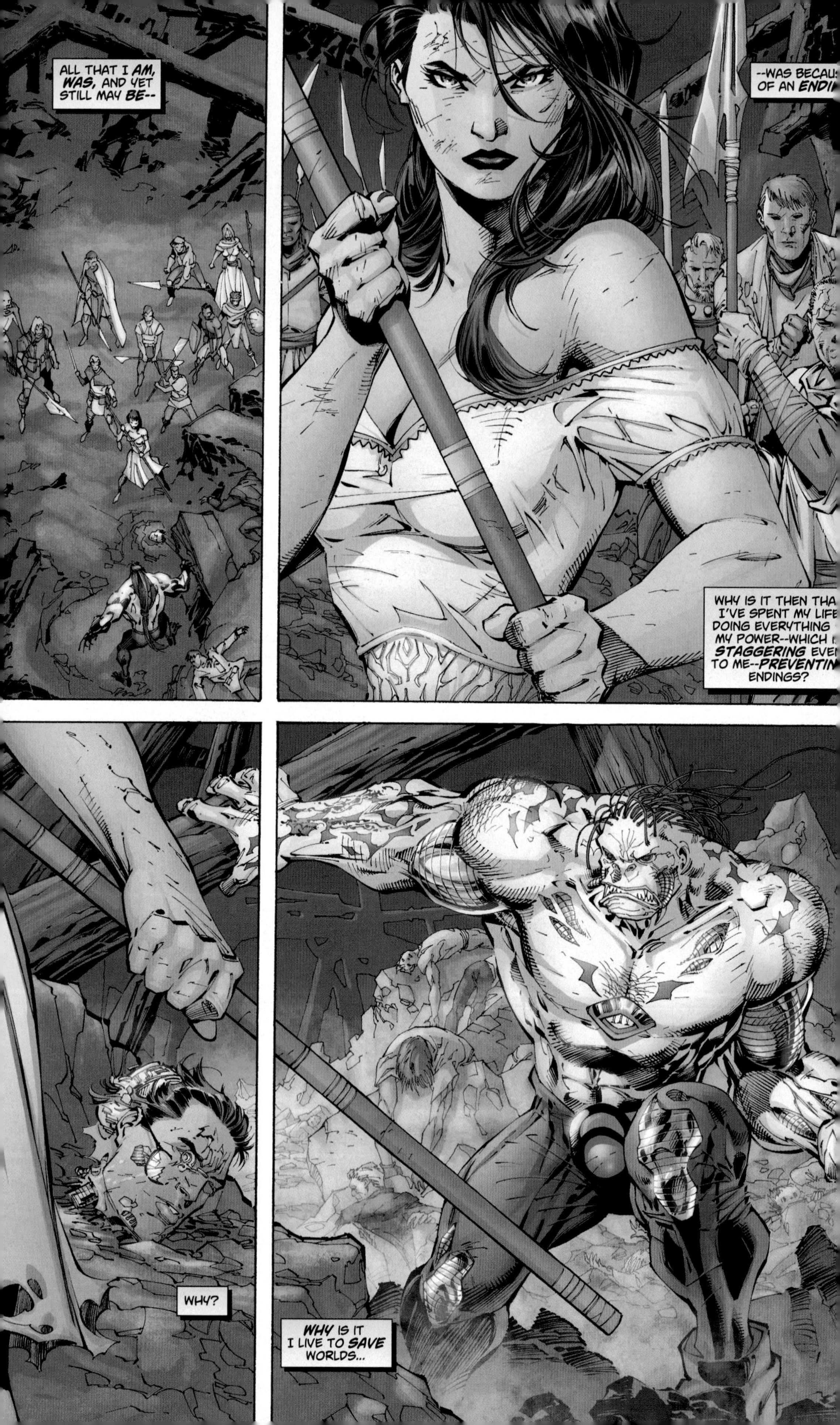

ALL THAT I AM, WAS, AND YET STILL MAY BE--
--WAS BECAUS OF AN ENDI
WHY IS IT THEN THA I'VE SPENT MY LIFE DOING EVERYTHING MY POWER--WHICH STAGGERING EVE TO ME--PREVENTIN ENDINGS?
WHY?
WHY IS IT I LIVE TO SAVE WORLDS...

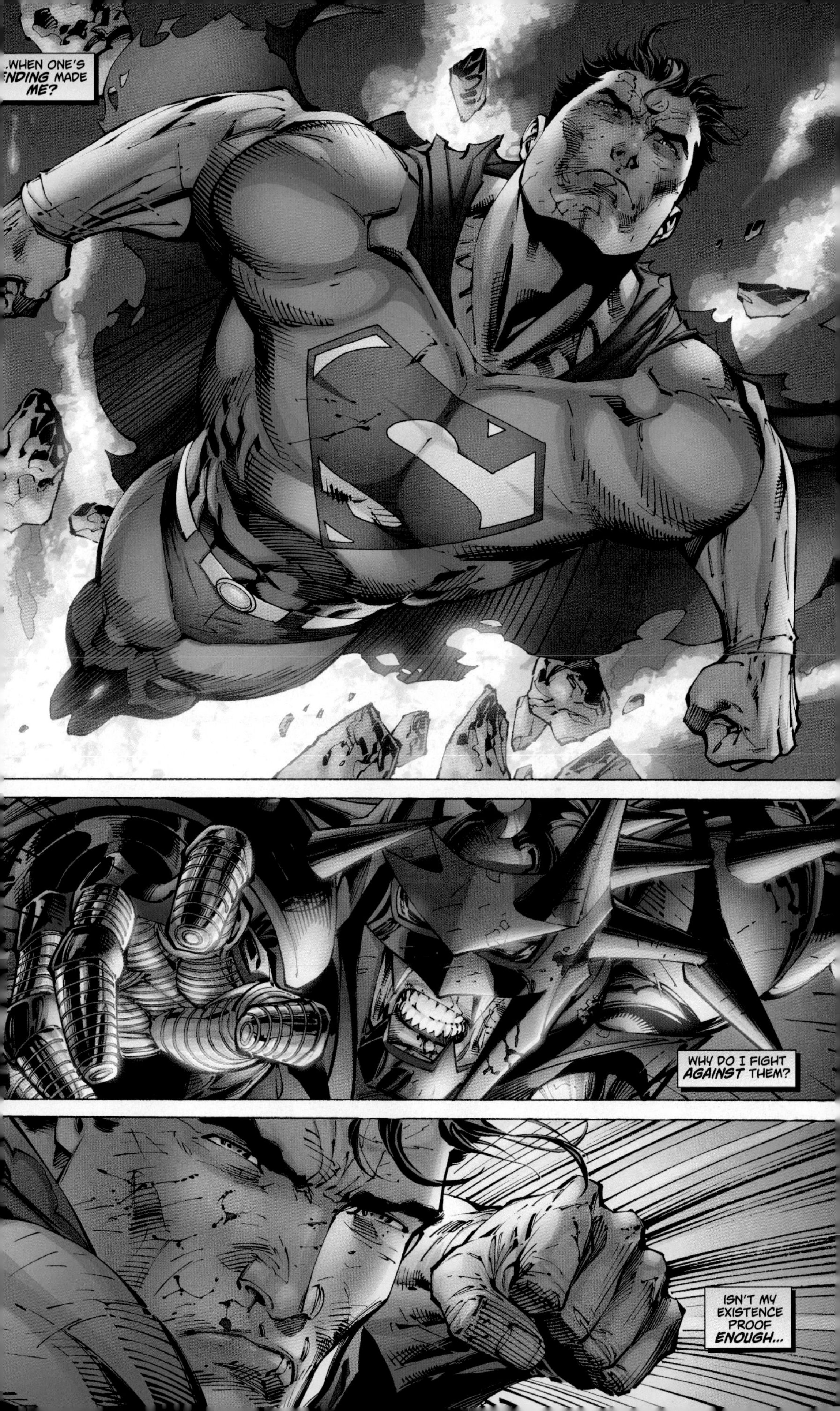
...WHEN ONE'S ENDING MADE ME?
WHY DO I FIGHT AGAINST THEM?
ISN'T MY EXISTENCE PROOF ENOUGH...

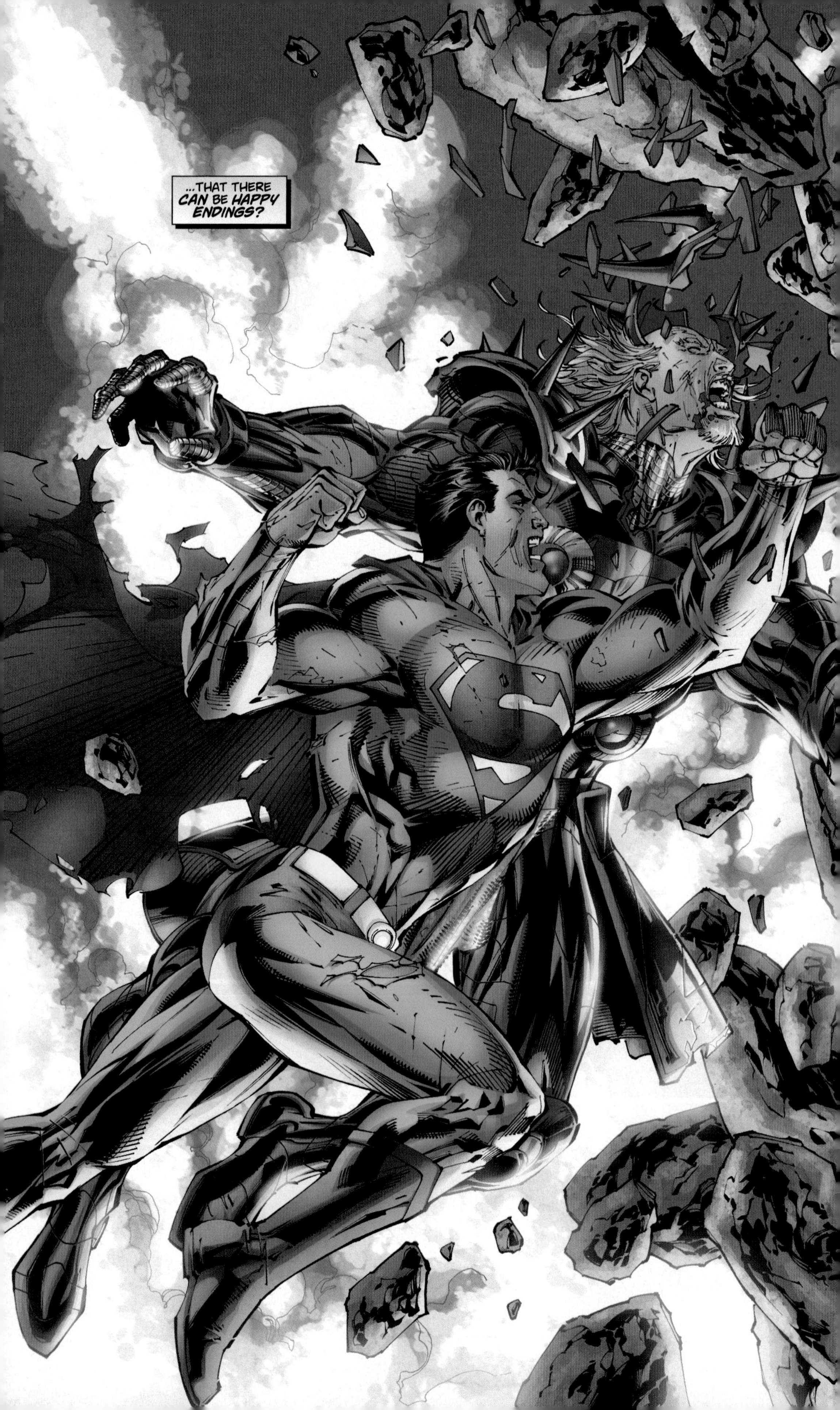
...THAT THERE CAN BE HAPPY ENDINGS?

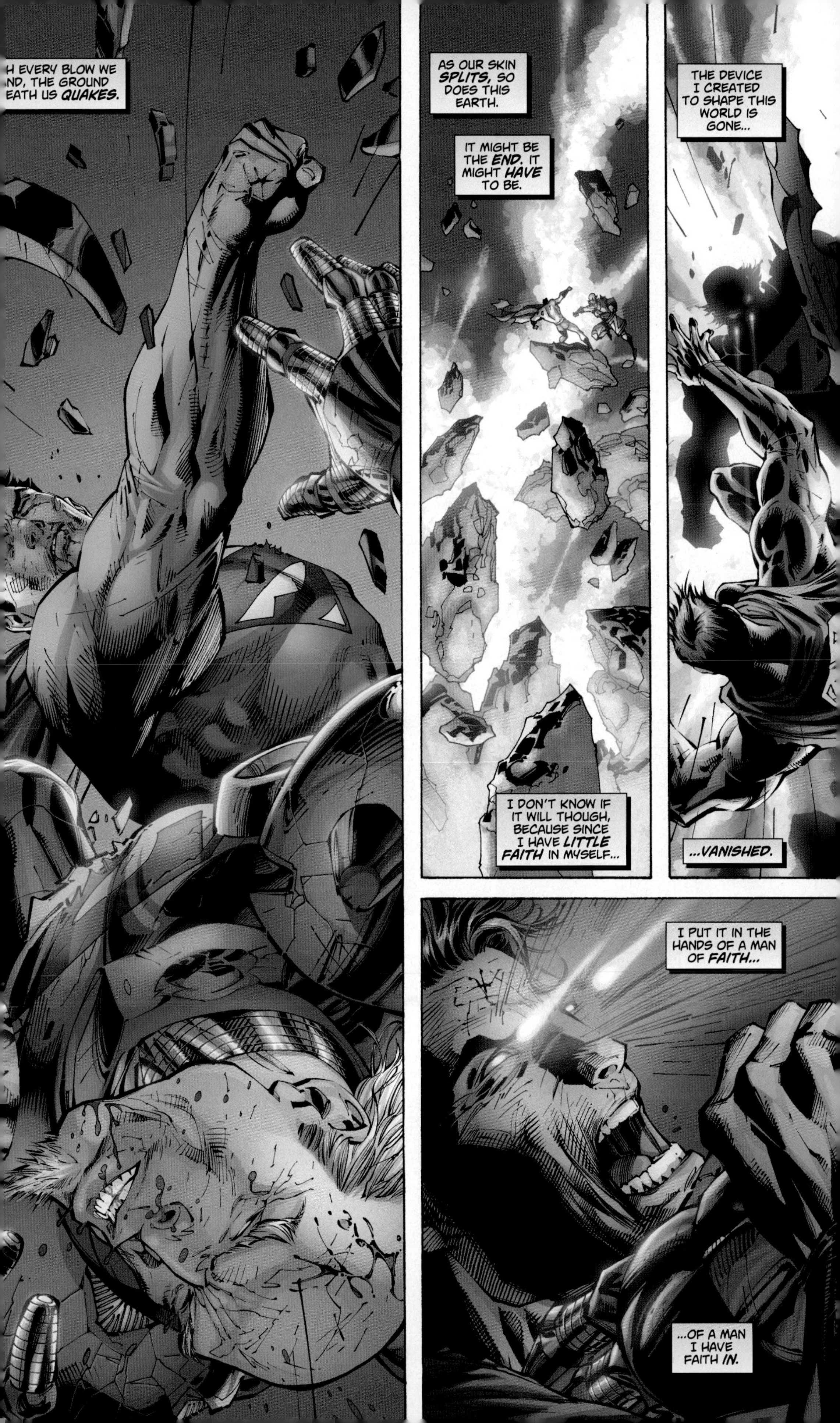

H EVERY BLOW WE
ND, THE GROUND
EATH US QUAKES.
AS OUR SKIN SPLITS, SO DOES THIS EARTH.
IT MIGHT BE THE END. IT MIGHT HAVE TO BE.
THE DEVICE I CREATED TO SHAPE THIS WORLD IS GONE...
I DON'T KNOW IF IT WILL THOUGH, BECAUSE SINCE I HAVE LITTLE FAITH IN MYSELF...
...VANISHED.
I PUT IT IN THE HANDS OF A MAN OF FAITH...
...OF A MAN I HAVE FAITH IN.

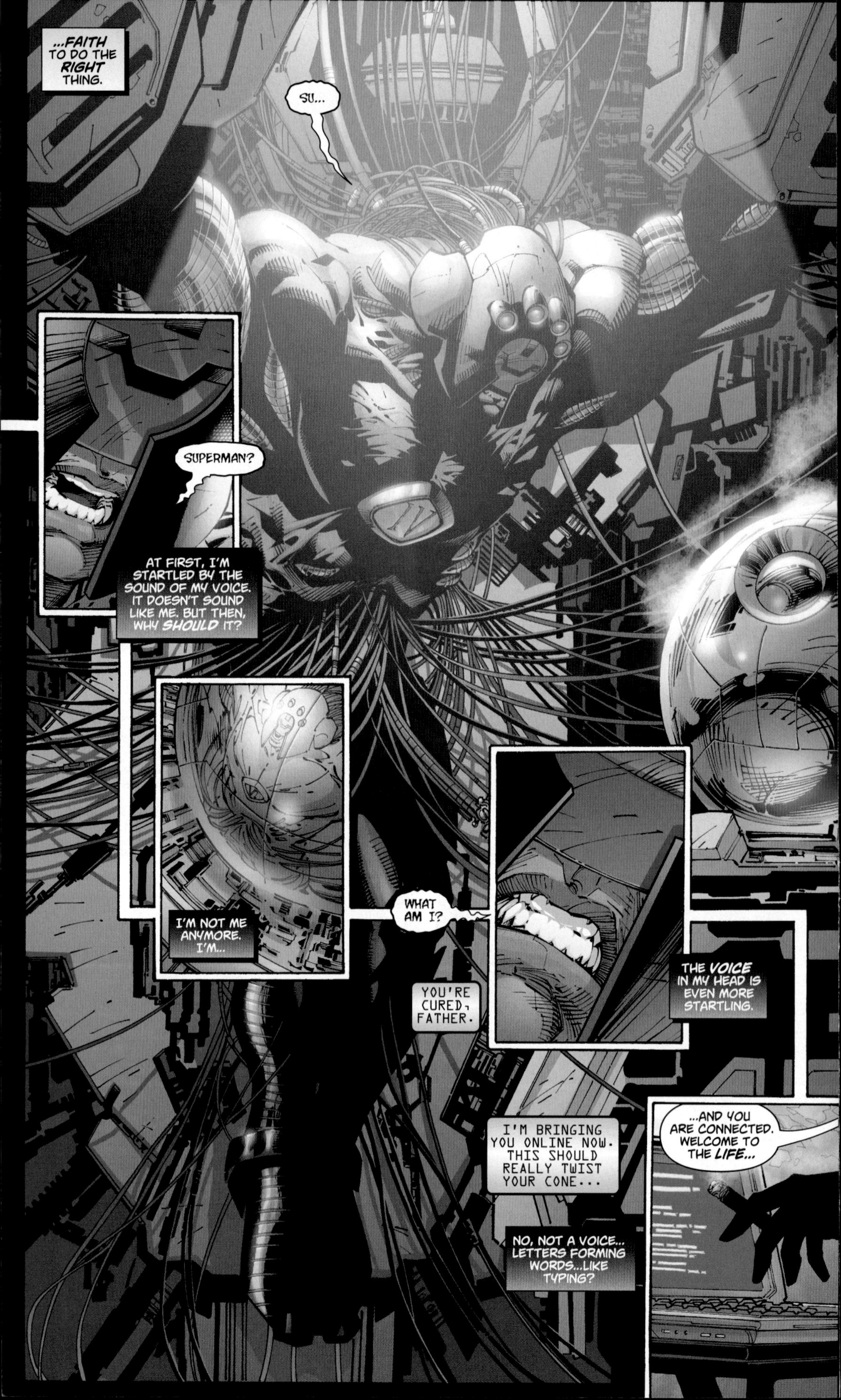

...FAITH TO DO THE RIGHT THING.
SU...
SUPERMAN?
AT FIRST, I'M STARTLED BY THE SOUND OF MY VOICE. IT DOESN'T SOUND LIKE ME. BUT THEN, WHY SHOULD IT?
I'M NOT ME ANYMORE. I'M...
WHAT AM I?
THE VOICE IN MY HEAD IS EVEN MORE STARTLING.
YOU'RE CURED, FATHER.
I'M BRINGING YOU ONLINE NOW. THIS SHOULD REALLY TWIST YOUR CONE...
...AND YOU ARE CONNECTED. WELCOME TO THE LIFE...
NO, NOT A VOICE... LETTERS FORMING WORDS...LIKE TYPING?

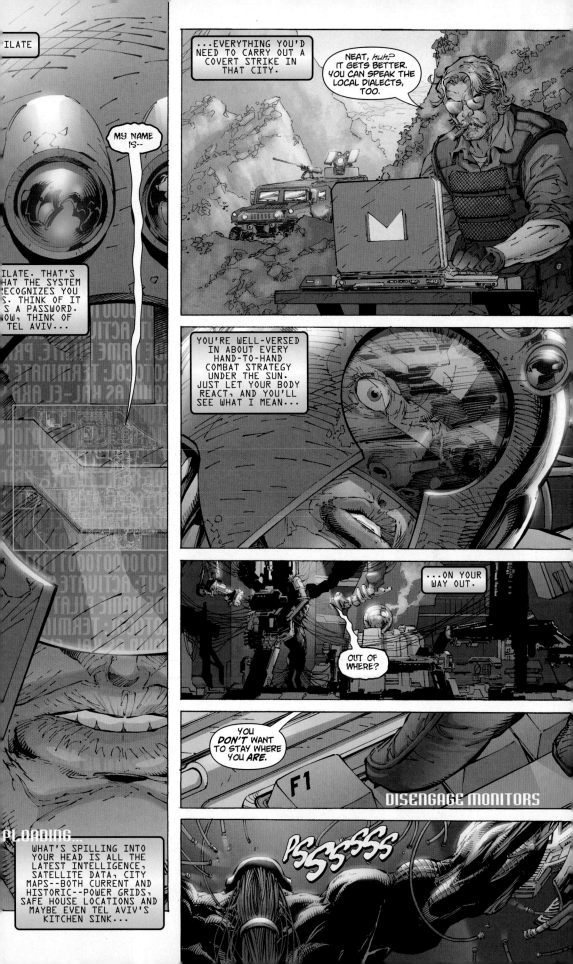

...ILATE

MY NAME IS--

...ILATE. THAT'S [W]HAT THE SYSTEM [R]ECOGNIZES YOU [A]S. THINK OF IT [A]S A PASSWORD. [N]OW, THINK OF TEL AVIV...

[U]PLOADING...

WHAT'S SPILLING INTO YOUR HEAD IS ALL THE LATEST INTELLIGENCE, SATELLITE DATA, CITY MAPS--BOTH CURRENT AND HISTORIC--POWER GRIDS, SAFE HOUSE LOCATIONS AND MAYBE EVEN TEL AVIV'S KITCHEN SINK...

...EVERYTHING YOU'D NEED TO CARRY OUT A COVERT STRIKE IN THAT CITY.

NEAT, *huh?* IT GETS BETTER. YOU CAN SPEAK THE LOCAL DIALECTS, TOO.

YOU'RE WELL-VERSED IN ABOUT EVERY HAND-TO-HAND COMBAT STRATEGY UNDER THE SUN. JUST LET YOUR BODY REACT, AND YOU'LL SEE WHAT I MEAN...

...ON YOUR WAY OUT.

OUT OF WHERE?

YOU *DON'T* WANT TO STAY WHERE YOU *ARE.*

F1

DISENGAGE MONITORS

PSSSSSSS

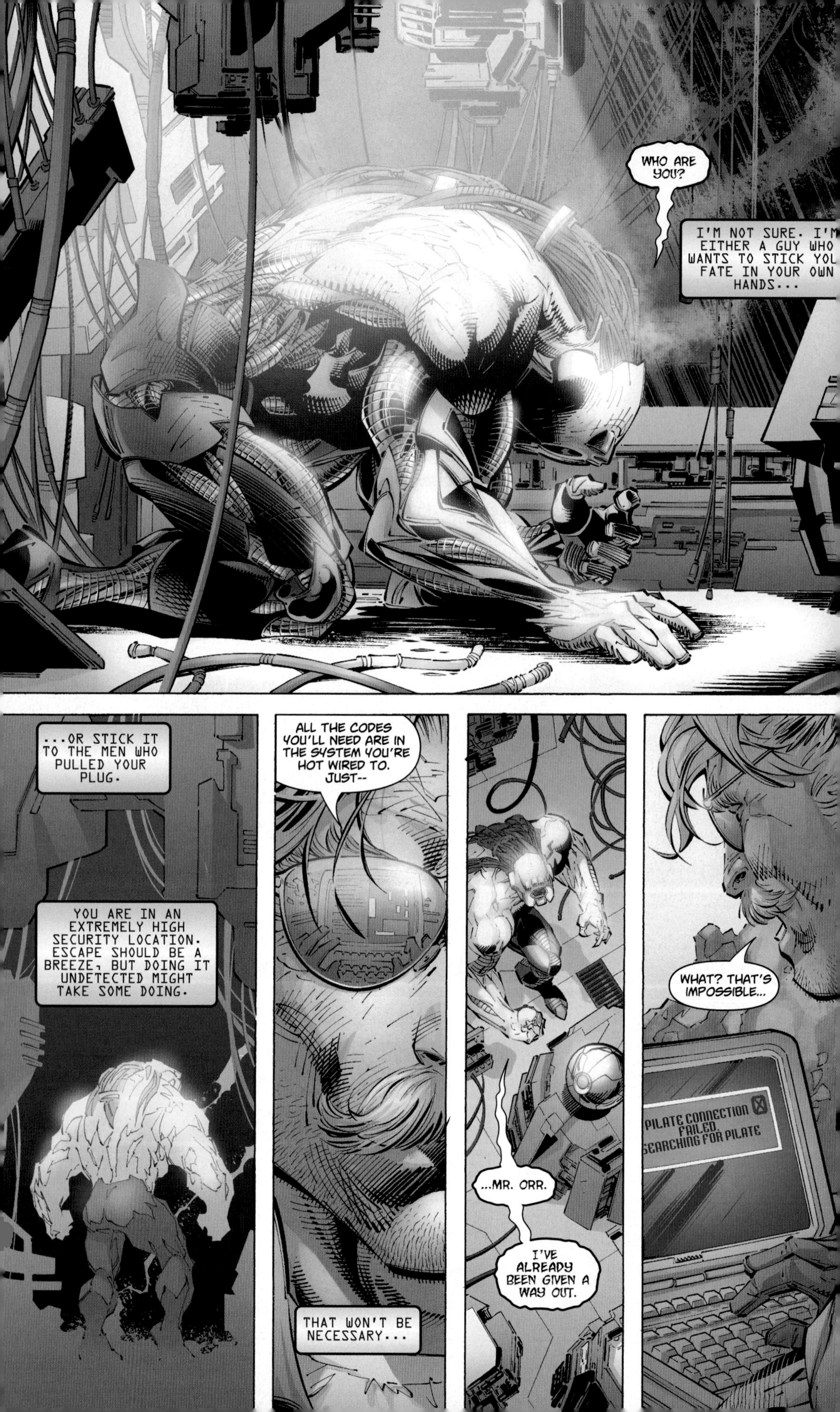
WHO ARE YOU?
I'M NOT SURE. I'M EITHER A GUY WHO WANTS TO STICK YOUR FATE IN YOUR OWN HANDS...
...OR STICK IT TO THE MEN WHO PULLED YOUR PLUG.
YOU ARE IN AN EXTREMELY HIGH SECURITY LOCATION. ESCAPE SHOULD BE A BREEZE, BUT DOING IT UNDETECTED MIGHT TAKE SOME DOING.
ALL THE CODES YOU'LL NEED ARE IN THE SYSTEM YOU'RE HOT WIRED TO. JUST--
THAT WON'T BE NECESSARY...
...MR. ORR.
I'VE ALREADY BEEN GIVEN A WAY OUT.
WHAT? THAT'S IMPOSSIBLE...
PILATE CONNECTION FAILED. SEARCHING FOR PILATE

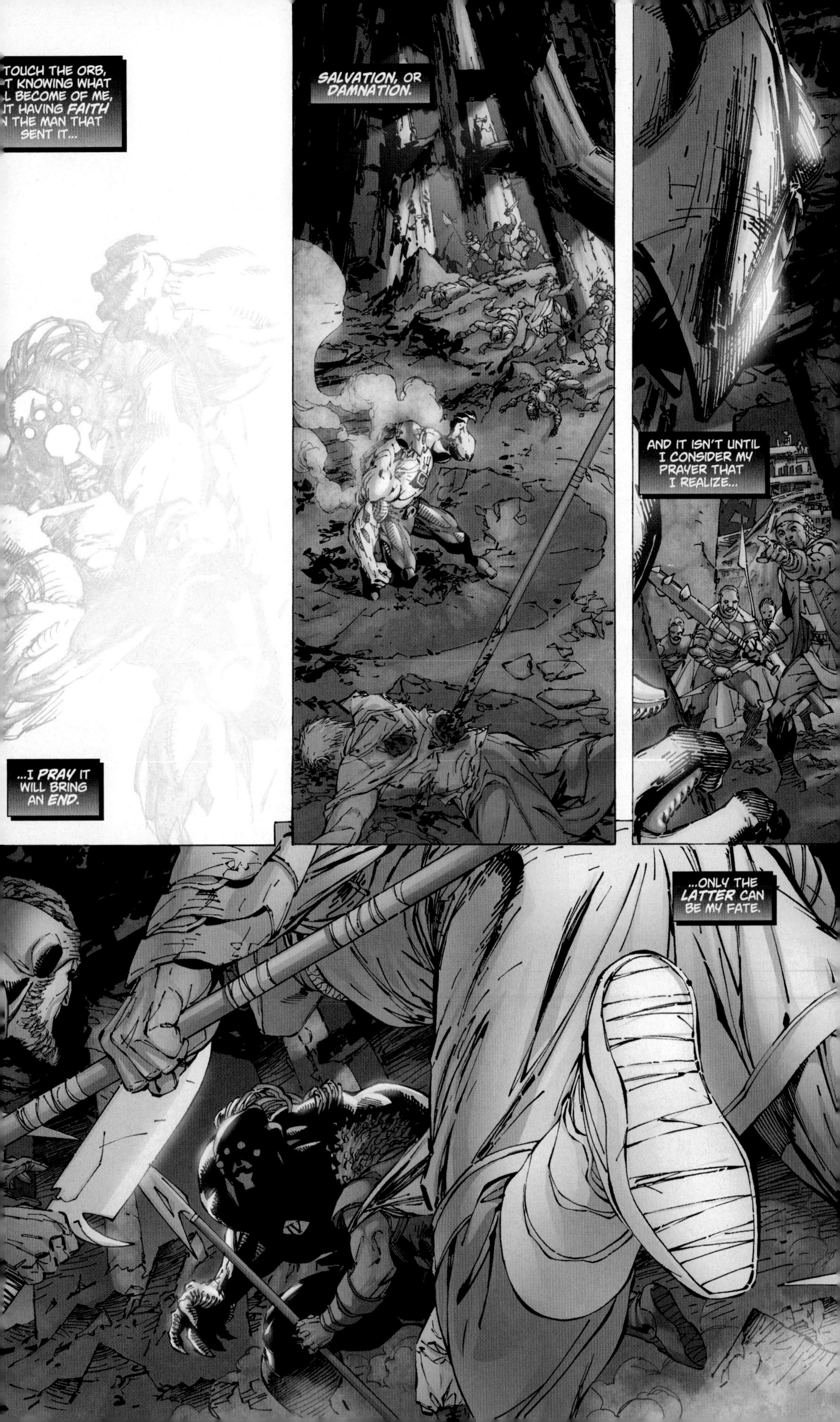
TOUCH THE ORB, T KNOWING WHAT L BECOME OF ME, IT HAVING FAITH N THE MAN THAT SENT IT...
...I PRAY IT WILL BRING AN END.
SALVATION, OR DAMNATION.
AND IT ISN'T UNTIL I CONSIDER MY PRAYER THAT I REALIZE...
...ONLY THE LATTER CAN BE MY FATE.

FINALLY, SON OF JOR-EL...

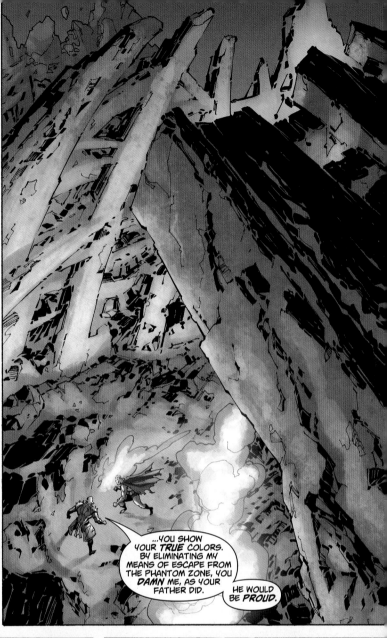

...YOU SHOW YOUR **TRUE** COLORS. BY ELIMINATING MY MEANS OF ESCAPE FROM THE PHANTOM ZONE, YOU **DAMN** ME, AS YOUR FATHER DID.

HE WOULD BE **PROUD**.

GENERAL, MY NAME IS KAL-EL...

...AND MY FATHER WOULD DO EVERYTHING IN HIS **POWER**--WHICH WAS **STAGGERING**-- TO **STOP** WHAT IS HAPPENING TODAY...

...THE **DESTRUCTION** OF A WORLD.

AND **I WILL** AS WELL.

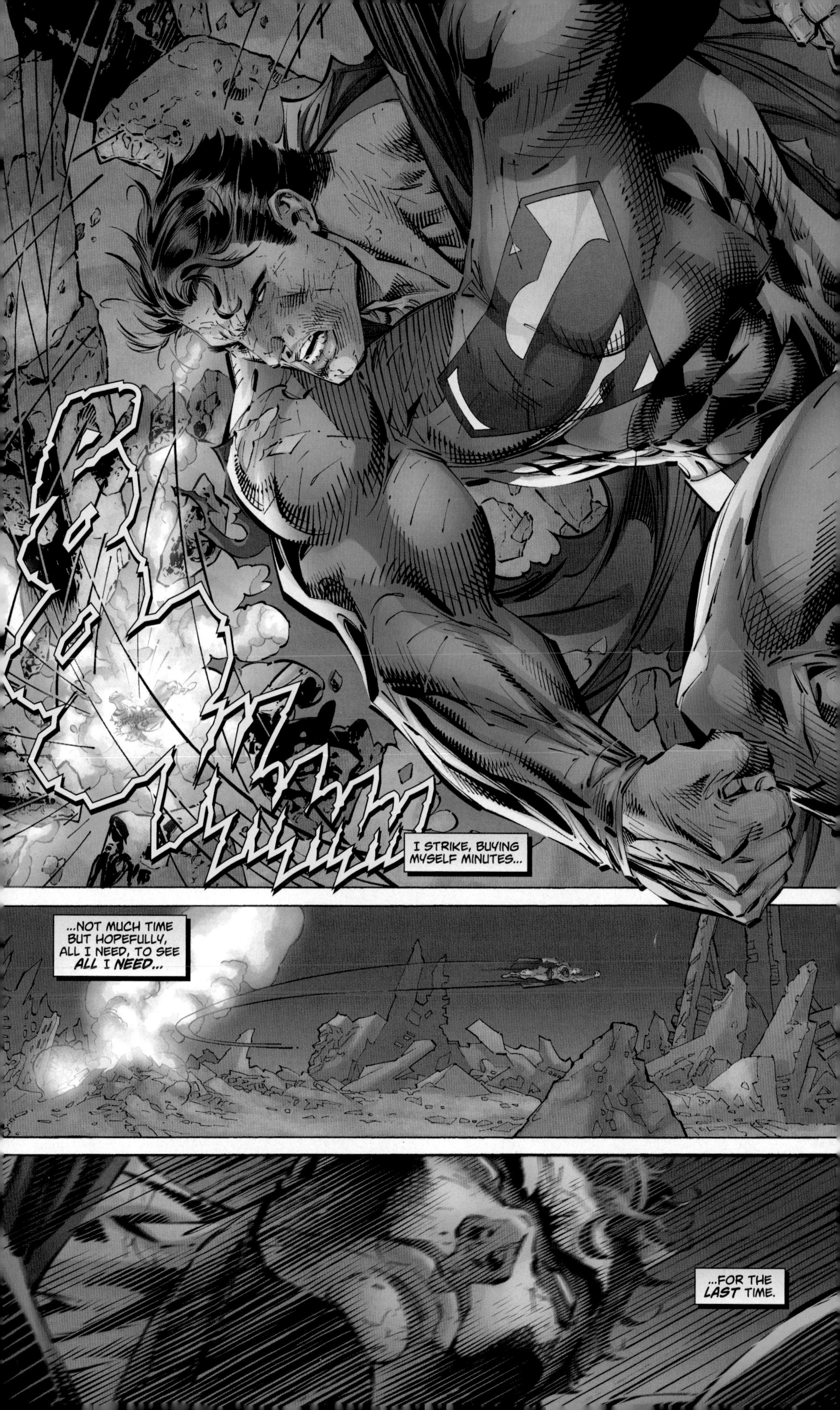

I STRIKE, BUYING MYSELF MINUTES...
...NOT MUCH TIME BUT HOPEFULLY, ALL I NEED, TO SEE ALL I NEED...
...FOR THE LAST TIME.

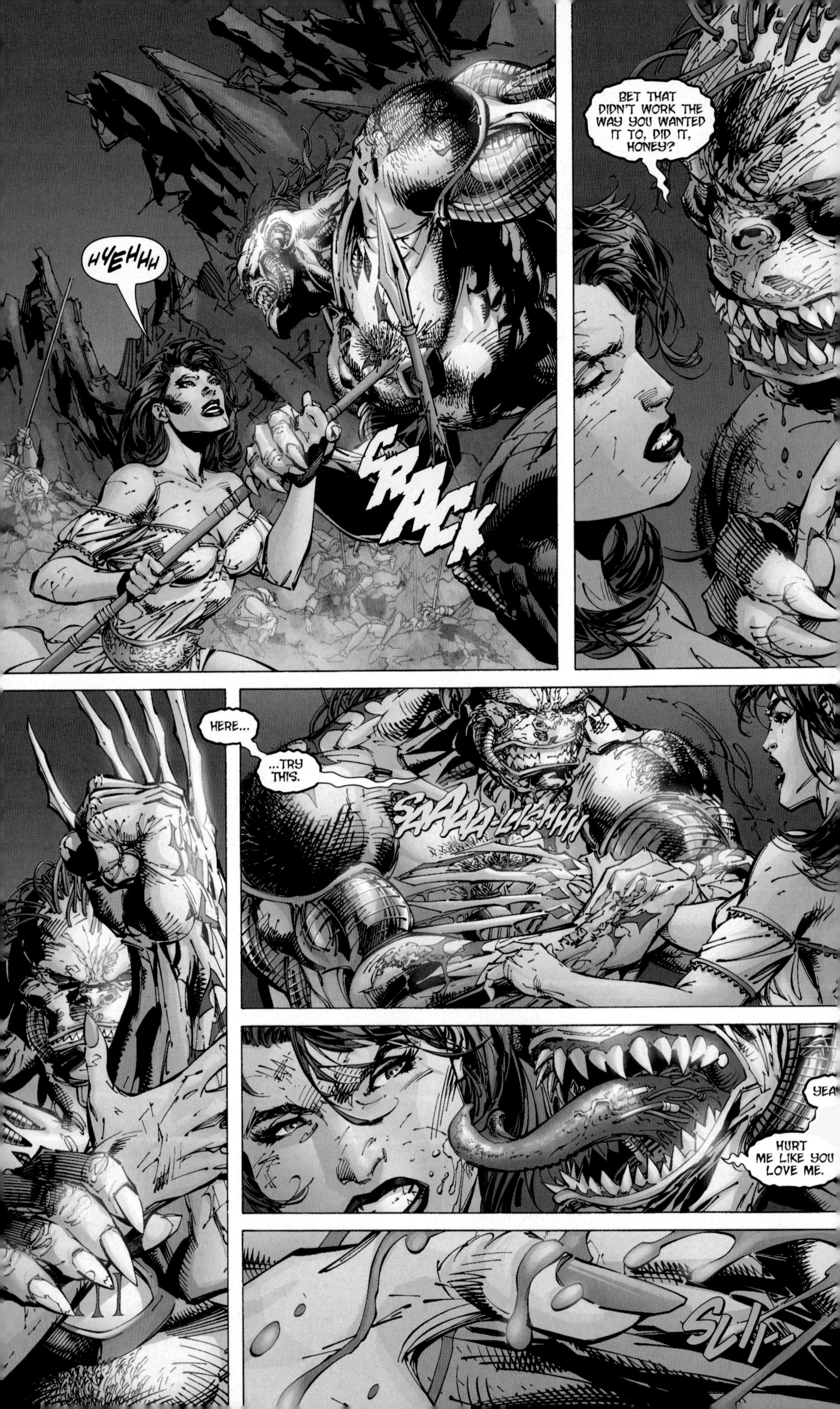
HYEHHH
CRACK
BET THAT DIDN'T WORK THE WAY YOU WANTED IT TO, DID IT, HONEY?
HERE...
...TRY THIS.
SNAAAA-LISHHH
YEA
HURT ME LIKE YOU LOVE ME.
SLIT-

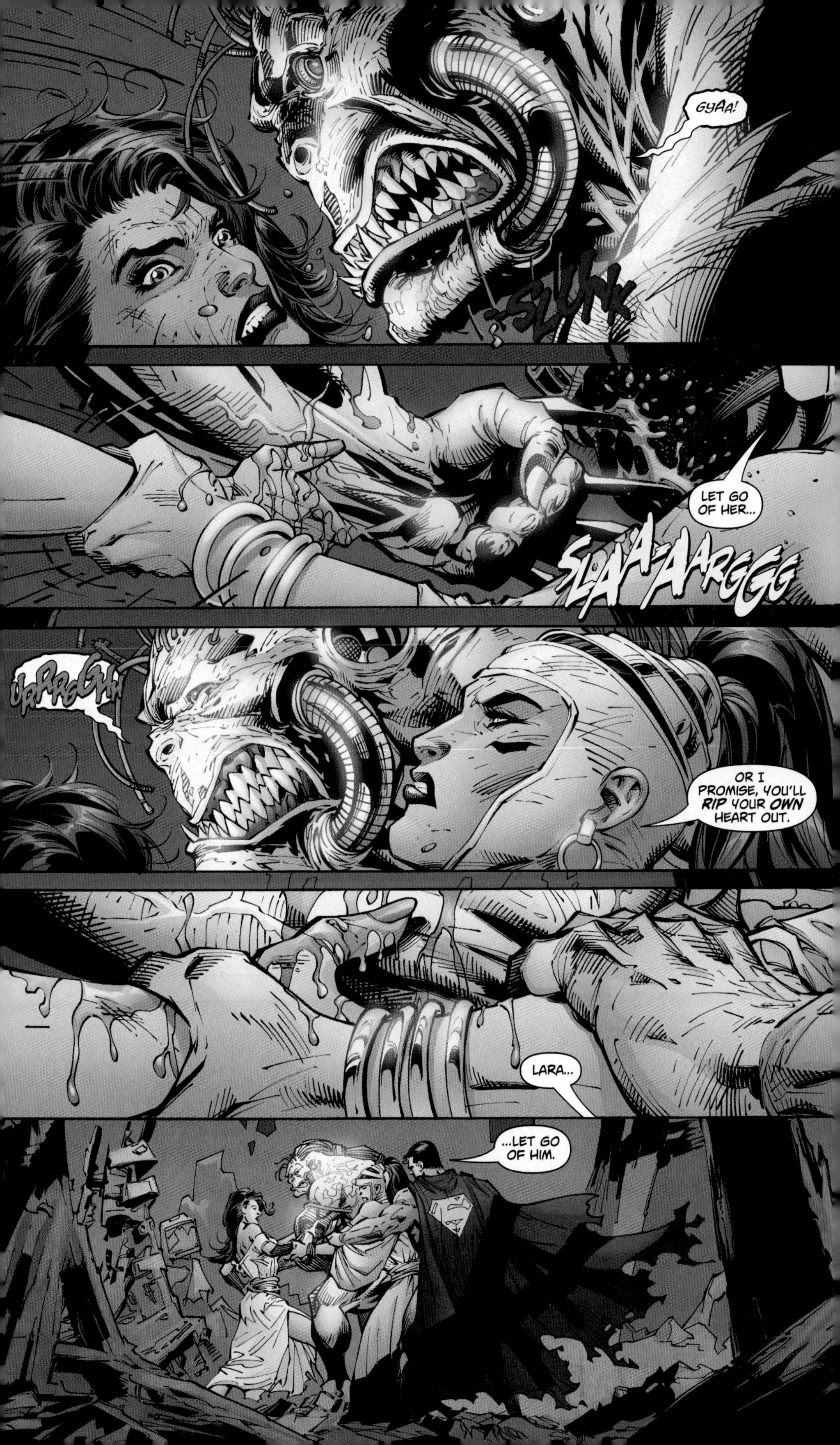
GYAA!
SLUNK
LET GO OF HER...
SLAA-AARGGG
URRRGGHH
OR I PROMISE, YOU'LL *RIP* YOUR *OWN* HEART OUT.
LARA...
...LET GO OF HIM.

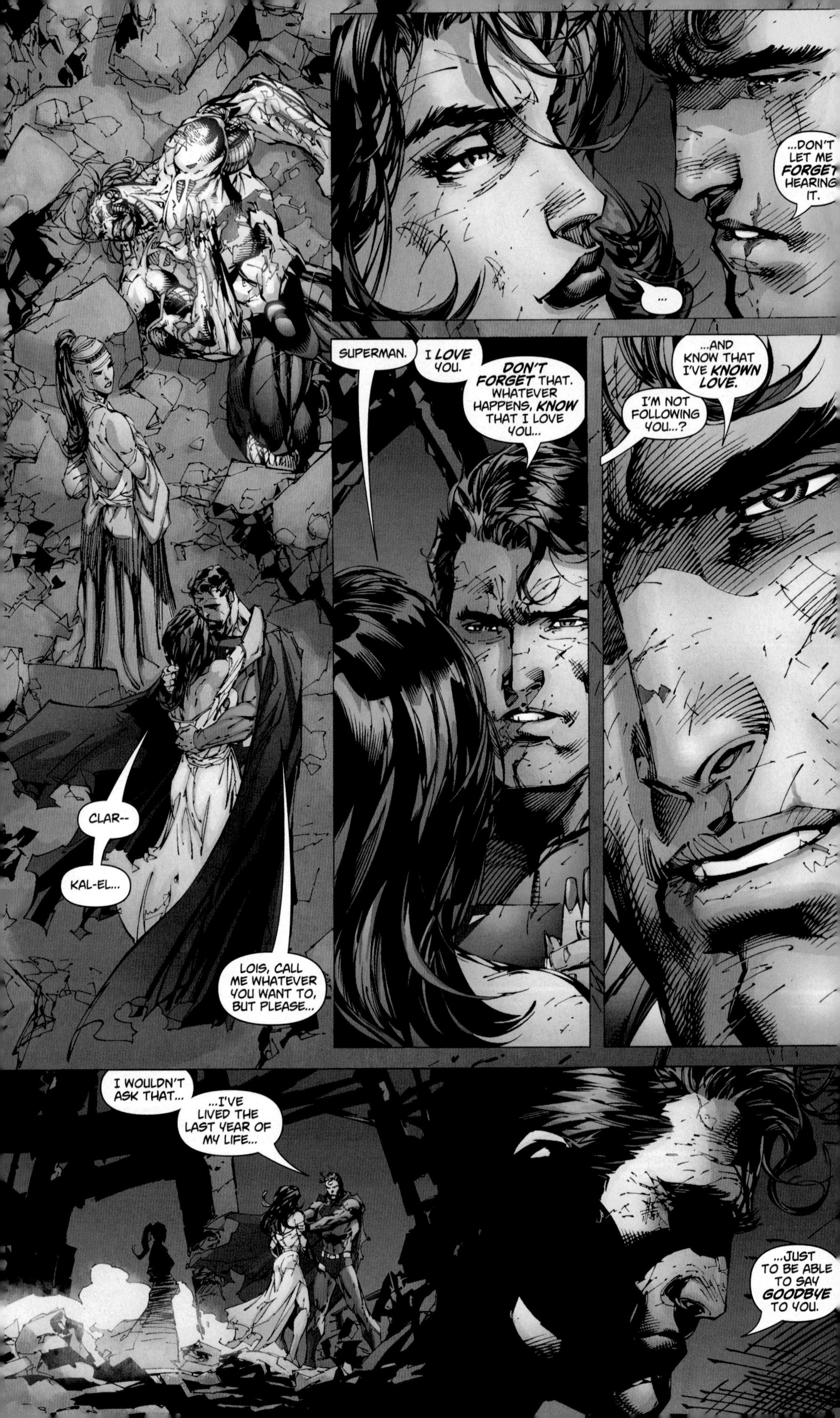
...DON'T LET ME FORGET HEARING IT.
...
CLAR--
KAL-EL...
LOIS, CALL ME WHATEVER YOU WANT TO, BUT PLEASE...
SUPERMAN.
I LOVE YOU.
DON'T FORGET THAT. WHATEVER HAPPENS, KNOW THAT I LOVE YOU...
I'M NOT FOLLOWING YOU...?
...AND KNOW THAT I'VE KNOWN LOVE.
I WOULDN'T ASK THAT...
...I'VE LIVED THE LAST YEAR OF MY LIFE...
...JUST TO BE ABLE TO SAY GOODBYE TO YOU.

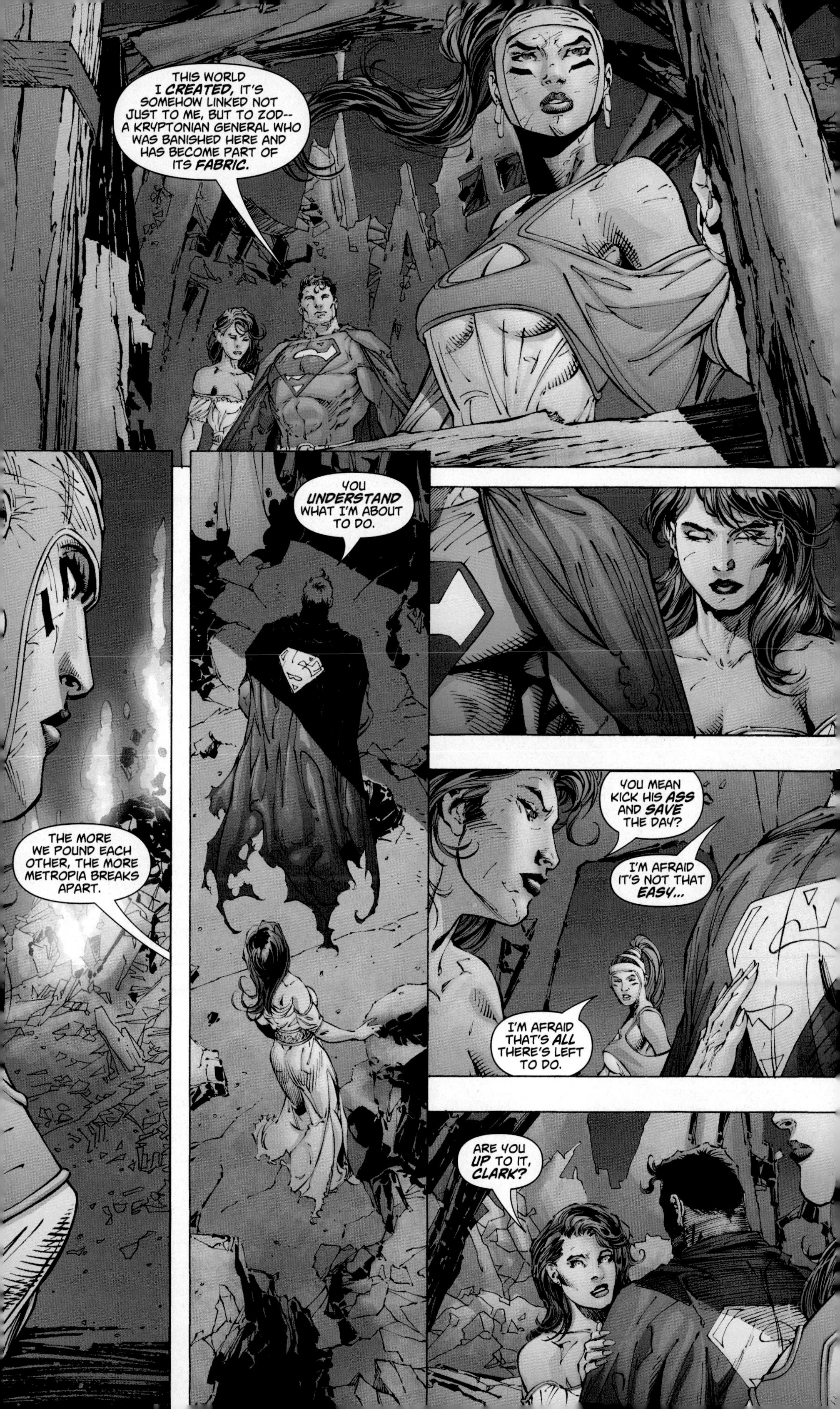

THIS WORLD I CREATED, IT'S SOMEHOW LINKED NOT JUST TO ME, BUT TO ZOD-- A KRYPTONIAN GENERAL WHO WAS BANISHED HERE AND HAS BECOME PART OF ITS FABRIC.
THE MORE WE POUND EACH OTHER, THE MORE METROPIA BREAKS APART.
YOU UNDERSTAND WHAT I'M ABOUT TO DO.
YOU MEAN KICK HIS ASS AND SAVE THE DAY?
I'M AFRAID IT'S NOT THAT EASY...
I'M AFRAID THAT'S ALL THERE'S LEFT TO DO.
ARE YOU UP TO IT, CLARK?

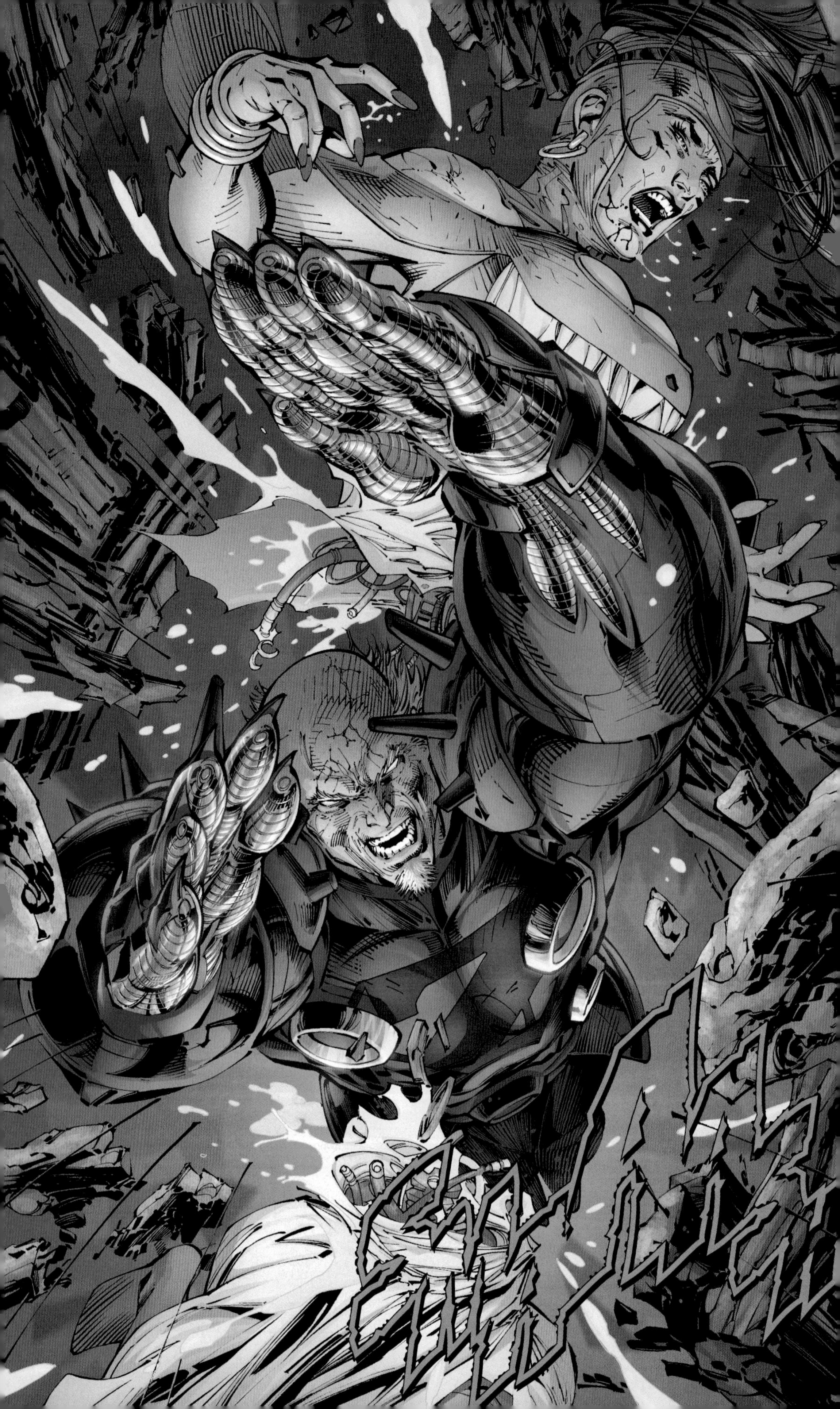

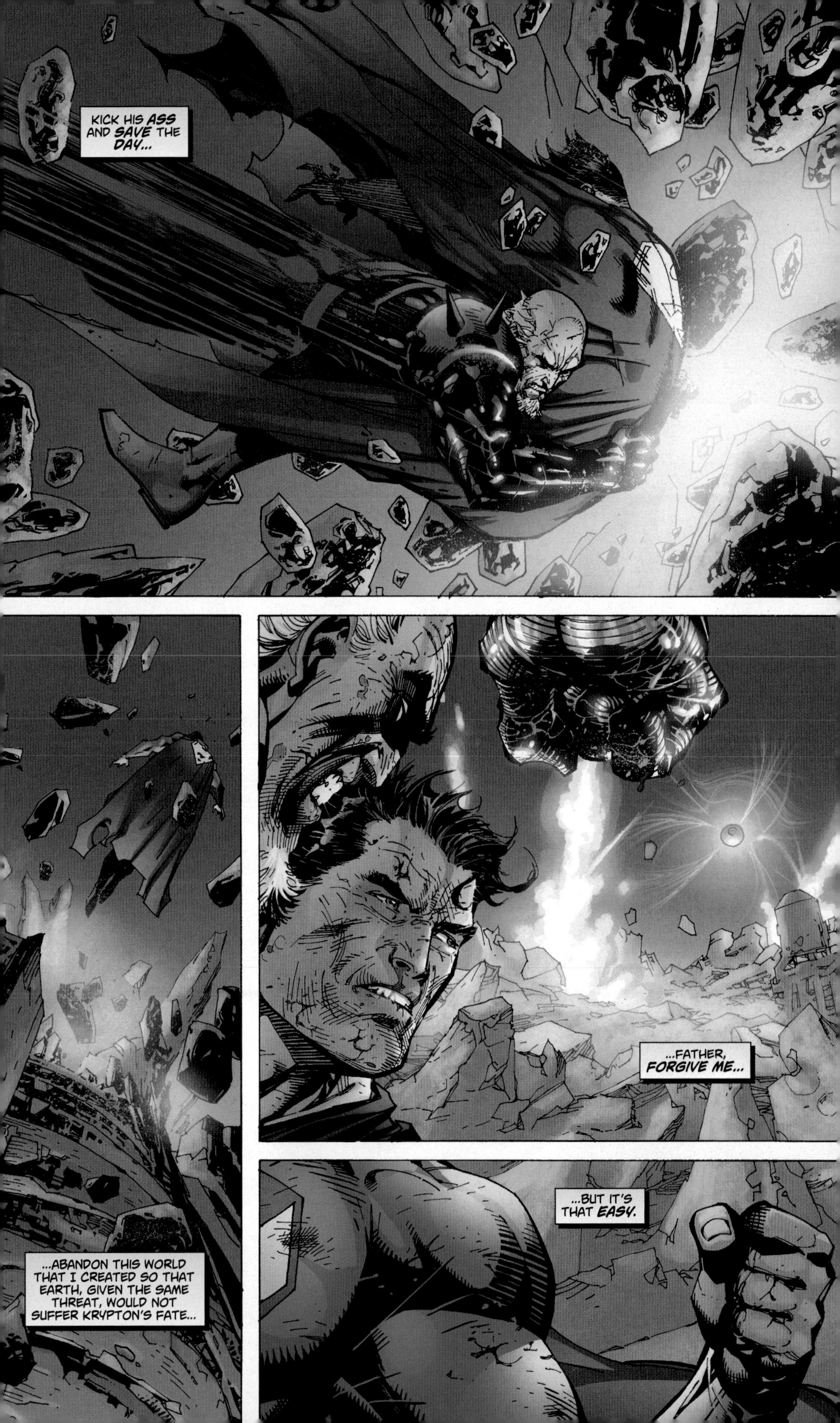
KICK HIS ASS AND SAVE THE DAY...
...ABANDON THIS WORLD THAT I CREATED SO THAT EARTH, GIVEN THE SAME THREAT, WOULD NOT SUFFER KRYPTON'S FATE...
...FATHER, FORGIVE ME...
...BUT IT'S THAT EASY.

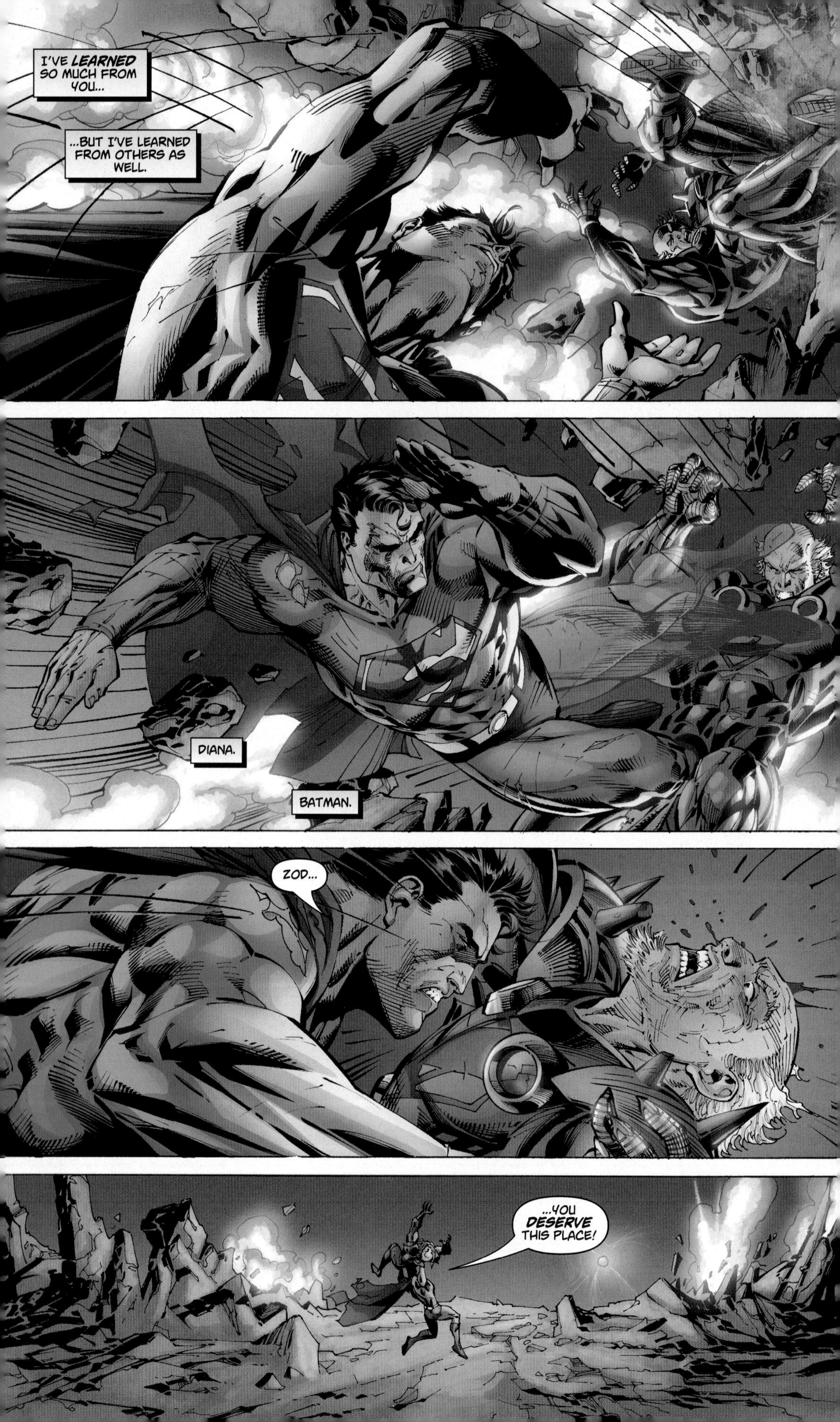
I'VE **LEARNED** SO MUCH FROM YOU...
...BUT I'VE LEARNED FROM OTHERS AS WELL.
DIANA.
BATMAN.
ZOD...
...YOU **DESERVE** THIS PLACE!

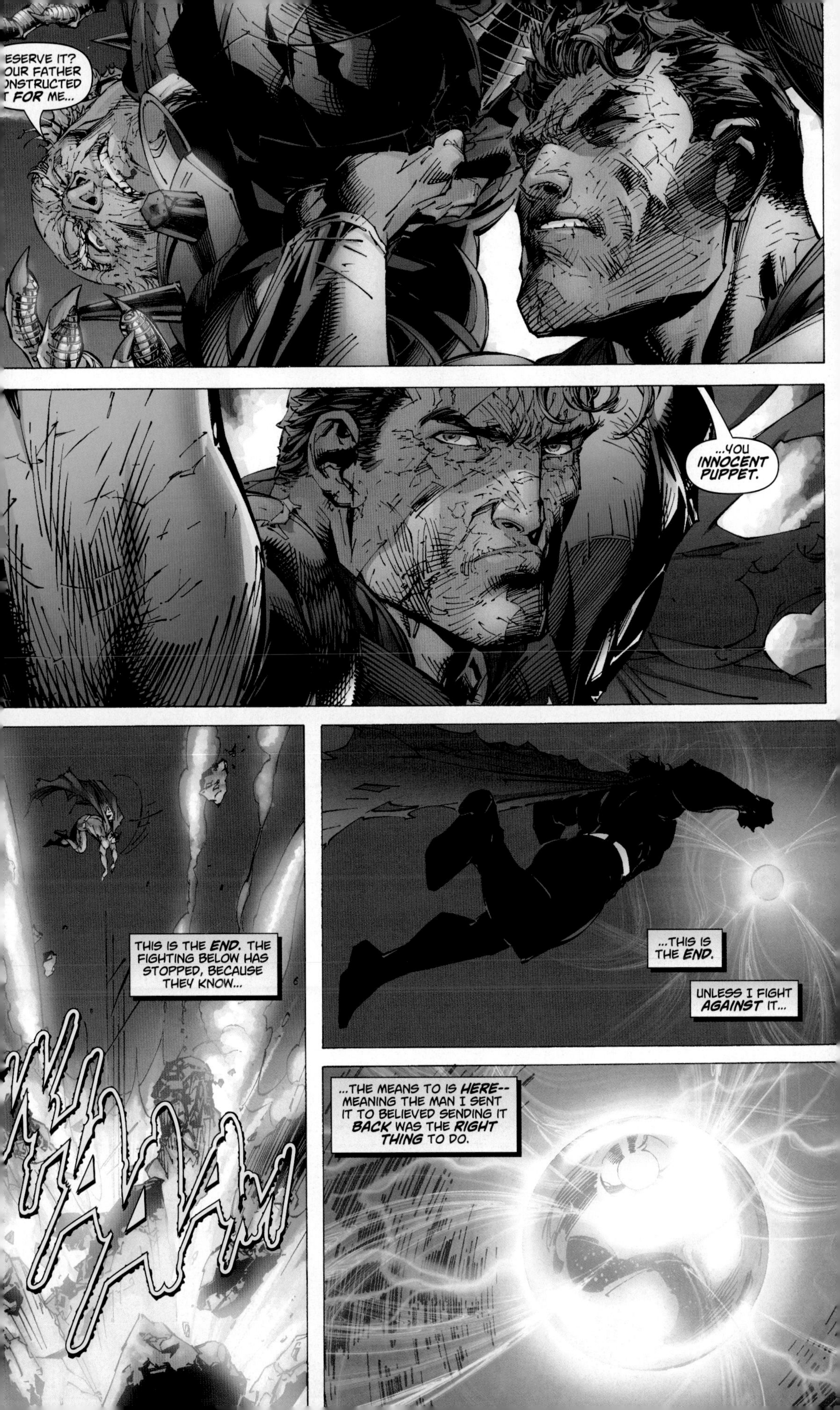
ESERVE IT? OUR FATHER ONSTRUCTED T FOR ME...
...YOU INNOCENT PUPPET.
THIS IS THE END. THE FIGHTING BELOW HAS STOPPED, BECAUSE THEY KNOW...
...THIS IS THE END.
UNLESS I FIGHT AGAINST IT...
...THE MEANS TO IS HERE-- MEANING THE MAN I SENT IT TO BELIEVED SENDING IT BACK WAS THE RIGHT THING TO DO.

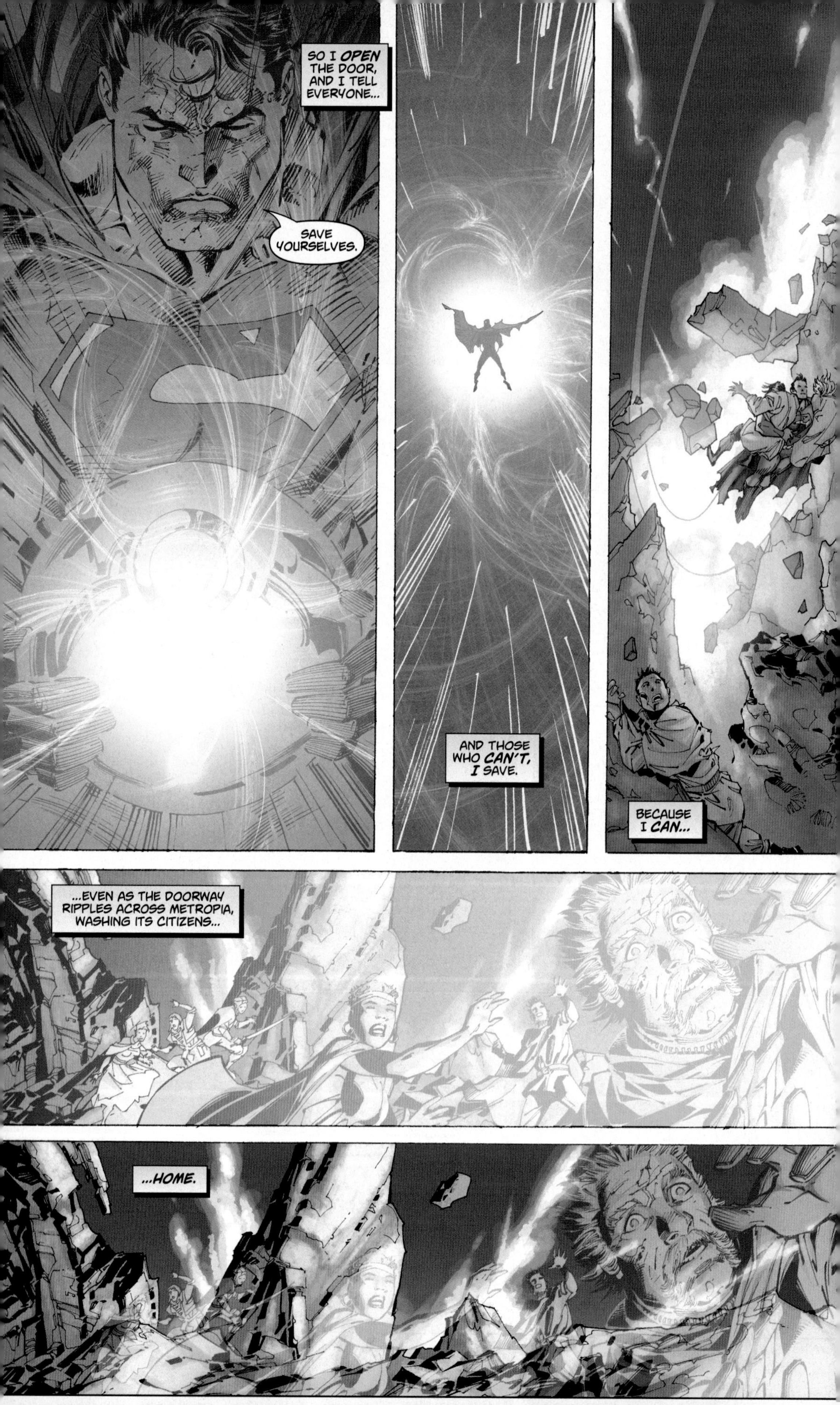
SO I OPEN THE DOOR, AND I TELL EVERYONE...
SAVE YOURSELVES.
AND THOSE WHO CAN'T, I SAVE.
BECAUSE I CAN...
...EVEN AS THE DOORWAY RIPPLES ACROSS METROPIA, WASHING ITS CITIZENS...
...HOME.

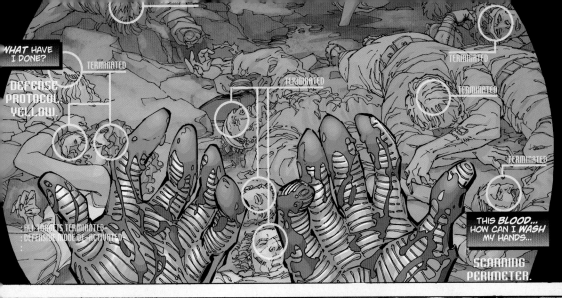

WHAT HAVE I DONE?

DEFENSE PROTOCOL: YELLOW

TERMINATED

TERMINATED

TERMINATED

TERMINATED

TERMINATED

ALL TARGETS TERMINATED. DEFENSIVE MODE DE-ACTIVATED.

THIS *BLOOD*... HOW CAN I *WASH* MY HANDS...

SCANNING PERIMETER.

WATER TOWER 10 METERS NNE. STRUCTURE COMPROMISED.

I ALWAYS BELIEVED *HELL* WAS JUST A STORY, IMAGINED BY THOSE WHO NEEDED SOMETHING TO DISTRACT US FROM THE HELL THEY CREATED IN *REALITY*.

BUT I'M *IN* HELL... *REAL* HELL. AND *DAMN* ME, IT'S OF MY *OWN* DESIGN.

HOW DO I GET *OUT?*

INITIATING PILATE TO EYE IN THE SKY LINK-UP.

NO RESPONSE. RECONNECTING...

ALERT. DEFENSE PROTOCOL: ORANGE

SUPERMAN?

DEFENSE PROTOCOL: RED

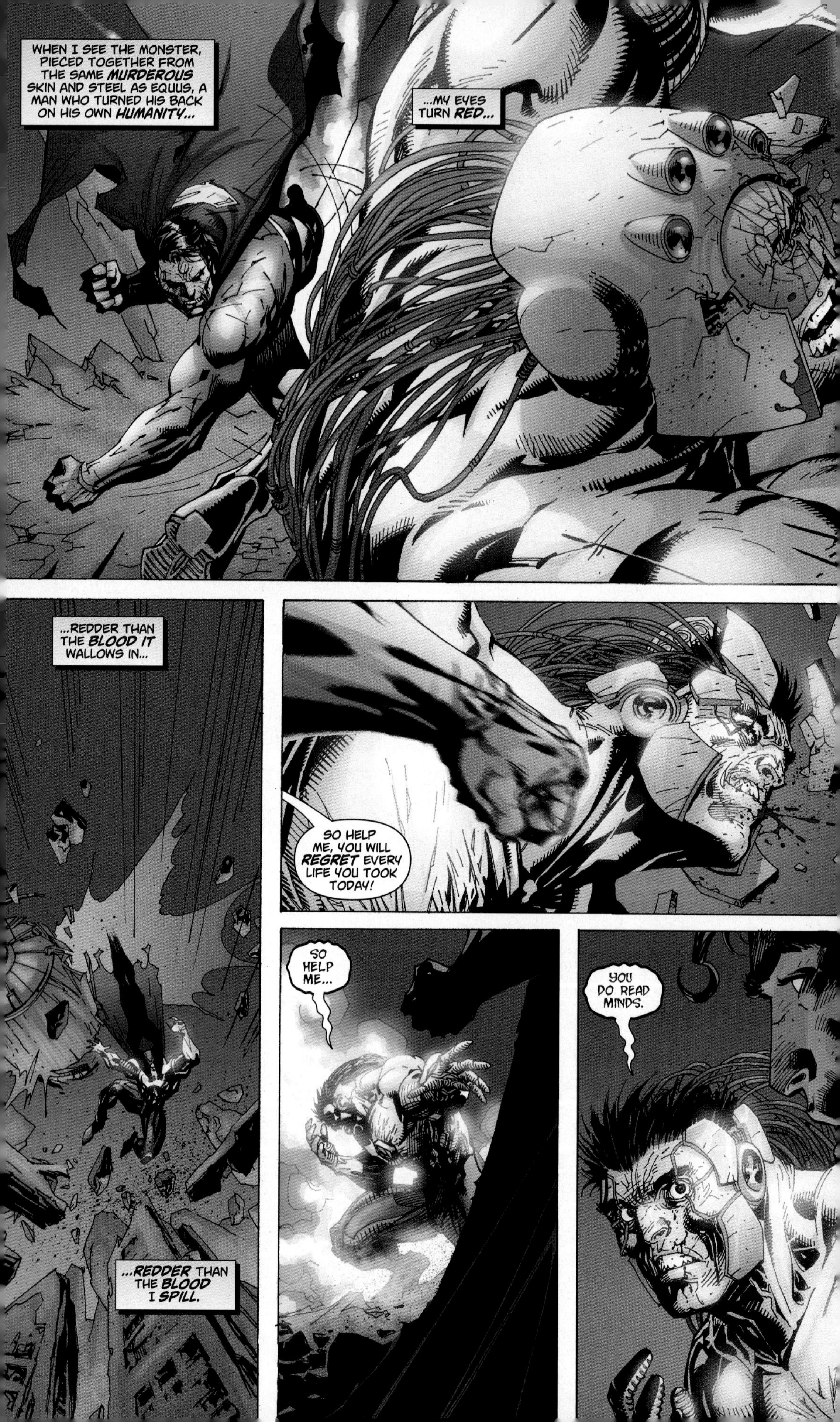
WHEN I SEE THE MONSTER, PIECED TOGETHER FROM THE SAME MURDEROUS SKIN AND STEEL AS EQUUS, A MAN WHO TURNED HIS BACK ON HIS OWN HUMANITY...
...MY EYES TURN RED...
...REDDER THAN THE BLOOD IT WALLOWS IN...
SO HELP ME, YOU WILL REGRET EVERY LIFE YOU TOOK TODAY!
...REDDER THAN THE BLOOD I SPILL.
SO HELP ME...
YOU DO READ MINDS.

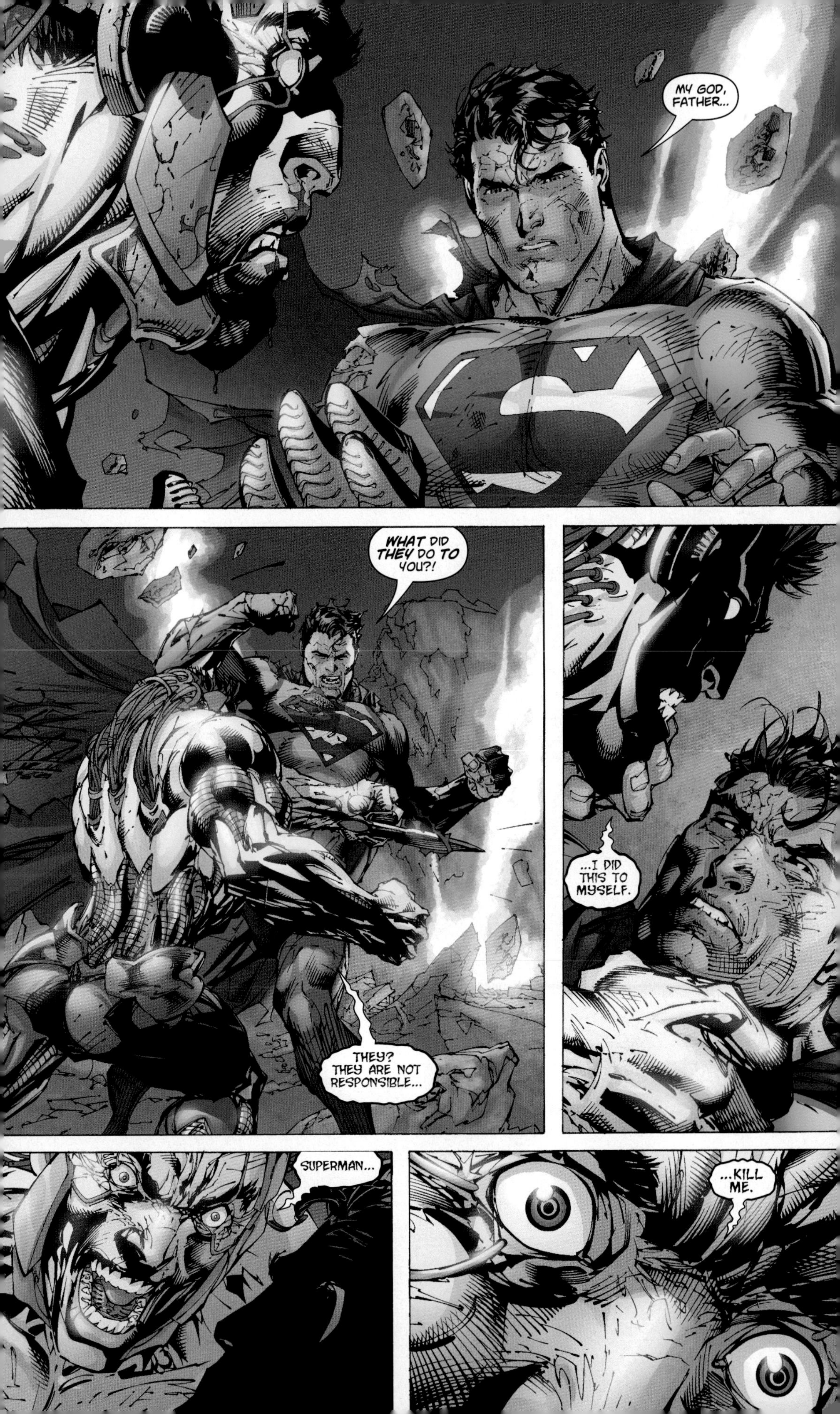
MY GOD, FATHER...
WHAT DID THEY DO TO YOU?!
THEY? THEY ARE NOT RESPONSIBLE...
...I DID THIS TO MYSELF.
SUPERMAN...
...KILL ME.

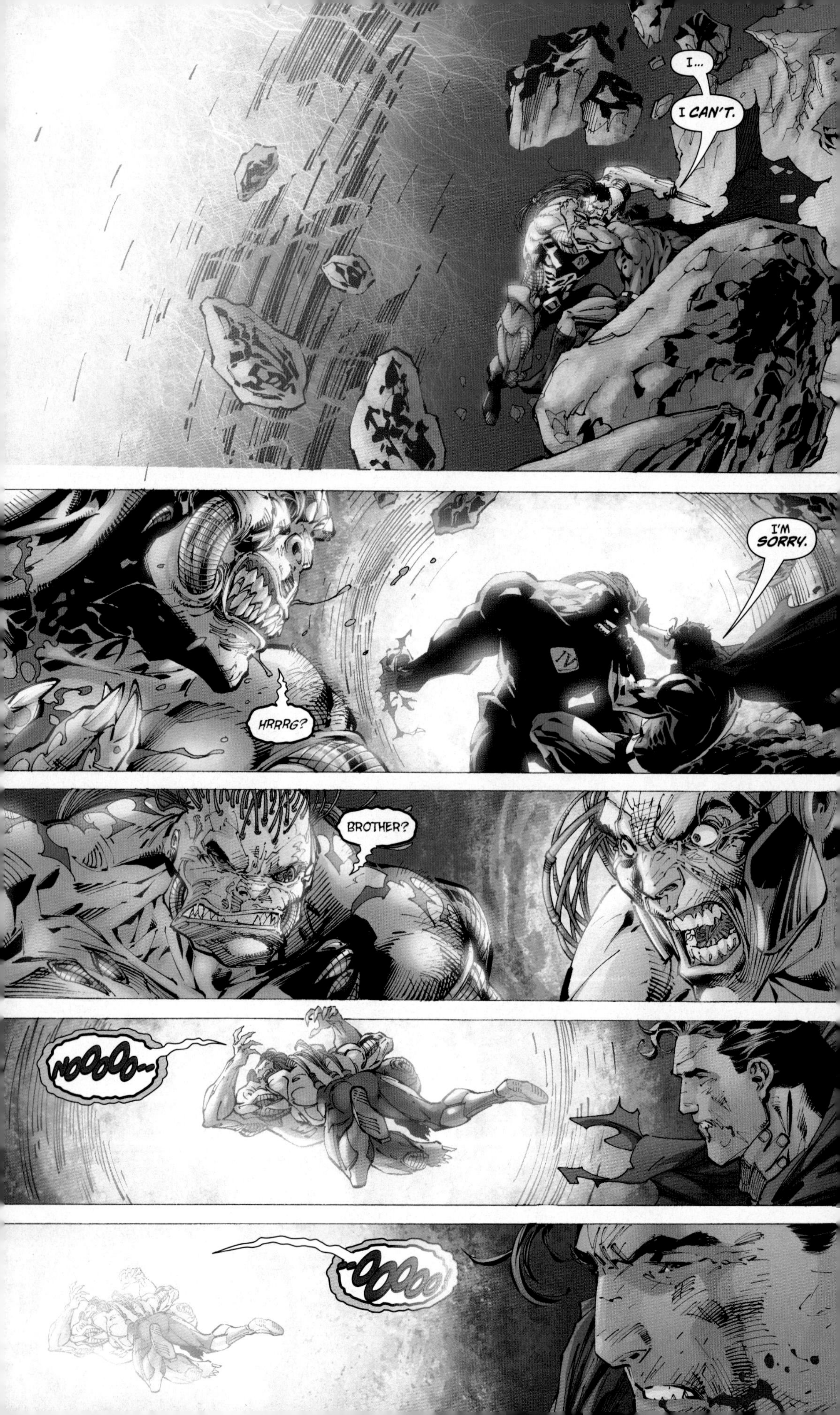
I...
I CAN'T.
I'M SORRY.
HRRRG?
BROTHER?
NOOOOO--
--OOOOO

WHAT DOES IT MEAN WHEN A MAN WHOSE LIFE IS BUILT ON *FAITH* SACRIFICES IT BY *SAVING* HIS OWN LIFE?

SUPERMAN...

...SAVE ME.

AND WHAT DOES IT MEAN WHEN A MAN IS WILLING TO SACRIFICE HIS OWN LIFE FOR WHAT HE *BELIEVES* IN?

ZOD...

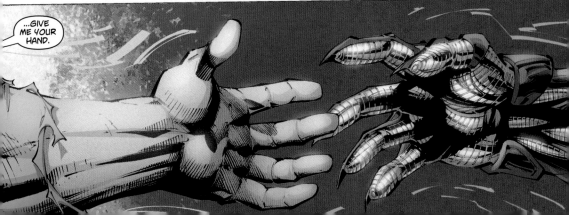

...GIVE ME YOUR HAND.

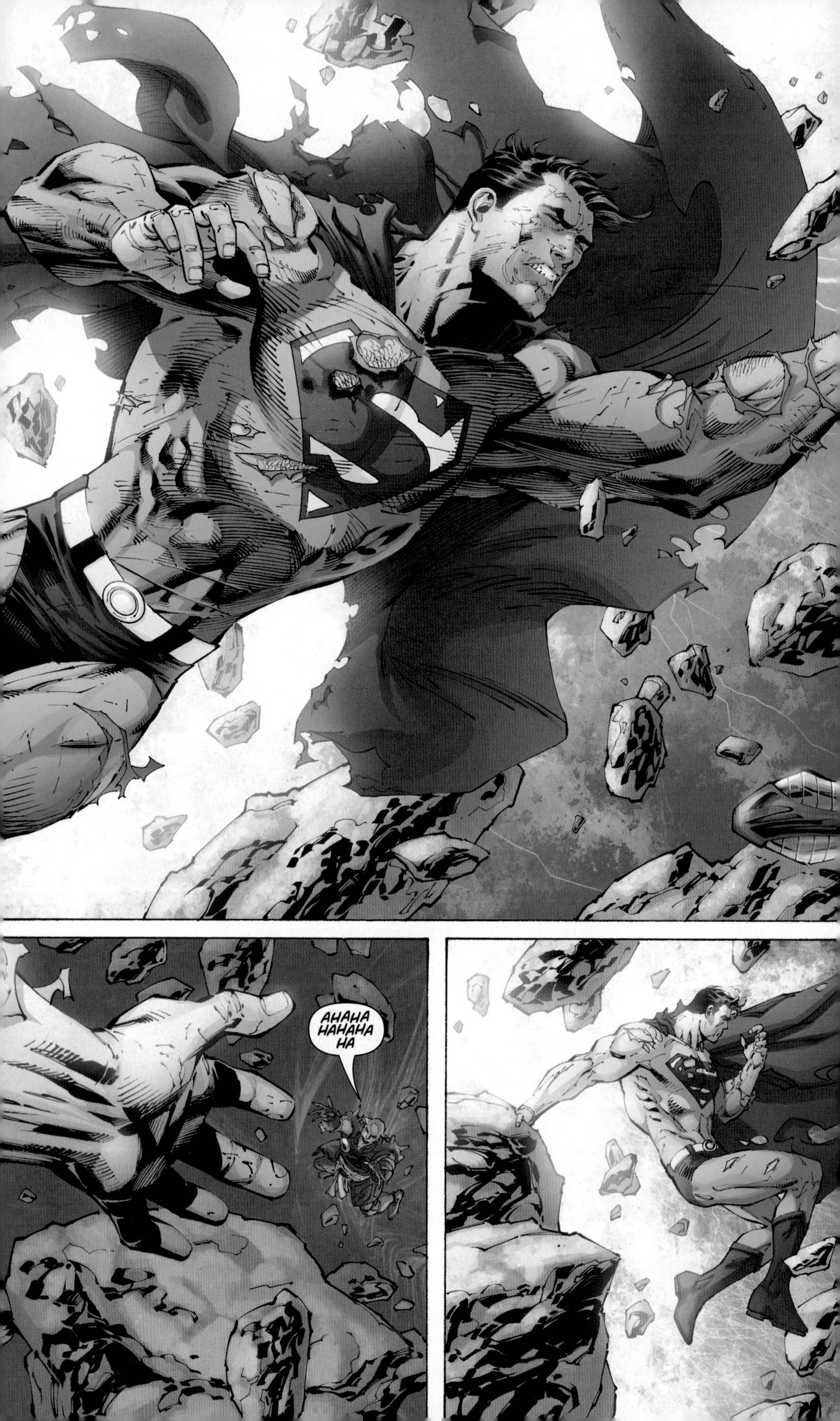
AHAHA HAHAHA HA

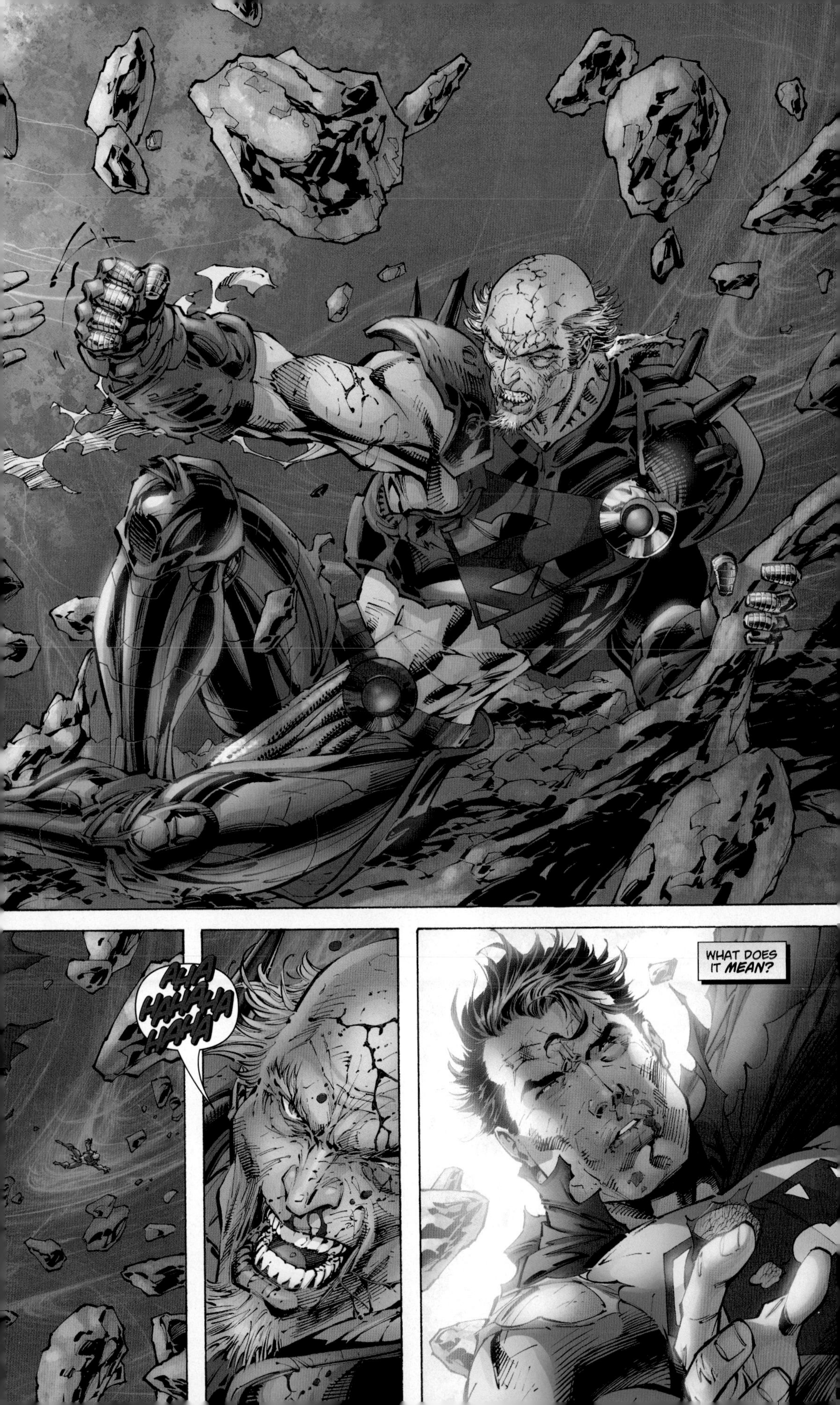
AHA HAHAHA HAHA
WHAT DOES IT MEAN?

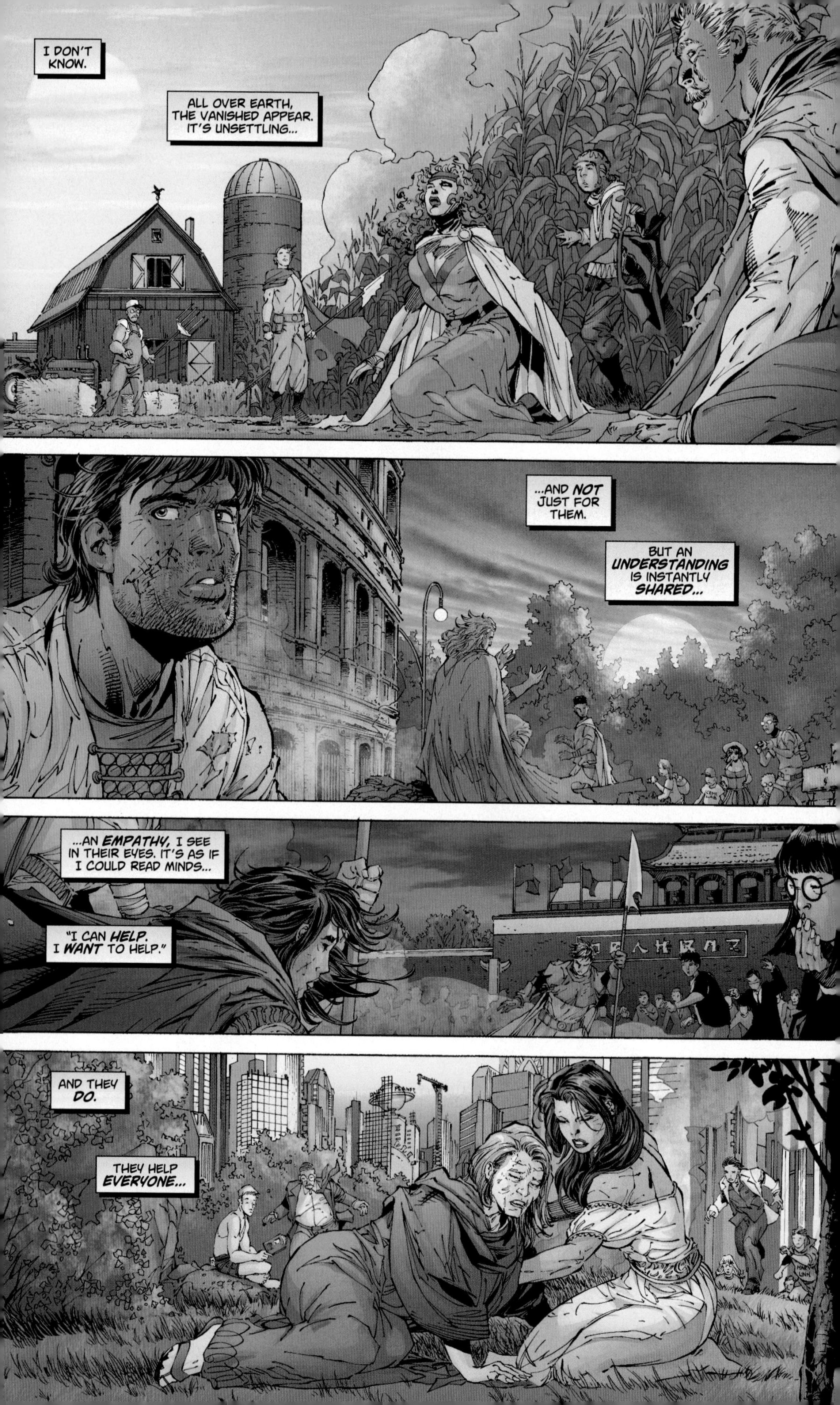

I DON'T KNOW.
ALL OVER EARTH, THE VANISHED APPEAR. IT'S UNSETTLING...
...AND **NOT** JUST FOR THEM.
BUT AN **UNDERSTANDING** IS INSTANTLY **SHARED...**
...AN **EMPATHY**, I SEE IN THEIR EYES. IT'S AS IF I COULD READ MINDS...
"I CAN **HELP**. I **WANT** TO HELP."
AND THEY **DO**.
THEY HELP **EVERYONE...**

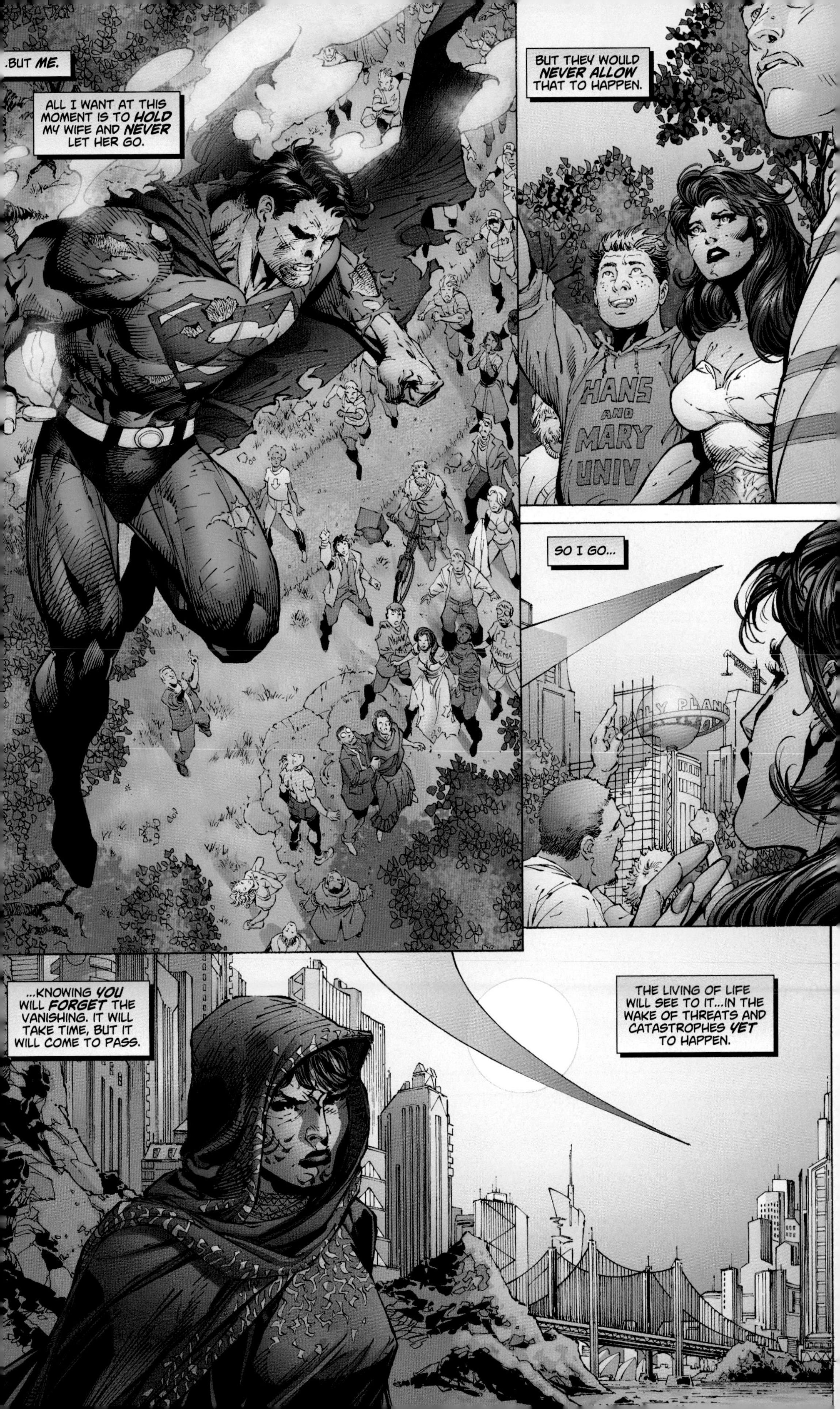

...BUT ME.
ALL I WANT AT THIS MOMENT IS TO HOLD MY WIFE AND NEVER LET HER GO.
BUT THEY WOULD NEVER ALLOW THAT TO HAPPEN.
HANS AND MARY UNIV
SO I GO...
DAILY PLANET
...KNOWING YOU WILL FORGET THE VANISHING. IT WILL TAKE TIME, BUT IT WILL COME TO PASS.
THE LIVING OF LIFE WILL SEE TO IT...IN THE WAKE OF THREATS AND CATASTROPHES YET TO HAPPEN.

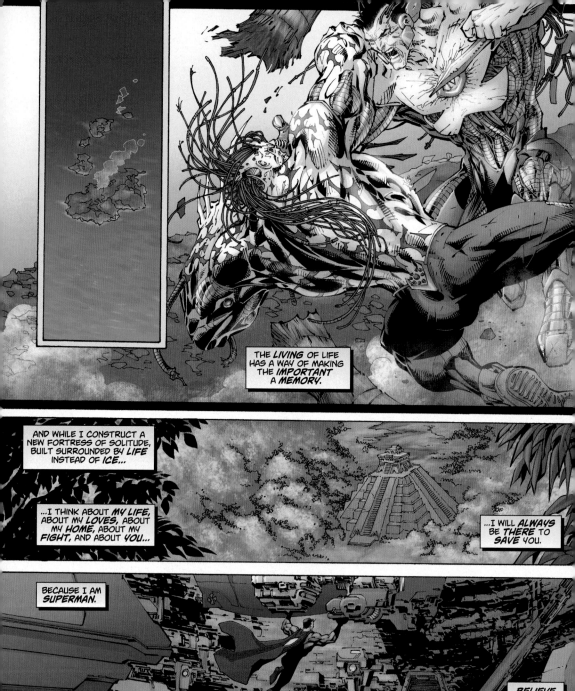

THE *LIVING* OF LIFE HAS A WAY OF MAKING THE *IMPORTANT* A MEMORY.

AND WHILE I CONSTRUCT A NEW FORTRESS OF SOLITUDE, BUILT SURROUNDED BY *LIFE* INSTEAD OF *ICE*...

...I THINK ABOUT *MY LIFE*, ABOUT MY *LOVES*, ABOUT MY *HOME*, ABOUT MY *FIGHT*, AND ABOUT *YOU*...

...I WILL *ALWAYS* BE *THERE* TO *SAVE* YOU.

BECAUSE I AM *SUPERMAN*.

BELIEVE THAT, UNTIL THE *END*.

THE END.

I WONDER, WHEN *IT* COMES...

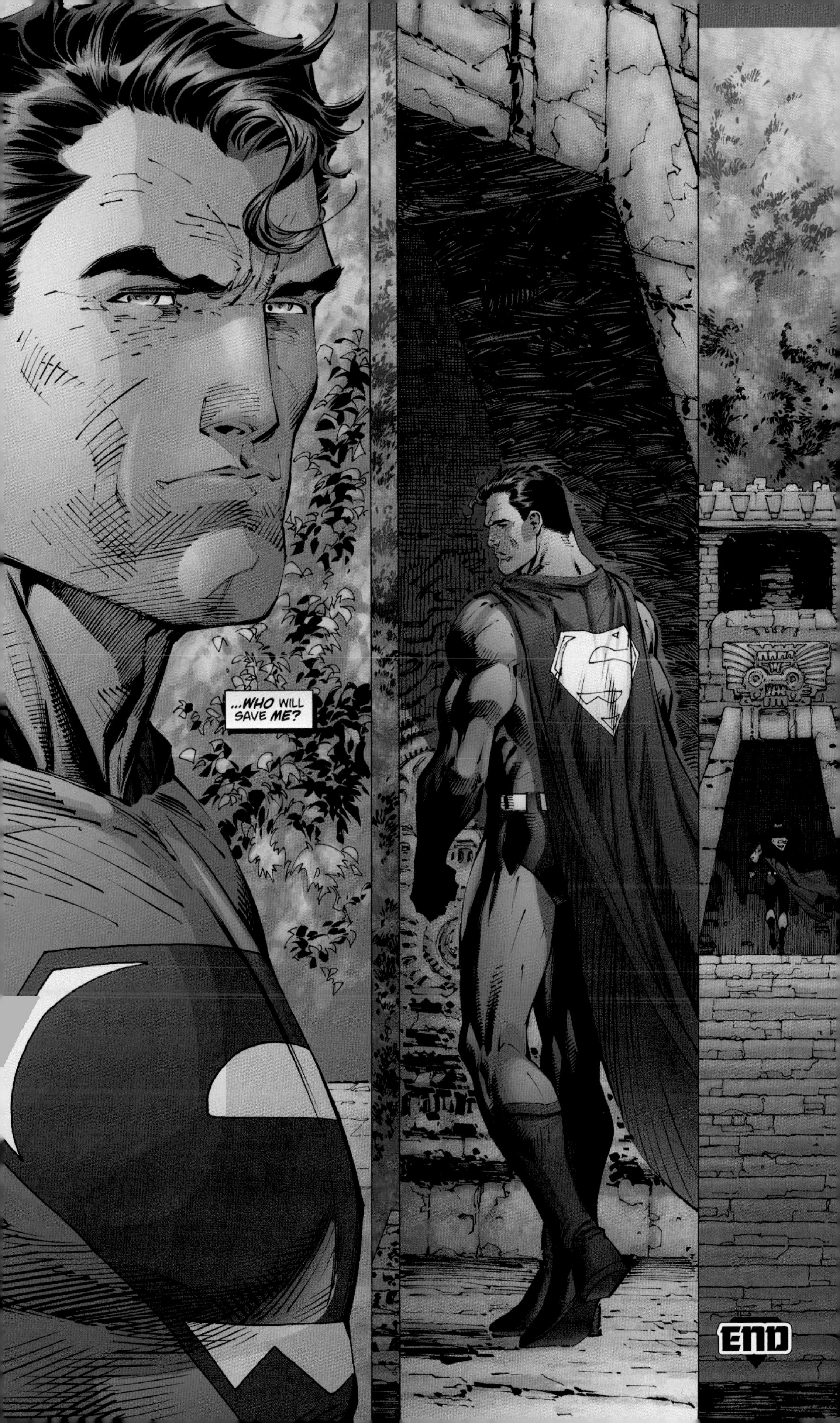
...WHO WILL SAVE ME?
END

SUPERMAN: FOR TOMORROW VOL. ONE

collection cover art by Jim Lee & Scott Williams with Alex Sinclair

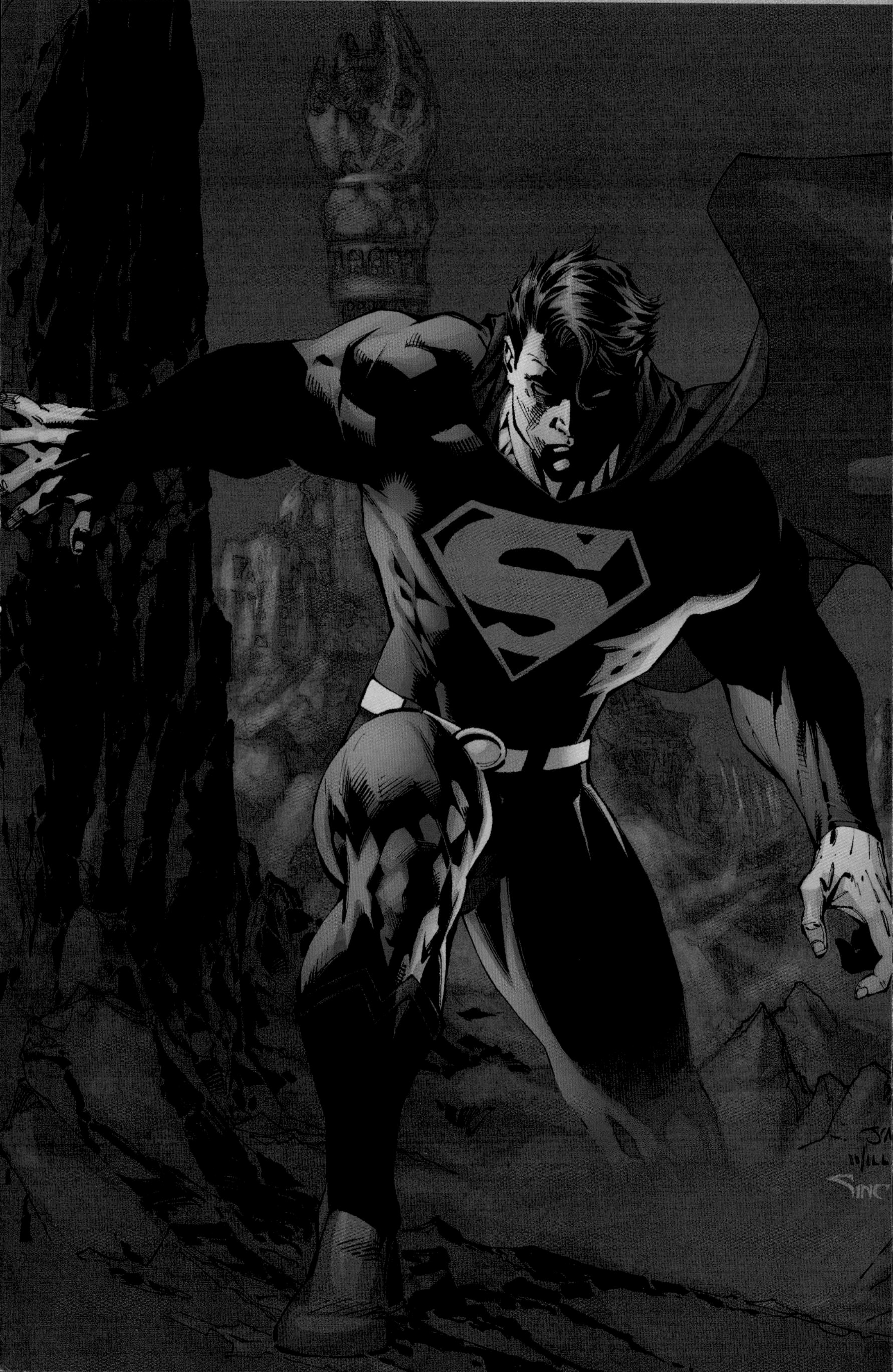

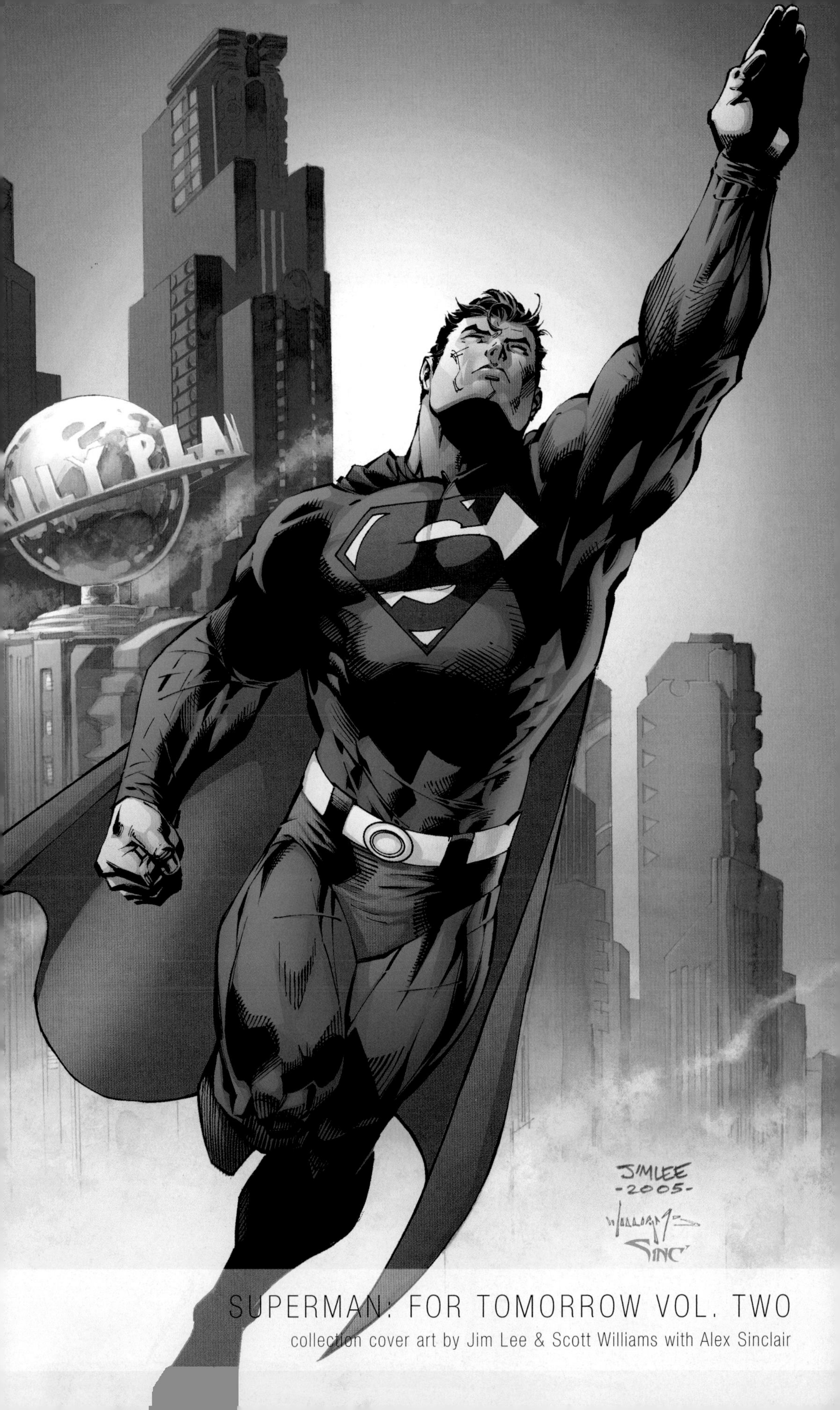
JIMLEE
-2005-

SUPERMAN: FOR TOMORROW VOL. TWO

collection cover art by Jim Lee & Scott Williams with Alex Sinclair

SKETCHBOOK
by Jim Lee

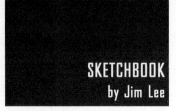

During the BATMAN: HUSH run, I had a chance to draw Superman but I didn't always feel comfortable working with the character. Working up sketches before diving into sequential work gives me a chance to ask different questions and explore different answers. In other words, it's a chance to experiment with different looks, different takes on the character before making the final decisions on the pages themselves. His costume is more challenging to draw than, say, Batman because of the primary colors and because it's fairly unadorned with gadgets or doohickeys. Big belts, collars and masks make it easier to draw characters because they hide seamlines, hide details and give the artist more elements to play with.

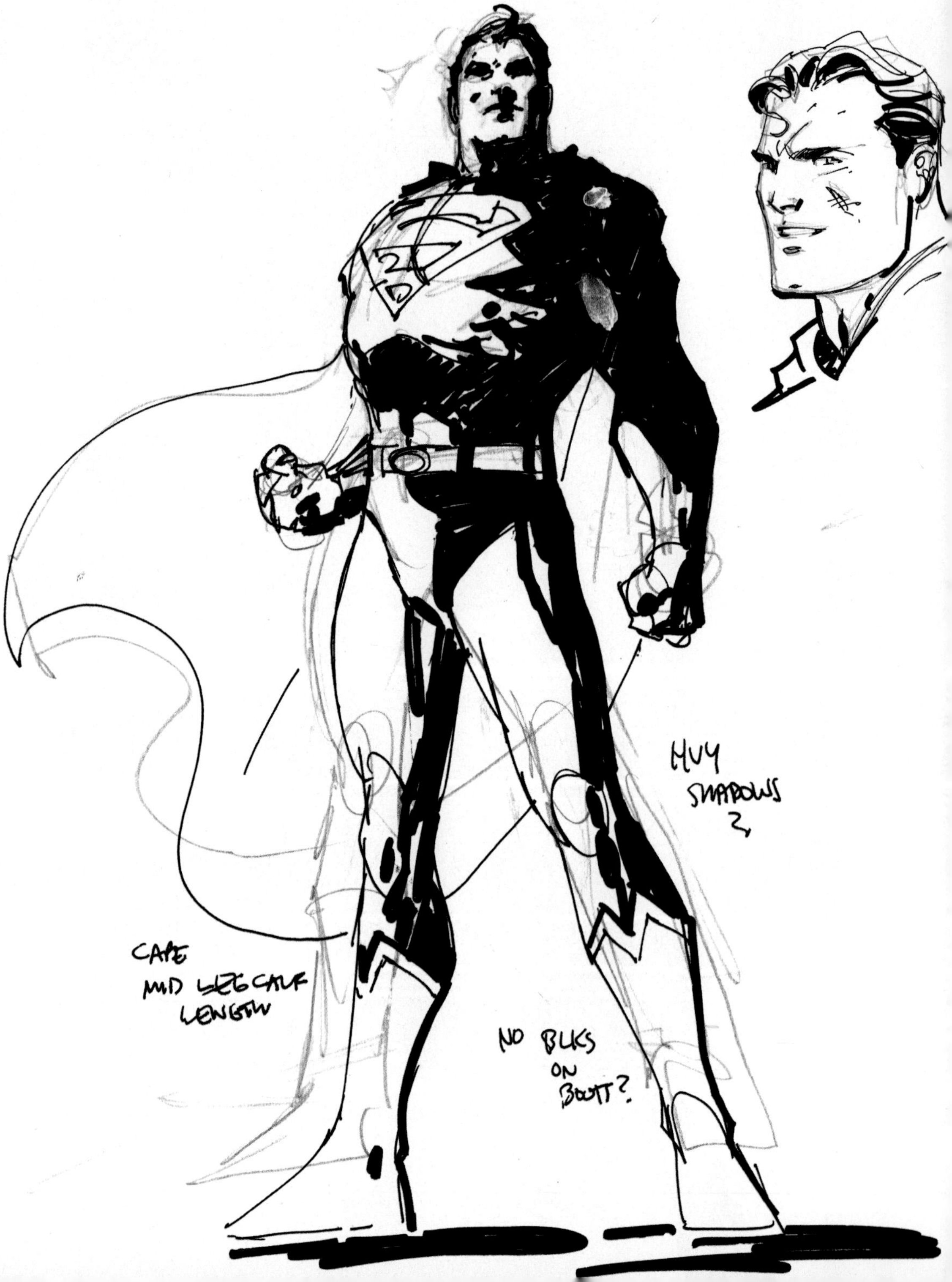
HVY
SHADOWS
?
CAPE
MID LEG CALF
LENGTH
NO BLKS
ON
BOOT?

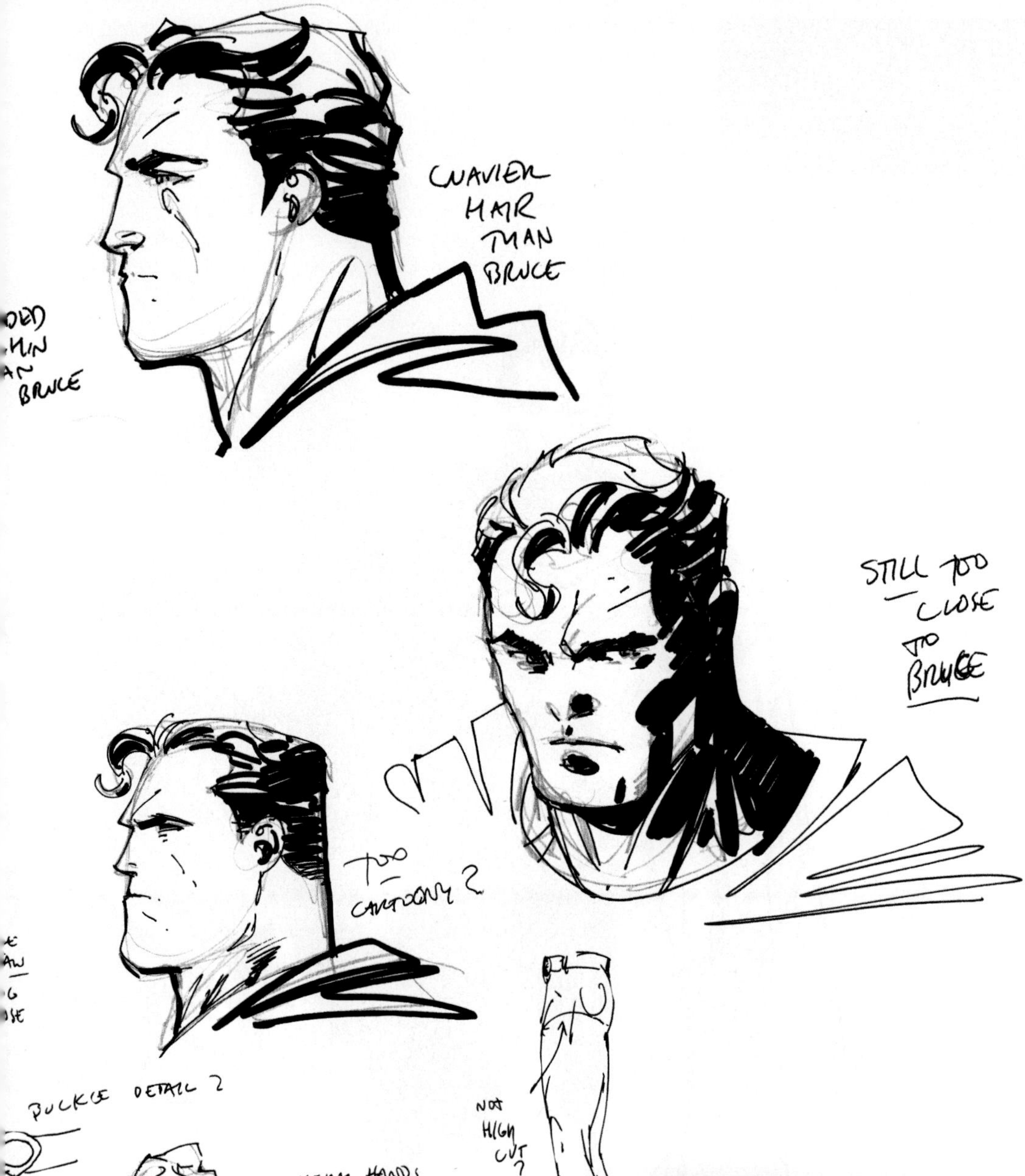

CLEANER HAIR THAN BRUCE
STILL TOO CLOSE TO BRUCE
TOO CARTOONY?

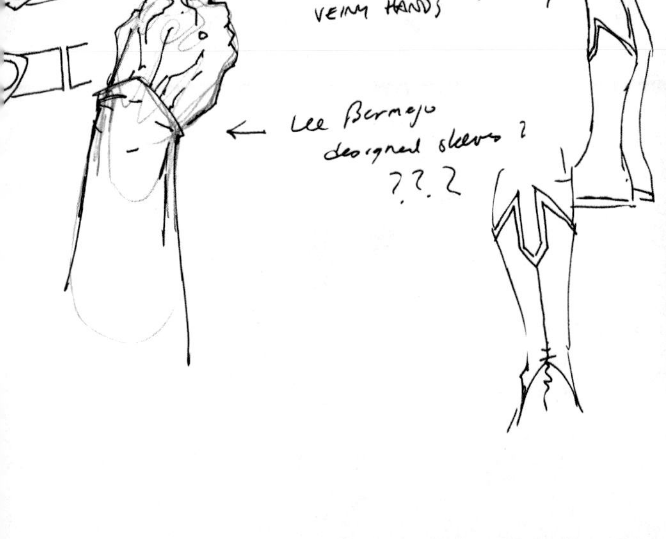

BUCKLE DETAIL?
VEINY HANDS
NOT HIGH CUT?
Lee Bermejo designed sleeves?
???

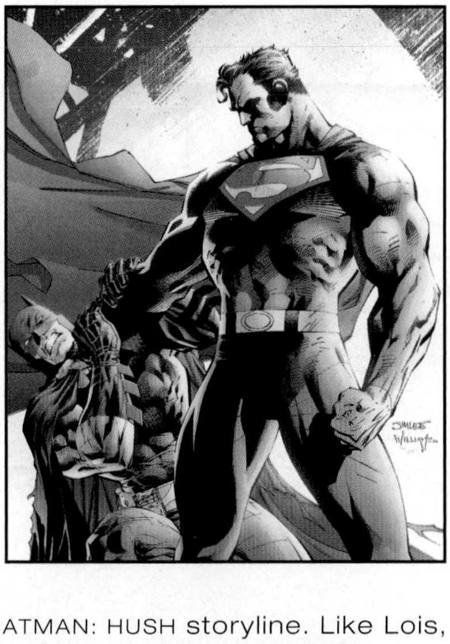

BATMAN #612 art by Lee, Williams and Sinclair.

Jim's work on Kal-El during the BATMAN: HUSH storyline. Like Lois, the artist wasn't satisfied with the look of the Man of Tomorrow.

SKETCHBOOK

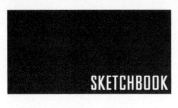

For the most part, Superman's costume is a nude body with lines at the wrist, collar, waist, legs and thighs. The cape is the only element you get to play with, either as a hiding element or to create a different overall silhouette for the character. In any design or drawing, if you are going to add shadows, you have to decide whether the shadow only affects certain colors — say, Superman's blues or his blues and reds — or if it will be more like real-life shadows and cut across any and all elements — for example, Superman's chest emblem. The problem with the latter is that you are then obscuring his world-famous chest symbol which is probably the most powerful element of his costume.

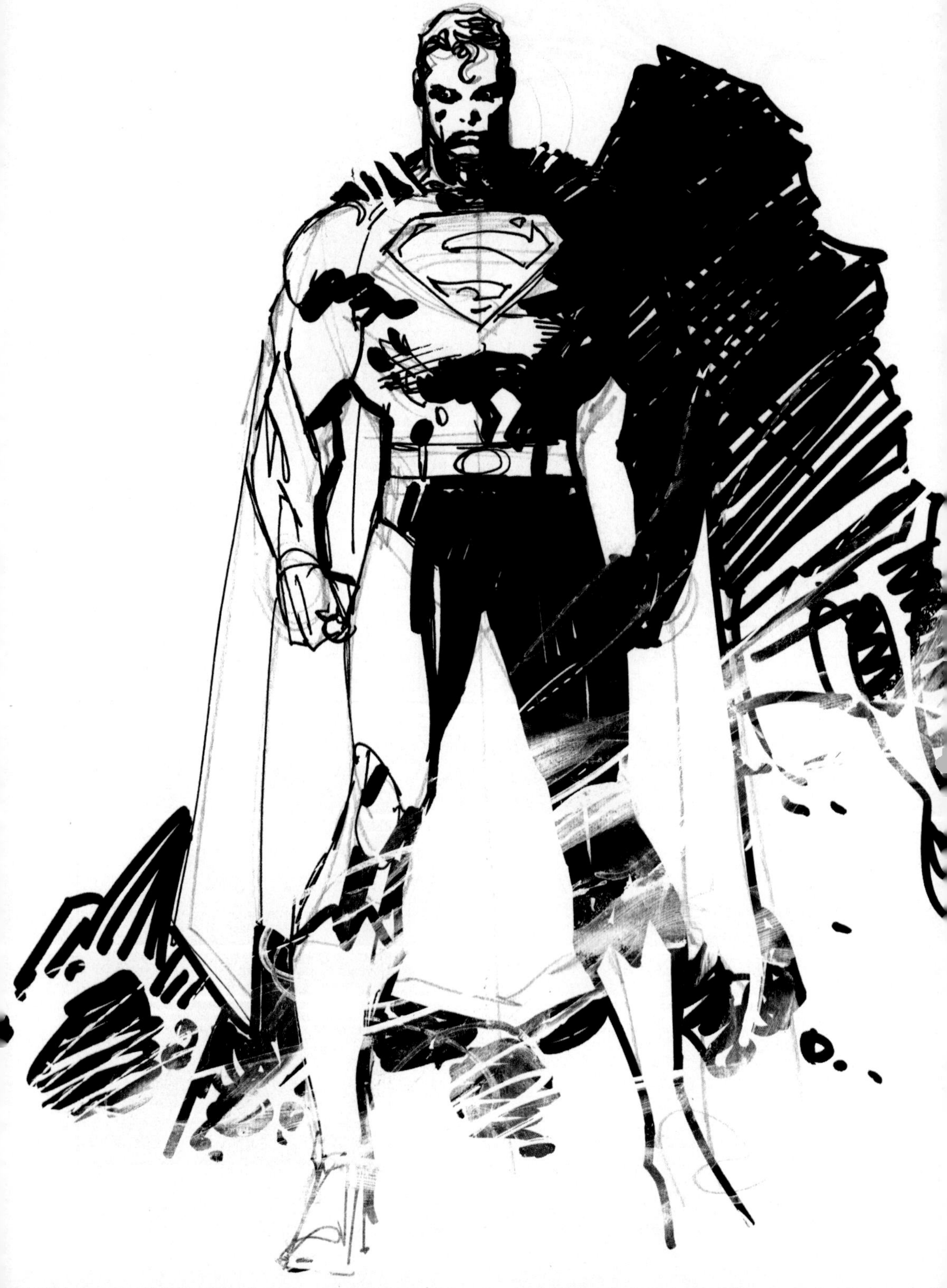

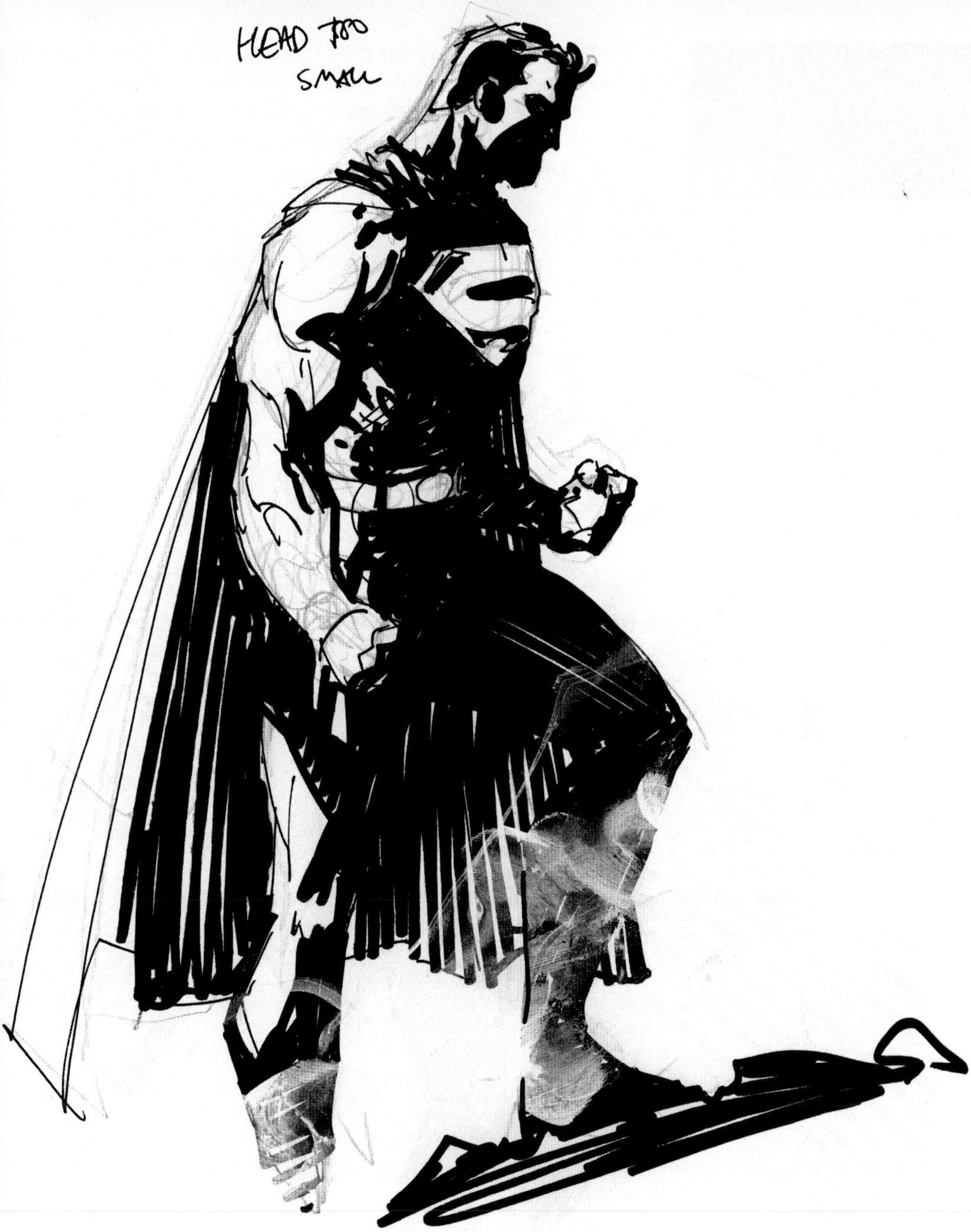
HEAD TOO
SMALL

Most people imagine Superman to be always in the light, that he is not as darkly shadowed a character as, say, Batman. But I wanted to challenge that notion, reverse it a bit and start throwing some serious blacks onto Superman's costume. In the process, I found if I kept the cape free of shadows, it would take on a luminescent quality, as if it were glowing behind him. Other times, when it would be shadowed, I could drop Superman's body silhouette into his cape, giving him a more mysterious, ominous look. He may be the preeminent good guy Super hero, but where does it say he can't look intimidating? He should look elemental when necessary, like a force of nature. The blacks help anchor his body and at the same time give his demeanor, his essence more gravity. Considering the storyline Brian has written, it is a sense of foreboding and seriousness which seems appropriate. The poses should remain heroic, classic, iconic; but the lighting, the shadowing can play against the imagery for interesting results. Sometimes I use the blacks just to frame the Superman "S" logo, because that is what gives the character's image its power. And it allows the primary red and yellow to really shine forth. Rather than obscuring and hiding the primariness of the colors — colors which are more or less out of favor in this day and age, at least for costume colors for heroes — the framing plays up the contrast for its fullest impact.

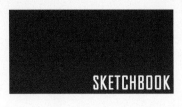

I also tinkered around with certain elements of his costume which I may gradually modify over the course of the run. Rather than start with these slight modifications, they may happen more organically as the series progresses. Just like in Hush, I imagine the Superman I draw in the final chapter will be very different from the first. Not just costumewise but in terms of the body's proportions, his sense of mass and in his lines. It's part of the fun of working on a regular book — finding the character as you do the work. In many ways, he actually finds you as the creative process unfolds.

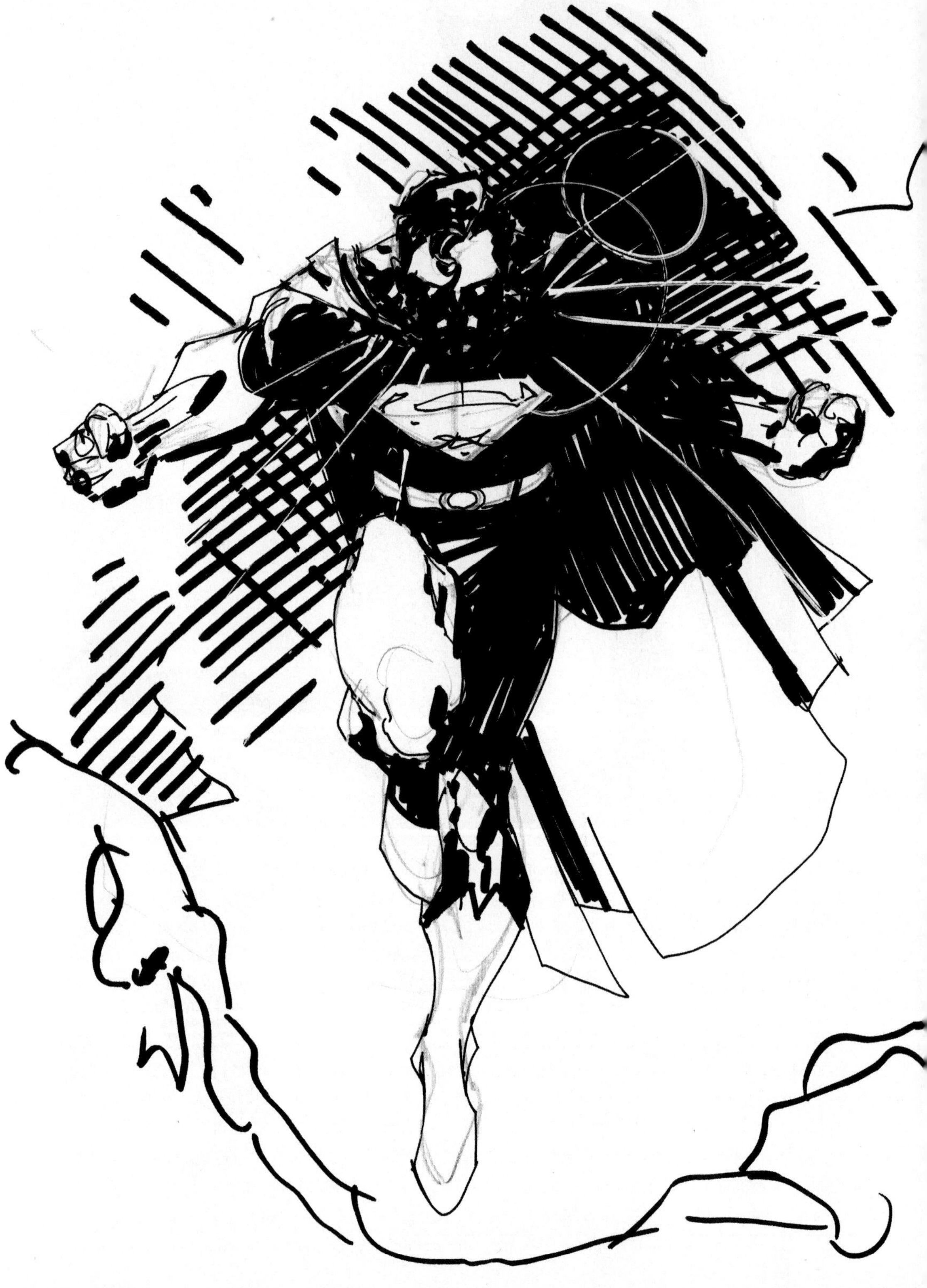

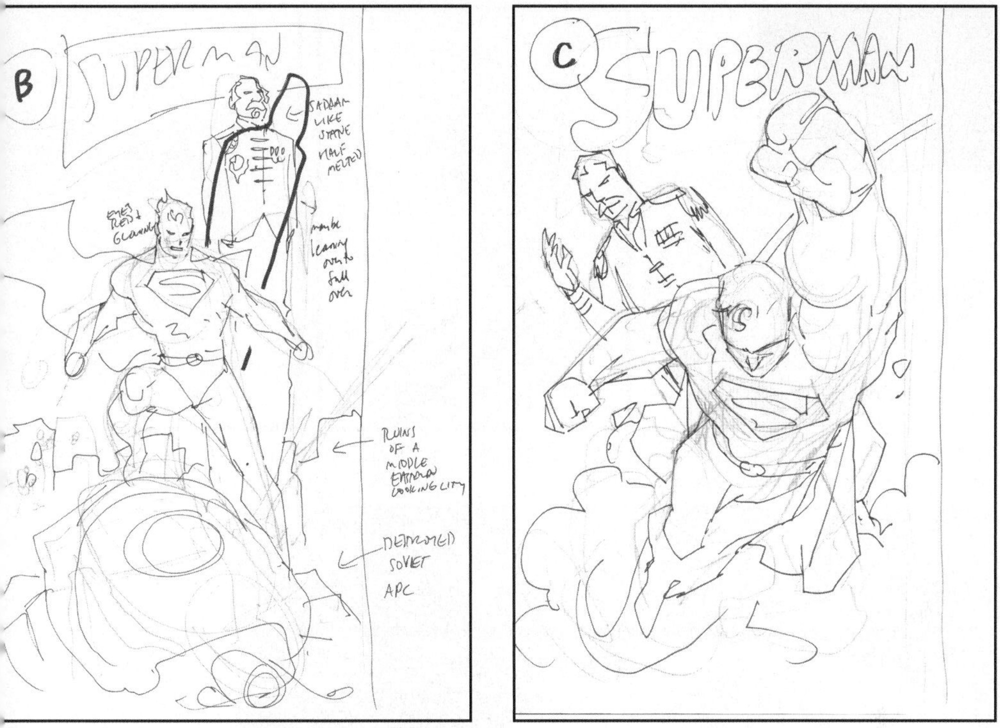
B
SUPERMAN
SADDAM LIKE STATUE HALF MELTED
RUINS OF A MIDDLE EASTERN LOOKING CITY
DESTROYED SOVIET APC
C
SUPERMAN

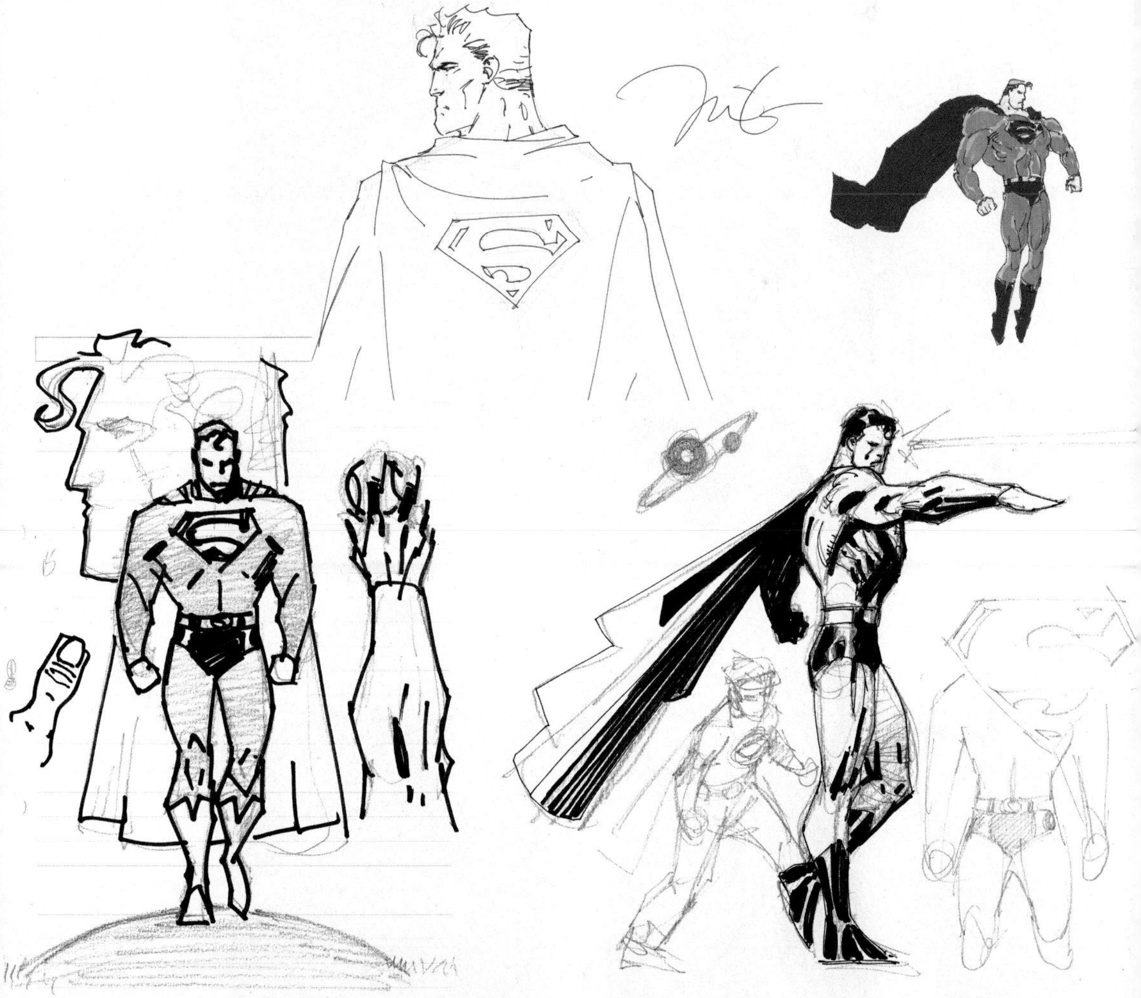

TOP: Rejected cover sketches for SUPERMAN #208
BOTTOM: Various Superman doodles

JIM LEE'S STEP-BY-STEP

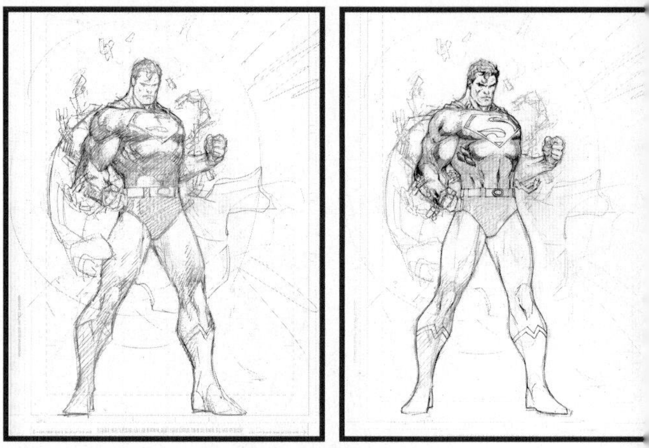

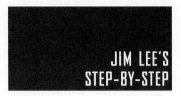

Various stages of an original drawing by Lee — an homage to Neal Adams' Superman #233 cover.

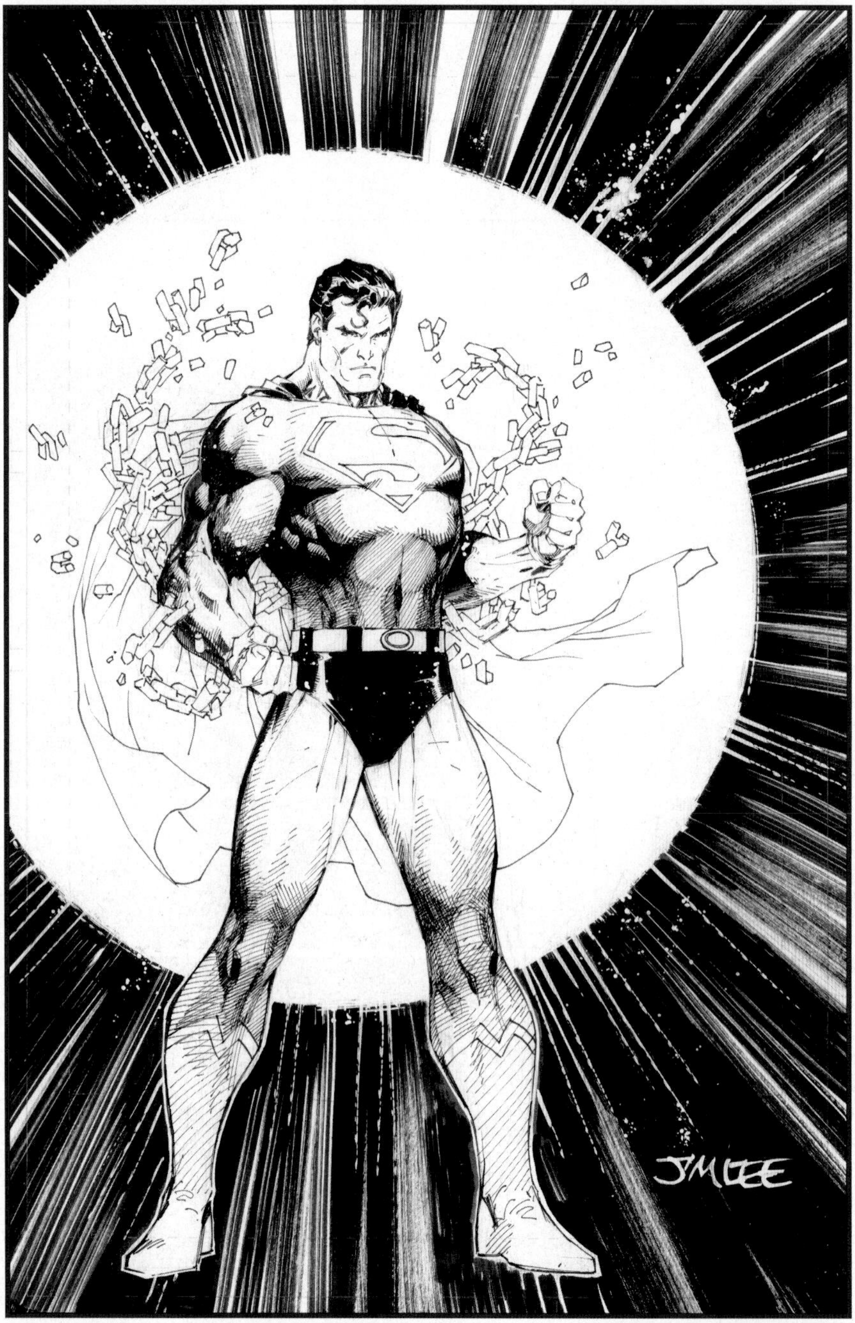

From Brian Azzarello's script, Jim starts with a rough thumbnail of the page, which he eventually translates into tightened pencils in preparation for inking.

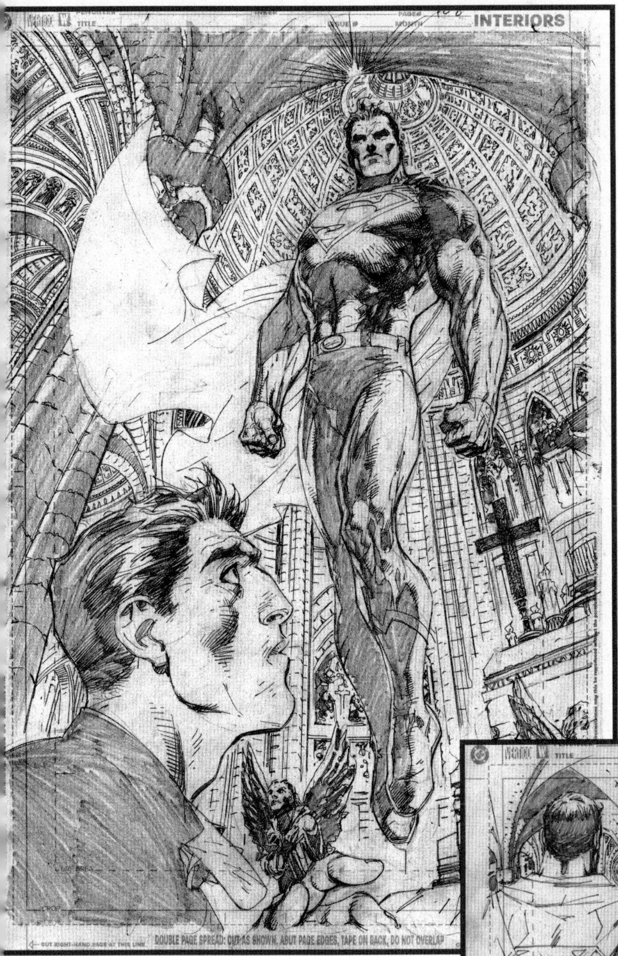
INTERIORS
DOUBLE PAGE SPREAD: CUT AS SHOWN, ABUT PAGE EDGES, TAPE ON BACK, DO NOT OVERLAP

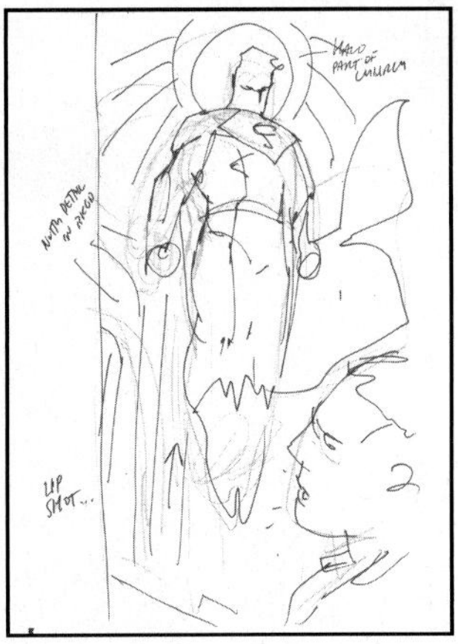
LIP SHOT...

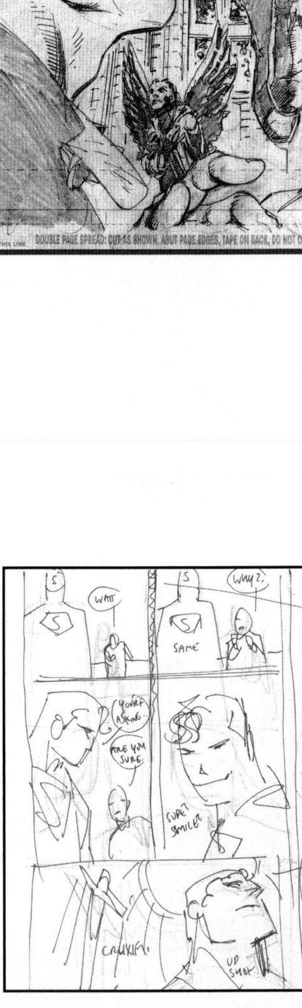
WAIT
WHY?
SAME
YOU'RE ASKING...
ARE YOU SURE
UP SHOT

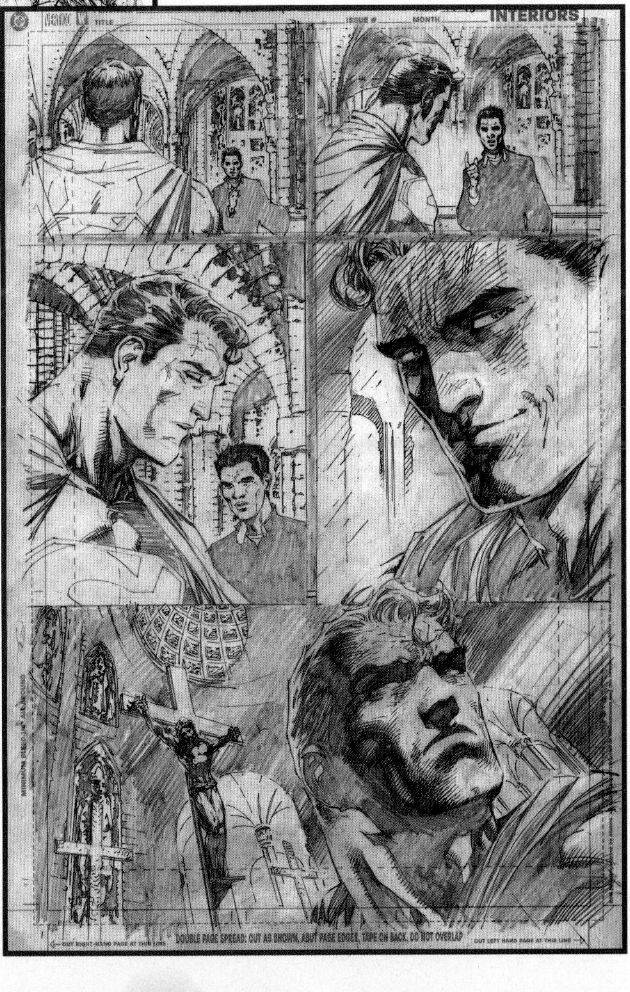
INTERIORS
DOUBLE PAGE SPREAD: CUT AS SHOWN, ABUT PAGE EDGES, TAPE ON BACK, DO NOT OVERLAP

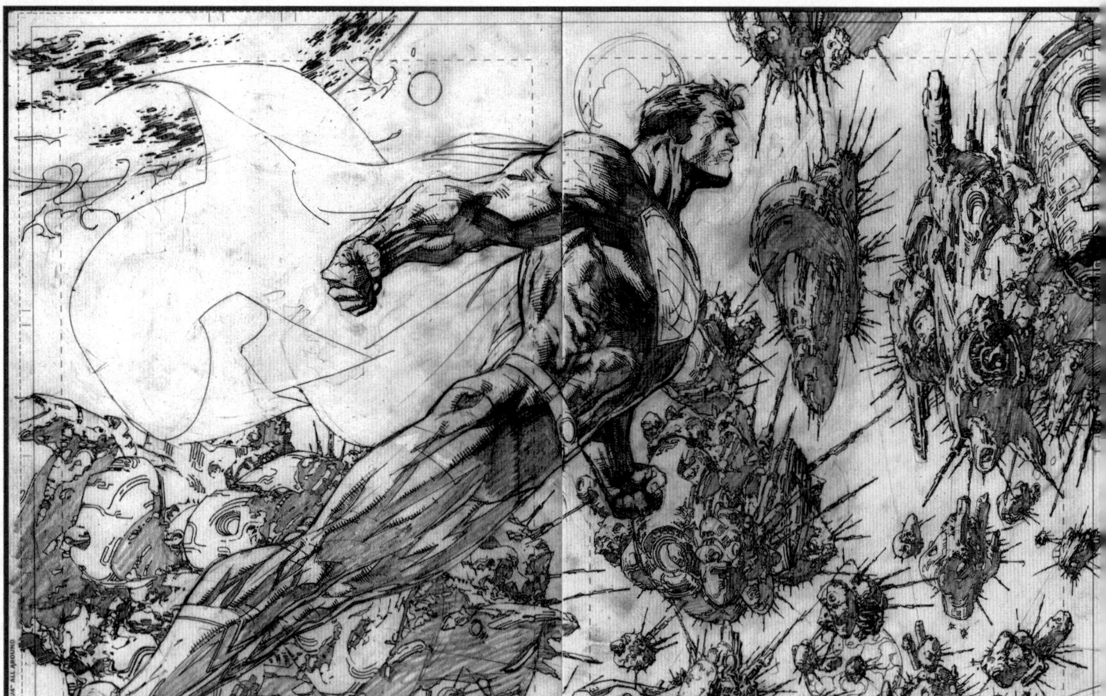

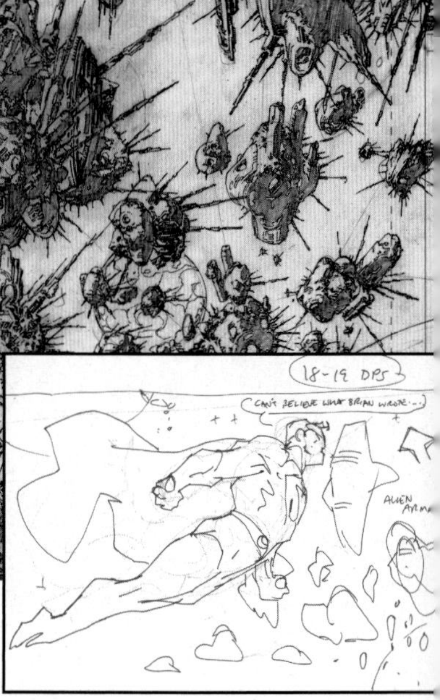
18-19 DPS
CAN'T BELIEVE WHAT BRIAN WROTE...
ALIEN ARMA

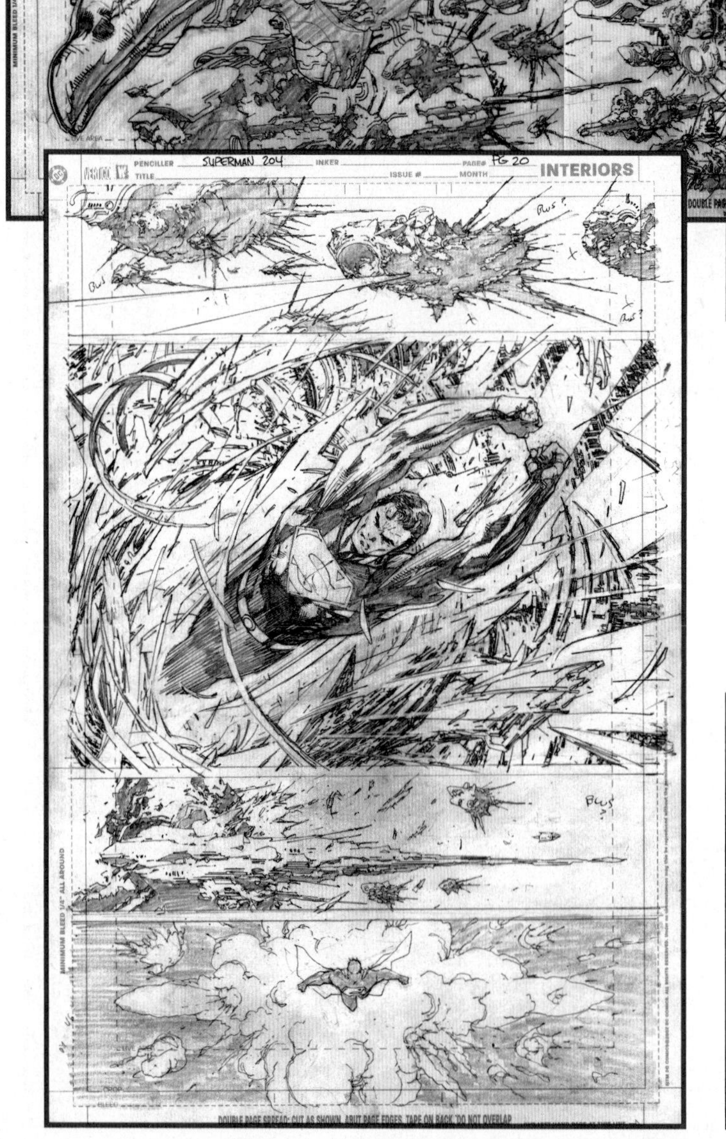
PENCILLER SUPERMAN 204
INKER
PAGE# PG 20
TITLE
ISSUE #
MONTH
INTERIORS
MINIMUM BLEED 1/4" ALL AROUND
DOUBLE PAGE SPREAD: CUT AS SHOWN, ABUT PAGE EDGES, TAPE ON BACK, DO NOT OVERLAP

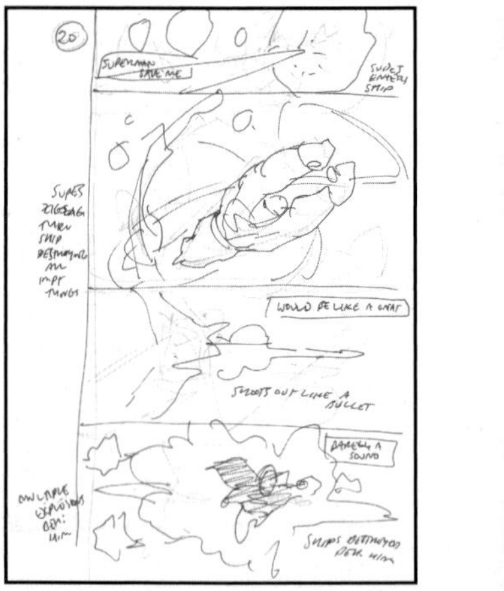
20
SUPERMAN SAVE ME
SUPES ENTERS SHIP
WOULD BE LIKE A GNAT
SHOOTS OUT LIKE A BULLET
BARELY A SOUND